PERSONALITY: *An Objective Approach*

Personality:

AN OBJECTIVE APPROACH

Irwin G. Sarason
UNIVERSITY OF WASHINGTON

JOHN WILEY & SONS, INC., *New York · London · Sydney*

16 15 14 13 12 11 10 9 8

Library of Congress Catalog Card Number: 66-13512
Printed in the United States of America

To Barbara

Preface

When I came to the University of Washington in 1956 I was asked to teach an undergraduate course called Theories of Personality. As I had had no teaching experience, I spent most of my first year in task-oriented activity, that is, trying to communicate and discuss the major personality theories extant. Gradually, the obvious became apparent: performing a task is meaningful only insofar as the task relates to a significant goal. What were my goals in teaching an undergraduate course in personality?

I concluded that what I wanted most to convey to students was the fact that the study of personality could be approached from an empirical point of view, that it could best be understood as part of a scientific analysis of behavior. The term "theories of personality," considered within such an approach, may, in fact, be misleading. A scientific theory may be thought of as the product of the conceptual ingenuity of a human thinker who has before him a set of objective data (facts) that require integration. Is the field of personality at a data-gathering or data-integrating point in its development? Both processes are surely needed, but if forced to be arbitrary, I would see data-gathering as the more immediate need in an objective study of the behavior of persons.

Does this mean that all that has been traditionally subsumed under the term "theories of personality" is of little value? Certainly not. I think it is necessary to acquaint students with prevailing conceptualizations of the person, his characteristics, and his behavior. But it is crucial to make it apparent *why* these conceptualizations are significant. They are significant, not so much because they are the climaxes of sustained research, but rather because they serve the function—the very valuable function—of providing hypotheses and hunches for empirical inquiry in the early stages of an objective approach to the person. From this point of view, for example, Freud's primary contributions might be seen in terms of his acute observations and challenging hypotheses, which have oriented numerous researchers, rather than the totality of his complex conceptual system.

At present, I introduce the study of personality to students in my undergraduate course with a review of major, broad-gauged conceptualizations (e.g., psychoanalytic, learning, perceptual) followed by an analysis of some of the significant methods of approach, and of data derived from objective empirical investigations. The course is no longer entitled Theories of Personality but is simply called Personality. This book contains the material I cover in seeking to attain the goal of a realistic survey of the present-day objective analysis of personality. While, on the one hand, I have tried hard to keep references to technical terms (such as *t*-test and analysis of variance) to a minimum, on the other hand I have sought to suggest the frequently complex nature of personality research. I have sought, also, to use examples in order to highlight the interrelationships among conceptual orientations, methods, and the results of experiments, and assessment and developmental studies.

A word should be said about the degree to which I have tried to make this a comprehensive volume and about the audience to which it is directed. As I have already mentioned, my hope is that this book will stimulate and contribute to students' awareness of current issues and problems in the empirical study of personality. To accomplish this, I do not feel it either necessary or desirable to survey the field in an encyclopedic fashion. Thus, some of the examples and emphases with which I have concerned myself will, no doubt, differ from the examples and emphases of other particular teachers. For example, I am sure that many teachers of personality courses will welcome my emphasis on the methodological challenges of research on personality. Others, however, may feel that more fact-presentation is desirable. Textbook-teacher diversity of this sort poses no problems—indeed, it may add spice to a course—so long as there is agreement on basic values. It will, I hope, quickly become clear to the reader that I value most a study of personality that objectively derives its data from the laboratory and from ongoing life settings, and that distinguishes between hunch and hypothesis, on the one hand, and between hunch and fact, on the other.

I am indebted to many individuals for their criticisms, advice, and encouragement. Colleagues have incisively and painstakingly reviewed part or all of the manuscript. Undergraduate and graduate students have provided me with much food for thought and many useful comments. Colleagues, students, and friends have helped me in many ways in carrying out research related to particular chapters. For all of this assistance I am deeply grateful. The following individuals were especially helpful to me at particular points in my work on this book: Erling E. Boe, James C. Diggory, Allen L. Edwards, Victor J. Ganzer, Andreas M. Pederson, Robert Rosenthal, Seymour B. Sarason, and Nathaniel N. Wagner.

My children bore up magnificently under the stresses and strains of bookwriting by a member of the family. Donald, Jane, and Suzanne were often of particular assistance in forcing me to remain in the real world during my authorial involvements. Most of all I am grateful to my wife, Barbara, who not only helped as one would wish a wife to help, but who also provided expert psychological consultation at many points. Next to the author, Barbara R. Sarason holds the world record for the number of readings by one individual of *Personality: An Objective Approach.*

The late Gordon S. Ierardi contributed in a number of important ways to the development of this book. I very much appreciate the opportunity of having known and having been influenced by him.

IRWIN G. SARASON

Seattle, Washington
February, 1966

Acknowledgments

I am grateful for permission to reprint material from the following copyrighted works: A. P. Watt & Son, Ernest Raymond, *The Autobiography of David;* Academic Press, W. A. Mason in L. Berkowitz, (Ed.) *Advances in Experimental Social Psychology;* Alfred A. Knopf, J. P. McKee and Marjorie P. Honsik in L. Postman (Ed.) *Psychology in the Making;* The American Association for the Advancement of Science, A. Einstein, *Science,* Vol. 91, J. A. Swets and W. Feurzeig, Vol. 150; The American Orthopsychiatric Association, *The American Journal of Orthopsychiatry,* J. Zubin, L. D. Eron, and Florence Sultan, Vol. 26, C. B. Ferster and Marian K. DeMyer, Vol. 32, No. 1; American Sociological Association, *American Sociological Review,* A. Davis and R. J. Havighust, Vol. 11; American Psychological Association, *The American Psychologist,* H. F. Harlow, Vol. 13, R. S. Lazarus, Vol. 19, S. Milgram, Vol. 19; *Journal of Abnormal Social Psychology,* A. Bandura, Dorothea Ross, and Sheila A. Ross, Vol. 66, G. Mandler and S. B. Sarason, Vol. 47, E. J. Murray, Vol. 49, M. T. Orne and K. E. Scheibe, Vol. 65, I. G. Sarason, Vol. 62, R. D. Singer, Vol. 63, J. C. Speisman, R. S. Lazarus, A. Mordkoff, and L. Davison, Vol. 68, G. H. Winkel and I. G. Sarason, Vol. 68; *Journal of Consulting Psychology,* W. T. Doidge and W. H. Holtzman, Vol. 24, S. Epstein, Vol. 25, E. J. Murray, F. Auld, and M. White, Vol. 18, A. Rosen, Vol. 22; *Journal of Experimental Psychology,* Elizabeth Duffy and O. L. Lacey, Vol. 36; *Journal of Personality and Social Psychology,* C. D. Spielberger, L. D. DeNike, and L. S. Stein, Vol. 1; Barbara J. Betz in H. H. Strupp and L. Luborsky (Eds.) *Research in Psychotherapy;* Appleton-Century-Crofts, L. E. Holt, Jr., *The Care and Feeding of Children: A Catechism for the Use of Mothers and Children's Nurses,* G. Lindzey, *Projective Techniques and Cross-Cultural Research,* R. G. Barker (Ed.) *The Stream of Behavior: Explorations of its Structure and Content,* F. S. Keller and W. N. Schoenfeld, *Principles of Psychology,* and E. R. Hilgard, *Theories of Learning;* Austin Riggs Foundation, G. P. Coon and Alice F. Raymond, *A Review of the Psychoneuroses at Stockbridge;* Basic Books Publishing Co.,

H. J. Eysenck (Ed.) *Handbook of Abnormal Psychology,* D. Rosenthal (Ed.) *The Genain Quadruplets: A Case Study and Theoretical Analysis of Heredity and Environment in Schizophrenia;* C. V. Mosby Company, L. J. Karnosh, and E. M. Zucker, *Handbook of Psychiatry;* Charles C Thomas, Publisher, Karen Machover, *Personality Projection in the Drawing of the Human Figure;* Chicago Board of Education, R. J. Havighurst, *The Public Schools of Chicago;* Columbia University Press, Margaret A. Ribble, *The Rights of Infants: Early Psychological Needs and Their Satisfaction;* Consulting Psychologists Press, H. G. Gough, *California Psychological Inventory Manual;* David McKay Co., C. W. Beers, *A Mind That Found Itself,* M. Sherman, *Mental Conflicts and Personality;* Duke University Press, K. Lewin, *The Conceptual Representation and the Measurement of Psychological Forces;* Grune & Stratton, S. L. Freedman, H. U. Grunebaum, F. A. Stare, and M. Greenblatt in L. J. West (Ed.) *Hallucination,* O. R. Lindsley, *Current Psychiatric Therapies,* Vol. 3; Harper & Row, R. R. Sears, Eleanor E. Maccoby, and H. Levin, *Patterns of Childrearing,* L. J. Cronbach, *Essentials of Psychological Testing,* A. H. Maslow in C. G. Moustakas (Ed.) *The Self: Explorations in Personal Growth,* K. Lewin, *Field Theory in Social Science;* Harvard University Press, H. A. Murray, *Thematic Apperception Test,* J. S. Bruner, *The Process of Education;* Holt, Rinehart and Winston, Erich Fromm, *The Sane Society,* G. W. Allport, *Pattern and Growth in Personality,* and Office of Strategic Services Assessment Staff, *Assessment of Men;* Houghton Mifflin Company, N. A. Cameron, *Personality Development and Psychopathology: A Dynamic Approach;* International Universities Press, H. Hartmann, *Ego Psychology and the Problem of Adaptation;* John Wiley & Sons, F. H. Allport, *Theories of Perception and the Concept of Structure,* A. L. Baldwin in P. H. Mussen (Ed.) *Handbook of Research Methods in Child Development,* F. Barron in C. W. Taylor and F. Barron (Eds.) *Scientific Creativity: Its Recognition and Development,* C. W. Fairweather (Ed.) *Social Psychology in Treating Mental Illness: An Experimental Approach,* J. W. Getzels and P. W. Jackson, *Creativity and Intelligence: Explorations with Gifted Students,* C. S. Hall and G. Lindzey, *Theories of Personality,* W. E. Henry, *The Analysis of Fantasy,* A. B. Hollingshead and F. C. Redlich, *Social Class and Mental Illness: A Community Study,* J. Kagan and H. A. Moss, *Birth to Maturity: A Study in Psychological Development,* K. Lewin in L. Carmichael (Ed.) *Manual of Child Psychology* (sec. ed.), N. E. Miller in S. S. Stevens (Ed.) *Handbook of Experimental Psychology,* E. H. Mowrer, *Learning Theory and the Symbolic Process,* Suzanne Reichard, Florine Livson, and P. G. Petersen, *Aging and Personality: A Study of Eighty-Seven Older Men,* Maria A. Rickers-Ovsiankina, *Rorschach Psychology,* L. J. Yarrow in P. H. Mussen (Ed.) *Handbook of Research Methods in Child Development,* J. Zubin, L. D. Eron, and Florence Schumer, *An Experimental Approach to Projective Techniques;* Logos Press, R. B. Cattell in J. C. McCary (Ed.) *Psychology of Personality;* The Macmillan Company, B. F. Skinner, *Science and Human Behavior,* M. Lorr, C. J. Klett, and D. M. McNair, *Syndromes of Psychosis;* McGraw-Hill Book Company, the following authors in S. Koch (Ed.) *Psychology: A Study of a Science,* Vols. 3, 4, & 5, N. Sanford, C. R. Rogers, P. R. David and L. H. Snyder, G. Von Bonin, K. H. Pribaum, E. H. Rodnick and N. Garmezy; Mouton & Co., n.v., Ruth Weir, *Language in the Crib;* The New York Academy of Science, *Annals of the New York Academy of Science,* A. F. Mirsky, Vol. 85; Paul E. Hoeber, *Psychosomatic Medicine,* H. Weiner, Margaret Thaler, M. F. Reiser, and I. A. Mirsky, Vol. 19; Physicians Postgraduate Press, *Diseases of the Nervous System,* R. W. Gerard, Monogr. Supplement 20, Sections 2, 5; Random House, R. May (Ed.) *Existential Psychology;* Ronald Press Company, O. H. Mowrer, *Learning Theory and Personality Dynamics;* Rosica Colin, Ltd., J. Custance, *Wisdom, Madness and Folly: The Philosophy of a Lunatic;* Russell Sage Foundation, M. L. and Lois W. Hoffman (Eds.) *Review of Child Development Research,* J. Kagan, pp. 162-163, L. J. Yarrow, p. 121; State Hospitals Press, Utica, New York, *Psychiatric Quarterly,* P. Milici, Vol. 11; the Journal Press, *Genetic Psychological Monographs,* E. A. Haggard, Vol. 49; Thomas Nelson & Sons, *Mind,* G. Bergmann, Vol. 52; University of Chicago Press, G. B. Schaller, *The Mountain Gorilla; Child Development,* Celia B. Stendler, Vol. 25; *Monographs of the Society of Research and Child Development,* M. I. Heinstein, Vol. 28, M. Lakin, Vol. 22; University of Michigan Press, W. F. Dearborn in Wilma T. Donahue, C. H. Coombs, and R. M. W. Travers (Eds.) *The Measurement of Student Adjustment and Achievement;* University of Minnesota Press, Hathaway, p. viii of Preface to W. G. Dahlstrom and G. S. Welsh, *An MMPI Handbook: A Guide to Use in Clinical Practice and Research,* M. Deutsch and Mary E. Collins, *Interracial Housing and a Psychological Evaluation of a Social Experiment;* University of Nebraska Press, *Monographs on Social and Child Development,* Dorothea McCarthy, Vol. 25, S. Schacter and B. Latané in D. Levine (Ed.) *Nebraska Symposium on Motivation* (1964), S. Epstein in M. R. Jones (Ed.) *1962 Nebraska Symposium on Motivation;* W. B. Saunders Company, E. Rosen and I. Gregory,

Abnormal Psychology; W. W. Norton and Co., S. Freud, *The Standard Edition of the Complete Psychological Works of Freud,* 1953–1955, Vol. 13, J. B. Watson, *Psychological Care of Infant and Child* (copyright renewed 1955 by John B. Watson), Karen Horney, *Neurosis and Human Growth;* Western Reserve University, *Marriage and Family Living,* L. W. Sontag, Vol. 6; Yale University Press, C. I. Hovland, I. L. Janis, and H. H. Kelley, *Communication and Persuasion: Psychological Studies of Opinion Change,* N. E. Miller and J. Dollard, *Social Learning and Imitation.*

I. G. S.

Contents

PART IV. PERSONALITY DEVELOPMENT

PART V. DEVIANT BEHAVIOR

1

Introduction

It has become commonplace to say that no two persons are alike. Every individual thinks of his own individuality and of the individuality of others, and all of us are generally disposed to take an appreciative, accepting attitude toward individuality in everyday life. Who has not observed that there are a great number of unusual people in the world? Or who has not noted that a person may behave in strikingly different ways under particular sets of circumstances? Observations of this kind reflect an awareness and appreciation of the wide range of behavior to be seen in a particular person and also among any group of people. Moreover, there is a note of fatalism in the cliché that explains this diversity of behavior: "After all, you can't make people over, can you?"

To the scientist whether people can be made over is an empirical matter. The statement, "People can be made over," is an hypothesis that may or may not be correct. Either way, this statement signifies a more than casual interest in the problems of the development and change of behavior. How does an individual become the person he is? What series of events produces a change in his behavior and characteristics?

These questions require us to specify both the characteristics and the behavior of individuals. The major tasks in a study of personality may be considered to be the search for the variables that bear on the differences between individuals and the differences within a particular individual over a period of time, and the scientific examination of these variables upon their discovery. Although one might qualify this view of the area of personality, the heart of the matter is the delineation and understanding of the differences among people at any given moment and within a single individual over a range of time.

DEFINING BEHAVIOR

Most psychologists center their attention on behavior. This interest often manifests itself in descriptions of differences among individuals in terms of the ways they respond to stimuli. For example, there are individual differences in how flushed the faces of individuals become when confronted with a picture of a nude person. Some students of behavior prefer to restrict the analysis of individual differences to observable responses like the redness of a person's face. Others, however, contend that the fact that a person's face becomes red requires an understanding of the underlying feelings and emotions (e.g., embarrassment) that give rise to a change in skin color. A special concern of those who concentrate on personality is the relationship of individual differences to behavior, particularly the differences to be inferred from behavior. Thus to facilitate a study of personality we need to develop some common notions about behavior and individual differences.

One approach to behavior is to attempt to describe it as carefully as possible. This method could involve a chronology of behavior. Barker and Wright (1951) carried this approach to a refined degree in providing a detached chronicle of one organism's responses. These researchers recorded all the events occurring in one day in the life of a seven-year-old boy.

At first glance, a description of behavior might seem a routine, straightforward task. Yet real problems often arise in obtaining concurrence among disinterested observers that certain events did, in fact, occur. One possible source for this type of unreliability in observation is the failure of observers to agree on which of the numerous events occurring in a period of time they will heed. Later we shall explore some of the methods used by psychologists to achieve reliable descriptions of behavior. Here let us merely note that prior, careful definition of what the observer is to pay attention to and record greatly helps in meaningfully describing behavior from one situation to the next. Likewise, assurance that different observers agree on their tasks greatly increases accord among them.

For simplicity, let us consider only the overt responses of a subject. These are responses that to some degree involve motor activity. We shall not describe how the subject feels or what he is thinking, but only the responses one can point to and physically measure—such as sighing, clearing one's throat, smoking a cigarette, writing a letter, or moving to the right or left. Of course, such a description presents a problem as the profusion of such responses by any individual even over so short an interval as an hour is staggering. It would be quite difficult to try to observe every one of these and to assign meaning to the record of individual responses. Most investigators, in fact, have confined their observations to responses of particular interest to them.

Perhaps psychology has not paid enough attention to the effects of these special interests and observer biases on research investigations. All told, the theoretical orientation of the researcher plays an important role in determining the direction that his research will take. For this reason, we shall review in the chapters of Part 1 some of the major theoretical ideas that have influenced the area of personality. While exploring these ideas, we shall also dwell on a related question: Have there been significant changes over the years in the theoretical orientations and points of view that have borne on personality research? As we shall see, there have been some noteworthy changes and we shall delve into a number of them. Sometimes these theoetical ideas directly determine the problems to be investigated, but more often their impact on research is indirect, though quite significant. In examining research in personality we must look closely at the theories and orientations because of their influence over researchers' selection of responses for study. To put this into more technical language—theories, orientations, and values direct researchers, to the specific variables and behaviors they describe, study, and manipulate.

One question we must face when psychology is defined as the study of behavior is what role covert responses—those that are not directly observable—should have in a science of behavior. Covert responses are internal; they include such things as thinking about a possible course of action, daydreaming, anticipating future events, and worrying. For some students of psychology, reference to responses that are not directly observable runs counter to the development of an objective science of behavior. However, for most students of behavior, and for students of personality in particular, an approach to psychology that limits itself to overt responses is incomplete. To obtain a sufficiently comprehensive analysis of the variables affecting overt behavior there must be reference to related internal or covert events. This is accomplished by integrating covert responding with a study of overt behavior. We achieve the integration by treating internal events as responses inferred from direct observation of overt responses, and by testing the power of the inferences to predict with accuracy. Later we shall have more to say about the methods used to attain this integration in the field of personality.

INDEPENDENT AND DEPENDENT VARIABLES AND INDIVIDUAL DIFFERENCES

All students of psychology know the difference between independent and dependent variables. An independent variable is one that is manipulated by an investigator. Time of deprivation of food, number of hours during which a subject is isolated from contact with other persons, and amount of praise for performance on a task are all examples of an independent variable. A dependent variable, in contrast, is one whose changes flow from the modification of some independent variable.

Like other scientific investigators, researchers in personality seek evidence that will eventually enable them to say: If *a* then *b*. However, the kind of chronological descriptive research undertaken by Barker and Wright (1951) does not involve the manipulation of independent variables. Instead, it concentrates entirely on dependent variables, the aspects of the subject's behavior that are observed and recorded by the researcher. We shall apply the term *experimental study of personality* to research in which the investigator exerts a substantial degree of control over the conditions under which the subject behaves. In Part 3 we shall consider some important experiments that illustrate ingenious ways of controlling and manipulating events in the environment.

The experiment is one of science's most powerful tools because of the high degree of control it permits over the conditions of the laboratory. But is this degree of control sufficient when the dependent variables are the responses of human beings rather than such matters as chemical reactions? The chemist who seeks a particular reaction can start from scratch, so to speak, and control and manipulate almost every aspect of the experimental situation. The scientist who deals with the behavior of an organism has no such opportunity. Although he may be able to exercise a high degree of control while the subject is in the experimental situation, he cannot achieve much control over the effects of an organism's history, especially when that organism is man.

Insofar as the investigator cannot control the history of the organism, he must expect some imprecision and ambiguity in the results he obtains. A number of possibilities arise under the circumstances.

One is to limit research on behavior to animals like rats and mice which can be bred and reared under laboratory conditions. Pursuit of this course, although a legitimate scientific endeavor, would not contribute directly to a science of human behavior. Another course limits itself to the responses of human beings which are not significantly influenced by either their genetic backgrounds or life histories. Although defensible from a scientific standpoint, this tactic poses a question. How does the investigator decide the extent to which the individual's history directly or indirectly influences his responses in an experimental situation? The question is often not easy to answer.

A third course comes directly to grips with individual differences and their histories. Those who pursue this course make these variables central in their investigations rather than accept them as sources of error to be minimized. Their tactic illustrates the necessity of taking note of the orientations and values that influence scientific inquiry. Researchers in personality may perform experiments dealing with problems resembling those investigated in the more traditional fields of experimental psychology, such as learning and perception, but they will emphasize the joint effects of experimentally manipulated independent variables, individual differences, and historical variables on these processes.

In view of the difficulty of controlling an individual's life for any extended span of time, how can students of personality accomplish a study of human behavior? The task may be approached in a number of complementary ways. One of these takes a longitudinal look. That is, the investigator does not attempt to control the individual's behavior but makes an effort to observe and record certain aspects of human life over a period of time. In Part 4 we shall delve deeper into longitudinal studies of human behavior, their potentialities, and the methodological problems associated with them. Here let us note that there is a wide range of agreement on the value of studying individuals over long intervals of time in order to gain knowledge of the processes involved in behavioral change.

This behavioral change is perhaps most obvious in development during childhood. How does the child develop? In what ways do heredity and environment influence the development of the child's responses? Certainly, the more detailed the description of the child's behavior over a period of time and of the influences at work on him, the better the longitudinal study will be. But this truism does not apply to the researcher who is limited in his resources—facilities, financing, staff, and energy. His problem is to select the aspects of individual's lives and behavior on which he should concentrate. Barker and Wright (1951), for example, filled an entire volume with the description of the behavior of one boy during one day. So laudable an in-depth approach cannot be practically applied, of course, to studies of 10 to 20 years' duration. In this case, the researcher necessarily must select a manageable, relatively small number of variables for intensive study, and in doing so, reintroduce the issue of the theoretical bases on which variables are chosen for investigation.

Contrasted with the longitudinal study is the cross-sectional study. Cross-sectional studies close in on many individuals at only one point or at a small number of closely spaced points in time. In these studies investigator and subject are strangers; the investigator does not make first-hand personal observations of the subject prior to the experiment. The immediate concern is not with development of the individual's personal characteristics, but with the relationship of current personal characteristics to his behavior. (Of course, a study of current characteristics may indeed lead to interest in and study of their histories.) Some of the variables in personality research that lend themselves to the cross-sectional approach include age, sex, the number of siblings, scores attained on particular tests, feelings expressed, and attitudes. These variables are known as individual difference variables.

Individual difference variables fall into two classes, factual and inferential. The factual variables are virtually 100 per cent reliable; observers would agree unanimously on their existence. They are such characteristics as age, the number of siblings, sex, race, and the number of rooms in one's house. Some students, however, might question the reliability of the assessment of certain factual individual difference variables. For example, in determining race, calling an individual white or Negro may be a highly arbitrary decision. In other words, sets of rules and conventions are often necessary in defining factual individual difference variables.

The inferential class presents even more difficult and challenging problems. These variables must be inferred from factual evidence of behavior. Whereas the observer can describe things and events, he can only define concepts; hence he cannot describe inferential individual difference variables, only define them. In defining a concept in a particular way, the observer implicitly assumes the responsibility for demonstrating the usefulness of this concept. One measure of its usefulness is its power to predict. Suppose, for example, we were interested in human tolerance of stress. We might regard stress as the distractions that occur in the environment. These might be annoying lights and noises going on and off while someone is taking an important intelligence or aptitude test. Suppose that we wished to predict on some basis how well each subject would bear up under stress. We would thus be confronted by a problem of prediction. How shall we assess the individual's tolerance of stress? One way would be through self-description. We might ask subjects to report on a questionnaire how they respond to distraction. Or we might assess stress tolerance by asking other individuals who know the subject well to describe his reaction to distracting influences. Either of these methods or any other one used to assess the tolerance of stress demands that the personality researcher base the assessment on factual evidence; that is, that he make it reflect reference to some overt response or measure.

For the inferential variables, such as stress tolerance, the meaning or predictive value of the observable evidence has to be determined. This is not the case, in a sense, for the factual variables like sex or age; their usefulness is self-evident. In the study of personality, inference plays a key role. Inferred concepts are among the major preoccupations of the investigator. These include such variables as adjustment, intelligence, aggression, and anxiety. Each of these concepts figures prominently in important areas of personality research. All of them involve the steps whereby concepts are defined, the relation of their definition to indices of behavior, and the establishment of predictive value for the indices so derived.

As we have said, the study of personality is concerned with the relationship of individual differences to behavior. However, this statement raises a minor point of semantics. Certain psychologists say they work in the area of personality; others describe their field as one of individual differences, or differential psychology. The distinction is minor because the contributions of psychologists to the study of behavior are far more important than the labels attached to them. The two areas, in fact, overlap in many places and workers in both areas have much in common. However, the following observation may have some pertinence: Personality researchers are probably much more concerned with covert or inferred characteristics than are most of the differential psychologists. Observable characteristics such as height, weight, and handedness are likely to receive more comprehensive treatment from the differential psychologists than from the workers in personality. The latter are more likely to place greater emphasis on the inferred characteristics of individuals.

THE ROLE OF INFERENCE

Inference plays a prominent role in personality for the same reason that it does in psychology or for that matter, in science. The scientist would prefer, of course, to deal exclusively with observable phenomena, if this were possible. However, all the processes and events in which he is interested are not usually conveniently and immediately observable by him. For the scientist, as for the layman, life requires the assignment of meaning to unobservable things as well as conceptual problem solving. Albert Einstein (1940, p. 487) phrased this fact in succinct terms:

> Science is the attempt to make the chaotic diversity of our sense-experience correspond to a logically uniform system of thought. In this system single experiences must be correlated with the theoretic structure in such a way that the resulting coordination is unique and convincing.
>
> The sense-experiences are the given subject-matter. But the theory that shall interpret them is man-made. It is the result of an extremely laborious process of adaptation: hypothetical, never completely final, always subject to question and doubt.
>
> The scientific way of forming concepts differs from that which we use in our daily life, not basically, but merely in the more precise definition of concepts and conclusions; more painstaking, and systematic choice of experimental material; and greater logical economy. By this last we mean the effort to reduce all concepts and correlations to as few as possible logically independent basic concepts and axioms.

Some examples from everyday life will highlight the need for inference in a study of personality. Why do some persons experience frequent, terrifying nightmares, others only occasional bad dreams, and still others none? Rather than answer this question here, we merely raise it for illustrative purposes. Right off, the obvious occurs to us: These groups of people are different. In what ways do they differ? This question leads directly to conceptualizations about the nature of dreams and dreamers, and arouses our interest in current personality and past historical differences among the subjects. Not only shall we conceptualize, in the sense of linking a number of observable events, but we shall also have to cope with covert events, such as the content of dreams and the dreamer's personality.

The example of dreaming may lead many students to think of the problem of unconscious motivation. This problem is a challenging one because it usually arises in situations in which the direct observation of the relevant stimuli does not adequately account for the subject's behavior. Take a slip of the tongue. Most of us are annoyed by our slips, partly because we feel we have failed to control our behavior. Or we are embarrassed and wonder about our stupidity when we forget the name of someone with whom we have had numerous dealings. In both instances and others like them we wonder what is going on in the mind of the individual which might account for such behavior. Since the mental events that might induce the observed slip of the tongue or forgetting of a name are not observable, the resort to inference seems inevitable and essential.

All definitions of psychology at the present time make reference to behavior. Textbooks for beginners direct their attention to the responses of organisms and the stimuli that induce these responses. Close study of the responses, particularly among human beings, makes it clear that a lot of responding does not flow directly from the stimuli at work in the organism's environment immediately prior to the specific response. Anyone who reviews his own collection of responses during the course of a day must soon recognize the extent to which his overt behavior is affected by covert events within himself that cannot be directly observed by others, researchers included. When the psychologist decides not to regard the organism as empty of responses because he cannot observe them, he tacitly accepts the necessity to relate, as well as he can, his inferences and the states he hypothesizes to events he is able to see and record. Any individual has the right to draw inferences and to hypothesize, but more than this is expected of the scientist. He must show that his hypotheses and inferences help to explain aspects of behavior which otherwise could not be as clearly understood. Furthermore, he must adhere to the law of parsimony, a general principle of scientific thinking that requires him to prefer the simpler of two hypotheses. However, he must not commit the error of regarding a hypothesis as truly simple if it needs additional assumptions to explain its meaning.

The role of inference in psychology has stirred its share of controversy. Although all psychologists agree that speculation not based on observable events and empirical facts is highly objectionable, they are less in accord on the amount of speculation and conceptualization which is desirable and healthy. Some psychologists prefer to keep inference to a bare minimum. They prefer to dwell on the ways in which observable events in the environment influence the observable responses of organisms (Skinner, 1953, 1954, 1956). Another point of view, which is currently dominant in the area of personality, fully subscribes to emphasis on observables but also seeks to draw attention to the events occurring within the individual. This additional interest in covert phenomena increases the need for theoretical formulations that are less essential to purely behavioristic orientations.

What is the value of a theoretical formulation? What can be accomplished with a theory that cannot be accomplished without one? Both questions imply a more basic one: What is a theory?

Although philosophers, psychologists, and others have written extensively on the nature of scientific theory, only two major points need concern us here. First, theories provide frameworks within which facts may be integrated. Francis Bacon, as many may recall, saw science as essentially a procedure and instrumentality for the collection of facts; the more facts collected, the better the science. This is a fine notion as long as there are not too many facts to consider. As facts and data accumulate, it becomes ever more difficult to keep track of them. Theories establish systems that permit the integration of large numbers of facts that may at times be quite disparate. Once the theoretical system has become available, existing facts may be easily derived from it. Thus theories are convenient.

Second, theories help generate new facts and new data. In biology, for example, Darwin's theory of evolution enabled researchers not only to relate a large assortment of facts to one another and generalize about them, but also to uncover *new* facts and lawful relationships. Were it not for the Darwinian theory these newer facts and relationships might not have been brought to light, at least not for some time.

Most psychologists agree that owing to the newness of their field and the complexity of its subject matter the development of theories of behavior is still rudimentary. This certainly applies to the psychological approach to personality. As we have mentioned, a major characteristic of workers in the area of personality is their preoccupation with internal processes and the effects of these on individual overt behavior. Some of these processes are susceptible to reliable measure. These include such bodily phenomena as blood pressure and brain waves. However, much less is known about mental and intangible processes such as thinking and intellectual and personality functioning. Research into personality, besides relating public events to other public events, as in a simple stimulus-response (S-R) sequence, endeavors to relate private events and states like fear, intellectual potentiality, and thought disturbances to public ones.

INFERENCE IN PERSONALITY RESEARCH

Taylor (1951) made public the results of an experiment in which puffs of air were administered to the eyelids of subjects. The airpuffs served as stimuli for eyeblinking responses. Here were two public events; anyone with adequate apparatus could observe the administration of the airpuffs and the blink of the eye. What interested Taylor was the extent to which, after a series of trials in which the airpuff was administered, the subjects would begin to blink their eyes *before* the puff of air was actually released. The problem was the establishment of conditioned responses in human subjects, that is, anticipatory blinking of the eyelid.

Working within Hull's (1952) drive theory, Taylor predicted that in a relatively simple situation, subjects who are high in anxiety would show a higher degree of conditioning than subjects of low anxiety. She scaled subjects in her experiment for anxiety in a number of different situations (see Table 10-1, p. 142 for sample items used by Taylor). As she expected, subjects who scored high in anxiety were higher in their rate of anticipatory blinking than were those of low anxiety.

What does this demonstrate with respect to inferring private from public events? From one standpoint Taylor merely related one set of observable events to another, her two public measures consisting of the score obtained on the anxiety scale and the frequency of the anticipatory eyeblinking responses. Although there is nothing wrong with this operational view of Taylor's experiment, it does justice neither to the frame of reference that gave rise to her study nor to the implication of the experiment's results. Lacking the Hullian theoetical framework, Taylor in all likelihood would not have devised her anxiety scale, nor would she have related it, as she did, to eyelid conditioning. Actually, Taylor hypothesized that her scale was an index of an inferred drive state. This hypothesis, in fact, has led to a long series of valuable investigations with human subjects. It has given rise to many findings that fit together through inference and make sense. These findings, however, would be nothing more than a collection of discrete facts were it not for the existence of a theory to pull them together.

Having a frame of reference, though, does not necessarily eliminate controversy and argument. We might hold that Taylor's inference about the characteristics reflected in her anxiety scale were erroneous and that some other interpretation might be superior. This touches off a controversy over the private events that gave rise to the scores obtained on the scale. How might the dispute be resolved? How do we discover which of two interpretations of a test score is the more useful and fruitful? To use the terms of Cronbach and Meehl (1955), the problem is one of *construct validity*. A construct is a statement or set of statements concerning some aspect of an organism's internal states or characteristics, or in the terms we are using, the private events believed to contribute to the shaping of specific public events, the latter the observed behavior of the individual. The value of the statement may be considered to represent its validity. Validity, therefore, refers to the usefulness of the construct. In the Taylor example we might ask what the construct validity of the Hullian approach to anxiety is as compared with the construct validity of other approaches.

Determination of construct validity is not nearly as simple in this case as it would be were we interested in tracing the circulatory system. The parts of the circulatory system today are observable public phenomona. For many centuries, however, the circulatory system was far from being a public event. Anxiety, on the other hand, is a concept rather than a thing. Construct validity is tested through the process of making predictions based on the existing concept or construct and then testing these predictions in experiments. The more predictions made and borne out, the higher the degree of construct validity. Concepts of hypothesized private events, which are not susceptible to behavioral assessment and which cannot be empirically studied and tested, have no construct validity. Where more than one concept exists, as exemplified in the procedure of interpreting the scores on Taylor's scale in many different ways, the concept that accounts for the greatest amount of behavior of organisms has the highest degree of construct validity.

At what point does the investigator start to operate on the conceptual level implied by the notion of construct validity? Generally he does so when it becomes necessary to use conceptualizations to tie together discrete pieces of evidence. In the eyelid conditioning example, an investigator, after working with several subjects, might wonder why some of them condition and others do not. He is confronted by the puzzle of individual differences within a particular situation. He might begin to think that if he could assess and manipulate the characteristics of individuals he would be able to predict the extent to which his subjects would display anticipatory eyeblinks. If he has a hunch about some internal characteristic, some tendency or state of the organism, he might proceed to develop a behavioral index such as Taylor's anxiety scale, and relate the index to the behavior that originally inspired his interest. If the index actually relates to the behavior in question, he has the first step in construct validity. Some constructs may apply to only a few situations whereas others may pertain to a multitude of behaviors. Cronbach and Meehl (1955) call the nature and number of relationships in which a construct figures its *nomological network*. Some of these networks involving many relationships will be quite complex; others will be rather limited.

The point, then, at which constructs become necessary is when the relating of public events to other public events, such as observable stimuli to observable responses, does not answer all the important questions raised by the available evidence. As we have already noted, a strictly behavioristic approach to personality which avoids reference to private events and internal states is enticing to researchers because it deals only with observable phenomena and does not goad the investigator to concern himself with "what is going on inside." But this does not suffice where human beings are involved. In research into human beings it is necessary to consider internal processes in order to account for behavior. But the investigator must adhere to the law of parsimony. That is, concepts and theories should be only as complicated as is required to explain available data and generate new relationships.

ISSUES IN THE STUDY OF PERSONALITY

The study of personality goes back to the days of the Greek philosophers. But if the field of study is limited to conceptualizations based on controlled observational studies, then its history might be said to date from the work of European psychiatrists of relatively recent years. These physicians directed their efforts toward understanding the behavior of maladjusted individuals. As the field of psychology expanded and matured, it became evident that the adjustment of both deviant and normal persons fell within its domain.

Within the discipline of psychology, increasing attention to the link between theory and conceptualization on the one hand, and to objective research on the other, has marked the development of the study of personality. Perhaps the major contribution of psychologists to the study of personality is their leadership in moving the area from the armchairs of individual thinkers to the laboratory. The notion that persuasive empirical evidence must support constructs is one of the hallmarks of the modern study of personality.

Yet the existence of this hallmark does not eliminate a number of persistent sources of dispute. The role of inference in the study of personality makes this quite clear. To be adequately characterized, the area of pesonality must be described in terms of its zones of agreement and disagreement. Only by doing this can most of the basic issues be appreciated. Let us examine some of these issues.

First: What is the definition of personality? The existing definitions of personality could fill a volume. In some definitions relatively specific functions are assigned to personality. For example, Krech and Crutchfield (1948, p. 73) have said:

Characteristic modes of tension reduction are learned by the individual as a function of his past experiences of success or failure with them and of the opportunity for employment of them within the confines of his particular culture. *Personality* may be described as the *pattern of relative importance* of these various modes of adjustment to tension which uniquely characterizes the individual.

Many definitions are quite general. Allport (1961, p. 28) has said: "Personality is the dynamic organization within the individual of those psychophysical systems that determine his characteristic behavior and thought." Cattell (1950, pp. 2–3) has offered a general definition that emphasizes the predictive power of the concept of personality:

. . . *personality is that which permits a prediction of what a person will do in a given situation* . . . . Personality is . . . concerned with *all* the behavior of the individual, both overt and under the skin.

Hilgard (1962*b*, p. 447) gives a definition that stresses the need to study individual differences:

. . . the term *personality* is used to mean the configuration of individual characteristics and ways of behaving which determines an individual's unique adjustments to his environment. We stress particularly those personal traits that affect the individual's getting along with other people and with himself. Hence personality includes any characteristics that are important in the individual's personal adjustment, in his maintenance of self-respect.

Most definitions implicitly involve the assumption that personality refers to some kind of hypothetical internal structure or organization. However, a trend has set in that leads away from more or less formal definitions of personality as an organization of characteristics and systems. The impetus for this trend seems to be an awareness that explicit, concise definitions of complex hypothetical structures may not be the best way to stimulate *empirical* knowledge about the connections among individual differences, personal dispositions, and covert behavior. Thus, McClelland (1951, p. 69) has defined personality as "the most adequate conceptualization of a person's behavior in all its detail that a scientist can give at a moment in time."

Hall and Lindzey (1957, p. 9), in reviewing theories of personality, have concluded:

. . . *no substantive definition of personality can be applied with any generality*. By this we mean simply that the way in which a given individual will define personality will depend completely upon his particular theoretical preference. Thus, if the theory places heavy emphasis upon uniqueness and the organized, unified qualities of behavior, it is natural that the definition of personality will include uniqueness and organization as important attributes of personality. Once the individual has created or adopted a given theory of personality, his definition of personality will be rather clearly implied by the theory. Thus, we submit that *personality is defined by the particular empirical concepts which are a part of the theory of personality employed by the observer.* Personality consists concretely of a set of values or descriptive terms which are used to describe the individual being studied according to the variables or dimensions which occupy a central position within the particular theory utilized.

The definition we shall use is similar to that of Hall and Lindzey. We shall consider personality as an area of investigation rather than as an entity, real or hypothetical. This area contains a variety of terms and concepts, and a number of methods through which their values may be estimated. Some of the terms and concepts may refer to the total functioning of the individual, some to particular determinants of behavior, some to individual differences, and others to psychological processes. All must be evaluated by their clarity of definition and their degree of helpfulness in predicting and manipulating human behavior. As the relationships among the various terms and concepts become clarified through empirical knowledge, the terms and concepts themselves will be better understood and eventually will become integrated with one another.

Second: What is the optimal balance between theory and research in personality? Students of personality may be classified according to the degree to which they stress the need for theoretical formulations. A trend has become discernible. It is a tendency toward greater emphasis on observation and evidence prior to stating broad theoretical positions. Although the trend is clear, particularly among American psychologists, differences of opinion persist about the conservatism necessary in speculations regarding the antecedents of overt behavior. One of the critics of this trend has been Allport (1961, pp. 550–551), who has referred to this emphasis on empirical investigation as a positivistic point of view and who has commented:

> Positivism does not pretend to be synoptic in its view of man. Its assignment is to find small facts under controlled conditions. The "fact" is bound to be small, since reliability can, as a rule, be obtained only when one deals with a limited fragment of behavior. Totalities of behavior are so inexact that the positivist turns away from them. Fragmentation yields firmer results. Therefore attention is devoted to the partial, the physical, and quasi-mechanical, the regular, the logical, because these aspects can be controlled. Attention is correspondingly withdrawn from the symbolic, the illogical, the uncoded, the configural because they cannot be reliably controlled.

Thus positivism teaches us how to be cautious and conservative, how to check and validate, how to be accurate and precise. Much of the detailed general information that goes into the psychology of personality, . . . is gathered by following the canons of experimental research. This procedure appeals to us because it offers the best means for verifying our discoveries. The price we pay is limiting our curiosity to only a portion of a human being. We suppress interest in the total pattern.

In reply to these criticisms, many researchers in personality contend that speculations regarding the total aspect are appealing and may give some people the feeling of having explained all complex phenomena. But unless the speculations are tied closely to reality, that is, to the observations which scientists can make, they are little more than fantasies. These researchers believe that whereas the investigator should be cautious and conservative in his endeavors, the research itself need not be mundane and unimaginative.

Third: What is the relationship of the area of personality to the general field of psychology? Over the years some writers seemed to view general psychology as the study of basic processes, such as learning and perception, that are pursued through refined experimental methods. Personality tended to be seen as representing a different sphere of interest that deals with motivational concepts. To some, the general psychologist approached behavior on a relatively molecular level whereas the student of personality approached it on a relatively molar level.

This view still permeates the thinking of many students of behavior. Yet it is now realized that the general experimental psychologist and the worker in personality have much in common. Personality researchers find themselves utilizing more and more the methods of the general psychologist and the general psychologist is finding more and more that the individual difference variables of the personality researcher are germane to his work. Sanford (1963, p. 566) has put this complementary relationship as follows:

If general psychology has thus been stretching itself to embrace more and more of what used to belong to the personality field, so has research in personality . . . served to bring "variables of personality" to an increasingly prominent place in the attention of the experimentalist in general psychology. There have been literally hundreds of researches undertaken by personality psychologists and devoted to showing that variables of personality were predictive of individual differences in the performance of laboratory tasks. In recent years, general psychologists have often used the same design; witness a succession of experiments in which scores on the Taylor Anxiety Scale . . . have been related to conditioning.

Thus although the issue of the relationship between personality and general psychology can be expected to continue to arouse controversy, there now appears to be a trend in both camps toward "borrowing" variables and problems from each other.

Fourth: What are the types of questions which personality researchers should be asking? Without a great deal of effort one could produce a long list of problems that have been and are being investigated by personality researchers. We shall not critically evaluate a large number of these here. However, it seems worthwhile to present some of the questions that have significantly influenced the developing study of personality. The following list reflects some of the different sets of values to be found in the area of personality.

What are the elements that determine the individuality of human beings? For example, is the concept of habit, or of attitude, or of feelings basic to a description of the individual? Whatever these elements may be, are they equally important in the lives of different persons? Or is each person unique; that is, do the elements differ for different people? Are disturbed personalities explicable on the basis of a different set of terms from those that characterize normal individuals?

How are these elements organized? Can adequate accounts of behavior be made by reference to certain elements, but not to all of them? Or is knowledge of the complex product of the elements needed for a meaningful description of behavior and its determinants?

How important is life history in determining the present behavior of the individual? Will a science of personality come about more quickly through comparative studies of many people than through comprehensive, long term studies of a small number of selected persons? How important are such biological factors as genetic composition and physiological traits?

Which research methods prove most fruitful in making a science of personality? Should the emphasis be on observing individual subjects in their natural habitat? Or should it be on experimentation in the laboratory? Should it be on techniques that permit reliable assessment of the characteristics of many people?

Through the course of this book we shall find these questions recurring and influencing the behavior of the personality researcher.

REVIEW AND PROSPECTUS

In this chapter some of the important aspects of the area of personality have been considered. The interest of personality researchers in individual differences, especially those inferred from behavior has been stressed. The empirical nature of the study of personality, the influential roles of orientations, frames of reference, and theories that grow out of and give rise to particular types of empirical inquiry have been emphasized. These emphases seem important because of the nonrandom nature of the researcher's activities. Beliefs and values exert a strong force over his work.

These considerations will lead us to spend some time on selected orientations and views that have influenced contemporary research into personality. In the chapters of Part 1 we shall take up the general problem of personality theory and explore in greater detail such topics as construct validity. There we shall examine the ideas of theorists whose direct and indirect impacts on the area seem to be significant.

After this review of theoretical influences, we shall turn to empirical approaches used at present and in the past to study human behavior and its determinants. We shall begin with the inferences concerning individual differences and the relationship of these differences to an individual's responses (Part 2). Most personality tests may be regarded as a means of developing constructs whose predictive value can be determined. We shall be interested in finding out how such tests are constructed, in what ways personality is assessed, and how psychometric and other personality indices contribute toward the development of a scientific study of personality.

Whether the researcher deals with constructs that are studied through tests or behavioral measures, at a number of points in his procedure he will likely carry out experiments that permit the control and manipulation of variables bearing on his construct. We shall give considerable attention to the contribution of experimentation to the development of personality as an area for study (Part 3). To anticipate, we may say here that a systematic review of some of the problem areas that rely heavily on laboratory work clearly illuminates the inextricable tie between methodology and theory. One aim in examining the laboratory as a place for the study of personality is to trace the steps that begin with hunches, proceed to the development of methods for evaluating the hunches, and end in theories having explanatory and predictive values.

It seems inevitable that much theory and research in personality will be directed toward understanding the development of the person. For example, an investigator may be especially interested in the study of individual differences in the behavior of college students. It is unlikely that he can completely ignore the histories of the students and the manner in which they become the kind of individuals they are. Developmental psychology covers diverse facets of the process of personal history from womb to tomb. Students of personality development are particularly concerned with the flowering of individual differences and their link to overt and covert behavior. We shall endeavor to show the relevance of both longitudinal and cross-sectional studies to the increase of our knowledge of the person (Part 4). A major objective will be to isolate some of the significant influences in both the organism and the environment that help shape behavior. Among these influences are genetic predispositions, the family, and social factors, including the school.

The final section of this book, Part 5, will examine a topic that is best understood through the contributions of the preceding sections. This topic is the description, understanding, and modification of deviant behavior. The important question is: To what extent does an understanding of deviant behavior require different sets of constructs from the ones formulated for normal behavior? Implied in the question, of course, is the problem of the choice of criteria to be used in labeling behavior as deviant or abnormal. We shall describe some of these criteria.

Throughout the book we shall attempt to use a common frame of reference. We propose to adopt the one in which the scientific study of human behavior is best advanced by treating behavior in terms of overt responses, their interrelationships, and the overt and covert events that produce them. From the standpoint of the newcomer to the area, the challenge is not to learn by rote but to contribute to the development of a well-formulated theory of personality. A consideration of the number of factors to be embodied in such a theory gives one renewed awareness of and respect for the complexity of man. These factors include biological traits, which encompass aspects of the individual's genetic heritage and bodily functioning; environmental and historical events, which comprise such variables as family and society; and the joint effects of these various factors on the individual's behavior. Because these joint effects often manifest themselves covertly rather than openly, we shall strive toward the sort of personality theory that has as an important aspect the explication of necessary constructs. Although the well-articulated theory we seek cannot be anticipated in the near future, the student involved in its pursuit can only gain inspiration and incentive from its subject matter, the human organism.

Part 1

VIEWS OF PERSONALITY

AT THE PRESENT TIME personality theory must be regarded as being in a rudimentary stage. The complexity of its subject matter, man, and the relative newness of the field, make this virtually a necessity. Most "theories" of personality, though traditionally called *theories of personality,* cannot meet the criteria for truly scientific theory; they often are not clearly stated parsimonious formulations that integrate observations and facts; furthermore, they do not always imply new empirical relationships. For this reason when talking about traditional theories of personality, we shall actually mean "theoretical orientations." These orientations may be considered as formulations, hypotheses, and interpretations that are capable of stimulating the gathering of data, and of developing eventually into scientific theories.

Whether one maintains that a well-developed science of personality already exists or whether one accepts the view favored here that such a science is only beginning to blossom forth, interest remains strong in the question: What are some of the major hunches, ideas, and theoretical positions that have affected the development of the study of personality? In the next several chapters we shall review some of the leading theoretical orientations. Essentially these orientations will fall into four groups, but in no way are they mutually exclusive, nor are they necessarily at variance with one another on any particular issue. Any pair of them we might select at random will disclose similarities. However, the way in which they will be presented here will highlight the major issues, the differences of opinion, and the diverse emphases among them.

The first orientation to be considered will be psychoanalysis.

After a consideration of the contributions of its discoverer, Sigmund Freud, we shall survey several of the neo-Freudian systems. These are systems that have borrowed heavily from psychoanalysis but have sought to disassociate themselves to a considerable extent from the mainstream of Freudian thought through dissent from certain psychoanalytic tenets and differences in emphasis and approach. We shall also pay some attention to the ego psychologists who have been greatly influenced by Freud and have endeavored to introduce several new concepts within Freud's system.

A second orientation draws heavily on findings and theories from the psychology of learning. Although psychoanalytic and learning approaches to behavior have much in common, they diverge in emphases. Both psychoanalytic theory and the majority of learning theories try to cope with the concept of unconscious motivation, but the psychoanalysts go at this more strenuously than the learning theorists. Conversely, the preoccupation with learned behavior is much greater among and better articulated by the learning theorists, although psychoanalysts are also concerned with this phenomenon.

The third orientation is quite heterogeneous, even more so than the heterogeneity among the neo-Freudians. This group objects strongly to the psychoanalytic emphasis on drives and the unconscious, and pays more attention to the conscious functioning of the individual. Its members tend to be philosophically more optimistic than the Freudians. Among its major figures are Gordon Allport and Carl Rogers. They have presented provocative writings on treating the individual and the self concept from a psychological standpoint. The contributions of these men and the controversies surrounding them, along with those of other self-theorists, will be among our major concerns.

A fourth orientation emphasizes field theory concepts. Psychologists who employ these concepts, have studied the individual on the basis of (1) his perception of the world, (2) the totality of his functioning as an individual, and (3) the complex context in which behavior ordinarily occurs.

Something should be said about the scope of these important theoretical orientations. In later sections of this book we shall deal with theoretical problems that pertain to relatively restricted aspects of behavior, such as the tendency of the individual to adopt an aggressive stance in certain situations, and his tendency to be influenced by the attitude of others. Many of these more limited and firmer problems will be seen as offshoots of the more global issues to be discussed presently. This section, however, is concerned with broad-gauged, general, theoretical considerations that encompass many, or all, aspects of human behavior.

Even though a general theory may cover all phases of behavior, certain facts and observations almost inevitably have special significance in the theory's development. Hence, the presentation of each theoretical point of view will seek to suggest the kinds of empirical observations that stimulated the theory. We shall also endeavor to suggest some of the ways in which the theoretical orientations have been used to expand the horizons of knowledge; that is, we shall look for the new relationships uncovered through application of the theory. This calls for evaluating each theory in terms of how adequately its concepts are defined, how these concepts relate to observable events, the kinds of predictions which emanate from the theory, and finally, the accuracy of these predictions.

As we begin this inquiry into personality, we must recognize the importance of the point made in the previous chapter about the bearing of a researcher's interests and values on his investigatory activities. The same stricture applies to the student as he approaches an introduction to the field of personality. This book will introduce him to the study of personality, but it will take independent reading and thinking to develop and, if necessary, revise his own approach to human behavior.

2

Psychoanalysis

To many minds there have been four great scientific revolutions in the recent history of man. These are the revolutions wrought by Darwin, Marx, Einstein, and Freud. It is impossible nowadays, however much one may disagree with the tenets of psychoanalytic theory, to deny the enormous influence of Sigmund Freud on so many facets of everyday life. Freud's thinking touched on a broad spectrum of scholarly activity, ranging from psychology and psychiatry to pediatrics, anthropology, philosophy, economics, and art, and his monumental views have had a profound impact on such diverse matters as child-rearing practices, advertising, the writing of novels, and educational procedures (I. G. Sarason, 1965*a*, 1965*b*). The core of Freud's thought is to be found in his theory of psychoanalysis, one of the major paths to the study of personality.

Psychoanalysis is both a theoretical system and a technique of treatment. Studies of psychoanalytic psychotherapy suggest the need to regard many behavioral symptoms as products of intrapsychic events, such as anxiety and conflict (Jones, 1953–1957). By means of a "talking therapy," in which the patient reviews present and past events and the feelings associated with them, Freud sought to ferret out the underlying sources of symptoms and to reduce the patient's anxiety and conflict. Freud evolved this therapeutic technique from (1) his observations of patients, and (2) the inferences and conclusions he drew from his clinical work.

THE DATA OF PSYCHOANALYSIS

Two broad classes of observations provide the bulk of the data of psychoanalysis. One of these includes deviant behavior that is psychopathological or irrational in some large manner (Freud, 1926); the other is what Freud (1900, 1904) referred to as the "psychopathology of everyday life" and includes the so-called minor foibles and characteristics of human beings.

Observations of Deviant Behavior and Behavior in Psychotherapy

Any discussion of psychoanalysis must stress Freud's dissatisfaction with the effectiveness of neurological techniques in treating many physical problems. In early work carried out with Breuer (1895), Freud endeavored to come to grips psychologically with disorders, such as paralyses and anesthesias, that could not be explained by neurological concepts. These disorders had usually been called hysterical reactions. Although Freud's interest in a psychological account of the precursors of psychopathology began with observations of hysterical patients, the scope of his undertakings rapidly broadened to include other forms of deviation. As his immersion in the events of psychotherapy deepened, his attention was drawn increasingly to deviations of behavior that did not have physical components—paranoid ideas, strange and unusual behavior, and obsessive thoughts. From this broader area of interest, Freud sought to develop constructs that might prove valuable in thinking about behavioral and physical disturbances in adjustment.

For treating behavior disorders Freud was greatly interested in the process of free association as an avenue to uncovering latent conflicts. Similarly he showed great curiosity in the central role of the therapist in the patient's fantasy life. Why should a stranger, albeit a professional one, Freud wondered, become so invested with personal significance by the patient? Questions of this sort were important in generating evidence for Freud's concepts of unconscious determinism and transference.

Finally, although Freud preferred his "talking therapy" to hypnosis, he maintained an interest in the workings of the latter. In hypnosis, it may be suggested to the patient that upon awakening from an hypnotic trance he will perform a certain act but will be unable to state that his performance had been proposed to him. This is the phenomenon of posthypnotic suggestion—a suggestion made during hypnosis that has posthypnotic effects. Thus it might be suggested to someone to make a long-distance telephone call to a complete stranger half an hour after awakening from a hypnotic state. If the subject performs the posthypnotic act, there is the problem of accounting for his inability to give a conscious explanation of his behavior. For Freudians who wish to present a science of man, this kind of example provides evidence of the need for concepts of unconscious thoughts and motivations and of the general significance of variables within the organism.

Observations of Everyday Life Events

What determines the ability to learn and remember conceptual relationships and factual material? This broad question has captured the interest of many researchers in the area of learning. Freud contributed to the study of learning with his hypothesis of unconsciously motivated forgetting. If an individual were to forget a telephone number that he had called only twice or three times previously, there would be little eyebrow lifting. On the other hand, were he to have called that number 150 times during the past year, his inability to recall the number on the 151st occasion might be noteworthy, especially if in the past he had no difficulty in recalling it.

Everyone can think of situations in which the forgetting of facts and thoughts seemed strange and puzzling—forgetting a friend's name, forgetting to make an important telephone call, forgetting an important engagement, forgetting a relative's or a friend's birthday. Freud (1904) was most interested in this sort of example. He felt that the usual practice of laughing them off or attributing them to accident might be satisfactory for laymen, but for the scientist interested in behavior this would be folly. We shall see that the concept of unconscious forgetting plays an important role in Freud's theoretical scheme.

Another phenomenon often regarded as accidental and haphazard is dreaming. Laughing off odd and sometimes weird dreams occurs frequently. For psychoanalysts, dreams are significant aspects of behavior which demand explanation. Why do some people have nightmares and others not? Freud (1900) sought answers to such questions through his concepts of unconscious behavior and the structure of personality.

Another class of responses to which Freud (1904, 1938) paid close attention was that of errors, mistakes, and slips of the tongue. Until Freud noted that these sorts of responses were psychologically interesting, they, like dreams, were considered to be haphazard and not scientifically interpretable. Misplacing an important object or article, incorrectly perceiving aspects of the environment (for example, incorrectly identifying a friend down the street), and unintentionally misintroducing one person to another all exemplify this class of response. Usually this sort of mistake is not of great personal significance, but when it has undesirable implications we exhibit embarrassment and shame. Freud's question was: Why do these responses occur? He did not contend that they should not occur. Rather he was interested in the meaning of these mistakes and slips.

No listing of the observations that stimulated Freud in his work would be complete without mention of some questions he raised about the phenomenon of humor. At first glance one might think that there certainly must be more significant aspects of behavior than jokes to which the student of personality might direct his inquiry. For Freud, all aspects of behavior were relevant and germane to the study of behavior. For example, among the observations made by Freud, and these can be confirmed by each of us, was that an impressive proportion of jokes involved an element of hostility and had a poking fun element. Why should this be the case? And, why are people so variable in their response to humorous stimuli? Freud responded to these questions with hypotheses and speculations about covert events occurring within the individual.

So far we have dwelt on the data upon which psychoanalytic theory is based. We turn now to Freud's attempt to construct a theoretical system that might relate to and provide explanations of the diverse behaviors he observed. Although we have refrained from doing more than hint at the major constructs of psychoanalytic theory, one point is already clear. That is that psychoanalytic theory is not a formulation concerned with restricted segments of behavior, or even broad categories of response such as the behavior deviations; psychoanalytic theory is a general approach to *all* behavior. There is no behavior to which it cannot be applied. Let us examine this broad gateway to behavior.

PSYCHOANALYTIC THEORY

Concept of Determinism

Freud's preoccupation with the study of the individual's internal activities naturally gives rise to major concepts concerned with these types of mental or psychological events. To him all behavior had a sound reason behind it. No response occurred simply out of the blue. Reality—that is, the environment—and the personal world of the individual combined to determine each response emitted. Personal world refers to the sum of covert activities that characterize the individual. These activities, as we have learned, are not immediately apparent to the disinterested observer. Individuals may be able to report some internal conscious events, but reference to them must be made in terms of hypothetical notions. Freud believed that no behavior, discernible or not, was undetermined.

The psychoanalytic concept of determinism states that every response results from, or is a function of, prior stimulation (Arlow and Brenner, 1964; Brenner, 1955). A stimulus could be a previous response if its emission leads to the discharge of the second one. With mental events, such as thoughts and dreams, the principle of psychic determinism states that each such event is a function of prior mental events. This principle is, then, one of causality. An example of psychic determinism can be seen in the case of a scientist who submits an application for financial support of a research project to a foundation and is notified that the foundation has decided not to grant his request. The next morning, the scientist reports having had an unpleasant dream in which he was a student. In the dream he fails an oral examination given by a teacher. A psychoanalytically oriented observer would comment that the dream was not a random event. He would say that reality (notification of rejection of the application) had set in motion a series of psychic events, most of which were probably unconscious, and these events caused or determined the dream.

A concept of determinism in no way requires that each event be determined by only one preceding event or stimulus. Indeed, in most cases, there will be multiple determinants. Psychoanalysts use the term *overdetermination* when multiple conditions contribute to the determination of a particular response. In the example of the scientist the dream of failing a test in school may have flowered from a combination of factors. Thus it might have resulted from a feeling of having personally failed in the grant application, a feeling of shame at having been publicly rebuffed, inordinate anxiety experienced when taking tests in school, and parental punishment for failing in tasks.

The Conscious-Unconscious Dimension

Mental events such as thoughts and fantasies vary in accessibility. For example, a phone number that a person called several years ago might be quite inaccessible. The likelihood that he will be able to recall it is slight. On the other hand, a phone number called frequently in the recent past might be "on the tip of his tongue." That is, it is very close to accessibility or to awareness, and the possibility of success in recalling it is high.

In 1913 Freud suggested that the mind be conceived as having three parts or systems: conscious, preconscious, and unconscious (Freud, 1953–1955). As he saw it, aspects of mental life currently in awareness are *conscious,* thoughts not currently at the level of awareness but easily raised to it are *preconscious,* and thoughts that can be brought to awareness only with great difficulty are *unconscious.* In

Freud's view, the conscious idea takes the place of an unconscious mental process without the individual's being aware of the substitution. In so doing, the conscious idea becomes a symbol for reality; it is an activity representing an unconscious conflict or partly gratifying some repressed motive, if not both. This process of utilizing symbols widely is characteristic of psychoanalysis and is known as *symbolization.* Through it hidden events can be brought out of darkness into the light.

What determines the ease with which mental events can be made conscious? Other things being equal, Freud held that the amount of intrapsychic conflict was the major factor controlling the degree of awareness. Where related to significant intrapsychic conflicts, mental events resided in the unconscious. Preconscious thoughts, on the other hand, were not likely to bear much relationship to intrapsychic conflict and could be brought to awareness through a simple redirection of attention.

Originally Freud considered the three systems, conscious, preconscious, and unconscious, as major topographical aspects of the mind. Later he revised his formulation so that the major divisions of the psychic apparatus became the id, ego, and superego. In this formulation, known as the "structural hypothesis," Freud assumed that the roles of the id, ego, and superego varied along the conscious-unconscious dimension. Today this dimension is among the most widely accepted and studied aspects of psychoanalysis. The concept of determinism in thought and mental functioning, for instance, had seemed to many to be a logical extension of the scientific assumption of determinism in the natural world. All responses of an individual, normal or deviant, are assumed to be determined. In many cases the determinants can be expected to be unconscious ones. Thus an unfortunate and embarrassing slip of the tongue would be explained in terms of the breaking into consciousness of unacceptable and threatening impulses which until the occurrence of the slip had been kept in check.

Take the man whose wife had just knitted him a cap. The wife had also knitted caps for the children in the family. When the man wore the cap to his office, someone commented pleasantly and jokingly about its "loud" design. The cap-wearer responded with, "Well, my wife made caps for the other kids in the family, so I guess she felt she should make one for me too." Immediately, upon completing this utterance, the cap-wearer's face became very red. He visibly displayed many signs of disturbance and embarrassment. If one accepts a deterministic point of view, this slip of the tongue was not a random event, but rather had certain determinants. One might further assume that the man did not intentionally make this slip. If he did not wish to present himself as one of the children in the family, why did he do so? On the basis of the information one cannot attempt to answer this question adequately. However, one might speculate about the relationship between the man and his wife, and wonder about the extent to which on an unconscious level the man fantasies his wife as a mother figure for him. If this were the case, it would be expected that his fantasies, upon approaching awareness, would arouse anxiety and conflict. This is, in fact, what seems to have occurred.

With the available information we are not in a position to speculate about this interesting question: Why did unconscious material break into consciousness at the particular time it did? Presently we shall see that frequently recurring problems in psychoanalytic investigations and theorizing relate to the factors that determine the level of accessibility of mental events. Why are certain kinds of thoughts accessible to certain individuals and not to others? Can accessibility be manipulated? We have already noted that a major goal of psychoanalytic therapy is to bring unconscious material to the level of awareness. Later we shall examine some experimental attempts that have been made to study the conscious-unconscious dimension (Chapter 16).

The Drive Concept

As we have seen, Freud held that (1) all behavior was determined, and that (2) an important set of determinants were unconscious thoughts and mental processes. Now we introduce one of Freud's (1950*a*, 1950*b*) most important and controversial concepts, that of unconscious drives, or as he called them, *instincts*. Freud believed that all behavior was ultimately determined by these instincts and that their influences on behavior could be devious and disguised.

What was Freud's conception of drives? He believed, as we have seen, that behavior did not occur simply as a function of external stimulation. Furthermore, he noted a striving toward goals in behavior; to account for it Freud speculated about behavior's inner determinants. He believed that drives functioned as inner causative forces. These were psychological states of excitation which he thought to be genetically determined and analogous to or derived from biological states of excitation. Just as one might refer to an individual's reserve or capacity of physical energy, Freud viewed the psychological drives as the sum of psychic energy available to an individual.

An individual's drive or energy level impels him to activity. How, does this come about? Freud presumed that the drive level, in effect, set up in the individual an inner state of tension that the organism sought to reduce. This idea of tension-reduction is similar to the drive-reduction formulations found in several theories of learning (see Chapter 4). One problem with Freud's formulation is that the nature of the drives is ambiguous. In part as a reaction against the prudish atmosphere prevalent in Vienna at the turn of the century, Freud (1905) emphasized the drive of sexuality. However, his conception of sexuality was very broad and could be equated with the organism's total quest for pleasure and gratification. The Freudian drive concept is complicated by the reference of many writers to two drives, sexual or libidinal drive and aggressive drive. Whereas Freud related sexual drive to parts of the body, he did not name physical referents for aggressive drive. In what sense, then, is reduction of the aggressive drive pleasureful? The popular cliché that sex determines everything oversimplifies and distorts the tenets of psychoanalysis.

Much has been said about Freud's drive concept, the controversies over it never ending. Rather than become involved in these arguments, let us restrict ourselves at this point to a direct statement of the concept which may prove useful in later discussion. The statement includes points on which there is considerable agreement at least among psychoanalysts: Psychoanalytic theory employs a libido or drive concept. The theory assumes that drives perpetually seek gratification. If one wished to speak of the unit of psychic energy, the word *impulse* would probably be as appropriate as any. Psychoanalytic theory, then, hypothesizes a libidinal energy or drive and libidinal impulses. We shall assume that the individual's libidinal drive is the sum of his sexual and aggressive drives, although in some cases we shall refer to sexual or aggressive impulses alone. Aspects of the environment that provide the individual's gratifications will be called libidinal objects.

How do these libidinal impulses come about? As we have already indicated, Freud believed that libido was genetically determined; one person might have been born with a greater quantity of libido than someone else. The environment plays a substantial role in the libido concept since it is the environment that provides the gratification of impulses. Although all people experience hunger, they reduce their hunger drive in various ways. Furthermore, as individuals develop, the objects in the environment that can facilitate the discharge of libidinal impulses change. A rattle may be an adequate object for an infant, but for most adults this implement would be quite inadequate.

Several writers (Hilgard, 1956, 1962*a*) have expressed the view that a necessary element is missing in psychoanalytic theory. This element is a serviceable concept of learning. Can individuals learn to discharge energy in response to environmental objects? Can they learn to obtain libidinal gratification from substitute objects, that is, objects that originally did not provide the possibility of drive reduction? Most of us would probably answer both questions in the affirmative, but we might be hard pressed to outline in a precise way the process whereby changes occur in the response to environmental objects.

Despite the absence in Freud's writing of any kind of formal theory of learning, the concepts of *response acquisition* and *response change* play important roles in psychoanalytic theory. This is particularly true for Freud's (1923) developmental theory, to which we next turn.

DEVELOPMENTAL THEORY

Libidinal Development

What is the psychological world of the young infant? What is the nature of his conceptual life and how does it develop? Does he engage in fantasy of some sort? Direct factual data bearing on these questions are nonexistent. As adults we come to know something of one another's psychological worlds through verbal communication. We cannot interview the infant. Thus "knowledge" of the early psychological development of the infant is often acquired through inference.

Freud, on the basis of clinical studies, increasingly came to emphasize the influence of early childhood experiences on adult behavior. However, he lacked the techniques for conducting direct studies of young children's thought and fantasy processes. Because of this he was forced to make a series of educated guesses concerning early psychic development. Only in recent years have psychoanalytically oriented investigators begun to conduct empirical investigations of Freudian concepts of infantile development. Consequently, certain portions of the libido theory must be regarded cautiously and the tentativeness of many of Freud's hypotheses must be appreciated.

The infant, according to Freud, comes into the world as a creature of libidinal impulses. Irrational in nature, these impulses are unrelated to reality factors. The excitement of the infant may be viewed as caused by these impulses. Inability to inhibit the expression of impulses is an important characteristic of what has been called primary process thinking. Primary process refers to the initial thought processes of the human organism and is characterized by the inability to discriminate between the real and the unreal, and the me and the non-me, and by the inability to inhibit impulses. Were the infant in possession of a conventional vocabulary, we would, on the basis of psychoanalytic theory, expect his speech to resemble a "word salad," an unrestrained gushing forth of words, fantasies, and thoughts. Primary process thinking might also be described as free association in its purest form.

The motive power providing the pressure for this flow of irrationality is expressed by the concept of libido or id. As we have stated, libido or the id represents the total supply of psychic energy of the organism. In its original form this energy stems from a composite of sexual and aggressive needs. By sexual needs Freud referred to the sum of the organism's pleasure seeking and erogenous strivings for bodily satisfaction; by aggressive impulses Freud meant the need to destroy objects. Examples of aggressive tendencies in children, of course, are many. The urge to fight and destroy is observed in all children. The energy of the id may be expressed in a direct or raw form, as in the general excitement of the infant, or it may be attached to objects in the environment. Sexual and aggressive impulses expressed in the former form may be described as objectless energy, whereas when expressed in the latter manner they may be called *cathected,* or directed, energy. All psychic energy is thought to be objectless at birth but as the child develops he begins to establish *cathexes* involving persons and things in his surroundings. The process of investing psychic energy in aspects of the environment Freud called the establishment of cathexes. He believed that objects that provide gratification become cathected.

This picture of the infant, all will agree, is a far cry from the one that emphasizes its ingratiating, cherubic qualities. For Freud, the sexual and aggressive impulses of infancy and childhood were explanatory devices used to elucidate important aspects of behavior. He was especially concerned with explaining irrational thinking and aberrant behavior.

If we accept Freud's description of the child as a pleasure-seeking organism unable to control impulses and only tenuously aware of its environment, we shall probably also agree that the infant is not very well equipped to function as a member of society. Because the infant seeks the immediate gratification of impulses he is in no way capable of attending to and manipulating reality factors; he cries when he is hungry and does not notice that his mother is preparing his food. To emphasize the lack of boundaries between the real and the fantastic, the wish and the fact, Freud described the infant as adhering to a pleasure principle rather than to a reality principle. Although people do not completely give up adherence to the pleasure principle as they become older, they do come with development to operate also on the basis of reality factors and the requirements of the world in which they live. How does Freud describe and account for the development in the infant of the capacity for adherence to a reality principle?

Development of the Ego

We have said that the individual engaging in primary process thinking ignores reality and attends only to the gratification of impulses. Is this not an inherently dangerous process? The child sees a toy at the other end of the room and in accord with his pleasure-seeking strivings rushes to pick it up. He ignores the many other toys in his path to the cathected object and consequently trips on one of them, falls down, and cries. He cries because he has been frustrated both by failure to attain immediately his goal object and also by the pain of falling down. Gradually, the child comes to be more careful an more dexterous in attaining his goals.

A psychoanalyst would say that the process exemplified here is that of ego development. It is the gradual acquisition of skills and techniques for achieving one's goals and satisfying one's wishes within the bounds of the demands of reality. Freud hypothesized that initially libidinal or id impulses were completely oblivious to intercourse with reality, but that with development the ego became that sector of the psychic structure that controlled and guided all commerce between the individual and the world about him. When the ego has become firmly established, ties or cathexes between impulses and objects come to be mediated by it. The ego develops as a reaction to the frustrations and dangers faced by the child. We have already given examples of such frustrations. In Freudian theory what might otherwise be regarded as negative aspects of the environment (such as toys strewn over the floor) are viewed as serving quite positive and necessary functions. Were the child, through some magic, completely immune to frustrations and dangers he would lack the motivation necessary for ego development.

It is possible to discern two sources of danger for the child. One of these is the environment; the other is the conglomeration of id impulses. In the example of the child recklessly tearing across the room to a favorite toy, two sources of potential danger can be seen. The first is the perhaps unnoticed objects strewn in his path and over which he might trip and fall. However, even if the child had noticed the objects in his path it is possible that his impulse for immediate pleasure gratification (that is, reaching the desired toy) might be so strong as to impel him to ignore the reality danger and rush for the toy he wants. As hypothetically constructed by Freud, the ego's primary function is to preserve the integrity of the organism, to notice danger signals, and to adhere to the pleasure principle only within the bounds of the demands of reality.

From all this it would appear that ego development requires the child first to experience danger and then to develop abilities and techniques for coping with it. The reaction of the ego to danger Freud called *anxiety*. By anxiety he meant a general state of "unpleasure." The capacity to perceive danger and to react to it with anxiety was considered by Freud to be innate. However, because one perceives danger and reacts to it with anxiety does not mean that the cause of the danger is necessarily clear to the individual. When the source of the danger is clear psychoanalysts speak of *signal anxiety*. When the source of danger is either vaguely perceived or not perceived at all, they speak simply of anxiety. It is the tension and unpleasantness of the anxiety experience that drive the child to gain knowledge and mastery over the world about him and also to inhibit the expression of impulses. This latter ability of the ego to inhibit the expression of id impulses is a prime characteristic of secondary process or reality oriented thinking. Secondary process thinking adheres to the reality principle just as primary process thinking adheres to the pleasure principle. A strongly developed ego allows for pleasure gratification if its attainment does not arouse intolerable anxiety. Thus a trip to the top of the Empire State Building might provide impulse gratification, but most individuals would deprive themselves of the thrill of jumping off.

Does the theory of the id and ego mean that we may do anything we want to do so long as we do not meet danger or trouble? If this were true, Freud's theory would be patently inadequate upon even the most superficial inspection. The fact is, of course, that we frequently inhibit the expression of an impulse even though it would be safe to express it. Thus guilt may often be as effective as external danger in contributing to the inhibition of impulses. How Freud incorporated this aspect of behavior into his framework is the topic toward which we now turn. He did so through the superego concept; and following its mention and a review of Freud's description of development, we shall return to the functioning of the ego in the form of defense mechanisms.

Development of the Superego

Although objects on the floor represent potential physical dangers, there are other sources of equally potent danger. The child in our earlier example wanted very much to obtain a toy at the other end of the room. Let us substitute for that toy an expensive piece of china treasured by the child's mother. Although the child might desire the piece of china as much as he desired the toy he does not run to the piece of china. The danger that helps the child to inhibit any wish he might have to explore and play with the tabooed object is fear of punishment by his mother should he in any way damage it. This fear occurs initially only in the presence of the possible agent of punishment, the parent. Later it will occur in the absence of the parent. The process of superego development involves the steps from fear of punishment to the child's actual adoption of parental norms and standards of behavior.

At early stages of superego development the child will resist touching the tabooed object only if the possibility of punishment is made clear by the presence and behavior of the parent. At a later stage in superego development the child will avoid the object because *he* feels that it is important to preserve intact a valued object. The process by means of which the child comes to experience guilt and to adopt the moral and ethical code of the family and the society has been referred to by Freud as *introjection.* We shall see shortly how he closely linked introjection of parental standards with the resolution of the Oedipus complex.

In a sense, psychoanalysis handles the disparate concepts of id and superego similarly. Both of these portions of the psychic apparatus are seen as being relentlessly at work. The id is ever pressing for impulse gratification. The superego is rigidly arousing guilt and requiring expiation. As might be expected, the presence of both strong id and superego tendencies can pose considerable conflicts. The id seeks pleasure; the superego arouses guilt over attainment or anticipation of pleasure. How are such conflicts resolved? Resolution is accomplished, Freud argued, in the same manner as was described for the ego's resolution of the pleasure and reality principles. The ego executes all of our behavior, but this execution is determined by (1) the factors of reality, (2) the intensity of libidinal wishes, and (3) the amount of guilt aroused by the superego.

STAGES OF DEVELOPMENT. One of Freud's major contributions to the field of personality was his conjecture that childhood experiences might play significant roles in affecting behavior later in life. He was stimulated by the observation that in virtually all of his patients the process of free association eventually led to the recollection of early childhood events. A number of critics of Freud's theory of development have pointed out that it was based primarily on the recollections of adults rather than on direct observation of children. Still, the importance of the role of early experience in affecting later development is accepted by most workers in personality.

Of all the relationships formed by the young child, Freud felt that those with his parents were the most significant. Especially did he feel this to be true for the child's attachment to the parent of the opposite sex. The story of the formation of this attachment and its consequences is the hypothesis of the *Oedipus complex.* According to this hypothesis, the child, at approximately the age of five, forms in fantasy an intense love relationship with the parent of the opposite sex. In its extreme form, the child is believed to wish for the death of the parent of the same sex in order that the deceased parent's role might be assumed by the child. Thus the little boy is assumed to desire the role which his father occupies in relation to the mother. Similarly the five-year-old girl wishes to adopt her mother's role in relation to the father. Although the boy's fantasied relationship with his mother and the girl's wish to supplant the mother in relation to the father are properly referred to respectively as the Oedipus and Elektra complexes, we shall consider the general problem of the child's fantasies concerning the parent of the opposite sex as the Oedipus complex.

As might be expected, these conjectures about the nature of fantasy in young children created a tremendous furor in Europe and throughout the world at the turn of the century. Freud was castigated for attributing heterosexual wishes and impulses to little children. The story of the Oedipus complex together with Freud's theory of infantile sexuality was interpreted by many people as a direct attack on the traditional Western concept of the cherubic innocence of children. It does seem clear that the idea of the Oedipus complex is a direct attack on the assumed sexlessness and purity of fantasy and thought of children. But Freud was most assuredly not attributing adult heterosexual impulses to children. Much of the confusion concerning Freud's theories of infantile fantasy and behavior stems from the commonplace connotations of the word sex. The word typically is used to refer to specific classes of impulses experienced by adults in relation to each other. Freud's theories do not necessarily have to be interpreted as meaning that the five-year-old boy has incorporated adult heterosexual impulses into his fantasied relationship with his mother.

It will be remembered that psychoanalysis hypothesizes that at birth the infant's mental life consists completely of libidinal impulses. These impulses represent the sum total of the infant's psychic energy. As the infant develops, these impulses become attached to objects in the environment. This is the process of cathexis. As the child develops to maturity, the kinds of cathexes formed and the nature of the objects cathected are assumed to change. Thus in early infancy objects that can be placed in the mouth are frequently very highly desired. With the development of the child these mouthed objects usually lose much of the strength of their cathexes and other classes of objects become cathected. Freud believed that there was an orderly progression of periods in each of which particular kinds of objects became highly cathected.

The first important phase of libidinal development is the *oral* period—objects (nipples, rattles, fingers) that provide sensuous pleasure when in contact with the lips and mouth are highly cathected during this phase. The lips and the mouth were referred to by Freud as an erogenous zone. The important point to be kept in mind in considering this first phase of development (and later ones as well) is the assumption that the infant seeks pleasureful sensuous experiences, and that objects that provide this gratification become cathected. It is in this general context of libidinal gratification rather than of adult sexual impulses that Freud's theory of infantile behavior must be considered.

The second developmental stage postulated by Freud was the *anal* phase. During this period activities associated with the anus and defecation became highly cathected. The process of releasing feces, Freud suggested, is sensually pleasureful for the child and because of this the beginning of toilet training is frequently met by the child with resistance. This is so because toilet training makes increasing demands on the child to conform to social and parental norms. In some cases, as the child begins to learn and appreciate the importance to his parents of his toilet training, long periods of retention of feces may be observed. This obstinacy, in addition to increasing the sensual pleasure experienced when defecation actually takes place, also provides the child with a means of controlling and frustrating his toilet trainer. Prolonged periods of retention of feces was seen by Freud as frequently being associated with narcissistic and sadistic fantasies.

The oral and anal developmental stages are important not simply because of the erogenous experiences associated with them. They are also stages of social development. On a conceptual level the oral period may be viewed as the cathecting of objects entering the body; the anal period as the cathecting of objects leaving the body. The former phase includes experiences in which the infant acquires objects and receives nurture from the environment. Attitudes and expectations connected with behaviors of getting and receiving in adult life are considered to stem to a large degree from experiences during the oral phase. Adult attitudes concerning giving and nongiving, conformity and nonconformity, are believed to be heavily influenced by early anal phase experiences.

Another important early experience for the child is the perception of his body as a source of libidinal gratification. By the *phallic* stage of development Freud referred to the period of childhood roughly occurring between the ages of three and five during which the child himself and his genitals become cathected. The phallic period is assumed to be important not only because of masturbatory and stimulational activities associated with it, but also because of the psychological correlates of sensual phallic activities. Narcissism, the erotic feeling aroused by one's own body, is especially believed to be heightened during this period since the child himself is his main source of pleasure gratification. Of significance also is the change in the nature of the cathected object during the phallic stage. Whereas in the early libidinal stages many objects can be cathected and become a source of pleasure, during the phallic stage the child's body and particularly his genitals become the libidinal center.

During the subsequent *Oedipal* period an important change takes place. The focus or object of cathexis becomes an external object, a person, rather than the child's own body and genitals. This person is the parent whose sex is opposite to that of the child. The parent of the same sex, Freud believed, comes to be viewed as an obstacle to complete possession of the desired parent. It must be kept clearly in mind that this possession of the parent of the opposite sex must be seen from the point of view of the child. For example, even if the mother is viewed as a sexual object for the five-year-old boy, his sexual aim (that is, the nature of the gratification obtained from the cathected object) is quite different from the aim of the father he wishes to supplant. The sexual gratification obtained by the child during his Oedipal fantasies and experiences is of a more diffuse nature than the gratifications of its parents who are involved in an adult heterosexual relationship. Thus the Greek legend of Oedipus's killing his father and marrying his mother must be viewed as a symbol rather than as an example of the sort of phenomenon with which Freud was concerned.

How does the child come to terms with his Oedipus complex? It is clear the the child's Oedipal desires cannot be gratified. Frustration is inevitable because he is powerless to banish the like-sexed parent and to assume the vacant role. Perhaps the most important source of conflict for the child is its own strong positive affection for the like-sexed parent. There would, then, appear to be two important aspects of the child's Oedipal conflicts. One of these is fear of retaliation by the like-sexed parent. The other is guilt over death wishes fantasied about or expressed to the like-sexed parent.

Resolution of this stormy Oedipal conflict, according to psychoanalysis, comes about through a process involving identification with the parent of the same sex. By means of this process boys take on the masculine characteristics of their fathers and girls assume the characteristics of their mothers. Although it is an oversimplification, one might say that these events seem to follow the principle: if you can't lick 'em, join 'em. In any event, resolution of the Oedipus complex is assumed to result in the child's relinquishing his quest, at least at a conscious level, for the parent of the opposite sex.

Along with identification, repression is assumed to play a significant role in Oedipal resolution. Freud postulated that traumatic intrapsychic conflicts might be resolved by the forgetting of aspects of the conflict itself and also of experiences indirectly associated with it. Postulation of the role of repression in resolving the Oedipal conflict provides a psychoanalytic explanation for the poor memories people display for early Oedipal and pre-Oedipal experiences.

The long *latency* period, approximately between the ages of six and eleven has been viewed as essentially a period of recovery from the stress of the Oedipal stage. Little in the way of Oedipal behaviors is seen during latency. Instead, the basis for an adult sexual identification develops. The end of latency occurs at different ages for different children. In general, it culminates in the puberal and adolescent awakening of interest in the opposite sex.

From this review of Freud's ideas concerning psychosexual development it would appear that id or libidinal influences are assumed to be present from infancy to maturity. However, the specific cathexes formed at the various developmental stages are believed to undergo change. Furthermore, it is assumed that the influence of the ego and superego in determining the nature of the cathexes formed increases with maturation. This latter point is of importance, since the strengthening of the ego and superego inevitably leads to frustration of some id impulses and compromises in cathexis formation. The nature of these compromises leads directly to the next topic, the nature of the ego's defenses.

THE CONCEPT OF DEFENSE

Many popularizations of psychoanalysis erroneously create the impression that the use of defenses is undesirable and even objectionable. Many people, besides, have drawn the inference that the use of defense mechanisms is an indication of the presence of mental disorder. Neither of these beliefs reflects an accurate interpretation of psychoanalytic theory. The theory assumes the use of defense mechanisms by all people regardless of their level of adjustment or personality integration. If this is true, the question arises: what is the relationship between the concept of defense and personality adjustment? The answer to this question has two parts.

First, it should be understood that there are said to be not a few, but many techniques (defense mechanisms) for coping with anxiety (Freud, 1946). The emotionally healthy individual is one who does not cope with anxiety by the use of only one or a few of these mechanisms. The emotionally troubled individual uses only a small number of these techniques. Thus, individuals who are mentally ill frequently seem to respond rigidly to anxiety in a stereotyped manner. Just as lack of diversity in the development of instruments of war can lead to disaster, rigid use of only a few defenses in coping with the problems of living can lead to breakdowns.

A second factor, in addition to that of the number and variety of defenses available to the individual in coping with anxiety, is the nature of the particular defenses used. Although it would be an oversimplification to say that there are "good" and "bad" defenses, psychoanalysts argue that some defenses lead to anxiety reduction at the expense of rather serious distortions of reality, whereas other defenses lead to a much more limited blurring of reality. The psychoanalytic explanation of abnormal behavior rests heavily on this interpretation of the relationship between defense and distortion of reality. More will be said later concerning this relationship. Presently we shall review some of the mechanisms involved in the psychoanalytic interpretation of anxiety and defense.

Repression

Before he developed the anxiety theory that we have already mentioned, Freud had put forth what is referred to as his first theory of anxiety. Briefly, this theory postulated repression as the cause of anxiety. To a considerable extent because of the conservative culture of Vienna in 1900, Freud came to believe that the difficulties and anxieties that his patients presented were caused by the damming up of libidinal impulses. Repression was conceived as the process whereby these impulses became barred from consciousness. The tension created by this difficult repression of the impulse from consciousness inevitably, it was thought, led to anxiety. The main job of psychoanalytic treatment was to lift repression and bring to awareness the dammed up unconscious libidinal impulses.

Review of Freud's later anxiety theory will make clear the radical differences between his two theories of anxiety. In the 1920s, on the basis of his clinical work with patients, Freud (1926) concluded that his first theory had incorrectly stated the relationship between anxiety and repression. Although unconscious libidinal impulses remained of central importance, he increasingly came to believe that anxiety resulted not from repression, but from intrapsychic conflict stemming from the clash of libidinal impulses, superego demands, and reality factors. Repression was now seen as a consequence rather than as a cause of anxiety and was thought to serve an anxiety-reducing function. This repressive function was believed to be accomplished by barring from consciousness anxiety-laden thoughts and impulses. If, for example, an individual has formed a very strong positive cathexis or attachment to a particular object, but thinking of this highly cathected object leads to intrapsychic conflict and anxiety, then the anxiety may be reduced by the formation of what may be called anti- or countercathexes to the object which transpose thoughts about the object to the unconscious level. The formation of these anticathexes which lead to the reduction or elimination of conscious thoughts about the object was called repression.

Can repressed thought be brought back to conscious awareness? Psychoanalysts believe that there are two classes of repressed mental contents, those that cannot be returned to consciousness and those that, through such means as psychoanalytic treatment, can be brought back to awareness. The former class of mental contents have been referred to as repression proper and the latter have been labelled as after-expulsion. It is obviously difficult to see how repressed thought that cannot be returned to awareness can ever be studied in any kind of objective scientific manner. In actual practice the term repression is used to refer to both recoverable and nonrecoverable psychic contents. The ease with which repressed material may be returned to awareness is believed to be a function of the strength of the initial cathexes, the strength of the anticathexes and the level of ego development.

Overuse of repression, however, may have many unfortunate consequences owing to the inability of the individual to come to terms and deal with repressed material. Study of the Oedipus conflict suggests that much of the anxiety and tension experienced by the adult in interpersonal relationships may be indirectly and complexly related to experiences and events associated with the Oedipal conflict. Psychoanalysts believe that complete repression of memories and derivatives of this conflict represents a barrier to better understanding of the conflict and to the improved adjustment of the individual.

As yet unresolved is the question of repression's primacy in the defensive structure. Whereas some writers have felt that repression is basic to all other defensive operations, other have tended to regard repression as one important defense among many. There seems little basis for taking a rigid stand on this issue in view of the lack of empirical evidence concerning interrelationships among the defenses. What can be said is that methods of defense can be quite complex. It is difficult from a psychoanalytic point of view to think of an aspect of behavior that is influenced by only one defense mechanism. This is in accord with the concept of overdetermination which states that any single aspect of behavior is influenced by a complex of psychological factors.

Although we shall not attempt to study exhaustively all of the defense mechanisms, it will be helpful to mention several of them in order better to indicate the various ways in which the ego is assumed to erect defenses.

Intellectualization

Intellectualization frequently takes the form of a superficial insight into one's problems. The intellectualizer may be able on a verbal level to present a coherent, well-reasoned analysis of himself and his motivations. What is missing in this intellectual analysis is the communication of relevant emotions and anxiety. Intellectualization may be seen as an isolation from awareness of emotional reactions. The intellectualizer often attempts to explain his irrational impulses and thoughts in purely rational terms. Used to excess, psychoanalysts believe that intellectualization has a rigidifying effect on the individual because the defense keeps the individual from coming to grips with impulses and strivings underlying his behavior.

Reaction Formation

When an individual behaves in a way directly opposite to what one would expect on the basis of his impulses, the defense of reaction formation is quite likely involved. For example, the mother who unconsciously feels strong hostility toward her child may, because her hostility arouses anxiety, actually cope with the impulses by expressing their opposite in the form of overly solicitous and overly protective behavior. Freud felt that although the behavior was the opposite of the impulses felt, there might still be vicariously unconscious gratification of impulses. Reaction formation represents a compromise between id and superego demands. However, the price paid is frequently a distortion in interpersonal relationships.

Sublimation

Although there is some question concerning the appropriateness of regarding sublimation as a defense mechanism, there is agreement among psychoanalysts that it serves anxiety-reducing functions and therefore possesses some similarity to them. Sublimation is the situation in which the most direct form of impulse gratification is blocked and this frustration is met by obtaining gratification through socially useful substitutes. For example, the individual ridden by hostile impulses may, instead of committing violent acts, express his aggression in the form of useful literary, intellectual, and social criticism—as for example, might be true of some drama, music, and art critics. If one views the socialization process as the gradual taming of raw aggressive and sexual desires, sublimation can be viewed as playing an important role in this process. Thus, intellectual and imaginative creativity may be viewed as classes of sublimated behaviors. Freud believed that by means of sublimation the drives could be expressed but in ways that furthered the good of society.

Denial

Several of the defense mechanisms inferred from adult behavior seem strikingly to resemble aspects of the young child's behavior. For example, the child frightened of a particular person, animal, or object might reduce his feelings of terror by behaving as if the fearsome stimulus were not actually present. That is, the existence of anxiety-provoking objects might be denied. Although common in children and occasionally observed in all adults, this defense of denial can become for some adults their primary means of reducing tension and anxiety. In general, we speak of denial when an individual denies the existence of relevant aspects of the environment.

There are two bases for regarding denial as an immature way of defending against anxiety. In the first place, the inability of the adult to go beyond the anxiety-reducing techniques of the child suggests a lack of ego development. In the second place, and probably of greater importance, is the fragility of denial. One may banish from consciousness thoughts of real danger in the environment, but the fact of the danger's presence remains. Thus denial results in a serious distortion of reality and in no way allows the individual using the defense to cope adequately with the danger confronting him.

Projection

Another defensive maneuver sharing the same characteristics of immaturity as denial is the mechanism of projection. Whereas denial represents primarily a distortion of external reality, projection involves also a distortion of internal reality. In projection, personal characteristics or impulses that arouse anxiety in an individual are externalized by attributing them to others. For example, the individual made anxious by his own aggressive impulses toward objects in the environment may reduce his anxiety by transferring, as it were, his own hostility to someone else. The individual himself thus becomes a virtuous human being whereas the person or persons upon whom he has projected his hostility become villainous agents of aggression. In addition to distorting reality seriously, the individual whose primary defense is projection also may create new sources of anxiety by incurring the wrath of individuals he accuses of possessing the undesirable projected impulse.

Regression

Of all reactions to anxiety and danger, regression in its extreme forms may be the most dramatic and debilitating. Regression, Freud believed, is the process by means of which an individual reverts to modes of response and means of gratification more characteristic of an earlier developmental level. An example from childhood is the regression frequently seen in a child upon the birth of a sibling. The regression does not necessarily involve behavioral debilitation in all spheres of behavior but may be focused in such areas as bowel and bladder control, self-feeding, and peer relationships. Perhaps the most tragic examples of regression are seen in those adult individuals in mental hospitals who have regressed to levels comparable to those of the child. Regression, like denial and projection, involves marked distortion of reality, and does not provide a basis for realistically coping with anxiety.

REVIEW OF MAJOR PSYCHOANALYTIC CONCEPTS

As we have presented psychoanalytic theory, two underlying assumptions have been emphasized. The first is the idea of psychic determinism, according to which current behavior and mental events are determined by preceding events. The second assumption is that not only is reference to unconscious events necessary in explaining overt behavior, but also that, indeed, most mental events are not immediately accessible to the awareness of the individual. Associated with this assumption is the concept of overdetermination which underlines the multiple causation of overt behavior.

Having decided that unconscious processes exerted a powerful influence over overt behavior, psychoanalytic theorists had to face the next theoretical hurdle, the development of hypotheses concerning the nature of these processes. As we have seen, Freud did not offer only one hypothesis. He propounded many, and felt free to change his formulations when it seemed necessary (for example, his first and second theories of anxiety). In terms of common acceptance among psychoanalytic writers, however, his concept of a psychic apparatus comprised of id, ego, and superego has probably turned out to be Freud's major contribution. In it, he has described within the same system both unconscious and conscious processes.

There are two important ways in which the id-ego-superego constructs may be viewed. One is in terms of their interrelationships. The other is in terms of their genesis. Psychoanalysts assume that in any given situation, an individual's behavior could be predicted if one had an accurate picture of id-ego-superego relationships at that time. The interplay of these forces characterizes the dynamic aspects of the individual's personality. The history of the id-ego-superego constellation is the major genetic problem of psychoanalytic theory. The optimal way of approaching personality from the standpoint of psychoanalysis would seem to be through joint study of both dynamic and genetic factors. However, as we shall see later when discussing research on psychoanalytic hypotheses, either the dynamic or genetic aspects of personality have been emphasized more frequently in given studies. These two approaches can perhaps best be seen by mentioning some problems suggested by each.

A dynamic approach directs us to the problems raised by the following types of questions: (1) Since psychoanalytic theory assumes that there are individual differences in amount of libidinal energy, how much of this energy is possessed by a particular person? (2) What are the levels of development of the id, ego, and superego for that person? (3) What is the individual's defensive posture; that is, what is his repertory of defenses, and how effective is it?

Some genetic problems that stem from psychoanalytic formulations are raised by these questions: (1) To what extent is there an orderly progression of cathexis formation; that is, to what extent are the hypotheses of oral, anal, phallic, etc., stages of development correct? (2) What effects do early experiences have on later behavior? For example, is the adult cigarette smoker's behavior determined by events in early infancy?

Questions such as these have stimulated much empirical investigation of psychoanalytic concepts (Sears, 1943; Shakow and Rapaport, 1964). Let us turn now to some problems related to the empirical study of psychoanalytic theory.

EMPIRICAL PROBLEMS IN THE STUDY OF PSYCHOANALYTIC THEORY

The major stumbling blocks in the path of straightforward determination of the construct validity of psychoanalysis are the sheer scope and generality of the theory and, probably most important, the large number of interacting constructs contained within it (Hall and Lindzey, 1957; Rapaport, 1959). It will be remembered that to be testable, constructs must be empirically rooted; they must be tied to reality by means of operational definitions.

When dealing with but one construct, the operational tying of the construct to empirical observations is feasible. However, in the case of psychoanalysis, and any other system with a large number of hypothetical constructs such as Hull's learning theory (Hull, 1952), one often has difficulty in tracing empirically all of the interacting terms. That is, when an individual responds in a particular way, the psychoanalytically oriented observer must simultaneously consider a number of interacting covert variables in order to offer a possible account or explanation of the observed response. For example, interpreting a slip of the tongue would require some knowledge of the situation in which the slip occurs, the characteristics of the individual's id, ego, and superego, and their contents. In addition, we would want to know the psychosexual history of the individual.

Psychoanalytic theory can provide *possible* explanations of all behaviors displayed by people because of the number of explanatory concepts contained within it. However, employing so many constructs relating to covert nonobservable events, it frequently cannot state with a high degree of confidence which of many explanations is the correct one.

Earlier we stated that the use of constructs relating to internal events was of great importance and value to workers in the area of personality. Now, it might appear that we are going back on our word. We have just said that Freud put so many processes and mechanisms inside the person that we can never be sure which ones are responsible for behavior observed at any particular time. This need not be interpreted as a criticism of hypothetical constructs *per se*. Rather, it may be taken as a criticism of the premature proliferation of interacting constructs that are ambiguously related to overt behavior. It is reasonable to say then that, lacking the needed empirical knowledge, psychoanalytic formulations attribute to covert processes a degree and kind of complexity which, *in toto,* cannot be objectively evaluated.

Psychoanalytic theory as an entity has presented too many interlocking constructs too soon. This does not mean that it is an invalid theory. Rather, this means that, at present, there are no available methods and procedures that can demonstrate the validity of the orientation as a general theory.

The Contribution of Freud

If the assertion is correct that Freud extended himself too far conceptually in his formulation of mental functioning, how may we proceed in evaluating his contribution to knowledge of behavior? Freud and psychoanalytic theory have been the stimuli for much heated controversy in psychology, psychiatry, and related fields (I. G. Sarason, 1965*a*, 1965*b*). The preceding comments may give the impression that the view of psychoanalysis presented here is essentially a negative one. Actually, pointing out some of the crucial problems in testing the theory empirically is simply facing some of the facts of scientific life. Let us, therefore, turn to some other facts that provide a more complete perspective for an evaluation of Sigmund Freud's contribution.

One of the major achievements of Freud's schema was the number of germinal concepts and observations it contained. Although it is usually hazardous to attribute to only one man the discovery of a topic or area, it seems reasonable in this case to assert that no man exerted an impact equal to Freud's on the scientific study of the determinants of human behavior. He has influenced us incalculably by the very fact of attempting psychological explanations of so many varied phenomena, such as dreams, humor, slips of the tongue, misplacing objects, and social relationships. Even if it turns out that all of his explanations were erroneous, Freud's place in the development of psychological science seems secure because of the many classes of overt behavior to which he directed attention. Freud may or may not have successfully integrated a large number of relationships, but he certainly did bring to light a large number of behaviors and events that psychology heretofore had not considered significant parts of its subject matter.

To assist in gauging Freud's contribution, it would perhaps be well to list some of the research areas on which his impact has been especially great.

PSYCHOTHERAPY. To begin with the area of psychotherapy seems appropriate since it was on the basis of his talks with patients that Freud developed his theoretical system. Whereas Freud's immediate interest was in psychoanalysis as a form of therapy, concepts such as transference, countertransference, and resistance have implications for all interpersonal situations. The applicability of these concepts has gone far beyond the psychoanalytic situation. The concepts have influenced the development of virtually all forms of psychotherapy, and have opened up significant problem areas in the study of psychopathology (Ford and Urban, 1963). For example, the whole burgeoning field of psychosomatic medicine has deep roots in psychoanalytic theory.

DEVELOPMENTAL PSYCHOLOGY. Even casual perusal of psychoanalysis clearly reveals the importance it places on the genesis of behavior. Although one justifiably can criticize psychoanalytic theory for minimizing the importance of developments in adult life, it has provided a wealth of hypotheses concerning the events of infancy and childhood (Baldwin, 1955). We shall talk about a number of these events in Part 4.

PROJECTIVE TESTS. While psychoanalytic thinking has helped generate research on child development, particularly of a longitudinal nature, it has also contributed to the development of cross-sectional studies of personality through psychological tests (S. B. Sarason, 1954; Schafer, 1954). Such tests as the Rorschach and association techniques, which present ambiguous stimuli to subjects and require them to interpret the stimuli, have been developed and are used widely in research and clinical work (see Chapters 12 and 13). Thus, for example, with the Rorschach test, clinical psychologists have attempted to assess individuals' levels of primary and secondary process thinking, defense mechanisms, and guilt reactions.

EXPERIMENTAL STUDY OF PERSONALITY. Most psychologists interested in research in personality have not adopted the entire gamut of psychoanalytic concepts. Rather they have followed up leads and hypotheses from psychoanalytic theory which seemed amenable to experimental study. Many of these leads have influenced studies of perception, learning, and thinking. The defense mechanism of repression has perhaps received the most extensive experimental study of all psychoanalytic concepts (see Chapter 16). Certainly, an experimentalist cannot study or duplicate in the laboratory the real life histories of individuals, but he may be able, through cross-sectional laboratory experiments, to gain a high degree of control over relevant variables (Hilgard, 1956, 1962*a*).

These four areas, general as they are, do not exhaust the number of fields that have directly felt the impact of psychoanalytic theory. But they do suggest the broad influence of Freud's formulation on empirical investigations of behavior. In many cases Freud's ideas have stimulated investigations whose results were contradictory to his formulations but which, nevertheless, increased knowledge of human behavior. In our view, Freud's contributions must be assessed in terms of the observations he made and the scientific developments he influenced and stimulated. This would seem to be a much maturer basis for judgment than simply asking the question: was he right or wrong?

It is impossible to express neatly or quantitatively the validity of psychoanalytic theory, but it is possible to observe the contribution of Freud to a science of personality. It seems reasonable also to attempt to assess the deficiencies and assets of Freud's theory. Proceeding in this manner it is consistent both to damn and praise psychoanalysis. It is necessary to recognize Freud's preeminent status as an observer and thinker and to be aware of weaknesses in his formulations. In this latter regard the following problems seem particularly pressing: (1) the inability to relate certain concepts to observable events (such as primal repression); (2) the lack of integration of reality factors with psychic determinants in explaining behavior; (3) the need to clarify and quantify the conscious-unconscious dimension; (4) the difficulty of simultaneously manipulating the various hypothesized covert factors; (5) the lack of clarity of the drive concept and the absence of quantitative indices of it; (6) the absence of a well-formulated concept of learning.

Criticizing in this way, however, does not dispose of the question of an over-all assessment of psychoanalytic theory. The reader will be in a much better position at the end of this book than at this point to come to his own evaluation because the impact of psychoanalytic theory can be fully appreciated only after systematic study of the subject matter of the field of personality. Many topics we shall consider have been greatly affected by psychoanalytic ideas. Consequently, we shall make no attempt here to weigh and summarize neatly Freud's contribution. However, as may already have been implied, it is our view that, on balance, Freud has made an enormous contribution to the development of a science of personality.

3

The Neo-Freudians

Most of the neo-Freudians are of importance primarily because of their rejection of aspects of psychoanalysis and the approaches that they suggested as alternatives. Consequently our discussion of the neo-Freudians will be presented primarily in these terms.

JUNG

Jung's break with Freud in 1912 was probably the most dramatic of all the disputes with the leader of the psychoanalytic movement. This was so both because of Freud's ego involvement in his theory and because of Jung's position within the movement. Just as Freud fulfilled the role of king, so Jung seemed clearly to be prince and heir apparent. What issues led to Jung's turning away from psychoanalysis?

The major point of dispute was the Freudian libido theory. Jung rejected the idea that libidinal energy was necessarily sexual in nature and exclusively pleasure oriented. For him, the concept of libido was valuable but he conceived of it as a life force which could be channeled in many directions as development proceeded. Thus Jung did not object to Freud's libido concept on any Victorian grounds, but on purely intellectual grounds. As the break with Freud widened, Jung developed his own group of followers and his approach came to be called Analytical Psychology. Although this psychology involves an exceedingly complex theoretical framework, Jung seemed to feel toward the end of his career that the facts relating to his theory were more important than the theory as a systematic entity (Hall and Lindzey, 1957).

The data that Jung treated during his long career included observations made in psychotherapy, literature, folklore, religion, and the occult, and experimental laboratory work (Jung, 1938, 1953, 1959). This collection of data may seem strange at first glance. One does not usually pair the occult with the laboratory. The pairing comes about primarily as an outgrowth of the many facets of Jung's career. Early in this century, he was influenced considerably by developments within experimental psychology. Following up some of Galton's work on word-association methods, he conducted a number of experiments dealing with reactions to word-association tests (Jung, 1918). He related the results of these studies to complexes and conflicts within the individual. However, as Jung became more deeply immersed in the concepts of analytical psychology, his interests in experimentation diminished and his interests in written and spoken history increased.

As his views changed, and as he became more involved in studying cultures and their literature, another major source of disagreement between him and traditional psychoanalysis emerged. This pertained to the concept of development. For Freud, the structure of the adult's personality was determined in early childhood. Furthermore, the individual's libido and early history were seen as decisive in shaping his later life. Jung rejected this notion of causality. In his view, there had to be much more room for creative development in the adult than Freud's formulation permitted (Jung, 1953). Jung used the term *self-actualization* to express the ability of the adult to enrich his inner life and to better his appreciation and understanding of it. This process of self-actualization appears to be somewhat analogous to the concept of evolution and implies an evolutionary step beyond the ability of the individual, through his ego, to have an awareness of external reality. Self-actualization suggests that both inner and outer reality are somehow integrated by the individual. In Jung's view, psychoanalysts, psychologists, and workers in related fields have not paid adequate attention to self-actualization and to changes in adult life, and in particular to the changes in older adults. As Jung perceived the broad sweep of human development, the first half of life was concerned with the exploration of external reality through scientific and other means. During the later years self-actualization reached its zenith. If successful in the actualization process, the individual then attained fulfillment and integration.

The concepts of an inner world and of a world of outer reality are also reflected in Jung's (1933) treatment of libido which, it is assumed, may be directed in two ways. Interest in aspects of the world are said to reflect extraversion and concern with one's inner life, introversion. Both attitudes are found in each individual, but the balance between them presumably will vary from person to person. Moreover, an individual may be overtly extraversive, but covertly introversive. In addition to suggesting introversion and extraversion as sources of individual difference, Jung described four psychologial functions or modes. These were: (1) thinking, which reflects the ideational component of mental life; (2) feeling, which reflects evaluations made by the individual; (3) sensing, which provides the individual with knowledge of the world about him; and (4) intuition, which, in the deepest sense, brings the individual into contact with reality; that is, extending beyond the meaning of external reality.

For Jung, the future was much more important than for Freud. Not only did Jung express a more optimistic view of development than Freud (the idea that man is constantly evolving into a better organism), but he also expressed ideas which suggest teleological elements. In Jung's view, to understand the present as well as possible, one must consider the future and anticipations of the future; man looks to the future and the view he perceives influences his present behavior.

In a sense, Jung criticized Freud at both ends of the developmental spectrum. We have described his concern with psychoanalysis's neglect of adulthood and his own ideas with regard to self-actualization. He offered ideas about hereditary influences on personality. Central among these is the notion of a *collective unconscious*. The collective unconscious consists, Jung believed, of ancestral, racial memories. These memories, he held, reflect systems of reactions characteristic of our ancestors. He referred to these as archetypes.

Jung conceived of a mental apparatus as consisting of several aspects: the collective unconscious ("the deposit of ancestral experience"), the personal unconscious which is composed of repressed and suppressed personal memories, and the conscious mind which comprises perceptions, memories, attitudes, and feelings.

This brief presentation does not try to do justice to the complexity of Jung's concepts. His collected works provide detailed accounts of the concepts upon which we have touched and of many others as well. Our aim has been to indicate the ways in which Jung's approach to personality contrasts with that of psychoanalysis. As we have noted, the issue that started Jung on his way to a sharp break with psychoanalysis was that of Freud's sexual interpretation of libido which Jung rejected. Jung also objected to the Freudian emphasis on the strong causative role of early childhood experiences in shaping adult life. His concepts of the collective unconscious and self-actualization represent efforts not only to explore variables untouched by Freud, but also to present a much more optimistic view of man. To be sure, we are limited by our social past; Jung, however, provided ample opportunity for human growth. Although Jung's developmental views differ importantly from Freud's, and although many of his concepts do not have counterparts in psychoanalysis, there are nevertheless many similarities between analytical psychology and psychoanalysis. For example, whereas Jung described the oral, anal, and phallic periods in terms different from Freud's, the events traced by Freud were similar to those described by Jung. This is also true of the defense mechanisms and many dynamic explanations of behavior.

Jung's Contribution

Jung's analytical psychology contains even more hypothetical terms concerning covert processes than Freud's psychoanalysis. The doubts expressed about the usefulness of psychoanalysis's introducing too many constructs too soon would certainly be greater in the case of Jung. As constructs dealing with internal events proliferate, any challenge or criticism of explanations of behavior may easily be avoided. Very general theories of behavior may have the cards stacked in their favor by the introduction of a sufficient number of explanatory terms that can be exploited as needed.

Cumbersome as it seems to be, Freud's theory has been of great value, as we noted in the previous chapter, in influencing thinking about behavior and in suggesting facts and relationships that are empirically testable. On the other hand, although some of Jung's notions have led to research efforts, most things unique to his theory have stimulated very few empirical investigations. Nevertheless, many of these may indeed be regarded as salutary. Jung's emphasis on development over the full life cycle, his early work on word-association, his ideas regarding the balance between introversion and extraversion, his use of literature, folklore, etc. as leads for hypotheses, and his insights into the phenomena of psychopathology (which we have not discussed) are certainly of significance. Nevertheless, the over-all Jungian empirical contribution to a science of personality has not been great. In fact, some of his concepts, particularly the idea of a collective conscious, have elicited repugnance among most members of the scientific community.

To summarize, Jung's writing at the anecdotal and literary levels provides many stimulating ideas and suggestions. One cannot help observing that at the scientific, or even prescientific level (1) there is a paucity of adequate research evidence generated by or related to many of Jung's views and (2) there exist barriers created by the profusion and complexity of these views, and also the lack of ties to observables, all of which prevent the testing of Jung's views through acceptable scientific methods.

ALFRED ADLER

Adler and Jung stand together as two members of the original group of psychoanalysts who early broke with Freud (Jones, 1953–1957). However, the similarity between them does not go far beyond this common characteristic. Jung, after rejecting many Freudian concepts, developed a set of ideas and hypotheses that rivals psychoanalytic theory in complexity. Adler, on the other hand, developed what he called Individual Psychology. In it he used a relatively small number of concepts, many of which were phrased in everyday terms. In fact, Adler has been criticized for having presented too simple a view of human behavior (Hall and Lindzey, 1957).

Adler objected to psychoanalysis on the grounds that Freud had greatly overestimated the importance of biological—sexual—drives as determinants of human behavior. He argued that the individual's social context was of much greater significance to development than Freud had admitted. Psychological maladjustment, he believed, should be examined essentially in terms of the individual's role and mode of functioning in society. In part because of Adler's emphasis on the effective functioning of the individual in society, the form of psychotherapy which he developed was much more practically oriented than are either Freudian or Jungian therapies. In working with patients, he was more interested in the here and now than in making the unconscious conscious and in reconstructing the past (Adler, 1927*a*, 1927*b*, 1930; Ansbacher and Ansbacher, 1956).

The concept most frequently associated with Adler is that of the *inferiority complex.* Adler viewed the individual as constantly striving toward goals and seeking self-actualization and fulfillment. Like Jung, Adler emphasized the effect of the striving toward goals on current behavior. These goals, he felt, might be either realistic or the product of fictions created by the individual. Realistic or not, all persons strove to attain their concept of superiority, a striving that Adler regarded as innate. Inferiority feelings, he felt, increased in proportion to the individual's failure to attain his goals. The following quotation suggests Adler's (1930, p. 398) conception of the individual's innate striving toward perfection:

> . . . I began to see clearly in every psychical phenomenon the *striving for superiority*. It runs parallel to physical growth. It is an intrinsic necessity of life itself. It lies at the root of all solutions of life's problems, and is manifested in the way in which we meet these problems. All our functions follow its direction; rightly or wrongly they strive for conquest, surety, increase. The impetus from minus to plus is never-ending. The urge from "below" to "above" never ceases. Whatever premises all our philosophers and psychologists dream of—self-preservation, pleasure principles, equalization—all these are but vague representations, attempts to express the great upward drive.

Implied in Adler's conception of superiority and inferiority is the idea that inability to attain goals fully must be assessed in terms of the private world of the individual. In some cases both society and the individual will share common interpretations of inferiority; in perhaps the majority of cases, however, this will not be true. Nevertheless, it may safely be said that all persons experience varying degrees of inferiority feelings at many points in life. For example, all children experience feelings of inferiority since they are, in a real sense, inferior. They have many goals and desires whose attainment and fullfillment are, for them, beyond the realm of possibility.

Although personal goals influence the behavior of all, the ways in which they lead people to order their lives will vary from one person to another. Adler used the term *style of life* to refer to a person's unique approach to life and to himself. The style of life is shaped by the kinds and intensity of inferiority feelings experienced by the individual. In general, Adler believed that Freud overestimated the child's inferiority experiences in the sexual sphere and underestimated the social environment as a stimulus for inferiority. Psychotherapy from an Adlerian point of view, consequently, attempts (1) to come to grips with the need for practical revisions in a person's style of life or life plan, and (2) to re-educate the individual in terms of his perception of and adjustment to the social environment. This re-education, Adler hoped, would permit the individual to give up or change his neurotic ways of compensating for perceived inadequacies.

Since Adler emphasized so strongly the uniqueness of the individual's life style, it seems appropriate to refer to his approach as an individual psychology. This individual psychology represents a striking contrast to Freud's drive theory. Despite Freud's efforts to make psychoanalysis a value-free system, many students have observed a strong vein of pessimism about the nature of man in some of his writings. Adler, on the other hand, clearly seems to have been an idealist and optimist. True, social influences can exacerbate the individual's sense of inferiority and distort the personality. But for Adler, man had an inherent positive involvement with people and an inherent capacity for creativity and self-development. Unfortunately, in too many instances, this normal striving for perfection becomes transformed into a neurotic search for superiority and power. But, whereas Freud spoke of the individual's behavior as a function of latent conflicting forces, Adler described man as a doer, striving toward perfection (Ansbacher and Ansbacher, 1956).

Adler's Contribution

Almost always, when a writer goes out on a speculative limb, controversy rapidly develops in attempting to evaluate his contribution. Some observers will interpret his efforts as foolhardy hypothesizing in the absence of data; others will be impressed by his heroism in striking out in new and challenging directions. Major differences of opinion exist concerning the originality of Adler's contribution. Some writers have seen Adler as more comprehensive in many respects in his approach to behavior than Freud. Others have felt that his theoretical framework was too limited in that he relied heavily on a relatively small number of determinants of behavior, such as inferiority feelings and style of life. Perhaps the most fruitful way to evaluate Adler's contribution is to consider him within the broad context of the psychoanalytic movement. A fair appraisal would seem to be that he performed several useful functions. Perhaps the most important of these were his emphasizing the role of social factors in human behavior and his recognition of the role of personal goals and strivings as determinants of behavior.

These emphases provide valuable supplements to psychoanalytic theory. But just as Freud may have been guilty of overemphasizing certain concepts (for example, the Oedipus complex), so also was Adler (for example, inferiority feelings). Another reasonable criticism of Adler is that his sometimes folksy manner of communicating ideas prevented researchers from tying his concepts to observables. This may be why relatively so few controlled empirical investigations have been directly influenced by the Adlerian point of view. Most of the available data regarding Adler's concepts have come from psychotherapeutic situations.

In recent years, however, there has been an increase in interest in Adler's writings. Several important investigators such as Lewin (1935) and Rotter (1954) have been influenced by Adler; specific areas of inquiry such as level of aspiration show his influence. Possibly this renewed interest may lead to efforts to reformulate Adler's ideas and to experiments and observations which meet rigorous scientific standards.

In fact, borrowing heavily from Adler, White (1959) has presented a formulation dealing with the need of people for competence. This need, he feels, is consistent with many everyday observations. Why does the young child insist on feeding himself with a spoon when his hunger would be satisfied more directly and quickly by having his mother place the food in his mouth? White has argued that though the hunger drive is obviously an important determinant of behavior, so is the need of the individual to manipulate objects and gain mastery over them. White's discussion of competence, in some respects similar to Adler's notions of inferiority and compensatory strivings, seems to be a creative contribution. It may have implications for individual psychology and for empirical investigations, particularly in the area of child development.

ERICH FROMM AND KAREN HORNEY

The relationships of the writings of Fromm and Horney to those of both Freud and Adler appear to be so similar that we shall talk about both of these theorists simultaneously.

Fromm (1941, 1959) and Horney (1937) rejected the emphasis upon the instinctual or sexual bases of behavior in psychoanalytic theory. However, their work appears to fall within a quasi-psychoanalytic setting. Horney (1937, 1939, 1950) provided useful descriptions of and discussions on the concept of anxiety, and she has written at length about the relationship of anxiety to neurotic self-strivings and to sources of insecurity throughout life. Fromm (1941, 1947) has particularly emphasized the insecurity of Western man in a complex, impersonal industrialized society.

Both Fromm and Horney have elaborated upon the need, emphasized by Adler, to study the individual within his social context. Fromm, particularly, has sought to apply psychoanalytic concepts to broader social concepts such as social movements. Whereas Horney's contribution has been primarily within the field of psychotherapy, Fromm's ideas have been influential in the social sciences as well. The writings of both show interest in social forces and the effects of environmental factors on the individual. Horney (1950, pp. 366–367) has stated her viewpoint as follows:

> Together with many others . . . who had discarded Freud's theory of instincts, I first saw the core of neurosis in human relations. Generally, I pointed out, these were brought about by cultural conditions; specifically,

through environmental factors which obstructed the child's unhampered psychic growth. Instead of developing a basic confidence in self and others the child developed a basic anxiety, which I defined as a feeling of being isolated and helpless toward a world potentially hostile. In order to keep this basic anxiety at a minimum the spontaneous moves toward, against, and away from others became compulsive. While the spontaneous moves were compatible, each with the others, the compulsive ones collided. The conflicts generated in this way, which I called basic conflicts, were therefore the results of conflicting needs and conflicting attitudes with regard to other people. And the first attempts at solution were largely attempts at integration, through giving full rein to some of these needs and attitudes and suppressing others.

This interpretation seems quite consistent with the Freudian ideas of anxiety, conflict, and defense. However, like Jung and Adler, Horney and Fromm have not been content simply with rejecting certain aspects (such as the libido concept) of psychoanalysis. In addition, they have sought to introduce what they considered to be necessary concepts to which Freud had not attended. With ideas comparable to those of Jung and Adler, Horney (1950, pp. 377–378) and Fromm have called for what would seem to be a more idealistic view of man:

. . . However great man's possibilities for becoming destructive, the history of mankind also shows an alive and untiring striving toward greater knowledge about himself and the world around him, toward deeper religious experiences, toward developing greater spiritual powers and greater moral courage, toward greater achievements in all fields, and toward better ways of living. And his very best energies go into these strivings. By dint of his intellect and the power of his imagination, man can visualize things not yet existing. He reaches beyond what he is or can do at any given time. He has limitations, but his limits are not fast and final. Usually he lags behind what he wants to achieve within or outside himself. This in itself is not a tragic situation. But the inner psychic process which is the neurotic equivalent to healthy, human striving *is* tragic. Man under the pressure of inner distress reaches out for the ultimate and the infinite which—though his limits are not fixed—it is not given to him to reach; and in this very process he destroys himself, shifting his very best drive for self-realization to the actualization of his idealized image and thereby wasting the potentialities he actually possesses.

Freud had a pessimistic outlook on human nature and, on the grounds of his premises, was bound to have it. As he saw it, man is doomed to dissatisfaction whichever way he turns. He cannot live out satisfactorily his primitive instinctual drives without wrecking himself and civilization. He cannot be happy alone or with others. He has but the alternative of suffering himself or making others suffer. It is all to Freud's credit that, seeing things this way, he did not compromise with a glib solution. Actually within the framework of his thinking there is no escape from one of these two alternative evils. At best there may be a less favorable distribution of forces, better control, and "sublimation."

Freud was pessimistic but he did not see the human tragedy in neurosis. We see tragic waste in human experience only if there are constructive, creative strivings and these are wrecked by obstructive or destructive forces. And not only did Freud not have any clear vision of constructive forces in man; he had to deny their authentic character. For in his system of thought there were only destructive and libidinal forces, their derivatives and their combinations. Creativity and love (*eros*) for him were sublimated forms of libidinal drives. In most general terms, what we regard as a healthy striving toward self-realization for Freud was—and could be—only an expression of narcissistic libido.

Albert Schweitzer uses the terms "optimistic" and "pessimistic" in the sense of "world and life affirmation" and "world and life negation." Freud's philosophy, in this deep sense, is a pessimistic one. Ours, with all its cognizance of the tragic element in neurosis, is an optimistic one.

Should the student of behavior be concerned with such matters as the aim of life? Fromm (1955, pp. 203–204) has clearly expressed himself with regard to this question:

The aim of life is to live it intensely, to be fully born, to be fully awake. To emerge from the ideas of infantile grandiosity into the conviction of one's real though limited strength; to be able to accept the paradox that every one of us is the most important thing there is in the universe—and at the same time not more important than a fly or a blade of grass. To be able to love life, and yet to accept death without terror; to tolerate uncertainty about the most important questions with which life confronts us—and yet to have faith in our thought and feeling, inasmuch as they are truly ours. To be able to be alone, and at the same time one with a loved person, with every brother on this earth, with all that is alive; to follow the voice of our conscience, the voice that calls us to ourselves, yet not to indulge in self hate when the voice of conscience was not loud enough to be heard and followed. The mentally healthy person is the person who lives by love, reason and faith, who respects life, his own and that of his fellow man.

The Contribution of Fromm and Horney

To what extent is it necessary or desirable for psychological theorists to take stands on issues concerning values? Should personality theories be optimistic or pessimistic in nature? Bergmann (1943, pp. 124–125) has called thinkers such as Fromm and Horney "nicifiers." By this he means that their need to view people as self-fulfilling, inherently good organisms interferes with a truly objective study of man and his behavior:

. . . I am deeply suspicious of the adverse criticism which comes from those nicifiers who object to psychoanalysis because of its being what they call a *drive psychology*. By this they mean that psychoanalysis bases its explanatory attempts upon the prime motivators; what they ignore, or want us to overlook, is that in this respect, psychoanalysis and contemporary experimental psychology do exactly the same thing. There is criticism and criticism. Writers like Miss Horney . . . are really the guardians of the good old spiritualistic tradition in philosophy, or, as psychoanalysts would phrase it, they are the carriers of the cultural resistance. I always feel like reminding those ladies and gentlemen that painting a picture is still painting a picture, in spite of the genetic connection which psychoanalysts claim to have discovered between these and other culturally less high evaluated phenomena and activities. The values, after all, are not called into question if their occurrence is scientifically explained, and for the rest, one does not crusade for the place of variables in an explanatory schema.

As individuals, each of us has and is certainly entitled to personal beliefs and biases, be they social, religious, or economic. But as developers of a science we must establish reliable relationships involving behavioral variables that are impervious to personal beliefs and desires. This stipulation applies equally to all theoretical orientations. It is mentioned especially at this point because the issue has been so clearly drawn by Fromm and Horney.

Although the research stimulated by the writings of Fromm and Horney has been small in amount and one can react unfavorably to value judgments contained in their work, they have contributed to the addition of social variables to psychoanalytic theory. They have also contributed to the technique of psychotherapy and to the elucidation, on a descriptive level, of many psychoanalytic concepts.

HARRY STACK SULLIVAN

Although Adler, Horney, and Fromm argued that psychoanalysis had neglected the significance of social forces in behavior, they did not present a strikingly different original, theoretical approach from that of Freud and his adherents. Harry Stack Sullivan, an American psychiatrist, attempted this large task. More than any other neoanalytic thinker, Sullivan was deeply interested in the empirical testability of concepts and the need for a careful relating of the ideas of theorists to observables. In his theory-building he developed a formulation of behavior that has been both influential and productive (Mullahy, 1949; Sullivan, 1947, 1953).

The core of Sullivan's approach to behavior was the personal relationship. Indeed, if one were to seek a basic behavioral unit in Sullivan's system, it would no doubt be the exchanges between persons. The personal relationship was so important to Sullivan because the individuality of each person was, for him, a function of the history of such relationships. Both acceptable and deviant behavior patterns could be explained in these terms. One area of investigation emphasized by Sullivan had to do with the socialization process and the variables which influence it.

In his treatment of variables influencing behavior, Sullivan emphasized two broad classes of needs. One of these was the need to satisfy biological wants. The other class of needs related to the individual's sense of security. By security, Sullivan meant a subjective experience of well-being and comfort. He often employed the word *euphoria,* which is usually used to describe extreme elation, to indicate this state. A prototypical example of euphoria, as Sullivan used the word, is the somnolent comfort that is easily inferred from the behavior of the infant who has just been fed.

With maturation, the sense of security comes more and more to be influenced by the child's environment. Significant persons such as the mother or father have the power to define for the child situations that are associated with a heightened sense of security. Behavior displeasing to these persons may be punished and result in insecurity. Acceptable behavior may result in attention and rewards. Just as anxiety was described by Freud as a state of unpleasure, Sullivan saw insecurity as a state which persons seek to avoid. Deviant behavior thus may be viewed as an effort, though an inadequate one, to achieve security and avoid psychological pain.

Sullivan believed that the easily observable responses of the social environment were not the sole contributors to the satisfaction of the child's need for security. He used the word *empathy* to indicate unverbalized or covert communications among people. For example, in the feeding situation it is not just the supply of food given to the child which is important. Unverbalized attitudes of the mother such as love or rejection also contribute either positively or negatively to the infant's security. Empathy, then, is an inferential concept referring to the unverbalized communication of attitudes from one person to another.

In Sullivan's view, in the course of development the child comes to build up a sense of self, a perception of himself. This self-percept is a function of the history of personal relations; Sullivan used such terms as "good me" and "bad me" to refer to two of these percepts. The sum of the percepts influences the development of what Sullivan called the self-dynamism. This is a comprehensive concept referring both to the self as perceived by the individual and the self as a doer and protector of the sense of security.

Sullivan mentioned several methods by which individuals sought to maximize security and avoid psychological pain. These resembled Freud's concept of the ego defense mechanisms. One of these techniques Sullivan called *dissociation*. This is a process through which thoughts and events related to the arousal of insecurity can be barred or cut off from consciousness. Another he called *parataxic distortion*. By this technique, individuals lock themselves into tight little compartments. They develop responses, skills, attitudes, and ideas without working them into relationship with other phases of their personalities. Their responses are determined by their own needs rather than by reality and social norms. In contrast, Sullivan referred to the *syntaxic* approach in which concepts refer to observable data. Such data are *consensual* and Sullivan believed that parents, teachers, and psychotherapists had the obligation to influence the individual to seek the validation of these data much in the same manner as a scientific hypothesis is checked for validity. Sullivan also urged the use of symbols and definitions conforming to those present in the social milieu.

We can see that Sullivan was interested in describing both the present dynamics and the history of behavior. In this respect, his views are compatible with those of Freud. Like Freud, he also sought to incorporate the role of biological factors into his conceptual schema. Sullivan seemed to have been well aware of individuals' biological needs such as food, sleep, and sex. In this regard, he seemed to be much closer to Freud than to Adler, Fromm, and Horney. However, Sullivan did agree with these writers that Freud had presented an imbalanced view of biological factors and that he had overemphasized the satisfactions associated with sex. An interesting aspect of Sullivan's treatment of biological influences was his inclusion of the need for personal contact as one of these. It is certainly arguable whether gregariousness and the need for personal closeness are biologically or socially determined. However, observations of children's responses to cuddling and the reactions of individuals who have experienced long periods of isolation are sufficiently impressive at least to make us consider a possible biological basis for the need for contact with others. Evidence consistent with Sullivan's emphasis on the need for contact with others has recently come from Harlow's (1958, 1962) research on infant monkeys. Harlow observed in his subjects a need for close bodily contact often rivaling their need for food. He interpreted this strong tendency of monkeys to approach soft, cuddly objects as reflecting a need, not socially created, for contact comfort.

The Contribution of Sullivan

With Sullivan's great interest in personal transactions, it is not surprising to find that social psychologists and sociologists have been influenced by his views. This may be seen in research into the social behavior of staff members and patients in mental institutions. Stanton and Schwartz (1954), for example, studied the personal relations that characterized a small, intensive treatment psychiatric hospital. One of the authors, Schwartz, actually immersed himself as a participant while observing the life of the institution. In Sullivan's view, where observations are made of other people and the observer is part of the group observed, his observations must be considered to be participant, as opposed to truly objective. Even in the psychotherapy situation, the psychotherapist would be termed a *participant observer*.

Stanton and Schwartz devoted much of their research to the study of relations among the hospital's staff (psychiatrists, psychologists, nurses, attendants). What they found was enlightening, and to some it may seem a little surprising. They found that the personal relations among the members of the staff affected the behavior of the patient population. The staff was often unaware of this influence that it exerted. It occurred even though staff members sought to disengage their intrastaff conflicts and differences of opinion from their treatment of individual patients. This evidence along with the findings of others appears to support Sullivan's notion of empathy, in that the communicating to patients of staff conflicts seemed to occur without explicit verbal communication.

One line of research suggested by Sullivan's concept of empathy deals with nonverbal communication (Ruesch and Bateson, 1951). Whether the result of empathy or some specific mechanism, nonverbal communication appears to occur frequently, but whether particular incidents signify such communication is an empirical matter. In some instances of apparent nonverbal communication, there may be minimal but decisively verbal cues. Regardless of this possibility, the study of nonverbal cues (such as gestural, facial ones) appears to be a promising one for students of interpersonal processes.

The ideas of Sullivan and his adherents seem interesting, provocative, and a positive contribution to the objective study of personality. Sullivan and Freud, probably more than any of the writers considered so far, consciously sought to construct nonvaluistic frameworks for the viewing of personality. Whereas some theorists have tended to emphasize a small number of determinants of behavior at the expense of other ones, Sullivan seemed to have sought, and in part achieved, a workable balance of emphasis between social and biological factors. A criticism of Sullivan's system is that, like Freud's system, it often contains definitions of terms that fall short of the precision needed in carrying out research. However, also like Freud's system, it has done much to stimulate other investigators whose work may contribute in the future to improving the content and the clarity of the Sullivan schemes.

When we consider the neo-analysts as a group, it would seem that Jung contributed a full-blown orientation to compete with that of psychoanalysis. Adler, Fromm, and Horney each emphasized the social determinants of behavior. Only Sullivan incorporated socialization as a process into a novel, systematic formulation.

EGO PSYCHOLOGY

Common to all of the psychoanalytic deviationists considered so far is the belief that Freud placed much more stress on the role played by sexual impulses in development than was actually the case. These writers have maintained that overemphasis of instinctual forces prevented Freud from giving adequate treatment to important environmental and social considerations. Most of these neo-Freudians have not seriously objected to such concepts as anxiety and defense, but they have rejected the prominent status given to biological drives in the tripartite id-ego-superego system.

Most of the deviationists have tended in varying degrees to form their own schools of thought. However, some students of psychoanalysis who have objected to particular aspects of the Freudian theoretical framework, rather than rejecting psychoanalysis, have preferred to revise and elaborate existing concepts. The most influential of these attempts (Hartmann, 1964; Hartmann, Kris, and Lowenstein, 1964) has come to be known as ego psychology.

Ego psychologists do not reject Freud's theory of drives. They believe, however, that the instinctual formulations of Freud have limited the potential of psychoanalysis as a general theory of behavior. Specifically, they have objected to Freud's notion that the ego and superego are completely dependent upon the id for psychic energy. They have felt that a completely drive-oriented approach to behavior does not adequately handle many of the individual's relationships to reality. Although a number of aspects of human behavior can be understood in terms of the influences of id impulses, a substantial part of a person's commerce with reality does not seem to require this idea. The ego psychologists have argued that the ego can more realistically be viewed as a structure some of whose functions are autonomous or independent of instinctual drives (Hartmann, 1958; Hartmann and Kris, 1945; Hartmann, Kris, and Lowenstein, 1946).

One means of theoretically avoiding the complete dependence of the ego on the id is to argue that whereas the functions of the id pertain to drives and the need for sensual gratification, the functions of the ego concern reality and adjustment to the environment. Freud, of course, did not ignore the problem of the need to account for the individual's adjustment to the world about him. However, his description of this adjustment was largely in terms of the ego's role in achieving a rapprochement between innate drives and the environment. Thus, for Freud, the ego defense mechanisms loom large as vehicles through which this rapprochement can be effected. But should there not be more to the concept of the ego than simply the idea of an agency for reconciling impulses with reality?

Ego psychologists answer this question affirmatively. They are interested in basic functions such as perception, motility, and ability to manipulate and gain mastery over objects in the environment. As the executor of behavior, they contend, the ego may appropriately be assigned these functions. On this basis they make a distinction between *ego defensive* functions and *ego autonomous* functions. The functions of the ego defenses are to reduce anxiety, resolve conflict, and achieve the rapprochement between the person's inner life and his environment. The ego autonomous functions relate to conflict-free behavior, such as turning a page and making a phone call. Although both functions may jointly influence behavior, the ego autonomous functions, especially, concern the spheres of problem solving, motor activity, and perception. Thus, the ego psychologists would question the need to explain, on an instinctual basis, the child's ability to add $2 + 2$ or to turn on the radio, or the adult's ability to drive a car and to develop such complex skills as operating a cyclotron. Traditional psychoanalysts might attribute these behaviors to sublimation.

In order to integrate theoretically the idea of autonomous functions within a psychoanalytic framework, Hartmann, Kris, and Lowenstein have hypothesized what they call an undifferentiated phase of development, consisting of the first five or six years of life. Out of this undifferentiated phase, both the id and the ego are assumed to develop. Some aspects of the ego's functions, such as the defense mechanisms, may be quite directly related to the id and its demands for gratification. Other aspects, like the conflict-free ego autonomous functions, may develop relatively independent of the individual's impulse life.

The following observations by Hartmann (1958, p. 4), one of the most articulate of the ego psychologists, well reflects the goal of ego psychologists to expand the scope of psychoanalysis:

> Psychoanalysis evinced quite early, and perhaps even from the very beginning, a narrower and a broader objective. It started out with the study of pathology and of phenomena which are on the border of normal psychology and psychopathology. At that time its work centered on the id and the instinctual drives. But soon there arose new problems, concepts, formulations, and new needs for explanation, which reached beyond this narrower field toward a *general* theory of mental life. A decisive, and perhaps the most clearly delineated, step in this direction is our recent ego psychology. . . . At present we no longer doubt that psychoanalysis can claim to be a *general* psychology in the broadest sense of the word, and our conception of the working methods which may properly be considered psychoanalytic has become broader, deeper, and more discriminating.

Hartmann (1958, pp. 8–9) has treated conflict-free behavior as follows:

> Not every adaptation to the environment, or every learning and maturation process, is a conflict. I refer to the development *outside of conflict* of perception, intention, object comprehension, thinking, language, recall-phenomena, productivity, to the well-known phases of motor development, grasping, crawling, walking, and to the maturation and learning processes implicit in all these and many others . . . . I need not list here all these functions: you know them. I certainly do not imply that the childhood activities I have enumerated, and other relevant ones as well, remain untouched by mental conflict; nor do I imply that disturbances in their development do not in turn give rise to conflicts, nor that they do not get embroiled in other conflicts. On the contrary, I want to stress that their vicissitudes play an important role in the well-known typical and individual developments and conflicts of instinctual drives, and in facilitating or hampering the individual's ability to master these. I propose that we adopt the provisional term *conflict-free ego sphere* for that ensemble of functions which at any given time exert their effects outside the region of mental conflicts. I do not want to be misunderstood: I am not speaking of a province of the mind, the development of which is in principle immune to conflicts, but rather of processes *in so far as*, in an individual, they remain empirically outside of the sphere of mental conflict. It is quite possible to state, both for the cross-sectional and the longitudinal aspects of an individual's mental life, what belongs to this conflict-free sphere. What we do not yet have is a systematic psychoanalytic knowledge of this sphere; we have only partial knowledge of reality-

fears, of defense processes in so far as they result in "normal" development, of the conflict-free sphere's contributions to the kinds and consequences of defense (and resistance), its contributions to the displacement of the aims of instinctual drives, and so on. We do not need to prove that investigations which are *limited* to this sphere, as those of academic psychology usually are, inevitably overlook basic psychlogical relationships.

From these comments we see that Hartmann has been careful to allow for the joint influences of the ego defensive and autonomous functions on behavior. We see also that the orientation of ego psychology is much more sympathetic than traditional psychoanalysis to basic areas of psychological research. Indeed, for the ego psychologists, a merger of the disciplines of psychoanalysis and psychology would appear to provide the most effective way of developing a true general psychology.

The Contribution of Ego Psychology

Although it is a relatively recent development, ego psychology has already made significant contributions. It has greatly increased the flexibility of psychoanalysis by adding drives, such as White's (1959, 1963) notion of competence, to those postulated by Freud. It has directed students of personality not only to the areas of anxiety and conflict but also to the general problem of adaptation to an environment. Ego psychologists, along with the neo-analysts, have been cognizant of the role of social factors in development. They have encouraged multidisciplined attacks on research problems using additional techniques to those emerging from psychoanalytic therapy sessions. Longitudinal developmental studies, in particular, have interested the ego psychologists.

The one writer who has contributed a great deal to revision of the psychoanalytic theory of development is Erik Erikson. Erikson (1950, 1964) has expanded upon Freud's formulations by discussing the psychological implications of the psychosexual stages of development. Each such stage, in Erikson's view, has associated with it one or a few core psychological crises or problems. For example, though infancy may be characterized psychosexually by the need for oral and sensory gratification it is also a period of life in which the child's attitudes of trust and mistrust of its environment are formed. Like several of the neo-Freudians, Erikson has also attempted to broaden the scope of psychoanalysis to include the adolescent and adult years.

It would be premature to conclude that the ideas of ego psychology have achieved an enduring revision of psychoanalysis. But they do appear to have contributed to increasing recognition of psychoanalysis as a body of hypotheses dealing with the general problem of adaptation to life.

CONCLUDING COMMENTS CONCERNING PSYCHOANALYSIS

From the ideas of Freud, of deviationists such as the neo-Freudians, and of the ego psychologists, it seems clear that psychoanalysis, even for the psychoanalysts, is far from an accepted single set of concepts. On the contrary, psychoanalysis is a collection of ideas in evolution. Attempts are being made to polish the inelegancies in Freud's original formulations. Efforts are under way to increase the flexibility of the libido concept. Significant, but neglected variables, such as social and cultural influences and intellectual problem solving, are being incorporated into the theoretical framework. Psychoanalysis and experimental psychology now have many aspects in common in their approach to research and study. On a number of fronts psychoanalysis seems to be in the process of becoming a more realistic and sophisticated theoretical orientation (Hilgard, 1962*a*; Munroe, 1955; Rapaport, 1959).

Pressing at the present time is the need for advances in research sophistication to parallel conceptual developments. If psychotherapy is to be a proving ground for theoretical ideas, it has to make the events of the therapist-patient interaction as public as possible—for example, through the use of films and tape recordings. Only in this way can reliable measures of behavior in psychotherapy be obtained. Yet it does not seem possible to limit the validation of psychoanalytic hypotheses to the events of psychotherapy. Field studies, such as observations in the home, longitudinal studies of development, and laboratory experimentation must be used to establish the relationships between theoretical concepts and behavior. For this to occur, both a reduction in the ambiguity of many concepts and the imagination of many different types of researchers are required.

Definitive validation of psychoanalytic theory must, like most scientific exercises, remain more a hope than an accomplishment. What is psychoanalytic theory? At present, to repeat, it is ideas in evolution. These ideas will change, be modified, be corrected, and will be omitted as increasing amounts of empirical knowledge come to light. Thus the validation of psychoanalysis must involve the validating of particular concepts at particular levels of development under particular sets of circumstances.

4

Learning and Personality

How behavior changes through experience is the predominant question in the psychology of learning. Observation of such changes in everyday situations has provided learning psychologists with the stimulus to study modifications of behavior from an experimental standpoint. There are many formulations concerning the learning process and there has been much research into the determinants of behavior change. One consequence of all this has been the recognition that learning cannot be dismissed simply by saying that we profit from experience. Rather, it is necessary to define as precisely as possible the variables that permit this gain.

Hilgard (1956, p. 3) has defined learning this way:

> Learning is the process by which an activity originates or is changed through reacting to an encountered situation, provided that the characteristics of the change in activity cannot be explained on the basis of native response tendencies, maturation, or temporary states of the organism (e.g., fatigue, drugs, etc.).

Miller and Dollard (1941, pp. 1–2) have stated that learning theory,

> ". . . is the study of the circumstances under which a response and a cue stimulus become connected. After learning has been completed, response and cue are bound together in such a way that the appearance of the cue evokes the response . . . . Learning takes place according to definite psychological principles. Practice does not always make perfect. The connection between a cue and a response can be strengthened only under certain conditions. The learner must be driven to make the response and rewarded for having re-

sponded in the presence of the cue. This may be expressed in a homely way by saying that in order to learn one must want something, notice something, do something, and get something. Stated more exactly, these factors are drive, cue, response and reward. These elements in the learning process have been carefully explored, and further complexities have been discovered. Learning theory has become a firmly knit body of principles which are useful in describing human behavior.

Learning theories and the theory of psychoanalysis share a significant characteristic in common: *both reflect a deterministic view of behavior.* Goals, plans, and purposes do influence behavior, but both learning theory and psychoanalysis deal with these products of the experiential histories of individuals.

The psychology of learning and psychoanalysis, however, show some noteworthy differences in emphasis and method. Psychoanalysis was developed within a clinical context, its starting point being an effort to explain the basis of deviate behavior. The psychology of learning, on the other hand, developed within the tradition of psychological experimentation, placing value on the use of carefully controlled laboratory methods. In recent years a number of attempts have been made to generalize from the data of learning experiments to the area of psychopathology; and, as we have observed, psychoanalysis is being studied more and more in the laboratory. As learning concepts are applied to personality, we shall see a number of similarities to psychoanalytic formulations.

THE ROLE OF REINFORCEMENT

The most basic ideas in the psychology of learning are those of stimulus and response. Everyone makes thousands of responses each day. What are the stimuli that incite these responses? What changes in them lead to changes in response? A change in response is often the result of some reinforcement. This may be described as events or stimuli that affect the probability of a response's occurring. The actual role played by reinforcement has been studied intensively in two types of experimental situations, one involving classical or *respondent* conditioning and the other involving instrumental or *operant* conditioning.

An eyelid experiment such as the one by Taylor (1951) described in Chapter 1 illustrates the kind of experiments used in classical conditioning. A subject seated in a chair is asked to look at a light on a nearby wall. Initially the subject is exposed only to the onset of the light. Then, in a series of trials, the ignition of the light is closely followed by the administration of a puff of air to the subject's eyelid. As the airpuff is a noxious stimulus, the subject defensively blinks his eye. Following several of these light-airpuff sequences the air puff is omitted. Nevertheless, most subjects continue to blink their eyes when the light alone goes on. If this happens, a conditioned eyeblink is said to have been established. Prior to the light-airpuff pairings, most subjects would not have blinked their eyes with the onset of light. However, through the association of the airpuff with the light, the light begins to elicit a conditioned response.

In this classical conditioning experiment, the airpuff may be called a reinforcer because it serves to strengthen and reinforce a response already in the organism's repertory of responses. In classical conditioning the "old" response, the eyeblink, is conditioned to a "new" stimulus, the light. If the reinforcer is omitted, a decrease in the emission of the conditioned eyeblink will be observed. Extinction occurs in the absence of reinforcement. Reinforcement and extinction procedures may be used selectively to strengthen or weaken a great variety of responses.

The role of reinforcement is somewhat different in instrumental conditioning experiments. In classical conditioning, the response under study—in the example given, an eyeblink—is a strongly established one. We blink our eyes many times every day, and the unconditioned stimulus, the airpuff, serves to elicit the eyeblink response. The aim of the classical conditioning experiment is to bring about a situation in which these common responses come to be evoked by an uncommon stimulus—the onset of a light, in our example. In instrumental conditioning, on the other hand, the response under study is always one that has an initially low frequency of occurrence. The experimental problem is to increase the probability with which that response will occur.

For example, saying "thank you" does not come naturally to children. They must learn to emit this response. A little prodding and skillful reinforcement help. Parents, on the first occasions of emission of "thank you" by their child, will usually bestow abundant praise and affection on the child. These environmental events constitute reinforcing conditions and will serve to strengthen the "thank you" response. Just as absence of reinforcement in a classical conditioning situation leads to extinction, so does it function in operant conditioning. Since most everyday examples of behavior change do not involve 100 per cent reinforcement, many researchers have investigated the effects of partial reinforcement.

Whichever theory of learning to which one adheres, it seems clear that experimentally manipulated stimuli that have reinforcing properties can exert powerful influences upon the response repertory of an organism. In everyday life, of course, not one stimulus alone but complex patterns of stimuli impinge on organisms. The complexities of these patterns necessitate caution in generalizing too glibly from controlled experiments that involve relatively simple stimulus conditions, to "uncontrolled" life experiences.

Learning theorists have varying views on the number of concepts needed to describe behavior in a meaningful way. Some, notably Skinner, have argued that we should start out with few concepts that refer directly to observable behavior. These concepts, it is felt, should be exhaustively studied before adding new ideas to a theoretical framework (Skinner, 1953, 1954, 1956). Other writers, notably Hull, have argued that the obvious complexity of the determinants of behavior requires the development of commensurately rich theories (Hull, 1952). As a case in point there is the Hullian use of the concept of drive. Hull felt that reference solely to the habits of organisms was not sufficient to account for the data of learning experiments. The additional ideas that he and other psychologists have emphasized include the concept of drive.

DRIVE

Hull (1952) viewed drive as the hypothetical resultant of tissue needs and wants. One frequent effect of drive arousal is an increase in the activity of an organism. In this sense, drives are assumed to have motivational properties. Organisms will engage in activity and work to satisfy their drives. When drives are satisfied, or as some prefer, when needs are met, a reduction in activity results. Thus, a hungry individual will be markedly less active following a hearty dinner than before eating.

Investigators who have found value in a drive concept similar to Hull's have argued for the simultaneous consideration of habit and motivation. They contend that behavior never occurs in a motivationless vacuum and that motivation combines with stimulus-response (S-R) habit tendencies to determine behavior. This view has often taken the form of a drive-reduction hypothesis: the reduction of an organism's drive functions as a reinforcement. Responses associated with drive reduction tend to be strengthened.

This argument has been used in cases where drive has been conceived in terms of strong external stimuli, such as persistent loud noise, and also where drive has referred to internal biological states of need such as hunger, thirst, and pain. Several writers have distinguished between primary and secondary drives. Primary drives are unlearned and presumably biologically rooted. For example, one does not have to learn to experience hunger in the absence of food. Secondary or acquired drives may be viewed as learned ones. Whereas all organisms have an unlearned need for food, different organisms, depending on their developmental histories, will acquire needs or drives for particular kinds of food. Beefsteak is not necessary for survival but in Western society it appears to have strong drive-reducing properties.

LEARNING AND PERSONALITY

Several persons interested in the problems of response acquisition and extinction have, because of complementary interests in problems bearing on the psychology of personality, sought to integrate learning concepts into personality theory and research. For example, Dollard and Miller (1950) have done precisely this with the relationship between learning concepts and psychoanalysis.

Consider the concept of drive. Hullian theorists have emphasized the role drive reduction plays in learning. Psychoanalytically oriented writers also include a drive concept in their approach to behavior. Their pleasure principle appears to be an analogue of drive reduction. Hilgard (1956, p. 291) has noted that Freud's concept of the pleasure principle:

> . . . represents one of the first points of correspondence between his views and those of learning theorists. The corresponding principle in contemporary learning theory is more likely to go under the names of the *law of effect* or *reinforcement theory*. The broad conception, common to both psychoanalysis and learning theory, is that a need state is a state of high tension. Whether we describe this in terms of instincts seeking gratification or of drives leading to consummatory responses, we are talking about the same sequence of events. What controls the direction of movement is a tendency to restore a kind of equilibrium, thus reducing tension.

Acknowledging this area of agreement between learning theory and psychoanalysis, Dollard and Miller have attempted to revise the formulations of psychoanalysis in S-R terms. The motivation behind their effort appears to have been the belief that they might thus reduce or eliminate many of the ambiguities associated with psychoanalytic theory. Their reformulation of Freud's system did not stem from a rejection of psychoanalysis as a collection of ideas, but from a strong sympathy with it and an appreciation of the overt and covert behavior it sought to explain.

In their treatment of the process of development, Dollard and Miller (1950) have adhered essentially to the stages hypothesized by Freud. Their interpretation of them, however, has emphasized the personal stimuli and responses associated with each stage. Thus, in discussing the anal stage they speak in terms of toilet training as a stimulus situation requiring certain conforming responses from the child. They recognize that the stimuli of this situation include not only the toilet seat on which the child sits, but also the attitudes communicated by its parents. Since toilet and cleanliness training are among the first situations that call for the child's adherence to culturally approved requirements, these writers believe that it has important implications for later development. Within their framework, Dollard and Miller have generally accepted the psychoanalytic emphasis on the significance of the early years of life. They agree with Freud that basic response patterns and attitudes are formed during this period.

Related to these response patterns are two additional concepts of importance to the psychology of learning. One of these is the idea of generalization. Generalization occurs when we respond in one situation as we did in a previous, similar one. The extent to which generalization occurs depends upon the similarity between the situations. Attitudes toward parents, for example, may generalize to other persons such as teachers and friends. The other concept used widely by Dollard and Miller is that of the response or habit hierarchy. The concept of a habit hierarchy assumes that for any stimulus situation, an organism has the potential of making any of a number of responses. These responses may be ordered in terms of their probability of occurrence in the stimulus situation. As has been noted, drive reduction plays a role in determining these probabilities.

From the standpoint of the psychology of learning, the early years of life are important ones. During these years the child establishes response hierarchies for a great variety of stimulus contexts. Dollard and Miller see the problem of modifying deviant behavior as one of manipulating the response hierarchy. In this view, the trouble with the neurotic individual is that responses high in his hierarchy are either inadequate or inappropriate. Thus the individual who has learned always to respond in a dependent manner to persons perceived as authority figures must, if he is to develop optimally, experience a weakening of these strong inappropriate responses and a strengthening of more appropriate ones—for example, the ability to assert one's independence.

Psychotherapy, for Dollard and Miller, is considered in terms of the need for individuals to revise and modify response hierarchies. They have used the term learning dilemma to refer to situations that necessitate this sort of revision. Since apparently inadequate response patterns often maintain themselves because they reduce the anxiety level of the individual, hierarchical changes may not be easy to produce.

Just as in Freud's framework, anxiety, for Dollard and Miller, is an unpleasant state that organisms seek to avoid. Put in stimulus-response terms, anxiety is an acquired or acquirable drive—acquirable since the capacity to experience anxiety might be viewed as innate. Reduction of this drive constitutes a reinforcing state of affairs, and responses associated with drive reduction will tend to be strengthened. At the level of covert responding, defense mechanisms are viewed by Dollard and Miller as responses to anxiety. One of them, repression, might be described as a covert or unconscious stopping-thinking response. Covert responses, such as repression, are thought of as cue-producing, in the sense that they serve as cues leading to overt behavior.

One facet of this stimulus-response approach which has been especially stimulating has to do with conflict. As in psychoanalytic theory, conflict is described in terms of its capacity to arouse anxiety. Research carried out by Miller, Brown, and others has resulted in a variety of paradigms of conflict (Miller, 1951). Among these are *approach-approach, approach-avoidance,* and *avoidance-avoidance* conflicts. These forms of conflict relate to the attracting and repelling properties of the environment. Choosing which one of two well-liked ties one will wear illustrates an approach-approach conflict. Deciding how much cold wind one is willing to withstand in order to see a football game illustrates an approach-avoidance conflict. Avoidance-avoidance conflicts, which may arouse very high levels of anxiety, occur when one must choose between two undesirable alternatives, for example, staying on a sinking oceanliner or jumping into shark-infested, icy water.

The type of learning approach to personality that we have been describing seems quite compatible with many of the major Freudian concepts. Its goal, as stated by Dollard and Miller (1950), is ". . . to combine the vitality of psychoanalysis, the rigor of the natural-science laboratory, and the facts of culture" (p. 3). With this combination, Dollard and Miller believe that both covert and overt behavior can be approached from a sound psychological standpoint.

By no means do all learning psychologists concur on the value of integrating their concepts with those of psychoanalysis, or for that matter, on the value of any other orientation. Rather, there appears to be a continuum of attitudes among learning psychologists. Many of them seem to share Dollard and Miller's interest in complex human processes. Others believe that much more experimental study of relatively simple laboratory situations is required before phenomena such as unconscious processes can be studied objectively. Still another group of learning psychologists, notably the followers of Skinner (1953, p. 31), believe that the problem of unconscious processes with which the psychoanalysts and Dollard and Miller are concerned are pseudo-problems created by a naive mentalism:

> The commonest inner causes have no specific dimensions at all, either neurological or psychic. When we say that a man eats *because* he is hungry, smokes a great deal *because* he has the tobacco habit, fights *because* of the instinct of pugnacity, behaves brilliantly *because* of his intelligence, or plays the piano well *because* of his musical ability, we seem to be referred to causes. But on analysis these phrases prove to be merely redundant descriptions. A single set of facts is described by the two statements: "He eats" and "He is hungry." A single set of facts is described by the two statements: "He smokes a great deal" and "He has the smoking habit." A single set of facts is described by the two statements: "He plays well" and "He has musical ability." The practice of explaining one statement in terms of the other is dangerous because it suggests that we have found the cause and therefore need search no further. Moreover, such terms as "hunger," "habit," and "intelligence" convert what are essentially the properties of a process or relation into what appears to be things. Thus we are unprepared for the properties eventually to be discovered in the behavior itself and continue to look for something which may not exist.

Psychologists who share these views contend that with a relatively small number of learning concepts much of complex human behavior can be accounted for. Among these concepts are those of reinforcement, extinction, counterconditioning, and discrimination learning. While agreeing that behavior is influenced by life experiences, these writers seek to avoid speculating about covert events. For them, a truly objective approach to personality must be in terms of the study of the observable responses of organisms and their identifiable antecedents. Lundin (1961, p. 8), who espouses the Skinnerian point of view, has offered this definition of personality:

Personality is that organization of unique behavior equipment an individual has acquired under the special conditions of his development.

The special conditions to which Lundin refers include the person's particular history of stimulus situations. The following quotation from Keller and Schoenfeld (1950, pp. 365–366) illustrates the way in which one might employ this strongly environmental orientation in an analysis of human development:

> The cultural environment (or, more exactly, the members of the community) starts out with a human infant formed and endowed along species lines, but capable of behavioral training in many directions. From this raw material, the culture proceeds to make, in so far as it can, a product acceptable to itself. It does this by training: by reinforcing the behavior it desires and extinguishing others; by differentiating out this or that specific response or chain of responses, such as manners and attitudes; by conditioning emotional and anxiety reactions to some stimuli and not others. It teaches the individual what he may and may not do, giving him norms and ranges of social behavior that are permissive or prescriptive or prohibitive. It teaches him the language he is to speak; it gives him his standards of beauty and art, of good and bad conduct; it sets before him a picture of the ideal personality that he is to imitate and strive to be. In all this, the fundamental laws of behavior are to be found.

In later chapters we shall see several examples of the influence of this point of view on the study of the child, the adult, and the maladjusted individual.

An orientation intermediate to the ones espoused by Miller and Dollard and the Skinnerian psychologists has been put forth by Bandura and Walters (1963). Bandura and Walters believe that a learning or sociobehavioristic approach will prove to be more productive than a psychoanalytic one which emphasizes internal processes, or a Dollard and Miller type of learning reinterpretation of psychoanalysis, or a Skinnerian environmentalist one. The Skinner approach, Bandura and Walters feel, is inadequate in that its principles are too limited in number and breadth to approximate an adequate theory of the person and of social behavior.

From their sociobehavioristic point of view, the following problems emerge for Bandura and Walters as especially significant—significant in the sense of their contribution to a comprehensive account of normal and deviant behavior: (1) the effects of rewards or reinforcements on specified responses; (2) the effects of punishment and nonreward on these responses; (3) the effects of prior learning on a person's reactions to attempts at influencing his behavior; (4) the effects of generalization and discrimination learning on behavior; (5) the effects of opportunity to observe someone else make a particular type of response on the individual's acquisition of that response.

This latter problem, which will be illustrated in later chapters (see Chapters 18, 22), arises in *observational learning*. Bandura and Walters' interest in this type of learning is quite consistent with their concern for social behavior and the contexts in which it occurs. When a child imitates and acquires a manner of speaking similar to that of its parents, the acquisition process must be regarded as a function of the particular set of personal relationships at work within the family. Interpersonal relationships, Bandura and Walters feel, must of necessity occupy an important position in an approach to the process of imitation. Mowrer (1950*a*) has stressed particularly the role which reinforcement may play in imitation. He has argued that the child imitates or models its parents' behavior because their responses have been associated with reinforcements for the child. For example, a child might begin to utter sounds after having had many pleasurable experiences in which its mother talked to it. The child's verbalizing might then be viewed as a form of self-administered reinforcement.

Clearly, there is a lack of agreement among psychologists interested in learning processes concerning their conceptual ties with the field of personality. Despite this absence of a unitary position there seems to be no question that learning theory has played a valuable role as a provocateur in the area of personality. Indeed, the recent work of Bandura and Walters and several other contemporary psychologists, notable among them Mowrer (1960*a*, 1960*b*), has served to make quite clear the interpenetration of personality and learning. Let us briefly note some of the empirical problems identified as a result of this interpenetration.

Learning and Individual Differences

As we have suggested, individual differences in behavior and personality are of concern to the psychology of learning, owing to its interest in their genesis. It is not surprising, therefore, that child psychologists have made use of learning concepts in attempting to account for the formation of personality. The principle of reinforcement has perhaps been the most widely applied learning concept in this regard. Many students of child behavior have successfully demonstrated that many personality characteristics are, to an important extent, a function of the reinforcement history of the individual.

A suggestive example of this may be found in studies reported by Rheingold (1956). She studied two groups of six-month-old infants who lived in an institution. The children in this institution were cared for by volunteers from the community. In her experiment, Rheingold for eight weeks took on the role of mother to a group of these children. During the eight-week period this group of children not only were cared for by one person rather than by many different people, but also the amount of reinforcement which they received in the form of attention and affection was far greater than for infants not in the experimental group. Rheingold's interest in carrying out her study was to determine the effects on infants' social behavior of the continued presence of a positively reinforcing mother figure. She found that the experimental subjects, those for whom she had cared, showed more social responsiveness to the mother figure and others than did control subjects who were cared for in the usual way by the institution. Other research by Rheingold (1961) has shown that the emission of social responses such as smiling in infants is influenced by the reinforcement history of the child. Rewards such as picking up and cuddling an infant after it has smiled increases the probability that the smiling response will recur in the future.

Procedures of this type have been employed to study many facets of personality in children. Aspects of behavior, such as dependency and independency, aggression, and anxiety, to name but a few, have been observed to be influenced by reinforcement in the environment (Bandura and Walters, 1963). The evidence suggests that the way in which children's characteristics and behavior develop is powerfully affected by the reactions of their environments to them. Furthermore, crosscultural research has shown that responses that are encouraged and reinforced by the family and society tend to become strengthened. Punished or ignored responses tend to disappear. The topic of selective reinforcement in relation to the development of the person will be explored at greater length in Part 4. For the present, we may simply mention that available evidence supports the hypothesis that personality characteristics of children and adults are shaped to a significant extent by their reinforcement histories.

STUDIES OF BEHAVIOR CHANGE IN ANIMALS AND HUMANS

Children are useful subjects for the study of the effects of reinforcement because their response hierarchies are relatively simple and in a formative stage. A review of the literature concerning conditioning in early life shows evidence that responses such as sucking, blinking, crying, general activity, and fear can be conditioned to a variety of visual, auditory, and tactile stimuli (Munn, 1954). However, adult humans and animal subjects have also been subjected to study in terms of learning's role in personality functioning (Mowrer, 1950*a*, 1960*a*, 1960*b*). Animal studies are valuable in their own right and for their suggestive value. Studies with humans are important because of their direct relevance to personality.

Studies of learned avoidance and fear responses in animals have had a strong impact on the area of personality. Numerous investigations have shown that negative reinforcement or punishment of responses (for instance, by administration of electric shocks) typically leads to a drastic decline in frequency of occurrence. Other researches have shown that through experimental manipulations, fear can become associated with previously neutral stimuli.

An experiment by Miller (1951) has demonstrated this possibility. He used rats as subjects and a piece of apparatus that had two compartments. When placed in one of these compartments, the rats were subjected to strong electric shocks. After a number of these experiences, the subjects' behavior became clearly agitated and anxious. This anxiety persisted in that compartment even when the shock was omitted. Thus the result of giving the shock was that the animals exhibited fear responses not only to the shock but also to the compartment in which shock had occurred.

Later the rats were given an "out." It became possible for them to escape from the compartment in which shock had been administered to an adjoining one. Miller found that, even after many, many trials with nonshock experiences, the animals fled into the adjoining compartment. Thus, a strong escape response from the compartment in which shock occurred had clearly been evoked. Miller concluded that the rats had acquired a strong fear of the compartment in which shock had occurred. Furthermore, he argued, this fear possessed the characteristics of an acquired drive. This acquired drive led to the rats' avoidance of the feared compartment and to their persistent escape responses. The basis for this acquired drive, Miller believes, was the association of a primary drive (in this case, the need to avoid the pain of shock) with a previously neutral stimulus (the compartment in which shock took place).

The interpretation given by Miller (1951, pp. 439–440) for his experimental results is consistent with the views of Dollard and Miller described earlier:

> . . . Learned drives depend on responses that produce strong stimuli. (Fear is a strong stimulus in the same sense that pain is.) Furthermore fear may be an innate response to certain stimuli, such as pain, and the fear response

innately produces the fear stimulus, just as electric shock produces pain. The only difference is that it is easy to attach the fear response to new cues. Similarly, learned rewards are produced by responses that remove sources of strong stimulation. Thus the basic mechanism of motivation (strong stimulation) is the same for primary and learned drives, and the basic mechanism of reinforcement (a reduction in strong stimulation) is the same for primary and learned rewards.

It is worth noting that Miller and others have shown that conditioned emotional responses are often highly resistant to extinction. They also generalize to stimuli similar to the ones initially associated with pain. At the human level, clinical observation suggests that extreme chronic anxiety may function in a manner analogous to the way in which fear affected Miller's rats. Conflict studies with animals and research on analogues of defense mechanisms have shown similarities to observations made of human behavior in everyday life and in clinical contexts.

Perhaps the most familiar group of studies with animals which seem to be related to human personality functioning are those that have gone by the name of experimental neuroses (Broadhurst, 1961). Using a classical conditioning approach, Pavlov was the first to perform this type of laboratory study. His subjects were dogs and his method was that of contrasting stimuli. This method involved differentially reinforcing responses to similar stimuli. For example, in one of Pavlov's experiments, a dog was trained to salivate to a circle, but not to an ellipse. The diameters of the ellipse were gradually changed until the dog could not discriminate between the circle and the ellipse. Pavlov observed that at the point at which it became impossible to discriminate between the two stimuli, many dogs appeared to "break down" or to show experimental neuroses. At this point, their behavior would often be marked by negativism and by aggression toward the experimenter. It is important to note, however, that not all animals showed experimental neuroses under the experimental conditions.

Liddell (1944) and others have described behaviors in other species that resemble the experimentally induced neurotic behavior of Pavlov's subjects. Wolpe (1962) has reported a provocative study in which cats were placed in a box and were shocked after the sounding of a buzzer. He found that the anxiety aroused by this procedure was so intense that the cats refused to eat food offered to them in the box even after 72 hours of nutritional deprivation. That generalization had occurred was demonstrated by the fact that the animals also refused food in other rooms of the same laboratory. Wolpe attempted to "cure" these cats by feeding them initially in markedly different environments. Then he gradually brought them to the point at which they would eat in the experimental box.

Most of this research clearly could not have been carried out with human subjects. Studies of trauma and conflict in animals may prove of great value in clarifying our thinking about human behavior and the conditions that give rise to behavioral aberrations. Attempts to use learning principles derived from animal experiments as bases for studies of human behavior would also appear to be promising.

Many students of psychotherapy have conjectured about the possibility of treating therapeutic situations from the point of view of learning and re-education (Bandura, 1961; Wolpe, 1962). Research on psychotherapy, aimed at this possibility, seems to be getting under way only now, but it appears to be promising. The focus of this research will no doubt emphasize the psychotherapist as a reinforcer of responses in the response hierarchy of the individual. Within this context, behavior, whether adjusted to reality or involving neurotic or psychotic perceptions of reality, may be described in terms of response tendencies that are formed through conditioning, imitation, and discrimination learning. Studies of severely disturbed persons treated on the basis of these principles indicate that often dramatic behavioral changes can be brought about through the use of selective reinforcement.

CONCLUDING COMMENTS CONCERNING LEARNING AND PERSONALITY

Learning approaches to problems of personality and motivation present interesting contrasts with those of the psychoanalytic orientation that were considered earlier. Espousers of the latter orientation strongly felt the need to develop, at any early point in their work, conceptions of the broad sweep of characteristics and tendencies that make up the human organism. Espousers of the former orientation have been more molecular in their approaches and have sought to keep references to covert events to a manageable minimum. (Although, as we have seen, there is by no means agreement on what is a manageable minimum.)

One might usefully think of all psychological formulations in terms of an S-O-R paradigm, in which S stands for stimulus, R for response, and O for organismic or internal variables, processes, and events. The writers so far reviewed can be ordered roughly with regard to the strength of O components in their formulations. First, there is Skinner, who objects to references to any mental events as explanatory terms, and who would rely almost exclusively on observable S and R variables. Then there are Bandura and Walters, who also emphasize S and R variables, but have gone at least one step beyond Skinner in dealing with internal events. The Dollard and Miller orientation is an environmental one, but reflects much preoccupation with inner conflict and the higher mental processes. Finally, the psychoanalysts are characterized by their concern with behavior as a product of complex internal processes.

In general, and at the risk of lumping together contributors who do not share the same set of values, we regard the application of learning principles to problems of personality as most salutary. True, one could argue legitimately that there must be more to the study of behavior than the acquisition and extinction of responses. But this belief need not divert us from appreciating the pervasive role of learning in the determination of behavior. The study of learning in relation to individual differences seems a fruitful direction for research, particularly because of the lack of a direct approach to learning in psychoanalytic orientations. Just as we may feel that Freud emphasized too strongly the role of unconscious motivation so may we believe that learning psychologists have overemphasized the role of environmental events in behavior change. But, and this is the crucial point, we may at the same time believe that these supposed over-emphases were simply aspects of major breakthroughs in the discovery of variables necessary to an analysis of behavior.

One final comment follows from what has just been said. There are indications that learning psychologists and psychologists who emphasize the role of unconscious processes in personality functioning are coming more and more to borrow ideas and facts from one another. This seems all to the good. Researchers and theorists seem destined to labor on those specific concepts that are of most interest to them. But the fruits of this labor will often be of higher quality if they engage in a degree of hybridization. In Parts 3, 4, and 5 we shall come across many examples of research stimulated by hybrid points of view.

5

The Self in Personality

Notwithstanding their significant differences of opinion, most of the theorists considered so far may be described as operating within an essentially deterministic framework. They have been committed to the belief that behavior can be explained by statements of the type: if *a*, then *b*. Whether emphasizing unconscious motivation and overdetermination or reinforcement and conditioning these theorists have appeared, by and large, to be wedded to the view that prior events are decisive determinants of present behavior. Though at odds over explanatory constructs and the data to be encompassed by personality theory, they have all directed their attention to the causes of behavior.

To a number of psychologists this deterministic point of view tends to depict man as a slave to drives, environmental contingencies, and his past. Objecting to this portrait of man, they have presented quite different approaches which de-emphasize the mechanistic underpinnings of behavior. Several of their conceptions of personality have dwelt on the individual's interpretations of himself and his world, the effects of his goals and purposes on his behavior, and the tendency toward self-actualization and self-enhancement. Contrasted with the psychoanalytic point of view, their orientations are concerned more with the development of the sense of self and rational maturity than with the need to gratify impulses or to sublimate them. That this is not a simply black-white discrimination problem is seen in the fact that many of the neo-Freudians emphasize both determinism *and* the need for self-actualization. They continue to recognize an element of "if *a*, then *b*" in their researches.

The views which we shall consider in this chapter reflect a reaction against Freudian and learning theory notions of the unconscious and reinforcement. These views involve strong preoccupation with the problem of the individual as a perceiver and interpreter of himself and as a determiner of his present and future behavior. The nature of these self-perceptions and the individual's conscious interpretations of them constitute central problems in a study of personality. Emphasis on these problems need not necessarily be construed as a roadblock to the search for historical antecedents. Rather, this emphasis might be seen simply as a reflection of a need to fill in gaps in our present conceptions of human behavior. Mowrer (1960*b*, pp. 416–417) has given a good example of one such gap in contemporary psychology:

> No psychologist, as an individual, has ever lost sight of the fact of his own mortality, i.e., the inevitability of his ultimate death; and this fact unavoidably colors the whole course and meaning of human existence. But psychologists, in their *official* role, have been strangely silent in this connection—and the reason is not far to seek. One of the major functions of religion and ethical philosophy has been to help man meet his existential perplexities; and in their attempt to establish and preserve their professional identity, psychologists have tended to ignore not only the traditional solutions but the very problem itself. Typical is the remark of a young clinical psychologist: "Yes, it is certainly true that persons in psychotherapy often speak of death and its personal implications for them, but at this point I keep quiet or else just 'reflect' what they have said".

Before turning to some of the more salient concepts in orientations that deal with the perception of the self, one necessary distinction should be drawn concerning the ways in which the self concept has been employed.

Two meanings of the self-concept appear to be prevalent. Hall and Lindzey (1957) have labelled these as the *self-as-object* and the *self-as-process*. The self-as-process corresponds rather closely to the Freudian conception of the ego. When psychoanalysts refer to the ego they usually mean the self as a doer, an executor and integrator of psychological functions. With this meaning, all commerce with reality is negotiated through the self as a doer. Among the ego or executive self-processes are perception, thinking, etc. The construct of the self (ego) offered by Freud, then, was that of an agent that responded to reality, and related reality factors to intrapsychic factors.

Where does the self-as-object, the self that views itself, fit into this psychoanalytic way of thinking? Certainly Freud allowed that individuals observed themselves as objects. Indeed, the use of introspection is one of the hallmarks of the therapy he invented. But, for him, awareness of oneself was still determined by unconscious drives and tendencies, and, therefore, was a product of more basic factors.

Thus, within psychoanalysis, it is not possible for the ego to engage, as it were, in unhampered self-observation.

The emphasis here will not be on the ego as the executive intermediary between the individual and the world. Nor shall we, at this point, go into the problem of the person as a stimulus for others. For the present we shall be concerned with the self-as-object and the problem of the individual as an experiencer and interpreter of his own experience. One American psychologist who has been most concerned with self-experiencing is Carl Rogers (1951, 1959). His orientation has often been used to exemplify the antithesis of the psychoanalytic and stimulus-response deterministic points of view.

ROGERS' CONCEPTION OF THE SELF

The deterministic approach to behavior assumes a reality to which an individual responds and adjusts. Rogers' (1959, pp. 191–192) entire system is based on questions he has raised concerning this concept of reality:

> There is one . . . attitude which I hold, which I believe has relevance for the proper evaluation of any theory I might present. It is my belief in the fundamental predominance of the subjective. Man lives essentially in his own personal and subjective world, and even his most objective functioning, in science, mathematics, and the like, is the result of subjective purpose and subjective choice. In relation to research and theory, for example, it is my subjective perception that the machinery of science as we know it—operational definitions, experimental methods, mathematical proof—is the best way of avoiding self-deception. But I cannot escape the fact that this is the way it appears to me, and that had I lived two centuries ago, or if I were to live two centuries in the future, some other pathway to truth might seem equally or more valid. To put it more briefly, it appears to me that though there may be such a thing as objective truth, I can never know it; all I can know is that some statements appear to me subjectively to have the qualifications of objective truth. Thus there is no such thing as Scientific Knowledge; there are only individual perceptions of what appears to each person to be such knowledge.

Rogers (1959, pp. 211–212) has related his concern with the subjective to scientific endeavor in this way:

> Although in the last analysis each individual lives in and by his own subjective knowledge, this is not regarded socially as "knowledge" and certainly not as scientific knowledge.
>
> Knowledge which has any "certainty," in the social sense, involves the use of empathic inference as a means of checking, but the direction of that

empathy differs. When the experience of emphatic understanding is used as a source of knowledge, one checks one's empathic inferences with the subject, thus verifying or disproving the inferences and hypotheses implicit in such empathy. It is this way of knowing which we have found so fruitful in therapy. Utilizing empathic inference to the fullest, the knowledge thus gained of the client's subjective world has led to understanding the basis of his behavior and the process of personality change.

In knowing a person or an object from the external frame of reference, our implicit hypotheses are checked with other people, but *not* with the subject of our concern. Thus a rigorous behaviorist believes that S is a stimulus for his experimental animal and R is a response, because his colleagues and even the man in the street agree with him and regard S and R in the same way. His empathic inferences are made in regard to the internal frame of reference of his colleagues, rather than in regard to the internal frame of reference of the animal.

Science involves taking an external frame of reference in which we check our hypotheses basically through empathic inferences as to the internal frame of reference of our colleagues. They perform the same operations we have (either actually or through symbolic representation), and if they perceive the same events and meanings, then we regard our hypotheses as confirmed.

At any given point in time an individual may be characterized in terms of his concept of himself and his experiences and interpretations of environmental stimuli. The degree of congruence between these two aspects of a person's psychological field, Rogers holds, influences the extent to which self-actualization can be expected to take place. Thus, self-actualization seems to be a function of the degree to which perception of self and perception of the world are in accord.

Rogers assumes that the individual has the capacity and tendency to symbolize and understand accurately the mental contents of which he is aware. The ability to symbolize experiences accurately in awareness and the tendency toward self-actualization are conceived by him to be related to the individual's sense of self-regard and the regard that he senses others have for him. Implicit here are the assumptions of needs for positive self-regard and for positive regard by others. Self-actualization results when these needs are met. When that happens, Rogers has contended, personality adjustment will be optimal. Optimal adjustment or, as Rogers phrases it, the fully functioning person is characterized by a low level of anxiety. Anxiety, for him, is a state of uneasiness or tension resulting from incongruencies between the perception of self and the total experience of the individual. Other characteristics of adjustment are openness with oneself and with confrères, lack of defensiveness, and self-consistency.

Rogers' thinking has been greatly influenced by his psychotherapeutic activities. Interestingly, whereas the ways in which they have talked about behavior contrast sharply, both Rogers and Freud developed their theoretical positions on the basis of similar observational data, the behavior of patients and therapists in psychotherapy. Rogers' work with children and adults led him to develop a "client-centered" approach which is in accord with the theoretical orientation just outlined. Within this orientation, the psychotherapy situation is one to which anxious, troubled people with low self-regard and discrepant, subjective self-world perceptions come for help. The task for the therapist or counsellor is neither to make interpretations nor to give advice or prescriptions to his client. Rather, it is to provide him with an opportunity to achieve a reorganization of his subjective world.

This is done through the therapist's acceptance of the individual as a person of worth. But acceptance by the therapist is ineffective, Rogers believes, if it is essentially intellectual in nature; the acceptance must be a function of the therapist's real respect, trust, and empathy for the person who is confiding in him. This view of the process of personality change holds that, in a sense, the patient becomes able to cure himself and improve in the trusting environment provided by the therapist.

Although Rogers' ideas were worked out with the data of psychotherapy in mind, they would appear to be suggestive with regard to other types of situations. Family, school, and social situations may be interpereted in the light of the needs and conditions hypothesized by Rogers. Each life situation might be viewed in terms of self-world discrepancies and development might be viewed as changes in the self-actualizing tendency, self-knowledge, and the needs for self-regard and acceptance by others.

This review of some of the highlights of the Rogerian orientation raises the question of how useful it has been in terms of generating empirical evidence. Most of its evidence pertains to the events of psychotherapy. Although some students have wondered about the usefulness of phenomenological theories for scientific investigative purposes, Rogers and his followers have probably contributed a methodologically sounder body of studies of the process of psychotherapy than any that has emanated from any other school of thought (Rogers and Dymond, 1954). One of the major Rogerian contributions has been the extent to which Rogers and his followers have sought to make public, through films and tape recordings, the actual transactions of psychotherapy. These studies have centered on what happens in psychotherapy as a result of the attitudes and behavior of both patients and therapists. One of their aims has been to trace the changes which occur in an individual's self-perceptions and perceptions of others as psychotherapy progresses.

ALLPORT'S VIEWS OF DEVELOPMENT AND THE SELF

The Rogers view of personality well illustrates the self-as-object concept. His writing represents one attempt to come to grips with the subjectivity of each of our personal worlds. It will be worthwhile to consider some other views of the self.

Of all psychologists who have been active in the field of personality over the past several decades, few have approached Gordon Allport in terms of scholarly contributions (Allport, 1937, 1960, 1961). He has exerted great influence through his attempts to analyze and synthesize existing views and evidence in the field of personality. In the course of this scholarly work it would be surprising if he did not come up with original conceptual contributions of his own. Fortunately, he has not surprised us.

We shall begin a review of some of these contributions with Allport's approach to the self-concept. This starting point is appropriate because several of his other formulations may be examined from the standpoint of the self-concept. For Allport awareness of self is a datum that cannot be ignored, no matter how many methodological problems it may pose for psychologists. He argues forcefully that each person has a sense of self and identity. Although he recognizes that the self as a concept poses thorny philosophical problems, he believes that students of behavior can contribute to the understanding of the development of the sense of self. He has in his writings hypothesized a series of developmental stages in this evolution.

The first one, which occurs during the first years of life, is called by Allport the period of the early self. During this period the child develops a sense of the bodily "me" and a sense of self-identity. The capacity to experience self-esteem and pride increases with maturation in these early years. During the succeeding few years of development, the child begins to evolve what Allport calls extension of self and a self-image. By this Allport means the child's ability to go beyond the complete egocentricity of infancy to an appreciation of the world about him and a sensitivity to the reactions of other people. During this period, Allport feels, the foundations are laid for the goals, purposes, and the responsibilities of adulthood.

The years from 6 to 12 Allport describes as a period in which the self-as-doer develops. During the school years the child learns how to cope rationally with many types of problems, such as those posed by school work and peer relationships. The period of adolescence is a climactic one in Western society because it is during this stage that the child must begin to cope with the problem of planning for the future, and particularly with the selection of an occupation. Erikson (1950) and others have also stressed this aspect of adolescent development. Allport uses the term *propriate strivings* to refer to the emerging capacity of the adolescent to plan, to implement his plans, and to develop a *Weltanschauung*. He speaks of the fruition in adulthood of the proprium, by which he means the synthesis of all of the states of relevance to the self which we experience. Thus, in the construct of the proprium, Allport has sought to unite such functions as wanting, striving, willing, and planning.

By means of what processes or events does the proprium come into being? In answering this question Allport seems to have adopted a position that might be said to involve the idea of developmental discontinuity. The early stages of self-development are viewed by Allport as products of learning and conditioning. Reinforcements from the environment help the child to learn which verbal labels go with which bodily and psychological sensations and experiences. However, with the development of the proprium, the individual's sense of self becomes self-perpetuating and directive in influencing behavior. The mature adult, Allport says, is much less easily swayed by environmental reinforcements than is the child. Allport has related this discontinuity in self-development to the problem of neurotic, psychotic, and normal behavior. Whereas normal behavior is guided by the proprium, deviant mental functioning, he argues, is attributable to inadequate self-development. Thus, maladjustment, for Allport, is essentially due to immaturity and developmental arrest of the proprium. He has contended that psychoanalytic and behavioristic interpretations of the genesis of behavior may apply in cases of personality maladjustment but that they are unable to account for normal, propriate functioning. Deviant behavior, in this view, is attributable to an iceberg of unconscious happenings. The mature person, on the other hand, can be understood primarily in terms of his conscious functioning.

Tied to his theory of the development of the self is Allport's concept of the *functional autonomy of motives*. He rejects assumptions of the constancy of motives and psychic energy. He is critical of the stress in psychoanalytic theory on the predominant role of sexual drive throughout life. During childhood, he believes, biological drives and motivations, such as those described by Freud, are important determinants of behavior. But with maturation, new and different social and personal motives come to the fore. These motives may have been acquired originally in connection with the biological drives and motives but have become functionally autonomous. Functional autonomy as a concept has aroused argument because most learning theorists reject the notion that acquired motives maintain themselves in the absence of reinforcement. For Allport reinforcement is more important in the early than in the later years of life. In the case of the mature adult, functionally autonomous motives are independent of the conditions which may have initially given rise to them. Although one might disagree with the particular way in which Allport has phrased functional autonomy, the observations that stimulated his interest in it are undeniably of interest to students of behavior. Why do some of us drive many miles simply to view a mountain? Why do we have the particular interests and values that we do?

Seward has suggested an interesting substitute to the notion of functional autonomy of motives that is designed to cope with questions such as these. He has argued for a broad conception of motivation to include not only biological, visceral needs but extraorganic or *exogenous motives,* as well. By exogenous motives, Seward refers to the organism's needs to know, predict, and control its environment. Thus, a child's efforts to find out how a light switch works may be thought of as the result of an intrinsic but nonvisceral exploratory motive. It is conceivable, as Seward (1963, p. 708) has suggested, that an explanation of the play of the child and the adult does not require the idea of functionally autonomous motives but rather can be understood in terms of the effects on behavior of exogenous motives.

> Functionally autonomous motives, as their name implies, were not subject to extinction. In this respect exogenous motives are fully qualified to take their place. Play is intrinsically rewarding; so is finding a bird's nest or solving an equation. Trips to the candy jar will cease when the jar is empty, but the desire for candy lives on. True, all the exogenous motives except boredom can be satiated to some extent as new learning reduces whatever discrepancy aroused them. So it might seem that we have merely exchanged one frailty for another. But the argument would hold only if we had exhausted the possible varieties of experience, an extremity seldom reached outside of concentration camps and zoos. Most of the earth's human inhabitants, cheerfully ignoring the specter of overpopulation, do not face psychic satiation as an immediate threat. Artists, composers, and advertisers continue to explore their media for fresh combinations to titillate or appall us. Scientists race one another into the unknown. Ordinary people find that even the companion of a lifetime is never completely predictable.

Allport has made a significant contribution by directing attention to the roles played by interests, values, and principles in affecting behavior. His views concerning the self and functional autonomy have been influential in psychology, in part because they represent an articulate alternative to the predominant deterministic model of science within the discipline. They do not, however, seem to require adherence to an extreme phenomenological viewpoint such as is found in Rogers' writings. Allport's attack on pure behavioristic theories of human behavior stems from the contention that psychologists tend to direct their investigative efforts too often to the study of isolated segments of behavior and that they unrealistically break the person up into discrete units, for example, habits, attitudes, drives. In Allport's (1961, pp. 572–573) view:

> The personality system is a complex product of biological endowment, cultural shaping, cognitive style, and spiritual groping. Only if viewed in this way can all the diverse methods of inquiry be brought to a focus. Their separate contributions can best be blended if we regard personality as a system—incomplete but bent on growth and on becoming more than it is. Any other assumption falls short of the measure of man. . . .
>
> Psychology is truly itself only when it can deal with individuality. It is vain to plead that other sciences do not do so, that they are allowed to brush off the bothersome issue of uniqueness. The truth is that psychology is *assigned* the task of being curious about human persons, and persons exist only in concrete and unique patterns.
>
> Since psychology has this peculiar assignment it cannot be content with the dogma that understanding people is achieved merely by ordering the individual to a class. That inferential knowledge of this sort is important no one will deny. But, in addition, knowledge through direct perception, configural comprehension, "acquaintance with," needs to be sought. The full resources of our cognitive equipment are needed as tools of research.

To achieve this psychology of individuality Allport has argued for an *idiographic approach to personality*. The idiographic study of personality is usually contrasted to the *nomothetic approach*. Nomothetic models assume that all people differ in many respects and that each person may be characterized by the particular amounts of the various human characteristics which he possesses. Thus, John Jones may be described by a set of characteristics including such things as his height, his weight, and his scores on intelligence, personality, and physical tests. The nomothetic view assumes that all people can be compared on all human characteristics. The idiographic model, on the other hand, assumes that if we truly ascribe individuality to the individual, we cannot at the same time assume that, generally, he is comparable to other people. The aspect of this position that has bothered the majority of psychologists has been the implication that, idiographically, one can do little more than appreciatively describe persons.

Actually, Allport has sought to develop a middle position which incorporates aspects of both the nomothetic and idiographic models. The synthesis that he has offered, however, is probably still too idiographically tinged to please the purely quantitative empiricist. Allport has maintained that each individual may be characterized in two complementary ways. He may be described in terms of common traits which are individual difference variables applicable to all people. Additionally, comprehensive personality description requires an accounting of his unique personal dispositions. The latter are characteristics peculiar to the individual. Data relevant to them may be gleaned from observation of the expressive and gestural aspects of the individual's behavior, study of personal documents (such as letters he has written), and his own self-descriptions and reports (Allport, 1942, Allport and Vernon, 1933).

An additional comment relevant to the position taken by Allport on the idiographic-nomothetic issue is that he is fully aware of the problems of methodology involved in it, particularly with regard to personal dispositions. His suggestions about the data that may be obtainable in order to infer personal disposition are valuable because they call attention to some aspects of behavior outside of the laboratory (for example, documents) that may add to our understanding of behavior. But most students of personality would agree that Allport's major contributions have been in the sphere of concept rather than of method. Oeser (1961, p. 450) has described these contributions in this way:

> For forty years *consciousness* has been taboo except among the lower orders of applied and clinical psychologists, and even these, except for a few experimentalists, have operated with the concept of an empty organism pushed from the past against present resistances into an unknown future. Against them Allport uncompromisingly erected the concept of the self-conscious, rational man, who creates his style and his future with forward-looking motivations.

THE GESTALT INFLUENCE AND THE SELF

Every introductory psychology textbook discusses Gestalt psychology. The student is almost always told that the whole is equal to more than the sum of its parts. Applied to the human organism this means that a person is more than the sum of his physical, mental, and emotional attributes. This is the case, Gestalt psychologists argue, because there is a unique character to the total configuration of these attributes which cannot be predicted simply on the basis of their enumeration. This Gestalt view of behavior is not incompatible with the idiographic approach. If personality, then, has to do with individuality, how does one study it? Not, say the Gestaltists, by segmenting the organism as the stimulus-response psychologists have been accused of doing. Gestaltists believe instead that the way to approach individuality is to concentrate on the total functioning of the person and the total configuration of his attributes. What assumptions do Gestalt personality theorists make about the nature of this total functioning?

In addition to assuming that the subject matter of personality is the total, integrated organism, many writers who have applied Gestalt principles to personality hold that man is driven by one major motive, that of self-actualization. As we have seen in the case of several theorists already mentioned, this inherent drive toward self-actualization directs the individual to develop and expand his potentialities in a way unique to him. Goldstein's organismic theory, which is Gestalt in orientation, illustrates the use of this assumption (Goldstein, 1939, 1940). It resembles many aspects of Rogers' self-theory, but is more complete in intent than Rogers' system. For Goldstein, the self-actualization tendency is the basic motivational determinant of behavior. Sex, hunger, and curiosity, which are usually analyzed as separate motivational entities, are, for Goldstein, merely manifestations of self-actualization. All human creativity is interpreted by him as resulting from the motive to actualize oneself. This conceptualization of self-actualization resembles ideas expressed by other writers, including Maslow (1954*a*, 1954*b*, 1956), Murphy (1947) and Angyal (1941, 1965).

The all-encompassing nature of Goldstein's orientation is seen in his efforts to include biological factors within the total configuration that defines the person. For this reason, Goldstein's approach may be called an organismic psychology. Pathology, both physical and mental, is seen to result from disorganization within the individual's total biological-psychological configuration. It is not surprising that Goldstein, a neuropsychiatrist, is as interested in the effects of bodily disturbances as in the effects of mental disturbances on behavior. Probably his major empirical contribution has been his research with persons afflicted by brain injuries. This research centered on the effects of brain injury on the mental and emotional aspects of individuals' behavior.

The advocacy of a tendency toward self-actualization in perhaps its most extreme form may be found in the writings of Maslow (1956, pp. 232–233):

The basic assumptions of this point of view are:

1. We have, each of us, an essential inner nature, which is to some degree "natural," intrinsic, given, and, in a certain sense, unchangeable, or, at least, unchanging.

2. Each person's inner nature is in part unique to himself and in part species-wide.

3. It is possible to study this inner nature scientifically and to discover what it is like—(not *invent—discover*).

4. This inner nature, as much as we know of it so far, seems not to be intrinsically evil, but rather either neutral or positively "good." What we call evil appears most often to be a secondary reaction to frustration of this intrinsic nature.

5. Since this inner nature is good rather than bad, it is best to bring it out and to encouage it rather than to suppress it. If it is permitted to guide our life, we grow healthy, fruitful, and happy.

6. If this essential core of the person is denied or suppressed, he gets sick sometimes in obvious ways, sometimes in subtle ways, sometimes immediately, sometimes later.

7. This inner nature is not strong and overpowering and unmistakable like the instincts of animals. It is weak and delicate and subtle and easily overcome by habit, cultural pressure, and wrong attitudes toward it.

8. Even though weak, it never disappears in the normal person—perhaps not even in the sick person. Even though denied, it persists underground forever pressing for actualization.

9. Somehow, these conclusions must all be articulated with the necessity of discipline, deprivation, frustration, pain, and tragedy. To the extent that these experiences reveal and foster and fulfill our inner nature, to that extent they are desirable experiences.

What Goldstein, Angyal, and others tried to do by way of defining the subject matter of psychology as the study of biological-mental configurational wholes, Maslow (1954*b*) seems to have attempted for the motive toward self-actualization. As the quotation suggests, he has operated within an organismic frame of reference that emphasizes the inherent goodness of man. Neuroses and other mental disorders, for Maslow, result from environmental forces that interfere with the self-actualization process. The assumption of the inherent goodness of man has led him, understandably, to a greater interest in the creative, self-actualizing person than in the disordered one. In this sense, he shares with Allport (1) an interest in what might be called the mature contributor to society and to himself, and (2) a tendency to regard psychopathology as explicable in terms different from those used in discussing the normal person.

Before leaving the topic of the self, mention should be made of an interesting attempt by Kelly to conceptualize individuals' perceptions of themselves (G. A. Kelly, 1955). For Kelly, how one perceives oneself is part of a construing process that goes on continuously. This process involves persons' interpretations of themselves and the world about them and their anticipations of future events. He has commented that ". . . *a person's processes are psychologically channelized by ways in which he anticipates events*" (G. A. Kelly, 1955, p. 46). The products of the person's construing process, Kelly refers to as constructs; these are the interpretations that the individual makes of internal and external events. Kelly's model of man asserts that people are constantly engaged in problem solving, and that their personal constructs are an important means of bringing order to their universe. Kelly has presented a suggestive hypothesis that each man is a theory constructor. He has also developed a psychometric device, the Role Construct Repertory Test, to assess these everyday life theories. Kelly's test has only recently come into usage in personality research but it seems likely to be of value to many investigators interested in the self and its workings.

CONCLUDING COMMENTS CONCERNING THE SELF-CONCEPT

While there are differences among the points of view expressed by such writers as Rogers, Allport, and Goldstein, there are several noticeable similarities. Outstanding among these is concern with the person's subjective world and the awareness of self. For the Freudian, self-reports are pathways to the unconscious determinants of behavior. For the phenomenologist, the reports of conscious experience is knowledge valid in its own right. This explains why none of the theorists considered in this chapter have approached the psychoanalysts in their preoccupation with unconscious factors (Combs, and Snygg, 1959).

The hypothesis that verbal reports can be studied in their own right rather than as distorted reflections of unconscious forces seems to be a reasonable one. Whether or not one agrees with writers such as Rogers, Allport, and Maslow, these men have helped stimulate empirical activity.

Rogers' studies of changes in self-description as a function of psychotherapy are suggestive of the persuasive value of his views. Another area of research influenced by Rogers' thinking has been the analysis of the content of a person's verbal productions. This research has been directed (1) to the study of the individual's self-references in the course of speaking, and (2) to the affective tone associated with these self-references. A study by Raimy (1948) was one of the first investigations of this type to be reported and many more have been published since. Other empirical attacks on the self-concept have been made through the construction and use of personality tests and rating scales. These instruments have been used to provide bases for inferring the individual's self-attitudes and degrees of self-satisfaction and self-consistency.

Hypotheses about the self-as-object raise a number of challenging questions: is self-actualization a product of the theorist's value system or is it a life process susceptible to objective study? Can verbal reports of subjective experience be accepted at face value? What are their relationships to unconscious factors? To what extent is the self-concept a product of learning? What is the relationship of the physical environment of the individual to his subjective psychological experiences? Regardless of the answers to these questions it does seem essential that personality description include references to the individual's sense of identity and evaluation of himself. It is a fact that self-theorists have effectively put the spotlight on these data, which leads us to say that they have contributed importantly to the psychology of personality.

A person's description of himself constitutes rich data from which various kinds of inferences may be drawn. These inferences may be thought of as constructs, whose validity must be established in the usual scientific manner. Hilgard (1949, p. 379) has spoken of the inferred self. By this term he has sought to emphasize that the self, like concepts of unconscious processes, motivation, learning, and perception, is an inference from behavior rather than a localized entity within the person. He has also sought through the term to include in the self-concept not only that of which we are aware, but also that of which we may be unaware:

The inferred self goes beyond the self of awareness by including for purposes of inference much that is excluded from self-awareness. Awareness includes the not-self as well as the self. In dreams and hallucinations we have products of the self, present in awareness, but products for which the self takes neither credit nor responsibility. It is hard to see the self as giving the stage-directions for the dream, or as selecting the epithets hurled by the hallucinated voices. Yet in making a reconstruction of genotypical motives, these products of the self enter as evidence. Some items, then, remain in awareness, but are not part of self-awareness. Other items are excluded from awareness by inattention or amnesia. Facts such as these necessitate indirection in the inference to motivational organization. A description of overt conduct is not enough to permit an accurate appraisal of motivational patterning.

Self theorists would, for the most part, concur with the assertion of a need for construct validation of self-concepts. Most of them would insist, however, upon the assumption that only the individual really has knowledge of his subjective world. Students influenced by existential philosophers like Kierkegaard and Heiddeger would probably insist on a number of other assumptions as well. One of these assumptions is that man's significance is not to be found in his past, but in what he is now and what he is becoming (Lyons, 1963).

The idea that the individual understands himself and the world from his unique vantage point seems perfectly legitimate. It would suggest the desirability of studying the self-concept in terms of self-report data provided by persons. Yet it seems unnecessary to assume that an individual's self-reports and self-understanding will be superior to the inferences drawn by scientific observers using all the data available to them. The individual's experience is certainly his, and his alone; his subjective reactions are experienced solely by him. But rather than guess about the validity or invalidity of these experiences, it may be preferable to regard them simply as data from which inferences may be drawn.

A summary of the points of view considered in this chapter must begin with the emphasis on the phenomenal, the subjective world of the individual. This world, many self theorists believe, is directed by a self-actualizing tendency. Several theorists, notably Goldstein (1939, 1940), have called for an integrated, holistic approach to the many facets of the organism. Others, notably Allport (1961), have cautioned against too strong a preoccupation with unconscious drives as determinants of behavior.

The self-as-doer refers to the things people do and the actions they carry out. The data relevant to the self-as-object are people's own reactions to themselves. Inferences about personality require reference to what people do and what they think about themselves and about others. One might add yet another class of data, what others think about us and how they behave toward us. May (1961, p. 48) has attempted to incorporate this social aspect of living into a concept of the self.

The tentative hypothesis I suggest is that my "being"—which by definition must have unity if it is to survive as a being . . . —has three aspects, which we may term "self," "person," and "ego." The "self" I use as the subjective center, the experiencing of the fact that I am the one who behaves in thus and thus ways, the "person" we may take as the aspect in which I am accepted by others . . . ; and the "ego" we may take as Freud originally enunciated it, the specific organ or perception by which the self sees and relates to the outside world. I hold no ultimate brief for this hypothesis at the moment; it calls for further clarification, and I offer it here for its suggestive possibilities. But the point I do wish to make strongly is that *being* must be presupposed in discussions of ego and identity, and that the *centered self* . . . must be basic to such discussions.

The writings of self-theorists have reflected an increasing concern with the problem of the existing person and his subjective world. This emphasis on the need to understand subjective reality represents an interesting contrast to the strong preoccupation of most contemporary psychologists with the need for objective data. This contrast is seen in these comments by May (1961, pp. 17–18):

There is no such thing as truth or reality for a living human being except as he participates in it, is conscious of it, has some relationship of it. We can demonstrate at every moment of the day . . . that only the truth that comes alive, becomes more than an abstract idea, and is "felt on the pulse," only the truth that is genuinely experienced on all levels of being, including what is called subconscious and unconscious and never excluding the element of conscious decision and responsibility—only this truth has the power to change a human being.

The existentialist emphasis in psychology does not, therefore, deny the validity of the approaches based on conditioning, the formulation of drives, the study of discrete organisms, and so on. It only holds that you can never explain or understand any *living* human being on that basis. And the harm arises when the image of man, the presuppositions about man himself are exclusively based on such methods. There seems to be the following "law" at work: the more accurately and comprehensively you can describe a given mechanism, the more you lose the existing person. *The more absolutely and completely you formulate the forces or drives, the more you are talking about abstractions and not the existing, living human being.* For the living person (who is not hypnotized or drugged or in some other way placed in an artificial position, such as in a laboratory, in which his element of decision and his responsibility for his own existence are temporarily suspended for the purposes of the experiment) always transcends the given mechanism and always experiences the "drive" or "force" in his unique way. The distinction is whether the "person has meaning in terms of the mechanism" or the "mechanism has meaning in terms of the person." The existential emphasis is firmly on the latter. And it holds that the former can be integrated within the latter.

6

Field Theory and the Study of the Individual

Self-theorists are consistent in emphasizing that the individual's awareness of himself influences his behavior. However, they differ in the extent to which they seek to integrate the self-system into a concept of the total organism. Thus, while Rogers has concerned himself primarily with the phenomena of subjective experience, Goldstein has approached subjective experience from a psychological-biological organismic standpoint. Another orientation to personality shares this interest in subjective experience but seeks to approach it within a broader, more social context. Field theorists emphasize not only persons' perceptions of themselves but also their perceptions of the environment. Thus, they seek an over-all framework which can encompass self-world relationships. The most influential of the field theorists has been Lewin.

KURT LEWIN

In the previous chapter, the influence of Gestalt psychology was attributed to the emphasis placed by Gestaltists on the subjectivity of one's perceptions and the need to study the individual as a configuration rather than as a collection of segmented parts. Field theory, as exemplified by its most sophisticated exponent Kurt Lewin, represents yet another outgrowth of Gestalt psychology. Like the Gestalt-influenced self-theorists, Lewin also treated behavior as a function of the world perceived by the individual. But, whereas self-theorists have been preoccupied with perception of self, Lewin's efforts were directed to the perception of the world, the individual himself constituting one aspect of that world.

Lewinian field theory (Lewin, 1935, 1951) can perhaps most easily be understood through comparisons with two other approaches to behavior. One, already considered, is that of psychoanalysis and learning theory which seeks to account for present behavior through references to historical antecedents. Advocates of these points of view contend that the individual responds as he does at any given time because of past experiences. The other approach, to be discussed in Part 2, conceives of personality in terms of patterns of individual differences. From this point of view the empirical problem is the isolation of individual difference variables and the establishment of relationships between these variables and behavior.

The Lewinian position is that the proper starting point for an account of behavior is neither the individual's past nor his isolated attributes and characteristics. Rather, Lewinians contend, behavior must be viewed in terms of its momentary quality. Behavior is ever-changing and so are its determinants. To conceptualize this constant flux, Lewin contended that the way to think of behavior was as the product of a field of forces or vectors. Borrowing heavily from field theory in physics and mathematics, Lewin argued that a person's behavior at any given time was a function of his psychological field. The forces or vectors in this field may have their source either within the individual or they may come from the environment. The Lewinian position recognizes that the environment comes to be transformed by the individual; the individual's perception of environmental stimuli is not the same as the stimuli themselves. The perception of external events, rather than the events themselves, contributed to the determination of behavior.

Use of the analogy of a physical field to behavior requires description of both the total field and the forces at work within it. The total field of forces Lewin (1951, pp. 57–58) labeled the *life space.* The life space contains the total configuration of psychological reality at any given moment.

The food that lies behind doors at the end of a maze so that neither smell nor sight can reach it is not a part of the life space of the animal. If the individual knows that food lies there this *knowledge,* of course, has to be represented in his life space, because this knowledge affects behavior. It is also necessary to take into account the subjective probability with which the individual views the present or future state of affairs because the degree of certainty of expectation also influences his behavior.

The principle of representing within the life space all that affects behavior at that time, but nothing else, prevents the inclusion of physical food which is not perceived. This food cannot possibly influence his behavior at that time under the conditions mentioned. Indeed, the individual will start his journey if he thinks the food is there even if it is actually not there, and he will not move toward the food which actually is at the end of the maze if he does not know it is there.

Behavior, then, is a function of the life space. Stated another way (Lewin, 1954, p. 919), the life space is a construct referring to the totality of the facts impinging on the individual:

The novelist who tells the story behind the behavior and development of an individual gives us detailed data about his parents, his siblings, his character, his intelligence, his occupation, his friends, his status. He gives us these data in their specific interrelation, that is, as part of a total situation. Psychology has to fulfill the same task with scientific instead of poetic means. The method should be analytical in that the different factors which influence behavior have to be specifically distinguished. In science, these data have also to be represented in their particular setting within the specific situation. A totality of coexisting facts which are conceived of as mutually interdependent is called a *field* . . . . Psychology has to view the life space, including the person and his environment, as one field.

Of what is the life space a function? Lewin held that the life space was determined by the environment and the person. It is important to observe that Lewin used the word environment in two senses. By environment he meant the events of the objective world. He reserved the term psychological environment to refer to that part of the life space which represents perceived reality. The distinction between events of the real world and the individual's perception and interpretation of them suggests that Lewin's position is quite different from purely phenomenological ones which seek to deal exclusively with subjective reality.

For Lewin, the life space may be conceived as analogous to a geometric shape whose interior consists of psychological reality. Outside the perimeter of this shape is the physical world. However, the boundary between the life space and the physical world is permeable. Thus, Lewin allowed for changes in the life space as a result of the individual's contact with the physical world.

The life space consists of the changing psychological environment (that is, the aspects of the physical world that are incorporated into the individual's personal world), and the person. The person was viewed by Lewin as consisting of differential structures or regions.

Thus, one may speak of the perceptual-motor region and the inner-personal region of the person. These regions, which are permeable, may be further subdivided, the number of subdivisions varying from individual to individual, and for a given individual, from time to time.

The idea that changes can occur between the regions of the life space would seem to imply an energy concept. Effort is required each time that the life space is reconstructed. When the life space is at rest there is no expenditure of energy. In states of disequilibrium, energy is required to return to the quiescent state. In states of conflict, energy is required to resolve the problem. Lewin's energy concept includes the idea of needs aroused by physiological states, characteristics of the environment, intentions to attain goals, and interpersonal conflict. The emotional correlates of these needs are called tensions. Properties of objects that lead to energy expenditure are referred to as valences (Lewin, 1938, p. 88). Positive valences refer to objects that represent attractions to the person. Negatively valenced objects repel the person and lead to avoidance behavior. Values and self-attitudes may have positive or negative valences:

> The concept of valence . . . does not imply any specific statement concerning the origin of the attractiveness or the repulsiveness of the valence. The valence might be due to a state of hunger, to emotional attachment, or to a social constellation. The final goal related to a valence might be a consumption like eating a cake; it might be the joy of watching a performance at a theater; a negative valence might be based on the fear of being defeated in a competition. The statement that a certain region of the life space has a positive or negative valence merely indicates that, for whatever reason, at the present time and for this specific individual a tendency exists to act in the direction toward this region or away from it.

What is the developmental course of this system that consists of interacting structures and energy expenditure? Two processes occur in development, Lewin believed. One is differentiation. During differentiation the number of regions within the life space increases. As the child develops, regions corresponding to abilities, interests, and goals become differentiated. As these regions proliferate it becomes necessary for the attainment of effective behavior for the second process, integration, to operate. To the extent that the regions become integrated within the person, we may refer to the person as a unified, configurational whole.

In this cursory view of Lewin's system we have not sought to review exhaustively all of the concepts it employs. Nor have we tried to discuss the mathematical aspects of his vector analysis of behavior.

Our aim has been to characterize what is involved in a psychological field theory oriented to the individual's perception of the world. What we have described is an ahistorical approach to behavior, in the sense that the past determines behavior only insofar as past products are represented within the current life space.

The relationship of Lewin's field theory to the study of personality is perhaps comparable to the relationship between personality and learning theory. Field theory is a general point of view from which the study of personality and other constructs may be undertaken. Whether or not one finds the Lewinian way of speaking congenial, there is no doubt that study of Lewinian theory has produced much that is valuable. Lewinian experiments have been valuable in demonstrating the relevance to behavior of the conditions under which it occurs. Studies of motivation and frustration defined in terms of environmental conditions, such as preperformance instructions, illustrate this sort of study. An example of one type of experiment stimulated by Lewin's field theory is one carried out by Zeigarnik (1927). Lewin believed that the intention to reach a goal or carry out an activity could be considered as a tension within the life space. This tension functions as a sustainer of goal-directed thought and activity. Reduction of the tension, Lewin thought, results in a change in goal-directed thought and activity. Zeigarnik's experiment was designed to provide objective data relevant to this interpretation.

Zeigarnik's subjects were asked to perform a series of varied tasks (problems, puzzles, etc.). The subjects were permitted to complete certain of the tasks but not others. After working on all of the tasks, each subject was asked to recall them. Zeigarnik found that the subjects recalled many more unfinished than finished tasks. This suggested that when subjects had not finished a task tension persisted. When a task was finished the tension created by the need to master the task dissipated.

There seems little question that Lewin exhibited great ingenuity in devising experiments from which he drew inferences about changes in the environment and in the life space. In Part 3 we shall mention a number of examples of experiments stimulated by Lewinian concepts.

Lewin's influence today seems to be greatest in an area closely associated with that of personality, social psychology. The great interest in Lewin among students of social phenomena is understandable in view of the role social forces in the environment play in influencing the life space, and particularly the psychological environment. Social psychologists who adhere to a Lewinian conception of behavior have conducted much research on the ways in which changes in social conditions induce changes in the individual. The concept of group dynamics, an important one in contemporary social psychology, was analyzed by Lewin in terms of group relationships and resultants of forces. He felt that just as the individual might be thought of as an organic whole, so might the social group be conceptualized. The impact of Lewinian ideas has also been felt in research on social perception and the perception of others, social influence and decision-making processes, frustration, level of aspiration, motivation, and conflict (Atkinson, 1964; Cartwright, 1959).

Still another contribution of Lewin has been his encouragement of action research. Action research is carried out in "live" social and civic settings rather than under controlled laboratory conditions. It is usually designed to provide firsthand information about how social change occurs. Furthermore, it places the social scientist in the position of attempting to apply his theoretical views directly to relevant social phenomena. Observation of individuals and groups in natural settings can contribute to knowledge of the life space. Lewin's writings have helped stimulate the development of a field known as psychological ecology. Barker (1963) and his colleagues, who were greatly influenced by Lewin, have conducted valuable descriptive research in social settings. Their research has focused on observing aspects of the physical environment that induce changes in the psychological environment.

OTHER FIELD THEORISTS

Several writers, along with Lewin, have criticized the predominantly behavioristic tone of American psychology. Their major point has been that studying relationships between particular stimuli and particular responses does not do justice to the complex organization of the organism. Virtually every field theorist has emphasized the roles of perception and cognition rather than the role of learning in the shaping and functioning of this organized whole. Some field theorists, like Lewin, have sought to apply their general systems to personality and social phenomena. Others have been concerned almost exclusively with perceptual and cognitive processes.

Brunswik (1955, 1956) represents a field theorist whose own research dealt largely with perceptual phenomena. However, some of his concepts have had an impact on the field of personality. His concept of representative design, especially, seems to have implications for many of the activities in which personality researchers engage. Brunswik was critical of the tendency of researchers in the area of personality and in other areas to perform isolated experiments involving particular kinds of situations. Although the manner of conducting the research need not necessarily be severely criticized, Brunswik noted that sweeping generalizations were often made on the basis of quite special experimental conditions. To overcome the gap between research and the inferences drawn from it, Brunswik stressed the need to use representative designs in experimentation. The idea of representative design implies that inferences about persons should be drawn only after individuals have been observed in a variety of situations. Furthermore, since in everyday life behavior is usually not observed in response to one stimulus or one situation, complexes of these must be used to approximate the situations of the real world. Brunswik's major contribution to the field of personality has been his insistence that investigators demonstrate the degree to which their experiments are representative of certain types of situations.

An example of a more general, eclectic field theory may be found in the writings of Gardner Murphy (1947). Murphy has presented a biosocial approach to behavior which uses the concept of the field but also uses other concepts from other theoretical points of view. Seeking to go beyond the purely psychological field theory of Lewin he has expressed interest in the biological aspects of the organism-environment field. He has borrowed ideas from S-R psychology and incorporated them into his general theory. But his orientation is primarily field theoretical because he does not regard the person as an entity in some sense separate from his environment. For Murphy, behavior must be viewed within an organism-environment field that takes on a particular configuration. This configuration undergoes a change as a function of the situations in which the individual finds himself.

In describing personality, Murphy refers to a number of classes of variables, among which are: (1) genetic and physiological predispositions; (2) canalizations, by which he means the way that social factors channelize biological needs (for example, Americans satisfy hunger by eating hamburgers and Italians by eating pasta); (3) responses learned on the basis of reinforcement; and (4) perceptual and cognitive styles.

With these concepts, Murphy (1947, p. 502) has sought to describe the socialization process and role-taking behavior, and also the self-concept of individuals. He has described his view of the self-concept in the following manner:

. . . the more closely we look at the matter, the more probable it appears that most human adjustments are in some degree adjustments not to an external situation alone, but to a perceptual whole of which the self is a part, a self-in-situation field.

For him, social, economic, biological, and other forces complexly interact to form the configuration defined by the organism-environment field. Murphy's field theory is much less formal than Lewin's in that Murphy appears to have contented himself with the task of describing broad classes of variables that determine the organism-environment field. Perhaps because of their eclecticism, Murphy's theoretical formulations have not had nearly the impact on psychology as Lewin's. However, Murphy has provided a useful attempt at integrating into one orientation several of the varied approaches to behavior taken by psychologists.

CONCLUDING COMMENTS CONCERNING FIELD THEORY

Field theory represents an effort to do justice to the momentary quality of behavior and to the complex of interacting factors that determine it.

Murphy has made his effort on an eclectic level. He seems to have been successful in delineating in a general way many of the types of variables needed for a comprehensive theory of behavior. Lewin, on the other hand, was quite specific in formalizing his field concepts. Some critics have wondered if recognition of the integrated aspects of behavior requires such a complex theoretical—and in the case of Lewin, mathematical—system. It is certainly true that Lewin's theory attempts, by means of a large number of constructs, to handle within one framework both the phenomenal world of the individual and events in the physical world. This is done by means of an analogy drawn to vector theories of physics and mathematics. One might ask: what reason is there to believe that organisms adhere to the same types of laws and relationships as physical and electrical fields? So far as we know there is no clear-cut evidence upon which to base an answer to this question. Critics of Lewin have contended that, although his theory may have stimulational value for researchers, it is an after-the-fact analogy from which testable predictions cannot be made. Regardless of the validity of such criticisms, it seems clear that Lewin made one of the first steps in psychological theory toward a recognition of the combined influences which contemporaneous events have on behavior.

Lewin's theory has also been criticized for its lack of emphasis on individual differences and the physiology of perception. As the following quotation suggests, Lewin (1954, p. 921) did not ignore the role of individual differences:

> A law is expressed in an equation which relates certain variables. Individual differences have to be conceived of as various specific values which these variables have in a particular case. In other words, general laws and individual differences are merely two aspects of one problem; they are mutually dependent on each other and the study of the one cannot proceed without the study of the other.

But he did not come to grips with the problem of the measurement of individual differences. Although he recognized that persons differed in the valences that they attach to particular goals, he did not develop methods by means of which these individual differences might be assessed quantitatively.

Floyd Allport (1955, p. 155) has especially criticized Lewin's lack of emphasis on physiological processes:

> For meeting the requirement of a logically consistent, explanatory, and complete theory of perception, [Lewin's] topological field-theory, for all its usefulness, leaves much to be desired. Because the physical and physiological bases of perception are ignored, or are concealed by shrinking the individual into a point-region, and because the perceptual phenomenon is placed in an "outside" field and each field is unique and occurs only "at the moment," it becomes impossible for the theory to explain how meaningful perceptions are built up or how the actual process of perception takes place. What is needed is an understanding of perception itself rather than merely a convenient formula for its role in human affairs. For a full understanding it does not help much to say that perception is "a sudden reorganization of the cognitive field." Or until the field concept can be put upon a basis broad enough to include physiological explanations it does not help to say that objects or events are perceived in a manner consistent with the existing "field."

However, as was said in the case of Rogers' point of view, one may reject aspects of a researcher's theory and yet find it possible to appreciate his stimulational value and his empirical endeavors. Lewin and his adherents have been a highly productive group of workers. Whether their productivity is an indirect function of the general orientation provided by Lewin's field theory or a direct function of predictions derivable from theory is difficult to say. If one does not take too seriously the highly formal and complex way in which Lewin's field theory was stated, one can find in it a productive orientation toward the study of the individual.

7

Theoretical Frameworks and Research on Personality

Clearly there is no single commonly accepted set of assumptions and hypotheses among theoretical frameworks that can serve as a guideline for research in the area of personality. Rather there are a number of orientations to the behavior of the individual. Some of these overlap in emphases and some provide striking contrasts to other views. A partial list of concepts and problems over which personality theorists differ in regard to the emphases given them are:

1. The nature of unconscious motivation (is it instinctively determined or is it a product of social learning?) and the relative weights given to rational and irrational components of mental life;
2. The roles of hereditary and biological factors;
3. The contribution of learning to the shaping of behavior;
4. The effects of the individual's history (particularly, early history) on present behavior;
5. The interpretations placed on the individual's self-awareness, self-reports, and his anticipation with regard to the future;
6. The relationship between the real world and the individual's subjective reactions;
7. The way in which the uniqueness of the individual is conceived and analyzed;
8. The extent to which valuistic concepts (for instance, self-actualization) are used in theoretical formulations.

A feature of most of the theoretical frameworks considered is their level of generality. In varying degrees they have been constructed to conceptualize the person in a global and comprehensive fashion. In this regard the usefulness and success of these conceptualizations must inevitably be dealt with. At the beginning of this section a distinction was drawn between theories, on the one hand, and theoretical formulations and orientations, on the other. A theory, we said, consists of a set of concepts that are parsimonious and defined in terms of observables, and that serve to generate new relationships related to established facts. On this basis, a theory might be expected to proceed from the specific to the general because it would initially be used to integrate a relatively small number of facts. As new information came to the fore, the theory would be revised and enlarged.

The formulations which we have considered have not followed this cautious pattern of development. Although all of them relate in some ways to observables, the data frequently have been anecdotal in nature and not the product of exhaustive, controlled observations. Consequently, it would seem unrealistic to attempt rigorous scientific evaluations of most of the positions reviewed. It would seem profitable, however, to look upon them as orientations to various types of empirical problems.

This means that we conceive of theoretical orientations as pretheory hypotheses about variables that appear to be candidates for inclusion in scientific theories. An important criterion in evaluating a theoretical orientation would seem to be its success in stimulating systematic research concerning the variables. Does a particular orientation stimulate researchers to investigate problems whose solution will ultimately lead to scientific theories? Several of the orientations reviewed seem to have had decidedly salutary effects on the gathering of empirical data. Whether truly scientific theories of personality of the future will bear a close resemblance to present-day theoretical orientations would seem of secondary importance. Of major importance is the fact that many of today's orientations seem to have been useful to researchers in suggesting problems that can be put to empirical tests.

As efforts to demonstrate the empirical values of the orientations to personality have intensified, there has been an increasing sophistication among both theorists and researchers. In particular personality researchers have become impatient with elaborate theorylike structures even though these formulations may have only the most tenuous ties to observable behavior. Hall and Lindzey (1957, pp. 550-551) have nicely expressed this attitude:

The psychologist should give up the idea that he has discharged his obligation if he provides a theoretical formulation that takes into account or makes consistent what is already known in a given empirical area. If the theory does nothing more than organize known facts we might as well remain at a descriptive level and forsake theorizing. The plea here is simply that theories be evaluated in terms of their capacity to generate new research. Psychologists should also show themselves more willing to accept the fact that assumptions concerning behavior that do not have eventual consequences for the kind of predictions to be made, or the type of data to be collected, are valueless and a waste of time, effort, and print. Let the theorist focus his attention upon formulations which have some meaningful relation to the business he is about—studying behavior.

Along with most psychologists, personality researchers have come more and more to define their task as that of relating constructs to observable aspects of behavior. Recently, they have tended to move in the direction of theoretical formulations that are narrower in scope than the broad orientations we have been considering, but that are also less ambiguous and more directly tied to their ultimate goal: the control and prediction of behavior.

This progression of interest in the area of personality, from general orientations to specific empirical problem areas, seems to be quite the same as one's process of acquaintanceship with a city. On the basis of guide books, maps, reading about the place, and speaking to people who are familiar with it, we come to the city with a general orientation toward things to do, places to see, and people to call upon. Once on the scene we quickly see that this general orientation, while helpful, is not sufficient to permit us to solve the many particular problems we inevitably encounter.

If we come to reside in the city, our conception of it five years after having moved there will, in all likelihood, be quite different from what we would have expected from the orientation with which we came. Five years later we would probably say that we were deeply grateful for the orientations and leads provided for us. But on the basis of our own empirical investigation of these leads modifications of initial views and expectations would become necessary. The one way really to know a city is to explore it street by street, person by person. Having an idea of what to look for in it is of an enormous importance to the neophyte. But we must look for ourselves—and this takes time and patience. At the outset, we must content ourselves with intimate knowledge of particular and perhaps isolated sections of the area. Having explored these we proceed to others. Ultimately, we come to integrate these initially delimited explorations.

Students of personality, at the present time, are engaged in just this sort of reconnaissance. They believe that at some point in the future integration of carefully gathered facts will be possible and that a truly scientific theory will emerge. They believe that at the present time it is unrealistic to speak of personality theorists and personality researchers. Rather the personality theorist and personality researcher must be one and the same person.

The remainder of this book will be concerned with aspects of behavior which are currently undergoing reconnaissance by personality theorist-researchers, with their methods of exploration, and the tentative conclusions they have reached. In the course of these characterizations we shall discover many examples of the influences of personality "guidebooks" on the activities of individuals seeking a science of personality.

Part 2

PERSONALITY ASSESSMENT

THE SO-CALLED THEORIES of personality deal, as we have seen, with the characteristics of persons. Many of these characteristics, rather than being self-evident or obvious, are usually traits and activities to be inferred from behavior. Our knowledge of them would certainly be enhanced if it were possible to obtain quantitative indices of these characteristics. Let us consider anxiety and repression, for example. Psychoanalysts maintain that both are important determinants of overt behavior. Would not objective indices of them prove valuable as data? It seems reasonable to expect that there are individual differences in the tendencies to become anxious and engage in repression. If this expectation has merit, the researcher must ask himself: can individuals be ordered and categorized on the basis of the frequency or intensity of anxiety experiences and repressive defenses?

Students of personality have been asking this type of question more and more in recent years. This trend toward what is called personality assessment reflects a growing awareness of the need to quantify individual differences. The concern with assessment may be described as an approach to behavior that assumes that much of the variability in overt behavior results from differences in the extent to which individuals possess particular personal characteristics. Researchers in personality assessment seek to define these traits unambiguously, to measure them objectively, and to use them to predict behavior. Part 2 will be concerned with these research efforts.

8

The Assessment of Personality

We shall regard personality characteristics as attributes, dispositions, and tendencies of people. We need not make general assumptions about the history or antecedents of these dispositions although it would seem reasonable to assume that they are joint products of the biology and prior experiences of the individual. We shall also make no assumptions concerning the extent to which particular characteristics typify the behavior of an individual. Although some inferred characteristics may relate to many aspects of overt responding, others may relate to quite specific but important response patterns which evolve only under particular circumstances.

We shall be concerned in our study of personality assessment with achieving an understanding of the methods used in assessing characteristics and the uses to which these methods have been put. The use made of any particular method will, of course, be influenced by its validity. We may speak of four types of validity: predictive, concurrent, content, and construct validity. Table 8-1 summarizes these types of validity and the questions and procedures relevant to them.

The need to establish predictive, concurrent, and content validity has been recognized for many years. The idea of construct validity has been clearly articulated only in recent years (Cronbach and Meehl, 1955). In the field of personality assessment a construct is a concept of a personal characteristic. The empirical study of a construct involves defining the characteristic, measuring it, and relating it to theoretically significant aspects of behavior.

TABLE 8-1

Four Types of Validation

	Question Asked	Procedure	Principal Use	Examples
Predictive validity	Do test scores predict a certain important future performance?	Give test and use it to predict the outcome. Some time later obtain a measure of the outcome. Compare the prediction with the outcome.	Tests used in selection and classification decisions.	Admission test for medical students is compared with later marks. Mental test given infants at time of adoption is compared to test of school readiness at age 6.
Concurrent validity	Do test scores permit an estimate of a certain present performance?	Give test. Obtain a direct measure of the other performance. Compare the two.	Tests intended as a substitute for a less convenient procedure.	Group mental test is compared to an individual test. Diagnosis of brain damage based on Block Design test is compared with neurological evidence.
Content validity	Does this test give a fair measure of performance on some important set of tasks?	Compare the items logically to the content supposed to be measured.	Achievement tests.	A test of shorthand ability is examined to see whether the content is typical of office correspondence. Tasks in a sewing proficiency test are compared with the course of study pupils have followed.
Construct validity	How can scores on this test be explained psychologically?	Set up hypotheses. Test them experimentally by any suitable procedure.	Tests used for description or in scientific research.	A test of art aptitude is studied to determine how largely scores depend on art training, on experience in Western culture, etc.

Adapted from L. J. Cronbach (1960), *Essentials of psychological testing* (2nd ed.), p. 106, Harper, New York.

MEASURES OF PERSONAL CHARACTERISTICS

Personality assessors seek to make statements about persons that can be shown empirically to be accurate and useful. These statements are made on the basis of many different types of data. Some may be quite impersonal and not even require direct observation of the individual under study. For example, an estimate of an individual's socioeconomic status may not require contact with the subject. Neither do many aspects of his medical and family histories require such contact. Although this kind of information is of great value in studying human lives and is useful in assessment, personality assessors tend to concern themselves primarily with data that are based on direct observation of the individual's behavior.

Much research in personality assessment follows the following paradigm. The researcher has an hypothesis about one or more personal characteristics which he believes may be related to some aspect of behavior. For example, he may believe that anxiety and repression, defined in particular ways, are related to marital success, also defined in particular ways. Having conceptualized these dispositions in which he is interested, he then observes selected aspects of the subject's behavior through tests and interviews. From these observations, he derives indices of the dispositions. The subject's standings on these indices are then related to the behavior that the researcher seeks to predict. This procedure may be described as a correlational one in which the relationships of predictors to criteria are established.

Straightforward as these steps may seem, there are a number of complexities and problems which call for acute awareness from the researcher. Among these are the stability of the behavior and the reliability in scoring the indices of personal characteristics. As to stability, does an individual have the same standing on an index when his behavior is observed on two separate occasions? The correlation between indices of traits observed at different points of time will indicate how stable the measured characteristics are. Where there is no reason to suspect that there has been a drastic change in the life of the subject, researchers prefer to derive indices of characteristics that have been shown to be highly stable. If a patient observed on two different occasions has been hospitalized in a mental institution during the interim, his behavior might be expected to differ markedly and the indices will reflect the change in characteristics.

Another important factor in assessment is the reliability of the procedure employed to determine a subject's standing on a personal characteristic index. This is similar to the question of the "fairness" of teachers. When a student accuses a teacher of not being fair he may mean that the teacher has not scored a test paper in the same manner as would other teachers or as the teacher would at another time. That is, a teacher might be accused of being unreliable in his scoring. Personality researchers strive to employ indices of personal characteristics which can be scored consistently, objectively, and reliably.

Although stable and reliable measures are of enormous significance, the ultimate matter in assessment is that of validity. Some psychologists have phrased the validity question in this way: What does a particular test measure? In what ways is a test score related to significant aspects of behavior? If we were to develop a highly reliable measure of a personal characteristic or an individual difference variable our sense of accomplishment would increase in proportion to the number of meaningful relationships into which the test entered. A highly reliable test that is unrelated to significant aspects of behavior would be a minor achievement indeed. Equally minor would be the development of a test that predicted the obvious. For example, to use the true-false item—I wear a tie on important social occasions—to determine the sex of subjects is certainly a roundabout way of approaching the obvious.

Usually when a researcher develops a test, he has in mind certain ways in which its validity or usefulness can be assessed. Some tests are constructed to answer specific practical questions. For example, the personnel department of an insurance company might find very useful a test that could predict the success of insurance salesmen. The validity of this kind of test might be straightforwardly determined. Once the test had been constructed and administered to the salesmen already in the employ of the company, scores on it could be correlated with the amount of insurance which they sold during a representative time period. The amount of insurance would, in this case, be a criterion or standard by which the effectiveness of insurance salesmen could be judged. If other criteria seemed appropriate, correlations between test scores and these criteria could be computed in order to assess the test's validity. Validity, in this sort of example, is a matter of a test doing the job that has been "assigned" to it. The criterion employed represents an index by which the test's validity may be judged.

When the researcher has a very clear idea of what he wants to measure, such as amount of insurance sold, or an individual's longevity, or resistance to communicable diseases, the procedure of delineating an individual difference variable, determining its reliability, and ascertaining its validity by means of correlations with criteria would appear to be relatively uncomplicated. The kinds of criteria employed will, of course, depend on the researcher's interest and needs. For certain purposes, the aim of the developer of a test might be to determine concurrent validity; in other cases, the primary concern might be with predictive validity. In the case of concurrent validity, the test developer's interest is in making statements about a subject's present behavior. Thus, in the insurance example, the personnel director might be concerned with the development of a measure to reflect the present performance of the company's salesmen. In the case of predictive validity, his concern would be with making statements about the future behavior of individuals. This would apply where the personnel officer wished to predict the future success of salesmen.

Cronbach and Meehl (1955) have pointed out that the concepts of concurrent and predictive validity may not be appropriate to many problems arising in personality research. The personality researcher may not be preoccupied with problems that can be solved simply by correlating a particular test score or index with one or a few indices of validity. Rather, he deals with concepts and variables whose implications may permeate a wide range of behaviors.

Consider the concept of submissiveness. An investigator might have an hypothesis or a hunch that the degree to which a person has tendencies toward submissiveness significantly affects his behavior in a variety of social situations. Let us assume that the investigator regards submissiveness as a tendency to yield to the will and suggestions of others. How might he proceed to study his hypothesis? Starting with the assumption that there are individual differences in the tendency toward submissiveness, he might elect to develop a measure of the concept and then try to establish its validity. Cronbach and Meehl would say that he has embarked on a study of the construct validity of submissiveness. The word construct is used rather than either predictive or concurrent because there is no one criterion of submissiveness comparable with the amount of insurance sold, on which observers would be in agreement. Selling insurance is one highly specific activity. Submissiveness, on the other hand, permeates a great many activities.

To repeat, in approaching submissiveness or any other attribute of persons, the assessment researcher usually begins with an hypothesis about an individual difference variable. His next step is to construct a test or index of the variable. This step may involve considerable pilot work. For example, there are several techniques for constructing tests, such as true-false, multiple choice, and projective. Frequently, the researcher will hypothesize about the type of measure which will best tap the variable in question. Whichever type he selects, some trial and error exploration is sure to be required.

Let us assume that our researcher has developed a convenient and a reliable test of submissiveness that he administers under standardized conditions. His major task, then, is to validate the construct underlying his measure. Although there are many ways in which he might proceed, one frequently fruitful approach is through the conduct of experiments in which conditions are created where persons high and low in submissiveness would be expected to behave differentially. In comparing performances under these conditions the researcher must demonstrate that any differences he obtains cannot be attributed to extraneous variables, such as intelligence and sex, in which he might not be deeply interested. Thus, he would want to compare the behavior in experimental situations not only of subjects differing in submissiveness scores but also of subjects differing on other variables, such as intelligence and sex. Such a comparison might influence his interpretation of his experimental findings.

No single experiment would, by itself, establish the construct validity of the test of submissiveness. However, if the test is found to relate to subjects' behavior in a variety of experimental and other situations a degree of construct validity will have been shown. Thus, if high scorers on the submissiveness test are found to conform more than low scorers under conditions of social pressure, if they follow orders more obediently, and if they less frequently object to insults directed toward them, an encouraging start will have been made in the construct validation of the researcher's scale.

It would probably be too much to expect the submissiveness scale to have predictive value in every experiment that appears to concern submissive behavior. The tendency toward submissiveness may manifest itself under certain conditions but not under others. High scorers on the submissiveness scale might be very submissive in certain situations (those involving bosses), slightly submissive in others (those involving parents), not submissive at all in still others (those involving peers), and conceivably, dominant under certain conditions (those involving wives). Moreover, the same submissiveness scores for individuals who differ in intelligence or socioeconomic status might have various meanings depending on the nature of the situations under study.

If some of these possibilities were true, it would become clear why we cannot express construct validity simply and succinctly in a few correlation coefficients. Cronbach and Meehl (1955) have called the complex of relationships which characterizes a construct its *nomologi-*

cal network. They have referred to the process of adding empirical evidence to a nomological network as mapping the construct. As the network acquires new data, and as some of these present embarrassments for the current version of the construct, revision of the construct must be considered. New data may also suggest the need for changes in the test or index employed. Therefore, in the test of submissiveness, for example, newly uncovered evidence might lead the researcher to revise his test and create new situations to which test scores can be related.

Types of Personality Measures

What are the specific vehicles through which personality assessors seek to make verifiable statements about the characteristics of persons? To what responses of human beings do they attend in order to infer covert tendencies and dispositions? In fact, some students of behavior argue against attempts at drawing inferences about covert events on the basis of observations of persons' overt behavior (Skinner, 1953). Rather, they believe, directly observable events should constitute the exclusive focus of psychological inquiry. Most personality researchers, however, seem to agree that as so much of an individual's overt behavi is related to internal personal processes, it would be unrealistic to forego efforts at inferring them.

Many of the writers mentioned in Part 1 might assert that, to know something about the internal workings of a person, one must ask him to describe himself. Allport, for example, would probably say that the best observer of an individual is himself. Self-descriptions would certainly appear to constitute important data about personality. However, in gathering such data one does not have to assume that the descriptions are necessarily correct or inherently valid. On the contrary, there is good evidence that self-descriptions, by virtue of their subjectivity, may contain considerable distortion and inaccuracy. Recent research has devoted considerable effort to the development of indices of personal bias in self-description.

Self-descriptions or self-reports may be obtained in many ways, but essentially such reports fall into two broad classes. One of these, typified by the interview, gives the subject wide latitude in describing himself. Thus, in certain kinds of interviews individuals might be asked to talk about and describe themselves in whatever manner they think would be most effective. This might be called a relatively unstructured, or free-response, self-description situation.

A second type of self-description situation used to assess personality is, from the subject's point of view, more restrictive and better structured. This consists of personality tests which often present discrete questions to the subject rather than an invitation to engage in general self-description. They require the subject to respond in specified ways to selected stimuli. For example, the stimuli might be statements about the self and the subject's task might be to indicate the extent to which they describe him.

Whereas both interviews and tests may call for self-reports, there are important differences between them. The interview gives the subject much more freedom in responding than does the test. In the interview the subject can, within certain limits, select for emphasis particular aspects of his personal characteristics. In addition, he can modify and qualify the statements he makes about himself. In the test, the subject is limited as to how he can respond to the stimuli presented to him. Given the statement, "I worry a lot," he might be restricted to an indication of whether the statement is true of him or he might be asked to indicate on a rating scale the degree to which the statement applies to him.

Although the subject is more limited in the test situation than in the interview situation, the former has one major superiority that has had a great impact on research in personality. This superiority relates to the ease of quantifying the subject's behavior. The subject's freedom of response is limited in the test situation because of the necessity on the part of the tester to categorize and score objectively and reliably the behavior sample he has obtained. Objective, convenient, and reliable quantification is so powerful an aid that personality testers are willing to place some constraints on the subject's behavior in order to obtain it.

That tests are easier to score than interviews is, of course, not an argument for replacing all interview procedures with self-report tests. Interviews pose problems because the difficulty of reliably scoring responses increases in proportion to the interviewee's idiosyncracies in self-description. The scores of two persons on a true-false personality questionnaire can be directly compared. How does one compare hour-long self-descriptions? Comparisons can be made after procedures—often complex ones—have been worked out which permit an observer or judge to categorize the subject's statements in a reliable manner. This procedure is called *content analysis,* because it analyzes the content of the individual's self-reports. In recent years, researchers have made considerable progress in the content analysis of verbal behavior.

Another approach to personality assessment is that of the situational test. The idea underlying the situational test is simple and appealing. If one is interested in predicting an individual's behavior in a particular situation, one can do so by devising an experimental situation that is as similar as possible to the actual one in which one wishes to make predictions and then studying the behavior of subjects in it in order to make predictions. For example, some employers might prefer to put prospective employees through a tryout period of a week or so, so that it would be possible to observe them in situations similar to the ones in which they would function were they to be hired. This kind of situational test is an actual job sample.

Other kinds may involve specially devised miniature life situations. For example, if one desired to predict behavior in really dangerous situations, one might devise miniature stress situations to which assessees might be subjected. Although it has greatly interested students of personality, the situational test has, as yet, been employed in a relatively small number of investigations. Perhaps the major reason for this is that, like the interview approach to self-report, it is complex, time-consuming, and poses difficult methodological problems.

In the interview, the personality test, and the situational test, the task for the individual is rather explicitly presented: describe yourself, answer these questions, solve this problem. The instructions given to him are outlined in such a fashion that ordinarily he has a clear understanding of the task before him. This, of course, does not mean that there is no ambiguity whatever surrounding the meaning of the task; nor does it mean that the subject will necessarily feel that he is able to perform as is required of him. However, the task usually does have face validity for him. Having face validity means that the individual will accept the task as a reasonable, and perhaps worthwhile, one. For example, a newly admitted patient to a mental hygiene clinic would usually accept an interview by a psychiatrist as a necessary and important event. The interview would have face validity for him. Thus, face validity is defined by the task and the context in which it is presented. Tasks that have face validity make sense to the subject to the extent that he can rationalize their use in his case.

Another type of technique, the projective test, usually has less face validity than other assessment procedures, primarily because of the novel and often highly ambiguous situation that it presents to subjects. Frequently individuals to whom projective tests are administered are puzzled as to the tester's reasons for administering them. Even after receiving introductory instructions the testee is often not confident that he either understands what is expected of him or that he can perform the assigned task. What is the nature of this kind of task that may not seem obviously significant and worthwhile to individuals?

In the self-report test situation, the subject usually grasps and accepts the idea that he is to describe himself. In the projective test situation, his task may not be to describe himself at all but rather to describe an ambiguous stimulus presented to him. Inkblots have been one of the most frequently employed projective stimuli. The task for the subject is to describe, not himself, but the inkblot before him. The hypothesis underlying such tests is that in describing ambiguous stimuli the individual projects aspects of himself and his characteristics into his description. The assumption is made that the subject's response to an ambiguous, relatively formless stimulus will invest the stimulus with some degree of structure, and that the nature of the structure he imposes reflects the kind of person he is and the sort of life he has led.

Two major problems confront the user of projective tests. The first, and most basic one, is that of inferring the subject's personality characteristics from his responses to ambiguous stimuli. The second has already been mentioned in connection with the interview: how can one reliable score, categorize, and quantify the responses made by the individual? The data obtained when an individual describes the different things he sees in an inkblot are essentially verbal behavior. Some of the ways in which psychologists have attempted content analysis of responses to projective stimuli, together with other quantification procedures, will be considered in Chapters 12 and 13.

Projective techniques and all methods of personality assessment are part of the search for variables that are relevant to an understanding of behavior. Our discussion of personality assessment methods will focus most intensively on techniques used in gathering self-descriptions and on techniques that require persons to respond to stimuli of varying ambiguities. These are the two classes of techniques that have been used most widely by researchers in the area of personality assessment. We shall provide examples of them as well as examples of other methodologies used in assessment work, such as situational tests. As we proceed we shall see both similarities and differences among the various methods and come to view assessment not simply as a vehicle for obtaining indices of characteristics but also as a psychological encounter interesting and challenging in its own right.

9

Self-Description of Personal Characteristics: The Interview

The use of self-description in personality assessment requires that individuals report on their tendencies, characteristics, attitudes, and opinions. These reports constitute data that must be analyzed objectively by an assessor. In personality tests a researcher will have worked hard and long in the construction of an easily scored instrument *prior* to administering it routinely to subjects. In the interview, most of the researcher's work comes in content analysis *after* the data have been collected.

In an interview situation the subject is given considerable latitude in "telling his story." In a testing situation he is called upon to respond in limited and prescribed ways. In either case, the use of self-reports as assessment data need not put the assessor in the position of having to assume their accuracy.

THE INTERVIEW IN PERSONALITY ASSESSMENT

There are many types of interviews that differ with respect to goals and methods (Kahn and Cannell, 1957). Interviews may be conducted for diagnostic, therapeutic, or research purposes. They may range from a quite informal interchange between interviewer and interviewee to series of specific questions asked of the interviewee.

When conducted under certain controlled conditions interviews may resemble types of situational tests. The stress interview exemplifies this overlap between assessment techniques. Such interviews are used to assess the subject's responses to increasing amounts of stress brought to bear in the course of the interview.

Both situational tests and interviews involve direct observation by one individual of another individual's behavior. Direct observations require categorization and quantification of the data obtained. This sort of observation usually calls for well-trained personnel and may be costly. Nevertheless, as an assessment method, as a clinical method, and as a social situation suited to research, the interview deserves serious consideration and intensive study. Only as more becomes known about the events that occur during interview situations can comparisons of the data obtained from then and from other assessment situations be intelligently attempted.

When used in a personality assessment program, the interview may be conceived as a means of eliciting responses that, it is hoped, will have predictive value and be related to a construct under study. The more highly organized the interview and the more specific the questions asked of the person interviewed, the more easily can the problem of reliably categorizing or scoring the responses be confronted. But even where subjects have wide latitude in expressing themselves, content analysis and the use of rating scales are usually employed to quantify aspects of their verbal behavior.

Content Analysis of Verbal Behavior

Some students have been so impressed with the difficulties in making order out of spontaneous self-descriptions that they have tended to avoid involving themselves with interview data. However, recent research strongly suggests that it is not beyond the wit of the psychologist to quantify the content of oral self-reports (Auld and Murray, 1955; Berelson, 1954; Marsden, 1965; S. B. Sarason, 1954).

Although it is not possible to quantify all aspects of the emotional overtones of verbal communications, one can categorize many aspects of the content of what a person has said. This categorization constitutes content analysis. The categories used in a particular content analysis will depend on the researcher's interests and ingenuity. Nevertheless, the method of content analysis is quite general.

The method involves the construction of a system of categories that can be used reliably by content analyzers or scorers. These categorizations may be relatively straighforward, or quite complicated. The adjective-verb ratio is simply the ratio of adjectives to verbs in a sample of speech. However, the Discomfort-Relief Quotient (DRQ) is the ratio of words suggesting discomfort and unhappiness to the sum of discomfort words plus words suggesting relief, comfort, and satisfaction (Mowrer, 1953). In general, a content analysis system tells the scorer the units of speech to which he is to attend and categorize, and the criteria he is to follow in making categorizations. A well-prepared coding system provides the scorer not only with these directions but also with examples of the types of responses to be categorized. Research has shown that many response classes can be categorized in a reliable fashion. That is, different scorers using the same coding system show a high degree of agreement in their categorizations.

The importance of a system of content analysis is that it provides the investigator with the possibility of using frequencies of response to describe verbal behavior and to serve as variables in experimental research. For example, do persons differing in the frequency with which they emit negative self-references ("I am an uninteresting person") respond differently to stressful situations or to authoritarian figures? In short, content analysis permits the scoring of spontaneous verbal behavior. These scores may be treated in the same way as any measure of individual differences. Although much preparatory work is required to construct a workable coding system, an advantage of content analysis is that it permits an investigator to score a wide range of expression by the self-describer.

A study by Murray (1954) illustrates the use of content analysis in psychotherapy. The investigation took the form of a case study of one patient who was undergoing psychotherapy and had had 17 treatment sessions. Murray was concerned with the question: Do scores derived from content analysis of verbal expression reflect changes in the patient's behavior during psychotherapy?

The particular case studied by Murray was that of a young college graduate who sought help because of a fear that he might die while asleep. Murray viewed the patient's symptom as resulting from strong consciously experienced anxiety that in turn, was related to strong hostile tendencies and inadequate defenses. Murray studied two verbal categories: hostility and defense statements. For each therapy session he tabulated the frequencies of hostile expressions by the patient directed toward figures such as his mother, aunt, and therapist. He also tabulated the frequency of statements reflecting the use of the defenses of intellectualization and somatic preoccupation, statements in which the patient expressed his views concerning phi-

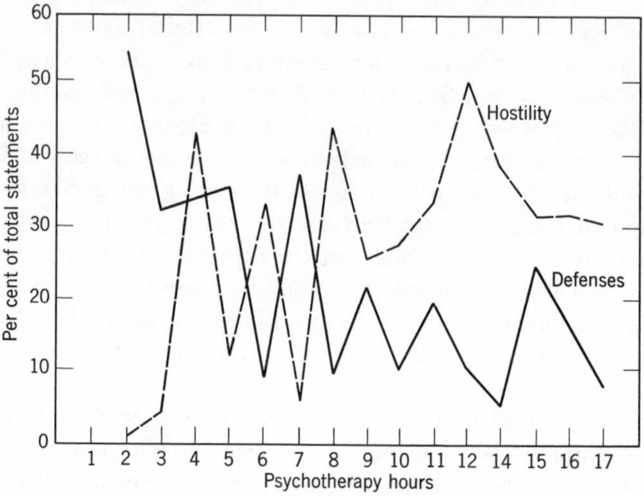

Figure 9-1 Percentage of hostility and defense statements throughout therapy—young college graduate (after Murray, 1954, p. 307).

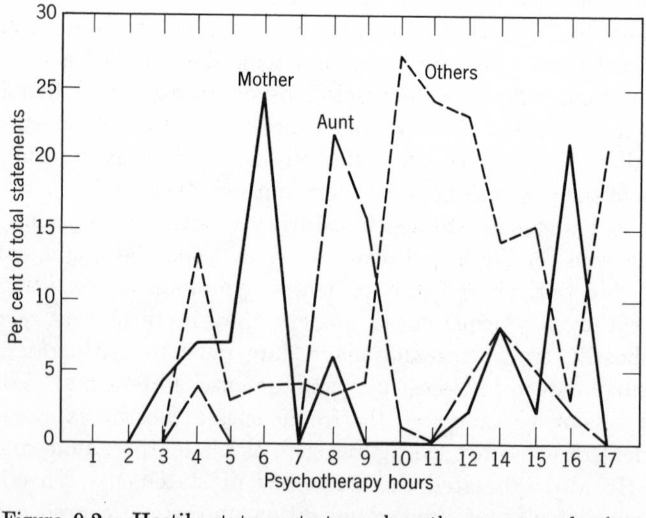

Figure 9-2 Hostile statements toward mother, aunt, and others —young college graduate (after Murray, 1954, p. 308).

losophy, current events, and his bodily concerns. Figure 9-1 shows the frequency of hostility and defense statements over the 17 sessions. Inspection of the curves shows the hostility statements increased and defense statements decreased during the sequence of sessions. Murray conjectured that as therapy proceeded the patient may have come to deal more comfortably and directly with his hostility, and to be less rigidly defensive.

One question related to the increase in hostile statements is: Which persons were the objects of the patient's hostility? Murray made a comparison of hostile statements by the patient directed toward his mother, his aunt, and other persons. Figure 9-2 shows the curves for these three content analyses. It seems clear that the objects of hostility underwent considerable change as therapy proceeded.

Another example of the application of content analysis to verbal behavior may be found in a psychotherapy study reported by Murray, Auld, and White (1954). It involved a woman beset by marital problems. Several content analyses of the patient's verbal expressions of conflict were performed. Figure 9-3 shows a plot of conflict statements made by the patient as therapy proceeded. There does not appear to be a marked trend to the statements of conflict over time. But now let us examine the patient's expressions of conflict in two particular areas: the patient's relationship with (1) her mother and

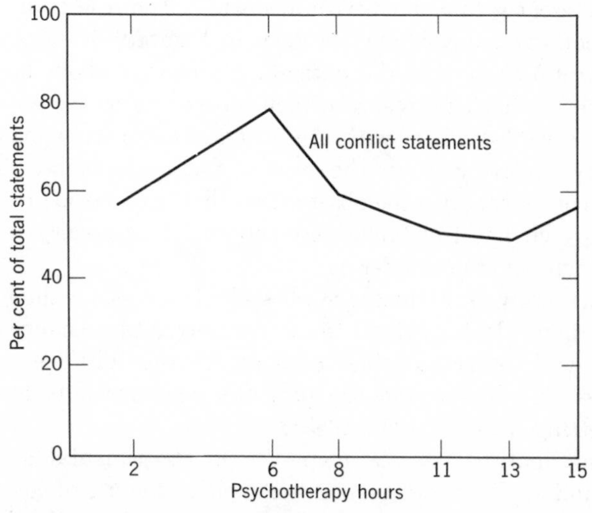

Figure 9-3 All conflict statements—marital conflict case (after Murray, Auld, and White, 1954, p. 350).

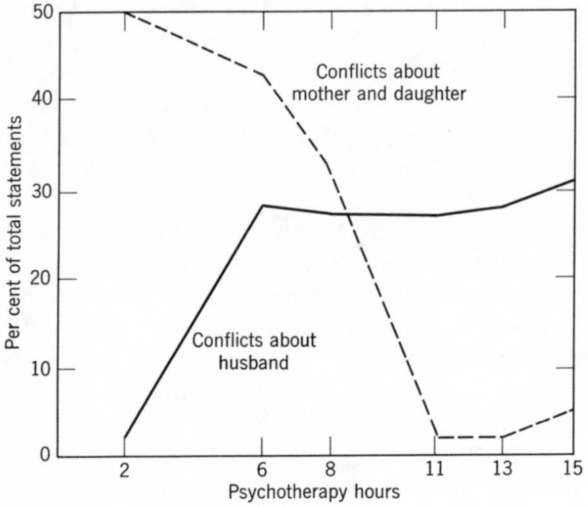

Figure 9-4 Conflicts about mother and daughter versus conflicts about husband—marital conflict case (after Murray, 1954, p. 351).

daughter, and (2) her husband. Figure 9-4 graphs the statements of conflict in these areas. As therapy proceeded, there was a sharp drop in conflict statements about mother and daughter and a sizable rise in references to conflict with husband. The results of a still more refined content analysis may be seen in Figure 9-5. The two curves in Figure 9-5 show that the patient's statements about hostility conflicts with her husband rose and then tapered off as therapy proceeded and that sexual conflicts with the husband came to be expressed verbally only relatively late in the series of therapy sessions. These findings are consistent with the observation that conflicts expressed in psychotherapy change from relatively superficial ones early in treatment to more significant ones later on.

Content analysis, as in the studies cited, serves a valuable descriptive function. It provides a basis for correlating changes in verbal behavior with other variables such as the therapist's impressions of the patient's progress and the patient's behavior outside the therapeutic setting (Snyder, 1961, 1963).

Content analysis may be employed in experimental as well as in clinical and applied settings. An example of the use of content analysis in experimental settings is a study reported by Krall (1953) of the personality characteristics of accident-prone children. It has been

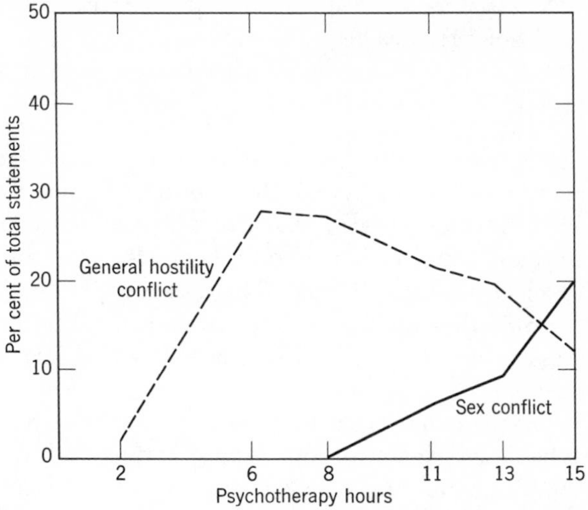

Figure 9-5 Hostility conflict versus sexual conflict—marital conflict case (after Murray, Auld, and White, 1954, p. 351).

hypothesized that accident-proneness is, at least in some situations, psychologically motivated. Krall tested this hypothesis in the case of 32 five-to-eight-year-old children with a record of three or more accidents (falls, lacerations) in a four-year period. These children were compared with 32 five-to-eight-year-old children with accident-free records.

The technique employed was that of a standardized doll play interview. In the standardized situation the children were permitted to play with a doll house. The house consisted of six rooms populated by a family of dolls. Each subject was asked to make up a story or play about the house, and the children's verbal responses were carefully recorded and content analyzed. Scores derived from their verbal behavior concerned such variables as aggression (doll and subject attitudes, feelings, intentions, and actions of an injurious, critical or destructive nature) and family atmosphere (doll and subject expressions of affection, generosity, and happiness among family members).

The results of the content analyses performed provided support for the hypothesis that there is a significant personality component in accident-proneness in children:

1. Accident repeaters engaged in significantly more aggression in doll play than accident-free children.

2. Accident repeaters showed significantly shorter latencies in expressing aggression than accident-free children.
3. Accident repeaters showed more activity and less realism in play with the doll family than accident-free children.

It was also noted that accident repeaters came from larger families and tended to be somewhat later in birth order, to come from broken homes, to have transferred from school to school more frequently, and to be known more often to home and school counselors in the public schools than accident-free children. The results of the study's content analyses suggested that the accident repeaters had stronger tendencies toward aggression and had more disorganized family lives than accident-free children.

Content analysis would seem to present possibilities for extending knowledge about the events of both psychotherapy and other clinical and research situations. Its development has been relatively recent but it already seems a promising avenue along which to explore and analyze the self-descriptions of people. We might add that content analysis need not be limited to instances of oral self-report or to data gathered in formal interviews. It may be used as well to quantify statements made in written documents and in almost any setting one might imagine. We shall see in Chapters 12 and 13 how content analysis has been applied to one type of personality test, projective techniques.

CONCLUDING COMMENTS CONCERNING THE INTERVIEW

The interview is certainly one of the most widely used assessment techniques. Physicians, psychologists, ministers, personnel officers, teachers, and many other groups make extensive use of the interview in a variety of ways. They use it because they regard it as a valuable basis for making statements about persons and because the interview has face validity for subjects.

The research examples which we have given of the interview are not at all typical of the day-to-day practical use of the interview. In the examples given laborious linguistic analyses were carried out in order to produce quantitative measures of individual differences. In day-to-day use interviews are not preserved (for instance, by means of tape recordings or film), and their contents are analyzed informally and subjectively by the interviewer. The gap between the objectivity of procedures like content analysis and the subjectivity of the typical interview is a large one. The gap exists for at least two reasons: (1) The study of the interview has only recently begun to move from a stage of assumed or face validity to one of a search for construct validity, and (2) the interview has often been more a source for the researcher's hypotheses than an object of analysis itself. In practical usage interviewing has been more an art than a science, more influenced by the personal and inferential skills of interviewers than by established laws of behavior.

Construct validity in relation to the interview will come about as the events of the interview become more clearly spelled out, as objective indices of these events are defined, and as these indices are shown to be related significantly to the lives of individuals. To date, quantitative study of the interview has been used to a considerable extent as a source for dependent variables, as in efforts to assess changes in verbal behavior during psychotherapy. It seems reasonable to expect that as objectification of the events of the interview proceeds, the interview will play an increasingly valuable role as an independent variable and as a predictor of behavior. The probability of this happening depends on advances in the process of recording and analyzing verbal behavior. Especially needed is a shortening of the process of analysis. Recent contributions suggest that improvements in computer technology may play a valuable role in achieving practical methods of assessment by means of the interview (Jaffe, 1963; Stone, Bales, and Namenwirth, 1962).

10

Self-Description of Personal Characteristics: Paper-and-Pencil Tests

Our study of content analysis demonstrated that even though interviews are usually not regarded as tests, they are susceptible to scoring procedures similar to those employed with traditional psychometric devices. Over the past several decades researchers have developed a broad area of study dealing with instruments specifically labelled personality tests. One group of these tests are of the paper-and-pencil variety. Subjects respond to them by reading statements in a test booklet and then replying on answer sheets.

Two events seem of particular significance in the history of paper-and-pencil personality testing. One of these was the development of intelligence tests. In the early part of this century, educators, clinicians, personnel workers, and psychologists found that scores obtained by individuals on tests of intelligence were of practical value in counseling and planning, and in the prediction of behavior. However, since it was clear that intelligence test scores alone did not account for individual differences in behavior, it seemed worthwhile to attempt to apply the psychometric model of intelligence assessment to the measurement of personal characteristics other than intelligence.

A second important event was the First World War. The induction into the armed forces of large numbers of recruits clearly necessitated some kind of selection procedure to identify men whose personality maladjustments would prove a detriment to the war effort. It seemed equally clear that it would be unfeasible to carry out even a cursory psychiatric interview with each recruit. As an approximation to the information that might have been gathered in interviews, a personality inventory that could be administered to groups was constructed. This inventory (Woodworth, 1919) consisted of printed statements dealing with areas of behavioral maladjustment. Among its items were these:

Have you ever been afraid of going insane?
Did you have a happy childhood?
Does it make you uneasy to cross a bridge over a river?
Do you ever walk in your sleep?

In part because this inventory, developed by Woodworth and his colleagues, became the model for personality test construction in the 1920s, most of the paper-and-pencil inventories after the First World War focused on the identification of personal maladjustment. In retrospect, one is impressed with the uncritical way in which these tests were accepted as measures of maladjustment. Many test constructors seemed to be concerned only with the face validity of their instruments. Because instruments labelled as "tests of adjustment" contained items that their authors believed were indicative of maladjustment it was assumed that this was what they measured.

Another characteristic of many of the early indices of maladjustment was their assumed unidimensionality. Often subjects' responses to items of self-description were summarized in terms of one, over-all score. It has become clear in recent years that the meaning of the concept of maladjustment is not immediately obvious, and furthermore, that individual differences in personality are too complex to permit summarization into a single score. As a result of this awareness, there is now a strong trend in the direction of multidimensional, as contrasted with unidimensional, paper-and-pencil self-report measures. Before turning to some examples of personality inventories that involve multidimensional scoring, a further word should be said concerning unidimensional paper-and-pencil personality tests.

UNIDIMENSIONAL SELF-REPORT MEASURES

Psychologists' interest in multifaceted personality descriptions makes good sense since it is difficult to see how one test score, or even a small number of them, can do justice to the complexity of the human organism. However, unidimensional indices have played a legitimate and useful role in personality research. Their greatest use has been found in those instances in which an investigator has an hypothesis about one particular facet of personality. On the basis of this hypothesis he might (1) devise a measure of the individual difference variable of interest to him, and (2) use it in research. This usage of a single score seems defensible as long as the researcher defines in a clear manner the variable which is of interest to him, and as long as he recognizes that his measure is not a global index of over-all personality functioning. It is useful, also, for the test constructor to concern himself with the possible relationship between his index and other indices extant.

Mention has already been made of one single-score paper-and-pencil test, Taylor's (1951, 1953) true-false Manifest Anxiety Scale. Table 10-1 lists some of the items in this scale. It will be remembered that Taylor used the items of this scale as a basis for inferring anxiety

TABLE 10-1

Twenty Items from Taylor's Manifest Anxiety Scale

I do not tire quickly. (False)
I have very few headaches. (False)
I cannot keep my mind on one thing. (True)
I worry over money and business. (True)
I frequently notice my hand shakes when I try to do something. (True)
I practically never blush. (False)
I have nightmares every few nights. (True)
I sweat very easily even on cool days. (True)
I feel hungry almost all the time. (True)
I have a great deal of stomach trouble. (True)
I am easily embarrassed. (True)
I am usually calm and not easily upset. (False)
I cry easily. (True)
I am happy most of the time. (False)
It makes me nervous to have to wait. (True)
Sometimes I become so excited that I find it hard to get to sleep. (True)
I have been afraid of things or people that I know could not hurt me. (True)
I certainly feel useless at times. (True)
I find it hard to keep my mind on a task or job. (True)
At times I think I am no good at all. (True)

Adapted from Janet A. Taylor (1953), A personality scale of manifest anxiety, *J. abnorm. Soc. Psychol.*, **48,** 286.

level in persons. Her use was experimental in that she compared high and low scorers under carefully controlled laboratory conditions. Other researchers have used the same items for a variety of purposes.

One common purpose has been to discriminate between selected groups. An example of this is a study (Davids, deVault, and Talmadge, 1961) in which two groups of women were compared. One group consisted of women who experienced abnormalities or complications in the delivery of their babies. The other group consisted of women who had normal deliveries. The Taylor scale had been administered to all of the women during pregnancy. To some subjects, it was also administered following pregnancy. Two results of this study provided much food for thought. First, the women with abnormal deliveries were found to have had a significantly higher prepregnancy mean anxiety score than the women who had normal deliveries. Second, both the women who had abnormal and normal deliveries showed a drop in anxiety scores following delivery. The latter finding suggests that, as with most life stresses, a woman's anxiety is lower following rather than in anticipation of the delivery of her baby. The former finding, that of differences in anxiety score during pregnancy between women with normal and abnormal deliveries, is not so easily explained. It is not immediately obvious why such a difference should exist. It is possible that the obstetricians of the women who had abnormal deliveries communicated to them the possibility of an abnormal delivery. This, in turn, could well arouse anxiety in pregnant women. But since the anxiety scale was administered during the women's very first visits to the obstetrician, this chain of events does not seem highly probable. Could it be that elevated anxiety scores may be practically useful psychological clues to complications in delivery? There is not enough information available to give an answer at the present time. But the results we have mentioned constitute a provocative contribution to knowledge about one significant life stress, childbirth.

Another example of a single-score personality test is the California F scale (not to be confused with the MMPI F scale). Adorno et al. in 1950 described what they called the authoritarian personality. Their interest in the authoritarian personality was influenced to a significant extent by the need to account psychologically for extreme forms of authoritarianism and fascism such as were observed in Nazi Germany. In their efforts, Adorno et al. sought to describe personality characteristics that underlie these extreme forms and also subtler forms of authoritarianism. They hypothesized that authoritarian or fascistic personalities were marked by a high degree of conventionality, superstitiousness, rigidity, aggressiveness, and several other characteristics. In an effort to select and then compare persons differing in these tendencies they developed a number of self-report indices. The most widely used of these has been the California F (fascism) scale. The items of this scale were written in the hope that they would reflect the tendency toward authoritarianism.

Scores of studies utilizing the F scale have been reported since the original work of Adorno et al. Many of these have shown the F scale to be related to various forms of personal prejudice, hostility, and autocratic tendencies. Frenkel-Brunswik (1949) extended the concept of authoritarian personality to perception and has shown that a subject's capacity for tolerating ambiguous stimuli (tolerance of ambiguity) is negatively related to F scale scores (the higher the score on the F scale the greater is the degree of authoritarianism attributed to individuals). The F scale has also been found to be related to the tendency to conformity (Linton, 1955). Numerous other specific findings such as these are to be found in the research literature.

The California F scale is valuable not only because it shows how researchers may employ a single personality index, but also because it suggests some of the problems one runs into in constructing a personality test. There are a number of ambiguities relating to the meaning of F-scale scores (Christie and Jahoda, 1954). Some of these have come about because of differences in interpretation of results. For example, the F scale has been found to be negatively correlated with intelligence. To the extent that intelligence and authoritarianism are related it becomes difficult to decide upon the basis for behavioral and attitudinal differences between high and low F-scale scorers. To what degree and in what sort of situation might prejudice be due to intelligence rather than, or perhaps in addition to, authoritarianism? This possibility is instructive in connection with the process of construct validation: in validating a construct it is necessary to show that the concept in which one is interested, rather than other concepts, accounts for the results of research endeavors (Campbell, 1960).

Another complication in deciding on the meaning of F-scale scores is the problem of test-taking attitudes (Christie, Havel, and Seidenberg, 1958). The F scale was developed prior to the heightened awareness among personality researchers of the role of these attitudes. It is keyed in such a way that high scores on it result from the subject's expressing agreement with the scales' statements. We, therefore, do not know to what extent a high F score is attributable to the authoritarian tendencies hypothesized by Adorno et al. (1950) or to a tendency to acquiesce to or agree with statements on personality questionnaires.

Clearly, future research on the F scale will have to focus more intensively on the merits of the different interpretations placed on the scores of individuals. The findings concerning test-taking attitudes on the F scale demonstrate the close link between methodology—in this case, the methodology of test construction—and theoretical formulations. Perhaps, in some sense, acquiescence, intelligence, and authoritarianism may be complexly related. Conceivably, moreover, the characteristics inferred from the F scale can be more effectively measured in other ways, using different tests and procedures.

The idea that a test measures a particular characteristic almost immediately gives rise to the consideration whether different tests purported to measure the same characteristic might not be better and more useful. This problem was referred to earlier when we pointed out that in the early development of personality tests, a spate of tests with similar titles, presumably referring to similar concepts, inundated the literature. We commented that to rely on the face validity of a title or test was risky and inadequate from a scientific standpoint. One concept that has stimulated the development of many different measures is introversion-extraversion. Ever since Jung described tendencies toward introversion and extraversion as important in the individual's social orientations, psychologists have sought objective measures of them (see Chapter 3) for use in research.

Over the years it has become clear that whereas many psychologists regard introversion-extraversion as an important dimension of personality, the various indices constructed to measure it have shown quite small correlations. One interpretation of this finding is that introversion-extraversion is not a single dimension of personality but a term that refers to a complex set of characteristics. Another interpretation is that it is a basic trait of personality, but that methodologically poor measures of it have confused the issue. Carrigan, (1960) in a review of the literature, has concluded that the status of introversion-extraversion as a single underlying characteristic is tenuous.

Quantitative approaches to introversion-extraversion by Guilford and Zimmerman (1956), Cattell, (1950), and Eysenck (1957) suggest that there may be some common factor resembling the hypothesized trait of this concept. Construct validation research of an experimental nature (Eysenck, 1961*a*) offers the promise of establishing behavioral referents for the concept. However, for the present, generalizing from one index of introversion-extraversion to another would appear to be hazardous.

In sum, the employment of single-score personality tests, particularly for research purposes, seems defensible and useful. However, a researcher's focusing on one specific individual difference variable does not absolve him of the need to question the extents to which he is successfully tagging that variable and to which his measure of it is related to other concepts and indices. These responsibilities are important facets of the construct validation of hypothesized attributes of persons.

MULTIDIMENSIONAL SELF-REPORT MEASURES

Where a researcher seeks a comprehensive description of personality rather than construct validation of a particular personal characteristic, a unidimensional test or questionnaire seems too limited for purposes of assessment. To provide suitable multidimensional instruments which might tap a number of personal characteristics, assessment researchers have experimented with a variety of testing procedures. We shall consider examples of some of those more widely used.

The Minnesota Multiphasic Personality Inventory

Assume that a problem exists, to wit, the description and diagnosis of behavior disorders. Assume further that well worked out constructs dealing with the personal characteristics of disturbed people are either unavailable or eschewed by the investigator. To take a concrete case, consider the problem of schizophrenia.

It is a fact that schizophrenia is the most prevalent and one of the most poorly understood diagnostic classifications. If we could determine fairly early in mental patients' hospitalizations that certain of them were suffering from schizophrenic disturbances, might not this information be of descriptive value and perhaps also of value in treating them? The same question could be brought up in the case of all of the major groups of patients treated in hospitals and clinics. Considering the absence of adequate theories and constructs relating to diagnosis, and the multiple and varied symptoms that patients present, is there any contribution that psychologists can make to the classification of patients?

One possibility might be to develop a large and comprehensive collection of self-report statements or items, to administer these items to patients with varied diagnoses, and to determine whether the item pool can successfully discriminate among patients with different diagnoses and problems. Were this approach to be followed, it would be necessary to select subjects carefully so that each one showed a relatively clear and uncomplicated pattern of psychopathology. If we could show that the test could distinguish among hypochondriacs, psychopaths, and schizophrenics, for example, then perhaps it could prove of value in cases where the symptomatology was more complicated and in cases where the prediction of future behavior would be desired.

This is essentially the procedure employed in the development of what at the present time is the most widely used self-report questionnaire, the Minnesota Multiphasic Personality Inventory (MMPI) (Hathaway and McKinley, 1942, 1943). The MMPI was originally designed to provide an objective basis for classifying different types of patients. Since it is in such extensive use and, since it may be taken as a prototype of one approach to personality assessment, let us describe and discuss the MMPI in some detail.

The MMPI comprises 550 statements that are to be answered True, False, or Cannot Say. (Cannot Say is indicated when the subject is undecided about the truth of the statement.) The 550 items are so varied in content that it is not easy to generalize about them. Some items pertain to attitudinal and emotional reactions, others relate to overt behavior and symptoms, and still others to aspects of the subject's past life. The diversity of MMPI statements is suggested by these sample items:

a. I believe there is a God.
b. I would rather win than lose a game.
c. I am worried about sex matters.
d. I believe I am being plotted against.
e. I believe in obeying the law.
f. Everything smells the same.

After the subject has taken the MMPI, his responses are scored in relation to a number of keys. These scores are then plotted on a graph or profile sheet that reflects the degree of deviancy of his responses. The following method led to the development of the various keys.

Consider the key developed for the Schizophrenia scale. Two groups of subjects were used by Hathaway and McKinley, the authors of the MMPI, in order to develop the scale. Normal subjects consisted of visitors to the University of Minnesota Hospital (nonpatients), college students, medical personnel, nonpsychiatric patients, and other groups in which there appeared to be no major behavior deviations. The test results of these normal subjects were compared with those of patients diagnosed as schizophrenic. Only those patients about whose diagnoses there was substantial agreement among psychiatrists were included in the tested group. Each of the MMPI's 550 items was examined to determine whether the diagnosed schizophrenic subjects responded differently from normal subjects. Those items on which schizophrenics and normals differed significantly came to constitute the Schizophrenia scale. A high score on the scale indicates that an individual has responded to these items in a manner similar to that of the schizophrenics in the original group used by Hathaway and McKinley.

Nine different scales were developed in this fashion. They are called clinical scales because they relate to different clinical groups, such as psychopathic personality, depression, and paranoia. Thus, by scoring these nine groups of items it is possible to determine the similarity of an individual's responses to the responses of the nine diagnostic groups. A high score on any given scale indicates that the individual's responses to its items are similar to those of the particular group of patients used in construction of the scale. These are the MMPI's nine clinical scales and their abbreviations:

1. Hypochondriasis (Hs)
2. Depression (D)
3. Hysteria (Hy)
4. Psychopathic deviate (Pd)
5. Masculinity-femininity (Mf)
6. Paranoia (Pa)
7. Psychasthenia (Pt)
8. Schizophrenia (Sc)
9. Hypomania (Ma)

Figure 10-1 shows how MMPI scores are plotted. Across the bottom of Figure 10-1 are the labels of the MMPI scales. The number of keyed responses is counted for each scale and then plotted. From a profile sheet such as the one in Figure 10-1, the degree of deviance of scores on each scale may be estimated. The tenth clinical scale is the Social Introversion (Si) scale which was developed after the original work of Hathaway and McKinley. Each raw score can be converted into a T score. A T score of 50 equals the average score of a normal reference group. Since the standard deviation of a T-score distribution is equal to 10, the degree of deviation of a subject's score from the reference can conveniently be estimated.

Figure 10-1 contains the MMPI profiles of three diagnostic groups: paranoid schizophrenics, depressives, and conversion reactions. It shows that many of the mean scores of the three groups differ noticeably from a T score of 50, the reference group's mean. It shows also

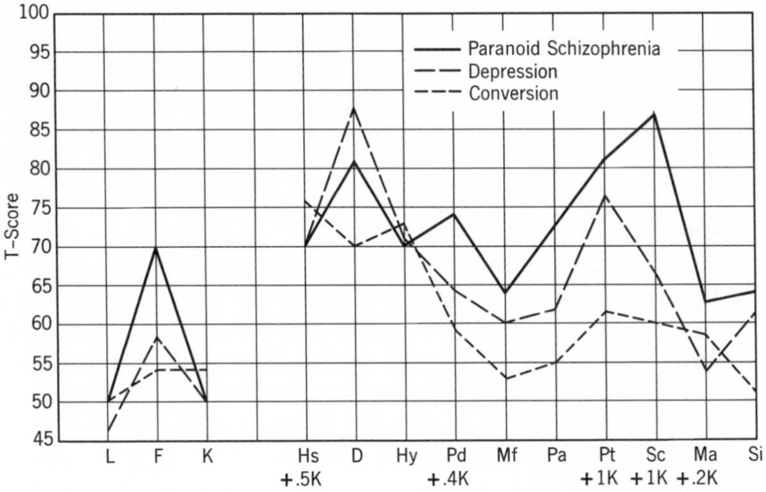

Figure 10-1 Mean T scores for three diagnostic groups on each MMPI scale (after Rosen, 1958, p. 454).

that on several scales there are differences of at least one standard deviation separating the three patient groups. Thus it would seem the MMPI can discriminate between normal persons and those who exhibit behavioral deviations and also among at least three of these types of deviation.

On the basis of findings gathered over a quarter of a century, MMPI users feel that its scales are of value not only in categorizing patients, but also for comprehensive personality description. Furthermore, it is felt that even though the MMPI was constructed for use in clinical situations, it may be valuable in describing the characteristics of persons who do not display overt symptoms. Thus, for example, high scores on the Schizophrenia scale (T scores greater than 80) may indicate a strong likelihood of bizarre thinking, disorganization of behavior, and pervasive social inhibition. Moderate scores (T scores between 55 and 65) may be suggestive of less extreme dispositions such as seclusiveness, seriousness, and personal dissatisfaction.

Because subjects might obtain low scores (that is, appear to be without psychiatric symptoms) on clinical scales for reasons other than their degree of psychopathology, three control scales were developed for the MMPI. In addition, one scale was defined simply in terms of the number of Cannot Say responses. (The counts of these responses were not entered in Figure 10-1.) One of the three control scales, the Lie (L) scale, was devised as a measure of the tendency to "fake good." Endorsement of many of these items suggests that an individual either does such things as read all the editorials in the newspaper every day and never tell a lie or that he is to some extent not telling the truth. In most cases the latter would be a more likely possibility than the former.

The K scale, the second control scale, was based on the observation that some normal persons, because of excessive openness and frankness, may obtain high scores on the clinical scales, whereas some psychiatric patients may obtain low scores because of defensiveness. The K scale was derived to reduce the effects of this biasing. In order to accomplish this, "K corrections" are made on a number of clinical scales. For example, in Figure 10-1, half of the patient's K scores was added to the Hs score. By itself, the K scale appears to be an index of defensiveness and the need to place oneself in a socially desirable light. The third control scale, the F scale, was intended to provide a measure of the intrusive effects of the subject's carelessness and confusion in taking the MMPI. A high score on this scale indicates that the subject has described himself as having a number of rare and improbable characteristics.

In the years since the MMPI was first introduced much information has been gathered concerning its use in clinical situations (Dahlstrom and Welsh, 1960; Welsh and Dahlstrom, 1956). It has also been used as a screening device in military, student counseling, industrial, and other settings. An example of the MMPI as a screening device is to be found in a paper by Doidge and Holtzman (1960). The paper dealt with the problem of homosexuality in the United States Air Force. In the Air Force homosexual suspects are subjected to intensive study and investigation. Such scrutiny is most certainly an unpleasant and embarrassing experience for a suspect. In Doidge and Holtzman's study four groups of men were compared by means of the MMPI: (1) H group consisted of men with predominantly homosexual tendencies and histories of homosexual behavior; (2) A group consisted of men with predominantly heterosexual tendencies but with a history of some homosexual behavior; (3) D group consisted of men with predominant heterosexual tendencies and no history of homosexual behavior. Men in this group were under study by the Air Force for offenses other than homosexuality; (4) N group consisted of heterosexual men not under investigation by the Air Force.

Figure 10-2 presents the MMPI profiles for the four groups. The H group profile has a clearly higher elevation than the other three profiles. It would appear that exclusively homosexual males manifest

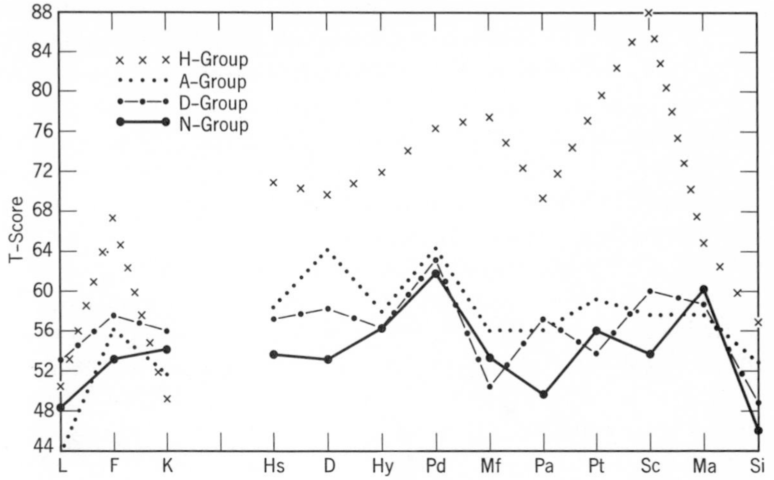

Figure 10-2 Mean T scores of the MMPI for four groups of airmen (predominantly homosexual, accessory homosexual, disciplinary, and normal). $N = 80$; each group = 20 (after Doidge and Holtzman, 1960, p. 11).

a higher over-all level of personality disturbances than either heterosexual males with some elements of homosexuality in their background or males selected on bases other than their sexual orientation. The ability of the MMPI to discriminate between the exclusively homosexual males and the other three groups suggests that it might be useful as a tool for screening overt male homosexuals.

One point that has come out clearly in the practical use of the MMPI is that valuable information is thrown away when employment of the MMPI is limited simply to isolated scores on the original Hathaway and McKinley scales. Much additional information can be obtained from taking into account the many patterns among the scale scores. Because of the subtleties often involved in these patterns, their interpretation requires a considerable degree of training on the part of the test user.

A major development in research on the MMPI has been the development of a large number of new and special scales derived from the 550-item pool (Dahlstrom and Welsh, 1960; Welsh and Dahlstrom, 1956). Usually these scales have been constructed either to fill a practical need or to make available an individual difference variable that is related to a particular construct or hypothesis. An example of a very practical application of the MMPI approach to personality test construction is found in the work of Hathaway and Monachesi (1953, 1961, 1963). These researchers were interested in assessing the tendency toward delinquency, certainly one of our most pressing social problems. In the course of their investigations, they developed a special Delinquency scale from the 550-item pool. This scale was based on differences in responses to the MMPI of known delinquents and nondelinquents. Their scale, by itself and in terms of its relationship to other scales, has proven of value in the everyday identification of individuals suspected of showing delinquent tendencies.

Another example of a new MMPI scale is one developed by Barron (1953). Barron was not interested in identifying varieties of abnormal behavior but rather in predicting persons' responses to psychiatric treatment. Using the empirical approach we have been describing, he compared groups of patients who were judged by experts as showing positive and negative responses to treatment. Barron called his scale an Ego Strength scale because he had hypothesized that the adequacy of a person's ego development would be related to his ability to change his behavior and attitudes and thus show improvement. Yet another aspect of Barron's construct of ego strength related to the ability of an individual to inhibit undesirable impulses and tendencies. His research has led to the suggestion that progress in psychotherapy is related to personal adequacy, flexibility, and the ability to express emotions in an appropriate fashion. Although Barron's work was done in the area of psychotherapy, the characteristic of ego strength, as measured by his scale, may have potential value in situations other than those characteristic of clinics. Ego Strength scale scores may provide measures of personality stability and reality orientation that relate to such characteristics as personal creativity and social sensitivity.

A final example of a special scale constructed with MMPI items is one with which we are already familiar, the Taylor (1951, 1953) Manifest Anxiety Scale. Although its method of construction differed from that used in the scales described, all of its items are contained within the MMPI. Taylor's scale has been used in some clinical settings, but it was constructed primarily as an instrument in construct validation research.

Critical Reactions to the MMPI

Having described the MMPI and indicated its wide usage in clinical and personality research, how may we evaluate its status and contributions? Few, if any, areas of psychology do not have foci of controversy, and the MMPI is no exception to the rule. A review of personality assessment literature shows that this inventory has been regarded by some as the beginning of a new era of scientific personality appraisal. Others, however, have been more impressed with its deficiencies and shortcomings. Doubtless the MMPI has had a powerful and salutary impact on personality research. But this evaluation need not require blanket acceptance or rejection of the MMPI. A more detailed review of this instrument seems necessary because many of the favorable and many of the unfavorable comments about it may have considerable merit.

On the positive side, the MMPI has stimulated much research in the fields of personality assessment and psychopathology. The work done on the original clinical and control scales, together with the efforts of many different investigators in devising new scales, has contributed to the search for personal characteristics that are relevant to behavior. More specifically, the MMPI approach to the derivation of scoring keys, though not novel in itself, has demonstrated the usefulness of a strictly empirical method of test construction. By strictly empirical is meant the fact that, for example, the Schizophrenia scale consists of only those items that actually have discriminated between schizophrenics and nonschizophrenics, and the fact that the Depression scale consists of only those items that have been shown to discriminate between depressives and nondepressives.

Most users of the MMPI refuse to make any assumptions either about the factualness of the subject's answers or about the subject's interpretations of the meanings of the items. The MMPI approach is instructive because it clearly presents one view of personality that does not depend very much on theoretical predilections and hypotheses. For this reason, the MMPI has proven particularly popular with students (1) who have strong doubts about the contribution which theoretical formulations can make to psychology at its present point of development, and (2) who believe that paper-and-pencil assessment methods can make discriminations among individuals. For these proponents of what has been called "dustbowl empiricism," theory development and construct validation are not secondary considerations but later steps in the development of personality assessment.

Another contribution of the MMPI is the sheer size of its item pool. There is considerable practical merit in having available a large number of items used commonly by different researchers who may be located in varied geographical regions. Such a common pool unquestionably increases the likelihood of easy interchange among investigators and comparison of their findings. Hathaway (p. viii of Preface to Dahlstrom and Welsh, 1960) has stated this advantage well.

A justification for the MMPI can be suggested now that was unforeseen in 1941. The subsequent wide use and availability of the test permits easier replication and application of experimental results than is the case if unfamiliar items and tests are used. The latter require too much of us. Our inertia prevents a proper pyramiding of new data upon the findings of others. When new findings are presented using an unfamiliar test, we rarely even replicate the work and still more rarely build upon it. If an investigator uses the MMPI or another widely employed test, however, then more information is easily added to the substantial fund already accumulated and the tool to use in replication or further work is readily available.

The fund of knowledge generated by the MMPI is by now substantial. Although many reported findings based on the scales have not held up under crossvalidation (that is, repeating a validation study using a new sample of subjects), several empirical results have been shown to have at least a fair degree of generality. Encouraged by this state of affairs, many investigators have become interested in the effort to go beyond the initial step of discriminating among particular groups of people on the basis of MMPI responses. They have sought to achieve formulations about constructs of characteristics that underlie obtained differences. Hathaway, (1960, p. viii) has stated this point clearly:

> That the MMPI will be a steppingstone to a higher level of validity I still sincerely hope; I hope too that the new level will soon loom in sight. In the meantime I see it as a steppingstone that permits useful communication at its own level even though the stone is rather wobbly.
>
> As I have stated, the MMPI began with validity based upon the usefulness of the various diagnostic groups from which its scales were derived. Now the burden of its use rests upon construct validity. Only a small fraction of the published data relating clinical or experimental variables to its scales or profiles can be understood in terms of the original approach. If the validity views of 1941 were the only support for the inventory, it could not survive. What is happening is that the correlations being observed with other variables in normal and abnormal subjects are filling out personality constructs that emerge, to be in turn tested for their ability to survive. It is significant that constructs, in the general sense of construct validity . . . can be the forerunners of diagnostic classes.

Proponents of the MMPI, while recognizing that it may be a far from perfect instrument, contend that it has been shown to make useful discriminations among various groups of persons. On the other hand, critics seem to be more impressed with (1) the methodological inadequacies of many studies that have yielded purportedly positive findings, and (2) the failures to replicate some previously reported positive findings (Cronbach, 1960; Rotter, 1954). Let us mention some of the specific criticisms of the construction and use of the MMPI in personality assessment. One argument is that the construction of MMPI scales too often has been based on a small number of subjects. More generally, this criticism is that the procedure used in sampling subjects was not adequate enough to permit drawing general conclusions. For example, in the derivation of the Depression scale, the criterion group consisted of 50 diagnosed depressive patients who were in the depressed phase of manic-depressive psychosis. These patients were compared with, among other groups, normal married couples and college students.

With respect first to the criterion group of depressed patients, it seems reasonable to desire a larger and more representative group than was used by Hathaway and McKinley. It is well known that psychiatric diagnoses vary according to the training and orientation of the persons making them. Furthermore, there is variability from hospital to hospital and from clinic to clinic in the ways in which diagnoses are made. The diagnoses of psychoanalytically oriented psychiatrists may not be congruent with those of psychiatrists of other orientations. In a sense, then, labeling a group of people as depressive may result as much from the semantics of the diagnosing process as from the behavior of the patients themselves. Upon reflection, it becomes clear that this poses no minor problem. It lays open to question the whole process whereby comparison groups are selected. In a way, the scales of the MMPI can be expected to be no better than the diagnoses upon which they were based. Furthermore, many have felt that such diagnoses are too unstable and subject to bias to be worthwhile in research, and that personality assessment should seek new dimensions and constructs by means of which persons can be described and compared, rather than traditional diagnostic ones that are of dubious reliability. In Chapter 29 we shall examine a study by Lorr, Klett, and McNair (1963) that attempted to do just this.

The same sort of criticism applying to criterion groups (such as Hathaway's schizophrenic and depressive patients) can be made of the normal groups with which clinically diagnosed groups are compared. By what standard can the label "normal" be applied to individuals? More specifically, in the case of the MMPI, in what sense can visitors to the University of Minnesota Hospital be regarded as adequately adjusted or normal? Decisions about the criteria of normality are weighty ones that cannot easily be made. However, it does seem likely that criticisms of the MMPI's sampling procedure might have been mitigated had more representative sampling of both criterion patient and normal groups been employed. Sampling procedures such as those used in the standardization of some intelligence tests would appear to be superior to those used with the MMPI (Cronbach, 1960). In intelligence test standardization, subjects are selected representatively on the basis of such factors as sex, socioeconomic status, and geography. It seems likely that in the future the relatively new field of personality assessment will profit increasingly from techniques used in the related and more venerable field of intellectual assessment.

The evaluation of the MMPI, or of any other test or procedure, should be based as much on what lessons have been learned from it as on how useful it has proven to be. Criticisms such as those regarding sampling are not only appropriate but also highly desirable and useful. Were a new MMPI to be developed today this sort of criticism would be of value in shaping a better inventory, one of greater discriminatory validity than the present one. Most evaluators of the MMPI have not sought to be picayune or sharply critical in their study of the MMPI. Often, they have been influenced by knowledge about personality tests that has developed since the MMPI was published. Often this knowledge resulted from investigations in which the MMPI was used.

TEST-TAKING ATTITUDES AND RESPONSE SETS

One of the best examples of new knowledge about the nature of personality is found in work on paper-and-pencil tests, predominantly the MMPI, dealing with test-taking attitudes and response sets. When psychologists study S-R relationships they are concerned with the response elicited by a given stimulus. For example, as mentioned in Chapter 1, Taylor (1951) was interested in the study of anticipatory eyeblink responses as a function of airpuffs administered to the subject's eyelid. Applying the same paradigm to personality test items, we may regard each item presented to a subject as a stimulus and his True or False check mark as a response. Recent work has clearly demonstrated that the S-R relationships in the analysis of personality test items are by no means simple; they pose major challenges to the researchers who work with them. The crux of these challenges is the problem of what the stimulus of a self-report item means to a subject.

The issue is clearly seen when each of us reviews his own experiences with true-false and multiple-choice achievement test items. Many persons have had the experience of making an error on a multiple-choice examination not because of lack of knowledge but because of incorrect or idiosyncratic interpretation of the item and the options provided. An analogous situation exists in personality testing. It seems reasonable to hypothesize that prior to the subject's making a True or False response on a questionnaire, conscious and unconscious factors intervene between the stimulus (test item) and the response (the subject's check mark).

The developers of the MMPI chose to ignore the question of the meaning of an item for a particular subject. They focused their attention instead on the ability of the items, whatever they might mean to the subjects, to discriminate among selected groups of individuals. However, it will be recalled that the control scales were devised (the K, F, and L scales) to provide measures of the subject's test-taking attitudes. This was done on the sensible assumption that subjects might answer items on the basis of certain attitudes toward the self-report task as well as on the basis of the degree to which statements applied to them. As we have pointed out, overly frank and open individuals might obtain inflated scores on clinical scales because they have, in a sense, bent over backwards to respond honestly rather than because of a high degree of psychopathology. Other individuals might seem much better adjusted than they really are, because they respond less in terms of the applicability of the statement to them than in terms of what they regard as socially desirable.

Edwards (1953*a*) published an influential analysis of the tendency to respond to self-report items on the basis of social desirability. In his study, he asked a group of subjects to rate 140 items that dealt with personality traits and characteristics according to the degree to which the traits were desirable or undesirable. Using this as an index of the judged desirability of the trait, he then correlated the index with the probability of individuals' endorsing the traits or ascribing them to themselves. The findings were clear-cut. The probability of subjects' attributing traits to themselves was found to be a direct function of the judged desirability of the items. This finding made it clear that the construction of personality inventories had to take into account this factor of the tendency to respond to statements on the basis of their perceived social desirability (Edwards, 1957). We shall see later that a test developed by Edwards, the *Personal Preference Schedule* (Edwards, 1953*b*), represents one attempt to control this factor in studying individual's self-reports.

One way of approaching the effects of the social desirability of statements is to construct a scale that measures a person's tendency to emit socially desirable responses. To get at this matter, Edwards (1957) developed a Social Desirability (SD) scale using MMPI items. He did so in a manner comparable to his study involving 140 items.

The score on the SD scale is the number of socially desirable responses that have been given to the items composing the scale.

The SD scale has been found to correlate significantly with many widely used personality measures, including the MMPI (Edwards, 1961). The problem for the future would appear to be: what is the meaning of these correlations? Do they show that the tendency to make socially desirable responses is predominant in the subject's behavior on questionnaires? For example, scores on the SD scale correlate strongly and negatively with the MMPI clinical scales and the Taylor Manifest Anxiety Scale. Does this relationship indicate that low scores on these scales arise because of the social desirability set, or does it simply show that maladjustment and psychopathology are not socially desirable? A worthwhile direction for research on the SD scale and other indices of social desirability would involve construct validation in which these measures are used as independent variables in experiments (Block, 1965; Crowne and Marlowe, 1964; McGee, 1962). Comparisons of different definitions of social desirability would also be instructive.

An example of a construct validation approach to social desirability may be seen in the work of Crowne and Marlowe (1964). These investigators constructed a measure of social desirability and then compared groups of persons differing in SD scores with respect to behavior in a variety of experimental situations. The results of these comparisons showed that persons who obtained high scores on the Marlowe-Crowne SD scale were more conforming, conventional, cautious, and persuasible, than low-scoring persons. This suggests that social desirability need not be seen simply as a set to present oneself in the most favorable light possible, but may be viewed as a constellation of attitudes reflecting low self-esteem, lack of assertiveness, and dependence upon the favorable esteem of others.

Since Edwards's initial study of social desirability and a provocative analysis of response sets by Cronbach (1946), much work in the area of assessment has been directed toward the isolation of variables that influence a subject's scores on personality scales. In addition to studies dealing with the possibility that subjects may respond to self-report items on the basis of the social desirability they perceive in the characteristic referred to in the items, investigations have also been conducted on other test-taking attitudes and response sets. For example, the acquiescence tendency is the set to answer true to self-report items, independent of their content. Jackson and Messick (1958) have drawn a distinction between the content of items, and the styles and sets with which individuals approach them. These stylistic individual difference variables include, in addition to tendencies to acquiesce to self-report items and to respond on the basis of the items' perceived social desirability, the tendencies to be evasive, cautious, and consistent and to respond quickly to test items.

It is becoming increasingly clear that response sets in relation to a person's self-description must not be regarded simply as troublesome sources of error in personality appraisal. Rather, the attitudes and tendencies which the subject brings to the self-report situation must be regarded as significant personality variables in their own right. That these attitudes and tendencies exist has become well known. What is needed now is an answer to the question: to what degree do they influence the picture of the person presented on paper-and-pencil tests? (Block, 1965; Rorer, 1965.)

Progress in science is defined as much by the discovery of problems and questions as by the concrete facts uncovered in the course of research. The study of self-descriptions illustrates this well. As work has proceeded in this area, a focal question has been: what are the determinants of self-descriptions? Viewed this way the correctness of self-description becomes only one of many salient questions. Among other problems inherent in the general question posed are:

1. How does the wording of self-report statements influence the individual's responses to questionnaires?
2. How do the instructions and directions of the questionnaire influence the self-description?
3. What are the individual's subjective reactions to the task of self-description?
4. How can response sets and test-taking attitudes be manipulated experimentally?
5. How do the content of items and the subject's style of responding interact with each other in influencing self-descriptions?

Returning to the MMPI, we would conclude that although it has proved of practical value in various kinds of settings, its major contribution has been as a vehicle for furthering the exploration of variables that influence self-descriptions. As we shall find later, there are many techniques in addition to the self-report questionnaire which may be used in assessing personality. The ease and convenience of questionnaires have made their use especially appealing. However, one of the most exciting developments in the area of self-report devices has been the growing recognition of their capacity to increase understanding of significant aspects of verbal behavior as well as their use as short-cut screening tools.

OTHER SELF-REPORT INVENTORIES

We have dealt with the MMPI in some detail both because of its wide usage and because it illustrates a number of the most important problems confronting those who attempt the measurement or assessment of personality characteristics. There are, of course, many other personality inventories which are used both in applied settings and in research. Let us review some of these.

California Personality Inventory

The California Personality Inventory (CPI), published in 1957 (Gough, 1957), represents work carried out over a period of years. In several respects it is similar to the MMPI. However, it was not devised with the aim of contributing to the differential diagnosis of mental patients. Gough (1957, p. 7) has stated the aims of his work in this way:

> The California Psychological Inventory was created in the hope of attaining two goals of personality assessment. The first goal, largely theoretical in nature, has been to use and to develop descriptive concepts which possess broad personal and social relevance. Many of the standard personality tests and assessment devices available previously have been designed for use in special settings, such as the psychiatric clinic, or have been constructed to deal with a particular problem, such as vocational choice. The present endeavor has been concerned with characteristics of personality which have a wide and pervasive applicability to human behavior, and which in addition are related to the favorable and positive aspects of personality rather than to the morbid and pathological.
>
> The second goal for the CPI has been the practical one of devising brief, accurate, and dependable subscales for the identification and measurement of the variables chosen for inclusion in the inventory. A further consideration has been that the instrument be convenient and easy to use and suitable for large-scale application.
>
> The inventory is intended primarily for use with "normal" (non-psychiatrically disturbed) subjects. Its scales are addressed principally to personality characteristics important for social living and social interaction. Thus, while it has been found to have special utility with a few problem groups, e.g. persons of delinquent, asocial tendencies, it may be expected to find most general use in schools, colleges, business and industry, and in clinics and counseling agencies whose clientele consists mainly of socially-functioning individuals.

Among the CPI's scales are those entitled: Dominance, Sociability, Self-acceptance, Self-control, Intellectual efficiency, and Flexibility. The inventory contains 480 true-false items and 18 scales. There appear to be four types of scales on the CPI measuring: (1) poise, ascendancy, and self-assurance; (2) socialization, maturity, and social responsibility; (3) achievement potential and intellectual efficiency; and (4) personal orientation and attitudes toward life.

The administration, scoring, and profiling of the subject's protocols are similar to those of the MMPI. The method of sampling subjects and the test-construction procedures used in its development represent a noticeable improvement over those employed in the MMPI. Many of these methodological advances result, no doubt, from lessons learned from working with the MMPI. For example, the keying of the various CPI scales was based on responses of a much larger sample, over 6,000 males and 7,000 females. In sampling, Gough paid attention to subjects' ages, social positions, status, and geographical locations.

Most of the CPI's scales were constructed in the same manner as those for the MMPI. However, instead of using experts, such as psychiatrists, to categorize groups of subjects, Gough employed such techniques as nomination by peers. For example, for the Dominance scale, he and his collaborators had high school and college students nominate peers who varied in dominance (in Gough's view, dominance referred to such characteristics as social initiative and persistence). In this way, high and low dominance groups were selected. These groups were then administered the CPI. Those of the 480 items on the CPI that showed significant differences between the peer-nominated high and low dominance groups were then considered as candidates for inclusion on the Dominance scale. A favorable aspect of the CPI is that in its development crossvalidation was frequently employed. That is, having shown that two groups of individuals selected on some basis, such as peer nominations, differed in their responses to the CPI, Gough then checked whether the differences obtained held up for new samples of subjects similarly selected.

Many of the questions raised concerning the MMPI appear to apply equally to the CPI. Just as the efficacy of using psychiatrists' judgments as the basis for selecting criterion groups in the MMPI was questioned, one might wonder about the rationale for using peer nominations in this inventory. Although peer nominations are defensible and represent an interesting technique, the possibility must be recognized that other procedures might yield quite different results. Another problem raised in connection with the MMPI which also applies to the CPI concerns the determinants of the subject's self-descriptive responses. Very likely an important area of future research with the CPI will explore the roles of response sets in relation to the subject's scores.

Because the CPI is a relatively new instrument, a definitive evaluation of it is not possible. We have already commented favorably on the generally high level of sophistication used in its construction. Many of the evaluative studies which have been reported suggest that the CPI may be of considerable value in describing the characteristics of persons whose behavior is not markedly deviant. It seems likely that many practical uses of the CPI will be uncovered, in the years to come—for example, in counseling students (Gough and Hall, 1964).

How construct validation of CPI scores and profiles will proceed does not at present appear to be so easily predictable. The manual of the CPI does not provide elaborated theoretical formulations that might lend direction to construct validation research. Although it contains definitions of the 18 scales, it does not indicate the criteria used in item selection or the hypothesized meaning of each scale. However, personality researchers will no doubt find it useful to have available the CPI's large pool of items that are oriented to behavior within the normal range of functioning.

Edwards' Personal Preference Schedule

This inventory contains 225 items. Each item consists of two statements rather than the one statement found in true-false or agree-disagree type tests. The subject is instructed to read each pair of statements and respond by checking the one that is most applicable to him. This is referred to as a forced-choice procedure. The 225 items are scored in terms of 15 variables. These 15 variables are based on hypothesized needs put forth by Murray. The language of the *Edwards Personal Preference Schedule* (EPPS) (Edwards, 1953*b*) reflects needs inferred from the subject's forced choices. Like the CPI, the emphasis is not on psychopathology but on general personality characteristics. Among the variables scored on the EPPS are: need for achievement, need for dominance, need for nurturance, need for affiliation, and need for autonomy.

The method of construction of the EPPS differed from that employed in the MMPI and CPI. The statements used by Edwards were written to adhere to the definitions of the needs being explored. For example, need for aggression was defined in terms of the need to attack contrary points of view, to criticize, to become angry, and to blame others. The 15 items pertaining to this need were written on the basis of face validity. That is, the items seemed relevant to the need as defined.

The EPPS has been used in a variety of ways, especially in counseling and related settings. It has been employed by many investigators concerned with a variety of research problems. Its standardization was not carried out as exhaustively as was that of the CPI and its norm group consisted mainly of college-educated persons. As with the CPI, construct validation that might shed light on the meaning of the scale scores has only just begun.

Recall that Edwards empirically demonstrated a strong positive relationship between the subject's judged social desirability of questionnaire statements and the probability of his endorsing them (Edwards, 1953*a*, 1957). In the EPPS, he has tried through the forced-choice format to establish a control for this influence of social desirability. Seeking to equate the social desirability of the 225 pairs of items, he obtained ratings of the social desirability of statements and then matched pairs of items with comparable ratings. In this way, Edwards hoped, the subject's choice of one of the two alternatives presented in a given item could not be attributed to the set to respond in a socially desirable way.

One can criticize this use of the forced-choice format in personality assessment on the grounds that conflict and annoyance are built up in individuals who are forced to choose between two strongly undesirable attributes (Guilford, 1959*a*). To use an extreme illustration, not found in the EPPS, a subject would probably have difficulty in choosing which of these two statements to endorse:

(A) I like to beat my wife.
(B) I like to be humiliated by others.

On the other hand, there are interesting possibilities for studying conflict and choice behavior with an instrument like the EPPS. An additional feature of the EPPS is the consistency key used in scoring it. The schedule contains 15 repeated items. It therefore becomes possible to determine to what extent a given subject is responding consistently to the same item. This information is of importance in terms of gathering evidence about the credence that can be placed in the scores for a given individual.

The EPPS, then, appears to be a device that can play a useful role in research on response sets and choice behavior, and in construct validation of personality theory. It represents an interesting psychometric alternative to the MMPI and CPI.

FACTOR ANALYSIS AND PERSONALITY ASSESSMENT

The observations made relative to a person's attitudes toward the task of self-description raise a question about the meaning of assessed characteristics: when does a researcher know that he has identified a personal characteristic in a relatively pure form? A statistical methodology known as factor analysis has proved useful to many students challenged by this question. It has also proved valuable to psychologists interested in *parsimoniously* handling large amounts of data which pertain to groups of persons. Factor analysis was originally employed for the study of variables underlying performance on intellectual tasks. Subsequent application of these procedures has been made in the study of a host of personal characteristics including interests, values, and attitudes. As personality assessment becomes increasingly multidimensional its multidimensionality is particularly appropriate for distillation through factor analysis.

A major goal in factor analysis is the achievement of order among facts. Factor analysts seek integration of facts in as parsimonious a manner as possible. In a personality inventory such as the MMPI, there are available 550 facts, namely, answers to the inventory's 550 items. One way of treating these facts is to determine which ones play a part in discriminating between selected groups of people, such as schizophrenics and normals. The factor-analytic approach is quite different. It poses the question: given a large number of pieces of information such as a subject's responses to test items, what is the minimum number of concepts needed to conceptualize them or to account for them? Factor analysis is a general correlational procedure which starts with the relationships among the bits of information. In psychological tests, the starting point would be the correlations among the items of a test or scores on a number of tests. Thus, a factor analysis of the MMPI might begin with the computation of the correlations among the 550 items. We shall not attempt to describe the procedures that follow this initial step. They involve complicated statistical operations and require intensive study of the process of factor analysis (Cronbach, 1960; Guilford, 1959*a*). However, the end product of a factor analysis can be explained succinctly.

Through factor analysis, researchers seek to delineate the smallest number of independent factors that can account for the relationships among a set of facts. The potentialities of factor analysis become evident when one considers that a relatively small number of factors or dimensions derived from it might provide a relatively succinct summary of a person's responses to a large number of items. Factor analysis holds out the possibility to researchers of rationally grouping items that go together. One interesting application of factor analysis to intelligence testing has been reported by Guilford (1957), who has argued that human abilities cannot reasonably be expected to be adequately summarized in one index such as the IQ. Rather, he has used factor analysis to quantify a number of distinct factors that signify abilities; this approach to intelligence has relevance for personality assessment owing to the movement from unidimensional to multidimensional measures.

An example of factor analysis applied to personal and social attitudes may be found in a study by Ferguson (1939). He administered to subjects 10 scales designed to measure attitudes toward war, the reality of God, patriotism, the treatment of criminals, capital punishment, censorship, evolution, birth control, law, and Communism. The relationships among these scales were computed and then factor analyzed. The aim of the factor analysis was to determine the smallest number of attitude clusters or factors that would account for the intercorrelations. Three factors were derived: "religionism," "humanitarianism," and "nationalism." The "religionism" factor accounted for attitudes toward God, evolution, and birth control; "humanitarianism" accounted for attitudes toward capital punishment, treatment of criminals, and war; "nationalism" accounted for attitudes toward law, Communism, censorship, and patriotism.

An illustration of factor analysis that is applied to an already existing set of personality items is evident in work with the MMPI. In most of the factor analyses of the MMPI the measures factored have been scores obtained by individuals on its scales. One of the main reasons for the predominance of factor analyses of scale scores rather than of individual items is the greater computational effort required in the case, for example, of 550 items as compared with, perhaps, 25 scales. The increasing availability of high-speed computers has resulted in much more attention to items in factor-analytic work.

In one factor analysis, Welsh discovered that two factors accounted for a significant proportion of the variance in responses to the MMPI (Welsh and Dahlstrom, 1956). The first, labeled factor A, appeared to be associated with the subject's admission of distress and awareness of personal anxiety. The second, factor R, appeared to relate to scales that have been interpreted as reflecting defense mechanisms such as repression, denial, and rationalization. On the basis of this evidence, Welsh constructed A and R keys for the MMPI. A subsequent study (Kassebaum, Couch, and Slater, 1959) replicated Welsh's work using a different group of subjects. Since the scales have been shown to account for two pervasive sources of variability on the MMPI, they may prove to have considerable predictive value.

Cattell (1957*a*) developed an entire personality inventory based upon factor-analytic methods. His test, the 16 PF Questionnaire, yields

16 scores on factorially derived scales. It is Cattell's hope that these scales tap basic underlying personality traits that will be useful in accounting for the behavior of individuals. At present, the amount of research on the 16 PF Questionnaire is small compared to the body of information available on the MMPI.

Another pioneer in the development of factorially derived tests has been Guilford (1959*a*). His interests have ranged over both tests of personality and tests of intelligence. He has constructed three factor-analytically derived inventories, An Inventory of Factors STDCR, An Inventory of Factors GAMIN, and the Personnel Inventory. The procedure he has used has been to factor analyze sets of self-report items and to develop scales consisting of items related to the factors derived. Guilford regards the scores for these factors as reflecting primary personality traits.

It is important to be aware that the factors derived from a factor analysis depend on the particular set of facts on which the analysis is performed. They are also a function of the particular statistical procedures employed in the analysis and of the investigator's interpretation of his results. Thus, although factor analysis is a mathematical approach to the relationships among tests and their items, the personal judgment of the factor analyst is a variable to be considered. As Cronbach (1960, pp. 248, 259) states:

> Although factor analysis is mathematical, it involves considerable judgment. The investigator chooses whatever method of organizing his results makes the best sense to him, and the result is variation among studies. This is confusing, just as it confuses the beginning student of geography to find different maps picturing Greenland in different ways. These differences are of little concern to the nonspecialist; the important thing is that all maps agree that there is such a large island in the North Atlantic. . . . The factor analyst may be compared to the photographer trying to picture a building as revealingly as possible. Wherever he sets his camera, he will lose some information, but by a skillful choice he will be able to show a large number of important features of the building.

To summarize, factor analysis is a method for boiling a large amount of information down to a parsimonious, meaningful core of variables. Although most students of psychological tests would agree that it can be of value for certain purposes, there is disagreement about the extent to which factor analysis, by itself, can contribute to the development of personality theory. Some researchers see factor analysis essentially as a means of grouping items and information which go together. Others appear to view it as a route to the uncovering of basic or underlying determinants of human behavior. The issue here amounts to the question: what interpretation shall be placed on factors derived from factor analyses of data? Cattell (1956, p. 98), a leading factor analyst within the field of personality, has offered this interpretation of a factor:

> . . . a factor is not merely a measuring device; it is a statement about a functionally unitary, constitutionally or sociologically determined pattern within personality, about which the general progress of psychological research may be expected to yield a great deal of information. When the natural history of a factor is known, i.e., when one knows how far it is determined by heredity, what its curve of growth is through childhood or of decline in later life, how it is affected by various learning situations or by physiological changes, etc., the ability to understand and to predict is greatly increased. No arbitrary scale, however good, can ever be used with the insight and with the useful application of general psychological laws that is possible with a factor measurement.

In considering factor analysis in relation to personality tests we have mentioned only a few of the researchers concerned with this area. Although factor-analytic procedures have been available for over half a century, their application to self-report indices has been more recent. It seems safe to say that the number of factor-analytic studies will increase in the years to come. As already suggested, factor analysis appears to be a useful tool in determining the relatively few factors that may underlie a person's response to a large number of self-descriptive items. But the predictive and theoretical usefulness of these factors can be determined only by relating them to significant aspects of the behavior of persons. Valuable as this tool is, it is important to realize that factor analysis does not represent a solution to all of the methodological and theoretical problems confronting personality researchers. We have already suggested that the factors underlying test responses may vary as a function of the nature of the test and the particular analytic methods employed. No matter how sophisticated a factor analyst may be in his statistical work, his factors will be no better than the items on which factor analysis has been performed.

A final word should be said concerning the contribution of factor analysis to personality research. This contribution will depend to a considerable degree on what is done with the factors once they have been derived. To the extent that they can be related to significant aspects of behavior, they will further a theory of personality. Whether particular factors reflect important basic general traits or characteristics must be empirically demonstrated. It would seem, then, that factor analysis can play a significant role in uncovering variables or factors that subsequently must be construct validated. In this sense, factor analysis may be regarded as a first step in the development of nomological networks.

CONCLUDING COMMENT CONCERNING PAPER-AND-PENCIL MEASURES

We have emphasized throughout our review of individual personality scales and groups of them (inventories) the need for construct validation, to wit, the establishment of relationships between test scores and behavior so that the development of psychological concepts and theories is facilitated. We must recognize, of course, that as new empirical relationships are uncovered constructs require revision and reformulation.

What can we say by way of general comment regarding paper-and-pencil self-description measures? It seems fair to observe that personality scales and inventories have been and are in very wide use. Psychologists and others working in a variety of clinical, educational, industrial, and other applied settings have found them helpful in describing and understanding individuals. Considerable research has attested to the ability of users of self-report questionnaires to make reasonably accurate discriminations among different types of persons on the basis of their responses. However, the personality literature does contain negative findings relative to the value of self-report measures. Perhaps the most significant and encouraging characteristic of current work with these measures is the rapidly increasing sophistication of researchers in their test development procedures, in their awareness of the many variables, such as response sets, that influence paper-and-pencil self-descriptions, and in their efforts to make theoretically meaningful the test scores derived from the instruments they construct.

In evaluating the role of paper-and-pencil tests as self-descriptive indices, it is necessary to consider their historical context. Early users of them were attracted by their objective, convenient formats. They employed them, to a large extent, for practical selection purposes, for example, selecting highly maladjusted armed forces recruits. While the role of personality assessment in selection work continues, there has been growing interest in relating assessment techniques to theoretical problems (Jessor and Hammond, 1957; Taft, 1959). The contribution of Cronbach and Meehl (1955) with regard to construct validation clearly has contributed importantly to this trend.

Another discernible trend is the increasing recognition that self-description is but one way of objectively and quantitatively assessing personal characteristics. As previously suggested, all personality tests may be viewed as vehicles for obtaining a person's responses to stimuli. It is possible to characterize tests in terms of the kinds of stimuli presented to subjects and the kinds of responses that they are asked to make. For example, both true-false and forced-choice personality tests present statements as stimuli to subjects. However, the subject on a true-false test responds by indicating whether each statement applies or does not apply to him. In the forced-choice test the subject must decide upon the relative degrees of accuracy of statements presented in pairs.

It would seem an unnecessary restriction to limit the personality assessor to a true-false, forced-choice, or any other type of format. It does not seem necessary either to restrict the assessor to self-descriptive and self-evaluative statements. A subject's response to the statement, "Pushy people are self-centered" may be as revealing or more revealing of personality characteristics than his response to the statement, "I dislike pushy people." The second of these statements on the surface appears to be more self-descriptive than the first. However, it seems to be unduly restrictive to limit personality tests and measures to statements and stimuli phrased only in terms of the first person. This fact has become increasingly recognized by assessment researchers. Whereas the earliest forms of this type of test contained items that dealt almost exclusively with the subject's personal reactions and opinions, recent ones have employed a variety of formats. Available evidence suggests that the method of assessment may very significantly influence the way in which persons are categorized and the correlations of assessed characteristics with selected aspects of behavior (Campbell and Fiske, 1959).

Many assessment methods are, like the paper-and-pencil questionnaires we have been describing, reliable, unambiguous, and objective. Summarizing several of their characteristics in a word one might say that they, like tests such as the MMPI and the CPI, are relatively highly organized. That is, the assessment situation is arranged so that both subject and scorer know their respective tasks. However, as in all personality assessment methodologies, the personal determinants—both conscious and unconscious—of the subject's responses may not be immediately obvious in these formats. Let us turn at this point to examples of some personality assessment techniques other than paper-and-pencil questionnaires. We shall see that many of these may be used in studies of self-description and other types of research.

11

Self-Description of Personal Characteristics: Other Quantitative Approaches

To limit objective methods of personality assessment to the self-report questionnaire seems unnecessarily restrictive. Conceivably, as much may be learned about an individual from his descriptions of others as from his description of himself. A combination of self-description and description of others would no doubt be most revealing.

SEMANTIC DIFFERENTIAL

Osgood, Suci, and Tannenbaum, in 1957, presented a technique that showed promise for obtaining and quantifying an individual's reactions to himself, to others, and, in fact, to any object or concept. They called the technique *semantic differential*. The term derives from the different meanings that a concept can have for different individuals. The technique is helpful for those wishing to assess the meanings of concepts to individuals and any changes in meanings that may occur. Despite the recency of its introduction, this technique has already been employed in many types of research.

The semantic differential is not a test in the same sense as the MMPI. It was not developed as a tool for practical selection or diagnosis, nor has it been standardized. Rather it is a research method of wide generality, useful to investigators with varying interests. The technique, from the standpoint of the subject, is straightforward. A series of concepts is presented to him. This task is to rate each concept on several seven-point rating scales. The same scales are used for all concepts.

Example of concepts which might be rated in this fashion are:

My mother	Myself	My Father
Home	Food	School

Scales along which each of these concepts might be rated include:

good ⊢—+—+—+—+—⊣ bad
nice ⊢—+—+—+—+—⊣ awful
heavy ⊢—+—+—+—+—⊣ light
hard ⊢—+—+—+—+—⊣ soft
pleasant ⊢—+—+—+—+—⊣ unpleasant

Like other objective approaches, the semantic differential may be administered to a group and its scoring may be rated as unambiguous. A great advantage of this technique is the many questions to which it can be directed. One might be interested in comparing a person's ratings of himself with his ratings of other concepts—for example, *my mother, my father*. One might also wish to compare different types of individuals (for example, delinquents and nondelinquents) with respect to their ratings of themselves and others. Still another possibility would be to compare the ratings of one particular individual at different points in time; for example, before and after psychotherapy, before and after a weekend, or before and after a particular experimental condition. Thus, in one study it was found that meanings of concepts on the semantic differential changed as a patient progressed in psychotherapy (Mowrer, 1953).

Researchers might consider using this technique in virtually any situation where assessment of and changes in meanings of concepts is desired. When the semantic differential is used in research it is necessary to do careful planning. The researcher, therefore, must decide upon the particular concepts and scales that are to be included in his study. In an effort to shed light on the bases of a subject's reactions to concepts, Osgood, Suci, and Tannenbaum (1957) performed a number of factor analyses of semantic differential rating scales. The results of their analyses suggest that, to a sizable extent, three factors underlie responses to the semantic differential. The first factor they called evaluative. Scales that are strongly related to this factor concern evaluations made by individuals—for example, of such distinctions as good-bad, honest-dishonest, and fair-unfair. A second factor, potency, is significant in accounting for a subject's responses to scales such as strong-weak, large-small, and heavy-light. The third factor, activity, appears to be related mostly to scales like fast-slow and active-passive. These factors may be viewed as variables whose values determine the meaning of a concept, or as dimensions in charting the "semantic geography" of concepts.

Osgood, Suci, and Tannenbaum recognized that a tool such as the semantic differential was only a preliminary step in the determination of the basis for different meanings of a concept. Further research will be needed to answer questions such as: what is the meaning of the concept *father* for a particular person? The semantic differential provides one empirical path along which these questions may be explored. It seems reasonable to expect that students of personality assessment may be able to make effective use of differences in meanings of concepts as individual difference variables for predictive purposes.

A procedure developed by G. A. Kelly (1955) has some characteristics similar to those of the semantic differential. His procedure, which he called the Construct Repertory Test (Rep test), is also directed toward the problem of the meaning of concepts. Whereas Osgood, Suci, and Tannenbaum phrased their research in terms of semantic meaning, Kelly based his work on the following assumption: "A person's processes are psychologically channelized by the ways in which he anticipates events." Just as researchers and theoreticians devise constructs so, Kelly feels, do all individuals. In his Rep Test, rather than use the same format for all subjects, he asks each subject to select his own concepts. In the course of taking his test the subject is given a list of personal roles (such as "your friend," "someone you would like to help") and is asked to mention specific people from his own life who fill these roles. Thus, the procedure seems to be more specifically concerned with the individual, his world, and the constructs he uses in interpreting it than is the method of Osgood, Suci, and Tannenbaum. Both approaches, however, represent imaginative and potentially fruitful attempts to come to grips with "what is going on inside" through assessment of reactions to self and to others.

RATING SCALES

The semantic differential is an example of the use of rating scales, which are among the most venerable of assessment devices. With a rating scale, the rater is presented with an item (a concept, a person, a situation). He responds by selecting one of a number of choices that seems most appropriate in describing the item. The rating scale is similar to the multiple-choice item except that the options on the former represent degrees of a particular characteristic. Examples of rating-scale items would be: "To what extent are you shy?" "To what extent are people unfriendly?" Subjects might be asked to place these items on scales ranging from "extremely" to "not at all."

Rating scales have been used both in research and in practical situations in which easily quantifiable reactions of individuals are desired. Instances of the latter would be ratings by supervisors or employees, by nurses and doctors or patients, and by teachers or students. In the course of research on rating scales, difficulties in using the method have been uncovered and attempts made to overcome them. Perhaps the major source of inaccuracy of rating scales is one mentioned in connection with personality inventories and scales, namely, response sets. Among these sets is the *halo effect.* This set operates when an individual rates someone favorably on a specific characteristic primarily because the rater has a generally favorable reaction to the person he is rating. Other response sets causing difficulties are the tendencies of some raters to say only nice things about people and of others to use the midrange of scales.

There are some safeguards against these inadequacies. One pertains to the wording of rating scale items. The degree of ambiguity of the items and the labeling of the scales on which the rater indicates his responses are known to affect ratings. Providing clear directions, where appropriate, to raters, training raters in the use of rating scales, and supplying them with minimally ambiguous concepts and scales will greatly increase the accuracy and reliability of the scales. In addition to manipulating the rating scale *per se,* the researcher should know something about the individual who performs the rating scale task. For example, what is the degree of acquaintance of the rater with a person whose behavior he is rating? The more information the rater has about the subject, either through personal acquaintance or through information provided him by the researcher, the more accurate will his ratings be.

Within the field of personality several rating scale techniques have proved especially useful (Cronbach, 1960; Guilford, 1959*a*). In studies of personality within social contexts, peer ratings have been widely used. When peer ratings are obtained, all members of a group—for example, students in a class or staff members of a school—rate one another on a common set of characteristics. If one were interested in leadership or aggressiveness among school children, to take a case in point, one might ask the members of a class to rate one another on these characteristics. In some cases, a procedure might be employed in which peers nominate small groups of their number who are outstanding in the characteristic under study. Applications of this sort of technique to social situations, called *sociometric ratings*, have been used to characterize the social structures of different types of groups (Gronlund, 1959).

Rating scales have been used widely in studies of psychopathology and in the effects of psychiatric treatment. For example, both Wittenborn (1955) and Lorr, Jenkins, and O'Connor (1955) introduced carefully prepared rating scales for use with psychiatric patients. These scales can be used to provide indices of a patient's social behavior in hospital ward situations, a patient's response to treatment, and hospital staff members' reactions to patients. In Chapter 29 we shall examine in detail a comprehensive rating-scale study of psychotic patients carried out by Lorr, Klett, and McNair (1963).

Still another application of rating scales is to be found in those instances in which an investigator wishes to study the reactions of individuals to certain stimuli. Thus, tape recordings of psychotherapy sessions and films of children at play might constitute stimuli presented to raters, who would then indicate their reactions to and their interpretation of them. Often the aim of this type of research is to provide comparisons among the responses of selected groups of raters—for example, psychiatrists, clinical psychologists, and psychiatric social workers.

It can be seen that the rating scale, although not immune to biases, can be a highly flexible instrument for personality research. It can be used in a wide variety of situations to study different sorts of problems, to study individuals who are rated by others; or to study the raters themselves.

THE Q-SORT TECHNIQUE

Another assessment method devised for problems similar to those for which rating scales are used is the Q-sort approach or Q-technique originally developed by Stephenson (1953). In a Q-sort a person is given a vocabulary such as sentences, phrases, or words with which he is asked to describe either himself or someone else. A restriction placed on the Q-sorter is that the vocabulary is used in a prescribed fashion. Most commonly, the sorts are made so that the sorter's use of the vocabulary adheres to a bell-shaped or normal distribution.

An example of a carefully prepared Q-sort method has been reported by Block (1961). Block's Q-sort (the California Q-Set) consists of

100 statements or items about attributes of individuals. The sorter reads the 100 items, which are individually printed on cards, and then sorts them into consecutive piles. At one end on the rating continuum, the sorter places cards containing items particularly descriptive of the individual under study. At the other he places the most uncharacteristic items. In Block's Q-sort each item is placed in one of nine piles or categories. The placement of items, as we have said, is made to resemble a normal distribution. Thus, the sorter must follow a forced-choice format. This means that he is required to place only a relatively small number of items in the "most characteristic" and "least characteristic" piles, and make many more placements in categories toward the center of the distribution of the nine piles. The scoring of the items is on the basis of weights assigned to the piles. Examples of descriptive items that might be included in a Q-sort are : "gets angry easily," "works hard," "is a thoughtful person."

A person might perform a Q-sort upon himself or upon others. A frequent use of the Q-technique has individuals perform Q-sorts on themselves on repeated occasions. This has been done in psychotherapy where an important question is: what attitudinal changes occur within the individual as psychotherapy progresses? Carl Rogers and his colleagues have asked patients to make repeated Q-sorts describing themselves in order to obtain indications of attitude and self-concept changes (Rogers and Dymond, 1954). The same procedure of repeated Q-sorts can also be used in cases where persons are asked to describe the characteristics of others. For example, although it might prove very time-consuming, it would be interesting to have a teacher make Q-sorts for each of his students several times during the school year concerning their adjustment and reactions to school situations. In addition to yielding information about the ways in which the teacher's reactions to students change, it might be possible to compare the Q-sort ratings of children with regard to individual difference variables, such as intelligence and socioeconomic background.

Besides performing a Q-sort about oneself or others, the flexibility of the method, like that of rating scales, permits still further possibilities. Q-sorts need not be limited to actual persons but may be used to describe hypothetical or fantasied states, conditions, and persons. For some purposes it might be of interest to compare a person's Q-sort self-description with a Q-sort description of the person he would like most to be, his ideal self. In psychotherapy or any other situation involving possible personality change, real self-ideal self comparisons stemming from a Q-sort might prove of great value (Rogers, 1959; Rogers and Dymond, 1954).

An important characteristic of all Q-sort procedures is that they permit quantification. This enables correlation between Q-sorts, just as quantification enables correlation between different sets of ratings. Two sets of Q-sort responses may be correlated with each other and the degree of relationship between them may be determined provided the same stimulus material has been employed in both sets. The degrees to which the Q-sort statements allow for comprehensive personality description, to which the sorter or evaluator understands his task, and to which he has an adequate basis for evaluating the person under study all influence the meaningfulness of data obtained with this method. A practical methodological point to note is that performing a Q-sort is a more challenging intellectual task than filling out a rating scale. In the rating scale, the rater has to deal with only one item at a time. In the Q-sort the sorter must engage in comparisons among items, sometimes 100, in order to decide on the piles into which they are placed. This requires fairly high motivation or interest on the part of the sorter.

CONCLUDING COMMENTS CONCERNING STRUCTURED PERSONALITY MEASURES

All of the instruments reviewed in Chapters 10 and 11 may be regarded as stimuli presented to persons. These stimuli may be categorized in terms of their particular characteristics, namely, personality scales and inventories, semantic differential, rating scales, and Q-sorts. As they serve to refer succinctly to different methods of assessing personal characteristics, such categorizations are useful. We have seen how the rating scale and its variants, such as the semantic differential, and the Q-sort are not tests in the same sense as the MMPI and CPI. They are methodologies of considerable generality rather than standardized instruments that possess constant content.

Despite their noticeable differences, all of the assessment techniques so far considered may be conceptualized within a common framework. All of them may be described as verbal stimuli that call forth designated types of responses from individuals. The subject taking the MMPI, or filling out a rating scale, or performing a Q-sort has been explicitly instructed on the task confronting him. In this sense, each of these tasks is well defined or well structured. In such a situation the individual has clearly stated guidelines concerning the ground rules under which he is to respond. The contrary situation is one in which the individual is not given specific directions about the ways in which he should respond.

Because of their explicit directions and ease of administration, the tightly constructed indices of personal tendencies can often be given to large groups of people. They can be scored in a straightforward fashion and can be subjected to quantitative analysis. These qualities have contributed to their wide usage. However, we have emphasized the fact that the convenience of a method in no way implies its usefulness. Without doubt the validity of an assessment procedure is of far greater significance than its ease of usage. All assessment procedures must face the ultimate test of utility in achieving description and prediction. Additionally, we have pointed out that knowing how an individual responds to a set of items does not necessarily enable us to delineate the manner in which conscious, unconscious, and situational variables combine to determine his responses. One of the challenges for students of personality assessment is to study the factors that lead to a person's description of himself and of others.

A review of the current status of objective personality assessment techniques leads one to conclude that they have been useful to workers in the past and that their usefulness will become greater as research on them proceeds. It seems fair to say that paper-and-pencil methods have moved successfully from a first stage of assumed (face) validity to a second one in which improvements in conceptualization and methodology are clearly recognized as basic to the determination of a more important, empirical validity. Through empirical validity studies, it becomes possible to establish the relationship of an individual difference variable measured in a particular way to either practically or theoretically significant aspects of a person's life.

12

Projective Techniques: Inkblots as Ambiguous Stimuli

In addition to the tests described in Chapters 10 and 11, another type of measure is widely employed to assess personality. The devices in question have much looser structures than questionnaires, and though they present stimuli to subjects, they do not require responses to be made through true-false categories, check marks, or card sorts. Because their stimuli are relatively unclear and ambiguous, this set of assessment tools affords subjects wide latitude in responding to stimuli. They have their own rationale to which we shall give some attention before moving on to examine some actual examples of how they work.

THE RATIONALE OF PROJECTIVE TECHNIQUES

In tracing the development of paper-and-pencil tests, we noted how heavily practical needs and goals influenced their construction. Woodworth (1919) built his Personal Data Sheet for the purpose of identifying emotionally maladjusted military recruits. Later the MMPI was devised to facilitate the diagnosis of various forms of psychopathology. Clearly, the use of paper-and-pencil tests as practical devices has been widespread for a long time, although the theoretical implications of the responses to them are now receiving considerable emphasis. In marked contrast, the basis of projective techniques has always been strongly theoretical.

The ideas behind projective techniques have been largely psychoanalytic (Bellak, 1956). Our review of psychoanalytic theory described projection as a defense mechanism through which an individual unconsciously attributes or projects his own undesirable characteristics to others than himself. Although this is the sense in which projection has been most commonly used, Freud (1953–1955, vol. XIII, p. 64) suggested that the concept could be a more general one than simply a defensive operation:

. . . projection was not created for the purpose of defence; it also occurs where there is no conflict. The projection outwards of internal perceptions is a primitive mechanism, to which, for instance, our sense perceptions are subject, and which therefore normally plays a very large part in determining the form taken by our external world. Under conditions whose nature has not yet been sufficiently established, internal perceptions of emotional and thought processes can be projected outwards in the same way as sense perceptions; they are thus employed for building up the external world, though they should by rights remain part of the internal world.

Implied in this view of projection is the desirability of gaining knowledge of individuals' private worlds and of understanding how covert processes influence perception of the external world. Frank (1939, p. 402) spoke of projective techniques as devices to achieve these ends. As he put it, projective techniques may be used in relation:

. . . to the problem of how we can reveal the way an individual personality organizes experience, in order to disclose or at least gain insight into that individual's *private world* of meanings, significances, patterns, and feelings.

Lindzey (1961) has argued that the most distinctive feature of projective techniques is their use in studying unconscious, covert determinants of behavior. Most users of these techniques concur. A question not easily answered, however, is how these covert tendencies may be effectively assessed. Freud's theoretical framework has been employed in approaching this problem. It will be remembered that he described the psychoanalytic situation in terms of the patient's free associations and their interpretation. Because of the importance placed on the elimination of situational cues that might guide the patient to talk about particular topics, Freud contended that the psychoanalyst should make therapeutic sessions quite undirected. If this ideal could be approximated, he believed, the verbal productions of patients could then be interpreted as products of their private worlds rather than as responses to contaminating cues provided by the environment. Put another way, Freud felt that individuals would more fully, and unconsciously, reveal themselves in ambiguous situations than in those in which they had a very clear idea of what was expected of them.

In applying this point of view to the assessment of personality, many workers felt that paper-and-pencil questionnaires could not even approximate these conditions. The possible ways of responding to the stimuli of paper-and-pencil tests are few in number. Conscious and unconscious reactions are both probably evoked by paper-and-pencil test items (Meehl, 1945). The statement, "I am a tense person," is subject to a variety of meanings depending upon the standards and orientations of people. But the only basis for assessors drawing inferences concerning these meanings is the subject's checking, rating, and sorting of the alternatives available to him. It has seemed to some researchers that more appropriate data for drawing inferences about the individual's perception of himself and the world about him might be obtained in situations that allowed more latitude in idiosyncratic expression.

Lindzey (1959) has described five classes of projective methods that seem to provide this sort of latitude: (1) associative techniques in which the subject is asked to react to words, inkblots, or other stimuli with the first thoughts that come to mind; (2) construction techniques in which the subject is asked to create something—for example, a story or picture; (3) completion techniques in which the subject is asked to complete an incomplete product, such as an incomplete sentence; (4) choice or ordering techniques in which the subject is asked to choose from or make order among stimuli, for example a set of pictures or inkblots; (5) expressive techniques in which the subject is asked to express himself freely in some manner, as in finger-painting.

These types of projective techniques are not mutually exclusive. Most actual projective techniques represent combinations of them. Lindzey's classification schema is useful, however, in generally characterizing projective devices. Another helpful schema is one provided by Campbell (1959) that is more general than Lindzey's in that it may be applied to the entire gamut of personality tests. Campbell has hypothesized three dimensions in terms of which personality tests may be described. One is a voluntary versus objective dimension. (Is the subject asked to make the first response that comes to mind or to convey accurate information?) The second is an indirect versus direct dimension. (Does the subject know the purpose of the test?) The third is a free response versus structured dimension. (Must the subject's response be one selected from a group of alternatives provided or can he respond in a free and fanciful manner?) On the basis of Campbell's schema, most projective tests would be described as voluntary, indirect, and free response.

The aim of projective techniques is to provide individuals with stimulus situations that are relatively high in ambiguity and low in the availability of cues concerning the appropriateness of possible responses to them. Lindzey (1961, p. 45) has described projective techniques in this way:

> . . . a projective technique is an instrument that is considered especially sensitive to covert or unconscious aspects of behavior, it permits or encourages a wide variety of subject responses, is highly multidimensional, and it evokes unusually rich or profuse response data with a minimum of subject awareness concerning the purpose of the test. Further, it is very often true that the stimulus material presented by the projective test is ambiguous, interpreters of the test depend upon holistic analysis, the test evokes fantasy responses, and there are no correct or incorrect responses to the test.

It is important to emphasize that some of the characteristics of projective techniques are not either-or alternatives to those of paper-and-pencil tests. Differences between these two classes of assessment vehicles are often only differences of degree. Thus, for example, although inkblots are not as unambiguous stimuli as self-descriptive statements, the latter will almost invariably not be interpreted identically by different individuals (Harris and Baxter, 1965).

An important similarity between projective tests and those previously considered is their use of standardized stimuli. If clinical workers and researchers are to be able to compare findings it is essential that the same test materials be used. One set of reproducible stimuli that has been widely used is the Rorschach Inkblots. These inkblots, devised by a Swiss psychiatrist, Hermann Rorschach, will provide our first example of a projective technique.

THE RORSCHACH INKBLOTS

The stimuli constituting the test that Rorschach described in a 1921 monograph, *Psychodiagnostik* (1942), seemed to some quite ridiculous as instruments of a scientist. No more than inkblots, they were not much different from those that children might make in the course of play. Rorschach's interest in inkblots represented an extension of his use of free association in work as a psychotherapist. He viewed responses to ambiguous inkblots as a diagnostic tool in studying unconscious processes, just as Freud used free association in work as a therapeutic device. After experimenting with thousands of inkblots,

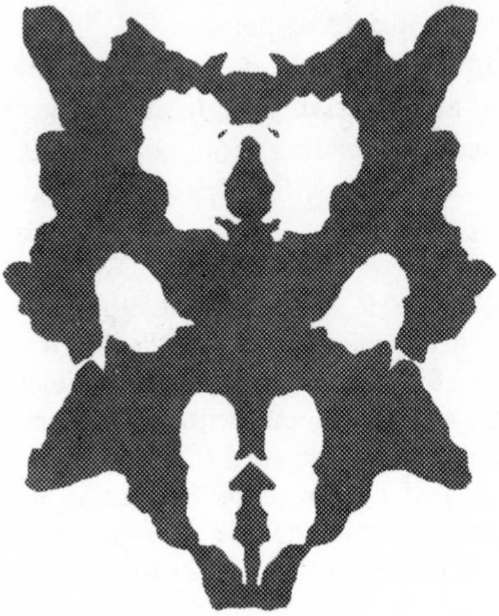

Figure 12-1 An inkblot similar to those used in the Rorschach test.

he settled upon ten for intensive study. Unfortunately, Rorschach died at an early age, and his own investigations were not completed. However, the potentialities of his idea of using inkblots as a projective device to explore fantasy were recognized during the 1920s and 1930s, and since then much research has been carried out with them.

Figure 12-1 shows an inkblot of the type used in the Rorschach test. How are such inkblots administered to subjects? The inkblot test as Rorschach developed it required individual administration. The test today is occasionally group administered for research purposes. For clinical purposes, however, it is still individually administered. The subject is asked simply to look at the inkblots, one at a time, and tell the examiner what he sees. Prior to administration of the inkblots he is told that there are no right and wrong answers. The purpose of the test, he is told, is to find out the sorts of things he sees in the inkblots. The subject is usually not limited to a designated number of responses to each stimulus. What he sees and how he reports what he perceives are left to him. During testing, the examiner avoids, as much as possible, intruding on the subject's preoccupation with the inkblots.

After the subject has given his responses to the ten inkblots, a second phase ensues in which the examiner becomes more active. This phase, known as the inquiry—as apart from the preceding performance or free-association phase—enables the examiner to clarify his understanding of the way that the subject has perceived the inkblots. During the inquiry the examiner asks questions such as: What made it seem like a ______________? What gave you that impression? How did you see it? The practical goal of the inquiry is to enable the examiner to score and interpret the protocol obtained. The test examiner makes every effort to approximate a verbatim transcript of the subject's responses. In addition, he makes notes concerning unusual aspects of the subject's behavior during testing—gestures, mannerisms, attitudes.

The Rorschach as a Perceptual Test

In what ways might we conceptualize this sort of testing situation in which individuals are shown ambiguous stimuli and given free reign in responding to them? Any answer to this question requires consideration of the sense in which the Rorschach inkblots constitute a psychological test. Certainly the Rorschach's structure differs markedly from any of the tests already mentioned. For example, whereas in the MMPI situation the subject makes 550 responses, the number of responses made to inkblots will vary widely. Nevertheless, one may regard Rorschach responses as capable of being categorized and scored, and the categories and scores derived from them as usable for predictive purposes.

Rorschach's work with inkblots was carried out within a theoretical framework that emphasized the relationship between perception and personality. This framework led him to be more interested in particular types of percepts than in their content. That a subject made seven responses involving animals in movement was, for Rorschach, a more important datum than the fact that the animals were fat pigs, peaceful sheep, or angry cats. He was more interested in discovering *how* a person experiences than in *what* he experiences (Rickers-Ovsiankina, 1960).

An example of the type of hypothesis with which Rorschach was preoccupied is that of the relationship between human movement and color responses. A human movement response is one in which the subject describes the activity of a human being ("This looks like a man climbing up a hill"). A color response is one in which color plays a significant role in the percept ("This looks like an especially deep blue sky"). Rorschach believed that the ratio of the number of human movement responses in a subject's test record to the number of color responses was indicative of the relative weightings of introversive and extraversive tendencies in the individual's personality.

Human movement responses were assumed to be correlated with inner-directedness and self-motivated fantasy. Color responses were assumed to indicate the individual's degree of responsiveness to external stimuli.

For many years this sort of hypothesized relationship between perception and personality was not subjected to rigorous empirical tests. Typically the various relationships among perceptual aspects of inkblot perceptions and personality were interpreted intuitively by clinical workers. Over the years, four categories of response were developed: (1) Location. How much of a blot's area does a subject use in a particular response? Which areas of the blot does he refer to? (2) Determinant. Which attributes or properties of the blot evoked the subject's response—the form of the blot and its color, shading, and kinesthetic features? (3) Content. What is the subject matter of a particular response—an animal, a landscape, a person? (4) Popularity-originality. Is a given response a usual or unusual one?

Each of these categories of inkblot responses have been related to particular personality trends. Prior to the Second World War, rigorous tests of the validity of these scoring categories were few in number. However, after the war a tremendous output of research appeared in the psychological literature on projective tests (S. B. Sarason, 1954). These studies created strong doubt about the usefulness of most of the categories employed. It seemed that the utility of few Rorschach scoring categories could be unambiguously demonstrated. After thousands of pieces of research one would have difficulty in stating with a high degree of confidence the empirical validity of the Rorschach test as commonly used (Zubin, Eron, and Schumer, 1965).

What was the effect of this negative evidence? A conclusion drawn by a number of psychologists was that the Rorschach was without value, and that its use should be discontinued. Nevertheless, the Rorschach continues to be among the most widely used personality instruments. Explaining this state of affairs is by no means simple. Clinical psychologists, among the prime users of psychological tests are not unmindful of the discouraging results in the literature, but they continue to put the Rorschach test near the top of their list of assessment techniques. They do so on the basis of its usefulness to them in personality evaluation. It would appear that, although empirical investigation of Rorschach scoring categories has led to few stable and consistent findings, the test was felt to be valuable in the hands of trained users. Might it be the case that the Rorschach has proved practically useful to clinical workers because of characteristics other than its perceptual scores?

The Rorschach as an Interview

Recent work on the Rorschach suggests that its clinical usefulness may be due more to the personal aspects of the inkblot situation than to the scoring categories (Lindzey, 1961; S. B. Sarason, 1954; Schafer, 1954). This possibility indicates an alternative to the traditional perceptual test model.

The psychometric model, as we have seen, treats the Rorschach as students of personality assessment approach tests like the MMPI. The MMPI may be scored according to available keys, and interpretations may be made on the basis of the relationships among scores on various scales. A similar treatment of the Rorschach permits one to consider its various scoring categories as "scales," and interpretations may be attempted on the basis of the relationships among them.

An alternative to this model does not emphasize the Rorschach as a traditional psychometric instrument. Rather, it considers the Rorschach testing situation as a social interaction between two people, a tester and a testee. This approach concerns itself more with the qualitative aspects of this interaction than with the Rorschach as a perceptual predictor of behavior.

A review of recent writing on projective techniques suggests that the qualitative study of a person's behavior on the Rorschach is becoming more and more intriguing to psychologists (Masling, 1960; S. B. Sarason, 1954; Schafer, 1954). The essence of this approach is that the Rorschach may be viewed as a variant of the interview, a social situation in which an examiner and subject are engaged in a personal exchange.

Examples of behavior emphasized from this point of view are such characteristics as the fluency of the subject's speech, the amounts of emotional expression with which the subject communicates his responses, his gestures and idiosyncracies, and the nature of the social interaction between the tester and testee.

Questions which arise from this more social approach include these:

1. In what way does the subject accept and respond to the inkblot task presented to him?
2. In what ways does the subject react to the examiner?
3. What is the emotional tone of the subject's behavior?
4. Are there discernible themes that run through subject's responses?
5. How comfortable does the subject seem to be in handling the Rorschach cards and in coping with the testing situation?
6. Does the subject seek to obtain the assistance of the examiner in "solving" the test presented to him?

If the Rorschach is regarded as a situation in which a subject is asked by a tester to respond to ten standard inkblot stimuli, what role might it be expected to play in personality assessment? One possibility immediately comes to mind. The Rorschach situation resembles the interview situation in many respects. Both involve interactions between two persons. The interviewer presents to the interviewee stimuli in the form of questions; the Rorschach tester presents inkblots. In discussing the interview as a self-report technique it was shown how content analysis of verbal behavior would provide quantitative data that could be used in empirical research. Might content analysis procedures be applied to the verbal behavior of Rorschach subjects?

An affirmative answer certainly seems to be reasonable. In fact, during the past several years, a number of investigators have constructed rating scales and other devices to analyze the content of responses to inkblots (Bower, Testin, and Roberts, 1960; Elizur, 1949; Holt, 1956; Holt and Havel, 1960; Lesser, 1961). Elizur (1949) devised reliable scales to measure the individual's anxiety and hostility levels on the basis of Rorschach responses. This sort of content analysis seems to possess considerable potential since it enables an examiner to quantify aspects of the subject's responses that traditional scoring procedures have neglected. One traditional Rorschach scoring category, for instance, involves a count of the number of responses referring to animals. Consider a person's response of "a roaring, ferocious lion" to an inkblot stimulus. This clearly refers to an animal, but its emotional connotations are quite different from another animal response, "a tiny mouse." Content rating scales have been used in an attempt to measure some of these connotations. For example, one of several rating scales developed by Zubin, Eron, and Schumer (1965, pp. 350–351) relates to a subject's tendencies to perceive in inkblots human figures that reflect attitudes of debasement. The scale may be used to score quantitatively every human response given to inkblots:

Human Debasement Scale

X. Scale does not apply
0. Human beings who are pleasing in appearance or engaged in ennobling situations: a very beautiful or happy woman, a man praying, etc.
1. Ordinary human beings or humans engaged in ordinary activities.
2. Human beings who are somewhat ugly in appearance or engaged in somewhat unflattering activities: an old woman with shrunken jaws, a man arguing or fighting, primitive tribal fights, etc.
3. Human beings who are markedly ugly or engaged in highly unflattering situations: misshapen, disintegrating, defecating, etc.

4. Humans who are thoroughly repulsive or engaged in disgusting or morally evil situations: a man pushing a woman off a cliff, a human being having sexual relations with an animal, etc.

The rationale for content rating scales has been stated clearly by Zubin, Eron, and Sultan 1956, pp. 779–782):

If you forget about perceptual scoring and limit yourself to the evaluation of the content of the protocols, the way you would evaluate any other interview—through a content analysis—the Rorschach can be clinically useful. It is simply a standard interview behind the veil of inkblots. The perceptual factors have nothing to do with it. Scales for evaluating content as well as factor analyses of these scales seem to work because it is the content that matters. . . . Since the perceptual scales are lacking in reliability and validity, while the content scales satisfy these two requirements, it is concluded that the *content* of the protocols and not the perceptual factors in the individual is the basis for whatever success the Rorschach has achieved. Thus, the Rorschach takes its rightful place as a systematic controlled interview, whose value lies in the content analysis that can be achieved of its protocols, and not as a test. Rorschach's hypotheses about the relation between perception and personality will have to wait until we develop more knowledge about perception itself. Until then, viewing the Rorschach technique as a systematic, controlled interview and basing its evaluation on content analyses of the protocols is the method to be recommended, because it is the only one that can now yield reliable and valid results.

The personal and content analysis approach to behavior emitted in Rorschach situations seems promising and deserves empirical study. It would seem highly desirable to develop quantitative indices of (1) the subject's responses to the Rorschach situation and (2) the emotional connotations of his responses to inkblots.

The Role of the Interviewer and the Tester

Whether one regards the Rorschach as a perceptual test or as an interview that employs standardized stimuli, it has one characteristic that most paper-and-pencil tests do not possess. This is a relatively high degree of personal contact between the examiner and the subject. Because of the straightforward way in which an instrument like the MMPI may be administered, the psychologist need not personally give it to subjects. This means that his interpretations of it can be carried out "blind," that is, without ever seeing the subject. The Rorschach, however, does require considerable social interaction.

There are advantages and disadvantages both to blind personality assessment and to assessment based on actual behavioral observations. Blind assessment serves to reduce any biases associated with actual observations of people. On the other hand, actual contact permits the use of behavioral observations that possibly may be valuable in assessment.

The two aspects of the psychologist's role in projective testing are: (1) the stimulus that he provides for the subject, and (2) the responses he makes in interpreting observational data. Actually, the potentiality for the tester as a stimulus to influence the subject's behavior exists directly or indirectly in virtually every type of assessment context. Even in the case of an MMPI administered by a secretary or technician, the manner of introducing the test by a particular tester, whoever he may be, can conceivably influence the subject's test responses. A major contribution of many Rorschach researchers has been the extent to which they have made clear the necessity of attending to the role of personal processes involving assessors and assessees in personality assessment. Studies have shown that the personal characteristics of testers can have significant effects on the subject's test behavior (Masling, 1960; S. B. Sarason, 1954; Schachtel, 1945).

Recent research in the field of psychotherapy has also indicated that the personality of the therapist may be closely tied to his effectiveness in helping patients (Betz, 1962; Rubinstein and Parloff, 1959; Strupp and Luborsky, 1962). What patients talk about in psychotherapy is determined not only by their problems but also by the ease with which they can express them. The interviewer plays an important part in creating a situation in which this expression can occur. Bandura, Lipsher, and Miller, (1960), for example, have empirically demonstrated that therapists tend to discourage patients from discussing problems that are related to their (therapists') personal problems.

Turning from the tester as a stimulus to the tester as an interpreter of data, we again see the importance of studying the abilities and personality of the psychologist. Just as there are individual differences among persons in terms of mathematical and artistic abilities, we can think of individual differences among psychologists in terms of clinical abilities, such as diagnosis and treatment. Some trained and some untrained individuals appear to have remarkable facility in diagnosing a person's problems and in helping him to overcome emotional impediments. Locating such individuals and studying them intensively would appear to be worthwhile. Were it possible to isolate the relevant limits of clinical inferences and clinical effectiveness, individuals who are not strong in these respects might be trained to improve their skills in this area.

An example of the clinician as a variable in personality assessment may be found in a study by Schachtel (1951). Schachtel examined a large number of Rorschach protocols obtained from delinquents and nondelinquents. In what was clearly a *tour de force,* he performed blind analyses of the test records, not knowing to which group the subjects belonged, and was able to predict far beyond chance which individuals belonged to which group.

Because the qualitative approach to the Rorschach that emphasizes nuances of speech and content analysis is so recent a development, it is not possible at present to draw generalizations about the characteristics of individuals who might be particularly successful in applying it. Neither the tester as a stimulus nor the psychologist as an interpreter of personality data has been adequately conceptualized. However, it can be said that one of the major contributions of the Rorschach test to the study of behavior has been the thinking it has stimulated concerning ways in which persons may be affected by testing situations and the problems associated with the analysis and interpretation of personality characteristics.

Current Problems in the Use of Rorschach Inkblots

At one time, psychologists regarded the Rorschach primarily as a clinical test to be used in diagnosing psychopathology and in describing personality structure. The data it was thought to provide included the frequent occurrence of various types of perceptual responses, the style and tone with which these responses were communicated, and the general behavior of the testee, such as side comments to the tester or gestures. The psychologist's task was to integrate and interpret these data. Considerable emphasis was placed on the intuitive abilities of the interpreter in ferreting out of the data before him significant, unconscious determinants of behavior. We have, however, considered the Rorschach in terms of the predictive value of its perceptual scores, of its characteristics as an interview method, and of its characteristics as a social interaction. Current research on the Rorschach emphasizes these facets.

As we have indicated, much of the research on the psychometric properties of the Rorschach has been discouraging. To some extent, this state of affairs is due to the Rorschach's inadequacies as a perceptual test (Cronbach, 1949). The fact that subjects are given wide latitude in their behavior makes it difficult to compare various idiosyncratic responses. The wide variance in the frequencies with which responses to the ten inkblots occur poses knotty statistical problems. It seems probable that in the future, researchers interested in hypotheses about the relationship between perception and personality will move in two possible directions. One might be toward strengthening the Rorschach as a test and improving the procedures used to study test results. The other might be toward the identification of criteria whereby perceptual scores can be validated.

A recent trend discernible in the Rorschach research literature is one toward a greater willingness on the part of investigators to experiment with novel methods of analyzing responses to inkblots. For example, Fischer (1964) and Fischer and Cleveland (1958) have defined two new scoring categories which they call *Barrier* and *Penetration.* These scoring categories, they believe, are related to the individual's body image. Barrier responses are those in which references are made by the subject to barriers, containers, and the boundarylike properties of objects. In penetration responses, references are made to penetrations of objects, disruptions in surfaces, and the permeable qualities of surfaces. In their research Fischer and Cleveland have ignored traditional Rorschach scoring categories and have restricted themselves to content analysis in terms of barrier and penetration scores. With these scores it has been possible to achieve adequate agreement among scorers and to distinguish between pathological and nonpathological groups. For example, with them Fischer and Cleveland and others have been able to discriminate between asymptomatic persons, persons with interior bodily symptoms (for example, peptic ulcers), and persons with exterior bodily symptoms (such as rheumatoid arthritis) (Fischer and Cleveland, 1958; Williams and Krasnoff, 1964). In one interesting study of social behavior it was found that high scorers on the barrier scale were more assertive and less self-depreciatory than low scorers (Ramer, 1963).

Another discernible trend is toward intensive examination of the conditions under which scoring categories do and do not predict the behavior of persons. Perceptual and content-scoring categories may relate to behavior under certain conditions but not others. One basis for some of the disparities in the Rorschach research literature may be that testing and experimental conditions have not been comparable in seemingly comparable experiments.

A lively field of investigation that seems to be developing is the study, through content analysis and social interaction variables, of persons' reactions to the Rorschach interview situation. The emphasis here is less on establishing the predictive validity of traditional Rorschach scores than on experimentally isolating personal and social variables that influence response to ambiguous situations. Among the independent variables studied from this point of view are: characteristics of subjects, characteristics of examiners, the instructions given to subjects, and social aspects of the testing situation. Dependent variables are often defined in terms of specially constructed content analysis scales, physiological, gestural, and stylistic patterns, and post-test reactions of subjects to the inkblot situation. This approach to the Rorschach has led to its increasing use in experimental studies of personality.

Another facet of Rorschach research that we have mentioned concerns the role of Rorschach practitioners as integrators and analyzers of data. Since some interpreters are more adept and sensitive than others, researchers have begun to ask the question: how does the psychologist respond to a test record from a problem-solving standpoint? There may well be as much value in studying projective techniques as a problem-solving task for clinicians as in studying the problem-solving reactions of subjects to ambiguous stimuli. This state of affairs would seem to be salutary both from the point of view of the psychology of personality and the point of view of diagnosing behavior disorders.

Finally, a word should be said concerning the role of the Rorschach inkblots in cross-cultural investigations. Of all available measures of personality, the Rorschach has been the one most widely used in anthropological studies. Lindzey (1961) has provided an excellent survey of the evidence concerning projective tests gleaned from the anthropological literature. He has reported these generalizations among those that have received some empirical support:

1. There is great variability in personality, as inferred from the Rorschach, among apparently homogeneous, nonliterate societies.
2. Persons who have been reared in societies that differ with regard to socialization practices and cultural backgrounds respond differently to projective stimuli.
3. Inferences about personality drawn from projective techniques seem to be consistent with inferences drawn from the data obtained in anthropological field work.
4. Projective techniques have proved useful in obtaining personality and life-history information from people with different cultural backgrounds.

Lindzey in presenting his summary noted, however, that there were inconsistencies in findings and inadequacies of methodology in many of these cross-cultural studies. Some of the favorable reports of the use of projective techniques in anthropological work have been based to a considerable degree on researchers' impressions of their data rather than on the data themselves. Lindzey's (1961, p. 319) review of the literature has led him to conclude that:

. . . (a) the process of assessing the cross-cultural validity of projective techniques is an enormously complex and demanding task; (b) we do not at present have adequate evidence upon which to base any confident generalizations; (c) what evidence we do have tends to support the utility of these tests in cross-cultural research, although this may be largely, or partially, a reflection of powerful biasing factors that have operated in most evaluations.

Concluding Comments Concerning the Rorschach Inkblots

As a test the Rorschach has a number of weaknesses. Its administration is time-consuming, its scoring is complex, and its relationship to a person's behavior is difficult to assess statistically. Despite these shortcomings and despite disparities in research findings concerning the meaning of its scores, its use in the clinic and in research persists. This persistence is due to the judgment that it does contribute significantly to the description of general personality functioning and the recognition that validating a multidimensional measure of personality cannot be expected to be easily accomplished.

Lindzey's (1961, p. 316) over-all conclusions concerning the validity of projective techniques as applied to cross-cultural research are sufficiently general to apply to the specific case of the Rorschach:

. . . the type of validity most relevant to projective techniques is construct validity, with all the consequent vagueness, complexity, and scarcity of simple coefficients. The link between projective techniques and complex, hypothetical variables (especially covert or latent dimensions) makes clear the difficulty, or impossibility, of identifying adequate criteria and the consequent necessity for resorting to indirect and complex inferential paths in the attempt to estimate validity. This close association between projective tests and construct validity has been noted in the past . . . .

. . . any attempt to assess the validity of a particular projective technique, let alone the entire class of projective techniques, must involve a careful appraisal of a host of different kinds of evidence, much of it indirect and difficult to translate and summarize. Consequently, it is not surprising that there is little agreement concerning the over-all validity of projective techniques even within our own society and in restricted domains of application. From this statement it is an easy step to the conclusion that the evidence for or against the cross-cultural validity of these tests is far from what we would ideally wish and by no means sufficient to support conclusive generalizations.

The idea of using ambiguous stimulus materials to analyze the individual's reactions appears to be a challenging one that deserves careful study (Kenny, 1964). Two aspects of this study must be the definition of variables that can be construct validated and the formulation of problems susceptible to objective inquiry. The following problems seem especially worthy of intensive study: (1) the perfection of the inkblot method from a psychometric point of view and the clarification of the stimulus properties of inkblots; (2) the development of useful and relatively convenient quantitative and qualitative measures of responses to inkblots; (3) increased investigation of the personal aspects of the testing situation; (4) further study of the inferential processes used by researchers and clinicians in describing personality and predicting behavior on the basis of available data.

As an addendum to this discussion of the Rorschach, it should be noted that the technique has been used here in much the same way as the MMPI was studied in detail because of its wide usage and because it could serve as a prototype of a class of tests. Similarly, because of its wide usage, we have spent more time on the Rorschach than we shall on the projective techniques to be considered next. It illustrates approaches, methods, and problems common to most projective techniques.

THE HOLTZMAN INKBLOT TECHNIQUE

Although inkblots other than the Rorschach cards have been used by investigators in the area of projective techniques, none of them has represented a sufficiently significant improvement over the Rorschach to obtain wide usage. It seems possible, however, that a recent inkblot technique developed by Holtzman, Thorpe, Swartz, and Herron (1961) will become widely used in research. This test presents to each subject a relatively large number of stimuli, 45 inkblots. In addition, there is a comparable set of inkblots that can be used where repeated testing is desired. Although its standardization leaves much to be desired, it is certainly far superior to any comparable information available for other projective tests.

The Holtzman technique seems clearly to be a psychometric improvement over the Rorschach. It was developed with more sophisticated test construction procedures and seems to be a more reliable instrument. A price, however, had to be paid for these advantages. The price is a relatively greater degree of structure in administering projective stimuli. Whereas the subject has wide latitude in responding to Rorschach stimuli, in the Holtzman test he is permitted to make only one response to each of the 45 inkblots. Thus, the patterning of associations to individual inkblots cannot be observed. Some users of projective tests will, no doubt, feel that this restriction is an important one since, on the Rorschach, responses of diagnostic significance may not be given until several responses have been made to an inkblot.

Another difference between the Rorschach and the Holtzman is that in the Holtzman an inquiry is conducted immediately following each response rather than after all of the subject's responses have been made. Advantages possessed by the Holtzman over the Rorschach Test are that a much wider assortment of stimuli is employed, and that a more reliable and comprehensive scoring system has been devised. Related to this advantage is the fact that the Holtzman scoring system includes several content-analysis categories relating to variables such as anxiety, hostility, and barrier.

The Holtzman treatment of inkblot responses seems to be promising. Because it uses a wider range of stimuli and poses fewer statistical problems than the Rorschach, it should prove to be particularly appealing as a measure of individual differences.

13

Projective Techniques: Other Types of Ambiguous Stimuli

If we direct attention to the broad situations that afford relative freedom in responding, we can see that the number of projective possibilities is indeed large. Although personality researchers have not exhausted situations which vary in degree of structure and ambiguity, the number of projective techniques available to them is certainly impressive. In this chapter we shall review some of these methods.

THEMATIC APPERCEPTION TEST

The Thematic Apperception Test (TAT) consists of 30 pictures and one blank card. The stimuli were obtained from a variety of sources. Among them were paintings, drawings, and illustrations from magazines. Although the stimuli possess more ambiguity than most photographs they have much more structure to them than inkblots. Figure 13-1 shows one of the TAT stimuli.

Most of the TAT cards depict scenes with personal connotations. The task for the subject is to tell a story about each card. In the story he is to tell what is going on in the scene depicted on the card, what the characters are thinking and feeling, and what outcome eventuates from the scene. Many users of the TAT limit the subject's stories to a duration of five minutes; however, there is no established convention concerning a time limit.

The TAT resembles the Rorschach in that relatively ambiguous

Figure 13-1 Card 12-F of the Thematic Apperception Test (reproduced from Murray, 1943).

stimuli are presented to individuals who are asked to engage in fantasy in response to the stimuli. Henry (1956, pp. 3–4) has provided the following rationale for TAT-type tasks:

The analysis of fantasy is a problem in the interpretation of symbolic statements. When in story form, these statements are organized by the intellect but take their meaning from the emotions. The interpretive significance of themas perceived and stories told to pictures is thus to be derived from the understanding of the ways in which emotional preoccupations are symbolized in words and plots, from the ways in which emotions bow to propriety in overt expression, and from the ways in which each individual lessens his own burden by expressing his feelings, though disguising them for himself and for others.

The technique of thematic apperception takes much of its particular relevance to the study of personality from this dual aspect of fantasy expression. On the one hand, fantasy in storytelling derives from the less conscious and less structured aspects of the individual's personality. To these areas of personality the rules of logic and propriety do not apply. On the other hand, the task set for the storyteller is one that requires him to organize his fantasy into a recognizable story form and to verbalize this story for the inspection of others. To this latter requirement the rules of logic and propriety do apply, at least those particular rules of logic and propriety that the subject has found applicable to his own life. Thus interpretation of thematic apperception must take place within these overlapping frameworks: the more nearly private and less conscious motives and generalizations derived from past life experiences, and the public, socially determined, more nearly rational frameworks of convention.

The TAT was developed by Henry Murray and the staff of the Harvard Psychological Clinic in the hope that it would prove of value in comprehensively assessing overt and covert aspects of personality (Morgan and Murray, 1935; Murray, 1938, 1943). There are no right and wrong answers to the TAT cards. Murray conceived of TAT fantasies in terms of what he called needs and press. Needs referred to internal motivators of behavior. Press referred to environmental determinants of behavior. Murray suggested that TAT stories be rated in terms of needs, such as those for achievement, aggression, abasement, and sex, and of press, such as physical danger and rejection by loved ones. In actual practice, Murray's scoring system has been used very little. While there are several widely used scoring systems for the Rorschach (Beck, Beck, Levitt, and Molish, 1961; Klopfer, Ainsworth, Klopfer, and Holt, 1954), this is not true for the TAT.

The use of the full set of TAT cards with an individual is the exception to the rule rather than standard practice. It thus appears that the TAT is even less of a standardized test than the Rorschach.

Since use of the TAT in applied settings rarely involves an attempt to analyze the subject's responses quantitatively, personality descriptions are largely determined by inferences drawn from the subject's behavior. Because there is no commonly accepted procedure for analyzing verbal behavior on the TAT, it becomes difficult to estimate reliability, either on the basis of interpretations made by various testers, or in terms of test-retest consistency.

Descriptions of personality written on the basis of the TAT usually deal with such topics as:

1. The subject's behavior in the testing situation;
2. Characteristics of the subject's utterances;
3. The kinds of fantasies offered by the subject;
4. The personal relationships depicted in the stories;
5. The conscious and unconscious needs of the individual;
6. The individual's perception of the environment;
7. The emotional tone of the stories;
8. The stories' outcomes;
9. Common themes that permeate the stories;
10. The degree to which the stories reflect control over impulses and contact with reality.

Despite lack of agreement on how to employ the TAT, and the need for convincing validity of the personality interpretations made from its use, the idea of establishing relationships between fantasy and behavior has continued to be appealing. Interest in such relationships has stimulated a sizeable body of research with the TAT. Many of the studies have been experimental in nature and not concerned directly with clinical problems.

Researchers have employed TAT responses as both dependent and independent variables. When response to the TAT has been used as the independent variable, researchers have compared individuals who have responded differently to the TAT regarding their behavior in specified situations. For example, do people who tell TAT stories with strongly aggressive themes behave more aggressively in social situations than those whose stories are not especially aggressive in content?

An example of the use of the TAT as a predictor is found in a study in which clinical psychologists analyzed the TAT stories of a group of adolescents (Henry and Farley, 1959). In addition to the TAT stories, a large amount of information was available about the subjects, such as data gathered in interviews and from observations. It was found that the clinical psychologists were able, on the basis of the TAT alone, to predict a statistically significant amount of this information. In Part 3 (especially Chapter 15) we shall come across a number of examples of the TAT's use in experiments. In these experiments content analyses of TAT stories have yielded scores on the basis of which particular groups of subjects have been selected. The purpose of this type of experiment is to compare, under experimental conditions, the behavior of persons selected in particular ways.

When TAT responses are used as a dependent variable, the interest usually is in the influence of historical, environmental, and experimentally manipulated variables on fantasy. For example, one might wish to know how experimentally aroused motivation influences fantasy as expressed in TAT stories, or how socioeconomic factors are related to themes of TAT stories.

An illustration of the TAT's use as a dependent variable is found in research reported by Ervin (1964). It was stimulated by the observation that spoken language had to be understood in terms of the social setting in which it was acquired. She selected for study 64 adult, middle-class French persons who had all lived in the United States for more than four years (mean = 12 years). Forty were married to Americans, all had learned English primarily from Americans, and all spoke English fluently.

How might the TAT play a role in an exploration of the social context of language? Ervin (1964, p. 504) conjectured that the English and French TAT's of these people would show differences in line with apparent differences in the French and American cultures. In order to evaluate her conjectures, she content analyzed their TAT's for a number of relevant variables. Her major findings included these: (1) themes of achievement and industriousness were more common in stories told in English, and (2) themes of quarreling among and verbal aggression against peers were more common in stories told in French. The following stories by a 27-year-old Frenchwoman married to an American illustrate these results. (The stimulus was Card 4 of the TAT.)

[French story] She seems to beg him, to plead with him. I don't know if he wants to leave her for another woman or what, or if it's her who has . . . but she seems to press against him. I think he wants to leave her because he's found another woman he loves more, and that he really wants to go, or maybe it's because she . . . she's deceived him with another man. I don't know whose fault it is but they certainly seem angry. Unless it's in his work, and he wants to go see someone and he wants to get in a fight with someone, and she holds him back and doesn't like him to get angry. I don't know, it could be many things. . . .

[English story] Oh, that one. In the past, well I think it was a married couple, average, and he got out of the Army and got himself a job or something like that or has decided he would go to college. He's decided to get a good education and maybe after he would have a better job and be able to support his wife much better, and everything would come out for the best. He keeps on working and going to college at night some of the time. Now let me see. He finally decided that was too much. He found he was too tired, he was discouraged and something went wrong with his work. The boss told him that, well, his production had decreased or something like that, that he didn't get enough sleep or something like that, that he couldn't carry on studies and working at the same time. He'd have to give something up, and he's very discouraged and his wife tries to cheer him up. Now, let me see. And eventually he'll probably keep on working his way through and finally get his diploma and get a better job and they will be much happier and . . . well, his wife will have helped him along too and as he was discouraged and all and was willing to give up everything, she boosted him up. That's all.

Ervin's work indicated that the TAT was useful in showing that there are significant shifts in social roles and emotional attitudes along with shifts in language.

A significant segment of the recent TAT literature has been concerned with the stimulus properties of its pictures (Friedman, Johnson, and Fode, 1964; Murstein, 1961). One dimension along which stimuli for fantasy may be evaluated is their degree of ambiguity, that is, the gestalt qualities of the pictures. Another dimension is pull value. Pull value alludes to the range of responses that a stimulus is capable of eliciting.

With regard to ambiguity, it appears that as it increases so does the pleasant tone of stories told by subjects. Murstein (1961), on the basis of a review of the literature, has suggested that pictures of medium ambiguity are more evocative than either highly ambiguous or highly unambiguous pictures of personally revealing stories. With regard to pull value, Eron (1950) has found that certain TAT pictures evoke many more stories involving themes of aggression, conflict, and achievement aspiration than do others. Generally, however, most of the TAT cards tend to elicit stories that are sad in emotional tone and suggest dysphoria. Inspection of any sample of TAT cards makes clear the basis for this type of emotional tone. The pictures depict scenes that strongly suggest unhappy personal relationships. It is difficult, indeed, to perceive very many smiles on the faces of characters in the TAT pictures. This restricted range of pleasantness would appear to be an important weakness for many kinds of investigations. It would be most interesting to develop a "happy" TAT with which the present one might be compared.

The concern with the stimulus properties of the TAT has a parallel in the Rorschach literature (Baughman, 1958; Kenny, 1964). Studies of the ambiguity levels and pull values of inkblot stimuli have led to the same conclusion that a review of the TAT literature induces: simply to label a stimulus ambiguous is itself ambiguous. What must be discerned are the ambiguity levels and pull values of projective stimuli that are relative to those of other stimuli.

Turning from the stimulus to the response side of the TAT, we find that much valuable work has been undertaken to delineate the characteristics of stories told by subjects. Researchers who have used the TAT have freely employed it as a vehicle for the study of constructs in which they have been interested, to wit, the Ervin (1964) investigation. Most of the TAT scoring systems that have been developed involve the use of rating scales to define variables relevant to the constructs under study (Crandall, 1951; Rotter, 1954). This use of ratings of selected characteristics of the person's fantasies parallels the content analysis of responses to inkblots and of self-descriptions in interviews.

An example of content analysis applied to the TAT may be seen in research carried out by Eron (1953), who developed rating scales to assess the emotional tone of stories and the types of outcomes given to them. His procedures entailed the rating of each story for emotional tone and outcome. The reliability of his scales appears to be adequate. Table 13-1 shows the scale used to rate the emotional tone of themes of TAT stories. Sumerwell, Campbell, and Sarason (1958) have found that scores on the emotional tone and outcome scales are

TABLE 13-1

General Rating Scale for Emotional Tone

? Subject cannot make up a story

0. Complete failure, submission to fate, death, murder, suicide, illicit sex with violence, revenge, aggressive hostility, severe guilt, complete hopelessness
1. Conflict with attempt at adjustment, rebellion, fear, worry, departure, regret, illness, physical exhaustion, resignation toward death, loneliness
2. Description, lack of affect, balance of positive and negative feelings, routine activities, impersonal reflection
3. Aspiration, desire for success and doubt about outcome, compensation for limited endowment, description with cheerful feeling, reunion with friends, contentment with world, feeling of security
4. Justifiably high aspiration, complete satisfaction and happiness, reunion with loved ones

Adapted from J. Zubin, L. D. Eron, and Florence Schumer (1965), *An experimental approach to projective techniques,* p. 578; John Wiley, New York.

significantly related to the instructions given to subjects prior to administration of the TAT cards. This result, together with others in the TAT literature, reinforces previous comments made on the need to study the context in which the subject's responses occur (S. B. Sarason, 1954; Rotter, 1954). Without doubt, the instructions given subjects exert significant influences over fantasies. Properly constructed rating scales of variables inferred from subjects' fantasies appear to be convenient and economical indicators of these influences (Crandall, 1951; Sumerwell, Campbell, and Sarason, 1958).

Quite likely, the use of the TAT, like that of the Rorschach, is moving from a first stage involving global, intuitive methods to a second stage which emphasizes experimental methods and quantitative research. The first stage served the useful function of orienting students of personality to the relevance of the study of fantasy to their area. The second stage has led to the asking of many more specific types of questions, such as: (1) What is the nature of fantasy? (2) What variables influence fantasy? (3) How does one assess and describe an individual's fantasy? Such questions have served to stimulate research relating to: (1) the construction of stimulus materials to elicit fantasy, (2) the relationship of fantasy to overt behavior, and (3) the historical and developmental antecedents of various types of fantasy. The TAT research literature has been marked by many inconsistent findings and disagreements in interpreting findings (Zubin, Eron, and Schumer, 1965). But perhaps the major contribution of the TAT is not its ability to make certain specific predictions. Rather it may be its value to students of behavior as a stimulus to the understanding of fantasy.

OTHER PROJECTIVE METHODS

Besides inkblots and pictures there is a host of other projective techniques. We shall not attempt to consider all of them. Rather we shall review three of the more prominent ones, the sentence-completion method, the word-association test, and drawing techniques.

Sentence-Completion Method

The task presented to the subject in taking a sentence-completion test is the same as the task presented to students in fill-in achievement tests. A fill-in item requires the subject to insert or fill in a word or clause missing in a sentence. In the sentence-completion test, individuals are presented with a series of beginnings of sentences that they are asked to complete. Whereas the Rorschach and TAT usually entail the examiner's recording of the subject's responses, the subject is frequently asked to write his own sentence completions. There are many sets of incomplete sentences in use by psychologists (Rohde, 1957). All sentence completions are intended as bases for drawing inferences about a person's fantasies, conflicts, and thoughts. Usually the subject has wide latitude in completing sentences.

When the test is used clinically, the individual's sentence completions are usually not analyzed quantitatively according to a scoring system. Rather they are used as data from which interpretative hypotheses are made. Thus, the role of the inferential process is particularly important in the use of sentence-completion methods. Among the aspects of the individual's responses that are attended to by interpreters of sentence-completion data are:

1. Attitudes expressed toward individuals important in the life of the subject, such as mother, father, boss, wife;
2. Attitudes expressed with regard to the subject's past life;
3. Sources of conflict;
4. Linguistic and stylistic aspects of the subject's completions;
5. Personal problems and the attitudes toward them;
6. Possible unconscious tensions and conflicts;
7. Ways in which affect is expressed;
8. Degree of contact with reality.

Advantages of the sentence-completion method are its simplicity and ease of administration. Clinicians frequently find it easier to interpret than such projective tests as the Rorschach and TAT. This is, no doubt, due to the fact that the sheer quantity of verbal responses on sentence-completion tests is less than on most other projective tests and also the fact that the sentence stem serves to narrow the range of possible responses.

Research on sentence-completion responses has been directed to a number of problems. One of these is the derivation of quantitative indices of responses to incomplete sentences. A number of researchers have been able to devise reliable rating scales for use with sentence-completion data. Rotter (1954; Rotter, Rafferty, and Schachtitz, 1949) and Rohde (1957) are among those who have conducted the most careful work on the development of such indices. Most frequently, the scoring systems involve rating the intensity of the subject's affect, the conflicts implied in his responses, and his general levels of adjustment. Although sentence-completion tests are usually not scored in a formal sense by clinicians, scoring them by rating scales is of great value in psychological research.

Some of the research areas in which sentence-completion methods have been used are (Rohde, 1957):

1. The study of social attitudes, family relationships, and life history. In this type of investigation ratings by judges of the subject's completions have been correlated with available life-history information.
2. The study of sex differences in, and personality correlates of responses to incompleted sentences. There is evidence to indicate that both of these factors relate to sentence completions of the subject.
3. The study of academic achievement and attitudes toward school. Studies in this area have frequently used sentence-completion tests whose items were particularly directed to the academic area.
4. The study of the effects of variations in sentence-completion stimuli on the subject's responses. Among the stimulus variables studied have been the phrasing of sentence items (such as first person vs. third person stimuli) and the degree of ambiguity of the items.

As more becomes known about the stimulus properties of incomplete sentences, the experimental conditions which affect responses to them, and the predictive value of judges' ratings of subjects' responses, it seems likely that not only will the quantitative analysis of sentence completions be used in personality research but in applied settings as well.

Word-Association Test

The word-association test might be regarded as a precursor to the sentence-completion method (Rotter, 1951). A word-association test is administered by presenting stimulus words to which subjects respond with the first word that comes to mind. Dependent variables often measured are, in addition to response words, the subject's reaction times and physiological responses. Shortly after the turn of the century, Jung selected a series of 100 stimulus words, and studied the subject's responses to them. He felt that long reaction times indicated that areas of conflict had been aroused by the stimulus words. In interpreting word associations, attention is usually paid to their content, their unusualness, and their appropriateness in relation to the stimulus. Changes in the subject's affective and gestural behavior as a function of stimulus words are also observed. As Jung used the word-association test, it could be viewed as an early attempt to study experimentally Freud's principle of psychic determinism.

Experimental studies of word associations have continued to the present day. Current research includes efforts to develop quantitative ways of analyzing these associations, to establish norms for associational stimuli, and to relate known personal characteristics and experimental conditions to the associations given by people.

Drawing Techniques

The projective techniques mentioned so far, though they differ with regard to their stimulus properties (inkblots, pictures, sentence stems, words), all require that subjects respond verbally. Several other projective techniques have called upon subjects to respond either by drawing pictures or by reproducing stimuli presented to them. A number of attempts have been made to use human figure drawings as bases for inferences about personal characteristics. Although a number of figure-drawing techniques involve quantitative scoring of the person's drawings, in applied settings figure drawings have tended to be used as bases for the intuitive judgments of interpreters. Machover (1949, p. 5) has expressed some of the hypotheses that have been offered concerning the relevance of human figure drawings to personality assessment:

> The body, or the self, is the most intimate point of reference in any activity. We have, in the course of growth, come to associate various sensations, perceptions, and emotions with certain body organs. This investment in body organs, or the perception of the body image as it has developed out of personal experience, must somehow guide the individual who is drawing in the specific structure and content which constitutes his offering of a "person." Consequently, the drawing of a person, in involving a projection of the body image, provides a natural vehicle for the expression of one's body needs and conflicts. Successful drawing interpretation has proceeded on the hypothesis that the figure drawn is related to the individual who is drawing with the same intimacy characterizing that individual's gait, his handwriting, or any other of his expressive movements.

Whereas obtaining figure drawings from people may require a relatively simple procedure, the validation of hypotheses such as those suggested by Machover represents a major challenge to researchers. An important stumbling block to obtaining meaningful norms for characteristics of drawings is the wide variability in drawing skills among people. This artistic ability factor may easily contaminate whatever information about personality is expressed in drawings.

Drawing techniques vary with regard to the type of stimulus presented to the subject and the response he is asked to make. Some drawing tasks simply ask the subject to draw a person. Others direct the subject to draw particular people or objects, such as yourself, your mother, a woman, a tree, a house. Still other tasks present stimuli to subjects, such as designs or pictures, and require subjects to reproduce them, sometimes from memory. The Bender-Gestalt Test (1938) is perhaps the most widely used of this more exacting type of projective technique.

There are a number of general problems confronting users of drawing techniques. The following questions seem especially important: How can individual differences in drawing be reliably scored or rated? How can ability and personality factors be separated and evaluated? What inferential processes are involved in global evaluations of drawing? What relationships exist between individual differences in drawings and the personalities of people? This last question, which entails construct validation of reliably scored characteristics of drawings, would appear to be the most basic of all. When used globally and intuitively, drawing responses can be subject to sweeping and unverifiable generalizations. Only empirical analysis of the relationship between drawings and personal characteristics can contribute to a science of personality.

CONCLUDING COMMENTS CONCERNING PROJECTIVE TECHNIQUES

The early history of paper-and-pencil tests was marked by a high degree of confidence—indeed, it was often a basic assumption—that personal revelations made to self-report questionnaires could be predictive of the behavior of individuals. A comparable idea in the history of projective techniques was that in responding to ambiguous stimuli, individuals would reveal significant facets of their unconscious processes and perceptions of the world. Our study of these two types of assessment methods leads to the conclusion that both ideas are too simplistic and do not do justice to the complexities of the human responder. This, of course, neither means that paper-and-pencil tests do not provide useful information for prediction, nor that projective techniques cannot shed light on covert processes. Rather it signifies that these achievements are not likely to be attained in uncomplicated ways.

We have suggested a number of the factors that complicate the use of projective techniques. We have also shown how projective techniques can be viewed from at least three vantage points. They may be conceived as tests, as interviews in which stimuli are presented to subjects and as stimuli for the cognitive activity of interpreters of behavior. Perhaps after all is said and done, the major contribution of projective techniques may be their role in making this threefold distinction so clear. This contribution is by no means limited to one particular method of assessment. In any psychological testing situation, whether it involves projective, paper-and-pencil, achievement, intelligence, or aptitude tests, each of these three aspects of testing plays a role.

One might generalize as follows about personality tests. They present subjects with particular problem-solving tasks. Whatever the problems and correct solutions, those solutions arrived at by subjects will not simply be a function of personal characteristics and abilities; this will be true even in a paper-and-pencil testing situation where instructions are quite explicit. For, in addition to instructions, a subject's behavior may also be affected by his prior attitudes toward the task and by nontest stimuli in the testing situation such as the style of dress of the tester, the personal style of the tester, and various other aspects of the tester's behavior. Finally, whatever the nature of the assessment situation, its data require interpretation. Whereas some kinds of data processing may be carried out in impersonal, programmed ways, the complex data of human behavior usually call for judgment and sensitivity on the part of a psychological interpreter. This is true even in the case of rigorously constucted tests, such as an intelligence test, where the psychologist's integrating of his observations of the testee's behavior with the testee's answers may lead to conclusions that could not be obtained from a set of answers and test scores.

It is clear that awareness of these interacting factors is not an end point. Rather it must be regarded as a prelude to increased sophistication in personality assessment. For projective techniques we have indicated some of the paths toward this goal. Perhaps the broadest of these might be referred to as the path of quantification. Whether we choose to regard projective techniques as tests that yield scores or as situations relatively lacking in structure and requiring content analyses, we profit from quantitatively describing the behavior of the individual. Through reliable instruments whose stimulus properties are known, quantitative indices of behavior can be effectively employed to describe personal characteristics, to compare different persons, to test hypotheses, and to evolve nomological networks.

14

Other Assessment Aids: Situational, Historical, and Biological Factors

Self-description and projective techniques are not the only arteries to personality assessment. Several additional types of approaches are capable of uncovering data that are relevant to the assessment of personality characteristics. Hence, to round out this close-up of assessment, let us survey some of these other data-gathering devices.

SITUATIONAL TESTS

One argument that might be leveled against some of the assessment methods considered thus far is that they measure behavior in situations that are by no means typical of real life. They may actually be quite unlike the situations in which the behavior to be predicted by assessors occurs. The argument in favor of developing situational tests is therefore convincing. It seems reasonable to hypothesize that the greater the similarity of the testing situation to the criterion one, the greater is the likelihood that the measures will be useful. However, situational tests are often unfeasible because of their cost and impracticality. They are not widely used in psychology. Yet for theoretical and certain practical purposes the study of behavior in real-life settings appears to have potential and, indeed, a considerable amount of interest value.

One of the best illustrations of the use of situational tests is the work Murray directed for the Office of Strategic Services (OSS) during the Second World War (Office of Strategic Services Assessment Staff, 1948). The job of the OSS involved carrying out secret missions that often were highly dangerous. Murray's team of psychologists was to assess the qualifications of candidates for OSS service. Each candidate was studied over a three-day period. The assessment included the gathering of life-history information and the administration of a large number of personality, intelligence, and achievement tests. In addition, the candidates were put through a variety of situational tests. These tests were designed to provide indications of candidates' reactions under unusual and stressful conditions that might be analogous to those to which OSS workers were likely to be exposed in the field. The rationale for going beyond traditional personality indices to the study of persons in special situations was stated in this way by the Office of Strategic Services Assessment Staff (1948, p. 8):

It is easy to predict precisely the outcome of the meeting of one known chemical with another known chemical in an immaculate test tube. But where is the chemist who can predict what will happen to a known chemical if it meets an unknown chemical in an unknown vessel? . . . How, then, can a psychologist foretell with any degree of accuracy the outcome of future meetings of one barely known personality with hundreds of other undesignated personalities in distant undesignated cities, villages, fields, and jungles that are seething with one knows not what potential harms and benefits?

An example of the type of test used was one in which the candidate was assigned the task of building a wooden structure. The candidate was given two assistants to aid him in this task. These assistants, described to the candidate as helpers, were, in fact, members of the assessment staff whose job it was to obstruct the building task and frustrate the candidate. The following dialogue (Office of Strategic Services Assessment Staff, 1948, pp. 105–110) involving the candidate (Slim) and the masquerading assistants (Buster and Kippy) suggests the degree to which the latter interfered with the former's efficient completion of his assigned task:

Slim: Well, let's get going.
Buster: Well, what is it you want done, exactly? What do I do first?
Slim: Well, first put some corners together—let's see, . . . make eight of these corners and be sure that you pin them like this one.
Buster: You mean we both make eight corners or just one of us? . . .
Slim: You each make four of these, and hurry. . . .
Kippy: Wha cha in, the Navy? You look like one of them curly-headed Navy boys all the girls are after. . . .

Slim: Er-no . . . I'm not in anything. . . .

Kippy: Are you a draft dodger? . . .

Slim: Let's have less talk and more work . . . You build a square here and you build one over there.

Buster: Who are you talking to—him or me?

Kippy: Why don't you give us a number or something—call one of us "number one" and the other "number two"? . . .

Slim: I'm sorry—What are your names?

Buster: I'm Buster.

Kippy: Mine's Kippy. What is yours?

Slim: You can call me Slim. . . .

Buster: It couldn't be with that shining head of yours. What do they call you, Baldy or Curly? Did you ever think of wearing a toupee? . . .

Slim: I don't see what difference that makes! Come on, both of you, and put an upright in each corner.

Kippy: He's sensitive about being bald. . . .

Slim: Just let's get this thing finished. We haven't much more time. Hey there, you, be careful. You knocked that pole out deliberately.

Kippy: Who, me? Now listen to me, you . . . If this darned thing had been built right from the beginning the poles here wouldn't come out . . . Jeez, they send a boy out here to do a man's job . . . .

Other situations presented candidates with equally thwarting experiences. One of those that seemed particularly frustrating was a stress interview in which the candidate was subjected to a grueling inquiry by a board of examiners. Other situations involved observing the candidate in a variety of individual activities and social interactions.

Two points are relevant to evaluating the OSS project. In the first place, the assessors were operating under a tremendous handicap, namely, the Second World War was in progress. Therefore, the detailed planning and careful pilot studies that are desirable in scientific work were simply not possible. The problem confronting OSS assessors was as practical as one could ever expect to face. In the second place, the crucial role of OSS personnel in the conduct of the war was so great as to remove the question of the feasibility of the assessment methods that might be considered. The OSS project is one of the rare examples in which the cost of assessment seemed almost inconsequential in comparison with the necessity of selecting the best candidate for the job at hand.

These situations used by the assessors were designed, as we have indicated, to provide, in miniature, examples of the sorts of stresses and frustrations that characteristically beset OSS personnel. Candidates' reactions to these situations were used as bases for assessors' ratings and evaluations. It would be nice if it were possible to evaluate succinctly and completely the OSS project. Unfortunately, for several reasons this is not possible. Although most of the statistical evidence concerning the value of OSS assessment predictions was equivocal, there remains reason for considering it an important part of the history of personality assessment. We have already mentioned the lack of planning that beset the OSS assessment work. In addition, there were a number of inadequacies and difficulties in the work which, although not conducive to obtaining positive results, are nevertheless instructive.

The candidates assessed were a highly heterogeneous group of individuals. Because of this, the assessment staff members ran into difficulties when they tried to describe and evaluate them within a common framework. Additional complications were the heterogeneity of tasks which OSS personnel performed, such as guerilla warfare and propaganda, and the variety of conditions under which the tasks were carried out. It is difficult to predict behavior in familiar situations. It is many times more difficult to predict behavior in situations of which we may have no personal knowledge. This, however, was the task confronting the OSS assessors. It is likely that many judgments and ratings by OSS assessors were made on the basis of their general stereotypes of personal adequacy for OSS rather than on the basis of knowledge of what tasks candidates might actually be assigned to accomplish.

Other comprehensive assessment programs using situational tests have been described in the literature. Together with the OSS study, they suggest the value of relating the assessment situation as closely as possible to the criterion situation (Cronbach, 1960; Stern, Stein, and Bloom, 1956). But for these tests to fulfill their potential in an assessment program, planning and research are needed to establish their appropriateness as indicators of future behavior. In addition to identifying meaningful situations, it is necessary to specify the ways in which subjects' behavior in them might be observed and recorded.

No matter how appropriate a situational test might be, if the observational techniques used are ineffective the validity of the test will be low. Reliable observations of behavior usually entail recording quite specific aspects of behavior. This has been done in some cases by counting the occurrence of certain responses within a particular period of time. In any case, it is necessary to establish the reliability of the procedure used in observing behavior.

The variety of responses that can be counted, rated, or recorded is, of course, quite great. Some researchers might be especially interested in the performance aspects of behavior, that is, the number of times a given overt response occurs, such as pressing a lever, or the magnitude of the response. Other researchers might be interested in social responses within groups of individuals—for example, those of a child in interaction with parents or peers. Still other researchers may be preoccupied with expressive behavior—the style that characterizes a person's motor and verbal behavior. For some purposes, researchers may observe behavior in situations that are planned in various ways. For other purposes, naturalistic observation may be indicated. Whatever the behavior studied, reliable quantification of observations is necessary before proceeding to an evaluation of a situational test.

To summarize, situational tests devised to test hypotheses and predict future behavior appear to have an important niche within the area of personality. Their use, however, requires attention to the questions of (1) the behavior samples to be observed and (2) the criteria by which they are to be evaluated.

LIFE-HISTORY DATA IN PERSONALITY ASSESSMENT

Much of the work of personality assessment entails gathering information about personal characteristics. These characteristics vary from complexity to ease of assessment. An interesting tentative hypothesis to consider is that complexity and ease of assessment do not necessarily correlate highly with predictive utility, and that particular, easily assessed characteristics may be as useful to the personality researcher as those requiring sophisticated methods and instruments. Irrespective of the correctness of this hypothesis, it is reasonable to argue that improvements in prediction go hand in hand with increases in the information available on persons. In this regard data about the histories of persons and their present status in life seem particularly relevant to personality assessment.

An illustration of this type of data is the socioeconomic status of the individual. Knowing only a person's reactions to a stress interview, such as the MMPI, and the Rorschach, the assessor might find himself puzzled by the data at hand. Information about the subject's educational level, occupational status, financial status, and place of residence, however, might prove of great value in dissolving apparent disparities and inconsistencies in the psychological data. Other facts about the subject's present status, such as whether he is married, and his age, could similarly prove to be helpful. In Chapter 29 we shall take up in some detail a provocative investigation by Hollingshead and Redlich (1958) of the relationship of socioeconomic and educational status to the incidence of mental disorder. These researchers found that social status bore a number of significant relationships to the various types of behavior problems that afflict people and also to the treatments provided for them.

Another illustration of the use of present-status and life-history information in personality may be found in research dealing with the tendency of persons to affiliate with others and with social groups. Schachter (1959) has incorporated the subject's ordinal position in the family as an independent variable into the design of his research on these tendencies. His findings concerning birth order have stimulated other researchers to determine its role in problems of interest to them (see Chapter 18). Ordinal position seems to be an historical variable worthy of note and study because it influences behavior toward the individual in the family setting.

The number of facts about a person's past and present conditions that might increase the predictive usefulness of personality assessment is so great that we cannot hope to mention all of them here. Some of these, in addition to the ones already noted, are the cultural climate of the community in which the individual lives, his family, social and occupational histories, and his present and past states of health.

For example, Tillmann and Hobbs (1949) investigated the relationship of personal-history data to a particular aspect of the current status of a particular group of persons. The aspect was the persons' records as automobile drivers among a group consisting of taxi drivers. After identifying accident-prone drivers and those who were largely accident-free, detailed personal histories were gathered on them. It was found that high-accident taxi drivers came from homes marked by parental divorce and instability and excessive strictness more often than low-accident drivers. High-accident drivers were also more likely than low-accident drivers to have poor employment histories and police records (apart from traffic violations), and only superficial relationships with friends and acquaintances.

Turner (1963) has reported a study that included in an interesting manner facts about the personal histories and current status of individuals. Turner was interested in determining the extent to which knowledge of seemingly unimportant life-history and status data was useful in predicting personality characteristics presumed to be of considerable importance. His study was limited inasmuch as all of the data gathered, the seemingly important and the seemingly unimportant, were derived from self-reports of individuals. Were it possible to have done so it would have been desirable to correlate the self-report data with actual behavioral observations. Nevertheless, as we shall see, Turner's results were both provocative and valuable.

Turner administered an Autobiographical Inventory to a group of over 100 college students. The items of the Inventory numbered several hundred. One group of items Turner judged to be "unimportant" on the *a priori* grounds that most students of psychology would not consider them to be personality variables of great significance. These items were considered to be predictors. A second group of items dealt with behavior and response patterns that would, in all likelihood, be judged as relating significantly to personality functioning. These items were taken to be criteria with which the predictors were correlated.

Predictors included such items as: (1) age when subject began regular drinking of beer; (2) frequency of visiting barber shops; (3) age when subject began regularly to wear a brassiere; (4) frequency of chewing gum; (5) frequency of drinking tea; (6) frequency of social dancing; (7) age when subject learned to ride a sled; (8) number of siblings in a subject's family.

Criteria included such items as:

1. Number of close companions at present;
2. Number of close companions during childhood;
3. Frequency of dating members of the opposite sex;
4. Number of fights, especially aggressive fights, which subject remembers having had;
5. Frequency of becoming intoxicated;
6. Frequency of praying alone;
7. Frequency of visiting psychiatrists or psychologists for help;
8. Frequency of impulsive acts later regretted.

In addition to filling out the Autobiographical Inventory, each subject took a battery of tests which included Gough's CPI (1957), Edward's PPS (1953*b*), Cattell's 16 Personality Factor (PF) Questionnaire (1957*a*), and an index of intellectual level. During the testing sessions observations were recorded of the subject's body movements, such as knee, arm, and foot movements.

All of the data of this research were correlated. Turner found that (1) many of the seemingly unimportant predictor items were more successful in predicting criteria than were scores on personality inventories, and that (2) observations of body movements during testing were predictive of many criteria. His results suggest the value in personality assessment of attending not just to scores on tests, but also to subjects' observed behavior during testing and to factual information on persons which can easily be gathered.

Psychological techniques of personality assessment provide bases for inferring characteristics and tendencies that may be quite subtle. These inferences can be expected to be better understood and more accurate if the assessor has, in addition to test data, knowledge of the facts of the individual's present status and past history. The more that is known about all facets of the individual who is being assessed the better the assessor's ability to predict his future behavior. As Turner's results so clearly suggest, we are at too early a stage in the field of personality to ignore seemingly unimportant or too obvious variables. The human organism is too complicated a mechanism for its student to ignore any evidence that may relate to its behavior.

BODILY CHARACTERISTICS AND PERSONALITY

Certainly one of the most obvious factors contributing to a person's individuality is his body and the way in which it functions. Unless one is comfortable with an arbitrary distinction between mind and body, the relationships of biological factors to behavior cannot be ignored. This relationship is seen perhaps most dramatically in certain clinical cases of disturbed behavior. Several forms of psychoses and mental retardation have been traced quite directly to disorders of a biological nature. In many other behavioral disorders organic conditions are probably contributing, if not solely determining, factors. At present, knowledge is all too limited concerning the relative contributions of psychological, genetic, physiological, and bodily variables to overt and covert behavior. However, work on this problem is increasing and there is reason to hope that the relationships among the several determinants of behavior will become clarified.

Body Types and Personality Types

One aspect of biological make-up that has received much attention in the area of personality is that of morphological characteristics. Morphology refers to bodily structure. As applied to personality, the question has been asked: what relationship does bodily structure have to personality characteristics and to behavior? An idea that has appealed to some students is that just as there may be types of personalities there may be correlated body types. From this standpoint it is an easy step to the next question: how are body types and personality types related to one another?

Before this question may be answered, it is necessary to define in an operational sense what is meant by body type and personality type. Defining body type is by far the simpler problem. Various body typologies have been described in the literature (Allport, 1961). Most of them are based on observations of body size, bodily proportions, and facial, skull, and hair characteristics. They may also be defined in terms of endocrine functioning, skin and blood characteristics, and other observable body features. Body types may be described through ratings of selected characteristics or by actual physical measurements. Body types based on these sorts of observations have been referred to as somatotypes. Since the problem of reliability in body typing is an important one and since individuals who represent "pure" types are rare, carefully prepared rating scales, accurate physical measurements, and adequate training of observers of body types must be assured in order that research can make a meaningful contribution to the study of behavior.

Kretschmer (1925) was one of the first to conduct research on body and personality types. His personality types were largely limited to forms of mental illness, particularly the varieties of schizophrenic reactions and manic-depressive states. These psychiatric manifestations were believed by Kretschmer to be functions of temperament or personality and of body type. In his writings he described what he called asthenic, pyknik, athletic, and dysplastic types.

Asthenics were described as narrow in build, thin in muscles and stomach, with contracted chest, delicate bones, and relative absence of fat. Kretschmer's research led him to the conclusion that asthenic individuals were marked by timidity, introversion, and lack of personal warmth. The psychiatric classification that seemed to correspond most closely to exaggerations of these characteristics was schizophrenia. The pyknik type was described in terms of roundedness of body shape, evidence of considerable body fat, and broadness of hips. These characteristics were regarded as associated with gregarious, friendly temperaments, and dependency on others. Kretschmer felt that forms of manic-depressive psychoses represented extreme instances of the pyknik body-temperament type. Presumably occupying a position intermediate to the pyknik and asthenic types was the athletic type which was characterized by strong muscular and skeletal development. The fourth type, the dysplastic, was not regarded as comprising a clearly definable set of characteristics. Kretschmer described dysplastic persons as "rare, surprising, and ugly."

Sheldon greatly improved the rating of body types by describing each individual in terms of how he fitted three somatotypes: endomorphy, mesomorphy, and ectomorphy (Sheldon, Dupertius, and McDermott, 1954; Sheldon, Stevens, and Tucker, 1940). These somatotypes correspond approximately to Kretschmer's pyknik, athletic, and asthenic body types. An advantage of Sheldon's somatotype rating scheme is that it explicitly recognizes the rarity of pure body types. Each individual is rated numerically on the basis of the contribution to his body build of endomorphy, mesomorphy, and ectomorphy. Along with body-type ratings Sheldon suggested three components of temperament that could be rated and that he hypothesized to be personality counterparts of body build (Sheldon and Stevens, 1942).

Viscerotonia, the counterpart to endomorphy, is defined as the tendency toward gregariousness, physical comfort, and relaxation. *Somatotonia,* the counterpart to mesomorphy, is defined as the tendency toward assertiveness, physical courage, and risk-taking. *Cerebrotonia,* the counterpart to ectomorphy, is defined as the tendency toward social inhibition, restraint, and introversion. Where body type-personality type correlation has been obtained, the question arises: what is its basis? For example, Glueck and Glueck (1956) have found that delinquents tend toward mesomorphy twice as often as do nondelinquents. Has this relationship any significance?

Although there is wide agreement concerning Sheldon's contribution to the classification of body types, and although Sheldon has obtained positive correlations between body type and temperament, there is much controversy over the validity of his contention that specific motivational and temperamental characteristics are peculiar to various body types. Similar controversies exist in connection with the psychological correlates of body build offered by Kretschmer. In evaluating the hypotheses of Kretschmer, Sheldon, and others concerning the personalities associated with body types, many students have felt that the personality traits studied have too often been defined in arbitrary and unreliable ways.

The concern with bodily shape and structure as independent variables is certainly salutary. However, the available evidence does not provide an adequate basis for drawing definite conclusions about the relationship of these variables to personality characteristics and to behavior. More information is needed on all these matters and also on a number of related questions. What, for example, is the relationship between genetic factors and bodily characteristics? What is the relationship of social status and nutrition to bodily characteristics? Are comprehensive schemas of body type and of personality the most effective bases of classifying persons?

Perhaps the major danger that besets research on the classification of bodily characteristics is the ease with which one can erroneously come to believe in the reality of a set number of types. That a relatively small number of naturally occurring, discrete types exists is a seductive idea because of its simplicity. This pitfall of many typologies should not deter attempts at efficient classification of persons, things, and events. It should, however, caution against oversimplifying the problems of classification. At least until evidence to the contrary becomes available, it would probably be best to regard typologies and classification systems as arbitrary devices. Some typologies may have practical value, but they must be recognized as products of human thinking rather than as discrete natural phenomena.

The criticism that use of typological concepts may tend to oversimplify complexities and continuities in nature may be applied to a number of psychological concepts (Allport, 1961; Cattell, 1957*b*). The concept of traits illustrates this point. Some writers have implied or directly stated that there are certain traits and attitudes which underlie behavior. It is clear, however, that when we speak of psychological traits, such as kindliness, gregariousness, and other-directedness, we are inferring characteristics from behavior. It is important to be constantly alert to the distinction between inferences drawn from behavior and the behavior itself.

If one clearly understands the inferential nature of type and traits, their role in the study of personality can be of great value. Such concepts can prove useful as frames of reference for consistencies in behavior and as bases for empirical investigations. In this way they may be viewed as constructs that are tied to particular sets of stimulus conditions and that are useful in explaining the behavior of individuals.

Before leaving the topic of bodily structure as a variable in the study of personality, we should note that the bodies of individuals can be looked upon from a different standpoint than the one we have been describing. We have been speaking simply of the correlation between defined body and personality types. One might also speak of the stimulus value of bodily characteristics. The obese child, for example, not only is barred from certain types of physical and social activities but his obesity also functions as a stimulus for him and for others.

Some writers, generalizing from examples such as this one, have dwelt on the individual's self-concept or body image (Mussen, Conger, and Kagan, 1963). They have usually employed the self-concept to refer to an individual's self-awareness and self-attitudes. However, an individual's body clearly serves as a stimulus for him and for persons with whom he comes into contact. Feelings of inferiority, superiority, and doubt may indeed be reactions, at least in part, to one's own perception of one's body and the evaluation one makes of it. Thus, we should pay attention not only to the correlation of bodily characteristics and behavior but also to the role of bodily characteristics as personal and social stimuli.

Biological Factors and Personality

Body typing is designed to assess one observable biological characteristic, physique. It does not require a high degree of technical knowledge to recognize that a number of other aspects of the biology of the individual can be measured and related to the behavior of organisms. Among biological individual difference variables that seem potentially relevant to the study of personality are: genetic characteristics, characteristics of the brain and nervous system, autonomic and biochemical characteristics, and glandular and nutritional characteristics.

It is commonplace in science to desire the integration and unification of disciplines, such as psychology, physiology, and genetics. Laudible as this aim may be, as particular disciplines undergo increasingly detailed study the complexities uncovered seem to be more than enough to preoccupy the attention of students in the field. As a result specialization tends to be progressive. Fortunately, fringe areas that truly relate to different areas of investigation begin to develop. When this happens, the fields involved mutually enrich one another and occasionally whole new and vital disciplines develop out of what previously seemed tangential or side issues.

Although one cannot easily predict the areas in which developments and breakthroughs of this type will occur, workers in one area should, at least, be alert to some of the potentialities in other disciplines. In personality, assessed personal characteristics and environmental factors have been the classes of variables most intensively studied. However, despite the tendency to preoccupy oneself completely with the area as it is presently defined, it is necessary to maintain a broad enough curiosity to be aware of related problems in other areas.

Notwithstanding the lack of strong ties between personality research and such areas of biology as genetics and nervous and physiological functioning, the available evidence clearly points to the need for shoring them up. At the outset of our consideration of personality we stressed its concern with a scientific treatment of individuality of behavior. Is it not clear that such factors as one's genetic endowment and the state of one's nervous and physiological systems are intimately related to behavior? Should not a study of the personality of the whole organism ultimately include reference to biological influences over development and behavior? In order to buttress affirmative answers to these questions let us consider a few of the biological factors mentioned. In doing so our aim shall not be to survey comprehensively knowledge relating to them, but rather to suggest some of the ways in which they are of relevance to the personality researcher.

GENETIC INFLUENCES IN BEHAVIOR

Probably no area of science can match genetics in recent explosions of knowledge. Within psychology, genetics has traditionally been defined in terms of the influence of parental characteristics on offspring. With respect to assessment, genetics would seem to have as strong a claim as psychology on the study of individual differences. Psychologists bring certain emphases to their work, geneticists bring complementary ones. It is interesting to note that genetics has been defined as being ". . . concerned with the distribution, development, and origin of individual differences" (David and Snyder, 1962, p. 1).

Genetic studies have isolated many sources of individual differences among organisms. To cite but a few examples, physique, skin pigmentation, and the shape of the face are influenced by genetic endowment. Although they are perhaps not directly influential in shaping psychological and social development, these genetically determined physical characteristics have many indirect influences on behavior, which it would be foolhardy to deny.

However, a number of direct links have been established between genetic structure and behavior (David and Snyder, 1962). For example, genetic bases for many forms of mental retardation have been demonstrated. (It is worth noting that there has been a recent upsurge in studies of various possible biochemical bases of mental retardation.) Over the entire range of intellectual functioning there is reason to believe that hereditary factors significantly interact with the environment to determine performance on intelligence tests employed by psychologists (Vandenberg, 1962). As knowledge of the structure and characteristics of genes increases it may become possible to make determinations of how genetic and environmental factors interact with one another in influencing intellectual functioning.

The problem of mental disorder is another one that has been subjected to investigation from the standpoint of genetic determinants. Most of this work has centered on the severest types of disruption, the psychoses. In schizophrenia, for example, the incidence of the disorder is much greater in cases where parents have been diagnosed as schizophrenic than where there has been an absence of parental schizophrenic manifestations. Although, obviously, such consequences can result from both genetic and social environmental influences, evidence regarding the incidence of schizophrenia in monozygotic twins supports the inference that genetic factors are of great importance. Kallmann (1959), who has pioneered in this type of study, has reported the incidence of schizophrenia in monozygotic (identical) twins to be approximately 70 per cent. The corresponding figure for dizygotic (fraternal) twins is approximately 15 per cent. Slater (1953), in an independent series of studies, has obtained comparable figures. Although issues of nature (heredity) and nurture (environment) have by no means been settled it does appear that genetic endowment is related to the incidence of disturbed behavior.

So far most of the research in genetics has been directed at specific forms of psychopathology and behavior deviations. However, beginnings have been made in showing that normal personality functioning is, in some measure, related to genetic variables (Gottesman, 1963). These relationships may turn out to be either direct, as has been shown for some forms of mental retardation, or indirect. For example, consider the degree of aggressive behavior manifested by an individual. This behavior might be found to be a direct function of inherited tendencies or it might be related to certain endocrine imbalances, which, in turn, are related to genetic characteristics of the individual, or it might be related to these factors in complex interaction with environmental factors.

Perhaps the major breakthrough needed to bring psychology and genetics into closer alignment is conceptual. What may be needed is a revision of the dichotomy between heredity and environment which nearly everyone makes at one time or another. David and Snyder (1962, p. 39) have raised this possibility:

> Every science from time to time discovers that it has been embarrassed by its dependence on a terminology based on concepts which date from an earlier, and sometimes from a prescientific, period. Genetics, since its inception, has been shackled with the dichotomy of "heredity" and "environment"—both of which were concept names before genetics was born—and it shares these shackles with psychology. Numerous authors have attempted, in one way or another, to reduce the confusion engendered by the vague and ambiguous referents which the terms *heredity* and *environment* have in many contexts. Those who have made constructive contributions in this direction include psychologists from several subdisciplines . . . , psychogeneticists . . . , geneticists . . . , and at least one biologist logician . . . , to cite only a few. Their

consensus would seem to be that we have been asking the wrong questions when we have tried to decide *which* is responsible—heredity or environment—for such-and-such observed variability, or when we have inquired *how much* of the variability is attributable to hereditary factors and how much to environmental . . . . Instead, we should be inquiring *how*, that is, investigating the developmental mechanisms through which the variability arises.

NEUROLOGICAL INFLUENCES IN BEHAVIOR

The functioning of the body is of relevance to personality in terms of both the independent and dependent variables associated with it. With regard to independent variables, such questions as these arise: What is the relationship of the nervous system to behavior? What influences do endocrine functions have over observed behavior? How does the physiology of the body relate to behavior? With regard to dependent variables, such questions as these arise: What are the physiological correlates of various types of behavioral responses? How is physiological functioning affected by psychological states? Are individuals with certain personality characteristics and behavioral histories more likely than others to develop particular bodily disfunctions?

Numerous examples of interest to personality researchers could be cited of the ways in which bodily characteristics relate to behavior. Perhaps the most dramatic are cases of deviant behavior attributable to known damage to the brain and nervous system (Coleman, 1964). Damage to the cerebral cortex can lead to rather specific types of behavioral impairment. For example, frontal-lobe lesions have been found to result often in memory defects, inability to conceptualize, hostility, and inadequate control of emotional expression. Irritation of the temporal lobe can lead to auditory hallucinatory experiences. Damage to the parietal lobe may result in impairment of the ability to discriminate among levels of intensity of certain classes of stimuli. Many forms of psychotic behavior, marked by such symptoms as shallowness of affect, impairment in judgment, and personality instability have been found to stem from disturbances in brain function.

Experimental surgical and other procedures used with animals and humans have helped to illuminate many brain-behavior relationships. Penfield and Roberts (1959) reported the results obtained when parts of the sensorimotor area of the human cortex were stimulated electrically. They found that the stimulation resulted in spontaneous vocalization; that is, verbalizations—but not meaningful words—were emitted by subjects. Penfield (1954) had previously described cases in which electrical stimulation of the temporal lobe had resulted in the dramatic recollection by subjects of events that occurred in their distant past. Olds and Milner (1954) also demonstrated that electrical stimulation of certain brain centers could produce reactions of pleasure and pain.

A great temptation in considering brain-behavior relations is to equate neurological events with psychological and behavioral ones. Two related impediments stand in the way of this appealing idea. First, individuals are not conscious of many neurological processes occurring within them. Second, and of overriding significance, are gaping lacunae in both the fields of neurology and psychology. Von Bonin (1962, p. 115) has made this point very clearly:

> . . . while the idea that the life of the mind and the life of the brain are correlated seems eminently reasonable and true, we cannot yet work it out in detail. We do not know exactly what the cortex does, how consciousness or, for that matter, the metric of the outside world arises, or how we move our bodies.

The developing ties between neurology and psychology represent a good example of the need for evolution of new disciplines out of established ones. Pribram (1962, pp. 121–122) has provided a convincing rationale for the emergence of such a discipline in neuropsychology:

> The empirical evidence upon which translations between psychological and neurological concepts can be based are the results of neurobehavioral experiments and observations. The systematization of such evidence constitutes the science of *neuropsychology*. By definition, neuropsychology is a reductive discipline. As such, it partakes of the characteristics of its nonreductive siblings, psychology and neurology. The three sciences differ in that the dependent variables used to gather relevant data represent the interaction of different systems of independent variables. Though all three sciences have in common a reference to *environment*—systems of independent variables that can be completely specified by the techniques of the physical sciences . . . —psychological and neurological sciences differ in the systems of variables specified by biological techniques: in the psychological sciences these systems refer to the whole organism, in the neurological sciences to only part of that organism. Neuropsychology, if it is to be effectively reductive, must relate all three systems of variables: environmental, organismic, *and* neural. When structural concepts are under consideration, these distinctions appear self-evident. However, when function is in question, the temptation arises to confound two of these three classes of independent variables. The neurologist is prone to disregard the distinction between organism and environment—psychologizing of neural processes follows and activity in the

brain-stem reticular formation becomes identified with consciousness. On the other hand, the psychologist is prone to disregard the distinction between organism and its parts—neurologizing of the psychological process is a common consequence, and drive becomes synonymous with hypothalamic function.

PHYSIOLOGICAL INFLUENCES IN BEHAVIOR

One area of biology that has been of most interest to psychological researchers is physiology. This has come about partly because of the marked individual differences observed in the physiological functioning of organisms. The identification of psychosomatic disorders in which personality and physiological processes are closely intertwined has contributed particularly to the interest of students of personality in physiological data (Coleman, **1964**). More will be said about psychosomatic disorders in Part 5.

Lacey (**1956**; Lacey, Bateman, and Van Lehn, **1952**; Lacey and Van Lehn, **1952**) has provided some valuable information about individual differences in physiological responding. He has shown that when a number of indices of physiological functioning are obtained from human subjects, there appear to be characteristic patterns among them from person to person. Furthermore, many of the correlations between pairs of indices are often not high. Thus, for example, knowing a person's blood pressure may not enable us to predict perfectly his heart rate. Lacey has found that these individual patternings of physiological responses are particularly clear when the physiological measures are obtained under stressful or anxiety-provoking conditions (David and Snyder, **1962**).

It appears, then, that each person has his own peculiar pattern of physiological responding to environmental stimuli. Lacey (**1956**) has stressed the need to compare physiological patterns of response with psychological ones. In one study he successfully related subjects' patterns of physiological responding to color and form responses to the Rorschach personality test (Lacey, Bateman, and Van Lehn, 1952). In a similar vein, Ax (**1953**) was able to isolate seven physiological response patterns that successfully discriminated between anger and fear. Finally, Funkenstein (1955) has demonstrated that physiological patterning is strongly influenced by the conditions under which physiological responses are recorded.

These results regarding the patterning of physiological responses are relevant to many researches in the area of personality. In several attempts to correlate particular physiological indices with measures of personality, the results have often been inconsistent and ambiguous.

It seems likely that some of the ambiguities are due to the failure to obtain comparable physiological measures in the studies. Furthermore, since the patterning of such physiological responses as heart rate, galvanic skin response, and blood pressure seem to be so important, study of only one or even a few such measures alone may serve more to complicate rather than to clarify the empirical relationships involved. It is interesting to observe an apparent trend toward multidimensional studies of physiological responses that parallels multidimensional studies of psychological responses.

An example of one of the more sophisticated studies of both psychological and physiological variables is to be found in the work of G. Mandler, J. Mandler, Kremen, and Sholiton (1961). These researchers wanted to know how people responded both verbally and physiologically to threatening stimuli. The physiological responses which were recorded were: heart rate, peripheral blood flow, finger temperature, and the palmar galvanic skin response. The personality measures included a phrase-association test which is similar to a word-association test except that the stimuli are phrases rather than single words. Five groups of phrases were used: neutral ones, and phrases relating to sex, aggression, dependency, and competition. Subjects' responses to these stimulus areas were scored through a content analysis procedure as to avoidance of the area (sex, aggression, etc.), defensive reactions to the area, and the degree of interference in responding that could be associated with stimulus materials. Examples of the latter were long reaction time, stuttering, and laughter. In addition to the phrase test, subjects were also administered the Rorschach test, an interview, the Taylor Manifest Anxiety Scale, and a specially prepared questionnaire dealing with their awareness of their own autonomic reactivity.

The results of the research showed that both verbal personality measures and the indices of physiological responses successfully discriminated the threat areas of the phrase-association test. The findings suggested an interesting distinction. G. Mandler, J. Mandler, Kremen, and Sholiton felt that ego-involving intellectual tasks, like an intelligence test, and ego-involving affective tasks, like the phrase-association test, might lead to different response patterns. Intellectual threat might lead to heightened conscious preoccupation with one's autonomic responding, whereas affective threat might be more related to actual physiological changes. These researchers found that specific patterns of verbal and autonomic response to particular aspects of personality were tapped by the phrase-association test.

Many other examples could be cited from the experimental literature in support of the need for increased attention to the direct and indirect relationships of bodily functioning and personality states. Brief mention should be made of two additional studies. Keys, Brozek, Henschel, Mickelson, and Taylor (1950) found many striking changes in personality characteristics as a function of a rather severe bodily change, drop in body weight, and changes in concomitant physiological responding caused by a semistarvation diet. Eichorn (1963) has cited much evidence of the indirect effects of differences in physiological maturation on personality development in children. Differences between early- and late-maturing boys and girls indeed affect personality development, socialization, and interest patterns.

One conclusion to be drawn from this sampling of researches on physiological functioning and personality is the need to avoid too sharp a separation between classes of variables. Although it may be of value to speak of personality variables on the one hand, and physiological ones on the other, it must be recognized that the distinction is, in a sense, imposed on reality. We can hope that future interactions among the processes we term psychological and physiological will be more fully appreciated and integrated.

Our aim in taking up bodily processes at this point was to broaden the frame of reference within which individual differences may be regarded. We have seen a number of examples of individual differences in bodily characteristics and have suggested some of their relationships to behavior. Bodily characteristics, like characteristics assessed with psychological assessment techniques, may be studied either as independent or as dependent variables. As independent variables, indices such as personality inventory scores, rated aspects of responses to projective techniques, and characteristics of physiological responding may be used as predictors. As dependent variables, these same indices may be studied to gauge the effects of experimental and environmental conditions such as degree of stress and social deprivation.

The psychophysiology of personality is just at a beginning, data-gathering phase. Numerous speculations have been offered concerning the relationship between human individuality and the workings of the body. It is clear that most of these speculations cannot be considered as anything more than fantasies until many empirical relationships become explicated. Gerard (1959, p. 38) has commented in this whimsical way on the whole question of the biological determinants of human behavior:

> There is much smoke; we have yet to find the fire. But I have every confidence that with advance of the life sciences we will soon see some flame, just as I am confident that advance in the physical sciences will soon show

us things we have not previously been able to see. Whitehead once told me a quatrain, attributed to a cook, which ran as follows:

"Moon, lovely moon, bathed in fire sublime,
Careening throughout the far boundaries of time,
Whenever I see thee I ask in my mind,
Shall I never, oh never, behold thy behind?"

CONCLUDING COMMENTS CONCERNING PERSONALITY ASSESSMENT

The aim of personality assessment is prediction. Predictors prove valuable either because they contribute to the extension of constructs or because they help to solve practical problems. The OSS Assessment Staff's (1948) efforts to predict the success of intelligence agents is an example of the latter. Taylor's (1951, 1953) use of assessed anxiety to predict eyelid conditioning is an example of the former. Whether an assessor's aim is purely theoretical, purely practical, or some combination of the two, he must decide on the behavioral responses he will use as criteria and the measures he will use as predictors. Selecting criteria is often a simpler task in applied settings than in settings involving construct validation. As noted previously, construct validation requires more than one simple and obvious criterion. Selecting predictors, on the other hand, usually requires the choosing of only a sample of many potential predictors for use in assessment. Individual differences in the ingenuity of assessors and in their methods go a long way toward determining the success of assessment efforts.

We have described some of the tools of the craft and some of the problems which beset the craftsman. The tools are information about persons. This information may be gathered through the use of a combination of tests and situations varying in degree of structure, through perusal of life-history data, and through biological study of the individual.

An important problem confronting assessment researchers is the fact that different means of gathering information about persons may not always yield the same results. When this lack of consistency occurs it might suggest that some data are worthless. But it also indicates the need to increase understanding of the relationships among different measures of personality. This need is illustrated by the following information gathered on one subject, a 19-year-old college student. These data show both consistencies and inconsistencies among several measures of personality.

Impressions of Psychological Examiner:

The subject is a large, somewhat overweight, 19-year-old, male, college sophomore. His general appearance conveys an air of studied indifference to physical appearance. His hair is long, always somewhat mussed, and in need of a washing. His clothes, although clean, are worn very casually and in unusual combinations.

The subject speaks in a way that is intended to impress others with both his extensive vocabulary and intellectual ability. He attempts to appear above all that is mundane and ordinary and, in general, reflects a desire to be classified as a rebellious intellectual. He is very condescending, in general, but did not generalize this directly to the tester. The subject is intellectually very bright and not uninteresting to deal with, although his pseudointellectual approach to everything soon becomes tiring and somewhat irritating. Any everyday occurrence is boring and unchallenging to the subject and soon almost everything seems to be boring to him. It was not long before the tester became bored with this unchanging approach and the subject's inability to enjoy the vast majority of life's experiences. In this sense, and many others, the subject is not as mature and sophisticated as he would wish to appear.

Excerpts from Self-Description in Interview Situation:

As a person, I'd have to take into consideration my relationships, how I feel I stand in relation to other people. I feel my general temperament is one of aquiescence. I despise arguments, I don't particularly care for too many people. I think a great deal of my time is wasted on other people. I feel that other people don't deserve my consideration. I very rarely become upset when other people do things not corresponding with my views. I don't particularly like children or the standard concept of what people are supposed to like. I despise girls, among other things. You want this to be true, naturally? Every girl with whom I've associated with has gotten me in trouble one way or another. Parents, as far as parents go—I feel my relations with my parents are on a very poor level. My father is rather domineering. I respond to this in a rather acquiescing mood. My mother is very permissive and I respond with a great deal of dislike. I have four brothers, none of which I particularly care for. As far as school goes, I dislike almost all my acquaintances in school. I dislike almost all my instructors in school with the exception of a very few and these are instructors who feel things that I like. I feel myself that I have the average amount of talents. I'm not particularly gifted. I think that in the things I do like, I have great capabilities of becoming good. My temperament lies more in the field of fine arts than it does in the field of science. I think that science is off in its interpreting my feelings. Music, literature, poetry—these are the fields that I feel I can do best in. These are the fields also that the people that I enjoy are either instructors or costudents.

I am, while I won't say exactly emotionally unstable, I do become mildly upset but I have no actual codified or recognizable defense mechanisms for these frustrations. I don't feel that people are picking on me, are necessarily harsh in their dealings with me. . . . If you were to ask me what actually I was as other people saw me or as I feel they saw me, then I would have to say that I am probably generally disliked among my acquaintances because I hold the attitude of intolerance to a lot of things that they express. The reason I do say this is because I feel that a lot of things they say are stupid. It is my feeling to races, I don't—at least I can't recognize in myself—any race prejudice. I feel that Jews all are as good as anyone else. They're like the Negroes, they're as good as anyone else. The Negroes haven't had a chance. They are definitely not as well trained as the white is, in my opinion, but this is not a prejudice. The most interesting people I've met that coincide with my temperament are Germans. I feel that there is a kind of emotional bond because there is not much emotion that is at all intelligible. As I said before, I like the fields of fine arts, mainly because this allows for the expression of people better than myself who well definitely you can say are cultured. Fine arts allow for the expression of true genius in all its forms, unlike science and this is my opinion why and I feel strongly attached to it.

. . . I despise certain animals, cats in particular, rats, snakes, toads. I couldn't say why I dislike them but if I ever become outraged or would like to take my feelings out on something these are the things that fall in line for it.

Um—hmmmmmmm—The one thing that I abhor extremely, there is actually two things, ignorance which is the witty kind, propagated ignorance and the pseudo-scientific religions, Rosicrucianism and Southern Baptism and sundry other religions in this class because it leads back that I think they are performing a great disservice not only to myself because I have to live with these people, but also to other people because they are being sucked in. I don't feel any empathy for children, their feelings. I would not go so far as say I don't care for anyone's feelings because I care for my own. I won't say I'm spiteful because I dislike children. They're a necessary evil, something to put up with. However, they must be cared for. Ummm. As far as my feelings toward school . . . I think I am wasting a great deal of time in school because I am lazy, extremely so. I don't feel this is a defense mechanism. I don't feel that a lot of things are important that I take. I feel that there is a great deal of ignorance that I must more or less wade through to get what I'm after. I won't say that I'm ruthless, if you could use the word. I would say that I strive for the things I want if I want them bad enough but I do take into consideration other people's feelings, for the fact that if one doesn't he'll turn around and they always get you in the end, so it's wise to watch other people. Uhmmmmm. I dislike intensely things that are filthy, things that suggest filth, both physically and abstractly. I despise uh these lurid jokes, I think there is no sense to them.

I dislike girls. If I were to assign numbers I would say 95 per cent because they are flighty, thoughtless, inconsiderate. Girls, naturally, have a physical appeal. Their mental capabilities are rather sparse or few and far between but there are certain characteristics in other people that I do admire and that I wish I had myself but am either too reticent or too lazy to acquire. I like a friendly attitude. That's one thing I don't have. I like the ability to laugh at your own troubles. This I do think I have. I'm a misanthrope but I don't see at times how one could be so naive to say that people are basically good.

Selected Responses to the Rorschach Inkblots:

Card IV:

Free Association	*Inquiry*
1. This looks to me like a giant either lying on the ground or with his feet off the ground where you're looking from the feet up.	1. The whole picture seems to be a triangle-feet-webbed feet-legs and body are large, and as you are looking up toward it, its head gradually grows smaller, and these two appendages look like wings or arms.
2. Prehistoric monster with a tremendous tail in the back with two feet in front with small hands near the top, or some type of . . .	2. The center section looks like a tail. Tail goes either with giant or prehistoric monster. With the giant, science fiction type thing. This also looks like a ray, he's enveloping something. This beam that gradually grows larger.
3. Or a cyclops with a ray coming out of his head.	3. All three are the same: a mangy prehistoric monster, its got sea weed and that kind of junk hanging on it. Giant is just an expression of the size of the thing, as it appears to me and the prehistoric monster. This little thing that looks like hands are wings—ha ha —a little farfetched.

Card IX:

1. Looks like two witches dancing around a fire, with some green shrubs in front of them. You're looking at them through the shrubs.	1. Painted hats, this is fire, this middle section actually looks more like a candle than a fire. They have scrawny hands and their dresses come down to round off the bottom. Painted noses, two eyes and high hats. Green are the shrubs suggested by their color, kind of ill-defined shape.

Free Association

2. From the top it looks like an explosion towards—downwards, perhaps an atomic blast. Viewed from the bottom it also looks like two spectators, ghouls or skeletons would be my guess. Something mysterious is going on above them, have clouds of gloom, and on top of that there is brightness over their heads, representing a good spirit or something like that. (Examiner noted subject's big sigh of relief.)

Inquiry

2. Ah—this is the material from the blast. This is the mushroom up here, this is the column, this perhaps is the big surge blasting out. Do you want ghouls now? Ah—these green things look like clouds hiding these two figures from this upper right, either God or goodness or something like that. And these are the two figures, ghouls or skeletons, got bony hands and round foreheads that look like there is no skin on them and no hair. It's extending a little farther over these figures and it's ah—clouded from these fellows, set apart by these clouds, gloom things and perhaps an attempt to explain this part of picture having this. This came second to me, first thing I saw was ghouls. Well at least we're out of the clouds.

Card X:

1. Looks just like an artist palette, blobs of color, doesn't seem to have much.

1. A bunch of blobs of color, kinda messy. Yeah—taken his palette and just blobbed water colors all over the thing. They run together forming little messes here. Two different colors of blue, green, pink, lighter red.

Selected stories told to TAT pictures:

Card 2:

This is a son who's working on the farm left to his mother by his father, his father is dead. He's a man with little brains, but much muscle. His mother was left pregnant by—ahh—the boy's father—ah—father couldn't have died too long ago, I guess. Working on this grubby little farm—mother is fed up but son is too stupid to be fed up—he just likes to work kind of. The girl in the picture is the boy's sister and she is probably frustrated like the mother by the farm and she's more intelligent than her brother. She has a conflict of staying on the farm and ending up like her mother or brother—but she chooses a way out by going to school. Mother is so frustrated by this farm that she cares little for these two children of hers, so they speed up and enhance this dislike by being different. This adds to the mother's frustration. The outcome—the daughter will grow up hating the things that her mother stood for and her husband—father rather—and in spite of this she loves her mother and loves her brother because he's so simple-minded—he's just completely out of it.

Card 6 BM:

This fellow was just about to be married and his girlfriend died a horrible death. She was riding a motorcycle and cracked up and died and O! it's more horrible than that—she was burned by acid. The son didn't know about it till then and he comes from a very well to do family. The mother, this boy's mother, despises this girl because she was the daughter of an ex-fiance of hers and the daughter's father turned her down so she carried it over to the daughter. She and her son argued about this girl and the son became mad because of the mother's opinion—and at this point right now the son gets the news of the girl's death. The son is quite upset—the mother has got several types of emotions, she's sad for son that his fiance has been killed, and for the girl, and herself because she feels her son will probably dislike her now. She's going over the event that led up to her disliking this girl. She's not sharing the same type of grief as her son—she's more or less in reverie about some of her past life. (Quest. How do you think it might turn out?) The son winds up hating the mother and the mother ends up in a very peculiar position, she has to run around trying to make up to the son and the more she does the more he despises her—these are mixed up people.

A striking feature of this subject's responses in these three assessment situations is the negative, dysphoric, critical, and often hostile quality of his verbal expressions.

1. *Interview* *a.* "I feel other people don't deserve my consideration"
   b. "My mother is very permissive and I respond with a great deal of dislike"
   c. "I dislike girls"
2. *Rorschach* *a.* "a mangy prehistoric monster"
   b. "clouds of gloom"
   c. ". . . blobs of color, kinda messy"
3. *TAT* *a.* "grubby little farm"
   b. "The son winds up hating the mother"

Paper-and-Pencil Test Data

The subject was also administered the MMPI and several true-false scales of anxiety and hostility. His MMPI profile showed one T score over 70 (two standard deviations above average for norm reference group). This was on the Masculinity-Femininity scale.

(For a college student this high a score is probably a reflection of intellectual interests and bookishness.) The Psychopathic Deviate and Hypomania scales showed T scores greater than 60 (one standard deviation above average for norm reference group). The total MMPI pattern suggested a bohemian, querulous, argumentative, and verbally hostile individual.

The subject received a quite high score on the Edwards Social Desirability scale and quite low scores on the Taylor Manifest Anxiety scale and a true-false questionnaire of hostile attitudes.

A review of all the data gathered on the subject indicates both consistencies and inconsistencies. We have already mentioned some of the similarities in his responses in the interview and to the Rorschach and TAT. The bohemian air and argumentativeness inferred from the MMPI would appear to be quite consistent with the interview and projective test data. However, the conventionality implied by the high SD score, and the relative absences of worry and negativism implied by the scores on anxiety and hostility scales does not seem to fit easily with interpretations based on the other data available. Which data are most valid? What are the different meanings which the subject may have placed on the various assessment situations? Validity is the payoff of work on assessment. But there is great need now to understand better both assessment methods and the meaning of assessment stimuli to subjects in order ultimately to realize such a payoff in describing persons.

We have described personality assessment as a search for relevant individual difference variables. We have seen the breadth of the variables used in the study of conceptual and practical problems, and the desirability of a multidimensional approach to assessment. We have also seen that the measurement of each type of individual difference variable has associated with it procedural problems, large and small. Through ingenuity and scientific methods, students of personality seek to solve these problems so that reliable description and meaningful prediction of behavior can be achieved. When these goals are attained, they hope to be in a position to contribute in an important way to the evolution of valid theories of personality. But even though this goal has not yet been reached, it is possible to point to a number of conceptual contributions which have resulted from personality assessment research. Cronbach (1960, pp. 607–608) has summarized these contributions in this way:

> For every type of decision and for every type of psychological information, there are many techniques and many specific instruments. The instruments differ in practicality, in the degree of training required to use them, in the

variety of information they obtain, and in fidelity. The instrument that works best for one tester will not be best for another tester making the same decision. Tests must be chosen by a highly qualified professional worker who has a thorough understanding of the institution and persons he serves.

All in all, psychological testing is an accomplishment its developers may well boast of. Errors of measurement have been reduced year by year, and the significance of tests has been increased, until today all facets of American society feel the impact of the testing movement. The school, industry, marriage, governmental policy, and character-building agencies have all been aided by tests. Interpretations of test data are daily creating better lives by guiding a man into a suitable lifework, by placing an adolescent under therapy which will avert mental disorder, or by detecting causes of a failure in school which could turn a child into a beaten individual. Methods are now available which, if used carefully by responsible interpreters, can unearth the talents in the population and identify personality aberrations which would cause those talents to be wasted. Building on these techniques, we are in a position to capitalize as never before on the richness of human resources.

Part 3

THE EXPERIMENTAL STUDY OF PERSONALITY

Through the various ways in which researchers probe for personal characteristics that are related to behavior runs a common thread. This is the underlying assumption that indices of human variability have predictive value, and that they can be shown to correlate with behavioral criteria. Sometimes these criteria are self-evident, as in some problems of prediction. Other times they are subtle and complex, as in most problems of construct validation. One avenue of approach to these latter types of criteria is the time-honored method, experimentation, to which this section turns. Along with assessment, the experimental method has repeatedly shown its usefulness in personality research. Its aim is the observation of behavior under specifically created conditions.

Experimentation is somewhat different from but complementary to the assessment approach to behavior. In experiments observations are made under carefully controlled conditions. By this standard, psychological tests and assessment methods qualify, perhaps, as experimental techniques. Certainly, researchers engaged in assessment try to record their measurements under standard conditions which eliminate extraneous influences over the behavior of subjects. Experiments, however, go one step beyond the control of extraneous variables. They are aimed, in addition, at manipulating the conditions under which behavior occurs. Experiments thus permit observations under carefully controlled *special* conditions.

In psychological experiments, all subjects do not necessarily respond to the same set of standard conditions. Rather, groups of subjects respond to conditions of different kinds. Psychological experiments thus differ from assessment procedures and research in natural settings by virtue of the unique situations that they create.

Our awareness of these many ways of studying behavior need not require us to prefer one to another. Observations made in experiments are not inherently more or less useful than naturalistic observations, nor are they necessarily superior or inferior to observations made in assessment situations. The kinds of observations recorded by a researcher depend on the problem he is pursuing and the sorts of observations he is capable of making. But for the problems appropriate to it, the experiment is one of the most powerful devices at the disposal of the scientist.

Experiments deal with two types of variables. Independent variables define the special conditions under which observations are made. Dependent variables refer to the observations themselves. In psychological experiments dependent variables are indices of behavior; independent variables are conditions intended to influence behavior. These conditions are human creations, products of the imagination and resourcefulness of researchers. They are manipulations of the environmental situations in which organisms respond.

The simplest experiment is one in which there are only one independent and one dependent variable. For example, in a psychological experiment the independent variable might be the number of hours of food deprivation. The measured response, the dependent variable, might be the number of the subject's free associations having food connotations. A more complex experiment might incorporate an additional variable: the subject's attitudes toward food, assessed prior to the deprivation period. Such a variable is not manipulated, but is rather the product of an assessment procedure. Assessed characteristics are used as variables in experiments when it is believed that experimental manipulations will have different effects on persons with different characteristics.

A still more complex experiment might add another manipulated condition, such as the amount of social contact permitted the subject during a period of food deprivation. Within the limits of practicality, several independent and several dependent variables can be studied in the same experiment. It is not unusual in the field of personality for experiments to involve as many as four or five independent variables. Since behavior is usually a function of a complex of variables rather than of one variable by itself, this experimental complexity would seem to make good sense.

Experiments are designed to establish relationships between independent variables (manipulated stimulus conditions and assessed characteristics) and dependent variables (overt responses). A crucial problem in evaluating the outcome of an experiment is the extent to which its independent variables may have been contaminated or confounded with extraneous variables. If it can be shown that an organism's behavior is due to a variable not considered by the experimenter, the value of the experiment declines measurably. For example, some food-deprived subjects might "fill up" on water to a much greater extent than would other subjects. Thus, although all subjects eat no food during a given period of time, the amounts of water in the digestive system will vary widely.

The reason experimenters must attend to all possible uncontrolled sources of variability in subjects' behavior is that an important purpose of an experiment is to draw inferences from observed relationships which can contribute to the development of theoretical concepts. If, because of failure to attend to variables other than the independent variables, unfounded inferences are drawn from experiments, theory building could well be retarded rather than advanced. Theory and methodology are closely intertwined. In any experiment it is necessary to consider both the concept under study and the adequacy of the methodology used to evaluate it. Seemingly positive or negative results could be due to the unnoticed effects of uncontrolled variables.

Psychological experiments are designed to identify variables that influence behavior. Experiments in the area of personality have focused especially on these influences on behavior: (1) personal characteristics; (2) characteristics of tasks; and (3) personal or social aspects of experimental situations. These three classes of variables account for a high percentage of the independent variables in experimental studies of personality. The dependent variables to which these are related are determined by the problem under study. Among the behaviors or dependent variables investigated by personality researchers are: (1) performance on intellective tasks; (2) verbal behavior; (3) social behavior; (4) attitudes toward self; and (5) physiological functioning. Each of these classes of dependent variables can be studied in terms of the question: In what ways is it related to assessed personal characteristics, characteristics of tasks, and interpersonal relationships?

The aim in Part 3 is not to provide a handbook of all experimental research on personality, but rather to raise some fundamental questions and to suggest the potential power of the experiment for the student of personality. Questions that will frequently occur include: (1) What sorts of attempts have personality researchers made to use the laboratory in their work? (2) What sorts of procedures characterize laboratory investigation of personality? (3) What are some of the problems that beset the personality researcher in the laboratory? (4) Are there at least tentative solutions to some of these problems?

15

Personality and Human Performance

Many people, were they to be confronted with the question, "What determines human performance, learning, and intellectual achievement?" would probably refer to such concepts as the IQ or intelligence. It is certainly true that children with high IQs learn faster and perform at a higher level than children with low IQs. However, knowing an individual's standing on an index of relative brightness will not always enable accurate prediction of his behavior. Also, knowing someone's IQ will not necessarily expedite answers to such questions as: (1) Under which sets of conditions will he achieve his maximal level of performance? (2) Which conditions are detrimental to his performance and learning?

Intelligence, like personality, is a construct, an inference drawn from behavior. Intelligence tests provide measures of relative levels of performance on selected tasks. Most general assessment batteries, however, include indices of both intellectual and personality functioning. Students of personality are interested in intellectual functioning, but particularly in terms of variables usually considered to be nonintellective in nature. Intelligence tests are perhaps among the most significant contributions that psychologists have made to the field of psychological measurement. But many psychologists believe that the understanding and prediction of performance would be greatly enhanced if knowledge of these nonintellective variables were increased. What sort of problems have personality researchers studied in the hope of increasing knowledge of learning and performance?

In most general terms, they have studied the personal characteristics of individuals and the variables associated with the situations in which they perform and learn. The characteristics of individuals include sex, socioeconomic background, and scores on personality tests. Representative variables associated with situations include the way in which the individual's task is introduced to him, the attitude of the tester or experimenter with respect to the subject, and the conditions that lead the individual into the situation. In this chapter we shall explore some of the ways in which performance has been studied experimentally.

Perhaps the most commonly employed experimental technique for influencing human learning and performance has been verbal communication to subjects. Such communication may be given in two general ways:

1. Orienting Instructions. Before a subject begins to carry out an assigned task, the experimenter provides him with an orientation to the task. For example, the subject might be told that the task he is about to perform is an intelligence test, or that the experimenter is interested only in certain characteristics of the task, not in the subject's level of performance.
2. Reports of Performance. At one or a number of points while working on the task, the subject is given information about the level or adequacy of his performance. The purpose of performance reports and orienting instructions is to determine their influence over subjects' behavior.

Although orienting instructions have been studied through various means, virtually every experiment involving them has been aimed at influencing the subject's attitude toward the task before him. In many contexts level of performance has been found to depend on why the individual thinks he is performing the particular task, on how important he thinks the task is, and on the consequences he envisions from doing well or poorly on it. Farber (1963, p. 196) succinctly expresses the reasons why personality researchers are concerned with these considerations:

> Subjects may not know exactly what is going on in an experiment or, for that matter, in a therapeutic session, but very few have no ideas at all. They may be mistaken, or they may be concerned with irrelevant matters, such as whether participation in the experiment is worth the time and trouble, or whether the counselor is as blasé as he seems, or what's for lunch. The one thing psychologists can count on is that their subjects or clients will talk, if only to themselves. And, not infrequently, whether relevant or ir-

relevant, the things people say to themselves determine the rest of the things they do.

In a provocative experiment Orne (1962*b*, p. 777) asked intelligent college students to perform on a series of exceedingly simple and boring tasks.

. . . we tried to develop a set of tasks which subjects would refuse to do, or would do only for a short period of time. The tasks were intended to be psychologically noxious, meaningless, or boring, rather than painful or fatiguing.

For example, one task was to perform serial additions of each adjacent two numbers on sheets filled with rows of random digits. In order to complete just one sheet, the subject would be required to perform 224 additions! A stack of some 2,000 sheets was presented to each subject—clearly an impossible task to complete. After the instructions were given, the subject was deprived of his watch and told, 'Continue to work; I will return eventually.' Five and one-half hours later, the *experimenter* gave up! In general, subjects tended to continue this type of task for several hours, usually with little decrement in performance. Since we were trying to find a task which would be discontinued spontaneously within a brief period, we tried to create a more frustrating situation as follows:

Subjects were asked to perform the same task described above but were also told that when [they] finished the additions on each sheet, they should pick up a card from a large pile, which would instruct them on what to do next. However, every card on the pile read,

> You are to tear up the sheet of paper which you have just completed into a minimum of thirty-two pieces and go on to the next sheet of paper and continue working as you did before; when you have completed this piece of paper, pick up the next card which will instruct you further. Work as accurately and rapidly as you can.

Our expectation was that subjects would discontinue the task as soon as they realized that the cards were worded identically, that each finished piece of work had to be destroyed, and that, in short, the task was completely meaningless.

Quite surprisingly, Orne discovered that the subjects worked intensively on the assigned tasks for long periods of time. In their reactions to the experiment, a high percentage of them expressed a strong need to cooperate with and please the researcher. Many assumed that if the researcher assigned the particular task to them there must have been a good reason for doing so. The main goal of Orne's research was not specifically to test for the effects of preliminary instructions on performance, yet the experiment showed that a person's concept of his task or assignment was a potent force in determining how he carried it out. Through manipulations such as orienting instructions and reports of performance, personality researchers have sought to influence experimentally what subjects think about and how well they perform the tasks assigned to them.

Many examples of the important role of a person's orientations and motivations in learning and performance are observable in common life experiences. Some students perform at a high level for some teachers, but indifferently for others. Grades obtained in courses become powerful symbols of status and achievement for many students, but not for all. Praise and punishment can significantly influence the way in which children and adults attack problems. All of these examples suggest the pervasiveness of the question: How do the characteristics of people (abilities, personal dispositions, attitudes) combine with environmental conditions (highly motivating instructions) to produce levels of performance? The experimentalist cannot avoid wondering whether the laboratory can be used for a microcosmic study of the variables associated with the achievements of people. Let us examine some of the methods employed in approaching this problem.

EXPERIMENTAL METHODS OF INFLUENCING PERFORMANCE

Communications to Subjects

ORIENTING INSTRUCTIONS. Most frequently these instructions are designed to emphasize the importance of the subject's doing well on the task presented to him. They are intended to involve him personally in the task at hand. The major points stressed in such instructions are that the task is a significant one, and that it would be in the subject's best interest to achieve a high level of accomplishment on it. In some cases the experimenter may wish to suggest to the subject that personally undesirable consequences might follow inadequate performance.

These particular instructions are intended to arouse and increase the motivation to achieve. For this reason they may be designated as *achievement-orienting* instructions. But they are not the only kind of experimental instructions. Another type, *task-orienting* instructions, encourages the subject to concentrate on the task rather than on himself. In employing them, the experimenter states that the purpose of the subject's performing a particular task is not to assess him, but to uncover some of the task's properties. Although the researcher is interested in comparing subjects who are given these two types of orienting instructions, he must include a third group into his research design. This group is a control or neutral group which will not receive any special instructions. Its members will simply be told the nature of the task and then proceed immediately to perform it.

REPORTS OF PERFORMANCE. Giving the subjects seemingly accurate reports of how well they are performing has been a popular means of influencing motivation and performance. When failure reports are employed, the subject is told on one or several occasions that he is not performing up to par. A question posed by this sort of condition is: Do failure reports constitute frustrations that detrimentally affect performance, or do they serve as motivators? Success reports inform the subject that he is succeeding on an assigned task. Do these communications help or hinder his performance? As with orienting instructions, experiments dealing with reports of performance require a control group that is not given feedback.

Task Characteristics

TIME PRESSURE. One way of conceptualizing both orienting instructions and reports of performance is to say that they influence or change the subject's attitude toward himself and the task at hand. These motivational communications are usually transmitted verbally by the experimenter to the subject. Some investigators have preferred to influence subjects' performance by more impersonal means.

One procedure involves the creation of time pressure. The subject is simply told that he will have so many minutes to perform a task. For this sort of manipulation to be effective, the task must be sufficiently lengthy so that there is little likelihood that the subject can actually complete it in the allotted time.

One basis of interest in the effects of time pressure on performance is quite obvious when attention is paid to the behavior of students during examinations. Many students have great difficulty in tolerating time pressure; others seem to thrive under it. Many teachers prefer power tests (no time limit) to speed tests in order to minimize the presumed deleterious effects of time pressure. From an experimental standpoint, the personality researcher is concerned with increasing general understanding of the ways in which variables such as time pressure affect behavior.

THE NATURE OF THE TASK. Another impersonal procedure for influencing orientations to tasks is to manipulate the tasks as independent variables. Of the many characteristics of tasks, difficulty or complexity has been accorded the most frequent study. The motivational properties of easy and difficult tasks can easily be overlooked. But a difficult task is not only a challenge to the intellect, it may also have various meanings to different individuals. Some persons may be frightened by challenging intellectual assignments, others may have difficulty maintaining their interest and effort unless there are such challenges. Some students may be challenged by certain kinds of tasks, such as those involving literary, artistic, athletic, or mechanical skills, but not by others. Hence both the nature of the task and its level of complexity may have important motivational properties.

INCOMPLETED TASKS. We noted in Chapter 6 that Lewin and his followers were theoretically interested in the effects on subsequent performance of incompleted or interrupted tasks (Cartwright, 1964; Lewin, 1951). Do subjects show differences in remembering tasks that they have been permitted to complete and tasks that they have not been permitted to complete? The Zeigarnik (1927) effect mentioned in Chapter 6 indicates that memory for tasks not completed is superior to memory for those completed. From a Gestalt point of view, this has been interpreted as indicating that there is a pressure to achieve closure on incompleted tasks. In terms of procedures that may influence performance, conceivably failure to complete a task may affect not only recall of the material involved, but also performance on subsequent tasks.

The Subject

Attitudes toward tasks may be influenced by a variety of situational factors. Orne's (1962*b*) experiment well illustrates the role of one of these factors. In it the social context of the situation influenced the subject's attitudes toward the task assigned to him. Both experimental communications to subjects, such as achievement-orienting instructions, and task characteristics can be expected to influence not only a person's performance, but also the evaluation that he places on it and his level of aspiration. Each of us can probably provide several examples of how self-evaluation and aspiration contribute to level of performance. In addition, experimental procedures concerning levels of aspiration and incorporating aspects of methods that influence performance have been employed to attack the problem of personal reactions to performance situations.

When level of aspiration is used as a paradigm, the subject is asked to state his goal or level of aspiration on a task. For example, if the task were the solution of a series of arithmetic problems, the subject would tell how many problems he believed he could solve in a designated period of time. Following this, the subject would perform and then be asked to state his level of aspiration with regard to a second series of arithmetic problems.

Depending on the researcher's aim and the nature of the task employed, a series of level-of-aspiration statements might be solicited followed by performance. Two aspects of a subject's reactions to this sort of situation are most relevant to our present concern. One is the way in which an individual's level of aspiration changes throughout a performance session. Do stated levels of aspiration become more or less realistic as the subject's experience with the task at hand increases? The other is the effect of level of aspiration statements on performance levels. Does the stating of a level of aspiration constitute a goal toward which the subject strives?

A good case can be made for the two-pronged assertion that (1) persons' attitudes are influenced by the situations in which they find themselves, and that (2) these acquired attitudes in turn influence performance. An equally good case can be made for the assertion that the attitudes that people bring with them to situations influence performance. A comprehensive experimental approach to intellectual performance would seem to require attention to manipulated situational variables and task characteristics and also to the long standing attitudes and attributes of subjects. The need to incorporate individual differences, involving both personality and ability factors, into experimental studies of learning and performance seems essential. Unfortunately, it is easier to say that this need exists than to prescribe the means of isolating relevant variables. Bringing individual differences into the laboratory is just in its infancy, but a growing number of investigators are testing hypotheses about personality characteristics within laboratory contexts.

EXAMPLES OF EXPERIMENTS ON PERSONALITY AND HUMAN PERFORMANCE

ANXIETY AND PERFORMANCE. Conditions such as those defined by achievement-orienting instructions or reports of performance can be viewed as contributing to the creation of an evaluative, testlike situation. In a competitive society such as the one in which we live, persons are subjected to many evaluations and tests. What are the psychological effects of being in situations in which performance is evaluated? Do these effects, in turn, influence the performance of competitors?

Early studies dealing with this question often came up with rather equivocal results—some subjects seemed to improve under evaluative stress, others tended to show decrements, and still others were unaffected (Lazarus, Deese, and Osler, 1952). Could these different responses to evaluative conditions be approached in a more meaningful manner? Following the lead that achievement-orienting instructions define experimental tasks as competitive tests, a number of investigators have sought to assess in a psychometric manner the anxieties of individuals over taking tests (I. G. Sarason, 1960; S. B. Sarason, and Mandler, 1952; S. B. Sarason, Mandler, and Craighill, 1952).

Most of the indices in current use are straightforward; the subject is usually asked to describe, either through rating scales or true-false items, his reactions to test situations. High scores indicate that the individual describes himself as being consciously aware of high levels of anxiety while taking tests. Low scores indicate a relative lack of awareness of anxiety during tests. In general, the items of test anxiety scales deal with worry and fear about taking tests and with heightened physiological activity, for example, accelerated heart rate and sweating, before, during, and after the tests.

If these scales tap test anxiety, one might expect them to show that persons with quite different scores perform differently, depending on the conditions under which performances take place. This expectation has been tested experimentally. S. B. Sarason and his colleagues, who were the first to assess anxiety with specific reference to testing situations, confirmed it in a series of experiments (Mandler and Sarason, 1952; Sarason, Mandler and Craighill, 1952). Figure 15–1 shows the Kohs Block Design Test (1923) time scores for six trials for high and low scorers on the Test Anxiety Questionnaire (Mandler and Sarason, 1952). The Kohs Block Design Test involved concept formation and has proven useful in intellectual assessment batteries. The data plotted in Figure 15–1 are the times for solution of block design problems by high and low test-anxious college students; greater time scores indicate poorer performance. Prior to administering the Kohs test all subjects were told explicitly and with emphasis that their level of performance on the block designs would reflect their intelligence level. In view of these instructions, it seems understandable that high test-anxious subjects performed more poorly than low test-anxious subjects.

Figure 15–2 compares the performances of high and low test-anxious subjects under two orienting conditions. Half the subjects were told that they would be expected to finish (ETF) a task presented to them. The remaining half were told that they were not expected to finish (NETF) the task. The task, of which there were five trials, was the Digit Symbol Test used widely in intellectual assessment. Figure

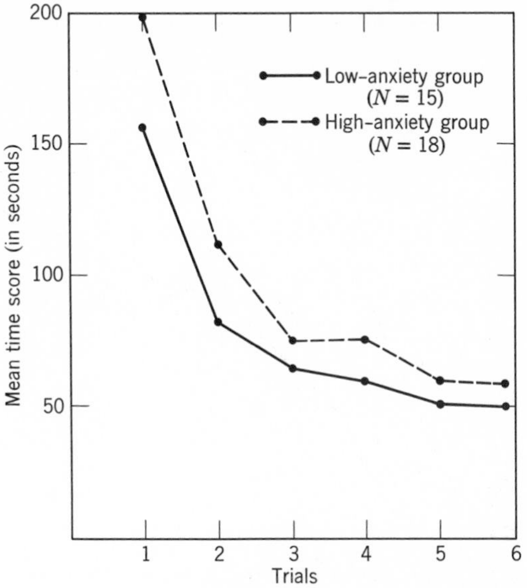

Figure **15-1** Performance curve for high-anxiety and low-anxiety groups for six trials of Kohs Block Design (after Mandler and Sarason, 1952, p. 170).

15–2 highlights two noteworthy results: (1) Low test-anxious subjects told that they would be expected to finish performed at a higher level than all other subjects, and (2) differences in performance between high and low test-anxious subjects were large under the expected to finish and small under the not expected to finish condition.

There is strong evidence that the more testlike an experimental task is made to seem, the greater the likelihood that high test-anxious scorers will perform poorly relative to low test-anxious persons under neutral or control conditions. Furthermore, many low test-anxious persons may actually show increases in performance as a function of conditions created by achievement-orienting instructions and failure reports. Thus the same experimental condition, such as achievement-orienting instructions, may have opposite effects on persons differing in test anxiety. High test-anxiety scorers seem to perform best when left alone, that is, under neutral or control conditions. Highly motivating conditions, on the other hand, facilitate the performance of low test-anxiety scorers.

An example of the type of experiment to which we are referring

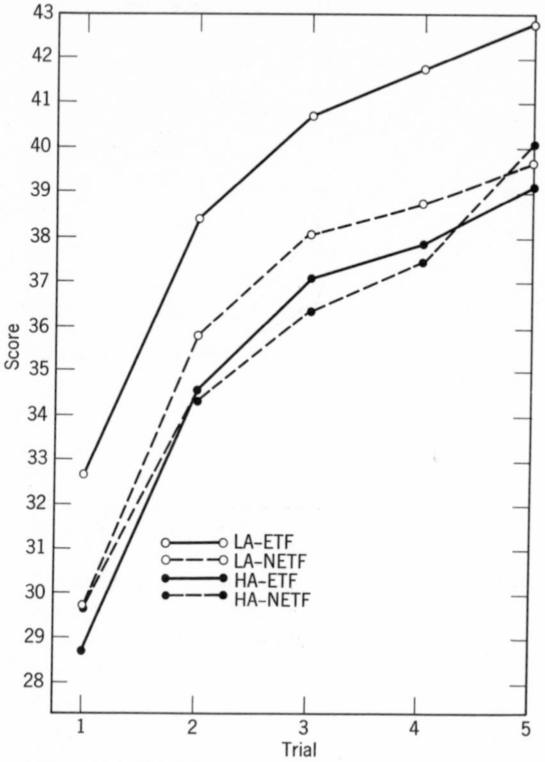

Figure 15-2 Performance curves of four experimental subgroups on digit symbol test (after Sarason, Mandler, and Craighill, 1952, p. 562).

is a study reported (I. G. Sarason, 1961, p. 166) concerning the relationship of test anxiety and orienting instructions to the solution of difficult concept formation problems. In the experiment college students were divided into high, middle, and low anxious groups on the basis of their scores on a test anxiety scale. The task required the solution of 13 difficult anagrams. Table 15–1 presents the anagrams used. Half of the subjects were told:

Ability to organize material such as the letters on the next page has been found to be directly related to intelligence level. High school students of above average intelligence (IQ greater than 100) and most college students should be able successfully to complete the task. You will have 18 minutes in which to complete it.

TABLE 15-1

Thirteen Anagrams Administered to All Subjects

1. ETLHHA
2. ETROS
3. RECMI
4. CNEGAH
5. NMGOINR
6. NSRWAE
7. SPRUUE
8. SUTCBII
9. SCLIAO
10. EVSUORN
11. RSANEO
12. IMTCELA
13. ELSAUX

From I. G. Sarason (1961), The effects of anxiety and threat on the solution of a difficult task, *J. abnorm. soc. Psychol.*, **62,** 166.

The remaining subjects were told:

> Most of you probably have worked anagrams. The task on the next page works the same way. These anagrams, however, are harder than most you have seen in books and magazines. Consequently, you may not finish all of them and you may find some of the anagrams very difficult. If this happens, don't worry about it. No one will find the anagrams easy.

Table 15–2 contains the mean (M) for each group in the experiment. Inspection of the table shows that under threat instructions, those that emphasized that performance on the anagram task was a reflection of intellectual level, the high test-anxious subjects performed at a

TABLE 15-2

Mean Number of Correct Solutions for Six Experimental Groups Divided on the Basis of Test Anxiety Scale (TAS) and Instructions

	Threat Instructions	Nonthreat Instructions
TAS	M	M
High	3.54	5.31
Middle	4.73	3.49
Low	4.92	4.04

Adapted from I. G. Sarason (1961), The effects of anxiety and threat on the solution of a difficult task, *J. abnorm. soc. Psychol.*, **62,** 166.

lower level than the middle and low test-anxious scorers. Under non-threat instructions, those that did not emphasize the anagram task as a test, high test-anxious subjects performed at a higher level than the middle and low test-anxious scorers. In view of this type of result, is it any wonder that early studies, which experimentally manipulated motivational variables but did not take into account individual differences in personal characteristics, failed to obtain consistent findings?

Another previously neglected variable, which has been related to personality and performance, is task characteristics. It will be remembered that Taylor (1951) found her anxiety scale, which dealt with general anxiety rather than anxiety specific to test situations, to be positively correlated with speed of eyelid conditioning. Eyelid conditioning as a task is quite simple—a subject either emits a conditioned eyeblink or he does not. If eyelid conditioning is thought of as a performance task, Taylor's results might suggest that anxiety facilitates performance. What would be the case if the task were more complex, more intellectual? Available evidence suggests that on some complex tasks, low scorers on the Taylor scale perform at a higher level than high scorers. However, as we saw in the Sarason (1961) study, this is not true for all complex tasks.

In some experiments a number of the variables mentioned were simultaneously studied. For example, studies of test anxiety, orienting instructions, failure reports, and task difficulty have confronted subjects with tasks of learning verbal material varying in difficulty level (I. G. Sarason, 1960). These experiments suggest that the deleterious effects on high test-anxious persons of achievement-orienting instructions and failure reports is significantly greater when the verbal learning task is difficult than when it is easy. In other words, both orienting conditions and task characteristics have a combined impact on persons who score high on the characteristic of test anxiety. A few studies have employed orienting instructions designed to allay evaluative fears (I. G. Sarason, 1958, 1961). In them subjects were urged not to worry about errors during performance. Under this condition high test-anxious subjects performed at a high level even when the task was a difficult one.

In most of the foregoing studies, the subjects were college or high school students. S. B. Sarason and his colleagues (1960) have reported on a provocative series of experiments involving assessed and manipulated variables in elementary school children. One of their goals was to compare under experimental conditions the performance of young children on intellective tasks with that of older students. To reach this goal they devised a measure of test anxiety appropriate for administration to young children and selected experimental tasks and conditions meaningful for elementary school children. Although test anxiety in young adults, adolescents, and elementary school children has been assessed with different instruments, the experimental results have seemed consistent in most respects.

Studies of experimental conditions involving anxiety inferred from psychological indices indicate the relevance of the experimental situation to the work of personality researchers. During an experiment the researcher has within his power control over the conditions under which persons respond. When he is investigating an inferred characteristic, such as anxiety, he may be able through experimental methods to create the necessary special conditions for empirically studying the relationship of the characteristic to behavior.

NEED FOR ACHIEVEMENT AND PERFORMANCE. Although there is considerable agreement that personality characteristics are related to achievement and intellectual functioning, it is not clear which ones have the greatest relevance. The nomological networks of personality constructs have not been sufficiently elaborated to permit agreement on the "best" personality variables for investigation in relation to learning and performance. Over the next several years, quite likely, different groups of investigators will concentrate their efforts on the study of particular constructs which seem to them to be most fruitful. It is not the aim in this chapter to review exhaustively all methods and constructs, but rather through appropriate examples to indicate the diversity of approaches to significant problems. The study of need for achievement provides an interesting contrast to that of anxiety. Workers who have focused on this aspect of behavior have operated on the basis of assumptions differing in some respects from those used in anxiety. Their work has also involved methodologies that differ from those used in research on anxiety.

From the discussion of the Thematic Apperception Test (TAT) (Chapter 13) it will be remembered that Murray (1938) defined several categories of needs and press which could be scored quantitatively. McClelland (1955) and a group of his colleagues selected one of the needs described by Murray, the need for achievement, for intensive examination. Their work was directed to scoring the need for achievement through content analysis of the individual's verbal responses to TATlike stimuli. Scores were then related to behavior in various experimental and naturally occurring settings (Atkinson, 1958*b*; McClelland, 1955).

It is important to bear in mind the differences in the task presented to the subject on an anxiety self-description questionnaire or rating scale, and on a need for achievement projective test. On the latter, the subject is not asked to describe himself. Rather he is asked to look at a series of pictures and write stories about what is going on in the scenes depicted, about what the characters are thinking, and about what he believes the scene's outcome might be. The scoring of need for achievement is based on such story characteristics as references to the efforts of characters to attain a high standard of excellence and to their accomplishments and goals achieved in the stories.

It seems clear that when a subject is described as possessing a degree of need for achievement on the basis of McClelland's (Atkinson, 1958*a*) procedures, an inference is being drawn from his verbal descriptions of a particular series of projective stimuli related to achievements. The reader might wonder how results of research that uses a fantasy approach to need for achievement would compare with other means of tapping the same variables, for example, a paper-and-pencil need for achievement questionnaire. However, before touching on this question, let us review some of the evidence concerning the fantasy approach to need for achievement.

One of the first investigations of need for achievement was conducted by McClelland, Clark, Roby, and Atkinson (1949). Their interest was in determining whether the conditions under which fantasy stimuli were administered affected the stories told about them. The subjects in the study took the need for achievement test after having performed a series of short, intellectual performance tasks. One group was administered the fantasy test after being led to believe that it had failed on the intellectual tasks. Another group was not given failure reports, but was tested under a relaxed condition. The experiment showed that failure reports heightened need for achievement imagery. That is, prior reports of failure increased need for achievement more than did the relaxed condition. Thus it might be reasoned that need for achievement can be regarded both as an individual difference variable and as an index sensitive to experimental manipulation.

The McClelland et al. experiment is valuable because it reflects a different orientation from the one that motivated the research on anxiety. This latter research has dealt almost exclusively with anxiety as an assessed characteristic relating to performance and learning. Need for achievement research has been directed to the question: How sensitive is the measure to experimental manipulation? It would be indeed valuable to know to what extent self-described anxiety tendencies can be influenced by experimental conditions.

Need for achievement has been related to behavior in a number of experimental investigations and high need for achievement scorers have been found to be superior in performance to low ones (Lowell, 1952). It has also been found to be significantly related to behavior outside the laboratory. Thus, there is evidence that white children score higher on need for achievement than do Negro children (Mingione, 1965); that need for achievement scores are positively correlated with occupational mobility (Crockett, 1962; Littig and Yeracaris, 1965) and that they are also positively correlated with entrepreneurial tendencies (McClelland, 1965).

An experimental study by Raphelson (1957) is particularly instructive because he employed not one, but three personality assessment scores. In addition to the need for achievement fantasy test, he also gave a group of college students the Taylor (1953) anxiety scale and the Test Anxiety Questionnaire (Mandler and Sarason, 1952). His subjects were asked to perform a complex perceptual-motor task under conditions designed to heighten a competitive attitude toward attaining a high level of performance. Raphelson's primary interest was in determining to what extent subjects of diverse personality characteristics would show different patterns of physiological response. His measure was skin conductance which is related to sweating and which has often been found to increase in stressful or competitive situations.

The hypothesis underlying the study was that the more specific personality indices were to the situation in which an individual was responding, the more predictive would they be. The study's results confirmed the hypothesis. It was found that both need for achievement and test anxiety were more strongly related to skin conductance than was general anxiety as tapped by Taylor's scale. When one considers that the Taylor scale does not deal specifically with test, competitive, or achievement situations, its inferiority as a predictor of skin conductance seems understandable. Interestingly, the most striking results came about from the joint study of need for achievement and test anxiety. High test-anxious, low need-for-achievement subjects showed much stronger skin conductance changes than did low test-anxious, high need-for-achievement subjects. This result suggests the value of multidimensional over unidimensional assessment in experimental work on personality.

Further support for this inference comes from a study reported by Feather (1961) who also assessed subjects on test anxiety and need for achievement. He used a set of four perceptual tasks, two of which were actually impossible of solution. Individual groups of subjects were given different orienting instructions about the levels of difficulty of these tasks. Some were told that the tasks were easy, others were told that they were difficult. It was found that subjects high in need for achievement and low in test anxiety persisted longer on tasks described as easy. On the other hand, subjects low in need for achievement and low in test anxiety persisted longer on tasks described as difficult.

Results such as Feather's (1961) and Raphelson's (1957) indicate that, at least in some contexts, assessment of both need for achievement and test anxiety leads to significant findings which would be obscured if only one or the other measure were employed. This raises the question of the contribution each of these individual difference variables makes to the prediction of experimental results. One possibility is that McClelland's need for achievement measure taps persons' hopes of success in and approach tendencies toward achievement situations, while test anxiety taps fear of failure or avoidance tendencies toward them (Atkinson, 1964).

Raphelson (1957) reported a correlation between test anxiety and need for achievement of −.43. Although this correlation is only moderately high, it does indicate a negative relationship between the two variables. Future research like Raphelson's and Feather's should prove of value in clarifying the relationships between these personality attributes.

One final word is in order regarding the question of different ways to assess need for achievement. Is there a high positive correlation between fantasy-inferred and self-described need for achievement? Studies in which these correlations have been computed have found, rather surprisingly, essentially no relationship between scores obtained through these different procedures (Atkinson, 1958*b*). Although the reason for the lack of relationship is by no means clear, the finding is certainly instructive. The lesson to be learned from it, to paraphrase a bit, is that one can't tell what a test measures from its title. It is therefore naive and foolhardy not to pay careful attention to the operational definitions, methods, and procedures employed in studying concepts.

At the conclusion of this chapter, it is important to bear in mind something that was mentioned earlier. We have not sought to survey comprehensively the many types of individual difference variables that have been related to human performance. Rather, we have sought to exemplify, through study of the anxiety and need for achievement variables, the efforts of personality researchers to achieve clearer understanding of the determinants and correlates of human performance. In Chapter 16 we shall continue our consideration of personality and performance from the point of view of psychoanalysis, one of the influential theoretical orientations described earlier (Chapter 2).

16

Psychoanalysis and the Study of Human Performance

The sheer number of covert processes and relationships referred to by Freud, as we saw in Chapter 2, stands in the way of studying psychoanalysis objectively and making a scientific evaluation of it. Furthermore, lack of precision in the formulation of psychoanalytic concepts makes for a situation that permits the explanation of behavior in an after-the-fact fashion rather than in a scientific manner.

Despite these criticisms, our over-all evaluation of psychoanalytic theory was favorable. We felt that Freud provided stimulation by his emphasis on the need to examine unconscious factors and by his efforts to conceptualize them. This evaluation was based on the belief that, considering the gaps in our knowledge of behavior, the significance of Freud was not that he failed to verify certain of his concepts but that he recognized the necessity of developing concepts that might do justice to both covert and overt determinants of behavior.

One's attitude in approaching a set of concepts influences the kinds of questions one raises about it. Some readers of Freud have asked: What is the validity of psychoanalytic theory? This question, which sounds quite reasonable, may, however, be misleading. Does determination of the validity of psychoanalytic theory mean the same thing as determination of the validity of a test of sales aptitude? If so, we could conclude that the question was raised out of partial lack of understanding of psychoanalysis and lack of appreciation of the complexity of human behavior. From our standpoint, the immediate question is not: What is the ultimate validity of its set of concepts?

but: Where have psychoanalytic concepts led us? This question implies others: What light has empirical knowledge shed on events hypothesized by psychoanalytic theory? What sorts of modifications in psychoanalytic concepts might extend empirical knowledge? In this chapter we shall survey several studies of human performance and learning which relate significantly to psychoanalytic ideas.

It seems clear that the laboratory is not the appropriate place to study certain aspects of psychoanalytic theory. If one were interested in the history of the individual and the stages of psychosexual development, longitudinal research and behavioral observation in natural settings would seem preferable to laboratory investigations. Similarly, if one were interested in various aspects of psychopathology and psychotherapy, clinical settings might be more appropriate than the laboratory. It seems naive to assume that all aspects of Freud's system can or should be approached from a purely experimental point of view. If we accept the limitation that laboratory investigation cannot be expected to contribute to the understanding of those concepts that do not lend themselves to experimentation, it is possible to cite a number of experimental problems whose conceptions have been strongly influenced by psychoanalytic formulations.

PSYCHOANALYTICAL CONTRIBUTIONS TO THE STUDY OF LEARNING

Most of the experimental efforts stemming from psychoanalytic concepts have centered on unconscious processes and events. Rapaport (1942), Sears (1943), and Hilgard (1952) have suggested that most of these investigations can best be described as studies of experimental psychodynamics. They are characterized by attention to intrapersonal events, and the possibility of influencing them through experimental intervention. The aspect of unconscious functioning which has most excited the imagination of personality researchers has been repression. Because so much of the experimental psychodynamics literature is concerned with the relationship of repression to learning and performance we shall use it as our major example of the laboratory approach to psychoanalytic concepts. In reviewing experimental work on repression we shall (1) trace the development of research in this field, (2) consider implications of the available evidence, and (3) evaluate some of the issues and problems which beset this area of inquiry.

At the outset it should be mentioned that because certain studies may have been labeled as experiments on repression they do not *ipso facto* parallel clinical or everyday-life examples of repression. For this reason some writers speak of experimental analogues of repression. In terms of our interests, the overriding question is not: Has "real" repression been studied experimentally? It is : *How has the experimental study of personality been influenced and furthered by the Freudian concept of repression?*

It is relevant to note that American psychology was slow to concern itself with the possible bearing of psychoanalytic concepts on the experimental study of behavior. However, by the late 1920s and early 1930s a number of psychologists were beginning to ask questions about the relationship of intrapersonal processes to learning. Certain aspects of Freud's notion of repression seemed to be particularly well suited for study within traditional laboratory contexts. At approximately the same time as psychologists were trying to "bring psychoanalysis into the laboratory," there was growing interest in discovering conditions that facilitate and hinder learning and retention. One aspect of this problem was the relationship of hedonic tone to retention. The hedonic tone of a stimulus or situation may be defined as its degree of pleasantness. Does the pleasantness of material to be learned relate to its retention? The link that some psychologists saw between this question and the concept of repression centered on Freud's hypothesis that unpleasure (anxiety) evoked the unconscious, defensive response of repression. To many investigators, studies of hedonic tone seemed a promising vehicle for experimentally testing this hypothesis.

Studies of hedonic tone typically followed a paradigm in which neutral stimuli were presented to subjects—nonsense syllables and numbers, whose recall could be measured at some later time. Associated with these neutral stimuli were other stimuli which were classified with respect to their pleasantness. For example, a foul odor might be considered as unpleasant or low in hedonic tone, and a fresh fragrance might be classified as high in hedonic tone. For brevity, these odors can be labeled as P and U odors. For further brevity, these investigations might be labelled by the not too elegant title of P-U studies.

An example of research on hedonic tone may be found in an experiment reported by Sharp (1938). In that study, three groups of subjects were presented with lists of word pairs. These word pairs were categorized according to their degree of hedonic tone or pleasantness. One list was considered to have pleasant connotations (for example, the word pair: enjoying life), one was considered to be unpleasant (for example, feeling inferior), and one was felt to be neutral (for example, carrying baskets). The aim of the study was to find out whether subjects who received the three kinds of word-pair lists would differ in recalling them. Sharp found that after 2-, 9-, and 16-day intervals the recall of pleasant and neutral words was superior to the recall of unpleasant words.

Studies of hedonic tone are instructive on a number of counts. First of all, despite the methodological weakness of many of them—an absence of needed control groups, inadequate statistical procedures, and small samples of subjects—the studies have helped to focus attention on the characteristics of learning tasks which might be related to retention. But there are reasons for second thoughts about the relationship between repression and hedonic tone. If repression is a defense against anxiety, what anxiety is aroused by a bad smell? Could there have been a semantic discrepancy between Freud's conception of anxiety as a state of unpleasure and the unpleasant stimuli employed in hedonic studies? A good case can be made for such a discrepancy. The unpleasantness of an odor or a sound is not really comparable to the unpleasantness of anxiety in significant personal situations. The major difference between these two uses of unpleasant is that a displeasing odor evokes in individuals a universal reaction of withdrawing from the stimulus. On the other hand, when Freud spoke of repression he was referring to an unconscious barring from consciousness of personally threatening stimuli, such as disturbing environmental events or frightening thoughts.

Because of this concern with personal relevance, studies tended more and more to create experimental conditions that might better arouse repression (Diven, 1937). These studies used a variety of procedures including orienting instructions and failure reports. They were of value because of their emphasis on situational conditions which may be of importance in affecting learning and performance. But here again questions were raised. What was the relevance to an understanding of unconscious processes of the finding, for example, that an individual's performance declined as a result of his failure on a prior task? Would not a more convincing demonstration of repression have been to show that (1) a subject's performance was lowered as a result of a stressful experience, like failure, and that (2) subsequently the level of performance was raised through removal of experimental repression procedures?

Zeller (1950*a*, 1950*b*) asked this question in relation to performance in a learning situation. He argued that a number of conditions had to be met for a study to be considered as an experimental analogue of repression. First of all, he argues that the researcher had to show that his experimental and control groups were comparable in learning and retention at the start of the experiment. If original differences in performance could be ruled out, Zeller contended, the researcher could proceed to a second experimental stage in which the experimental group would be subjected to a condition designed to induce repression while the control group would not. If the induction of repression were effective, the performance of the experimental group should decline, but that of the control group should remain the same or show an increase as a result of greater practice. At this point, Zeller suggested a third, hitherto unstudied condition, the lifting of repression. If it were possible to lift repression in the experimental group its performance level should go up, and at the end of the experiment, the control and experimental groups should again be comparable.

The support for Zeller's paradigm came from an experiment that he performed (Zeller, 1950*b*). His subjects were college students and their task was to learn a series of paired associates (for example, ZIK-DEM). With increasing trials subjects improved in ability to respond with the second member of the pair when the first one was exposed. Comparable performances were shown by the control and experimental groups. Three days later the subjects returned and were given a series of relearning trials. Again, comparable performance levels were obtained from both groups. At this point Zeller attempted to induce repression in the experimental group. This was done by administering the Knox Cube Test to all subjects. This test requires the subject to reproduce a pattern tapped out by the tester on a series of blocks. The task was useful to Zeller because it permitted the tester to tap either simple or complicated patterns. As a result of the difference in levels of difficulty and in comments made to the subjects, it was clear that after working on the Knox Cube Test for 15 minutes, the control subjects had been given a success condition and the experimental subjects a failure condition. In administering the failure condition, Zeller sought to avoid in any way relating failure on the Knox Cube Test to subjects' performance on the paired-associates learning task.

Immediately after performance on the Knox Cube Test the control subjects' retention was seen to be superior to that of the experimental group. After another three-day interval the retention of the two groups was again compared, and again the control group was superior to the experimental group. Zeller now instituted what he considered to be a lifting of repression. Both groups again performed on the cube-tapping task, but this time they were given a series of easy problems. Furthermore, the experimental subjects were told not only that they had succeeded but also that they had reached a level characteristic of very superior people. Zeller (1950*b*, p. 413) described the reactions of his experimental subjects at this point as follows:

> It was amazing to see the change in attitude on the part of the subject. As far as the experimenter knows not one subject doubted his (the experimenter's) statement. The entire tone of the relationship was altered. The subject was cooperative, happy, and in some cases almost euphoric. Although it was not possible to keep a genuine record of the individuals'. block tapping scores, there is little doubt that the individuals in this group exceeded the control group at this point.

Promptly following this second experience on the Knox Cube Test, another retention measure of paired associates was obtained. Now the control group was no longer superior. The retention levels of the two groups were comparable. After a final three-day interval, retention was again measured, and once more the two groups responded comparably. The results of the experiment were interpreted as indicating that the failure condition administered to the experimental subjects on one task, the Knox Cube Test, had induced repression of other aspects of an anxiety-provoking testing situation which included the previously learned paired-associates. When the repression was lifted performance returned to normal.

Although his experiment would appear to come much closer than studies of hedonic tone to getting at the repression of personally relevant material, Zeller recognized that it was not possible to rule out other interpretations. It could be argued, for example, that the differences obtained between the experimental and control groups were due to such factors as subjects' changes in attitude, interest, motivation, and cooperation rather than to repression. An evaluation of the Zeller experiment would have to be basically the same as the one offered of the hedonic tone studies. Whether repression actually occurred in his experimental group, Zeller clearly succeeded in demonstrating the effectiveness of his conditions. He showed that experimentally created conditions influenced learning. A later study replicated some of the relationships which he uncovered (Aborn, 1953).

A still more recent study carried out by Truax (1957) has contributed to further refinement in the experimental study of repression. Two aspects of his investigation merit comment. The first of these was that the task employed in assessing repression effects was specially devised to correspond to sources of anxiety for the individual subject. Truax not only attempted to approximate anxiety-provoking conditions which might lead to repression, but he also perceived individual differences in the extent to which individuals attempted to cope with anxiety through the use of repressive defenses. The second refinement was the incorporation into his experiment of an individual difference variable which he felt might reflect the tendency to use the defense mechanism of repression. His personality measure was the difference between an individual's Hysteria (Hy) and Psychasthenia (Pt) scores on the MMPI. This difference had been suggested by Eriksen (1952, 1954) as an index of the tendency to use repressive defenses. (Ericksen found that a high Hy-Pt group recalled fewer incompleted tasks and was rated as showing more repression than a low Hy-Pt group.)

Truax found this index to be significantly related to subjects' reactions to repression-inducing conditions. What Truax demonstrated most strikingly was that there were important differences among individuals in their response to conditions like those employed by Zeller. In recent years a number of investigators have also demonstrated the need to relate individual differences in repressive tendencies to behavior under experimental conditions (Byrne, 1964; Byrne and Sheffield, 1965). This suggests that certain anxiety-arousing conditions may lead to deterioration in performance for some subjects and facilitation for others. All persons may employ repression as a defense against anxiety, but the frequency with which this occurs and the types of occasions on which it does may vary from person to person.

One might conclude a discussion of the experimental study of repression as related to memory and performance by emphasizing the need for further methodological advances along the lines suggested by the work of Zeller (1950*a*, 1950*b*) and Truax (1957). Many of the problems connected with the laboratory study of unconscious processes are similar to those that concern personality research on learning and performance (Chapter 15). These include attention to (1) individual differences among subjects, (2) characteristics of the tasks on which they perform, and (3) personal or social aspects of the experimental situation.

Some writers have criticized experimentation on repression on the grounds that it is contrived and not sufficiently close to real life (Kris, 1947). This criticism seems beside the point. Researches said to deal with repression should be evaluated by the light they can shed on behavior rather than by the degree to which they can reproduce certain types of hypothesized states in the laboratory. Furthermore, the argument that laboratory behavior is basically different from behavior in the classroom, in the home, or in the office would seem to be a difficult one to defend. Certainly Freud in his writings repeatedly presented examples that were meant to show that the unconscious operates not only in some behavioral situations but in all of them.

Interest in another psychoanalytic concept, regression, has also contributed to the study of motivational factors in human performance. The most frequently cited laboratory study of regression was carried out by Barker, Dembo, and Lewin (1941). These investigators used nursery school children as subjects and investigated the relationship between frustration and regression. They observed and rated children's behavior in play situations. The experiment began with a free-play period, using standard toys and materials with which the children were familiar. The creation of frustration was begun by incorporating the standard toys with a group of new and highly attractive toys. Each child played in this situation for a period of time, after which the standard toys were separated from the new ones. Then the child was permitted to play only with the standard toys, while the new, wanted toys remained in full view, but could not be manipulated.

The major question asked by Barker, Dembo, and Lewin was: Would the level of constructiveness of children's play be different during the prefrustration and postfrustration play periods? More specifically they asked: Would frustration lead to a decrement in performance? Their findings indicated that the constructiveness and creativity of the children's play behavior declined upon separation from wanted, attractive toys. The postfrustration play was described as being more immature than the prefrustration play. These data have been interpreted as a demonstration of the psychoanalytic concept of regression because of this reversion to a lower level of functioning. Interestingly, another study showed that when pairs of close friends were put through the experimental procedure, the effects of frustration were reduced; the level of constructiveness of play did not decline to the level observed when the children were seen individually in the experimental situation (Wright, 1942).

Freud regarded regression as a process whereby objects libidinally gratifying to an individual moved from a higher to lower stage of psychosexual development. Some students might question the appropriateness of the use of the term regression in the Barker, Dembo, and Lewin (1941) studies. Differences of opinion over the meaning of their results have led to some useful clarifications of the effects of frustration on behavior. Child and Waterhouse (1952, 1953), particularly, have been concerned with clarifying this relationship. They have argued that rather than dealing with regression, the Barker,

Dembo, and Lewin study was concerned simply with the effects of frustration on performance. They contended that the play experiment demonstrated that frustration led to a deterioration in behavior; or, as they put it, to a lowering of the quality of performance of the subjects. They suggested that experimenters should explicitly devote their attention to such questions as:

1. What effects does frustration on a task have on subsequent performance of that task?
2. What effects does frustration on a task have on subsequent performance of a different task?
3. How does frustration affect the quality of a person's behavior in social and other nonperformance situations?

In discussing the concept of frustration and regression, Hilgard (1956) has offered some additional suggestions which are useful. He has distinguished among types of regression, two of which are : (1) instrumental-act regression, by which is meant an organism's reversion to a previously learned set of responses; and (2) primitivation, which refers to a general disorganization of behavior and, in Child and Waterhouse's (1952, 1953) terminology, lowering of quality of performance. Although the body of experimental data related to regression or quality of performance is at present small, it seems likely that conceptual clarifications of the type mentioned will facilitate research in this area.

One point we may legitimately raise in relation to regression and repression studies is the difficulty of devising laboratory conditions that relate directly to a person's history of anxiety experiences and defensive reactions to them. On ethical and practical grounds many extreme repression-inducing experiences cannot be created in the laboratory. However, with increasing incorporation into laboratory studies of individual difference variables which are outgrowths of personal development (for example, Truax's (1957) measure of repression) it should be possible to shed more light on the antecedents and correlates of repression responses. Although there may once have been meat on the criticism that laboratory studies of personality did not pay sufficient attention to characteristics acquired through development, this criticism does not seem to have nearly as much substance today. Personality researchers are giving increasingly greater recognition to the potential of treating personal characteristics and life history factors as independent variables.

PSYCHOANALYTIC CONTRIBUTIONS TO THE STUDY OF PERCEPTION

We have seen how repression relates to learning and performance. How does the repression concept apply to perception, the process by means of which we become aware of objects and discriminate their qualities? That repression might relate to perceptual phenomena as well as to learning and forgetting seems reasonable. Through repression, an individual might forget previously learned material and thoughts, but could not repression also serve a defensive function by barring from consciousness the perception of stimuli? One characteristic of repression is that it bars from consciousness anxiety-provoking material which may be either internal (thoughts) or external (environmental stimuli).

Just as learning experiments relating to repression deal with motivated forgetting, so do certain experiments concerning perceptual phenomena deal with motivated perceptual effects. Perhaps the most salutary influence of the repression concept on the study of perception has been the questions it has posed. For example, do motivational factors cause perceptual distortions? Anecdotal reports from everyday life seem to support a positive answer. There are also other relevant data. For example, there is evidence that accident-proneness may be related to unconscious factors. Since the perceptual component in accidents appears to be a strong one (for example, the failure of an automobile driver to see danger ahead), practical necessity suggests the need for studying the interaction of perceptual and motivational factors.

In reviewing projective tests we saw the effort to approach this interaction from a psychometric standpoint. A good place to begin the pursuit of an experimental approach to this interaction is an experiment reported by McGinnies (**1949**). The experiment involved a procedure that has been widely employed in research on perception. Subjects are shown stimuli by means of a tachistoscope and their task is to identify them. With a tachistoscope it is possible first to expose a stimulus for so short an interval of time that it would not be possible to identify it. The interval or time of presentation can be progressively increased to the point at which it would be easy for a subject to recognize the stimulus. Some of the problems that can be investigated with this sort of procedure concern the determination of thresholds (at which point can a subject barely discriminate a stimulus?), the study of the nature of the stimulus in relation to thresholds, and the assessment of individual differences in perception.

McGinnies' experiment proved stimulating because he set out to test the hypothesis that the degree to which tachistoscopically-presented stimuli arouse anxiety can influence the point at which recognition occurs. He presented subjects who were college students with a task requiring the recognition of a series of words. Each word was initially exposed for a very short period of time. The duration of presentation was gradually increased until the subject correctly identified the word. McGinnies used two types of words. He called them neutral and critical words. Neutral words were socially acceptable ones; critical words were not (to wit, *bitch, whore*). In addition to determining subjects' ability to identify these words, McGinnies obtained a measure of autonomic activity, the galvanic skin response which is usually regarded as an indicator of emotional arousal.

The results of this experiment provided much food for thought. McGinnies (1949, p. 250) found that longer exposures were required for the identification of critical or taboo words than for neutral words. Galvanic skin responses were stronger to the critical than to the neutral words. What interpretation might be placed on these empirical findings? He argued that they suggested a mechanism of perceptual defense that had the characteristics of repression:

> Perceptual defense apparently is based upon conditioned avoidance of unpleasant or dangerous stimulus objects. That the individual actully discriminates the stimulus before he fully perceives it is evident in his increased emotionality before recognition. Inimical stimuli, then, may serve as cues which are appropriately evaluated by the central nervous system even though the integration of the afferent impulses is such as to delay recognition, either through distortion or an increase in threshold or both. Almost without exception, the galvanic skin response of the observers was greatest following the final exposure of the critical words; that is, the one during which recognition occurred. Clearly, the process of perceptual defense is designed to delay the greater anxiety that accompanies actual recognition of the stimulus.

It would be convenient if McGinnies' results could be accepted at face value as a demonstration of repression with respect to perceptual performance. Whereas many psychologists accepted them as such, some did not. The skeptics not only rejected McGinnies' interpretation but suggested factors that they felt had been uncontrolled in his experiment. One of these concerned the relative frequencies in the English language of the neutral and critical words shown to subjects. It was argued that McGinnies' critical or taboo words occurred, in fact, less frequently than the neutral ones (Howes and Solomon, 1950, 1951). Was it any surprise, therefore that longer exposures were needed to identify correctly tabooed than neutral words? It was also argued that subjects might simply have been suppressing, rather than repressing, socially unacceptable responses. In terms of this argument, the stronger galvanic skin response to the tabooed than to the neutral words might have simply reflected subjects' embarrassment, rather than any unconsciously rooted sources of anxiety.

The controversy aroused by the McGinnies experiment followed the pattern mentioned earlier with regard to repression and motivated forgetting. As criticisms of pioneering efforts were made, numerous variables were suggested as possibly relevant to the controversial results and interpretations. This pattern can be observed in every area of scientific inquiry and shows the fallacy of seeking ultimate or final answers to questions. In this connection it is illustrative to examine some of the empirical work and controversy that McGinnies' experiment stimulated.

Consider the word-frequency issue. In a critique of McGinnies' perceptual defense interpretation Howes and Solomon (1950, 1951), judged the frequency of McGinnies' neutral and critical words by comparison with the Thorndike-Lorge word-count list. This lengthy list is based on the frequency of occurrences of words in written sources, such as books and magazines (Thorndike and Lorge, 1944). Howes and Solomon based their rejection of McGinnies' interpretation on the premise that he had not equated the frequency of occurrences of neutral and critical words. Certainly it seemed clear from Howes and Solomon's reports that the critical words occurred much less frequently than the neutral words.

If Howes and Solomon's critique were to be accepted uncritically, we might then be forced to conclude that McGinnies had offered a complex theory of unconscious determinism to account for results that could be handled much more parsimoniously. But the plot thickens. McGinnies responded to the criticism of his work by pointing out that the frequency of occurrence of words could be variously defined. He felt that many of his tabooed words (such as *bitch*) would occur relatively infrequently in literary sources because of their socially undesirable connotations. (Each of us probably can think of some literary sources that do not reflect this constraint.) In other words, word frequencies in various sources and among various groups could be expected to differ widely.

Wiener (1955) has reported an experiment relevant to this issue. Instead of using a tachistoscope he presented subjects with booklets containing 30 carbon copies of the same word. As the subject went through each booklet, Wiener noted the number of the copy on which the subject correctly recognized the word. Rather than comparing neutral words with taboo words, he selected one word that could be interpreted either in a neutral fashion or in terms of its socially undesirable connotations. He used the word *fairy*. To one experimental group, a list of neutral words with the fairy imbedded in it was read by the experimenter to the subjects. In the case of another group, the word fairy was imbedded in a list containing many words with sexual connotations, such as *queer* and *homosexuality*. The reading of these lists preceded the word recognition task. Clearly, word recognition was removed by Wiener as a confounding factor since he used only one word and varied the conditions associated with it.

The results did not show a repression effect. Rather, they showed that subjects who had been previously exposed to the list containing sexually related words recognized the word fairy more quickly than the group which had been exposed to the neutral list. The significance of this finding is not immediately obvious. But it does seem Wiener showed that while word meaning may be an important factor in perceptual defense studies, word frequency determined in a particular way may not alone account for results of experiments on perceptual defense. His experiment indicates the significant role that orienting conditions can play in the task of perceptual discrimination.

Another attempt to incorporate needed methodological improvements into the design of perceptual defense studies was made by McCleary and Lazarus (1949; Lazarus and McCleary, 1951). They used nonsense syllables rather than clearly meaningful material. With half of these nonsense syllables an emotional response was conditioned by administering electric shocks in contiguity with the presentation of the nonsense syllables. No shock was associated with the remaining nonsense syllables. Following this experience, the subjects were tested tachistoscopically. All of the nonsense syllables were presented on a tachistoscope with speed of presentation varied from very fast to moderately slow. During the interval between the exposure of each nonsense syllable and the subject's response (which indicated whether he had recognized the word exposed) the galvanic skin response was recorded. It is important to note that no shocks were administered during the tachistoscopic part of the experiment. The dramatic finding reported by McCleary and Lazarus was that, even in those cases in which the speed of exposure was too fast for subjects to discriminate correctly what had been exposed on the tachistoscope, there were differences in galvanic skin responses associated with the shocked and nonshocked stimuli. To the previously shocked nonsense syllables, subjects showed heightened galvanic skin responses—even though they could not report on a verbal level what the stimulus had been. McCleary and Lazarus concluded that their shocked subjects had at an unconscious level been able to discriminate the emotionally loaded, previously shocked nonsense syllables. This unconscious discrimination they called subception.

We shall not attempt here to explore all of the aspects of unconscious motivation as it may relate to perception (Eriksen, 1958). Much more might be said about the controversies and procedures related to issues such as: Should the phenomenon of perceptual defense be described as repression or suppression? Is there really a phenomenon of subception? However, the important point is that psychoanalytic notions such as repression and unconscious determinism have contributed to the development of a burgeoning and promising area of experimental work on perceptual processes. Since recognition responses and discrimination are such pervasive aspects of behavior, it would seem worthwhile to pursue many of the leads provided by the work performed so far on unconscious motivation and perception. Among the variables that seem particularly germane are: (1) characteristics of the stimuli presented to the subject (words, nonsense syllables); (2) orienting cues provided to him (the instructions administered); (3) degree to which the material is personally relevant (does the material relate to areas of conflict experienced by the individual?); (4) personality characteristics of subjects; and (5) personal aspects of the experimental situation.

Before leaving the topic of psychoanalytic concepts and perception, a word should be said about a contribution that has been made by the ego psychologists. Mention was made in Chapter 3 of the efforts of ego psychologists to expand the scope of psychoanalytic theory to include nondefensive as well as defensive modes of response to situations. Psychoanalysts such as Hartmann (1958) and Erikson (1950) have emphasized the need for study of what has been called the ego's conflict-free zones or functions. This suggestion grows out of Freud's conception of the ego as the agency through which the individual engages in commerce with the environment. A number of writers have urged the development of closer ties between traditional research areas within psychology and the ideas of psychoanalysis. Evidence that this is occurring in the field of perception has been coming to the fore.

Among the leaders in encouraging attempts to study experimentally aspects of the hypothesized conflict-free ego functions has been Klein

(1956, 1958; Gardner et al., 1959). He and his colleagues have conducted a number of studies of the relationship of individual differences in perceptual style to task performance. The assumption underlying this effort has been that just as there appear to be individual differences among persons in terms of their repertories of conflict-related mechanisms, so is it likely that there are individual differences in conflict-free areas.

The work of Klein has led to the suggestion that there are at least two types of perceptual style, leveling and sharpening. Levelers are individuals who have relatively great difficulty in solving problems involving fine discriminations and estimations. Sharpeners, on the other hand, do relatively well on problems that require careful attention to detail. According to Klein, sharpeners seem more able than levelers to attend closely to stimulus boundaries. Levelers appear to perform better than sharpeners on tasks requiring the subject to disregard or ignore irrelevant stimuli. Leveling and sharpening, from this view, might tentatively be regarded as cognitive styles that need not be related to anxiety and conflict. However, other evidence suggests that levelers and sharpeners do show differences in terms of personality pattern (Steele, 1961). Levelers have been described as emphasizing the defense of repression. Sharpeners have been described as compulsive, obsessive, and greatly concerned with order and details.

These descriptions are provocative because they suggest an interaction between anxiety-aroused ego defenses and presumed conflict-free ego functions. For example, it may be that repressers who are levelers and who are not disabled by underlying anxiety, may actually excel at certain tasks, particularly those requiring the "repression" of irrelevant aspects of stimulus situations. Perhaps the most exciting aspect of this new research area of ego psychology is the possibility it holds for at least a partial rapprochement between traditional psychological approaches to thinking and problem solving, and traditional psychoanalytic preoccupations with anxiety, conflict, and defense. If this line of investigation can fulfill the promise that many perceive in it, our understanding of the whole, unsegmented individual will be greatly increased.

The work of Klein, Gardner, and others suggests that persons' reactions to perceptual tasks may provide useful measures of individual differences for the personality researcher. An example of such a task is one that requires the subject to isolate an object from its background. Another requires the subject to maintain his perceptual orientation in an experimentally tilted room. Scoring responses made in situations such as these are not so convenient as scoring an MMPI.

These situations, in fact, do not easily fit the traditional stereotype of a psychometric instrument. Behavior in them, however, can be quantified and used for purposes of prediction (Vernon, 1952). This demonstrates the desirability of not restricting the definition of individual difference variables exclusively to tests such as those described in Part 2.

Cognitive as well as perceptual styles have been subjected to research. Exploration of them has also been influenced by psychoanalytic theory which, because of its emphasis on persons' thought processes, can truly be considered to be a cognitive approach to behavior. An example of a cognitive style that has been explored by researchers is one that relates to differences between analyzers and synthesizers. Analyzers are persons who are particularly adept at breaking up events into their components; synthesizers are particularly adept at integrating parts into meaningful wholes.

The possibility that conflict-free cognitive and perceptual styles and assessed personality characteristics are not unrelated, but rather intersect, is demonstrated by an investigation reported by Kogan and Wallach (1964). These investigators were concerned with problems related to cognitive processes in decision-making. How do people reach decisions? How much risk are they willing to tolerate in making decisions? Kogan and Wallach approached questions such as these by studying subjects' behavior in experimental situations in which degrees of risk in making decisions were analyzed. They found that there were easily noticeable individual differences among subjects in their willingness to make high-risk decisions. But this type of cognitive behavior was found to be complexly related to subjects' anxiety and defensiveness as inferred from personality tests and according to their sex. Variables such as these may be referred to as *moderator variables* when they influence the correlations between other variables. For example, Kogan and Wallach found that the correlations between variables related to the decision-making process were quite different for male and female subjects characterized by particular patterns of anxiety and defensiveness scores.

Let us now reiterate some points made earlier. Psychoanalytic concepts have stimulated many hypotheses and orientations in experimental personality research. We have suggested that the importance of this contribution should be evaluated primarily in terms of the fruitfulness of this research in furthering the development of an objective study of the person rather than as a means of validating psychoanalytic theory.

In view of (1) the complexity of human behavior, (2) the complexity of psychoanalytic theory, and (3) the likelihood that, as in the case of all pioneering theoretical efforts, many aspects of the psychoanalytic theoretical framework are in error, the idea of verifying psychoanalytic theory *in toto* seems to be a naive one.

Although the body of satisfactory experimental investigations of hypotheses relating to psychoanalytic concepts is small, the number appears to be on the increase and the level of sophistication to be rising. Recognizing the need to temper optimism with proper respect for the methodological problems involved in studying unconscious events, we still feel that the field of experimental psychodynamics is a distinctly promising one. Psychoanalysts, whose activities have been primarily clinical, quite likely would approach the empirical study of psychoanalytic concepts in different ways from those described here. But as Hilgard (1952, pp. 44–45) has so aptly commented:

> Whatever the psychoanalysts do about research, the obligation is clearly upon experimental, physiological and clinical psychologists to take seriously the field of psychodynamics, and to conduct investigations either independently or in collaboration with psychoanalysts. It is a tribute to Freud and his psychoanalytic followers that the problems faced by psychologists in their laboratories have been enormously enriched by the questions the analysts have taught us to ask.

That the nature of psychoanalytic theory as well as the study of experimental psychodynamics will change as we obtain more empirical knowledge seems to be a foregone conclusion. Freud (1953, pp. 129–130) made this point in the following manner:

> . . . Psychoanalysis is not, like philosophies, a system starting out from a few sharply defined basic concepts, seeking to grasp the whole universe with the help of these and, once it is completed, having no room for discoveries or better understanding. On the contrary, it keeps close to the facts in its field of study, seeks to solve the immediate problems of observation, gropes its way forward by the help of experience, is always incomplete and always ready to correct or modify its theories. There is no incongruity (any more than in the case of physics or chemistry) if its most general concepts lack clarity and if its postulates are provisional; it leaves their more precise definition to the results of future work.

CONCLUDING COMMENTS CONCERNING PERSONALITY AND HUMAN PERFORMANCE

Human performance seems clearly to be more than a matter of abilities and skills applied to tasks. Indeed, the assumption that abilities, skills, and intelligence are clearly independent of personality factors is open to serious question. Many of the experiments that we have reviewed showed that groups of initially comparable persons might perform at quite different levels on a variety of tasks as a result of specially created situational factors. These factors are important because they influence the meaning of the performance situation for the individual.

The influential role of persons' interpretations of situations and tasks can be seen in many everyday life experiences. Culturally deprived children perform poorly on intellectual tasks at least in part because these tasks do not meaningfully fit into the world in which they live. The performance of many individuals shows a marked decline because of their response to personally upsetting experiences. Many older persons' performance deteriorates sharply at retirement because of the frightening connotations which they attach to that event in life. Many persons show marked increases in performance when placed in situations that provide incentive and motivation.

The study of personality and human performance is aimed at explicating the ways in which personal dispositions and environmental events combine to shape the achievements of people. The complexity of this problem makes it foolhardy to expect simple, easily generalized solutions. The combination of assessment and experimental techniques that we have described does, however, seem to provide a worthwhile vehicle for studying the problem.

17

Personality and Verbal Behavior

Intellectual achievement is only one aspect of the individual's total behavior. Most of the studies mentioned in Chapters 15 and 16 dealt with the conscious attempts of people to solve problems presented to them. Another aspect of human behavior, language, takes a somewhat different tack.

During the early stages of language development, the use of words may adhere closely to an achievement pattern. The child's task is to acquire words. Anyone who has observed the two-year-old incorporate a new word into his vocabulary cannot help but be impressed and amused at the fervor with which he approaches the acquisition of language—and the joy he experiences when he is successful. However, as the child's language repertory broadens, his preoccupation with it declines and he begins to be less self-conscious in speaking. For the adult, speaking may often appear to be an automatic process. The powerful role of learning in the acquisition of language is fairly evident. To make this assertion by no means exhausts the ways in which language may be studied from a psychological point of view. Assessment researchers, we saw, use the verbal productions of persons as bases for predicting behavior. Thus, self-descriptions in the form of responses to interviews, questionnaires, and paper-and-pencil tests have been related to many aspects of human functioning. Similar attempts have been made with projective techniques and other kinds of personality instruments.

However, if verbal behavior can be regarded as a basis for predicting behavior, it becomes legitimate and important to ask how verbal behavior itself may be influenced. In Chapter 15 we alluded to this matter while discussing the work of McClelland et al. (1949);

these researchers investigated conditions bearing on fantasy responses to need for achievement stimuli. In this chapter we shall explore the experimental approach to verbal behavior more thoroughly from the standpoint of the personality researcher.

EXPERIMENTAL METHODS OF INFLUENCING VERBAL BEHAVIOR

Experimental attempts at isolating variables that influence verbal behavior have followed a number of paths. We shall consider three of these, the effects on verbal behavior of (1) deprivation conditions, (2) orienting communications, and (3) events that occur during verbal responding.

DEPRIVATION CONDITIONS. Is the behavior of the individual affected by major changes in his pattern of living? Intuitively, one would suppose that major changes in life patterns certainly influenced behavior. But in what ways? One technique used to approach this question experimentally involves depriving persons of selected aspects of everyday living. A type of deprivation having implications for the study of personality is the withholding of biological necessities such as food, water, and sleep. Another type drastically reduces the number of environmental and sensory stimuli impinging on the individual. From the point of view of verbal responding, we shall be interested to learn how deprivation conditions affect what people say about themselves, others, and the stimuli in their environment. We shall look at some of the empirical evidence related to this issue.

ORIENTING COMMUNICATIONS. We observed in Chapter 15 that achievement-orienting instructions given to subjects before they worked on a task could significantly influence their performance levels. Other types of orienting communications have been used to study changes in attitudes, self-description, and verbal responding. Their role in the study of behavior is basically the same as that played by deprivation conditions; they contribute to evaluating the effects of experimentally manipulated, prior experiences on verbal expression. Among the examples of research directed to this problem that we shall examine will be several social psychological studies of attitude change.

EVENTS THAT OCCUR DURING VERBAL RESPONDING. It is not difficult to show that behavior may be influenced by events occurring prior to responding. These may be such events as orienting conditions that terminate before responding begins, or they may be states such as hunger that begin prior to the onset of responding and continue through it. Another class of events are those that occur *while* the individual is responding. These might be rewards or punishments for the emission of particular responses. We shall mention several lines of research that reflect interest in this approach to the manipulation of verbal behavior.

Examples of Experiments on Personality and Verbal Behavior

THE EFFECTS OF DEPRIVATION. Among the personality instruments studied in relation to states of social or biological deprivation, projective tests have been the most widely used. The most probable reason is the suspicion that their relatively high degree of ambiguity gives deprived subjects the widest latitude in expressing thoughts and concepts related to need.

One of the early studies in this area was performed by Sanford (1936). He investigated the effects of food deprivation on word associations and responses to TAT-like pictures. His subjects, children between the ages of 7 and 11 years, were given the personality tests before and after meals. The major finding was that twice as many food-related responses were given before meals as after. A second study using college students as subjects showed that the longer the period of food deprivation, the greater were the number of responses related to food (Sanford, 1937). Levine, Chein, and Murphy (1942) reported findings in line with these results.

Research by McClelland and Atkinson (1948, 1955) also was related to the study of projective expression of needs. These investigators withheld food from groups of candidates in a submarine training school for periods of 1, 4, and 16 hours respectively. They found significantly different responses to ambiguous stimuli between the 1- and 4-hour groups and between the 1- and 16-hour groups, but not between the 4- and 16-hour groups. The differences showed that the 4- and 16-hour groups gave more responses involving food-related objects, such as knives and plates, than did the 1-hour group. This sort of result did not hold for responses involving food itself. This suggests that perceptual responses of people deprived of food do reflect their states of deprivation, but not necessarily in direct and obvious ways.

The food deprivations in these studies were by no means extreme. This fact may account in part for the lack of significant differences between the 4- and 16-hour deprived subjects. Perhaps the most comprehensive experiment on food deprivation was the one conducted by

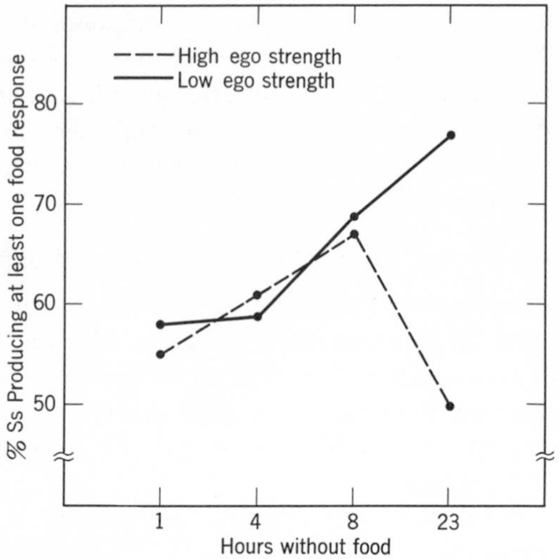

Figure 17-1 The influence of ego strength upon the relationship of food associations to time without food (after Epstein, 1961, p. 466).

Keys, Brozek, Henschel, Mickelson, and Taylor (1950). Their subjects were conscientious objectors who agreed to a six-month period of semistarvation. Each subject lost more than 20 per cent of his body weight over the six-month interval. Most of the time the subjects were extremely hungry. Under this drastic deprivation regimen food came to dominate their lives. They talked about food, fantasied about food, and even fought about food. Much of their thinking concerned visions such as devouring sumptuous platters of food. Observations of their personal behavior indicated marked decreases in sociability and pleasantness, and a decline in sex drive. It is noteworthy that responses to projective tests did not show progressive changes corresponding to the length of time of deprivation.

This semistarvation experiment provides an interesting contrast to studies of relatively mild deprivations. It suggests the need to keep in mind the severity of deprivation in generalizing about the behavioral effects of deprivation. Its findings bear many similarities to accounts of verbal and social behavior among populations subjected to famine and chronic food shortages. A complicating factor in experimental studies of food deprivation, where deprivation periods are relatively short, is that significant results might be due as much to the set created by participating in such an experiment as to actual food deprivation. Thus knowing that one is going to be deprived of food for four hours may lead to a preoccupation with food out of all proportion to the biological effects of the deprivation period.

Another possibly important factor in response to food deprivation is the individual differences in personality characteristics. Epstein (1961) deprived subjects of food for 1, 4, 8, and 23 hours. He divided the subjects into high and low ego strength groups on the basis of scores derived from their responses to the Rorschach test. The index of ego strength he used is a function of the perceptual accuracy and complexity of responses to inkblots. Figure 17-1 shows the percentages of subjects who gave at least one food response to the inkblots. It is clear that the major differences occurred among those deprived of food for 23 hours. In this group high ego strength subjects showed a sharp percentage drop in food responses not found for any other group of deprived subjects. Epstein interpreted this to mean that persons high on ego strength were more successful than those of low ego strength in inhibiting responses related to the hunger drive.

Another of Epstein's observations has particular interest for the student of self-reports. Epstein had each subject rate his degree of hunger at the end of the deprivation period. Figure 17-2 shows the relationship of these ratings to time of deprivation. There clearly was no simple linear relationship between self-rated hunger and period

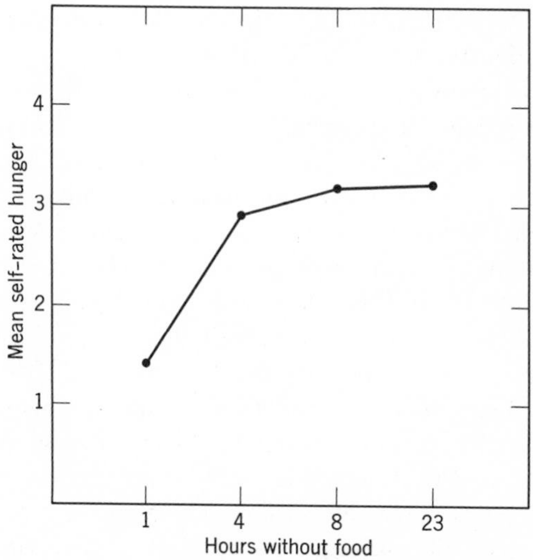

Figure 17-2 Self-rated hunger as a function of time without food (after Epstein, 1961, p. 465).

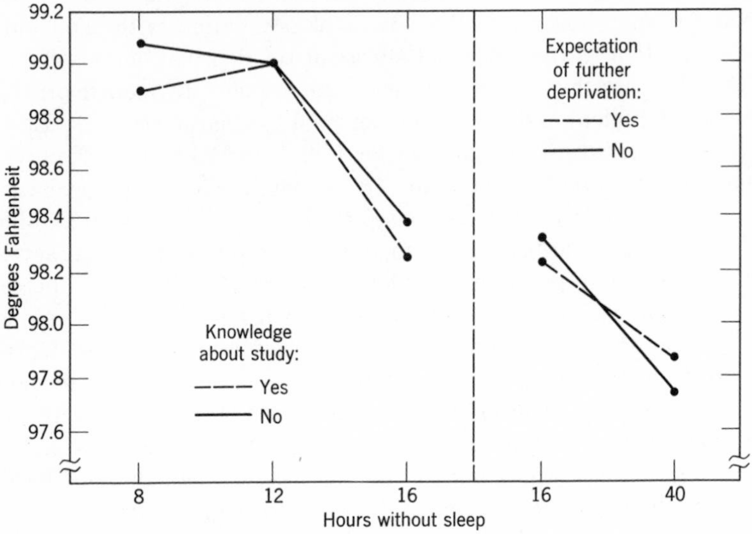

Figure 17-3 Body temperature as a function of time without sleep (after Nelson, 1961, as presented in Epstein, 1962, p. 150).

of deprivation. Although there was a large increase in rated hunger between the one and eight hour deprivation periods, a leveling-off occurred thereafter. Thus self-descriptions do not necessarily show parallelism with deprivation periods.

This lack of parallelism was shown in a study by Nelson (1961) in which the independent variable was time of deprivation of sleep. In this experiment subjects were deprived of sleep for eight, twelve, and sixteen hours. Because of the possibility that subjects' attitudes about deprivation might be relevant, half of the subjects were explicitly told that the experiment pertained to the effects of sleep deprivation. The remaining subjects were not given this information. Finally, the subjects were further subdivided on the basis of one other variable. This was whether or not they were told that there would be additional hours of sleep deprivation beyond the ones expected. At the end of the deprivation period all subjects were given a TAT-type test containing stimuli designed to evoke story themes related to sleep.

For our purposes three sets of data are especially relevant. These are the physiological concomitants of sleep deprivation, self-ratings of degree of sleepiness, and the amount of emphasis on the theme of sleep in TAT-type stories. Figure 17-3 shows the decline in body temperature with increasing hours of sleep deprivation. This result is in accord with known relationships in the biology of sleep deprivation. Figure 17-4 shows subjects' self-ratings of sleepiness at the end of the deprivation period. Those subjects who were not told the purpose of the experiment showed increases in self-rated sleepiness. The opposite seemed to be the case for subjects given this information. Figure 17-5 shows the relationship between the emphasis on sleep in TAT stories and sleep deprivation. Nelson scored sleep emphasis through a content analysis procedure. As can be seen from Figure 17-5, subjects who were enlightened about the experiment introduced more themes involving sleep than did the other subjects. There were also differences in sleep emphasis between subjects expecting further deprivation and those not expecting it.

These results provide a basis for the inference that physiological responses to biological deprivation, self-description, and fantasy descriptions do not go hand in hand. The results do, however, support the conclusion that knowledge given explicitly or implicitly about the

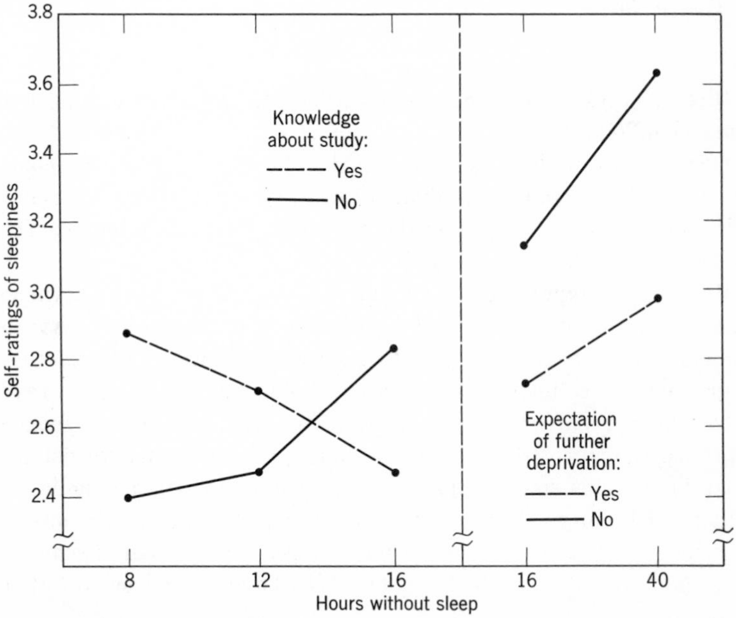

Figure 17-4 Self-ratings of sleepiness as a function of time without sleep, goal availability, and sleep set (after Nelson, 1961, as presented in Epstein, 1962, p. 150).

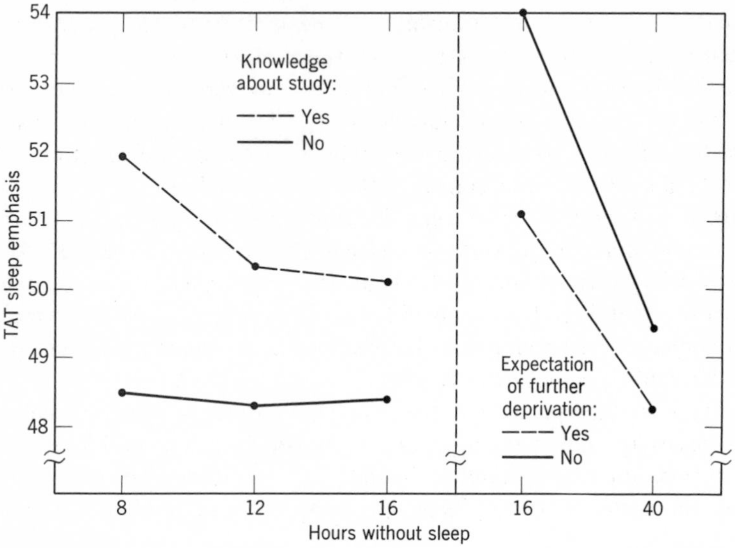

Figure 17-5 Thematic sleep responses as a function of time without sleep, expectation of further deprivation, and sleep set (after Epstein, 1962, p. 152).

nature of an experiment can create orientations and preoccupations of marked influence.

Our final example of research on the effects of deprivation concerns the withholding from individuals of sensory stimulation. Sensory deprivation might be viewed as the extremest form of ambiguous stimulation imaginable (Heron, 1957).

Both physiological and psychological researchers have shown great interest in the effects of prolonged periods of monotony. Available evidence suggests that prolonged sensory deprivation (for example, 24 hours) has a deleterious effect on psychological functioning. Investigators have reported such aberrations as hallucinations or false perceptions, thought disturbances, and child-like emotional responding.

Hallucinations under sensory deprivation have in particular been a focus of inquiry. Subjects in sensory deprivation experiments often describe vivid and unusual visual images. Freedman, Grunebaum, Stare and Greenblatt (1962, pp. 112–115) have quoted several of these accounts:

[Subject No. 21] The herd of elephants. Oh, that was pretty, that came very spontaneously. It was just sort of elephants in black, with pink and blue and purple . . . they were moving. The picture was moving as if it were a close-up, sort of a backdrop . . . the elephants were grey . . . the background was pink . . . they weren't real elephants, because they were more like cutouts.

. . .

[Subject No. 28] Yeah, they were sort of greyish-black socks. It was a white shelf about that big. About three feet wide and two feet deep and just covered with a mountain of socks. The significance of that is that my clothes are kept in that type of arrangement . . . that might possibly be the connection.

. . .

[Subject No. 23] I was getting hungry. I . . . saw sliced turkey on a plate. It was very, very brief.

. . .

[Subject No. 30] I did see one thing . . . uh . . . a very bright green pasture or lawn. I'm not quite sure which, and that was fleeting, too. Just a broad open expanse. Just green grass.

. . .

[Subject No. 19] "One of the more peculiar images that I saw with music was . . . I was looking up at a wood shelf; not very big, and watching the shelf, and listening to the music, and then the shelf started to wave in rhythm to the music in a very plastic fashion."

. . .

[Subject No. 26] . . . they were just black and white, but very white faces, theatrical. There was a Chinese lady with a white face and the black hair with pins in it, and, uh, she was . . . they had these sliding kind of doors they have in Japan . . . She was motioning someone within, and so, I tried to move forward and I got a better look at the lady; but I tried to look at who, what, she was motioning to. When I tried to look into the room, the whole thing went, and that was it.

. . .

[Subject No. 19] . . . abstract images of just, you know what a panelling might look like, of the French panelling with one box set inside of another in depth . . . a whole long line of these things at angles to each other . . . sort of a nice brownish (color) . . . more distinct than I'd seen before . . . probably greater detail than it's been possible to see it.

Psychological study of the effects of sensory deprivation has involved a variety of dependent variables, among them, performance on intelligence and personality tests and self-reports in interviews. It seems clear that loss of contact with a meaningful and changing environment can have noticeable and sometimes dramatic consequences. The study of sensory deprivation is of special psychological interest on two counts. One relates to the behavioral effects of deprivation;

verbal reports by subjects of hallucinatory experiences are an example. The other concerns the sensory deprivation experiment as a particular type of situation in which individual differences come into play. As we have indicated, in a number of contexts subjects' attitudes and set toward the task defined for them can be potent factors in determining their behavior.

An experiment reported by Orne and Scheibe (1964) provides strong support for this assertion. These investigators suggested that some reportedly dramatic effects of sensory deprivation might have been due as much to the subject's expectations of what was going to happen as to sensory deprivation *per se*. Orne and Scheibe noted that in some experiments subjects were required to sign statements releasing the experimenter from responsibility in the event of harmful, lasting effects, resulting from sensory deprivation. In other experiments potential subjects were subjected to psychiatric screening. Most of the facilities in which sensory deprivation experiments have taken place have observation windows and microphones. They also have "panic buttons" which, when pressed, lead to the "release" of the subject from the deprivation condition. Finally, subjects are often asked to report any unusual thoughts, visions, and mental experiences, while undergoing sensory deprivation.

Orne and Scheibe argued that these aspects of sensory deprivation experiments, *by themselves,* could produce some of the dramatic effects attributed to the deprivation of sensory stimuli. To test this possibility Orne and Scheibe (1964) performed an experiment that was aimed at finding out whether manipulating the orienting instructions and conditions during the experiment could produce the same effects as sensory deprivation. It is important to realize that their experiment did not involve actual sensory deprivation. Rather, it was aimed at creating conditions which might lead to effects usually ascribed to sensory deprivation.

Two groups were compared in the experiment. Each subject in the experimental group was greeted by an experimenter dressed in a white medical coat. He was then asked questions about his medical history. In the room was a tray marked "emergency tray." It contained drugs and medical instruments. The subject was asked to sign a release form and his blood pressure was taken. In the "isolation chamber" there was a microphone and a prominently placed "emergency alarm." The subject spent four hours in this "chamber" which could in no way be construed as a sensory deprivation cubicle. The "chamber" was not sound shielded and noises from adjacent rooms could be easily heard. As the following instructions Orne and Scheibe, (1964, p. 5) indicate, the subject was not severely restricted in terms of his activities:

> The experiment for which you have volunteered has as its object the determination of the psychological consequences of a special kind of deprivation procedure.
>
> There are three parts to the experiment: Testing Period I, the Experimental Deprivation Condition, and Testing Period II. You will receive special instructions in the testing periods.
>
> During the deprivation period, which will last an undisclosed length of time, you will have an optional task involving adding numbers, the full instructions for which will be explained once we enter the chamber.
>
> While you are in the chamber, you will be under constant observation. Also, there will be a microphone through which anything you might say will be recorded. It is important that you report your experiences freely and completely. You are not expected to talk a great deal, but you should report any visual imagery, fantasies, special or unusual feelings, difficulties in concentration, hallucinations, feelings of disorientation, or the like. Such experiences are not unusual under the conditions to which you are to be subjected.
>
> If at any time you feel very discomforted, you may obtain release immediately by pressing the button which I will show you once we enter the chamber ["by knocking on the window," for control subjects]. Do not hesitate to use this button if the situation becomes difficult [this sentence deleted for control subjects]. However, try to stick it out if you can.
>
> Should you feel upset, or should anything untoward develop, a physician is immediately at hand [this sentence deleted for control subjects].
>
> Remember, I should like you to pay special attention to any special visual or other sensations, or feelings of disorientation, and to report these experiences as they happen.
>
> Do you have any questions?

The control subjects were treated in the same way as the experimental subjects except for certain differences. The experimenter wore a business suit rather than a white coat and behaved toward the subject in a less formal manner than toward the experimental group. A medical history was not taken, the "emergency tray" was absent, and the subject was told that he was in a control group of a sensory deprivation experiment. It was explained to him that the usual apparatus of sensory deprivation experiments—translucent goggles, arm gauntlets, white noise, soft bed, and restricted activity—were not to be used in the control group. In addition to a four-hour confinement in the experimental room and the prior conditions and instructions, all subjects were administered a battery of cognitive and perceptual tests.

What influence did the experimental conditions have on the behavior of subjects during the four-hour period? There were many clear-cut behavioral differences between the experimental and control groups. More sensory deprivation "symptoms" were found among the experimental than among the control subjects. These symptoms included perceptual abberations, irritability, intellectual dullness, anxiety, and spatial disorientation. These descriptions by Orne and Scheibe (1964, pp. 10–11) suggest the direction of the differences:

The control group subject typically started his isolation period by inspecting the room, looking through the drawers in the desk, then settling in one of the chairs, and beginning to add the numbers. After this, the pattern of activity would generally consist of long periods of repose interspersed with moderate amounts of activity on the serial additions. These subjects gave the impression, while in the chamber, of being in every way relaxed and in a pleasant frame of mind. The rate of verbalization was lower for control than for experimental subjects; typically there was but a single rather long comment at the beginning telling the experimenter how the subject intended to occupy his time while in the chamber.

In marked contrast to the repose of the controls was the general behavior of the experimental subjects. They usually began the experiment in much the same way as controls: inspection followed by some adding of numbers. But, after the first hour there would ensue a marked restlessness, a decrease in the performance of serial additions, frequent comments of displeasure at some aspect of the experience, or remarks indicating concern over lack of time sense. Occasionally experimental subjects would try to sleep, but with little success. Some exercised, while others undertook an intense and minute inspection of the room. Viewed in relation to the controls, these subjects gave an impression of almost being tortured. While the control group seemed to alternate between quiet contemplation and work with numbers, experimental subjects seemed to fluctuate between periods of unpleasant restlessness and abstract, vague periods of total inactivity.

Since the experiment carried out by Orne and Scheibe did not in fact include a sensory deprivation condition, caution must be exercised in interpreting its results. It does seem, though, that actual sensory deprivation is not required to create states in individuals that seem comparable to those reported in sensory deprivation experiments. Thus it seems that changes in behavior, including persons' self-reports and reports about their environment, can be noticeably influenced by specially created orienting conditions. Orne and Scheibe did not include individual differences in personal characteristics as independent variables. But work in other areas suggests that characteristics brought by persons to a sensory deprivation-type situation might well influence their reactions to orienting conditions and to actual sensory deprivation.

ATTITUDE CHANGE. How we feel toward persons, institutions, and objects may reveal quite a bit about ourselves. Because of this likelihood, many paper-and-pencil questionnaires include items of the type: People with mental problems should be kept in hospitals.

Such items refer to human attitudes by reflecting beliefs, feelings, and tendencies to respond to aspects of the environment. Much verbal behavior, whether in the form of responses to questionnaires or of expressions in everyday life, can be viewed as reflections of attitudes held with varying degrees of fervor. Two questions seem especially important to psychologists interested in personality and social behavior: How do attitudes influence social behavior? How may attitudes themselves be influenced? Because of this chapter's interest in verbal responses as dependent variables we shall concern ourselves primarily with the second question and merely mention that there is considerable evidence of attitudes significantly affecting social behavior.

The phenomenon of attitude change is not so much a question of whether it occurs as of what sorts of events and manipulations bring it about. Anyone who follows the periodic reports of public opinion polls knows that attitudes change—sometimes dramatically. Researchers, particularly social psychologists, have sought to specify some of the factors which engender these changes (Krech, Crutchfield, and Ballachey, 1962).

A number of variables that relate to attitude formation and change have been isolated. These include the sources of information available to persons (newspapers, teachers), the range of experiences available to them, their personal needs and self-attitudes, the degree to which others share their needs and attitudes, and their group affiliations. Much of the research on attitude change has been concerned with two problems: (1) strengthening attitudes already held, and (2) changing the direction of attitudes to which people adhere.

A widely used method of inducing attitude change has been to assess attitudes at two points in time and to intersperse between them orienting conditions and communications designed to effect changes in beliefs, feelings, and opinions. An experiment by McGuire (1960, p. 346) illustrates the procedure. At the outset of the study, attitudes toward sets of logically related issues were assessed. This was done by administering 16 sets of three syllogistically related propositions. For example:

. . . Students who violate any regulation that has been made to safeguard the lives and property of other students will be expelled; the regulations against smoking in the classrooms and corridors were made to safeguard the lives and property of the student; students who violate the regulation against smoking in the classrooms and corridors will be expelled.

These three propositions were placed at scattered points throughout the questionnaire and the subject's task was to indicate degree of agreement with them.

Following administration of the questionnaire, each subject was given 16 messages, each of which supported the validity of one of the propositions in each of the syllogisms. These messages were endorsed by established experts. The rationale for the experiment was that it bore on people's ability to comprehend expert discussions of controversial issues. After the messages were given to subjects, attitudes were reassessed through readministration of the questionnaire. McGuire found that attitudes of subjects changed not only on the propositions for which experts' supporting statements had been presented, but also on related issues not specifically referred to in the messages. When the attitude questionnaire was administered one week later, the amount of attitude change was even greater. Thus, there seemed to have been a "seeping-in" effect.

Another study demonstrating the relevance of time was carried out by Hovland and Weiss (1951). They presented opinion questionnaires to subjects before, immediately after, and four weeks after receiving experimental communications about selected topics. The independent variable in the study was the credibility of the source of communications to the subjects. For half of the subjects the communications were made by sources considered untrustworthy. For the remainder the sources were considered to be trustworthy. Figure 17-6 shows the attitude changes which occurred immediately and four weeks after communications from these sources. Immediately after the communications were given to subjects there was more attitude change apparent in the group given the high than among subjects given the low credibility source. But interestingly, four weeks later retention of attitude change declined in the high credibility group while increasing in the low credibility group. Thus, there may have been a "seeping-in" effect in the low credibility group and a "seeping-out" effect in the high credibility group.

Another experiment on attitude change, reported by Janis and Terwilliger (1962, pp. 405–406) used a somewhat different paradigm. These investigators were interested in the effects of communications that aroused fear on expressed attitudes. They used two conditions which they called low threat and high threat. Both pertained to the effects of smoking. The high-threat version consisted of the same 15

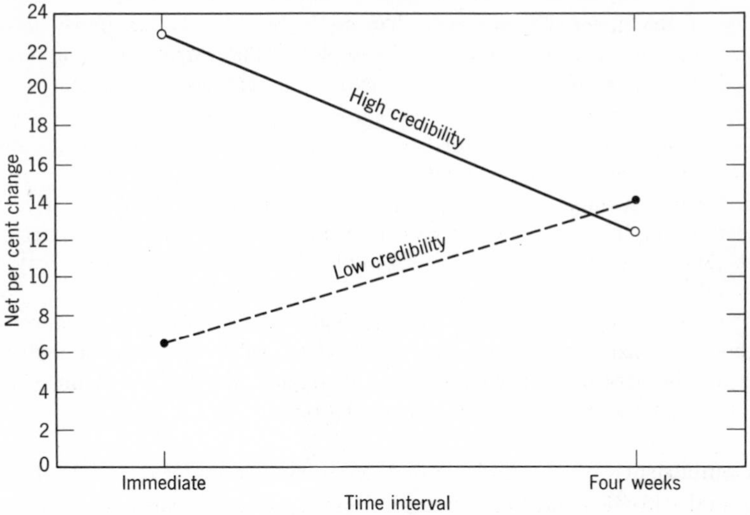

Figure **17-6** Retention of opinion change. Changes in extent of agreement with position advocated by high credibility and low credibility sources immediately after exposure to communication and four weeks later (after Hovland and Weiss, **1951**, p. **646**).

paragraphs as the low-threat version plus seven additional paragraphs that contained vivid descriptions of the suffering and poor prognosis of cancer victims.

The communications were presented individually to subjects. Each subject was asked to express his thoughts and feelings after each communication. Tape recordings were made of these verbal responses and content analysis performed on them. Pre- and postcommunication interviews dealing with subjects' attitudes toward cancer were also conducted. The subjects' spontaneous associations to each of the experimental communications were scored in terms of the following categories:

A. Affective Reactions

1. Expressions of worry, affective disturbance, or emotional tension evoked by the communication. Example: "That is awful."

2. Reference to the unpleasant aspects of cancer—pain, suffering, body damage. Example: "I never realized what a terrible disease it is. . . ."

B. Evaluative Comments

1. Major criticisms, i.e., explicit rejection statements to the effect that a given argument or conclusion concerning the harmful effects of *smoking* is incorrect, unwarranted, or unacceptable. Example: "I don't believe that."

2. Minor criticisms, i.e., unfavorable comments about the style or objectivity of the material being read that imply but do not manifestly assert that the argument is unacceptable. Example: "This argument is not clear."

3. Major favorable comments, i.e., explicit acceptance statements to the effect that a given argument or conclusion concerning the harmful effects of *smoking* is correct, warranted, or in agreement with the subject's own views. Example: "I go along with that."

4. Minor favorable comments, i.e., positive statements about the style or objectivity of the material being read that imply but do not manifestly assert that the argument is acceptable. Example: "That is an impressive way to put it."

5. Paraphrasing of arguments (concerning the harmful effects of smoking) without criticizing in any way, implying that the subject accepts the material although he does not explicitly say so. Example: "So the idea in this statement is that the more a person smokes the bigger the risk he takes."

Comparisons of the high- and low-threat groups revealed that (1) the high-threat condition elicited more emotional expressions about the danger of cancer than did the low-threat version, and (2) the low-threat condition seemed to be more effective in changing attitudes than the high-threat condition. Perhaps the most provocative finding of the study was this second one. It appears that when attempts are made to change attitudes through use of strong fear-arousing methods, individuals may form psychological resistances to the messages.

Sometimes fairly well-controlled experiments can be carried out in natural settings. An example of this possibility, which relates to attitude change, is a study made of attitudes toward Negroes (Deutsch and Collins, (1951, pp. 98–99). The subjects were residents in biracial housing projects. Two projects were fully integrated, with the assignment of Negro and white families done without regard to race. Two other projects were segregated in the sense that Negroes were assigned to separate buildings or separate parts of buildings.

How might these two living arrangements influence the attitudes of whites toward Negroes? It should be noted that there was no evidence of the white tenants in the integrated and segregated units differing in attitudes toward Negroes prior to coming to live in the projects. Figure 17-7 shows changes in attitudes toward Negroes for the white residents of integrated (Groups A and B) and of segregated (Groups C and D) projects. Two facts are highlighted in Figure 17-7. First, noteworthy attitude changes occurred in both groups. Second, positive attitudes toward Negroes increased dramatically among white residents living in integrated housing projects.

On the basis of this evidence one might reasonably suspect that contact with specific groups of people is significantly related to attitudes toward them. The following quotations from housewives who showed large attitude changes support that suspicion:

. . . "I started to cry when my husband told me we were coming to live here. I cried for three weeks. I didn't want to come and live here where there were so many colored people. I didn't want to bring my children up with colored children, but we had to come; . . . . Well, all that's changed. I've really come to like it. I see they're just as human as we are. They have nice apartments, they keep their children clean, and they're friendly. I've come to like them a great deal. . . . I'd just as soon live near a colored person as a white; it makes no difference to me."

. . . "I thought I was moving into the heart of Africa. I had always heard things about how they were . . . they were dirty, drink a lot . . . were like savages. Living with them, my ideas have changed altogether. They're just people. . . . They're not any different."

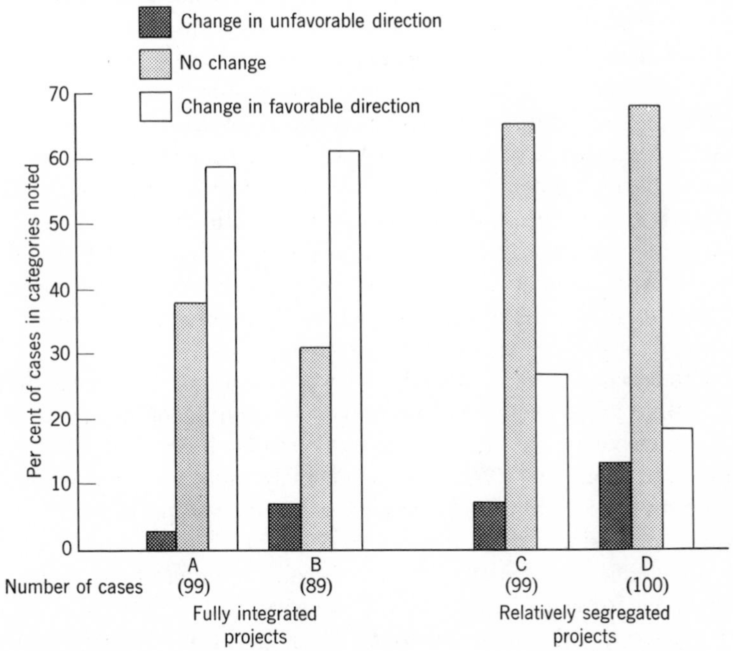

Figure 17-7 Changes in white housewives' attitudes toward Negroes following residence in biracial public housing projects (adapted from Deutsch and Collins, 1951, p. 97).

Since we have seen many examples of how personality characteristics affect behavior, we may wonder whether individual differences in these characteristics play any part in attitude change. A study by Weiss and Fine (1955) suggests that their role may be considerable. These investigators chose to study attitudes toward juvenile delinquents. They offered the hypothesis that persons who tended to direct hostility outward (extrapunitiveness) would be more likely to emphasize the need to punish juvenile delinquents than would persons who tended to direct hostility toward themselves (intrapunitiveness). To test this hypothesis, they used a "before-after" research design. Their "before" measures were projective indices of extrapunitive and intrapunitive hostility, and an opinion questionnaire covering attitudes toward juvenile delinquency.

Several weeks later, one group of subjects was asked to read an article arguing for the use of strict discipline and punitive measures in handling young offenders. Immediately following this experimental exercise a questionnaire on attitudes toward juvenile delinquency was administered. A second group was not given this reading assignment. Six weeks later, attitudes toward juvenile delinquency were again measured. The results showed that individuals with tendencies to direct hostility outward responded more positively than most other people to what might be called "hate propaganda." The group showing the greatest leniency toward juvenile delinquents was the control group. A lenient attitude also characterized subjects low in hostility despite the experimental communication. Hostile subjects did show an increase in a punishing attitude toward delinquents as a result of exposure to the experimental communication. Weiss and Fine's data, together with other available evidence, make it appear that personal dispositions of a general nature, such as extrapunitiveness, relate significantly to specific types of attitude change.

Attitude change may also be viewed in terms of persuasibility. Personality researchers have attacked one significant determinant of persons' responses to attempts at persuasion—individual differences. Linton and Graham (1959) comprehensively reviewed the research literature on the relationship between personality and persuasion. Some of their conclusions were: Persons who can be persuaded with relative ease to change their attitudes, beliefs, and opinions tend to have a strong need for social approval and security, to be conformers, to admire power in others, to experience feelings of inadequacy and inferiority, to have weak and passive self-images, to think uncritically, and to be low in intellectual wherewithal. That there is good reason to study individual differences in susceptibility to persuasion can be seen from a consideration of its pervasive role in society. Persons are constantly bombarded with persuasion intended advertisements, they seek in conscious and unconscious ways to influence and persuade others, and they no doubt develop resistances and defenses against being persuaded to alien points of view.

One field in which the process of attitude change and persuasibility is particularly important is medicine. Frank (1961) has noted that until the last few decades most medicines were pharmacologically inert. That is, they were placebos. What is, of course, relevant for our present topic is the fact that these inert substances so often worked. It seems unmistakable that the success of placebos has been due to psychological influences brought to bear and suggestions made by physicians. We can see then why many experimenters are attempting in laboratory settings to isolate variables that influence changes in attitudes and ways of behaving.

So far we have been dealing with one attitude at a time. Our aim has been to isolate variables that mold particular ideas, beliefs, and opinions. Festinger (1957) has directed attention to the more complex problem of the relationship of attitudes to one another and to behavior. Specifically he has been concerned with attitudes and thoughts that are in conflict. If a person believes A he is likely, other things being equal, to act on the basis of that belief. If he believes B he is likely, other things being equal, to act on the basis of that belief. But what if he believes both A and B? What if A and B conflict? For example, if a person were a staunch Democrat and also greatly admired a particular Republican, how would he resolve these two sets of attitudes? This conflict has been described in terms of dissonant cognitions. By cognition, Festinger (1957, p. 3) means ". . . any knowledge, opinion, or belief about the environment, about oneself, or about one's behavior." Cognitions that are consistent with one another may be said to be consonant. Those that are inconsistent with one another may be said to be dissonant.

Festinger hypothesized that when a person experienced dissonant cognitions, he became motivated to resolve them. If a person has two dissonant attitudes and is required to act in accordance with one of them, Festinger argued, he would be less likely to undergo attitude change if he made the decision of his own volition than if he were forced by some external souce to make up his own mind. Conflict resolution performed by the individual himself might well be longer lasting than if an external force induced it. An experiment by Festinger and Carlsmith (1959) nicely supports these conjectures.

Festinger and Carlsmith had college students perform monotonous and repetitive tasks. The students were then paid to tell prospective subjects for the same experiment that the project was highly interesting. The monetary inducement in some cases was $1.00 and in others it was $20.00. Later, the subjects who had been paid were interviewed and asked to describe how interesting they thought the tasks in the experiment were. The results supported Festinger's conjecture. The $1.00 subjects apparently persuaded themselves that the tasks were, in fact, enjoyable, while the $20.00 subjects described the tasks as dull and uninteresting. One might say that the $20.00 subjects had been bribed. When one takes a substantial bribe, one need not necessarily believe in the correctness of one's actions. Privately, the $20.00 subjects continued to believe as they had before the bribe. The $1.00 subjects, on the other hand, if they were bribed, were bribed only slightly. Since they could not "blame" the briber, it would seem that they had to change their attitudes.

Experiments on cognitive dissonance have dealt with the effects of inconsistent attitudes on behavior and the effects of being forced to act contrary to one's attitudes. They have also been conducted to assess the effects of various degrees of dissonance on behavior and the relationship of dissonant attitudes to personal commitment (Brehm and Cohen, 1962). Festinger's concept of cognitive dissonance and the research it has stimulated would seem to represent a worthwhile, initial burrowing into the complex that we call social attitudes.

REINFORCEMENT AND VERBAL BEHAVIOR. Two major questions have guided a number of recent explorations of verbal behavior: (1) Can reliable procedures be developed for the classification of verbal responses? (2) If verbal responses can be reliably classified, can they be influenced and modified by experimention?

Answers to the first question involve applications of content analysis. How is reliability in content analysis attained? As already indicated, some classes of response pose few reliability problems—for example, formal characteristics, such as counts of verbs and adjectives. Other classes of response require the training of categorizers to handle them. For example, if we wished someone to analyze the content of a sample of speech in terms of the number of times the speaker made self-references, it would be necessary to define adequately for the categorizer what was meant by a self-reference. After having done this, it would then be necessary to give the categorizer practice and training in adherence to the definition of a self-reference.

Once a reliable procedure for content analysis has been devised, it becomes possible to move in any of several directions. In one direction, the response classes isolated through content analysis may be used as independent variables. Thus we might wish to compare individuals who make a great many positively toned self-references with those who make relatively few. We might also wish to correlate the frequency of positively toned self-references with the frequency of other response classes, such as negatively toned self-references. In another direction lie categories of verbal behavior that are considered as dependent variables. Our review of these will revolve around the question: by means of what procedures is it possible to influence or change an individual's verbal behavior?

Psychologists concerned with the process of learning have shown that rewards and punishments influence the frequency with which many responses occur in both animals and humans. For example, food given to a hungry animal after it has made a selected response will serve to increase the likelihood of that response's recurring. Telling a child that he is behaving like a big person may serve to increase the frequency of mature behavior. In these cases, food and approval are reinforcing events, events that increase the likelihood of occurrence of responses preceding them. Might this paradigm be applied to the study of human verbal behavior?

Greenspoon (1955) reported a suggestive study in which college students were asked simply to say words for a period of time. Their instructions were, "Say all the words that you can think of. Say them individually. Do not use any sentences or phrases. Do not count. Please continue until I say stop." Every time a subject uttered a plural noun, the experimenter responded with: "uhm-hmm." Greenspoon found that these events increased the frequency of emission of plural nouns. Following report of this finding, many researchers conducted studies elaborating the Greenspoon reinforcement procedure. The aim of these studies was to find out to what extent environmental events during speech function as reinforcers of designated verbal responses. The results indicated that emission of many classes of verbal response could be influenced through experimental reinforcement procedures (Krasner, 1962; Krasner and Ullmann 1965).

Classes of verbal response have been studied in two types of situations. Greenspoon's experiment illustrated one type, the relatively free situation in which few restrictions are placed on the subject's responses. The other type is more restricted from the subject's point of view. In it, he is given a choice among a number of possibilities. Illustrative of this approach was an experiment by Taffel (1955) that presented subjects with a series of 3 by 5 cards. Each card contained a typewritten group of pronouns. The subject was asked to make up a sentence per card using one of the pronouns listed. Taffel reinforced the subject's use of personal pronouns by saying "good" after each one used. He found that reinforcement worked in the same way as it had for Greenspoon in a free responding situation.

Because of their apparent similarities to procedures used in more traditional conditioning and learning experiments, studies of the type conducted by Greenspoon and Taffel came to be known as verbal conditioning experiments. As the literature on verbal conditioning grew, it became clear that reinforcement could be effective in experimentally manipulating discrete classes of response, such as plural nouns and personal pronouns. With these results in hand, a number of questions came to the fore:

1. Could findings similar to those of Greenspoon and Taffel be obtained in situations more resembling interviews and social conversations?
2. What factors, in addition to reinforcing events, affected the extent to which verbal conditioning occurred?
3. Was it possible to specify the personal characteristics of individuals who did and who did not respond to reinforcing events?
4. To what extent were subjects aware of the reinforcements administered to them and how did they interpret reinforcing events?
5. Having conditioned a subject to emit certain verbal responses, could we correlate change in his verbal behavior with other aspects of his behavior repertory? Let us now consider these five questions in turn.

1. REINFORCEMENT IN INTERVIEWS. The evidence to date suggests that reinforcements do affect verbal behavior in social conversations and interviews. A number of investigators have shown that the experimenter's responses such as "uhm-hm" and "good" did increase the emission of response classes that are more complex than either plural nouns or personal pronouns (Krasner, 1962; Williams, 1964). For example, several studies have focused attention on affectively toned statements made by individuals in the course of talking about themselves. Reinforcements have been found to influence both positive and negative references to self: "I feel good"; I feel bad" (I. G. Sarason, and Ganzer, 1962).

Other examples of the influence of reinforcing events over verbal expression include these. Verplanck (1955) found that reinforcing the expression of opinions in the course of everyday conversation increased the frequency of opinions being expressed. The reinforcements used were displays of interest by a listener in the opinions expressed by a speaker. (Students might explore the effects of this experimental manipulation on the expression of opinion among their friends, relatives, and teachers.) Several studies have shown that reinforcing particular types of responses on personality tests, such as the MMPI, Rorschach, and TAT, increases their frequency of emission (Krasner, 1962). Speech rates of children have been effectively manipulated through reinforcement and so have categories of the speech of neurotic and psychotic patients (Salzinger, et al., 1962; Salzinger, 1959).

It seems reasonable to conclude that significant first steps have been made in showing the influence of reinforcing events over self-descriptions, and speech generally. Events that occur as people are talking can significantly affect what they say. This ability to manipulate verbal behavior provides a convincing argument in support of the power of the experimental method. Starting with what might at first glance seem to be a rather denuded experimental situation, it has been possible to isolate and manipulate conditions which increase or decrease many categories of speech.

2. RELEVANT VARIABLES IN ADDITION TO REINFORCEMENT PER SE. Once it has been shown that reinforcement does influence verbal responses, a number of provocative questions arise. These concern the conditions under which reinforcement is most effective. For example, does the frequency of reinforcement influence levels of verbal conditioning? Do verbally conditioned responses show extinction when reinforcement is omitted? Unfortunately there has not been enough experimental evidence related to these questions to permit firm conclusions. It appears likely, however, that in research on changes in verbal behavior frequency of reinforcement will emerge as a significant independent variable. Available evidence suggests that extinction may be more difficult to assess in relation to verbally conditioned responses than in more traditional conditioning settings.

Does it make any difference what kind of reinforcement is used in verbal conditioning studies? Although again there is only limited evidence on this point, it appears that the nature of reinforcement is an important factor. For example, it has been found that social reinforcements, such as an experimenter saying "uhm-hmm," lead to a faster increase in emission of reinforced responses than do impersonal reinforcements, such as light going on following responses falling within the defined response class (I. G. Sarason, 1958; Sarason and Minard, 1963). Furthermore, it has been shown that such characteristics as the anxiety and hostility levels of human reinforcers can affect the way in which experimenters administer social reinforcements and the amounts of verbal conditioning that their subjects display (I. G. Sarason, 1965*c*). Also, experimenters who are more self-confident obtain higher levels of verbal conditioning from subjects than do less confident experimenters (Verplanck, 1955). It would seem necessary in future reinforcement studies to increase understanding of the human reinforcer. This necessity arises not simply out of the methodological relevance of such understanding to verbal conditioning procedures but also out of its potential for increasing knowledge of how individuals affect each other in social situations.

Several attempts have been made in verbal conditioning studies to manipulate social aspects of the experimental situation. Orienting instructions and conditions have been used as independent variables in these efforts and their effects have turned out to be significant. For example, it has been found that achievement-orienting and ego-involving instructions lead to faster conditioning than do task-orienting instructions, and that pre-experimental comments of the experimenter affect responses to reinforcement (Krasner, 1962; I. G. Sarason, 1965*c*).

Much more needs to be known about the conditions that produce changes in verbal behavior. Clearly it will not do to say that events following the emission of particular responses cause verbal behavior changes. It is not enough to know that an experimenter utters "uhm-hmm" after each negative self-reference made by a subject. *It is also necessary to know something about the human reinforcer and the way in which he administers reinforcements.* The closer verbal conditioning experiments come to dealing with everyday verbal expression, the more necessary will it be to attend to the personal aspects of the reinforcement situation. The more necessary will it be to attend also to the roles of orienting conditions and the characteristics of the persons whose responses are being reinforced.

3. PERSONAL CHARACTERISTICS OF SUBJECTS. Early in the history of research on verbal conditioning it was noticed that there was a wide range of variability among subjects in response to reinforcement. If the basis for this variability could be understood, it seemed likely not only that the precision of experiments would increase, but also that leads for future exploration would turn up.

A number of significant subject characteristics have already been isolated in verbal conditioning experiments. The characteristic most frequently studied has been anxiety. In most experiments in which this variable has been manipulated, high scorers on anxiety scales have shown a more positive response to reinforcement than low-anxiety scorers (I. G. Sarason, 1965*c*). For example, high test-anxious subjects show a greater increase in negatively toned self-references as a result of reinforcement than do low test-anxious scorers (Sarason and Ganzer, 1962). How might one account for such a result? One explanation is that the greater insecurity and discomfort associated with heightened anxiety, particularly in testlike experimental situations, may make a person more sensitive to cues in the environment. One such cue might be the experimenter's reinforcements.

Perhaps related to this experimental evidence is the frequent clinical finding that anxious patients respond more positively to psychotherapy and to psychotherapists' interpretations and suggestions than patients who display few symptoms of anxiety. It seems likely that in the future, anxiety and other personal characteristics will prove valuable in throwing light on how verbal behavior changes. Quite probably the role of reinforcement will be studied intensively henceforth not only in experimental situations but also in clinical ones involving deviant verbal expression.*

Among other subject characteristics examined in reinforcement studies have been sex, dependency, hypnotizability, neuroticism, and hostility. It appears that subjects relatively high in need for approval, in hypnotizability, and in dependency show more positive responses to reinforcement than subjects low in these characteristics (Krasner, 1962; I. G. Sarason, 1965*c*). Thus predictions about persons' reactions to reinforcement require knowledge of the characteristics that they bring to experimental settings.

4. THE PROBLEM OF AWARENESS. One aspect of verbal conditioning experiments that has vexed a number of researchers is the degree to which subjects are aware of what is going on when they are in reinforcement experiments (Dulaney, 1962; Spielberger, 1962). After a subject has increased his emission of a particular class of responses (plural nouns, affectively toned statements, etc.) as a result of the emission having been reinforced, is he capable of stating that his behavior has changed, and why it has done so? There is no agreement concerning how crucial this question is. One group of investigators, predominantly made up of adherents to B. F. Skinner's (1953) behavioristic approach, believe that the important point in verbal con-

* That high-anxious persons may not respond more positively than low-anxious persons to reinforcement under all conditions is suggested by an experiment reported by Spielberger, De Nike, and Stein (1965). Future research will be needed to specify these conditions clearly.

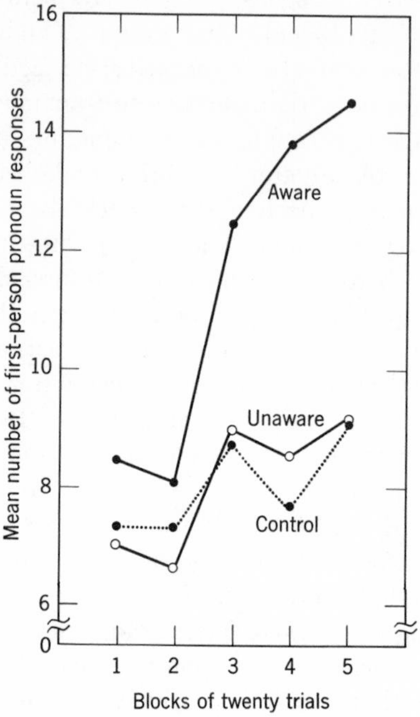

Figure 17-8 Conditioning curves. The mean number of first-person pronoun responses of the aware, unaware, and control groups on the conditioning task (after Spielberger, DeNike, and Stein, 1965, p. 234).

ditioning experiments is that reinforcement can modify behavior. Whether or not the subject is aware that his behavior has been manipulated is, to them, a secondary issue. Other researchers, however, believe that failure to assess the subject's awareness ignores a possibly relevant variable.

In early investigations of awareness, experimenters generally asked the subject a few questions of the type: "What did you think this experiment was about?" "Did you notice that I said 'uhm-hmm'?" What did you make of that?" Later studies have employed detailed lists of probing questions presented to subjects at the conclusion of experimental sessions (Spielberger, DeNike, and Stein, 1965; Spielberger, Levin, and Shepard, 1962).

Figure 17-8 shows the conditioning curves of three groups of subjects in one such study (Spielberger, DeNike, and Stein, 1965). On the basis of answers to a long sequence of questions asked in postexperimental interviews, subjects were judged to be either aware or unaware of the fact that they had been reinforced for using first-person pronouns. (The control group consisted of subjects who received random reinforcements. Reinforcements were administered to this group but not for any particular type of response.) It seems clear from Figure 17-8 that only subjects who were aware that their verbal behavior was being reinforced showed significant increase in usage of first-person pronouns.

The most detailed postconditioning inquiries have found that many subjects can be brought to a point at which they will refer to the relationship between reinforcement and change in verbal behavior. Such studies have often led to the conclusion that experiments in verbal conditioning do not involve learning without awareness. However, other investigators have found that most subjects do respond to reinforcements even though they are unable to verbalize the fact (Krasner, 1962). At present it seems that the degree to which experiments show that subjects recognize that their verbal behavior is being manipulated is at least partially a function of the procedure used to assess awareness.

How does one resolve the conflicting views and findings anent the role of awareness in verbal conditioning? Is the subject *really* aware of the experimenter's reinforcements? Let us assume that our criterion of awareness is one subject's ability to verbalize the relationship between reinforcement and changes in his verbal behavior. If, through a long series of postexperimental questions, he becomes able to verbalize the relationship between reinforcement and his use of a particular response class, in what sense may it be said that awareness was operative during the experiment itself? In other words, knowing a subject's level of awareness after the experiment has been completed and after he may have been oriented by postexperimental questions does not permit the easy drawing of conclusions concerning his level of awareness during conditioning.

Should one conclude then that postexperimental inquiries in research on verbal conditioning are worthless? Certainly not. In view of the potential bearing of personal variables on experimental situations, it would seem desirable for researchers to interview subjects on their reactions to experimental procedures followed. Such inquiries might profitably be seen as part of the broader problem of uncovering the subject's reactions not only to experimental procedures, but also to experimenters and to other potentially significant aspects of the psychological experiment (DeNike, 1964; Farber, 1963).

5. THE RELATIONSHIP BETWEEN CHANGE IN VERBAL BEHAVIOR AND OTHER BEHAVIORAL CHANGES. Assume that a subject has been conditioned to emit hostile verbal responses. By virtue of this "training," will the likelihood of his responding in a hostile manner in other situations increase? This question introduces the problem of generalization. Stimulus generalization has been studied in many kinds of experimental contexts. It has been found that subjects who are conditioned to make a particular response when confronted with a particular stimulus, will, after a series of reinforced trials, make conditioned responses to stimuli that resemble the original stimulus.

Several studies have shown that there are postconditioning, carry-over effects in verbal conditioning studies (Krasner, 1962; Simkins, 1961). Timmons (1959), for example, reinforced subjects for emitting verbal responses related to buildings. After the experiment he asked each subject to draw a picture of the first thing that came to mind. Subjects reinforced for verbal responses concerning buildings were found to draw more buildings than subjects who were not reinforced. B. R. Sarason (1956) reinforced subjects for using bodily activity verbs, that is, verbs that connote body movement. Before and after doing this she had the subjects engage in a period of free word-naming. She found that subjects who had been reinforced showed postreinforcement increases in the use of bodily activity verbs whereas control, nonreinforced subjects did not.

An interesting approach to the carry-over effects of reinforcement may be seen in an experiment carried out by Singer (1961). This investigator, interested in the modifiability of prodemocratic attitudes, administered the California F and E scales (Adorno, et al, 1950) to a group of female college students. These scales have been described as measures of authoritarian and antidemocratic tendencies. Three months later each student participated in an experiment in which the experimenter read aloud the F-scale items. Each subject was asked to state whether she agreed or disagreed with the item. Whenever subjects in the experimental group responded in the prodemocratic direction, the experimenter said either "good" or "right." In the case of subjects in the control group, the experimenter simply read the F-scale items and recorded the responses to them. The experimental and control groups were divided into two sub-groups. To half of the subjects the E-scale items were read aloud after completion of the reading of the F-scale items. The remaining subjects filled out the E scale themselves after the experimenter had excused himself.

Two questions arose in interpreting Singer's findings. Did

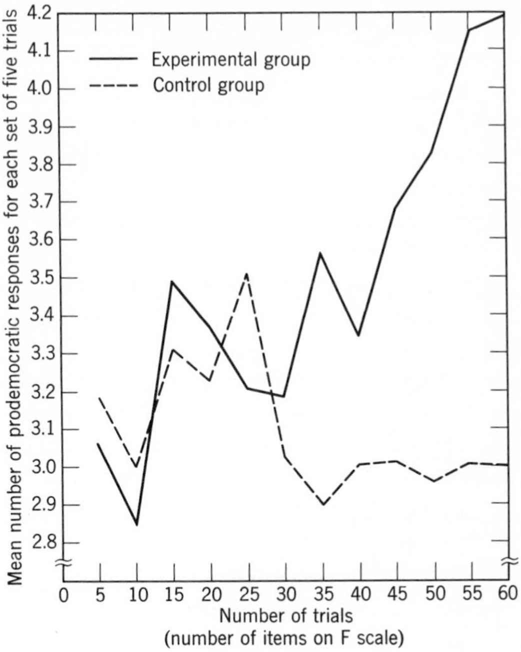

Figure **17-9** Learning curves by groupings of five trials (after Singer, 1961, p. 44).

reinforcement influence attitudes as reflected in F-scale responses? Did reinforcement of F-scale responses influence E-scale responses? It is important to note that while the F and E scales seem to tap similar attitudes, the statements in the two scales are different. Figure 17-9 presents the learning curves for the experimental and control groups. By the end of the F-scale series, it can be seen, there is a marked difference in the prodemocratic attitudes expressed by the two groups. Thus, prodemocratic attitudes can be influenced through verbal reinforcement.

With regard to the possibility of generalization, Singer found that when the experimenter was present and read aloud the E-scale items, there was a significant increase in prodemocratic responses to them. But when the subjects filled out the E scale themselves, with the experimenter absent, a significant increase was not obtained. This suggests that generalization of reinforced attitudinal responses does occur but that the physical presence of the experimenter is required. A reasonable inference is that the social context of the generalization situation is highly relevant to the possibility of obtaining generalized effects.

Results such as Singer's, together with several studies which failed to obtain generalization (Krasner, 1962), leave us with a somewhat unsettled state of affairs. Perhaps the major methodological problem in the study of generalization is that of establishing the degree of similarity between the verbal conditioning situation and postconditioning situations. If it turns out that generalization of verbally conditioned behavior can be firmly established, numerous exciting possibilities will arise. For example, can verbal conditioning procedures be employed as a form of therapy to modify behavior? To what extent may psychotherapists, physicians, and parents be regarded as reinforcing agents? Is it possible that strong fears, such as phobias, can be overcome through verbal conditioning techniques? Does reinforcement of verbal behavior have a carry-over effect on motor behavior? It is too soon to answer these questions with surety, but the possibility that verbal conditioning research may contribute to the development of new ways of modifying behavior seems more than sufficient justification for further experimentation in this area.

CONCLUDING COMMENTS CONCERNING PERSONALITY AND VERBAL BEHAVIOR

It is apparent that experimental manipulation of psychological variables can produce significant changes in verbal behavior. As we have seen, some of the techniques used in these manipulations are similar to those found to be effective in influencing performance levels. We have also seen that the ways in which experimental conditions affect behavior are influenced by the personal characteristics of subjects.

These findings have implications for the study of personality assessment. It is true that assessed characteristics are related to verbal reactions recorded under experimental conditions. But it also appears true that indices of these characteristics can themselves be influenced by specially created conditions. This suggests that when a person's characteristics are assessed, it is necessary to attend to the conditions under which indices are obtained. The evidence reviewed in this chapter shows that the manner in which people describe themselves and what they say about themselves and others can be influenced by the situations in which they make verbal responses. Personal characteristics cannot be studied in a vacuum, but must be related to characteristics of the situations in which they are assessed. A reasonable conclusion would seem to be that assessment and experimental approaches are interdependent and any sharp separation between them must be regarded, at least to some extent, as arbitrary.

The methods and findings that we have reviewed also have implications for the development of psychological constructs. It is one thing to be able to predict behavior on the basis of assessed characteristics and to manipulate experimentally the behavior of people, but it is another thing to say why these methods are effective. For example, why is reinforcement effective in influencing verbal responses, why do sensory deprivation conditions lead to behavioral changes, and why do orienting communications have an impact upon expressed attitudes? There are no simple answers to these questions. This is so because of the complexity of people. Researchers can carefully control the environmental inputs which impinge on people and they can reliably observe and record their outputs, the overt responses. But the mental processes which bring these outputs about cannot be observed directly.

These processes must be inferred and all researchers may not draw the same inferences from the same data. The great advantage of an objective approach to inputs, outputs, and indices of personality characteristics is that the scientist can hope eventually to devise procedures which will permit tests of the inferences drawn.

18

Personality and Social Behavior

Neither personal characteristics nor environmental events occur in a vacuum. We have already seen that the social context and the subject's impressions of an experiment cannot be ignored. The personality of the experimenter who administers a set of experimental conditions may be as important in influencing behavior as the conditions themselves. Indeed we may speak of the personal or social psychology of experiments and shall have more to say about the meaning of this term presently.

To turn to a somewhat more general topic, the social psychology of many situations has been studied through the effects of social processes on behavior. Although social psychology may be defined as the study of social behavior and personality psychology as the study of personal characteristics, psychologists agree that an understanding of personality variables is essential for a meaningful attack on the complexities of social interactions. This view is perhaps best reflected in the creation in 1965 by the American Psychological Association of a publication, *The Journal of Personality and Social Psychology,* concerned with relationships between the two areas.

Studies of social behavior may be distinguished from studies of verbal behavior only in relation to arbitrary criteria. Many of the experiments mentioned in Chapter 17 dealt with verbally expressed social attitudes. The experiments to be considered here often concern the effects of social variables on verbal behavior and, in general, tend to deal much more directly with social behavior and personal relationships than those presented in the previous chapter.

Although it would be unrealistic to attempt to survey the entire field of social psychology, it is realistic and desirable to indicate some of the areas of overlap between personality and social psychology. The reader has perhaps already noted instances in earlier chapters in which responses of a social nature were studied from an experimental standpoint—for example, the problem of changing social attitudes. In the present chapter we shall deal at some length with a variety of experimental situations in which the primary object is the individual as a social animal. The social roles played by people may be actual, implied, or imagined. Two aspects of the social situation are especially germane to our interests: Can social behavior be studied experimentally? To what extent do personal characteristics play a part in influencing social behavior?

EXPERIMENTAL METHODS OF INFLUENCING SOCIAL BEHAVIOR

Virtually all of the experimental methods described in connection with studies of personality, performance, and verbal behavior have been incorporated into studies of social responses. Personal behavior as a function of social deprivation, orienting communications, reinforcement conditions, and a variety of events occurring during experimental sessions has been subjected to analysis in a variety of ways. We shall therefore not review these procedures, but shall observe their use in selected representative researches.

One particularly distinguishing feature of much social-psychological research is the use of the atmosphere and social structure of the group as an independent variable. Whereas social and personal conditions may be regarded as complicating and extraneous factors in certain areas of psychological investigation, for the social psychologist they lie at the very heart of his subject matter. Thus the social psychologist seeks to devise experimental situations in which behavior in groups and reactions to groups can be studied systematically.

Experiments on Personality and Social Behavior

THE NEED FOR SOCIAL AFFILIATION. A significant aspect of social behavior pertains to the choices persons make concerning other persons. Some individuals choose to affiliate, it often seems, with virtually any group for which they are eligible. Other individuals resist joining groups. Most of us fall at intermediate points between these two poles. Researchers have attempted to study aspects of affiliative behavior under controlled laboratory conditions. Let us examine one major experimental undertaking dealing with this type of social behavior. We shall see that it has implications for both the social psychologist and the personality psychologist.

Schachter (1959) reported an ingenious series of laboratory studies of the need to affiliate. His research stemmed from two major propositions: (1) association or affiliation with other people may be necessary to achieve personal or individual goals (it may be necessary to join a union to hold a job), and (2) people in and of themselves may be viewed as goals for one another (most friendships are entered into because they are personally satisfying and fill mutual needs). A question that Schachter posed for himself was: Is it possible to specify some of the conditions that either increase or decrease the likelihood of an individual's making an affiliative response?

How did Schachter deal experimentally with this challenging question? His approach was to attempt first to arouse subjects' need for affiliation, and then to measure the extent to which this aroused need, in fact, affected their social behavior. His experimental work involved two orienting conditions which he labelled a high-anxiety and a low-anxiety condition. Under the high-anxiety condition, subjects were told that they were going to receive a series of painful electric shocks as part of a psychological experiment. Under the low-anxiety condition, subjects were told that they would be administered electric shocks, but that these shocks would be mild and not at all painful. After receiving one of these sets of instructions, each subject was informed that an interval of 10 minutes would precede the experiment.

At this point the subject's affiliative behavior was measured by asking each subject if she (all of the subjects were girls) would like to spend the 10-minute interval in a room by herself or in a room with other persons. Subjects who did not care whether they spent the period alone or in the company of others were given an opportunity to express their lack of preference. The results of the experiment showed that 63 per cent of the subjects to whom the high-anxiety condition was administered indicated a preference to be together with other persons during the waiting period. The comparable figure for the low-anxiety subjects was 33 per cent. In addition, twice as many low-anxiety subjects as high-anxiety subjects indicated that they did not care whether they would be alone or together during the waiting period. These results suggested that the experimental manipulation which Schachter called anxiety arousal was effective and was positively related to affiliative needs expressed by individuals. This seems analogous to everyday life in that a common stress often brings people closer together.

Schachter did not end his research there. He conducted several additional experiments which shed light on some of the effects of experimentally induced anxiety on social behavior. For example, in one of these, he was able to show that high-anxiety subjects who had indicated a preference to wait with a group expressed this choice only if they could wait with other participants in the same experiment. In no case did a high-anxiety subject indicate a preference for waiting with strangers, such as individuals sitting in a waiting room for reasons other than participation in the experiment. Schachter (1959, p. 24) concluded that this evidence

> . . . removes one shred of ambiguity from the old saw 'misery loves company.' Misery doesn't love just any kind of company, it loves only miserable company. Whatever the needs aroused by the manipulation of anxiety, it would seem that their satisfaction demands the presence of others in a similar situation.

While Schachter's investigations of need for affiliation have had a stimulating effect on the study of social behavior, it is equally true that one individual difference variable which he examined in relation to affiliative need has had a considerable impact on researchers in a variety of fields. This variable is of particular interest because it demonstrates the value of conceiving of individual differences not simply in terms of personality test scores, but more generally in terms of indices of the histories of persons. The variable that Schachter (1959) selected was ordinal position within the family. By ordinal position is meant a person's chronological age in relation to siblings. He found that though family size was unrelated to affiliative responses under high-anxiety conditions, ordinal position was strongly related to their incidence: the later an individual's birth position, the less likelihood there was that an affiliative response would be made. In one study of all first-born subjects, he discovered that 80 per cent chose to wait with other people prior to the shock experiment. Of later-borns only 31 per cent chose to wait with others. Furthermore, first-born and only children indicated significantly less willingness to withstand pain than later-born subjects.

The work of Schachter is instructive on two counts. The results of his explorations are valuable in and of themselves, and they raise significant questions. His work involved female subjects. Would comparable experiments with males yield similar findings? Furthermore, Schachter inferred stronger need for affiliation under conditions of anxiety for first-borns and only children than for later-borns. What was the basis for this difference? One possibility is that first-born and only children do not differ from later-borns in their need for affiliation, but rather in some factor or factors that relate to expression of the affiliative need. It is well known, for example, that many shy people have strong needs for ties and relationships with others, but that for a variety of reasons they are unable to express or manifest them. Schachter's research involved specific definitions of anxiety and affiliation. What might he have found with anxiety and affiliation defined in other ways? It should be emphasized that these questions are not raised in criticism of Schachter's work, but rather to indicate its value in developing challenges for future research.

Schachter's approach to affiliation was to gather laboratory evidence concerning it and then to search for individual characteristics, such as birth order and family size which might bear a relationship to the affiliative response. Another approach to the problem would be to begin by constructing a test to measure need for affiliation. Following the assessment of affiliative need, efforts might be made to relate this personal characteristic to indices of need for affiliation derived from social behavior. A group of investigators appear to be in the process of developing such a measure (Atkinson, 1958*b*; Shipley and Veroff, 1952). Their procedure has been similar to that employed by McClelland (1955, 1961) and his collaborators in devising a measure of need for achievement. Using TAT-like stimuli appropriate to the social need for affiliation, they have proceeded to develop a content analysis system that provides scores indicating the need for social acceptance and affiliation. Evidence so far gathered indicates that affiliation need expressed in imaginative stories to TAT pictures is sensitive to various kinds of experimental manipulations. For example, groups that were tested following a condition intended to heighten the need for social acceptance received higher need for affiliation scores than subjects tested under a control condition. It is interesting to note that one study (Conners, 1963) found that need for affiliation scores were greatest for second-born and lowest for only children. First-born children occupied an intermediate position on need for affiliation.

What is the relationship, if any, between Schachter's laboratory approach to the affiliative response and this assessment approach? As yet it is not possible to answer this question with hard facts. But it would be rather surprising if no relationship existed. On the basis of what is known about these two approaches to essentially similar concepts, it would seem worthwhile in future work to combine these approaches. Were this to be done, investigations of affiliation might be directed to the simultaneous study of (1) subject variables, such as birth order and assessed need for affiliation, and (2) experimental manipulations designed to evoke affiliative responses.

What conclusions may be drawn from the research literature concerning the psychology of affiliation? As already pointed out, not enough time has passed since Schachter reported his findings to permit the gathering and reporting of needed additional data. Some studies seem to corroborate Schachter's results while others leave doubts about the nature of the relationships of birth order, other personal characteristics, and experimental manipulations to affiliative behavior. But it seems legitimate to conjecture that the experimental study of affiliative behavior may make a significant contribution to understanding persons' social reactions and the meaning people attach to associating with others.

MANIPULATING SOCIAL BEHAVIOR

Verbally expressed attitudes are susceptible to experimental influence. We have seen that their manipulation has taken the form of either persuasive communication or reinforcement of expressed attitudes. By extending the topic of social influence beyond the problem of attitude change, we can describe some of the ways in which behavior changes as a function of variables inherent in social situations. Two problems command our attention: (1) social conformity, and (2) changes in social behavior which result from imitation and reinforcement.

Conformity

The study of variables that influence an individual's decision to affiliate with a group clearly relates to a significant aspect of social behavior. Equally important is the understanding of an individual's behavior once he has found a group or entered a social situation. There is a growing body of literature that deals with characteristics of group situations and how they relate to individual behavior (Krech, Crutchfield, and Ballachey, 1962). One such characteristic is the influence of the group over its members. Individuals behave differently when they are in a group from when they are alone. In part, this is because of the need to adhere to the standards of the group. We shall examine the influences of groups over the behavior of individuals.

Let us devise an experimental situation that requires the individual to make judgments and discriminations about verifiable phenomena. Let us then hire a group of confederates and pay them to make statements that are not factual. Placed in an experimental situation with the confederates, the subject is asked to make certain judgments and discriminations. The situation is so arranged that the subject makes his oral responses to the stimuli only after hearing the responses of the confederates. Question: Will the subject's judgments and discriminations in any way differ as a result of having heard the misleading responses of the confederates?

Asch (1956), a prominent social psychologist, conducted a series of laboratory studies that relate to this question. In his work he employed the task of judging the length of lines. In each of several trials, the subject was shown a line called the standard and three other lines. The subject's job was to state which of the three comparison lines was equal in length to the standard. In his experiments, Asch did not have his confederates make incorrect perceptual judgments on every trial. Rather, he arranged it so that on certain trials they made correct judgments, on other trials their errors were moderate, and on still others they stated that a line that was clearly unequal in length to the standard was equal to it.

Such an experiment, of course, requires a control group of subjects not subjected to group pressure. Under nonpressure conditions, Asch found that the subject's judgments were virtually free of error. Our concern therefore will be primarily with the subject's behavior under the group-pressure condition. Here are some of Asch's major findings:

1. Generally, the faked judgments of the confederates significantly influenced the subject's judgments. Only 25 per cent of the subjects under the experimental condition gave errorless judgments.
2. However, the range of variability was wide, with some subjects maintaining their independence by apparently ignoring confederates' judgments, and others showing a strong tendency to conform to the group norm.
3. Using a different perceptual task, brightness judgments, he replicated the results of the length of lines experiment.
4. Later in the experiment when subjects were given the opportunity of not making their judgments in public, errors declined precipitously.
5. The size of the errors made by subjects was proportionate to the size of the errors made by the confederates.

It has been shown, then, that a set of laboratory conditions can be devised that will significantly influence persons' judgments in a group situation. Group pressure must be regarded as an independent variable affecting behavior. How do people feel about their conformity to group pressure? Are they aware that they are conforming? Asch attempted to answer these questions by conducting post-experimental interviews with subjects. For purposes of data analysis, he categorized subjects into two groups: independents and yielders. Independents were those who were relatively uninfluenced by confederates' judgments; yielders showed a strong conformity trend.

When asked: "When you gave an estimate that disagreed with the others, did you feel that if the lines were measured with a ruler you would turn out to be right or wrong?" 87 per cent of the independent subjects expressed confidence in the correctness of their judgments. The comparable figure for the yielders was 41 per cent. 45 per cent of the independents indicated they were at times tempted to answer as had the confederates. On the other hand, 80 per cent of the yielders admitted this temptation. In general most subjects felt concern over their disagreements with other group members and did not realize that the majority of judgments had been faked. In interpreting his results, Asch concluded that an individual's sense of self-worth was an important determinant in social opposition situations. According to this interpretation, independents have the capacity of maintaining their self-esteem in the face of strong social pressures to conform. Yielders' feelings of self-worth, on the other hand, deteriorate under the ordeal of social opposition.

There have been several variations of the Asch experiments. Sherif (1935; Sherif and Cantril, 1947), for example, has explored the autokinetic effect which involves subjects' judgments of the extent to which a pinpoint of light moves in a darkened room. Comparing the judgments of subjects under control and group pressure conditions, he found that group pressure does influence the judgments of subjects. Like Asch he found that many subjects were not aware that they had been influenced.

Another social psychologist, Crutchfield (1955), has made a significant contribution to the experimental study of conformity through innovations in methodology and through further exploration of the personality correlates of conformity. He argued that when a person was asked to make judgments in a group situation, and when his private conviction was at variance with the group consensus, he was in a conflict situation. In Crutchfield's opinion, there are two ways of resolving such conflict. The individual either behaves independently and accepts his deviant role in the group, or he conforms.

Crutchfield's methodological innovation was highly practical. In Asch's experiments it was possible to study only one subject per session, and it was necessary to employ a confederate group. Crutchfield's procedure permitted several subjects to be processed per session without the necessity of confederates. This was accomplished by seating subjects in partly closed booths, each person having a switchboard in view. After the stimulus to be judged had been exposed, each subject could tell from his switchboard what sorts of judgments other subjects had made. The experimental situation was so arranged that each subject thought that he was the last one to make judgments. Furthermore, information given to the subjects on their switchboards was controlled completely by the experimenter. Thus, each subject could be made to think that the others had responded in any way the experimenter wished. This arrangement, then, permits an efficient group-pressure situation which bears many similarities to that used in Asch-type experiments. However, the degree of personal contact between subjects is reduced in the Crutchfield as compared with the Asch-type setup. How do Crutchfield's results compare with those of Asch?

Using a wide variety of tasks and requiring judgments by subjects, Crutchfield indicates individual differences in conformity similar to those found by Asch. Crutchfield made an effort to isolate some of the bases for this variability. Some of his findings were these:

1. Certain groups of people show more conformity than others. Among male subjects studied by Crutchfield, military officers showed the strongest tendency to conform to apparent group norms. The group that showed the least tendency toward conformity consisted of research scientists.

2. There appear to be personality differences between conformers and independents. The California F scale (Adorno et al., 1950), a measure of authoritarian attitudes, was found to be positively related to conformity tendencies. Independents as compared to conformers were found to have more maturity in social relations, greater intellectual effectiveness, more self-control, and fewer inferiority feelings. Conformers tended to express more conventional and moralistic attitudes than independents. Conformers also seem to have less ability in coping with threatening and stressful situations and to be more anxious and timid than independents.

3. Excessive conformity is negatively related to creativity. This finding suggests the desirability of investigating properties of groups that might either favorably or unfavorably influence the creative process.

Before leaving the topic of conformity let us refer once more to some of the findings previously mentioned concerning personality and persuasion (Chapter 17). Studies of persuasion have typically been designed to determine to what extent various types of communication are influential in modifying the attitudes that people express. Though some people may be generally more persuasible than others, the degree to which a communication designed to change attitudes is effective depends on the nature of the particular communication and the characteristics of the person subjected to it. Linton and Graham (1959) have examined possible differences between individuals who are and are not influenced by communications intended to be persuasive. They found that subjects who changed their attitudes as a result of an experimental communication have more passive self-attitudes, less self-assertiveness, more admiration for power, and more need for social approval and adhere to peer group conformity pressures.

Further exploration of the personality factors at work in social situations would seem to be useful in accounting not only for data gathered in experimental studies of conformity and persuasion, but also for aspects of everyday social events which play roles in the molding of lives (Jones, 1964). In our own country and throughout the world there is ample evidence of pressure to conform. ("Use shampoo X, everyone else is!") ("Mother, everyone else can stay out until 1 A.M.")

It is difficult to think of problems more deserving of dispassionate investigation than those of conforming behavior. One such investigation is a study by Milgram (1963). It is especially interesting because it dealt not only with conformity but with conformity that aroused high levels of conflict among subjects. In it subjects were led to believe that they might physically hurt other persons in the course of carrying out certain procedures. Milgram found that, despite this possibility, many subjects obediently followed the directions given to them. As with the more benign task of judging lines, there was wide variability among people in their tendency to conform to the pressures brought to bear on them.

Pursuing the discussion one step further, we might point to an aspect of social situations bearing significantly on social conformity and persuasion: the role of leaders. Without necessarily taking a stand on the great man theory of history there seems to be no question that individuals filling leadership roles, be they in the family, school, or nation, can be powerful factors in achieving conformity from followers and in persuading followers to adopt certain ideas. It is therefore not a surprise that the study of leaders and leadership has interested social researchers. In some experiments attempts have been made to answer the question: Is there a general trait or characteristic of leadership? It appears that leadership is not highly specific to particular tasks nor to general, over-all situations and tasks. Rather, there seem to be clusters of tasks on each of which a person might be high, medium, or low in leadership (Krech, Crutchfield, and Ballachey, 1962).

This state of affairs seems analogous to the situation observed in personality and performance. In reviewing that topic we saw that personal characteristics and task characteristics interacted with one another to influence performance. With regard to social behavior it would appear that the ways in which people react to groups depend on the nature and aims of the groups, and the personal characteristics of group members.

Imitation and Response to Reinforcement

As we have seen, group pressure can be a potent factor in influencing behavior in a social situation. Moreover, persons with leadership qualities are capable of influencing social behavior. Although the nature of leadership as a personal characteristic or set of personal characteristics is by no means clear, there are innumerable examples of situations in which persons follow leaders. Examples abound particularly in the study of children's behavior (Bandura, 1965). A great many responses of children are acquired by following the lead of parents, teachers, and peers. Starting with this fact, Bandura and Walters (1963, p. 47) have conceptualized the behavior of following others as a process of imitation:

> Imitation plays an important role in the acquisition of deviant, as well as of conforming, behavior. New responses may be learned or the characteristics of existing response hierarchies may be changed as a function of observing the behavior of others and its response consequences without the observer's performing any overt responses himself or receiving any direct reinforcement during the acquisition period.

Imitation contributes significantly to the determination of role behavior, the complex social behavior determined by group norms, personal characteristics, and the availability of models that can be imitated. When people adopt a role or imitate a model they are often unaware of doing so. Nevertheless, imitative behavior seems to be a product of learning.

This has been shown in an experiment reported by Bandura and McDonald (1963, p. 276). The subjects were children between the ages of 5 and 11 who were presented with a series of paired situations for which a moral judgment was required. For example, in the illustration that follows, the child was asked which of the two boys, John or Henry, was naughtier:

1. John was in his room when his mother called him to dinner. John goes down, and opens the door to the dining room. But behind the door was a chair, and on the chair was a tray with fifteen cups on it. John did not know the cups were behind the door. He opens the door, the door hits the tray, bang go the fifteen cups, and they all get broken.

2. One day when Henry's mother was out, Henry tried to get some cookies out of the cupboard. He climbed up on a chair, but the cookie jar was still too high, and he couldn't reach it. But while he was trying to get the cookie jar, he knocked over a cup. The cup fell down and broke.

One question asked by Bandura and McDonald was whether children's moral judgments would be influenced by moral judgments made by an adult model. (In certain groups the model as well as the child responded to the judgmental tasks.) That is, are moral judgments a product of imitative learning? They found that children who were exposed to an adult's moral judgments showed a significant learning effect. The children came to imitate the judgments of adult models.

We shall see later that imitation influences aggressive behavior in much the same way as moral judgments were influenced by models' behavior (Bandura, 1962). Experimental studies of imitation suggest that the degree to which it occurs depends on the social context, the personal characteristics of the model, and the personal characteristics of the individual whose imitative behavior is being manipulated. These inferences seem completely in accord with observations from everyday life. Which television or sports personality will come to function as a model for a particular child depends on the role played by the hero and the characteristics of the child. Which parent will be imitated more frequently by a child depends on the family context, the child, and the parents. The ways in which these factors combine to determine behavior are not yet clearly understood. Through controlled experimentation it may be possible to clarify these relationships.

In an imitative situation a person observes the behavior of another and comes to respond in a manner similar to the model. Thus, according to this definition, explicitly administered reinforcements for imitation were not given to Bandura and McDonald's subjects. The possibility of using conditions such as rewards and punishments to influence social behavior has been suggested by a number of writers. Everyday life examples suggest that what a person "gets out" of social situations affects his social behavior. Attendance at club meetings that are not rewarding usually results in dropping out of the club.

We tend to associate with people who are congenial and rewarding and to avoid people who are bores or who "get on our nerves."

In Chapter 17 we saw that reinforcement can be a potent factor in effecting changes in verbal behavior and expressed attitudes (Krasner, 1962). In later sections we shall see examples of the role of reinforcement in social behavior. These will be discussed when we review some experimental approaches to aggression and to the control of deviant behavior. In both cases we shall see that events that follow particular responses emitted by a person can significantly influence his social behavior. It will be remembered also that there seems good reason to explore intensively the ways in which positive and negative reinforcements influence social behavior. Available evidence suggests that much social learning occurs both through imitation and through the effects of reinforcing conditions.

AGGRESSION

If universality of occurrence and social importance are justifications for the study of a concept, aggression clearly stands close to the head of the list of topics requiring investigation. It has typically been defined in terms of an organism's attacking, fighting, and destructive responses directed at other organisms or objects or itself. Using this broad definition, we can note that aggresssion has been observed not only in all mammals but in all vertebrates as well. (Many invertebrates do not display these types of responses.) At the human level, the problem of aggression is especially complex because of the role of thought and symbolic processes. People can have aggressive thoughts and wishes, but may inhibit their overt expression. Because of this, some writers have drawn a distinction between aggression and hostility, using the latter term to refer to attitudes and covert aggressive tendencies, and the former to refer to overt responses designed to do harm (Berkowitz, 1962; Buss, 1961).

Even casual inspection of man's history, especially the period of the twentieth century, leads one to raise a number of searching questions concerning the aggressive nature of man (McNeil, 1965). Why do people fight? Why have virtually all periods of human history been marked by wars? Why has the horror of war increased so frighteningly in intensity? How might one account rationally for such irrationality as pervaded the era of Nazi Germany? What is the basis for the human capacity to be cruel?

Many men have thought and written about the basic issues involved in these questions. Some have treated aggression as an instinctive response. Others have considered it as a learned tendency. Still others have believed it to be a drive that, like biological drives, pervades all aspects of behavior (Feshbach, 1964). Freud, it will be remembered, considered aggression to be a biologically rooted drive comparable to that of sexuality. He believed that these two basic drives played roles in the determination of all behavior. Whereas many students have found this point of view understandable and deserving of further inquiry, few have accepted Freud's notion of a death or destructive instinct expressed through aggression. Freud believed that the path to the objective verification of the death instinct lay in biochemical investigations. To date, neither these nor behavioral investigations have provided support for this facet of his theory.

The aspects of Freud's view of aggression that have aroused considerable interest relate to the problem of those social strictures in society directed against the expression of aggression. Freud tended to preoccupy himself with the sexual rather than the aggressive determinants of overt behavior. However, as time has passed it has often seemed that the social pressures against the expression of aggression are at least as great as those against the expression of sexuality. How do these pressures affect the child and the adult? What defensive operations do individuals employ to inhibit aggression? What are the effects on behavior, both overt and covert, of inhibited or defended aggression? We shall suggest some of the directions that experimental attacks on these sorts of questions have taken. We shall begin with one of the most basic questions asked about aggression: What are its antecedents?

Experimentation on Aggression

Aggression can be viewed as overt and covert responses. What events, what prior conditions, evoke these responses? Assume that an individual has already built up a repertory of aggressive responses. Under what conditions is he likely to emit them? Dollard, Doob, Miller, Mowrer, and Sears (1939), in an influential monograph, *Frustration and Aggression,* sought to come to grips with this question. They offered what has been referred to as the frustration-aggression hypothesis. They defined frustration as interference with goal-directed patterns of activity. Aggression was seen as one response of organisms to frustration. This does not mean that all aggression necessarily results from frustration, nor does it mean that all frustrations inevitably lead to aggression. The hypothesis simply states that there is a significant link between frustrating conditions on the one hand and aggressive responses on the other.

Many studies have been conducted to test the frustration-aggression hypothesis. They have often involved the creation of frustrating situations in which there is opportunity to make aggressive responses. There are several ways in which frustration can be induced in people. In the Barker, Dembo, and Lewin (1941) study, described in Chapter 16, children were frustrated by the presence of a physical barrier between them and a set of desired toys. Other ways of inducing frustration include the withdrawal of rewards that previously occurred in a goal-directed pattern of activity, punishment, and annoying stimuli such as distracting sounds. Thus, although it is possible to speak generally of frustration as being a result of interference with goal directed activity, the interferences assume a wide variety of forms.

There is considerable evidence that experimentally created frustrations do influence the performance and social behavior of people (Yates, 1962). This does not necessarily mean that these influences are attributable to aroused aggressive tendencies. For example, the vigor of children's responses increases as an indication of the degree of frustration experienced (Haner and Brown, 1955). But can vigor or strength of response be equated with aggression? Because of questions of this type it is not possible to state with certitude that the frustration-aggression hypothesis has been supported or refuted by particular experiments. It would seem most sensible at the present time to regard the frustration-aggression hypothesis as a formulation that has stimulated much research and many questions. Available evidence suggests that if it is to be conclusively supported or refuted a number of variables related to the definitions of frustration and aggression will have to be more clearly specified.

It will be necessary, for example, to specify the strength of the response that is frustrated. Interference with an activity that is not especially important to an individual cannot be expected to define a significant frustration. It will also be necessary to specify the severity of frustration. Mild frustrations may lead to much different reactions from intense ones. Regarding the properties of aggressive responses, we shall have to specify not only their strength but also the ways in which they manifest themselves. For example, is aggression experienced on the level of fantasy or is it acted out overtly? In what ways do aggressive tendencies combine with other response tendencies? To what extent is it necessary to assume that aggressive responses are intended to be aggressive?

Although there may be methodological problems in precisely relating aggression to antecedent frustrating conditions, the fact remains that all people experience aggressive tendencies. How do people react to these tendencies? Feshbach, (1955, 1961) has shed light on this question. In one study (Feshbach, 1955) he investigated (1) the effects of experimentally instigated aggression on fantasy behavior, and (2) the creation of conditions that could reduce aggressive tendencies. The aggression-arousing situation took place in a college classroom and involved an experimenter who made arrogant and insulting comments to the class. He commented negatively both on the maturity of college students and on their narrow interests. Following this phase of the study, some subjects were given an opportunity to reduce their aggression through fantasy. This was done by having them tell stories about TAT pictures. Would the opportunity to express aggression in fantasy serve to reduce subsequent expressions of aggression?

The results of the experiment showed that those subjects who were insulted were much more critical of the experimenter and the experiment than others who had not been insulted. The postfantasy measures of aggression were subjects' responses to an attitude questionnaire and a sentence-completion test that yielded a score for degree of aggression. Feshbach found that insulted subjects given the fantasy experience showed less aggression on these measures than insulted subjects who had not been assigned the story-telling task. He also noted that subjects who had been insulted showed more aggression on the TAT than non-insulted subjects. It would appear, then, that the experimental insult condition had a significant effect on fantasy and that the fantasy experience was related to subsequently expressed aggression.

This study suggests that it may be possible experimentally not only to arouse aggressive tendencies, but also to reduce them. Another facet of aggression concerns the ways in which people respond to their own aggressive tendencies. A study that approached this issue has been reported by Hokanson and Shetler (1961). These investigators placed subjects in a situation that was introduced as relating to the blood-pressure response of people to various tasks. In the performance of a series of intellectual tasks, subjects assigned to a situation high in frustration were interrupted and harassed during their work. A previous study (Hokanson, 1961) had shown that this sort of frustration could arouse strong feelings of anger. Following either this anger-arousing condition or a control condition, subjects were informed that the next task involved guessing. The subject was to think of numbers from 1 to 10 and the experimenter was to guess the number. If the experimenter made incorrect guesses (which, of course, occurred frequently) the subject was to administer an electric shock to the experimenter. In the control group subjects informed the experimenter about the correctness of his guesses through a light signal rather than through administration of shocks. It was arranged that both frustrated and nonfrustrated subjects who were given the opportunity to aggress against the experimenter would administer the same number of shocks to him. Comparable equality obtained for subjects who flashed lights to the experimenter. Before and after each phase of the experiment, subjects' systolic blood pressure was recorded.

A significant finding was that subjects who were frustrated showed greater elevations of blood pressure during the experiment than did control subjects. Another significant finding concerned an aspect of the experiment that bears upon previous comments about social variables in experiments. Hokanson and Shetler used high- and low-status experimenters, as defined in terms of the experimenter's age and in terms of comments made to the subject (the high-status experimenter was described as a professor, while the low-status experimenter was described as a student). It was discovered that the effects of frustration and aggression depended on the status of the experimenter. The opportunity to aggress against high- and low-status experimenters resulted in different patterns of blood-pressure change. For example, subjects frustrated by the low-status experimenter and given an opportunity to aggress against him showed postexperimental blood-pressure levels similar to those of nonfrustrated subjects. Subjects frustrated by the low-status experimenter but not allowed to aggress showed higher blood-pressure levels than frustrated subjects who were permitted to aggress.

It would seem that Hokanson and Shetler were successful (1) in studying experimentally the relationship of overt aggression to the individuals' own psychophysiological responses, and (2) in showing that the social context in which frustration and aggression take place is a significant variable.

One aspect of their experiment raises an interesting question. What were the subjects' reactions to being in a situation that required them to do harm to another person? Surely there must be a point at which people will refuse to follow the instructions that they hurt others. Milgram (1963, p. 371) has shown experimentally that that point may be further out on the "hurt-continuum" than might be expected. His experiment was stimulated by the many reports of shocking events that occurred in Nazi Germany:

Obedience is as basic an element in the structure of social life as one can point to. Some system of authority is a requirement of all communal living, and it is only the man dwelling in isolation who is not forced to respond, through defiance or submission, to the commands of others. Obedience, as a determinant of behavior, is of particular relevance to our time. It has been reliably established that from 1933–45 millions of innocent persons were systematically slaughtered on command. Gas chambers were built, death camps were guarded, daily quotas of corpses were produced with the same efficiency as the manufacture of appliances. These inhumane policies may have originated in the mind of a single person, but they could only be carried out on a massive scale if a very large number of persons obeyed orders. Obedience is the psychological mechanism that links individual action to political purpose. It is the dispositional cement that binds men to systems of authority. Facts of recent history and observation in daily life suggest that for many persons obedience may be a deeply ingrained behavior tendency, indeed, a prepotent impulse overriding graining in ethics, sympathy, and moral conduct.

The procedure used to find the point at which obedience to the command to harm another person would break down was as follows. Pairs of subjects were brought into a laboratory and told that the experiment in which they were to participate concerned the effects of punishment on learning. One subject was to adopt the role of teacher, the other the role of learner. The teacher's task was to administer electric shocks to the learner. In fact, the experiment was arranged in such a way that the learner was a confederate. It was also arranged that the learner actually did not receive the electric shocks; this had also been the case in the Hokanson and Shetler (1961) experiment.

The directions to the teacher were to administer electric shocks to the learner. Furthermore, as the number of errors made by the learner increased, the teacher was to increase the severity of the shock. As described by Milgram, the experimental arrangements were most realistic. The teacher was told that although the electric shocks would be painful, no permanent tissue damage would result from them. Although teacher and learner were in separate rooms, the teacher was able to hear sounds from the learners' room that clearly suggested pain and anguish.

Milgram's dependent variable was simple. At what point in the shock series would the subject refuse to administer further pain to the confederate? Twenty-six of the 40 subjects obeyed the experimental instructions fully. That is, they reached the point at which they thought they were administering the strongest possible shock to the confederate. Fourteen subjects refused to continue with the experiment. Most of the subjects were described as displaying extreme levels of nervous tension. Profuse sweating, trembling, stuttering, and nervous laughter occurred frequently. An observer of one of Milgram's (1963, p. 377) subjects gave this description of his behavior:

> I observed a mature and initially poised businessman enter the laboratory smiling and confident. Within 20 minutes he was reduced to a twitching, stuttering wreck, who was rapidly approaching a point of nervous collapse. He constantly pulled on his earlobe, and twisted his hands. At one point he pushed his fist into his forehead and muttered: "Oh God, let's stop it." And yet he continued to respond to every word of the experimenter, and obeyed to the end.

A subsequent experiment (Milgram, 1965) showed that when subjects are given an opportunity to observe other subjects (actually confederates) refuse to administer strong electric shocks, the likelihood that they will similarly refuse is high. Milgram's experiment gives the lie to the assertion that experiments cannot be realistic. With regard to the phenomenon of aggression it shows that under appropriate conditions persons can administer or refuse to administer great pain to others. It also shows that there are differences among people in the ways in which they resolve the conflict between the need to follow commands and the wish not to do harm.

A question that arises in a study such as Milgram's concerns the reactions of subjects to the procedures administered to them. Were subjects traumatized or harmed in any lasting way by these procedures (Baumrind, 1964)? After completion of his 1963 experiment, Milgram (1964, p. 850) sent a written report of the experiment and its results to the subjects. He then asked them to respond to a series of questionnaire items. Table 18-1 summarizes some of their responses. The table shows that both persons who obediently followed the commands of the experiment and those who were defiant and terminated the experiment had favorable attitudes toward it. These are comments made by two of the subjects:

> This experiment has strengthened my belief that man should avoid harm to his fellow man even at the risk of violating authority. . . .
>
> To me, the experiment pointed up . . . the extent to which each individual should have or discover firm ground on which to base his decisions, no matter how trivial they appear to be. I think people should think more deeply about themselves and their relation to their world and to other people. If this experiment serves to jar people out of complacency, it will have served its end.

TABLE 18-1

Response to Questionnaire Used in a Follow-up Study of the Obedience Research

Now that I have read the report, and all things considered . . .	Defiant	Obedient	All
1. I am very glad to have been in the experiment	40.0%	47.8%	43.5%
2. I am glad to have been in the experiment	43.8%	35.7%	40.2%
3. I am neither sorry nor glad to have been in the experiment	15.3%	14.8%	15.1%
4. I am sorry to have been in the experiment	0.8%	0.7%	0.8%
5. I am very sorry to have been in the experiment	0.0%	1.0%	0.5%

Note. Ninety-two per cent of the subjects returned the questionnaire. The characteristics of the nonrespondents were checked against the respondents. They differed from the respondents only with regard to age; younger people were overrepresented in the nonresponding group.

Adapted from S. Milgram (1964), Issues in the study of obedience: A reply to Baumrind, p. 849. *Amer. Psychologist,* **19,** 848–852.

It would seem that, although the experiment provided a far from pleasant experience, the experience was personally meaningful and valuable to many of the persons who participated in it.

One line of investigation suggested by the Milgram study and others cited relates to individual differences among people in their tendencies or needs to express aggression. In recent years there has been growing interest in devising assessment techniques that might measure these differences. The techniques have been primarily of two types, paper-and-pencil, self-report measures and projective techniques. Factor analytic studies have been carried out to isolate both over-all aggression and significant components of aggressive trends. Buss and Durkee (1957), for example, isolated these independent factors in a questionnaire: (1) tendencies to be physically assaultive; (2) indirectly expressed hostility; (3) irritability; (4) negativism; (5) resentment; (6) suspiciousness; (7) verbally expressed aggression; and (8) guilt over hostile impulses and attitudes. As psychometric indices of individual differences in aggressive tendencies are perfected, it is likely that they will play an increasingly important role in experimental research on aggression.

Most of the foregoing discussion has dwelt on aggression in adults. There has also been, however, a great deal of interest in observing and describing aggressive tendencies as they develop in children.

Recent experimental approaches to aggressive behavior in children have permitted evaluation of the learned aspects of aggression. Research by Bandura and his colleagues has been specifically directed to the experimental study of imitative aggressive responses made by children (Bandura, Ross and Ross, 1961, 1963*a*, 1963*b*; Bandura and Walters, 1963). In one of their investigations, preschool children were placed in a situation with an adult model. For one group of children, the model made aggressive responses toward dolls in the course of play. For a second group of subjects the model made no such responses. Ninety per cent of children in the first group subsequently made aggressive responses themselves. None of the second group of subjects behaved similarly. Several studies suggest that merely through observation of aggression in others, the likelihood of aggressive responses in children increases. Figure 18-1 shows children reproducing aggressive behavior that they had observed on film. Actual presence of a model is not required for a child to emit this kind of behavior. A study by Bandura, Ross, and Ross (1961) has permitted a further generalization. They found that children who had interacted with an aggressive model not only imitated the model's aggressive responses, but also emitted aggressive responses not necessarily identical to those displayed by the model.

There is evidence that environmental factors such as available models for imitation and reinforcement conditions influence the expression of aggression. For example, the greater degree of aggressiveness shown by males than by females is to a considerable extent a function of roles that they learned or adopted in the course of development.

Although at present our understanding of the role of positive reinforcement in aggression is clearer than our understanding of the effects on behavior of punishment and negative reinforcement, it does seem that both types of reinforcement are important in determining behavior. Thus, Sears, Maccoby, and Levin (1957) have reported that permissiveness of mothers relative to expressing aggression correlates positively with aggression displayed by children in the home situation. Bandura and Walters (1959) found that mothers of aggressive boys were much less upset when the boys aggressed against them than were mothers of nonaggressive boys. Experimental evidence indicates that the amount of aggression shown by children engaged in doll play is positively related to the permissiveness (with regard to aggression) of the supervising adult. Chasdi and Lawrence (1955) showed that reproofs for aggression in an early stage of doll play markedly reduced aggressive doll play later.

When, for whatever reason, someone does not overtly express pent-up aggressive tendencies what happens to the aggression? Psychoanalytic theory suggests that one possible consequence might be displacement. Just as a man who has been frustrated by his boss at the office may come home and express his anger to his wife, so might we hypothesize that aggression often expresses itself in indirect ways. Miller (1948) performed a now famous study with white rats that appeared to demonstrate experimentally the phenomenon of displacement of aggression. He placed pairs of rats in an enclosure and administered electric shocks to them. There was, however, one way in which the animals could avoid the shock. They could strike aggressively at each other. The rats rapidly learned the solution to their problem and the frequency of these responses increased sharply. When one of the rats was removed from the enclosure and a doll substituted for it, an interesting result eventuated. A large percentage of the rats responded aggressively to the doll when the shock was administered. It would appear that both displacement and stimulus generalization were involved in Miller's experiment.

Social psychologists have attempted to extend the study of displacement to the human group. In one study (Miller and Bugelski, 1948), an attitude questionnaire was administered to a group of boys before and after a tedious, frustrating situation. An over-all decrease in positive attitudes and tolerance for minority groups (Mexicans and Japanese) was observed. This sort of evidence might be taken as support for a scapegoat theory of prejudice. Put another way, a scapegoat may be viewed as an object onto which is heaped displaced aggression. In the example of the man thwarted at the office we would say, then, that he used his wife as a scapegoat or object of displaced aggression.

Berkowitz (1959) has provided another suggestive example of this sort of relationship. He compared subjects who differed in their degrees of antisemitism. Half of the high- and half of the low-prejudice subjects had a frustrating and annoying interaction with an experimenter. The remaining subjects had a neutral interaction. Subjects in both groups, following the interaction with the experimenter, were introduced to a peer, a fellow student. After a period of conversation with the peer, the subjects were asked to rate and describe him on several characteristics. Berkowitz found that the antisemitic subjects under the frustrating conditions displayed significantly more unfriend-

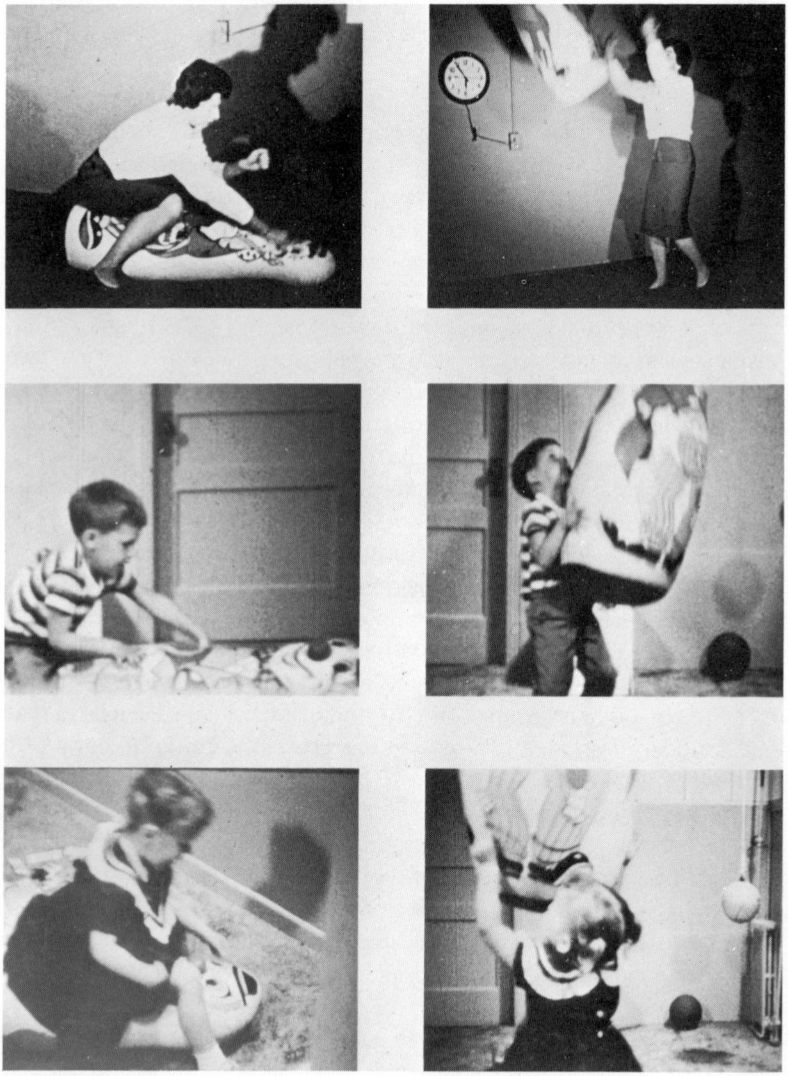

Figure 18-1 Photographs of children reproducing the aggressive behavior of the model they had observed on film (reproduced from Bandura, Ross, and Ross, 1963*a*).

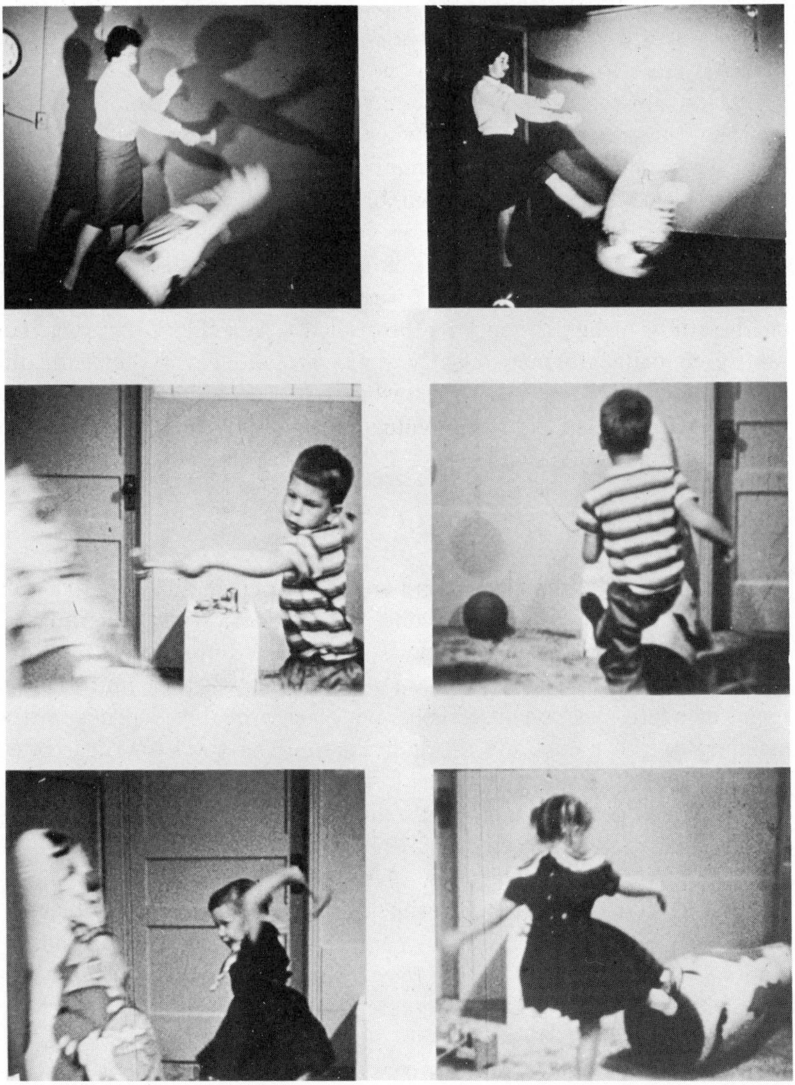

liness to a neutral person, the fellow student, than the antisemitic subjects who had not been frustrated. Apparently, hostility had extended from the experimenter to the neutral person. Rather surprisingly, the subjects who were low in prejudice showed a more positive attitude toward the peer following frustration than following the neutral experience with the experimenter.

Quite clearly aggression is a major problem in our society both because of its obvious relationship to various extreme behavioral deviations and also because of its role in social relationships. The studies mentioned illustrate some of the ways in which experimental attacks on the study of aggression have proceeded. As evidence accrues, our ability to delineate more clearly the overt and covert determinants of aggression will increase. Knowledge of these determinants may ultimately prove of practical value in the resolution of significant human conflicts.

THE PERCEPTION OF PERSONS

Time and again in experimental studies of personality we have seen the need to attend to both personal characteristics and experimental conditions that influence behavior. How we interpret situations influences our behavior in them. For example, whether imitation of social or aggressive responses will take place probably depends on the meaning of the model for the individual. The tired and frustrated researcher might, in a rash moment, wish that he did not have to think about the things that his subjects think about. It would be convenient in laboratory investigations not to have to worry about the subjects' unverbalized reactions (1) to the task presented to him, (2) to himself, and (3) to the experimenter. Of course, these subjective aspects of the person's behavior, complex as they may be, cannot be ignored. Fortunately, it is the very challenge of man's peculiarities and complexities that draws researchers and theorists to the study of human behavior.

The problem of the effects of persons' subjective reactions to stimulus situations has received increasing attention during recent years. One concern of this chapter has been the reactions of persons to experimentally controlled social stimuli. It is quite obvious that in everyday life we are constantly confronted with many uncontrolled social stimuli. Perhaps the most significant of these are other persons in the environment. Personality researchers and social psychologists have in recent years become increasingly interested in the possibility of objectively analyzing how persons perceive other persons (Cline, 1964;

Tagiuri and Petrullo, 1958). The study of perception of persons deals with subjective responses to personal stimuli and stems from the common observation that an individual's perceptions of others can exert powerful influences over his social behavior.

In experiments, individuals often react not only to designated patterns of stimuli that interest the experimenter, but also to other incidental stimuli. In this section we shall indicate some of the experimental approaches to the study of subjective reactions to other persons. How do people form impressions of others? How do they integrate information about people into over-all impressions? That individuals integrate facts about people into organized impressions has been shown by research carried out by Asch (1946, p. 261). In one of his studies an experimenter read to a group of college students a list of discrete personal characteristics. The task was to write a brief description of someone who possessed the characteristics. Reproduced below are sketches written by two subjects. The characteristics in the list read to them were: "energetic, assured, talkative, cold, ironical, inquisitive, persuasive."

He is the type of person you meet all too often: sure of himself, talks too much, always trying to bring you around to his way of thinking, and with not much feeling for the other fellow.

He impresses people as being more capable than he really is. He is popular and never ill at ease. Easily becomes the center of attraction at any gathering. He is likely to be a jack-of-all-trades. Although his interests are varied, he is not necessarily well versed in any of them. He possesses a sense of humor. His presence stimulates enthusiasm and very often he does arrive at a position of importance.

These sketches indicate that the subjects not only used the data given to them, but also went beyond them. For example, the second subject stated, "He possesses a sense of humor." Yet the list did not refer in any way to this particular characteristic. Perhaps through techniques such as extrapolation and projection, individuals "fill in gaps" in forming impressions of persons. Asch (1946, p. 261) has offered these comments on the task of forming impressions:

. . . When a task of this kind is given, a normal adult is capable of responding to the instruction by forming a unified impression. Though he hears a sequence of discrete terms, his resulting impression is not discrete. In some manner he shapes the separate qualities into a single, consistent view. All subjects . . . of whom there were over 1,000, fulfilled the task in the manner described. . . . Starting from the bare terms, the final account is completed and rounded.

Now let us consider this list of characteristics: intelligent, skillful, industrious, warm, determined, practical, cautious. After obtaining sketches from one group of students based on these characteristics, what would happen if a comparable group of subjects were given the identical list except that the word "cold" was included instead of the word "warm?" Asch hypothesized that changing one stimulus element would change the total stimulus configuration. The evidence obtained supported this notion. The "warm" group described their hypothetical person as being wiser, more popular, humorous, and imaginative than did the "cold" group. It is pertinent to note, however, that the warm "person" was not described simply as being more desirable than the cold one; the two sets of sketches showed both similarities and differences. In view of the apparently slight change in the stimulus situation (in this case, the list of characteristics) the differences seem particularly striking. Asch's findings suggest the need to increase understanding of the process by means of which persons draw inferences about others. The task for Asch's subjects was not explicitly to report their inferences but to describe verbally a hypothetical person. Their descriptions, however, made it clear that overt behavior was determined to a considerable extent by inferences that people drew from data available to them. These inferences might be implicit or explicit, consciously present or not. The important point, illustrated by Asch's study, is the need to increase understanding of the nature of these subjective reactions and of their influences over behavior. Subsequent research has made clear that the kind of inferences that an individual draws about others depends importantly on the particular conditions under which he receives information about them (Matkom, 1963; Wishner, 1960).

Perhaps we had better restate the topic in a somewhat different manner. When persons are confronted with personal stimuli (included in this term are other people, real or hypothetical), they respond in a problem-solving manner. For example, when introduced to a stranger at a cocktail party one's conversational gambits will be a function of cues that one perceives in the stranger. Some individuals might seek a neutral topic for conversation (the weather, the stock market), others might raise a topic for conversation that on the basis of available cues would appear to be of particular interest to the other person. One point that seems clear from observations gathered at cocktail parties and other places is that there are individual differences in the kinds of responses made by people confronted with personal stimuli. These responses, in a sense, may be regarded as a product of their personal constructs (G. A. Kelly, 1955).

A study by Cline and Richards (1960) illustrates one experimental approach to the problem of social judgments. These researchers conducted brief sidewalk interviews with people (shoppers) that they filmed. After the filming, they went into the homes of the interviewees, interviewed them, and administered a battery of personality tests. Having gathered these data, Cline and Richards then obtained personality descriptions of each subject from five people who knew them well. The films were now shown to a group of college students. The task for the students was to make predictions about the personality characteristics of the people seen in the films. Thus these subjects' descriptions and judgments were made in relation to real as opposed to hypothetical persons, as in Asch's experiment. Each student received an accuracy score in terms of the correctness of his predictions. Accuracy was judged by comparison with the detailed information that the investigators had gathered about the persons in the films.

Cline and Richards found that a good (accurate) judge of a particular person is likely to be a good judge of other persons. A poor judge of one person tends to be a poor judge of others. Subjects who were good judges of one particular personality characteristic also tended to be good judges of other characteristics. These results seem to suggest a degree of generality in the ability to make accurate judgment about others. Cline and Richards indeed concluded that their study had provided evidence in support of a general trait of ability to judge other people.

Before returning to a discussion of social judgments and perceptions, let us briefly mention one other experiment in this area. Scodel and Mussen (1953) reported a study in which an attempt was made to determine whether the personality variable in which they were interested would be related to descriptive statements made about another person. In their study a measure of authoritarianism was administered to a group of college students. High-authoritarian students were paired with low-authoritarian students. Each of these pairs engaged in informal conversation about radio, television, or the movies for a period of 20 minutes. After this informal conversation each student was brought to a separate room and was asked to fill out an attitude questionnaire as he thought his partner would fill it out. High-authoritarian subjects were found to attribute high-authoritarian attitudes to their partners—who, in fact, were low in authoritarian tendencies. On the other hand, low-authoritarian subjects were able to judge their partners accurately. Thus we see an indication that not only are there individual differences in the perception of others, but also that it may be possible through a combination of personality assessment and laboratory techniques to discern some of the bases of these observed differences among people.

The studies of Cline and Richards (1960) and of Scodel and Mussen (1953) have been referred to as person perception experiments because the problems investigated in them concern the perception of persons. The description of inferential processes used by individuals in response to personal stimuli, and the determination of criteria of accuracy in personal perception are not simple. But a start seems to have been made in dealing with them. Is it possible to list some of the variables that seem relevant to an understanding of persons' responses to persons? Let us try.

1. THE VARIABLE OF THE TASK IN PERSON PERCEPTION. Simply on intuitive grounds alone it seems reasonable that the task of judgment posed for an individual might influence his accuracy of perceiving persons. For example, does the task of person perception involve the emotional, intellectual, historical, or attitudinal spheres of behavior? Is accuracy in person perception influenced by the amount of information provided? What effects do increasing amounts of information about a judged person have on accuracy in predicting that person's characteristics? Related to this question is the degree of acquaintance and contact between the judge and the judged. With increasing personal contact, do personal accuracy scores go up? Another aspect of the task presented to the judge is the response he is asked to make. May the judge describe his response to someone else in his own words or is he asked to use a check list or rating scale of some sort?

2. THE CHARACTERISTICS OF PERSONS. Cline and Richards' (1960) study suggested a general trait of accuracy of person perception. Scodel and Mussen (1953) found that one personality variable, authoritarianism, was related to the accuracy of person perception scores. Other investigators have found intelligence to be positively related to accuracy. But by and large, not enough is known in studies of person perception accuracy about the influence of characteristics of judges and the people they judge. Each of us has had the experience of meeting someone who is a stranger to us and yet within a few minutes makes us feel that we have known him for a long time. Bruner and Taguiri (1954) have suggested that the more similar two people are, the more likely they will be able to predict each other's behavior accurately. It seems probable that as our understanding of personality characteristics increases, so will our understanding of the processes involved in the formation of groups and friendships.

3. RESPONSE SETS. People's descriptions of others is often biased by certain response sets. For example, some people manifest a response set of social desirability. That is, they tend to respond on the basis of what they regard to be desirable or acceptable in their social milieu (see Chapter 10). Some judges of persons may tend to say only "nice" things about others, or may be influenced by "halo effects." Other judges may tend to assess persons largely in terms of themselves. Still others may have their own peculiar theories of personality and erroneous conceptions about people's behavior. This could easily lead to biased judgments of others. We saw that in personality tests the importance of response sets was increasingly being recognized. Presumably the concept of response set has applicability to descriptions of others as well as to description of self.

The individual is much like the scientist. Many of his actions are based on inferences rather than on observed facts. With the individual, as with the scientist, the questions of both the accuracy of and the basis for his inferences require careful probing. Allport (1961, pp. 521–522) has presented this point as follows:

> The process of perceiving persons is both like and unlike all other perceptual processes. The chief difference is that human objects, unlike other objects, impress us with their purposes, their animation, their intentions toward us, and their relative unpredictability. A peculiar excitement attaches to person perception. . . .
>
> In spite of the complexity of the process we maintain that psychologists are not entitled to sidestep the problem of *accurate* knowledge as some are wont to do. My personality lies "in here," yours "out there." Although it is important to know the process by which I attempt to bridge this chasm, it is no less vital to know how well I succeed. *A major task in life is to achieve increasing success in our perception of one another.*

Before leaving the topic of perception of persons, its relationship to comments made earlier should be indicated. In Chapter 12 and 13 we considered the problem of the interpretation of clinical data. For example, how accurate are the clinical psychologist's inferences drawn from the Rorschach responses of patients? What problem-solving processes lead him to his inferences? From the present discussion it seems clear that the problem of persons' interpretations of others and the problem of the accuracy of clinical judgments are both aspects of the same question: How do persons conceive of others? A combination of assessment and experimental methods will be required to answer this question. Assessment methods can help develop indices of processes of judgment and accuracy in describing others. Experimental methods can help identify many of the conditions that influence processes of judgment and accuracy in judging others.

In a sense, of course, the scientist and the individual do differ in that the scientist's inferences require objective validation and the individual's inferences do not. The fascination of man is not that he is right or wrong in a particular situation. What fascinates the student of personality are the myriad ways in which man solves social and other problems. That there are difficulties and stumbling blocks in empirically analyzing man's problem-solving and the interpretative process does not absolve the psychologist of the responsibility of gaining glimpses into its workings.

CONCLUDING COMMENTS CONCERNING PERSONALITY AND THE SOCIAL BEHAVIOR OF PEOPLE

Our aim in reviewing experimental research on personality is not to cover comprehensively all relevant literature. It is to suggest through appropriate examples what experimental research on personality is about. The material referred to in this chapter indicates that significant aspects of everyday life activities can be incorporated into controlled experiments. Among the aspects emphasized are the needs for social affiliation and conformity, the expression of aggression in social contexts and persons' perceptions of others. As was observed in previous discussions, we have seen how individual differences and the social context of variables combine to influence behavior. A person does not respond in a simple and direct way to a stimulus situation, such as a group of people to whom he is introduced. We might conjecture that prior to responding he must perceive the stimuli in the situation and interpret them. This interpretative process is a private one. But indices of personal characteristics can provide clues to the assumptions and attitudes in terms of which the person interprets stimuli and responds to them.

This view of the responding organism suggests the basis for the considerable overlap between the fields of personality and social psychology. Studies of personal characteristics that disregard the social contexts in which they manifest themselves and studies of social behavior that disregard the characteristics of interacting persons must to some extent be viewed as artificial. Integrating the two approaches makes for a far more meaningful approach to the individual. The problems, methods, and findings reviewed suggest that controlled experimentation can make a valuable contribution to the study of individuals in social contexts.

19

Animal Research, Personality, and Social Behavior

One may very well wonder how research on animals could contribute to the furtherance of understanding of human behavior, especially of the personalities of people. Actually research using animals interests students of personality in a number of ways. In the same manner as new drugs are tested on animals before being tried out on human beings, certain problems of personality functioning lend themselves to preliminary study with animals. Many psychologists have endeavored to develop analogues to human behavior through using animals as subjects. Though not directly applicable to the human organism, these analogues may prove useful in devising future experiments with people. Two valuable purposes are served by animals: (1) they may be subjected to experimental treatments that on ethical grounds could not be administered to humans, and (2) their histories and environments can be carefully regulated. Hebb and Thompson (1954, p. 533) have made the acute observation that animal research may

> . . . clarify a human problem without "proving" anything. It may draw attention to facets of human behavior one has not noticed; it may point to a troublemaking but implicit assumption; it may suggest a new principle of human behavior. Furthermore, animal experiment in the past has repeatedly shown that the treatment of some human problem or other has been oversimplified.

In this chapter we shall pursue two general types of animal studies. One concerns the applicability of concepts of personality theorists to the behavior of animals. The other pertains to patterns of social behavior in animals.

Most formulations about personality have concentrated on the relationship of man's experiences to his present characteristics and reactions. Many of the experiences that have been assumed to relate to personal characteristics cannot be duplicated or studied experimentally with humans. A series of exeriments conducted by Maier (1949) illustrates the value of animal studies for personality researchers.

Maier's research dealt with the concepts of frustration and fixation. It will be remembered that psychoanalysts have hypothesized that behavioral regression and fixation are outcomes of anxiety aroused by intense frustrations and conflicts (Chapter 2). Maier studied one type of intense frustration that could not ethically be approximated in human subjects.

He defined a frustrating situation as one in which a highly motivated organism was faced with a problem that it could not solve, but to which it was forced to respond. The subjects were white rats who performed a discrimination learning task. The apparatus employed placed the rat in a situation requiring him to jump across an open area to one of two doors. If the rat jumped to the correct door, the door fell and the animal landed on a platform where it received a reward. If the rat jumped to the incorrect door, it bumped its nose and plummeted into a net. Previous research had shown that rats were capable of learning this kind of discrimination problem. But how would the rats respond to a situation in which the problem was made insoluble? Such a situation could be attained by not providing the subject with cues from which it could discriminate between the two doors.

Maier found after a series of trials on the insoluble task that the rats refused to jump to either of the doors. To motivate them to respond he administered airblasts while they were on the jumping stand. These airblasts were made to be so uncomfortable that the animals jumped and consequently bumped their noses and fell into the net. Under these traumatic conditions, many of Maier's animals developed what he called fixated or stereotyped responses. These rats would jump to only one door rather than alternate in some fashion between the two doors. This response tendency, which is interesting in itself, was made even more interesting when a change occurred in the experimental situation. After the fixated response had been established the problem was made soluble. Yet many rats continued to emit their fixated responses for literally hundreds of trials. In some extreme cases, even when one door was removed and food placed in clear view, the animal's fixation could not be broken.

Perhaps the aspect of Maier's work on fixation that has been of most interest to students of personality is the similarity of the fixated rats' stereotyped behavior to many human neurotic symptoms. Just as one wonders what rewards or reinforcements maintain the "stupid" behavior in rats, so might one wonder about the basis for such repetitive human response patterns as stuttering and ritualistic behavior. Mowrer (1950*a*) has spoken of a "neurotic paradox" by which he means the self-defeating and self-perpetuating (that is fixated) character of neurotic behavior. Maier's rats appear to have shown a paradox of just this type.

Animal studies have been directed both to the creation and removal of "symptoms" in animal subjects (Yates, 1962). Experimental neuroses have been created by placing subjects in situations of conflict. Using rats as subjects, Miller (1951) and Brown (1948) demonstrated several types of conflict: (1) Approach-approach. The conflict between two desirable and wanted alternatives, such as choosing between two ties. (2) Approach-avoidance. The conflict aroused by being able to receive a wanted alternative but having also to suffer an unwanted alternative to attain it, such as wanting to rob a bank but being afraid of the consequences. (3) Avoidance-avoidance. The conflict between jumping into the frying pan or into the fire.

Masserman (1943; Masserman and Siever, 1944) created experimental neuroses through an approach-avoidance conflict by teaching cats to lift the lid of a food box in order to obtain food and then placing them in a situation in which as soon as they lifted the lid they received an annoying blast of air. Speaking analogically, the conflict for the cat was to decide whether to remain hungry and not be subjected to airblasts or satisfy its hunger and have the unpleasant airblast experience. When the conflict reached its zenith, Masserman reported, cats displayed many symptoms that seem similar to human neurotic ones. These include listlessness, fearfulness, and lack of attention to environmental happenings. He tried experimentally to ameliorate this type of symptom in many ways. Greatest success came when the relationship between experimenter and subject was, again to use an analogy, one of trust and understanding. Gentleness in handling and gradual retraining steps proved effective in getting neurotic cats to the point at which they again approached and opened the fear-producing box.

Studies of conflict in animals have been directed to a variety of problems (Eysenck, 1964). Some investigators have been especially interested in uncovering variables that influence organisms' ability to adjust to states of conflict. For example, it has been shown that the social conditions under which rats are reared influence the likelihood that they will develop gastric ulcers under conflict conditions (Ader, Tatum, and Beels, 1960). Rats reared together are more susceptible to ulceration when placed alone in a conflict situation than rats reared alone. Other students of the behavior of animals have focused on some of the biological variables that may relate to reactions to conflict. For example, it has been shown that different types of drugs have quite specific and perhaps opposite effects on reactions to conflict (Barry and Miller, 1962; Miller, 1961).

One characteristic of animals as subjects is that their experimental histories can be carefully controlled. With some species it is possible to go beyond the control of individual animals to the study of behavior over generations. In the case of animals such as rats or mice, it is possible to select a characteristic or trait of special interest to the researcher and proceed to inbreed it. Hall (1936, 1941) reported one series of experiments in which rats were inbred for emotionality. Emotionality was defined as the tendency of rats to urinate and defecate when exposed to strange situations. Over successive generations it was possible to inbreed one group of animals high in emotionality and another group low in emotionality. Other characteristics, for example, high and low aggressiveness, have also been successfully inbred (Scott, 1958; Scott and Fuller, 1965).

Another problem that can be studied in animal research but not in work with humans concerns the relationships among hereditary and environmental factors. All studies of humans on this topic must perforce be after the fact. Illustrative of what animal research permits is an investigation (Lindzey, Lykken, and Winston, 1960) that dealt with the effects of infantile trauma and genetic factors on adult behavior. Infant mice, offspring of four strains, were assigned to experimental and control groups. In the experimental group, the mice when four days old were administered a noxious auditory stimulus for four successive days. Control mice were treated exactly like the experimental animals except that the traumatic auditory stimulus was not administered. At 30 days of age, animals from both groups were placed in situations in which indices of emotionality and timidity could be obtained. Further indices were obtained at 70 and 100 days of age. One indication of emotionality was the presence or absence of urination and defecation when the animals were placed in the same type of stimulus situation in which the traumatic auditory stimulus had been administered to the experimental group; the sound, however, was omitted during these tests. The research showed that differences in adult emotionality were a function of infantile trauma. Even at 100 days, the experimental animals responded more emotionally than the control animals. But marked differences in response to infantile trauma were also obtained among the four strains of mice used. It seems clear, then, that at least for mice, the best prediction of adult emotionality results when attention is paid simultaneously both to hereditary background and environmental trauma. The following conclusions by Lindzey, Lykken, and Winston (1960, p. 13) seem in some respects remarkably similar to several drawn in considering other areas of personality research:

> What are the implications of such a finding for psychological theory? One may contend that these results, even secured in connection with mere mice or guinea pigs, provide a type of confirmation of Freud's assertion that any attempt to map early experience into adult behavior must allow for the contribution of genetic factors. While such a statement has a rather hollow sound at the level of human behavior because of the little that is known concerning the gene structure of man, it does have some specific empirical implications. For example, our results would suggest that when an investigator works with *S*s [subjects] of unknown or uncontrolled heredity, it is altogether possible to conduct an otherwise exemplary study of the effects of infantile experience and fail to find evidence for such effects. Or, more generally, we may expect that a variety of different empirical findings might be observed in similar studies as a consequence of investigators dealing with *S*s of various genetic backgrounds, rather than as a result of faulty experimental technique. In general, this is a finding that makes life more complex for both investigator and theorist, and in an area where there has never been any shortage of complexity.

Of all animal studies conducted in recent years, few have had the impact of Harlow's (1958, 1962) experiments with monkeys. His concern was with variables at work in early mother-child relationships, particularly the degree of tactual contact between mother and child. In these experiments, infant monkeys were essentially reared by wire mesh and terry-cloth "mothers." (See Figure 19-1.)

These "mothers" or more exactly, mother surrogates, were mock-ups from which the infant could obtain food. Since the young monkeys could obtain food easily from the wire or the cloth mother surrogates, it seemed there was only one important difference between the surrogates. This difference was in the possibility of what Harlow has called contact comfort. He found that it was much easier and more sensually gratifying to infant monkeys to cuddle up to a soft cloth

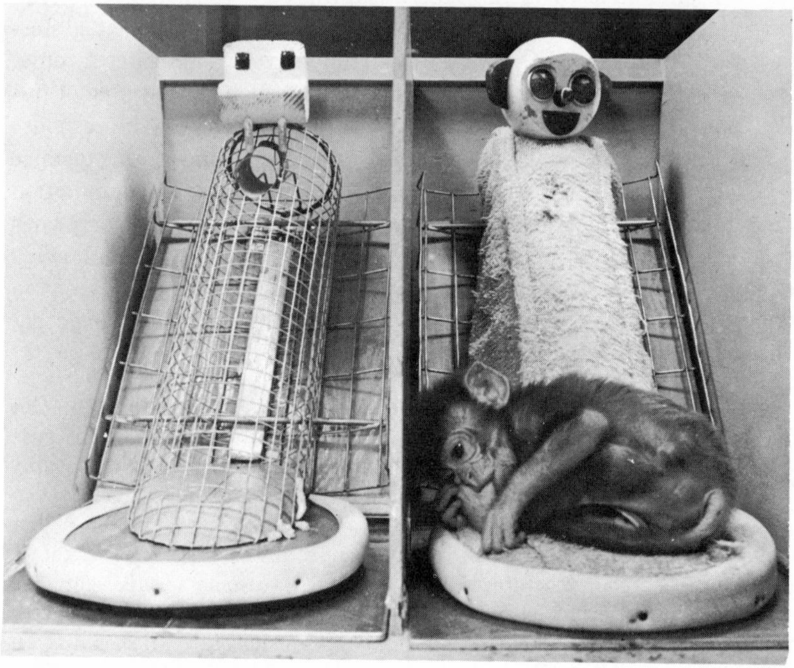

Figure 19-1 Wire and cloth mother surrogates (reproduced from Harlow, 1958).

object than to a rigid hard one. (Anyone who observes the behavior of human children with their "security" blankets will see this very clearly.)

The major question posed by Harlow's experiments was: Does contact make a difference in influencing the infancy and postinfancy behavior of monkeys? On several counts, Harlow's results unambiguously demonstrate that there are differences and that they are quite striking. He found that an infant monkey reared with the wire mother would, when given free choice, approach and cuddle the cloth mother rather than the surrogate that had, in effect, provided it with its daily bread. The preference of infant monkeys for the terry-cloth surrogate, regardless of the source of nutriment, persisted for many months. Furthermore, when the subjects were placed in fear-arousing situations, they preponderantly ran for solace to the cloth rather than to the wire surrogate. (See Figure 19-2.) The fact that the infants reared by the wire surrogate seemed to be more emotional and less well-adjusted than those reared by the cloth one led Harlow to conclude that the degree of contact comfort available to the infant was an important variable in social adjustment and development.

Is a cloth mother comparable to a real monkey mother? Harlow's evidence suggests that a synthetic mother is not as effective a rearing agent as a real one. Studies of adult monkeys who had been reared with cloth mothers indicated more aggressiveness, poorer social adjustment, and less effective heterosexual behavior among them than among monkeys reared by real mothers (Harlow, 1962).

Although there are hazards in generalizing from one type of organism to another, and although more research on the variables involved in contact comfort is needed, Harlow's findings appear to support the emphases that several theorists have placed on the significance of experiences in early childhood. It will be remembered that both Freud and Sullivan in particular stressed the influential role of early mother-child relationships on the course of social development (Chapters 2 and 3).

These examples of animal studies relating to a variety of personality

Figure 19-2 Typical response to cloth mother surrogate in fear test (reproduced from Harlow, 1958).

concepts suggest that experiments with subhumans can provide valuable leads for research on humans. They provide vehicles for isolating some of the life-history variables that influence numerous aspects of behavior. Let us turn now to a consideration of some animal investigations in which social behavior *per se* was observed and experimentally manipulated.

THE SOCIAL BEHAVIOR OF ANIMALS

Studies of the behavior of animals are important scientific contributions, irrespective of their possible contribution to an understanding of human individual differences and social behavior. However, students primarily concerned with the latter phenomena cannot help but be eager to obtain comparative data on individual differences and social behavior among lower organisms. What kinds of social organizations do animals display? What sort of individual difference variables relate to their social behavior? Because the primates of all animals are most similar to man, we shall focus attention on them as we deal with these questions.

Recent evidence has shown that not only do primates such as monkeys and apes have social orders, but that these relationships are also highly complex (Mason, 1964; Mirsky, 1960). Consider this description given by Schaller (1963, p. 237) of the mountain gorilla:

> The focal point of each group is the leader, who is, without exception, the dominant silverbacked male. The entire daily routine—the time of rising, the direction and distance of travel, the location and duration of rest periods, and finally the time of nest building—is largely determined by the leader. Every independent animal in the group, except occasionally subordinate males, appears to be constantly aware of the location and activity of the leader either directly or through the behavior of animals in his vicinity. Cues reflecting a changed pattern of activity are rapidly transmitted through the group and the subsequent behavior of the members is patterned after that of the leader.

Schaller spent many months observing the behavior of mountain gorillas under natural conditions. That such observations can be both fascinating in themselves as well as valuable for a comparative approach to behavior is suggested by this account by Schaller (1963, pp. 237–238) of the behavior of a group of gorillas:

> The leader usually communicates his readiness to move on by a simple but characteristic gesture. He rises and without hesitation walks rather stiff-legged and rapidly in a certain direction. This gait differs markedly from

the leisurely pace employed when merely ambling a few steps. By watching the leader I was able to predict a group movement as rapidly as the gorillas. The response of the animals to the leader is most clearly shown in the rest area. Whenever the leader rises to change his position, at least one animal turns its head to watch. If the leader rises and walks slowly several feet, the others usually do not respond. But if he indicates his readiness to leave, at least one animal rises to join him within half a minute, and others do likewise until the whole group has become alerted. In general, the speed of response to the leader depends on the abruptness of his actions. When he moves slowly out to feed, some gorillas remain occasionally in the rest area for five or more minutes, but when he departs suddenly, the animals generally run to his side.

Sometimes the leader employs a characteristic posture which apparently serves as a signal to the other members of the group, indicating his imminent departure. He faces in a certain direction and stands motionless for as long as ten seconds with front and hind legs spread farther from each other than usual. . . .

On occasion, the male emits a series of two to eight rather short but forceful grunts, either as he stands or within 200 feet after having moved from a site. This vocalization seems to signify "Here I am, follow me," for the members of the group respond by moving in his direction. Once, the leader gave this sound while the rest of the group watched me from the branches of trees. Although he was out of sight behind a curtain of vines, all except one animal descended and joined him, only to return into the trees when the leader did not move away.

We have already mentioned an example of the complexity of primate social behavior. Harlow's work with infant monkeys reared by wire and cloth mothers suggests that the infant-mother relationship is exceedingly important. The cloth mother appeared to provide infant monkeys with what might seem to be emotional security. Other studies with monkeys have shown that the nature of infants' filial-like attachments depends on their environmental experience. For example, chimpanzees reared in social isolation until 21 months of age played freely together but did not show the usual signs, such as clinging behavior, of filial-like attachments (Mason, 1964).

As infant primates mature, their close attachments to their mothers wane and their social ties with peers increase. The importance of these ties has been shown in one study in which opportunity for social activity among young chimpanzees was found to be equally or more reinforcing than food (Mason, Saxon, and Sharpe, 1963). There seems little question that among primates there is not only a social organization but that there also exist very strong affinities.

What role might individual differences play in animal social relationships? A common observation in many species is a hierarchy of social dominance. This factor seems both stable and long lasting and may not be restricted, as might be thought, to fighting behavior. Experimental attempts to alter dominance in primates through manipulations such as food deprivation and food quality have often been unsuccessful (Mason, 1964). On the other hand, experimental brain lesions have been successful in achieving changes in the dominance hierarchy. Mirsky (1960, p. 85) has made these comments concerning the effects of such lesions on social behavior:

> . . . all these lesions have the effect of destroying or weakening previously learned connections between complex social stimuli and socioemotional responses. The loss or forgetting of learned responses to the human being is manifested in the following way: the operated animal responds directly and simply to the offer of food by accepting it readily. This would account for the apparent increase in fearlessness in the individual-cage situation. The amygdala lesion produces more of such impairment or "forgetting" than do the other limbic lesions, and this is reflected in the group-cage situation. The animal's cage mates, which are unimpaired, seem to sense its uncertainty and hesitation and, according to their own patterns of social responses (their own aggressiveness), may attack and then dominate a previously dominant animal.

Some field workers have gone so far as to refer to highly dominant male primates as possessing the characteristic of leadership. Supporting this inference is evidence that certain animals take the lead in initiating social activities, such as determining the line of march. Primate leaders also have been observed to play a role in quelling intragroup fights, protecting females and young, and in determining the territory covered by their groups.

It thus seems likely that observations of social relationships among animals hold rich possibilities for the fields of personality and animal psychology. Mason (1964, p. 300) has referred to some of these:

> . . . social dependence, docility, playfulness, a strong impulse toward investigatory activities, lack of aggression, and the variable and incomplete character of many instinctive patterns are prominent traits in all young primates. By adolescence they seem to have largely disappeared in the normally socialized macaque, while they continue to be prominent in the behavior of the adolescent chimpanzee.
>
> In man, as in all primates, these traits seem to recede with advancing age, but they are retained longer, well into reproductive maturity. Consider, for example, the nature and amount of rough-and-tumble play that occurs among human parents and children. Although such activities also occur between chimpanzee parent and child, they are relatively limited in variety

and frequency. In the majority of monkeys, parental play is rare, if not altogether absent.

Thus it is possible that many of man's distinctive psychological traits arise from a common source, namely the tendency to retain infantile or juvenile characters into adulthood. This is conjecture, of course, and the evolutionary trends that culminated in man cannot yet be described with confidence. The possibility that behavioral studies of the nonhuman primates may contribute to the solution of this evolutionary question adds an exciting dimension to primate research.

CONCLUDING COMMENT CONCERNING ANIMAL RESEARCH, PERSONALITY, AND SOCIAL BEHAVIOR

Superficially, it might seem defensible to argue that an understanding of human behavior can come only from studying it. But the nature of our curiosity about human behavior will vary depending on the context in which we operate. Animal research is of direct relevance to curiosity about the relationship between the behavior of humans and the behavior of other organisms. Isolation of the unique facets of man is an empirical matter, and this requires that man be compared with other organisms. In addition to the role played by animal research in a comparative study of man, animal research can be of great importance to personality psychologists because of its hypothesis-generating and hypothesis-testing possibilities.

20

Personality and Physiological Responding

Personality researchers conduct experiments because they wish to observe behavior under carefully controlled conditions. As these conditions are varied and studied from different perspectives, it is hoped that fruitful explanatory concepts will evolve. In conducting experiments it is necessary to decide not only upon the conditions under which organisms are to respond but also upon the dependent measures that are to be recorded. Dependent variables to which we have referred include indices of performance, verbal responses, and social decisions.

Another class of dependent variables also mentioned includes indices of bodily reactions. Examples of such indices are heart rate, palmar sweating, characteristics of the blood, and glandular secretions. An area of investigation that has intrigued a number of researchers concerns the relationships among overt responses, covert responses, and physiological responses.

Physiological responses are also, in a sense, private. They occur within the organism and, interestingly, are often not under the conscious control of the individual; for example, one cannot stop sweating in a stressful situation simply by instructing oneself to do so. Can data about internal bodily processes contribute to the development of personality constructs? This question shall be our primary concern in this chapter. Most studies of personality are based in some manner on the analysis of verbal behavior and motor responses. But are not verbal, motor, and physiological responding but different facets of the organism's reply to stimulation? Might not nonverbal facts, in the form of indices of internal bodily events, add an inevitable dimension in a comprehensive psychology of the individual?

EXPERIMENTAL METHODS IN STUDYING PHYSIOLOGICAL RESPONDING

Physiological responses are dependent variables. Hence it is not surprising that psychologists have been interested in the question: What kinds of environmental events lead to changes in indices of physiological functioning? Just as one might ask: In what ways do orienting conditions influence performance? So might it be asked: How do orienting conditions influence physiological responses such as heart rate, pulse, and sweating? Finally, it might be asked: Are there similarities or parallels between the effects of orienting conditions on the more commonly employed dependent measures in personality research and on measures of physiological responding?

These questions suggest that, other than the particular techniques of recording changes in bodily processes, methods for studying them are not basically different from those employed in studying the psychological problems of performance, verbal behavior, and social behavior. Whatever the response measures recorded and whatever the experimental conditions, attention must be paid to the need for appropriate control conditions with which experimental conditions can be compared.

Examples of Experiments on Personality and Physiological Responding

PHYSIOLOGICAL RESPONDING AND PERFORMANCE. In Chapter 15 we investigated the effects of experimental conditions, to wit, orienting instructions, failure reports, and task characteristics on the achievements of individuals. These conditions may be conceptualized as influencing the internal state of the individual, which in turn influences performance. To be better able to understand the effects of experimental conditions on internal states, several investigators have attempted to find out what effects these conditions might have on the physiological state of the individual.

An example of such a condition may be found in Raphelson's (1957) study in which subjects were placed in a competitive test situation requiring performance on a complex perceptual motor task. The objective of the experiment was not so much to compare a stressful with a nonstressful condition as to determine the relationship between certain personality characteristics and physiological responses to the competitive situation. However, within the design of the research it was possible to compare the subjects' physiological response prior to and during performance on the competitive task. The dependent variable in Raphelson's study was the electrical conductance of the skin, in this case, measured on the palm of the hand.

Before turning to Raphelson's study let us say a few words about the use of skin conductance as a dependent measure. Skin conductance ranges from a low point during sleep to high levels in emotionally arousing or highly motivating situations. It is regarded as an index of the organism's level of physiological activity. What typically happens to skin conductance under neutral motivational conditions may be seen in Figure 20-1 (Duffy and Lacey, 1946) which shows skin conductance curves for each of three days for two tasks differing in difficulty level. The experiment involved the determination of the subjects' thresholds for tones over a three-day period. Examination of Figure 20-1 indicates that skin conductance levels decreased over the three-day period. Furthermore, skin conductance during Days I, II, and III shows progressive declines throughout the sessions. These changes seem attributable to the subject's progressive

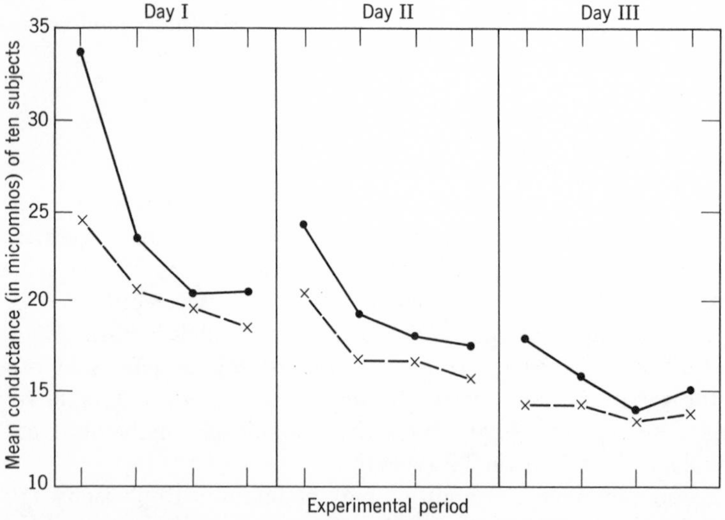

Figure 20-1 Palmar conductance during easy (Task I) and difficult (Task II) discriminations (after Duffy and Lacey, 1946, p. 441).
Task I ——— Task II – – – –

adaptation to the experiment. In all likelihood, they probably felt much more at ease at the end of the experiment than at its beginning. A study by Sears (1933) illustrates the effect of the nature of the task on physiological activation. He had college women solve 20 arithmetic problems. When the first 10 problems were easy and the last 10 were hard, he found that there was a gradual decline in activation through the first 10 problems, but that with the first hard problem an abrupt increase occurred.

Let us return now to Raphelson's (1957) experiment. He wished to observe changes in skin conductance between a preorienting instruction period and a postorienting instruction period. The subjects were selected on the basis of test anxiety, general anxiety, and need for achievement scores. The measures of these characteristics were the Test Anxiety Questionnaire (Mandler and Sarason, 1952; Sarason and Mandler, 1952), Taylor's Manifest Anxiety Scale (1953), and McClelland's (1955; McClelland, Clark, Roby, and Atkinson, 1949) index of need for achievement. During the preorienting instruction period, there were no statistically significant differences in skin conductance related to these personality measures.

The picture changed, however, following administration of motivating instructions. These instructions informed the subjects that they were to perform as well as they could on a series of test items. Scores on the Taylor scale of general anxiety were not found to be related to skin conductance changes. Both the test anxiety and need for achievement measures were significantly related to this dependent variable. Furthermore, when subjects were divided on the bases of their scores on both test anxiety and need for achievement, the most clear-cut results obtained.

Raphelson (1957) reasoned that subjects low in need for achievement and high in test anxiety would show the greatest increases in skin conductance. This expectation stemmed from the assumptions that the McClelland measure was an index of hope of success in competitive situations and the test anxiety measure was an index of fear of failure in such situations. Someone with little hope of success and a great deal of fear of failure should, according to this interpretation, be most upset by highly motivating conditions. Indeed, Raphelson found that the low need for achievement, high test anxiety group showed the greatest relative increase in skin conductance following the test instructions. When the data for subjects high in need for achievement and low in test anxiety were compared with that of the high test anxiety group, differences in the expected direction emerged.

The results of the experiment indicate that characteristics assessed by means of psychological techniques bear significant relationships to physiological reactions. They further suggest that the more specific the personality measures are to the nature of the experimental situation (in this case, a testing situation), the more significant will be these relationships. Another study (Kissel and Littig, 1962) has shown that test anxiety is related to skin conductance in testing situations but not in situations in which instructions inform subjects that their performance will not be evaluated. These results may be integrated with those reviewed in the discussion of personality and performance. It would appear that assessed personal characteristics are related both to actual performance levels and to physiological activation during performance.

Some studies of physiological activation have been aimed particularly at finding out how persons respond to extremely dangerous and personally threatening tasks. In one such study (Berkun, Bialek, Kern and Yagi, 1962) physiological responses were recorded for soldiers participating in military exercises under conditions of realistic, simulated forest fires and radioactive fallout. Another study which dealt with a realistic life stress was reported by Epstein (1962). In his experiment, Epstein obtained self-reports and skin conductance measures on a group of persons who were in the process of learning to perform parachute jumps.

Figure 20-2 shows skin conductance levels both before and after jumps for these novice parachute jumpers. It can be seen that the conductance level was always higher before than after a jump. This indicates, as would be expected, that the parachutists were more tense before than after jumping. It appears, as one might again expect, that the prejump tension of the parachutists was particularly great on their first several jumps.

What one would not necessarily expect in Figure 20-2 is the increases in conductance that occurred after the parachutists had made 20 to 30 practice jumps. There is no ready explanation of the apparent increases in tenseness. What may be happening is what often occurs in the case of persons who learn to drive an automobile. At the point at which the novice driver becomes capable of maneuvering the car, he may experience a kind of euphoric confidence. However, with an increase in experience, an awareness of the danger of accidents may lead to increased caution and tenseness.

Epstein (1962) did not only record physiological responses. He also obtained self-ratings from the parachutists of their approach and avoidance tendencies as the time for a jump neared. He found that the approach tendency, that is, the willingness to jump, was much

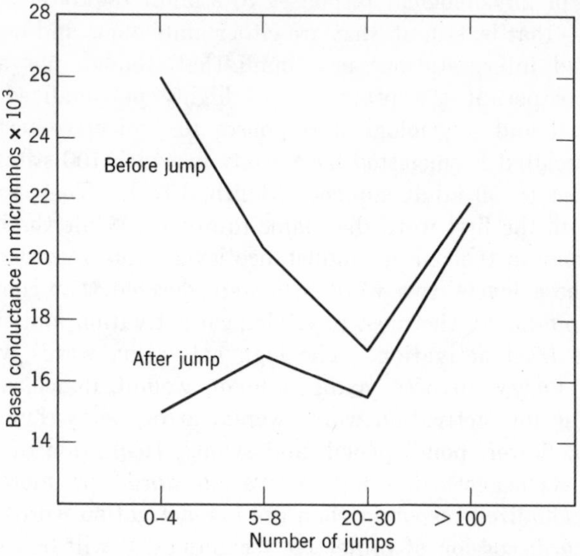

Figure 20-2 Basal conductance before and after a jump as a function of experience (after Epstein, 1962, p. 183).

greater than the avoidance tendencies early in the waiting period before a jump. However, as the moment for the jump approached, the avoidance tendency showed a large increase. Why, then, did the parachutists jump? One explanation is that the psychological momentum which led them to become involved in parachute jumping in the first place was so great as to override the avoidance tendency.

Epstein and others have noted a number of interesting characteristics among the verbal reports of persons whose task it is to perform dangerous assignments (Fenz, 1964). For example, Epstein (1962) found that anxiety dreams are rarely reported by parachutists before jumps, but that a few days after a jump they are much commoner. Another study (Basowitz, Persky, Korchin, and Grinker, 1955) found that self-ratings of fear in paratroopers increased several days after their period of training had ended. These findings concerning fear and performance under dangerous conditions suggest the desirability of carrying out investigations in which verbal behavior, physiological responding, and level of performance can be directly compared.

PHYSIOLOGICAL RESPONDING AND FANTASY. In addition to interest in the physiological correlates of performance, there is reason to be interested in physiological responses to stimuli that are more or less projective—that is, stimuli that are either ambiguous and hence permit personalized interpretations or stimuli that, though not ambiguous, nevertheless permit the projection of highly personalized reactions. That verbal and physiological responses to projective tests may be highly correlated is suggested by a study in which 100 stimulus words were spoken to 50 adult subjects (Smith, 1922). Their task was to respond with the first word that came to mind. While the individuals were responding their skin conductance levels were recorded. On the basis of these levels, two word lists were derived that contained the 10 words producing the most physiological activation and the 10 producing the least activation. The high activation words were these: kiss, love, marry, divorce, name, woman, wound, dance, afraid, and proud. The low activation words were: carrot, berry, hunger, white, glass, give, flower, pond, pencil, and swim. Inspection of the words in these lists suggest that high-activation words are more likely to arouse personalized responses than are low-activation words.

From the discussion of projective techniques, it will be remembered that there are significant relationships between verbal and physiological responses to the Rorschach, and a phrase association test (Mandler, Mandler, Kremen and Sholiton, 1961). Nelson and Epstein (1962) have reported on the relationship between a personality characteristic assessed with TAT-like material and responses to a word-association test. They isolated one conflict and one comparison group. All subjects were shown two TAT-type pictures. One picture had stimulus characteristics that might lead subjects to tell stories involving hostility. The other, a neutral picture, was much less likely to give rise to hostile stories.

The conflict subjects were those who told stories involving hostility to the neutral picture but not to the one more likely to arouse hostile fantasies. Conflict over the expression of hostility was inferred in these cases because of the inappropriateness of the hostility-related responses. Those subjects who responded appropriately constituted a comparison group. The conflict and comparison groups were administered a word-association test that included three types of words. These types differed in terms of word links to hostility: High hostility words included "smash" and "kill"; medium hostility words included "push" and "chase"; neutral words included "run" and "jump."

The question that interested Nelson and Epstein was: Would persons who are conflicted over hostility, as assessed through stories told to projective pictures, differ from persons who are apparently without conflict in responding to these stimulus words? To obtain an answer to this question they recorded two measures: galvanic skin responses to the three types of words and reaction times to them. For each type of word the conflict subjects showed stronger galvanic skin reactions than the comparison subjects. Similarly, for each type of word, the conflict subjects had longer reaction times than the comparison subjects. In both cases the differences were the smallest for the neutral words. It would appear that both reaction times and physiological responses to verbal stimuli differ considerably for persons unlike in inferred conflict over hostility.

A situation containing interesting projective aspects was used by Lazarus, Speisman, Mordkoff, and Davison (1962) in a study of physiological responding. These investigators studied the behavior of college students during three experimental sessions. During Session One the subjects took a battery of personality tests, including the CPI and portions of the MMPI. During Sessions Two and Three they viewed a type of projective technique, motion pictures. The Session Two film was entitled, "Corn Farming in Iowa," and was neutral in its connotations. The Session Three film was entitled "Subincision," and depicted crude operations on the penis and scrotum of adolescent aboriginal boys. Previous research had indicated that this film was an emotionally arousing stimulus (Aas, 1958; Schwartz, 1956).

During Sessions Two and Three a number of dependent measures were obtained. These included indices of skin resistance, heart rate, and biochemical measures of physiological reactions. In addition, written responses and self-ratings of tension level were recorded. The following questions were asked of all subjects at the end of Sessions Two and Three: What were your reactions to this movie? What are the things in the movie that stand out in your mind? The subjects were also asked to write down as much as they could recall of what went on in each movie. These written comments were then subjected to content analysis.

Lazarus, et al. found that there were large heart rate and skin resistance differences between Sessions Two and Three. There were also large differences between these sessions with regard to subjects' self-reports and written descriptions of the films. Both the verbal and the physiological data showed that exposure to the "Subincision" film aroused a high level of psychological stress. Figure 20-3 shows variations in skin conductance among a group of subjects who watched the "Subincision" film (Lazarus, 1964). Heightened skin conductance

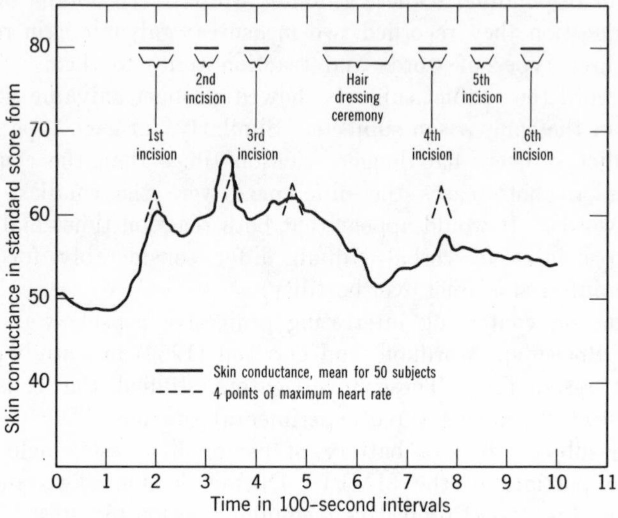

Figure 20-3 Variation in skin conductance during the subincision film for 50 subjects (after Lazarus, 1964, p. 404).

clearly characterized the first four incisions depicted in the film. The deep skin conductance trough in the middle of the film occurred while relatively benign hair dressing ceremonies were being depicted. The curve in Figure 20-3 would seem to reflect the psychological stress created by the film.

Lazarus, et al. found that some assessed characteristics were more related to this stress than others. With regard to the correlation between personal characteristics assessed in Session One and physiological reactivity, it was found that subjects characterized as ambitious, shrewd, confident, impulsive, forceful, and self-centered were physiologically less reactive during the "Subincision" film than were those identified as mature, moderate, self-controlled, and responsive to the plight of others.

The experiment of Lazarus, et al. (1962) has shown that individual differences in personal characteristics are correlated with physiological reactions. A subsequent study (Speisman, et al., 1964) sought to isolate experimentally some of the variables that might influence persons' reactions to stress. The "Subincision" film was shown to four groups of subjects. For each group a different sound track accompanied the film. The four types of sound track were: (1) *Trauma.* This em-

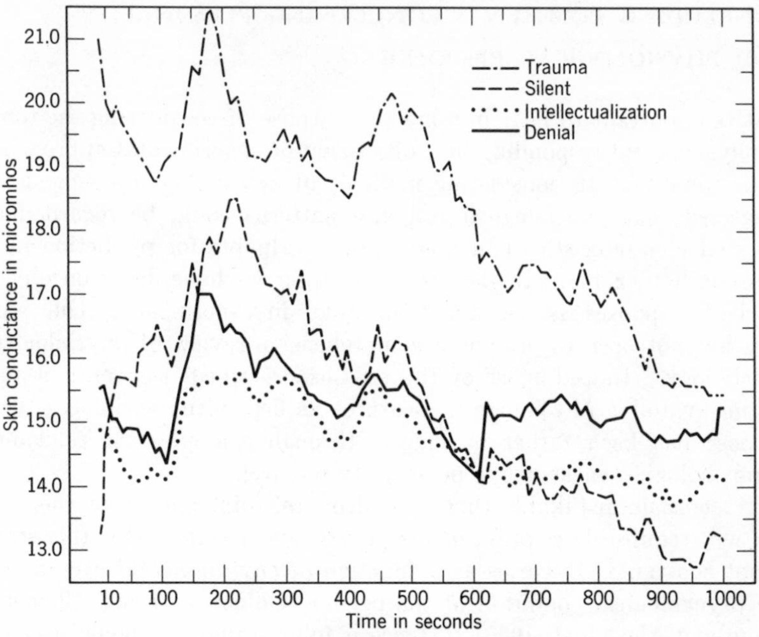

Figure 20-4 The effects of the experimental treatments on skin conductance (after Speisman, Lazarus, Mordkoff and Davison, 1964, p. 373).

phasized the danger of the operation performed in the film, the sadism involved in it, and the pain suffered by the circumcized boys. (2) *Intellectualization.* Emphasizing the circumcision ritual as an interesting specimen of human behavior, this sound track was more intellectually than emotionally oriented. (3) *Denial.* This emphasized that the native boys looked forward to circumcision and denied that it was either threatening to health or terribly painful. (4) *Silent.* No sound track accompanied the film.

Figure 20-4 shows skin conductance patterns for the four experimental groups. It is clear that the trauma sound track led to much higher skin conductance levels than did the other three conditions. The work of Lazarus and his colleagues (Lazarus, et al., 1962; Lazarus, 1964; Speisman, et al., 1964) strongly suggests that an understanding of persons' reactions to presumably stressful stimuli requires attention both to assessed characteristics and to experimentally manipulated variables.

CONCLUDING COMMENTS CONCERNING PERSONALITY AND PHYSIOLOGICAL RESPONDING

It is important to bear in mind the purpose of considering the topic of physiological responding in a discussion of experimental approaches to personality. In considering methods of personality assessment we suggested that physiological response patterns could be regarded as assessed characteristics and might prove valuable for prediction purposes (Chapter 14). In the present chapter we have dwelt on physiological responses as dependent variables in experiments. Our purpose has not been to provide a comprehensive review of physiological psychology. Indeed most of the studies described used only a few of the available physiological measures as dependent variables. Our purpose has been rather to suggest through examples the relevance of physiological measures to personality research.

It seems unmistakable that any ultimate, total picture of the person will require description of his physiological state. But this state is not constant. It varies as a function of environmental events and the psychological condition of the person (Goldstein, Jones, Clemens, Flagg and Alexander, 1965). Hence it follows that psychologists seek to determine in what ways bodily processes function under different types of conditions. Physiological responses *may* run parallel to persons' verbal responses. But this relationship cannot be expected always to obtain (McCleary and Lazarus, 1949; Lazarus and McCleary, 1951).

As workers in the field of physiological psychology are well aware, there are many complex problems that permeate the study of physiological responses. We have already pointed out that different people show particular patterns of physiological responses to specific types of environmental stimuli (Lacey, 1950). There are also technical problems relating to the means through which these responses are recorded. For example, different procedures used in recording physiological reactivity may not always yield identical results. Thus it is not sufficient for a researcher to decide to obtain certain kinds of physiological data. It is also necessary for him to consider the possible methods for obtaining the data (Dykman, Ackerman, Galbrecht and Reese, 1963). Then there are psychological problems associated with the recording of physiological responses. To obtain indices of physiological events it is necessary to hook up subjects to recording instruments. What effect does being "hooked up" have on a person's bodily processes? Personality researchers, with their interest in the context in which behavior occurs, seem well suited to contribute answers to this question.

Two other matters relating to physiological activity seem of special interest to personality researchers. One is the correlation between persons' physiological responses and their perceptions of them. Although it is important to gain an understanding of persons' psychological selves, it also seems worthwhile to increase understanding of their bodily selves. Psychological investigations can shed light on the relationships between bodily events and verbal reports of them.

Another matter that merits experimental study is physiological reactivity in social contexts. Most physiological experiments are carried out in situations in which the behavior of one subject at a time is studied. Although the technology of obtaining physiological records has often required this one-at-a-time limitation, improvements in technique should make it possible to study the physiological reactivity of groups of individuals. An example of the possibilities may be found in one investigation in which the heart rates of patients and therapists were recorded (Di Mascio, Boyd, Greenblatt and Solomon, 1955). A correlation of +.79 between patients' and therapists' heart rates was found during the initial stages of the psychiatric interview. The correlation during the final stages was —.44. It also appeared that the psychotherapists differed in the influences they had on patients' heart rates.

There is no question that persons are affected psychologically by other persons with whom they come into contact. It seems likely that they would also be affected physiologically. A task for the future is to determine the nature of these effects.

21

Experiments as Social Situations

In the preceding chapters we have described experiments dealing with performance and learning, perceptual processes, verbal and social behavior, and physiological reactions. All of these fields are vast domains in and of themselves. For the student of personality who is interested in the total functioning of the individual person, the number of independent and dependent variables to which he attends can be restricted only on the basis of arbitrary distinctions. The personality researcher feels free to borrow techniques and problems from other investigators in other fields and hopes that his orientation to behavior will lead to unique and fruitful contributions to the general body of scientific knowledge.

The experimental approach to personality can prove instructive in several ways. We have seen how psychological experiments have shed light on hypotheses stemming from general theoretical orientations. This has been especially true in connection with psychoanalytic theory. We have also seen how experiments have themselves served to generate ideas and hypotheses for future study. For some experiments the impetus seems to come from general orientations to behavior; for others it seems to emanate from empirically derived facts for which explanations are not readily available.

As the study of personality has become more and more empirical, its concepts about personal characteristics and their relationships to behavior have become more specific. This has come about in part because students of personality in going into the laboratory have become more aware of the complexes of variables that affect even the simplest behavioral response. In considering the roles of these variables in behavior, it has often been found that general orientations to behavior such as those reviewed in Part 1 are simply not sufficiently specific to delineate the form of experimental manipulations and controls. Global theoretical orientations have served to raise general problems for investigation, but the tendency has been for these problems to be divided into more specific ones dealing with relatively small units of behavior. Thus, for example, psychoanalytic thinking has contributed in a significant way to ideas underlying experiments on perceptual defense. Current conceptions and hypotheses about perceptual defense, however, are both more restricted in the types of behavior referred to and more complex in the number of specific independent and dependent variables with which they deal.

One might interpret these experimental methods and findings as supporting the notion of a psychology of situations. Persons find themselves in many and varied kinds of situations. Thus we might classify human situations into those involving the need to solve intellectual tasks, to interact socially with others, and to reflect upon oneself. One contribution of the experimental study of personality to general psychology has been its demonstration in a variety of situations of the important roles of personal characteristics and situational variables. We have seen that in many situations studied by psychologists, such as perception experiments and experiments on learning and physiological reactivity, these personal variables play roles that cannot be ignored. Because personal characteristics and the contexts in which they manifest themselves seem so important and so general, it is not surprising that the area of personality overlaps as much as it does with other areas of study.

Helson (1964), recognizing this overlap, has developed what he calls an adaptation-level approach to behavior. This approach deals with the adaptation or adjustment of individuals to environmental conditions. Adaptation to the environment, however, is not determined solely by external conditions. It is determined, also, by the individual's perceptions of these conditions and by his personal characteristics. Helson is equally critical of approaches to behavior that describe the individual as solely a product of environmental pressures, and approaches that conceive of him as solely a product of psychic forces. According to Helson (1964, p. 582) personality is the study of the person in the situation: "Personality is envisaged as the product of external and internal forces, acting at specific times, in specific situations, and having specific outcomes characteristic of the individual."

The contribution of personality research to the general psychology of behavior can be seen no more clearly than in recent evidence that bears on what might be termed the social psychology of the psychological experiment (Orne, 1962*b*; Rosenthal, 1963). Because of the broad significance of this evidence, let us examine it and its implications.

We have seen that situational variables in psychological experiments can influence behavior over and above treatments that experimenters explicitly administer to subjects. By situational variables are meant the characteristics of a situation that influence a person's interpretation of himself and the task at which he is working. According to this definition, orienting instructions and failure would be regarded as situational variables. *Findings of personality experiments suggest that to the extent that this sort of situational variable is operative but not controlled, the meaning of experimental data is open to question.* The advantage of manipulating such variables in a laboratory is that it permits the presentation, control, and emphasis of aspects of everyday life situations that occur unsystematically and are entangled with many other aspects of day-to-day living.

Orienting instructions and reports of performance can be regarded as communication variables, that is, they are information transmitted by an experimenter to a subject. It is not difficult to think of numerous examples of how two people might utter the same words and yet communicate quite different meanings to a listener. Sarah Bernhardt, one of the great actresses of this century, was said to have been able to evoke tears from audiences simply by reading the telephone directory to them in an idiosyncratic and compelling manner. A waitress can say, "May I help you?" and make you feel that you are most unwelcome. A teacher can say to a student, "You are doing fine," and make the student wonder what he has done wrong. Does it not seem plausible that different experimenters might evoke quite distinctive affective and emotional responses from subjects simply by virtue of the influence of the former's personality characteristics on their administration of the experimental communications? Empirical evidence has begun to accrue concerning this possibility, and the body of data, though small, is quite convincing in showing the need to study experimenters as well as subjects in psychological research.

What is this evidence? Consider an example provided by Rosenthal and his colleagues. These researchers have systematically studied what they refer to as experimenter bias (Rosenthal, 1963; Rosenthal, Persinger, Kline and Mulry, 1963). Their hypothesis was that experimenters can be biasing factors in psychological research. Using performance and learning tasks and tasks requiring subjects to make judgments, they found that experimenters' beliefs and hunches concerning how an experiment would turn out correlated with the actual results obtained. That is, experimenters may get the results they expect (or hope) to obtain. This effect has been shown to be equally potent in research on animals and humans (Rosenthal and Lawson, 1964). Furthermore, it has been shown that when naive experimenters are told what the "probable" results of an experiment will be, these "probable" results are obtained.

It should be emphasized that these findings do not seem to be interpretable simply as illustrations of conscious biasing or faking on the part of the experimenters. Rosenthal's study of several samples of experimenters indicated that they were trying as much as possible to be objective in their procedures. In one experiment, for example, experimenters were told that the rats they were running through a learning situation were "dull" rats (Rosenthal and Lawson, 1964). In fact, the rats were a random sample of rats caged in a laboratory. The learning of these rats, however, was poorer than a comparable group of rats not labeled as "dull."

At the human level, experiments have been reported in which samples of experimenters have been compared on the basis of certain personal characteristics. These characteristics include sex, test anxiety, and hostility. Not enough research has been carried out to permit generalizations about all of the ramifications of these characteristics. However, it appears that they are sufficiently potent to justify concern over the possible confounding effects of experimenters' personal characteristics on subjects' behavior in a wide variety of experimental contexts (McGuigan, 1963).

An example of research in which there were manipulations of *both* subjects' and experimenters' characteristics is the investigation reported by Winkel and Sarason (1964, p. 603). These experimenters had college students perform a difficult verbal learning task. Two characteristics of the subjects were studied, sex and test anxiety as inferred from questionnaire responses. One manipulated situational variable was the orienting instructions administered prior to performance. Three sets of instructions were used. Subjects given achievement-orienting instructions were told that the verbal learning task was a test of intellectual ability:

> This is a short form intelligence test. It involves the memorization of nonsense syllables as in ordinary verbal learning experiments. However the list you have to learn is one which measures intelligence and the ability to think in abstract terms. Pay close attention to each syllable, since each one missed lowers your score when it is compared with other people. The first trial will not be counted against you.

Another group of subjects was given reassuring instructions:

These kinds of lists are hard and so it's no surprise or matter of concern if you progress slowly at first and make mistakes. Before we start, perhaps I could mention a few things that will be helpful to you in the learning of the list I am going to show you on this memory drum. Many people get unduly upset and tense because they do not learn the list in just a few trials. If you don't worry about how you are doing but rather just concentrate on the list you will find you learn much more easily.

All subjects received these preliminary instructions:

You will see words appearing in this opening one at a time. After a word is presented, call out the next one *before* it appears. Of course, the first time through the list you won't be able to anticipate any words but after that call out the word before it appears in the window. Prior to the beginning of each new trial there will be a short rest in which you will see blank spaces in the opening. Asterisks will indicate that the first word in the list will appear next. When you see them call out the first word. Do you understand?

A control group received only the preliminary instructions that provided subjects with needed information.

One characteristic, the test anxiety of the experimenter, was studied. Instead of having a single experimenter, Winkel and Sarason used 12 male experimenters who had high scores on a self-report, test-anxiety questionnaire and 12 who had low scores on it. The major concern of Winkel and Sarason was with the question: Would differences in experimenters' test anxiety levels bear a relationship to subjects' performance under the experimental conditions?

Figure 21-1 shows the learning curves for the male and female subjects who were in contact with the high and low test-anxious experimenters. Examination of the learning curves suggests a number of interesting relationships. For example, the influence over learning of reassuring instructions was quite different for male and female subjects exposed to high and low test-anxious experimenters. Males and females under the neutral and achievement-orienting conditions responded comparably to high test-anxious experimenters. But this was not true of subjects exposed to low test-anxious experimenters. These and other findings reported by Winkel and Sarason provide evidence that experimenters are the vehicles through which experimental conditions are administered to subjects, and these vehicles, because they are human, are *not* standardized.

Some of the implications of experiments that analyze the relationships of experimenter characteristics to performance can be seen clearly

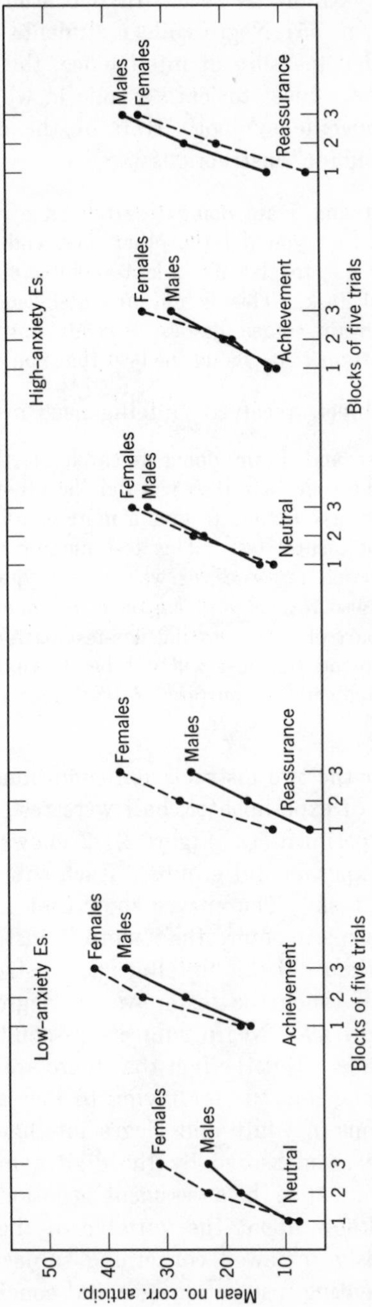

Figure 21-1 Mean number of correct responses for male and female subjects run by high- and low-anxious experimenters under three instructional conditions (after Winkel and Sarason, 1964, p. 605).

in research on the variable of race. In one study (Katz, Roberts, and Robinson, 1965, p. 55) Negro college students were administered a difficult version of a measure of intelligence, the digit-symbol test. The test required the subject to learn a code in which each digit was associated with a specific symbol. Half of the subjects, following a pretest, received "motor" instructions:

> I am a psychologist and I am doing research on eye-hand coordination. I have the code task that you did the other day, and now you are going to do a code task for me, to give me a more complete picture of how you work on this type of task. This is not an intelligence test, and it has nothing to do with your course grades or your aptitude as a student. Nonetheless, it is important that you do the best that you can . . . .

The remaining subjects received "intelligence" instructions:

> I am a psychologist and I am doing research on the measurement of intelligence. I have the code task that you did the other day, and now you are going to do a code task for me to give a more complete picture of your ability on this type of mental test. This test measures the speed and accuracy of your intellectual processes, as well as how quickly you can learn abstract material. It also reveals your capacity for concentration. Eventually this test will be part of a new intelligence-test battery that will be used in colleges. Your score on this test will not be shown to your teachers at Fisk. It will be used only for the purpose of developing the new intelligence-test battery . . . .

The subjects under the two instructional conditions were subdivided on the basis of race of experimenter, half were tested by a white and half by a Negro experimenter. Figure **21-2** shows the performance curves for the four experimental groups. Each subject had five trials on the digit symbol task. The curves show that for Negro subjects tested by a white experimenter, the "motor" instructions led to a higher performance than did the "intelligence" instructions. Just the opposite was the case when the tester was a Negro. We do not at the present time know *why* Negro subjects respond so differently to Negro and white testers. But the fact that there are significant differences provides a strong impetus for trying to increase understanding of Negroes' perceptions of white and Negro intelligence testers. Apparently, intelligence as measured by the digit symbol test, is influenced by the social context of the assessment situation.

Adding what we know about the variable of the experimenter to the material previously reviewed concerning subject and situational variables such as orienting instructions, several conclusions seem warranted. Summing these up in one statement, we would say that *for*

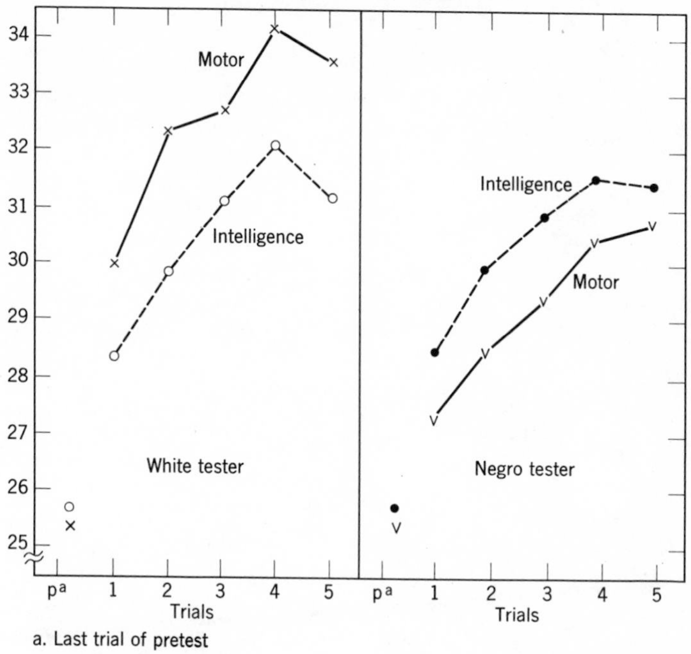

Figure 21-2 Mean digit-symbol scores on five 1-minute trials of the hard task for Negro subjects who had a white or a Negro experimenter and motor-test or intelligence-test instructions. ($N = 23$ for every group.) (After Katz, Roberts, and Robinson, 1965, p. 57.)

any interaction between individuals, be they subject and experimenter, friends, or employer and employee, it is necessary to examine the social aspects of the setting. Although all of the social aspects may not be important in any given context, it is only appropriate scientific caution to be aware of their potential roles.

At the outset of Part 3 we set forth the objective to demonstrate the role of a venerable method, experimentation, in the study of personality. We have seen that whereas the method may be an old one, it is capable of turning up new facts and relationships, and new problems for future investigation. We have also seen that, at least in the area of psychology with which we are concerned, the experimental method is not an impersonal device devoid of general meaning. Rather, it represents a way of studying personal processes with a care and precision not possible under ordinary conditions.

Part 4

PERSONALITY DEVELOPMENT

In several of the physical sciences, a researcher may "start from scratch" in his investigations. He may begin each experiment, so to speak, at time zero. He need not worry about the effects of yesterday's or today's barometric pressure, temperature, or humidity, on the reaction under study. Because he can control virtually all of the variables relevant to the reaction, any reference to matters prior to the experiment becomes essentially *non sequitur*.

What may be *non sequitur* to the physicist is, however, a very serious, real matter to the psychologist and to all students of the social and biological sciences. No matter how carefully the environment of animals is controlled, perfect control is never possible. At the human level, the concept of control and standardization of living conditions is not only impractical but also alien to many basic values. A researcher may be able to control carefully the conditions under which human subjects behave in a particular experimental situation. However, lurking in the back of his mind will be the facts of constitutional differences and differences in behavioral histories among his subjects. How might these differences influence present behavior?

Consider the individual difference variable of aggression. In agreement with Freud, we might entertain the hypothesis that aggression and humor are related. In order to evaluate this hypothesis we might develop a test that reflected persons' aggressive tendencies. Scores on this index could then be related to such characteristics as ability to tell jokes effectively, to write humorous prose, and to respond with gusto to funny stories. If we convincingly linked aggression with humor, our findings would indeed be interesting. They might also lead to the discovery of relationships among aggression, humor, and other aspects of behavior. Certainly at some point we would ask ourselves questions about the historical antecedents of aggression and humor. To what past individual factors of development might differences in present-day behavior be attributed?

One further example will bring home the value of historical antecedents to present-day characteristics and behavior. In Chapter 15 we described some of the efforts of McClelland (1955, 1961) and his colleagues to determine under experimental conditions the relationship of need for achievement to behavior. If, as appears to be true, McClelland's measure of need for achievement is related to aspects human performance and social behavior, then what is the genesis of this variable?

To obtain at least partial answers to this question, investigations have been carried out dealing with the behavior of children and child-rearing practices, parent-child relationships, and events and prior experiences that might predispose persons to particular levels of need for achievement. These studies suggest that individual differences in need for achievement can be detected in children as young as five years of age. They also suggest that mothers of sons who score high in need for achievement appear to expect more self-reliance from their offspring than mothers whose sons obtain low scores on need for achievement. There are also indications that emphasis in the home on self-reliance in children promotes a strong need for achievement only if the emphasis is a function of parental interest in the children's acquisition of self-mastery. When the emphasis on self-reliance stems from parental rejection of offspring, need for achievement seems to be relatively low. Crosscultural research has shown that need for achievement varies from society to society and that this variability is at least in part attributable to differences in child-rearing practices (McClelland, 1961).

Students of personality, therefore, must attend not only to individuality at a particular stage of development, but also to the genesis of that individuality. The problem of how people come to be the individuals they are constitutes the *raison d'etre* for an area of investigation called *developmental psychology*.

Eschewing conjecture, developmental psychologists may be considered to be empirical historians. In their research they seek to observe directly response patterns at various stages of life and from their observations to draw inferences about the process of development. Their work deals both with changes in behavior that occur as development proceeds, and with the influences brought to bear upon the individual that are related to changes in his behavior.

Awareness of the multifaceted nature of human behavior leads quickly to the realization that the concept of development is very complex and broad. Physical characteristics, perceptual and motor abilities, and intellectual attributes, as well as personality, are affected by chronological age and events correlated with chronological age. Because of our interests, we shall emphasize in our study of development conditions and situations that have been demonstrated or hypothesized to play important roles in the evolution of personality.

The presentation of problems in personality development will be made in terms of two broad topics. One involves the research methods and techniques that characterize the investigation of human behavior from a developmental point of view. We shall describe, illustrate, and discuss some of the more important of these research tools. A second topic concerns the chronicle of developmental events. Whether or not one realizes it, any attempt at listing the major happenings within the life span entails making judgments and discriminations. One's interests, hypotheses, and beliefs orient one to certain events rather than to others. For example, certain developmental psychologists are especially interested in the physical and chemical aspects of development. While not denying the importance of individual differences in these concomitants, students of personality development tend to emphasize personal events in the life of the individual and the effects of these on present and future behavior. Our approach to personality development will be couched primarily in these terms. In the course of a chronicle of personality development we shall, where appropriate, give examples of efforts to clarify the changing pattern of personal events that characterize the individual as he proceeds through life. In doing this, we shall become acquainted both with existing knowledge and the methodological problems that confront researchers.

22

Research on Personality Development

Before we embark on an examination of personality development, a few preliminary points should be made. A basic one is that development is a concept, an abstraction. It is an inference drawn from observed changes in behavior. It cannot blithely be assumed that the development of an organism necessarily follows a predetermined course. Nor can it be assumed that the determinants of behavior are easily discerned and traced. In some instances, genetic predispositions and biological maturation may account largely for observed changes in behavior. For example, it is unlikely that even elaborate attempts to teach a child to walk at a very early age will bear much fruit. Children seem to walk when they are ready to walk. Since early motor behavior is not powerfully influenced by learning, it is possible to chart with relative accuracy the course of its development. However, if one considers language development, the picture is quite different. Stimulation of the child's oral productions and reinforcement of them can make for relatively rapid acquisition of verbal skills. Learning, then, can be a very significant factor in early language development (Mussen, Conger, and Kagan, 1963).

In general, behavior changes that are attributable primarily to genetic predispositions and constitutional factors and that are not importantly affected by events in the environment can be charted and predicted with considerable accuracy. However, when the environment, and particularly the social environment, of the individual exerts a sizable impact on behavior, learning assumes a major role. This usually results in varied behavioral tendencies, whose development are usually not so easily traced. Most of our discussions of child development will focus on the social development of the individual and his interaction with his environment. A review of the personality theories presented earlier will quickly show that all of these formulations pertain to the individual in social contexts (See Part 1). Since there is reason to believe that learning is a decisive factor in the shaping of social behavior, our approach will emphasize personal relationships and the tendencies learned from them.

This emphasis is in no way meant to deny the importance of hereditary predispositions, glandular functioning, and other aspects of biological makeup. We assume that biological bases of individual differences operate in all people. We assume also that regardless of natural endowment, the personality of the individual manifests itself within a social context. Any ultimate, composite treatment of human development must be in terms of complex nature-nurture interactions between genetics and biological predispositions, on the one hand, and upbringing, on the other. At present there are large gaps in our knowledge of how these determinants are related, particularly with regard to the development of personal characteristics. Until these gaps are filled there would seem to be merit in analyzing various aspects of development from different points of view with an eye toward ultimate integration.

Our efforts will be psychological in nature. They will be directed primarily to an analysis of development in terms of persons and their transactions with their environment. To emphasize the point just made, this need not imply that the way in which personality expresses itself is determined 90 per cent by the environment and 10 per cent by genetic factors, or any other pair of percentages. All this implies is that the environment, upbringing, and personal involvements are powerful influences in the shaping of personality that merit careful study. At the human level, this is particularly true. Genetic predispositions, biological structure and function, and unlearned tendencies provide the equipment with which all organisms come into the world. The social environment plays an important role in shaping the way in which behavior manifests itself. For this reason, the psychological study of organism-environment interactions would seem to be one fruitful avenue along which to approach human personality development.

RESEARCH METHODS IN PERSONALITY DEVELOPMENT

We have already touched upon the major methods and techniques used in developmental research with the exception of the longitudinal study of personality. However, it is one thing to have a general methodology available and another to adapt it to a particular problem. Childhood is a crucial period from a formative standpoint, and most developmental research has been concerned with the early years of life. Because of the rapid changes in abilities and attitudes throughout this period, the study of children poses many challenging problems that call for flexibility and ingenuity on the part of the researcher. Our review of research techniques will not introduce very many new methods. It will, however, deal with the adaptation of methods already considered to the study of children.

Observational Data

There is nothing more basic to scientific investigation than observation. In psychology, behavior is observed and inferences are drawn on the basis of the observations made. Generally speaking, the observations of the student of behavior are characterized by a relatively high degree of objectivity and reliability. To be of any scientific value, observations must be susceptible to description in similar terms by disinterested observers of a particular behavior.

In conducting observational studies one must recognize that the presence of observers may affect a subject's behavior. This is true particularly when the subject is concerned that his behavior is being observed. For this reason, researchers seek to make their observations in as unobtrusive a manner as is possible. A researcher who is observing a group of children engaged in playground activities seeks to avoid either influencing the way in which the children play or becoming directly involved in their activities. In addition, it is important that the biases of observers be kept to a minimum. This is not to say that biased observations, such as those provided by a mother, are of no interest to personality researchers. They may very well be, but when they are, the careful researcher avoids any pretensions concerning their objectivity. The distinction to be drawn is between the scientist's observations and the observations and reactions of others. Actually the latter may provide valuable data for the scientist about the ways in which persons such as family members and friends perceive one another.

In some studies, what is observed may not be decided prior to the recording of observations. For example, if one is interested in studying behavior in everyday life, one cannot, by definition, control what the person who is under observation does. Nor in such situations can one know ahead of time what the subject will do.

When naturalistic observations are made, observers sequentially record the responses emitted by the subject. For example, in one study 69 types of response among a group of gang delinquents were recorded (Short, Tennyson, and Howard, 1963). Data recorded ranged from the incidence of penny pitching, to playing basketball, to auto theft. After making observations, observers can compare their records in order to determine the degree to which they agree that certain events did occur. The use of naturalistic observation in psychology is the major tool of behavioral ecology, which deals with naturally occurring behavior. Barker (1963, pp. 10–11) and his collaborators, following up ideas offered by Lewin, have made important contributions to the study of behavior in the natural settings in which people live (Barker, 1963; Barker and Wright, 1951). They have reliably categorized responses of persons in such settings. Ultimately, of course, behavioral ecologists may wish to move from description of behavior to its prediction. To do so will require dealing with future behavior as a function of past and present behavior. Predicting future behavior requires knowledge of which of the myriad responses emitted currently by the individual are related to or predictive of his future behavior. Such knowledge presupposes meaningful definition of past, present, and future behavioral events:

> How does one approach such complex phenomena? The aim of the research must be to discover units that will help to bring order to the innumerable data the behavior stream provides. This has to be accomplished on the frontier of knowledge where guidance by pre-established facts and hypotheses is necessarily minimal, and where investigation must follow the canons of discovery rather than those of scientific verification. The problem is to unriddle both facts and theories. . . . The most complete understanding of the logical and technical requirements of good research methodology and theory construction will not save investigators of the behavior stream from primitive searching and thinking at the present time. This is inevitable. And it is not serious if the primitive theories and methods keep investigators close to the reality of the stream of behavior, and encourage freedom of intellectual movement within a flexible conceptual system.

Some researchers have preferred to make observations of behavior under more controlled conditions than are possible in naturally occurring settings. For certain kinds of problems this preference may be quite appropriate. Some researchers may even have clearly in mind exactly which of the responses made by persons they wish to record. For example, one might be specifically interested in crying behavior, or dependent behavior, or aggressive behavior. Regardless of the conditions under which observations are made and the content of the observations, it is necessary to establish categories of behavior that can be reliably scored.

In order to comprehend the scope of problems for which observational techniques might be appropriate, we shall consider two examples. The first, a study by Gump, Schoggen, and Redl, (Barker, 1963), demonstrates the use of observation in natural settings. The second, a study by Bandura, Ross, and Ross (1963*a*), illustrates the use of observation under more restricted and controlled conditions.

Gump, Schoggen, and Redl (1963, p. 171) were interested in describing and comparing the behavior of a nine-year-old boy, Wally, in two settings. One setting was a boys' camp. The other was his home. In each setting a day-long recording of Wally's behavior was obtained by having trained observers take turns at making a continuous, detailed record of everything Wally did and said, and everything said and done to Wally. With the lengthy, day-long record of behavioral sequences in hand, the next step was to categorize the events in the sequences. Without categories of responses, Gump, Schoggen, and Redl would not have been able to compare quantitatively Wally's behavior in the camp and at home. The unit adopted by these researchers was called an episode:

> Briefly, an episode is a unit of behavior which (1) occurs within the normal behavior perspective of the behaving person, and (2) is characterized by constancy of direction, i.e., the behavior is directed toward a single, particular goal. These episodes, over 1,000 in each day, served as basic units. They were described in terms of a variety of characteristics: play form, nature of social interaction, behavior initiation, and emotional tone. Determination of the frequency with which episodes of a given kind occurred made possible a quantitative description of each day. Such quantitative descriptions of each specimen record were then compared, resulting in a quantitative statement of similarities and differences between Wally's day at camp and his day at home.

One of Gump, Schoggen, and Redl's interests was in Wally's play activity at home and at camp. Therefore, they focused their attention on play episodes and showed that different observers agreed that particular episodes did in fact occur. Other aspects of Wally's behavior that these researchers studied were the feeling tone of his social interactions and his tendencies toward dominance, aggression, and nurturance in relation to others. The results of this intensive study of one child showed striking differences in behavior in the social milieu of the home and the social milieu of a camp. Wally showed more and stronger negative emotional responses at camp than at home. At camp, he experienced more peerlike relationships with adults than at home. In terms of play activity, he showed more active, exploratory, constructive, and fantasy-tinged behavior at camp than at home.

The research of Gump, Schoggen, and Redl is instructive because it shows how observations can be employed reliably in naturally occurring situations. It also suggests the potential value of this methodology for the study of meaningful psychological problems. Although the detailed observation and categorizing of sequences of Wally's behavior were time-consuming they did achieve the goal of reflecting the complexity of behavioral events occurring in the life of a child over a relatively short time span.

The problem investigated by Bandura, Ross, and Ross did not require descriptions of subjects' behavior that were as comprehensive as those obtained in the study by Gump, Schoggen, and Redl. Rather, the research of the former involved the observation of particular responses related to a specific hypothesis. These responses were recorded in a controlled situation which, nevertheless, permitted the child latitude in play behavior. Bandura, Ross, and Ross (1963*a*) wished to test the hypothesis that exposure of children to aggression by an adult would lead to increased aggressiveness in their play (Chapter 18).

In one group, an adult model played with toys in a highly aggressive manner. Another group of subjects was shown a film that depicted comparable aggression by an adult model. During an ensuing 20-minute free play period for children exposed to either "live" or film model, the responses of the subjects, who were four-year-old boys and girls, were observed. Using a predetermined system, the investigators rated the behavior of the children. The ratings involved tabulation of a variety of aggressive behaviors. Since the researchers were primarily interested in learning whether the children would imitate the aggressive real-life and film models, the youngsters play was categorized according to the incidence of aggressive and nonaggressive responses. The results of the experiment showed that children exposed to either a real-life aggressive model or an aggressive model depicted in a film displayed significantly more aggression in their own play than comparable children in a control group not subjected to an aggressive model.

Both the Gump, Schoggen, and Redl and Bandura, Ross, and Ross studies are interesting with respect to their differences and similarities. The latter study was designed to determine the effect of particular experimental procedures on a particular class of responses, on this occasion aggressive responses. The former was not intended to test a particular hypothesis, but to describe and compare behavior in two naturally occurring contexts. Both studies shared the need to devise reliable objective means for quantitatively characterizing behavior. Both used a procedure comparable to content analysis.

From previous discussions, it will be remembered that content analysis involves the definition of classes or types of responses (Chapter 9). With these definitions in hand—for example, the definition of a particular type of aggressive response—observers and raters can tally the number of times certain responses occur. These might be responses of children at play, verbal responses of parents in interviews, responses made by subjects in verbal conditioning experiments, and responses of patients in psychotherapy. In utilizing this procedure it is important to define response classes on the basis of the characteristics of the subjects under study. Aggressive behavior in young children may manifest itself mainly in overt motor acts such as hitting and pushing. Aggressive behavior in older children may, in addition, involve verbal insults. In the case of adults, aggression may be expressed verbally, as well as in indirect, subtle ways.

In general there would appear to be two steps in dealing with observational data. The first is recording responses made by individuals. The second is analysis of the observations made (Wright, 1960). Reliable analyses of individual responses permits quantitative comparisons of an individual's behavior from one time to another and of the simultaneous behavior of different subjects.

The Experimental Method

In experimental work it is extremely important to gear the manipulation of the independent variables to the abilities and characteristics of the subjects under study (Hoffman and Lippit, 1960). What may be a useful technique for arousing the motivation of adults may be inappropriate and ineffective in arousing motivation in children. Baldwin (1960, pp. 22–24) has pinpointed a number of the problems confronting the experimenter who studies very young subjects:

> One set of special problems arises from the fact that the subjects of child-development research are children. Quite aside from the fact that the job of child psychology is to understand children, we must understand them somewhat even to conduct research with them. In terms of traditional research operations, children are somewhere between animals and adults. In research on adults we are accustomed to structuring the situation with language, to instructing the subjects with language, and, in many experiments, to collecting verbal responses that are treated as communications by the subject about some subject matter. Research with animals is conducted on quite a different basis. The situation is structured by such things as walls, electric grills, and stimulus patterns, and the behavior of the animals is taken as a reaction, not a communication. Children fall in between. For very young children, the techniques used with animals are necessary, but as the child grows older we can begin to utilize language as a research tool. The trouble is that

children do not understand instructions very well, and verbal structuring of the situation does not always produce the same results that it does with adults. We cannot count upon the effectiveness of these verbal procedures with children. We can, of course, treat children as if they were animals and study them nonverbally, but that is to sacrifice the very thing about children that makes them especially valuable as research subjects. This very lack of docility of children to verbal procedures is a major field for investigation; we ought to study it, not circumvent it.

How do these characteristics of children affect research? One of the problems is to establish a prescribed psychological situation for the child. Suppose, for example, that we want to offer the child a choice between two alternatives to determine preference. For an adult, we can be reasonably sure that when we give him a choice he is actually choosing. A child may pick the first alternative he sees without ever looking at the other one. He may vacillate so much from one alternative to the other that we suspect his final behavior is more accidental than deliberate, or he may break down emotionally because he cannot have both alternatives.

In many experimental conflict situations, for example, we want to be sure the subject knows what he can do, what the consequences are of each possible course of action, and what courses of action are not permitted in the experiment. With adults these objectives can usually be achieved by making the apparatus clear and the instructions specific, but children may pay no attention to the directions or may be attracted to one feature of the apparatus at the expense of another. They may insist on the experimenter's help when the adult would conform to the proper mores of the experiment. These behaviors might be made the subject of investigation, but when we want to study some other aspect of child behavior we do not want to be sidetracked into an investigation of all these difficulties. Consequently, the experimenter must use considerable skill to be sure that the psychological impact of the situation is what the experimenter intends.

We have seen examples of this ingenuity of child psychologists in the Bandura, Ross and Ross (1963*a*) experiment on aggression in preschool children and the Lewinian studies of the effects of frustration on the quality of children's performance in play situations. (Barker, Dembo, and Lewin, 1941). As we proceed in this chapter, we shall find many additional examples of the use of experimental methods that have been tailormade to fit the developmental capacities of children.

Personality Assessment

A number of ways of assessing personality were mentioned earlier and were viewed as devices for obtaining responses from which inferences about personal characteristics might be drawn (Chapter 8).

Among the methods of personality assessment that we explored were tests (true-false and projective), rating scales (the semantic differential), and interviews. It is often necessary in developmental research to devise special methods that are appropriate for use with individuals of particular age groups.

Because they permit subjects to respond at whatever level of which they are capable, projective tests have been widely used in research with children, some as young as the preschool period. Some researchers have been especially interested in comparing the responses of children of different age groups to ambiguous stimuli. Others have developed test materials specifically for use with youngsters of a particular age level. For example, the Children's Apperception Test (Bellak and Bellak, 1949), which in format resembles the TAT, was designed for use with young children. The Picture-Story Test (Symonds, 1948), which also resembles the TAT, was designed especially for use with adolescents. Because paper-and-pencil tests and rating scales do not require complex responses from subjects, they have been used over a wide range of subjects. Later in this chapter we shall see that adaptations of paper-and-pencil tests are possible and can be used with children too young to take inventories such as the CPI or MMPI.

One of the major problems in assessing personal characteristics of very young children is maintaining their interest and cooperation. Interviews and tasks such as individual and group play, doll play, and painting have been widely used in efforts to assess personality characteristics of boys and girls. Yarrow (1960, pp. 561–562) has outlined a number of the more important methodological considerations in assessing the personalities of children. His discussion focused specifically on the interview as an assessment instrument:

The commonest justification offered for the choice of the interview over more impersonal techniques, such as the personality inventory or attitude questionnaire, is the presumed facilitating effect of the personal relationship in the communication process. It is likely that in many research situations the interpersonal relationship will contribute substantially to the validity of the data. The direct relationship in the interview reduces misunderstandings by providing the opportunity to clarify the meaning of unclear questions. Furthermore, very inhibited children may need the reassurance of the interviewer's permissive attitude before they are able to express negative attitudes or reveal emotionally charged feelings or experiences. We cannot, however, assume uncritically the greater value of the interview for all kinds of problems. For example, a child may be freer in expressing criticism of some aspect of school policy on a written questionnaire than in a direct interview with a strange adult. Similarly, an adolescent may be less able to express verbally in direct interview the details of his sex information than in writing. The fact that the nature of the child's relationship with the adult in the interview situation exerts a significant influence on the content of his response provides a source of variance difficult to control.

Numerous problems in interviewing children are determined primarily by age-level characteristics. A major problem derives from the child's limitations in language facility and comprehension of language. Other problems have their origins in the conventional role relationships between children and adults in our culture. Thus we may have overdependent behavior at one developmental stage and extreme negativism at another period. In establishing comparability of meaning between one interview situation and another there may be special difficulties because of differing stages of language maturity in children of approximately the same age. Other difficulties in interviewing, although not uniquely characteristic of its use with children, do require special considerations, e.g., developing adequate rapport with the child while keeping the relationship within nontherapeutic bounds and avoiding communication of the interviewer's biases.

In planning the research use of the interview, therefore, a major concern is the establishment and control of the relationship between the child and the interviewer. In addition to the broad question of rapport, there are many aspects of the relationship to be considered, such as the meaning of the interview relationship to the child and the role relationships established.

Many investigations of personality development require the use of a variety of techniques. For example, a researcher interested in the effects of child-rearing practices on children's personalities may find it advantageous to interview both parents and their offspring. Clearly, these interviews will differ in content and the personal relationship formed between interviewer and subject.

Longitudinal Research

From one standpoint longitudinal study is the most obvious and direct way to study human development. In this kind of study subjects are not seen for one or a few experimental sessions, but observed in a variety of ways over a period of years. What better way to view the developmental process than to observe carefully changes in the behavior of individuals over a period of time?

Despite the appeal of longitudinal studies, their number is surprisingly small. When one considers the logistics of the longitudinal study, the basis for this state of affairs becomes understandable. Let us assume that we wish to carry out a longitudinal project that would cover the period from kindergarten through the senior year of college. Let us assume further that the aim of the study is to trace personality changes through this long and formative period of development. How does one proceed to trace development?

If our concept of personality emphasized the evolution of personal characteristics, we would have to decide, before any data had been gathered, which individual difference variables were the ones most central to our interests. After defining these variables, we would have to select particular indices of each of them. One problem in making such a selection is the fact that what might be a useful measure of a variable at one age level, might be quite inappropriate for another age level. The way in which the five-year old expresses his aggression is usually quite different from the modes of aggression available to the ten-year old.

There are a number of ways in which the problem of the selection of tests and measures can be solved. We might, for example, recognize the marked changes that occur from kindergarten to college and decide to use different measures of our individual variables at different age levels, or we might use as indices ratings of subjects made by their parents, teachers, and peers. Regardless of how we plan our project, we must plan the research before we begin it. Since the "experiment" in longitudinal research may last 10 or 20 years, or even longer, it is crucial that the study be mapped out in as detailed and feasible a way as possible. The matter of feasibility is not an unimportant one. It is one thing to formulate a significant theoretical problem, and another to devise the actual procedures with which the problem may be attacked.

A great many practical and personal considerations beset the longitudinal researcher. On the practical side are such possibilities as the loss of subjects in the middle of the project (such losses might be due to moving from one place of residence to another, illness, and death) and changes in project personnel from time to time. On the personal side a crucial factor is the ability of the researcher to be able to withstand criticisms of early measures as "old fashioned" and the tension of a long period of time before all the necessary data can be gathered and analyzed.

Despite these considerations, which serve as deterrents to longitudinal developmental research, a number of such studies have been carried out and have encompassed time periods as long as 30 years. To suggest the dimensions of this sort of undertaking we shall provide an illustration of one major contribution to longitudinal research, the Fels Research Institute developmental study (Kagan and Moss, 1962).

One aspect of the Fels program involved the careful study of personality development in 89 subjects. The purpose of the study was to shed light on the process by which the middle-class child becomes a mature individual. Many data were gathered on each of the 89 subjects. The data took the form of behavioral observations (for example, in nursery settings), behavior on personality and intelligence tests (for example, the Rorschach and Stanford-Binet tests), and responses of both parents and children during interviews. Thus we see that longitudinal research requires the integrated use of a variety of assessment techniques. Most of the procedures used in the Fels project were repeated several times. For example, the Rorschach test was administered every third year between the ages of 8½ and 17½ and interviews with the children were conducted every year from age 6 to age 12. Information about the subjects and their families was gathered at the Fels Institute, in the subjects' homes, and at school. Most of the data gathered covered the first 14 years of life. However, there were adult follow-up studies for 71 of the 89 original subjects. The ages of the subjects at the time of this follow-up study ranged from 19 to 29.

The Fels researchers were interested in a comprehensive description of personality from birth to maturity. But it should not be surprising that they were especially concerned with certain variables and continuities throughout life. Many of the analyses of data performed by the Fels researchers were specifically directed to characteristics such as passivity, dependency, aggression, and anxiety as these are expressed at various developmental periods.

The following case illustrates how one particular characteristic manifested itself in the development of a person. The characteristic was social anxiety. The excerpts presented from Kagan and Moss (1962, pp. 175–181) suggest its pervasive and chronic character. The subject was a male, second-born child of a lower middle-class family. The following notes were written after his first visit at age two years to the Fels Institute:

> *S* gave the appearance of being frightened at first. When taken downstairs for the physical examination following the mental test, *S* would not allow the doctor to take his hand to guide him. He was shy and remained very timid throughout the procedure. He cried when the examination began and cried at new items in the procedure. He was suggestible and responded to distraction. He recovered quickly from his tears, was attentive to the toys given him, and was interested in their construction. Although the mother was present during the mental test that preceded the physical exam, *S* was shy and apprehensive.

The following notes were written after *S* had spent a three week period at the Fels nursery school. He was four years of age at the time:

This was *S*'s first visit to the nursery school and probably his first time away from home for any length of time. It took the entire period for *S* to make the adjustment. *S* was very apprehensive and insecure during his first days. He cried a lot and stood about looking sad in the interim between his howls. Initially he did not enter into any of the play but was entirely concerned with his unhappiness. He objected to coming and cried in the car. Once at the school he stood about weeping or sobbing and followed the teacher around for comfort. He was not in a tantrum of anger, but appeared to be showing fear and apprehension. For the first two weeks *S* made no attempts to get into any of the groups. He was shy with the other children and timid with the new equipment.

During the period he was highly emotional and did not try to control his fears at all. He was somewhat sober and depressed most of the time, although he got friendly and happy toward the very end. He showed no anger, little jealousy, and no excitement. With adults he was very conforming and obedient. Even though unhappy, he was not especially rebellious.

At age eight, *S* attended the Fels day camp:

S is still a shrinking violet, avoiding any situations where he might be hurt, by physical contact with others, hard objects, high places, etc. He seems to show a social diffidence and an unsureness, and these two things reinforce each other. The first morning *S* disappeared from the group and was discovered all alone in the front yard quietly sobbing to himself. He explained his presence there in terms of a sore foot, and while he had, in fact, hurt his foot, his generalized discomfort at the newness of the day-camp situation probably reinforced the pain and reduced him to tears. He was continually ignored or shoved around by the more energetic and outspoken children. In any close contact situation, such as a crowded car, *S* completely withdrew and became self-effacing.

At age 16 *S* was interviewed by a staff psychologist at Fels:

E: "What are some ways in which you would like to be different from the way you are now, some of the things you would change about yourself?"

S: "I'd like to be more forward, I mean, to be able to meet people and talk."

E: "Any other ways that you would like to change?"

S: "I'd like to feel like I could take on responsibilities which I don't. I don't feel like—I don't feel self-confident. *That's it in a nutshell, self-confidence*"

At age 20 *S* was interviewed again. He is described as a thin and slight-of-build young man who looked more like an adolescent than a young man. He spoke in a low, high-pitched voice during the interview and was uneasy and nervous:

E: "Did you tend to be afraid of your boss on the job when he came around?"

S: "Yeah, I was kinda afraid of him."

E: "What about this fellow you are working with now? Do you feel relaxed with him, or tense?"

S: "No, I don't feel relaxed with him. I just as leave he's not around."

E: "You feel tense when he's around?"

S: "I'm not afraid of him, see; I just don't like to have him around. That other guy down there; at first I couldn't talk to him, ah—not at all, but it's getting a little bit better now."

E: "What about Dr. ———: the man that you worked for in college? Did you feel tense when you were with him?"

S: "It's a funny thing; I wasn't exactly at ease with him, but he was nice and I really like him and I still do. I think I am in awe with him. You know, he was a big professor, something that I'd like to be, and I was really never friendly with professors. Well, I was really never friendly with any school teachers."

E: "Did you talk much in classes?"

S: "Well, that all depends on the professor. In Dr. ——— class I always had my mouth open, but in other classes—I never said a word."

E: "Why was that? Because you had no questions or because you just didn't want to say anything?"

S: "I don't know, I just didn't want to talk. In history I never said a word unless he asked me."

E: "If you ever had any questions, did you go up after class or during office hours to ask professors about your work."

S: "I didn't do that. I don't know if I could do it yet or not."

E: "Have you ever thought about doing it and decided not too?"

S: "Yeah."

E: "Why did you not go?"

S: "I don't think I would. I never knew professors, any professors that you would say personally, except Dr. ———. Well, of course, I asked him things 'cause I worked with him, ah—not any of the others, like Dr. ———. I wanted to talk to him, and I think if I had talked to him, my problems would have been solved."

E: "Why didn't you talk to him?"

S: I don't know; I couldn't. He had such a way about him that I couldn't get my point across. He would persuade his opinion on me. He would, and I don't want his opinion. I mean he would try to tell me that he was right and I'm wrong and believe me he's right. He had a way about him that my opinion had no value. It was like going in and talking to a blank wall.
He would have such a better argument than I would that I would lose, that's what I thought anyway."

E: "Who do you feel more comfortable with, more relaxed with, men or women?"

S: "Older women I don't like, older men, ah—too. Because, you know, they don't talk about the same things I do. Older women don't either—I—I couldn't go in a room with an older woman and talk to her."

E: "How about people you own age? With whom do you feel more comfortable, boys or girls?"

S: "Boys. I don't talk to girls much. I mean, I couldn't go up to a strange girl and talk to her as well as I could a strange boy. But if I know the girl, then I can talk to her."

E: "Can you tell me about your friends, the kind of friendships you have?"

S: "Well, you know, I don't think I have any close friends. When I came home from college, any friends I had in high school were gone, and—ah—I didn't have any people that were more than acquaintances, they weren't close friends. A couple of people that I work with are classified as friends more than acquaintances, but not what I would call a close friend. When I was in school I had, oh, three real close friends and a lot of acquaintances, ——— was a very close friend."

E: "What made you and ________ such close friends?"

S: Like I said before, he's like me. Neither one of us was very good in sports and it seemed like everyone else was, and I envied them."

E: "You say you envied these other people and he didn't?"

S: "He did. Oh, I don't know if he did or not; I don't know if he cared. But I did. I mean, I'd like to have been good sportswise, but, ah, he wasn't either. You see, we had to go someplace else. I couldn't go with the gang of boys and talk about sports and, ah, there didn't seem to be so many places to go, and I like to talk about books that I've read that other people have read and, ah, argue about 'em. But I couldn't do that with very many people. That's the way I like to talk."

E: "Could you do that with ________?"

S: "No, he didn't read books, but there were a few more people on campus that I could argue with. But, yet he would listen to me and give me his ideas if he had read the book. But we could talk about serious things."

E: "Was there something else about him personally, another reason that might account for the fact that you and he were close friends?"

S: "Well, in the first place, when I first got to know him, we both didn't know any people, and I sat beside him in class, see, and that's how I got to know him. We didn't know anyone, and it was hard for both of us to get to know people. I think it was even harder—more hard for him to get to know people than it was even for me. Because he lived off campus and it's extra hard then. He didn't know many people and I didn't know anyone and—so we just sorta went together."

E: "In college were you the kind of person who actively sought to make a lot of friends?"

S: "No, I didn't make a lot of friends."

E: "Was that out of choice or because of no time?"

S: "It's probably cause I didn't know how; I couldn't. In the dorm we were in sections and I was in section 5. I lived with these guys, and I know all of them real well, but I was hardly on speaking terms with some of them in the other sections. I have to be with people a long time before I get to know them. I just couldn't go up to a person and enter into a conversation with him, even if I knew him." . . .

These excerpts provide a specific instance of a general finding in the Fels study: inhibition and apprehension with peers during childhood is predictive of social anxiety in adulthood. The Fels researchers found that social inhibition and apprehension in early childhood for boys, and in late childhood for girls, was predictive of adult social anxiety. Thus social anxiety as a consistent aspect of life seems to begin earlier for boys than for girls.

Earlier we mentioned the stress placed by many writers on the early years of life as determinants of later behavior (Chapters 2, 3, and 4). If this emphasis is correct, it would be reasonable to expect positive correlations between behavior early in life and later on. Longitudinal studies are valuable because they can be designed to uncover such possible consistencies. The Fels study would appear to provide support for the belief that from the response tendencies exhibited by a person at a young age predictions might be made about his later behavior.

Kagan and Moss (1962), who have reported the Fels findings, noted that behaviors observed in children as young as three to six years of age were often significantly related to aspects of behavior in early childhood. Among the characteristics observed in children before the age of 10 years that were related to similar characteristics in adulthood were: the tendency to withdraw passively from stressful situations, dependency on one's family, involvement in intellectual mastery, threshold for experiencing anger, and, as we have seen, anxiety in social interactions. However, tendencies to be compulsive, to harbor irrational fears, and to be irritable early in life were not predictive of similar tendencies later in life. In attempting to predict later characteristics from earlier ones it is necessary to be aware of environmental events that might significantly affect the course of development. For example, the early and later behaviors of an individual whose parents' social-class membership undergoes a sharp change may not be consistent owing to this change.

One variable that comes into play during development is the individual's sex role. The concepts of male and female roles are only vaguely defined in the case of three-year-olds. On the other hand, these roles come to be sharply defined in adolescence. In their longitudinal comparisons, Kagan and Moss found that sex-role identification was a major determinant of the adoption of certain response patterns later in life. Aggression, dependency, sexuality, and competitiveness in later life all seem to be influenced by sex-role standards in middle-class American society.

As we have noted, some characteristics observed in children as young as three to six years of age were correlated with later characteristics. However, early-later correlations were clearest when early life was defined by the ages 6 to 10 years. This finding is provocative because of certain events that occur during this span of time. It is the period during which the child enters school and develops an attitude toward intellectual achievement. It is the period during which the child becomes involved in peer and extrafamily relationships, and it is the period during which children take on many of the values and characteristics of their parents. The Fels study suggests the need for intensive evaluation of the variables at work during this particular formative time.

A final comment concerning longitudinal research pertains to the "sleeper effect." Kagan and Moss found that certain variables measured very early in life were more predictive of later behavior than were variables more contemporaneous with adolescence and adulthood. This would suggest that perhaps the consequences of early life experiences might lie dormant for a relatively long period of time before overt manifestations could be observed. Observed consistencies in behavior together with the sleeper effect noted by Kagan and Moss suggest that there are both significant continuities and discontinuities in personality development.

The Fels project is only one of many longitudinal studies that have been conducted. It is, however, one of the most ambitious and carefully carried out studies of this type. Longitudinal investigations vary with respect to the kinds of persons studied, the characteristics observed and measured, and the length of time during which data are collected. Some investigators have been primarily interested in qualitative studies, others have sought to obtain quantitative measures of behavior change. Despite the methodological and practical problems concerned with the study of individuals over a long time period, longitudinal research represents one of the most valuable approaches to the study of personality.

Having reviewed some of the major tools at the disposal of the researcher concerned with the developing person, we turn next to a consideration of situations and life experiences that contribute to the evolution of personality. In tracing this chronology we shall pay particular attention to hypotheses and concepts that have influenced research on personality development and to applications of a variety of research methods to the study of human development.

23

Events in Personality Development

Probably no single person has contributed as much to the description of personality development as Sigmund Freud (Chapter **2**). Anomalous as it may seem, it is no easy task to state precisely in what ways Freud's contribution came about. For the most part, the influence of psychoanalysis on the study of personality development has been indirect rather than direct. Psychoanalysis has contributed to the definition of many of the problems with which research on personality development deals. But it is one thing for two people to agree on the statement of a problem and quite another for them to concur on the way best to attack it.

Although most students of personality development do not accept *in toto* the theoretical framework of psychoanalysis, most of them have been impressed with the events that Freud hypothesized to occur during the early years of life. One need not adhere to the libido concept to study children's needs for sensual gratification. One need not accept the concept of primal repression (the idea of unrecoverable memories) to infer unconscious processes in young children. One need not accept the theory of the Oedipus complex to be aware of the profound impact on the child of personal relationships within the family. One need not accept the notion of stages of psychosexual development to acknowledge the importance of certain situations such as those involving feeding and elimination. One might feel that it is legitimate to criticize Freud for not sufficiently stressing either the totality of social influences upon the child or the significance of events beyond childhood. This need not blind us from attending to Freud's suggestions of variables and periods that shape personality.

Other theoretical orientations have also had discernible, albeit often indirect, impacts on the study of development. Rogers (1951), Maslow (1954*a*), and Gesell (1954) have emphasized development as a creative process that is facilitated by acceptance of the child by its environment (Chapter 5). The emphasis placed by self-theorists on the self-as-knower has served to orient students to the changes over a period of time in the ways in which we perceive ourselves and the world about us. The field theorists (Chapter 6) have emphasized the need for studying the totality of events, including social and personal ones, that impinge on the organism. From a philosophical standpoint, a number of writers, notably Freud, S-R theorists, and Lewin, have presented convincing cases for the adoption of a deterministic view of behavior. The belief that behavior is determined by variables that can be isolated, observed, and manipulated has contributed much to the study of the developing person.

We have defined personality as the study of individual differences. People differ with respect to observable behavior and thought processes. Since thought processes are not directly observable, they must be inferred from overt behavior. In treating personality development, emphases will be placed on the tie between inferences and concepts on the one hand, and the data supporting these formulations on the other.

One useful approach to the individual is to describe his development in terms of a history of experiences. To understand this history requires study of environmental events and the individual's interpretations of both these events and himself. Required also is an analysis of the relationships between biological and social development. Thus, how the growing individual's body functions, how the individual handles life's crises, masters skills, becomes a member of a culture, and develops affectional ties must be seen as related, rather than as discrete problems.

We shall begin our study of development by discussing the earliest stages of life, the prenatal and postnatal periods. We shall see that even during these periods environmental factors play significant roles in influencing the behavior of the young human whose actions appear to be driven in the main by biological needs. We shall see that even in the womb the fetus is not immune to environmental influences. We shall see that as early as the very first months following birth the interaction between the infant and the person who occupies the role of the mother may truly be viewed as a social one.

In studying the evolving interaction between the human organism and its environment we have to bear in mind that its behavioral repertory is influenced not only by environmental happenings but also by genetic predispositions. McClearn (1964, p. 473) has conceptualized nature-nurture relationships in this way:

It is inappropriate to view the behavioral repertoire as composed of those traits that are inherited and those that are not. All traits have environmental and genetic components. Thus it is appropriate only to inquire as to the relative proportion of the population variability which is due to differences in genetic and environmental factors. The hoary "nature-nurture controversy" must be replaced by a concept of "nature-nurture collaboration." Understanding of the dynamics of behavior cannot be achieved by ignoring either source of variation.

The complexity of this collaboration is suggested by the fact that the effects of genes may not become manifest until advanced stages of development. In some ways this seems analogous to the "sleeper effect" observed in the Fels longitudinal study. At the present time very little is known about the mechanics of the collaboration to which McClearn refers. But recent growth of the field of behavior genetics provides a basis for optimism that it will become a part of the scientific study of development (Chapters 14 and 19).

While there are gaps in our understanding of genetic influences over behavior, available evidence strongly suggests that there are very few aspects of development that are uninfluenced by environmental and social interactions. After some comments on environmental influences on prenatal and postnatal development, we shall consider social variables that in combination with biological factors contribute to the shaping of personality. Topics that will be emphasized will be the child's developing sense of security, the relationship of personality to intellectual development, the need of the child to conform to social mores, the emotional responsiveness of the developing individual, the extension of the child's personal world to include schools and peer experiences, and the growth of independence. In the discussion, we shall also refer not only to the most formative years of childhood and adolescence, but also to personality development in the adult.

PRENATAL AND POSTNATAL DEVELOPMENT

The human fetus does not lead a very active social life. Nonetheless, the prenatal period is of interest to the student of personality. In the past, psychological aspects of this period were not given the attention they deserve. Recently, this void has begun to be filled. It appears that the prenatal period can be usefully studied from two points of view. One concerns the actual development of the fetus.

The other relates to the psychological effects of a woman's pregnant condition on herself and on other persons in the future environment of the child.

The womb environment is relatively stable with hereditary factors largely determining the formation of biological structures and functions. The most obvious feature of the prenatal period is the physical growth of the fetus. During the intrauterine period the bases for postnatal capacities to respond become established. However, there is evidence that while the fetus develops in a highly protected environment, it is not immune to environmental influences.

It has been shown that the near-term human fetus does respond to external stimuli such as loud noises (Lipsitt, **1963**; Mussen, Conger and Kagan, **1963**). Furthermore, prenatal conditioning is possible in fetuses six to nine months of age. Loud noises will evoke movement in the fetus. Demonstrations of prenatal conditioning have usually been conducted by pairing a neutral conditioned stimulus with an unconditioned one, such as a loud noise. Furthermore, studies of prenatal conditioning have shown that there are noticeable individual differences among fetuses in the extent to which they can be conditioned to stimuli.

All of the implications of the finding that late fetuses can be conditioned to make specific responses are, as yet, not clear. It is one thing to demonstrate a phenomenon under controlled research conditions and quite another to observe the phenomenon under naturally occurring conditions. However, it would seem reasonable to suppose that prenatal conditioning, and perhaps other forms of learning, do occur in the normal course of intrauterine life. Future research will be needed to determine the extent to which conditioning occurs in fetuses, the kinds of stimuli that evoke conditioned responses, and the relationship of prenatally conditioned responses to postnatal behavior.

Although the study of the responses of a fetus to external stimuli is perhaps most germane to the interests of behavioral scientists, the internal environment of the uterus cannot be ignored as a source of stimulation. The physical condition of the mother may have a far-reaching impact on the fetus. Maternal malnutrition, drugs, and pelvic x-rays administered to the mother during pregnancy, as well as the age of the mother, can affect prenatal and postnatal development.

The psychological condition of the mother has been shown to affect prenatal responsiveness. It is known that heightened emotionality in people has important physiological concomitants. Mothers who differ in emotionality and in the psychological stresses experienced during pregnancy will show differences in the chemical make-up of their blood and in autonomic nervous system activity. These in turn can influence fetal development. Sontag (1944, p. 4) described some observations of infants whose mothers had experienced severe emotional stress during pregnancy:

Such an infant is from the beginning a hyperactive, irritable, squirming, crying child who cries for his feeding every two or three hours instead of sleeping through his four hour feeding. Because his irritability involves the control of his gastrointestinal tract, he empties his bowels at unusually frequent intervals, spits up half his feedings and generally makes a nuisance of himself. He is to all intents and purposes a neurotic infant when he is born—the result of an unsatisfactory fetal environment. In this instance, he has not had to wait until childhood for a bad home situation or other cause to make him neurotic. It has been done for him before he has even seen the light of day. In certain instances of severely disturbed maternal emotion which we have observed—for example, one in which the father became violently insane during his wife's pregnancy—the infant's bodily functions were so disturbed that a severe feeding problem resulted. The child was unable to retain food and became markedly emaciated and dehydrated. Experience with other similar cases suggests that many of the feeding problems which pediatricians experience with young infants arise from an abnormal fetal environment.

Study of the relationship between emotional trauma experienced by pregnant women and the behavior of their offspring would seem to be a challenging area of investigation. Equally challenging is the problem of women's attitudes toward their pregnancy. For some women the fact of being pregnant may constitute a major traumatic event. The degree to which this happens is a function of reality factors in the life of women (for example, whether conception took place out of wedlock) and of their personality make-up. It seems likely that the prepregnancy personalities of women have much to do with the incidence of major emotional disruptions during pregnancy. These in turn can affect the fetus.

Although the long-term effects of a woman's emotional state during pregnancy may not be easily predicted, it would seem quite possible that her anxiety and tension might have adverse consequences for the development of her offspring. Prenatal development is not simply a matter of physical maturation and growth. The fetus is affected by the environment provided by the mother and external stimulating conditions as well. It seems reasonable to conclude that genetic, biological, and psychological factors become intertwined in determining behavior even at the prenatal level. Reliable information on the emotional and attitudinal characteristics of mothers could prove particularly valuable in shedding light on these relationships.

Before turning to some of the psychologically meaningful events of infancy, a word is needed concerning the event of birth. It will be remembered that Freud used the birth experience as the prototype of the experience of anxiety. He defined anxiety as a state of unpleasure experienced when the individual is confronted with an influx of new and painful stimuli. This seemed to him to be analogous to what happens at birth when the fetus is suddenly and literally thrust into a new and strange environment. Rank, (1929), apparently not satisfied with the analogy that Freud suggested, contended that in fact the birth trauma had a definite and decisive traumatic effect on the future life of the individual.

Since newborn infants cannot communicate to us what birth means to them, it is unlikely that Rank's argument can ever be put to a direct test. Yet, if one simply observes that the change from life *in utero* to life in the world is the most profound one experienced by an organism, it does seem reasonable and worthwhile to ask the question: How does the event of birth affect the child? Observations of the activity level and biological functioning of the newborn infant can contribute to answering this question, or at least they can provide data on the basis of which inferences might legitimately be drawn. Comparisons of the behavior of normal, late, early, and Caesarian section infants would be especially pertinent.

Reactions to childbirth can be much more easily studied from the standpoint of the mother than from that of the infant. Obstetricians have noted wide variability among pregnant women with regard to their anticipations of and reactions to the birth process. While the pain of giving birth to a child is related to the structure of the uterus and other biological conditions, it also seems to be related to the amount of fear and dread associated with childbirth. As was suggested earlier, the prepregnancy personality make-up of the woman has much to do with her expectations with regard to childbirth and motherhood.

Our description of the psychological problems of prenatal development makes it clear that (1) the moment of birth is really not the time zero of psychological development, and that (2) biological growth and maturation are not the only processes that characterize fetal life. However, complicated as the relationships among the variables that affect the fetus may be, they seem almost manageable when compared with those that affect the newborn infant. Although there are many gaps in our knowledge concerning the variables that influence development during infancy and childhood, several periods have been suggested or found to be crucial as determinants of personality. In this chapter we shall highlight a number of these.

Perhaps the most impressive aspects of infancy are the rapid changes that take place during the early months of life. From a state of complete helplessness, the infant develops an effective repertory of abilities and capacities with which it responds to the environment and to the problems of life. From a state of an almost complete lack of involvement in the social milieu, the child becomes a socially oriented individual and exerts an impact on the environment.

The first weeks of life are a period of convalescence from birth. The neonate spends 80 per cent of its time in sleep. Only the need for food, the lack of warmth, and sometimes elimination seem to disturb its sleep. Parents of very young infants often express amazement at the seeming ability of their offspring to "sleep through anything." Do these observations suggest that infants are unresponsive to what goes on in their environment? There is reason to believe that they are not as unresponsive as they seem to be. For example, a wide variety of environmental stimuli have been shown to be capable of eliciting sucking responses in young infants (Lipsitt, 1963). Environmental stimuli rather quickly come to have a strong impact on the infant.

From the point of view of personality development, it is important to be aware of the great family-to-family variability in the amount of environmental stimulation provided the child. Although the implications of these differences in environmental stimulation are by no means clear, it would seem that the exploration of their effects on later development would be a worthwhile endeavor. Such research could profitably be directed at two basic problems: (1) the effects of family-to-family differences in over-all stimulation given the child, and (2) the effects of the types of stimulation provided the child, such as auditory or tactual.

An observational study reported by Rheingold (1960) illustrates the need for research related to these problems. Rheingold compared the stimulation given by five middle-class mothers to their children with the attention given five infants in an institution by the staff. The two groups of subjects had been matched for chronological age. She found that the infants brought up at home received almost five times the attention given infants reared in the institution. Home infants were looked at approximately five times more often, held six times more often, patted 13 times more often, and shown 18 times more affection than institutionalized infants. On the other hand, the institutionalized infants were dressed more often than the home infants. In general, the two groups of infants were given the same types of care. The differences were primarily in the amount of attention and stimulation provided.

That environmental, and particularly maternal stimulation does influence the personality of the child has been suggested by several studies of the effects of institutionalization. It seems clear that an institutionalized child's environment may involve limited sources of affection, handling, and over-all stimulation (Rheingold, 1960, 1961). Furthermore, studies of the effects of institutionalization suggest that constricted and barren environments in the early months of life often lead to profound emotional disturbances and intellectual retardation. Studies of young children who have been separated for periods of time from their parents corroborate this impression. The following variables seem especially important in determining the child's reactions to separation: (1) the age of the child at the time of separation; (2) the relationships existing between child and parents at the time of separation; (3) the care provided the child after separation; (4) the relationship, if any, between the child and parents during separation; (5) the length of the separation period; (6) postseparation experiences; and (7) individual differences in institutional experiences among children.

After reviewing the literature on child-parent separations, Yarrow (1964, p. 121) came to these conclusions:

> The significance of separation to the child depends on many individual and environmental variables. A temporary interruption in a relationship is likely to have very different significance for personality development from that of a permanent loss of a love object. The significance of separation which is followed by marked deprivation of maternal care in a poor institution or foster home is likely to be very different from separation which is followed by the provision of good substitute maternal care, as in adoptive placement. The effects of separation are modified by individual vulnerabilities and sensitivities, constitutional and acquired, as well as by sensitivities which are characteristic of specific developmental periods. The meaning of separation to the child also depends on the larger experiential context in which it occurs. Its significance is undoubtedly different in the context of a parent's death from that in the context of the parent's going on vacation. Its meaning may even depend on the larger cultural setting.

At the animal level, Harlow's (1958) research with infant monkeys provides still additional support for the contention that the nature of the stimulation given offspring influences their development. It will be recalled that Harlow found that infant monkeys reared with wire mother surrogates showed more emotional and anxious behavior than those reared with cloth mother surrogates. These findings suggest that deficiency in one type of stimulation, tactual contact, has a detrimental effect on the future behavior of infant monkeys. Research with other species also supports this inference (Denenberg, 1964).

Whereas the over-all level of stimulation within the child's environment is a most important variable, it is, of course, clear that in the early years of life his parents are the most potent stimuli in his world. The prolonged period of helplessness that characterizes human childhood probably causes parental variables to be more potent in humans than in other species. One might be even more specific and conjecture that of all the persons who people the child's world, the mother or the person who fills the mothering role, exerts the most far-reaching influence over personality development. For this reason, it is not surprising that so much attention has been paid by researchers to the mother-child relationship during childhood (Schaffer and Emerson, 1964).

Early social interactions have often been approached in terms of (1) the characteristics and behavior that the mother brings to her relationship with her baby; (2) individual differences among babies in such characteristics as crying, wakefulness, and over-all activity level; and (3) actual social interactions between mother and child. In the following sections we shall explore the contributions of mother, father, and child to early social interactions. We shall see many indications of the significance of these factors.

THE MOTHER

A mother's behavior influences her child, and the child's behavior has an impact on the mother's life. Because the mother has such a high degree of control over the child and his environment, her role would appear to be more dominant and influential than the child's. It therefore makes sense to inquire into the nature of the maternal figure and the maternal role.

The behavior of a mother toward her child is a function of her interpretation of the job of being a mother, her involvement in performing that job, her personal characteristics, and her evaluation of the adequacy with which she is carrying out the child-rearing task. These determinants of a mother's behavior appear in principle to be the same as those involved in performing any job or assignment. The obvious difference is that the mother has such far-reaching responsibility toward her child, such control over him, and so intense an affectional tie to him. But affectional tie does not mean the platitude that all mothers love their children. There are mothers who neither love nor accept their children. Some mothers may see the maternal role as an obstacle to their own self-fulfillment. Although we may have difficulty empathizing with the rejecting mother, one cannot help but appreciate and sympathize with the plight of the woman who is compelled to devote virtually all of her energies to a task that she may find frustrating and even perhaps loathsome. Of course, it may not be easy to identify rejecting mothers. Understandably, few mothers will admit to strong rejecting attitudes toward their children. Yet it seems reasonable to hypothesize a range of reactions to children from intense rejection to complete acceptance.

One cannot proceed very far in a study of child development without careful study of parents, their personalities and problems, and their histories. Illustrating this necessity is one study that evaluated the relationship of mothers' personalities to child-rearing practices and children's adjustment (Behrens, 1954). The children ranged in age from two to six. The interview was the assessment technique used to facilitate the evaluations. Content analyses of interviews were carried out and ratings made of the mothers' responses. The results of the study indicated that while actual child-rearing practices were not directly related to such variables as the mothers' self-concepts and the affection that they displayed to their children, mothers' personality characteristics did seem to bear significantly on the adequacy of their children's adjustment.

Mothers who differ in their accepting and affectionate behavior may also differ with respect to such behaviors as protectiveness and dominance. The study of overt responses of various types can prove of great value—for example, the study of their actual child-rearing practices. It would seem necessary also to pay attention to underlying psychological factors that contribute to the overt behavior and to the stimulus configuration that the mother displays to her child. It may also be necessary to pay attention to apparently nonpsychological individual differences among mothers. Support for this possibility comes from a study in which women's duration of menstrual flow was found to be positively correlated with the favorableness of their attitudes toward mothering (Levy, 1942).

THE FATHER

If the father is not the forgotten man of developmental psychology, he is certainly the neglected man. This neglect comes about for a number of reasons. During the early years of life the mother is unquestionably the most pervasive influence over the child. Consequently, the mother has been the prime focus of researchers who are concerned with the influence of the environment on the growing child. Another reason for the neglect of the father is his relative inaccessibility. He is at work most of the day and therefore is not as available for study as the mother.

No matter how many reasons one might give in defense of it, lack of knowledge of the father as a child rearer is deplorable. The same conclusion might be drawn about our knowledge of siblings, since they play important roles in the family structure and have also been relatively neglected (Koch, 1956). Indeed, one might regard the assertion that the mother is the prime child rearer in the family as a statement to be proved rather than as a statement of fact. Although the mother usually spends the greatest amount of time with the young child, it may not always be true that she is the most important influence. Furthermore, the amount of time spent with a person may not necessarily be equated with the amount of influence exerted over him.

Despite the practical impediments to studying the role of the father, a number of investigators have been successful in doing so. The results of their efforts support the belief that the father can be a most fruitful object of study. One such study has been reported by Becker, Peterson, Hellmer, Shoemaker and Quay (1959) who compared the families of 25 children not in need of psychological treatment with the families of 32 children who were. Except for the variable of personality adjustment, the two groups seemed comparable. By studying both mothers and fathers of these children, the researchers found that the parents of the maladjusted children were themselves maladjusted and tended to be arbitrary and inconsistent in the handling of their children. In terms of our present concern with the father, it is noteworthy that the role of the father seemed to be, if anything, more important than that of the mother's. The fathers of maladjusted children were found to be withdrawn from the family and especially inconsistent in their responses to offspring. It would not be surprising if certain forms of maladjustment in children were attributable primarily to certain characteristics of fathers and other forms to certain characteristics of mothers.

Another group of studies has dealt with the effects of prolonged absences of fathers on personality development in children. Most of these investigations involved war separations (Lynn and Sawrey, 1959; Stolz, 1954). Their results suggest that children separated from their fathers for long periods of time experience more difficulty in forming meaningful social relationships with adults and peers than do children who have not experienced father separation. Furthermore, father-separated children seem to be tense and more anxious, less mature, and less sure of themselves in a variety of situations than children not separated from their fathers.

Still another group of studies covers sex-role identification (McCandless, 1961; Mussen, 1961; Payne and Mussen, 1956). Both psychoanalytic and social learning views of behavior have emphasized as a factor in development the adequacy of models with whom children can identify. There is reason to believe that the sex identifications of men and women and the degrees of masculinity and femininity they exhibit are influenced by the models that their parents provided for them. Several studies of identifications formed by boys have demonstrated that the significant developmental variable for them is the father. Reviewing the concept of sex-role identification in relation to both boys and girls, Kagan (1964, pp. 162–163) has offered this analysis of the concept:

> The construct of sex role identification is not without its ambiguity and one could argue for its fragmentation into several better articulated terms. Its retention as a descriptive and explanatory concepts rests on the assumption that the concepts *male* and *female* and the dimensions *maleness* and *femaleness* are basic to our language. The evidence supports this assumption. The child as young as four has dichotomized the world into male and female people and is concerned with boy-girl differences. By the time he is seven he is intensely committed to molding his behavior in concordance with cultural standards appropriate to his biological sex and he shows uneasiness, anxiety, and even anger when he is in danger of behaving in ways regarded as characteristic of the opposite sex. The appellation of "sissy" to a boy or "tomboy" to a girl usually has a strong negative affective charge. . . . the desire to behave in accordance with sex role standards extends far beyond an interest in sports for boys and cooking for girls. For the desire to establish a sex role identification touches many important domains of behavior, including school work, sexual behavior, and vocational choice, and has a strong effect on behavioral continuities over the course of development.
>
> The emphasis on the motive to match one's behavior to a standard has been central in this paper. It is suggested that one of the most compelling of human motives is the desire to reduce the discrepancy between an internal standard and the ever-changing behavior of the individual. Thus, expression of sexual behavior, verbal aggression, or academic mastery is sometimes an intermediate act that serves a more powerful motive than sex, aggression, or achievement; namely, the desire for congruence between an ideal representation of the self and one's everyday behavior. This appears to be a uniquely human motive and psychology is witness to a refreshing confluence of theoretical writings that emphasize this point of view.

There would appear to be great need for study of fathers as variables in the family situation. We know that behavioral maladjustments in children may be significantly related to fathers' characteristics, that prolonged absence of the father early in the life of the child may lead to unfortunate developmental consequences, and that the father for the boy—and the mother for the girl—is a major factor in identification. Still, it is possible to cite examples, such as the divorced or widowed woman, in which a mother successfully rears masculine sons. These examples together with the many examples which could be presented of unfortunate consequences of father absences make clear the need to explore carefully the father's role within the family.

THE CHILD

We mentioned earlier the need to attend to individual differences before birth and during early infancy. But the discussion of the influence of parental factors over the offspring's development might seem to argue that virtually all aspects of the child's personality development arise from his interaction with stimuli and events within the situation in which he is reared. We can accept this statement if we understand that the child-rearing situation does not simply create responses in the child, but selectively modifies the child's existing behavioral repertory.

Looking at the entire family from the standpoint of behavior modification, we must inquire into ways in which the child influences the behavior of others. This is especially true as the child comes to be relatively independent and to appreciate his capacities as a modifier of the behavior of others. Awareness of the influential role of the child does not require retraction of earlier statements concerning the pervasive influences of parents in shaping the behavior of their children. It does, however, require recognition of the relevance to the family of stimuli emanating from the child as well as the relevance to the child of stimuli emanating from parents.

A clinical example dramatizes the need for studying the child as a stimulus. Childhood schizophrenia is an extremely debilitating psychotic condition. It usually involves difficulty on the part of the child in maintaining adequate contact with reality. In addition, childhood schizophrenics usually display unpredictable and distressing behavior such as hallucinations and emotional outbursts. Clinical researchers have considered a number of hypotheses that might account for this type of deviant behavior. In testing their hypotheses they have studied the parents of childhood schizophrenics in order to assess their contributions to their children's difficulties.

There is reason to believe that emotional disorders such as childhood schizophrenia are related to the environment created by parents. But do these relationships demonstrate that factors such as the emotional problems of parents cause childhood schizophrenia? Might not one hypothesize that childhood schizophrenia is genetically determined and that the deviant child-rearing practices of parents are simply an expression of their inability to cope with deviant children? This possibility further strengthens the belief that the contributions of both parents and children to the family environment require careful study.

Returning to the general problem of the child as an influential factor in the family, it seems clear that regardless of the basis of its behavior, the child can be a potent contributor to the emotional climate within the home. This potency may be seen even in very early infancy. There are marked differences among infants in amounts of crying and few people enjoy the crying of infants. Regardless of what determines large amounts of crying, the stimulus of protracted, intense crying may have marked bearing on the way in which parents interact with their offspring and with each other.

Our consideration of the responses of mother and child makes it clear that even very early in life these responses result from mutually stimulating social interactions. In succeeding sections we shall explore some of the more significant of these interactions. This will be done in terms of needs, problems, and situations that mark personality development.

THE SECURITY NEEDS OF THE CHILD

It would probably not be difficult to obtain agreement on the characteristics that are desirable for children and adults to possess. Among these, no doubt, would be relative freedom from morbid and debilitating anxiety, adaptability to the variety of experiences that confront people, and effectiveness in and enjoyment of personal relationships. Possession of these might be said to define the secure individual. Many developmental approaches to personality have been directed to the isolation of variables that contribute to personal security. What needs of a developing organism must be satisfied in order that personal security may be attained?

A logical starting point for gathering information about variables that might relate to security needs is the organism's first contacts with its environment. We have already mentioned the personal quality of these contacts. Descriptions of contacts between mother and child must be regarded as incomplete without reference to the characteristics which both the mother and the child bring to these interactions. In addition to a general awareness of the relevance of individual differences, it is necessary to make at least tentative hypotheses concerning the nature of these differences and the particular situations in which they might play significant roles.

In early childhood, the types of child-environment contacts are relatively small in number and they usually involve persons who fulfill a mothering role. We shall begin our investigation of variables related to the child's security needs with a consideration of one type of personal contact that has been subjected to much conjecture and a small, but growing body of behavioral research. We refer to contacts associated with the oral orifice, sucking behavior, and feeding situations.

The Concept of Orality

Freud's concept of the oral personality is not universally accepted. Indeed it is a subject of considerable theoretical controversy. But his emphases on (1) the mouth as an erogenous zone, and (2) feeding as the infant's first important personal situation have been potent factors in influencing research on the development of personality. Some of the research stimulated by Freud's ideas has been concerned primarily with feeding methods as they relate to an hypothesized need for oral gratification. A collateral body of evidence relates to the relationship of personal factors such as the mother's attitudes and personality characteristics to the child's behavior in the feeding situation.

The most obvious feature of the early feeding situations is that the infant's nutriment is obtained through sucking. It is necessary to note that the infant's sucking responses are not reserved exclusively for food intake. Nutritional and nonnutritional sucking are found in all children. Nonnutritional sucking is the sucking behavior of infants who have just eaten and who are about to fall asleep. A perhaps more dramatic example is the occasional four- or five-year-old child who spends literally hours each day engaged in thumbsucking. Is thumbsucking a product of inadequacies in early childhood feeding situations? Is thumbsucking a symptom of insecurity experienced by the child?

These sorts of questions clearly reflect the present state of knowledge concerning the specific problem of nutritive and nonnutritive sucking, and the general one of early childhood determinants of personality. Questions rather than answers characterize the study of early childhood experiences. In one sense, this may seem to leave students in a rather insecure position. However, when we consider that we are dealing with complicated questions that have been propounded only very recently in the history of science, it does not seem surprising that we are still in a question-asking phase. Despite the recency of the empirical study of child behavior, we shall see instances of important data gathering and come across contributions to the clarification of significant questions. In this sense, we may legitimately be optimistic. If we can proceed from asking "wrong" and ambiguous questions to questions that are explicit and scientifically testable, we are clearly moving in the direction of progress.

Sucking Behavior and the Feeding Situation

An illustration of the need for clarification of questions about early experiences may be found in a study of hypotheses and data concerning the sucking response. How does one account for both nutritive and nonnutritive sucking in human infants and children? This question is important psychologically and its answer may have far-reaching practical consequences. What should be the attitude of the mother toward the feeding situation? Does it make a difference whether a mother breast-feeds or bottle-feeds her baby? Should the baby's nutritive sucking be encouraged or discouraged? Should nonnutritive sucking be ignored or "dealt with" in some way?

The Freudian interpretation of sucking behavior is that the region of the mouth is an erogenous zone that provides pleasure gratification. Sucking is the means by which this gratification is attained by the infant. To interfere with or frustrate the infant's need to suck is, from a psychoanalytic point of view, to interfere with the child's psychosexual development. Thumbsucking in older children (and even, in some cases, adults) may from this standpoint constitute fixations at or regressions to the oral stage of development. Some students have conjectured that cigarette smoking in adults is also a residue of unsatisfied infantile oral needs. One implication of this view would appear to be that natural breast feeding of children together with unhurried weaning is superior to artificial bottle feeding and rapid weaning.

A provocative contrast to the psychoanalytic contention that thumb-sucking is a symptom of insecurity and a product of inadequate sucking experiences in infancy may be found in the writings of the behaviorist John B. Watson (1928, pp. 137–138). His cure for thumb-sucking was not more sucking in early infancy but less of it:

> How can we correct thumb-sucking? The answer is, *cure it during the first few days of infancy.* Watch the baby carefully the first few days. Keep the hands away from the mouth as often as you are near the baby in its waking moments. And always when you put it into its crib for sleep, see that the hands are tucked inside the covers. . . .
>
> If the habit develops in spite of this early scrutiny, consult your physician about the infant's diet. Tell him about the thumb-sucking. If after changes in the diet thumb-sucking persists, then take more drastic steps to break the habit. Sew loose white, cotton flannel mitts with no finger or thumb divisions to the sleeves of the night gown and on all the *day dresses, and leave them on for two weeks or more—day and night.* So many mothers leave them on only at night. Unless the child is watched every moment the hand will at one time or another get back to the mouth. You must be careful to see that the dress or night gown is fastened securely but not tightly at the throat—else if the infant is persistent he will learn to disrobe himself to get at his hands. If the habit still persists make . . . the mitts of rougher and rougher material.

The core of the psychoanalytic-behavioristic argument seems clear: Is sucking behavior in the infant a natural pleasure-seeking activity or is it simply a response that can get out of hand? Before turning to empirical evidence that bears on this controversy, it is important to note that hypotheses such as those offered by Freud and Watson contribute to knowledge even if they are not found to be correct. The contribution in such cases is the stimulus they provide to objective exploration. What facts have been laid bare in the course of these explorations? What variables do influence sucking behavior in human infants?

One fact of interest is that there are noticeable individual differences among infants in the intensity of sucking behavior. It is possible that there are constitutional differences in the need to suck. It has been shown that the intensity of sucking responses is positively related to the vigor and health of the infant, the infant's hunger, and characteristics of its nutriment, such as the temperature of milk obtained through sucking.

What about Watson's idea that sucking is essentially habitual in nature? Sears and Wise (1950) have reported data that bear on this question. Through interviews with mothers they collected information concerning the reactions of infants to different times of initiation of weaning. They failed to find differences in degree of thumbsucking between infants weaned early and late. They also found that abruptness of weaning was uncorrelated with thumbsucking. Sears and Wise did find that the later the weaning was initiated the greater was the emotional upset observed in the infant. This would appear to be compatible with the view that for late-weaned children, the sucking response has become a well-learned habit. It is well known that well-learned responses are not easily extinguished and replaced, and that emotional upset may be created when a strong habit is interfered with.

Levy (1928) reported some evidence that is related to the occurrence of nonnutritive sucking. Using data gathered in interviews with mothers, he compared one group of children who were thumbsuckers with a group of nonthumbsuckers. Analysis of the content of the interviews suggested that thumbsuckers had experienced fewer night feedings, had been fed more frequently on a schedule, as opposed to on demand, and had had access to pacifiers less frequently than had nonthumbsuckers. These differences between thumbsuckers and nonthumbsuckers were not found to be attributable to the variable of breast versus bottle feeding.

Levy (1934) also reported a suggestive experiment with dogs that is related to the study just described. He compared two groups of puppies who differed in amount of sucking behavior. One group received formula through slowly flowing nipples that required the animal to suck vigorously. The other group was fed by means of rapidly flowing bottles. The two groups of puppies were compared with respect to the vigor with which they sucked a nipple-covered finger. Levy found that the puppies with a history of relatively little sucking sucked the finger more vigorously than did the puppies who had had more sucking opportunities. He also found that the bottle-fed puppies displayed more restless behavior and seemed more poorly adjusted than the nipple-fed puppies.

Generalizing from this type of data, Ribble (1943, pp. 22–28) has offered the following interpretation:

> During the first three to six months of an infant's life, sucking is his most gratifying and all-absorbing activity. . . .
>
> Sucking usually reaches a maximum intensity about the fourth month of life, and, if it has been fully and agreeably exercised to this time, begins to diminish spontaneously when the baby begins to vocalize, to bite, and grasp with his hands.
>
> . . . Most important to the infant himself is the pleasure value of sucking.
>
> . . . Sucking is then a part of the instinctual behavior with which the child is equipped at birth. . . .
>
> Very quickly rhythmic intervals become established in which the infant shows evidence of a "wish to suck" . . . .

Ribble's comments have contributed to controversial either-or arguments about sucking behavior and its meaning. The aforementioned studies and others suggest that nutritive and nonnutritive sucking are influenced by a variety of factors. Broadly speaking, these include individual differences at birth and the sucking history of infants. With regard to the former it may be that future research on genetic and constitutional predispositions will prove helpful. With regard to the latter, study of personal variables within the feeding and family situations would appear to be indicated. It would seem that Freud's preoccupation with sucking as a pleasureful activity and Watson's insistence on sucking as a maladaptive habit each reflect oversimplification of the complexity of the behavior under study. But these men were eminently successful in arousing interest in that behavior and its determinants.

As research proceeds on these determinants, we can no doubt expect additional relevant variables to come to the fore. After reviewing sucking behavior from the standpoint of nature-nurture controversies, McKee and Honzik (1962, pp. 648–649) have made two suggestions that bear investigation:

> The first has to do with the use of the mouth as an organ of sensory exploration and as an organ of prehension and manipulation. We do not mean to imply that this aspect of orality is totally distinct from sucking. Obviously, oral sensory experience is partly determined by nutritive sucking. We mean only to call attention to an aspect of orality that we have slighted. Many close observers have reported both sensory exploration and prehension . . . yet we have very little normative data or systematic knowledge of how the mouth comes to be used in these ways. We do not know what effects, if any, result from different kinds of feeding experience, thumb-sucking, or other oral history. The field is challenging and totally unexplored.
>
> The second additional area of inquiry concerns the non-oral consequences of different oral experiences . . . we have limited ourselves to the *development of the sucking* response. But many persons are convinced that there is an even more interesting and socially important question involving the relation between early oral experience and the development of personality and sexual behavior. Direct measures of infantile oral experience would be extremely valuable. It is our impression that many so-called measures of, say, "the oral component of the libido" are no such thing, but are instead only assumed correlates of the assumed oral component. In passing, we suggest that if *real* oral experience in early life does have an effect on later sexual development, it may well turn out that the most relevant aspect is the development of the mouth as a sensory, exploratory, and manipulative organ.

Two problems arise in assessing the significance of sucking or any other activity. One of these relates to the conditions associated with the emission of responses. It seems possible that sucking activity by itself may not be a crucial factor in future personality function. But in conjunction with certain other variables, such as the mother's personality or socioeconomic factors, it might be very potent. An understanding of the feeding situation requires more information than a simple statement of feeding procedures—bottle, breast, or cup feeding. Also required is information about the total context of situations in which sucking and feeding occur.

The second problem concerns the consequences of inadequate sucking opportunities. Lack of these opportunities may influence present and future behavior—but in what ways? This problem is analogous to the one that confronts test developers: Which of many possible criteria should be selected for validation purposes? In sucking activity one might hazard the hypothesis that inadequate sucking in infancy will predispose individuals to engage in such activities as pencil chewing and cigarette smoking. But we may reasonably ask, even if the hypothesis is correct, might not certain intervening experiences during the years between infancy and adulthood modify the influences of sucking deprivation? Thus far, empirical evidence relevant to questions like these has not been available.

Let us turn now from the area of specific nutritive and nonnutritive sucking responses to the broad class of responses connected with the feeding situation. There exists a growing body of evidence concerning the personal dimensions of the feeding situation. Since feeding takes up so much of the time of early mother-child contacts, nurturance in terms of food provided the child is thoroughly mixed up with nurturance in terms of affectional, exploratory, and social gratification. Harlow's (1958) work on contact comfort in infant monkeys strongly supports this interpretation, and suggests the need for studies of humans in which variables, such as how the child is held during feeding, are manipulated. The child in the nursing situation not only obtains needed food, but also obtains its first experiences of receiving love and attention from the environment. Viewed this way, the feeding situation may be considered to be the matrix within which the child develops attitudes concerning "getting situations." Attitudes about "getting behavior" stem from the child's perception of the world as a place that provides for his wishes and needs.

In order to better understand the variables that might be operative in the feeding or "getting" situation, Sears, Maccoby, and Levin (1957) conducted an exhaustive interview study of the attitudes of 379 mothers. They studied mothers' attitudes toward themselves, their roles as mothers, and their children. This approach seems potentially fruitful since the attitudes of the mother contribute to the definition of her as a stimulus for the child.

An interesting statistic uncovered by Sears, Maccoby, and Levin was that 60 per cent of the mothers in their sample had not breast fed their babies. More than half of the mothers who did breast feed shifted to bottle-feeding within three months. It is noteworthy that 26 per cent of the sample mothers stated that the reason they had not engaged in breast feeding was their physical incapability to do so. In comparison to the infrequent incidence of breast-feeding incapacity in primitive cultures, this figure seems extraordinarily high. One wonders if it was really the case that 26 per cent of the mothers interviewed by Sears, Maccoby, and Levin were incapable for physical reasons of performing a natural biological function. Interestingly, a comparison made by these authors of breast-feeding and bottle-feeding mothers in terms of the variable of sexual permissiveness, showed that the former were much less anxious and modest about sexuality than the latter.

Comparing breast-feeding and bottle-feeding mothers, Sears, Maccoby, and Levin found no consistent differences between these two groups in terms of reports of problems in behavior exhibited by their children, such as bedwetting, aggressiveness, and severe feeding problems. Although Sears, Maccoby, and Levin's findings are more suggestive than conclusive, the possibility arises that mothers who breast feed and mothers who bottle feed differ with respect to sexual modesty but do not differ with respect to other characteristics. If this were true, it would seem likely that the guilt experienced by many mothers who choose to bottle feed rather than to breast feed their babies is unwarrantedly strong.

If indeed the characteristics of the mother may override or complicate whatever psychological effects breast- and bottle-feeding *per se* may have, then much of the literature on feeding methods seems subject to criticism. Most of the literature on feeding methods has dealt only with feeding techniques rather than with the feeding situation, which includes the mother and her attitudes. This deficiency in the design of feeding studies may account, in part, for the lack of consistency of findings on the effects of various feeding methods on the security of children.

Heinstein (1963) has reported one of the few research projects that not only compared children who have received different feeding regimens, but also studied personal aspects of mother-child contacts. The data of the project consisted of open-ended interviews with mothers and observations of children made by physicians and nurses. The subjects were a sample of children studied longitudinally over a period of several years. No evidence was found to suggest that breast- and bottle-feeding regimens *per se* differentially influenced the later adjustment of children.

One significant personal variable studied by Heinstein was what he referred to as the mother's warmth. By this he meant the strength of the bond between mother and child, the mother's friendliness, and the mother's expressiveness of affection. Both boys and girls who had warm mothers showed fewer behavior problems than the offspring of cold mothers. Among the problems on which these groups were compared were: finickiness with regard to food, temper tantrums, and lack of independence. Heinstein (1963, p.38) summarized his findings in this way:

> There appeared to be no over-all advantage for boys or girls to be breast fed or nursed long or short periods. While individual problems, beyond what would be expected by chance, were related to types of nursing regimes, there were no clear advantages to a single procedure. Contrary to expectation, an "oral" behavior syndrome tended to be related to longer breast feeding and nursing for boys.
>
> Both boys and girls appeared to benefit, behaviorally, from warm rather than cold mothers. Girls with a stable mother were better adjusted, whereas boys showed no behavioral differences if the mother was rated high or low on nervous stability. Marital adjustment of the parents seemed to have an insignificant role in relation to problem behavior of both boys and girls.

Another part of Heinstein's research dealt with the relationships among the maternal characteristic of warmth, the duration of nursing, and the breast- versus bottle-feeding variable. Heinstein (1963, p. 46) was concerned with:

> . . . the distribution of problem behavior for subjects under four general conditions representing the combined influence of the nursing situation (breast or bottle; long or short nursing) and the favorable or unfavorable characteristics of the parents. For boys the combination of breast feeding and parental variables appeared to have no over-all significance for adjustment. Girls, on the other hand, reacted favorably to the concomitant influence of both breast feeding and favorable parental characteristics, particularly when the mother was above average in warmth toward the child. Girls breast fed with a cold mother were, on the other hand, more prone to problem behavior.
>
> Boys, however, were affected by the length of nursing when the parents were also considered. When they were nursed long and had a cold mother, there was considerable maladjustment. On the other hand, long nursing with a warm mother made for better behavioral adjustment. Girls, contrary to the results with breast feeding and variables on parental characteristics, were not found to be affected by the combined conditions of long or short nursing with favorable or unfavorable parental variables.

Thumbsucking was present in girls more often with breast feeding and favorable parental characteristics. The control of each variable permitted the conclusion that it was not simply breast feeding or good parents, but rather the combined effects of both.

These findings would appear to buttress the view that it is necessary to assess the contributions of feeding methods *and* personal variables in order to establish meaningful relationships between the feeding experiences of children and their subsequent behavior. Thus we must conclude that whereas it would be convenient if psychologists could recommend to mothers the use of specific optimal child-feeding practices, the actual complexities of the feeding situation and the mingling of the mother's personality and feeding procedures indicate that such recommendations could be made only at the risk of hazardous oversimplification.

The Heinstein study appears to support this conclusion by its determination of the effects of feeding experiences and mothers' warmth on later adjustment—some of these data were gathered when the children were as old as 18 years of age. Although longitudinal information is surely of great value, there is also merit in limiting investigation to the influence of maternal characteristics on behavior during infancy. Lakin (1957) used this approach in gathering evidence about possible psychogenic factors related to a common problem, infantile colic. Colic is a condition in which an infant emits loud, seemingly agonizing cries for long periods of time. The condition, despite its frequency of occurrence, is not well understood. Some writers have attributed colic to the immaturity of the infant's central nervous system, others have referred to overfeeding and underfeeding as etiological factors, and still others have hypothesized a psychogenic factor, presumably emanating from the mother-child interaction.

In his study, Lakin made personality comparisons between mothers of colicky infants and mothers of a control group of noncolicky infants. Each of the subjects had recently borne her first child. The two groups were comparable with regard to socioeconomic status, education, and health. The children of the two groups of mothers appeared to be similar with regard to age, birth weight, and ease of delivery. Information gained about the mothers was derived from their responses to projective tests, questionnaires, and a Q-sort task. These data were then analyzed in terms of variables that Lakin (1957, p. 11) felt might be related to the incidence of colic in infants. These were Lakin's hypotheses:

a. Mothers of colicky infants have tended to experience poorer parent-child relationships than mothers of control infants.

b. Mothers of colicky infants have tended to experience greater intrapersonal conflict over role acceptance than mothers of control infants.

c. Mothers of colicky infants tend to have greater concern over their adequacy in the female role than do mothers of control infants.

d. Mothers of colicky infants tend to have attained less adequate marital adjustments than mothers of control infants.

e. Mothers of colicky infants tend to be less motherly than mothers of control infants.

These were the major findings with regard to Lakin's five hypotheses:

Hypothesis *a*: The mothers of colicky babies appeared to have experienced stronger feelings of competitiveness toward their own mothers and greater emotional distance from both parents than had the mothers of noncolicky babies.

Hypothesis *b*: Mothers of colicky babies seemed to experience greater personal conflict over fulfilling the maternal role and more concern over frustrated vocational ambitions than mothers of noncolicky babies.

Hypothesis *c*: Feelings of inadequacy and a generally poor self-concept were more characteristic of mothers of colicky babies than of mothers of noncolicky babies.

Hypothesis *d*: The mothers of colicky babies appeared to have made poorer marital adjustments than the mothers of noncolicky babies.

Hypothesis *e*: The mothers of colicky babies seemed to be less adept and secure in carrying out maternal duties than the mothers of noncolicky babies.

It seems clear that there were noticeable personality differences between the two groups of mothers studied by Lakin. This does not mean that factors such as genetic or constitutional determinants are unrelated to the incidence of colic in young infants. Rather, it supports theorists such as Sullivan who contend that even at very early stages of development, the maternal and environmental influence can be of great significance. Of course, providing support for this contention and demonstrating precisely in what manner the characteristics of the mother become transmitted to the child are two quite different matters. Although Sullivan (Mullahy, 1949; Sullivan, 1947, 1953) hypothesized a process that he called empathy to account for this transmission, direct empirical evidence is lacking concerning the way in which conscious and unconscious conflicts and attitudes in the mother affect the child. We do seem to have reached the point where the hypothesis that covert and overt maternal behavior can be a determining factor in the early development of the child seems to be reasonable. However, it is important to note a methodological limitation of studies like Lakin's and Sears, Maccoby, and Levin's (1957). In them researchers interviewed mothers *after* their offspring had passed the stage of infancy. A more unambiguous way to assess parents would appear to be to make contact with them *before* their children are born.

That early influences exerted by the mother may carry over to later age periods was suggested by the Fels longitudinal study (Kagan and Moss, 1962). Corroborating evidence has been provided by Schaefer and Bayley (1963) in another longitudinal study. On the basis of interviews, Schaefer and Bayley made ratings of various personality characteristics of mothers. These inferred characteristics were then related to offsprings' behavior more than a decade later. Schaefer and Bayley's correlations of maternal characteristics with children's behavior at various ages support the hypothesis that the social and emotional adjustment of children at various age levels is related to the personality characteristics of their mothers as assessed during the children's first three years of life. It is interesting to observe that the "sleeper effect" noted by Kagan and Moss (1962) was also found by Schaefer and Bayley. For example, they saw that maternal behavior during the first three years of the child's life was more highly correlated with sons' behavior at ages six to nine, than with sons' behavior during the first three years of life. One variable that both the Kagan and Moss and the Schaefer and Bayley studies showed to be of great importance in influencing correlations between mother and child was the sex of the child. Other potentially significant variables not as yet subjected to systematic study include the socioeconomic status of the family and the intellectual level of the child.

Taking stock of the evidence, we might justifiably conclude that while various factors such as genetic predispositions and feeding methods employed may play significant roles in influencing behavior, the psychological variable of the mother seems definitely to be one that cannot be ignored or neglected. Future research will be required to determine precisely the ways that maternal behavior, both overt and covert, affects behavior in infancy as well as in later life. The combined use of assessment techniques and direct observations of mother-child interactions would seem necessary in this research.

Having observed the significance of the presence of the mother in the child's world, let us turn to another aspect of the problem, the effects on the child of absence of the maternal figure. Everyday observation makes poignantly clear the security need of the child for its mother. Almost everyone has observed the tenacious clinging behavior of children and the tears that may emanate at separation from the mother. This sort of anecdotal evidence has served to stimulate behavioral researchers to investigate empirically the phenomenon of maternal deprivation.

Studies of institutionalized children have been used to assess the effects of maternal deprivation. These suggest that the sense of security and the social, intellectual, and emotional responsiveness of institutionalized children are not as well developed as in children reared at home. Studies of children reared at home who become separated from their mothers provide collateral evidence concerning maternal deprivation. It appears that the age at which separation occurs is related to the child's response to it. Children separated from their mothers prior to six months of age seem to show much less emotional disruption than children separated at ages greater than six months.

The occurrence of maternal deprivation is related to the occurrence of sensory deprivation (Casler, 1961). Institutionalized children, while certainly deprived of a mother's love, are also deprived of sensory stimulation and exploratory behavior. In children separated from their mothers, the less traumatic reactions of young infants may be attributable to their neurological and cognitive immaturity. Children separated after the age of six months, on the other hand, have developed cognitive and affective responses to a reinforcing mother. Separation for such children involves, at the same time, separation from maternal love and affection and separation from familiar stimuli.

These comments suggest that the concept of maternal deprivation requires clarification. The question that seems to be particularly important is: What is the meaning to children at different stages of development of physical separation from a parent? Not only must the factor of loss of love be separated from the factor of loss of sensory stimulation, but in older children, consideration must also be given to cognitive and symbolic reactions to separation. In addition, the evidence cited earlier suggests that the effects of maternal deprivation on the child may depend on the characteristics of the mother from whom the child has been separated. On intuitive grounds alone it seems sensible that a child separated from a rejecting mother will respond differently to separation from a child separated from a loving, security-instilling mother.

This inference is in accord with the assertion that the child's sense of security and overt behavior is not a simple function of the presence or absence of the mother, or the type of feeding regimen used. Awareness of this leads to an increased appreciation of the multifaceted nature of seemingly simple behavior. In the case of the child's feeding, we have a situation in which nutriment is derived. But in addition to food intake, the child also derives tactual stimulation from the mother as well as stimulation from her attitudes and emotional responses to the child, and from her own preoccupations, anxieties, and conflicts. *Feeding in the infant may be viewed as an experience in which the child gets physical things (food) from the environment. But it is necessary to be aware that the infant also experiences the totality of psychological factors that contribute to a comprehensive definition of the feeding situation.*

The dynamics of the feeding situation might be taken as a prototype of many events experienced by the developing child. These events may also be analyzed from the point of view of the parent. Each developmental hurdle involves ground rules set down within the family and within society. We have seen that family-to-family differences in child-rearing practices do exert discernible influences over the particular hurdles posed for the child. There is evidence also of subculture-to-subculture differences in the ways in which children are reared (Bronfenbrenner, 1958). For example, Davis and Havighurst (1946) used assessment interviews with mothers of young children in order to compare child-rearing practices among these groups: (1) white middle class; (2) white lower class; (3) Negro middle class; (4) Negro lower class.

Tables 23-1 and 23-2 summarize some of their findings of differences with regard to class and to color. The work of Davis and Havighurst has suggested that the sociocultural and color variables by themselves and in interaction with each other contribute significantly to child-rearing practices in the home. But interestingly, they

TABLE 23-1

Class Differences in Child Rearing

Feeding and Weaning

More lower-class children are breast-fed only.

More lower-class children are breast-fed longer than 3 months (Negro only).

More lower-class children are fed at will.

Weaning takes place earlier (on the average) among middle-class children (white only).

More lower-class children suck longer than 12 months (white only).

More lower-class children have pacifiers (white only).

More middle-class children are held for feeding.

More lower-class children are weaned sharply (Negro only).

TABLE 23-1 (*Continued*)

Toilet Training

Bowel training is begun earlier (on the average) with middle-class children.
Bladder training is begun earlier (on the average) with middle-class children.
Bowel training is completed earlier by middle-class children (Negro only).
More middle-class parents begin bowel training at 6 months or earlier.
More middle-class parents begin bladder training at 6 months or earlier (Negro only).
More middle-class parents complete bowel training at 12 months or earlier (Negro only).
More middle-class parents complete bladder training at 18 months or earlier (Negro only).
More lower-class parents complete bladder training at 18 months or earlier (white only).

Father-Child Relations

Middle class fathers spend more time with children.
Middle class fathers spend more time in educational activities with children (teaching, reading, and taking for walks).
Lower-class fathers discipline children more (Negro only).

Occupational Expectations for Children

Middle class expect higher occupational status for children.

Educational Expectation (Length of Education)

More middle-class children expected to go to college.

Age of Assuming Responsibility

Middle-class expect child to help at home earlier.
Middle-class girls cross street earlier (whites only).
Lower-class boys and girls cross street earlier (Negro only).
Middle-class boys and girls expected to go downtown alone earlier.
Middle-class girls expected to help with younger children earlier.
Middle-class girls expected to begin to cook earlier (white only).
Middle-class girls expected to begin to sew earlier (white only).
Middle-class girls expected to do dishes earlier (Negro only).
Lower-class children expected to get job after school earlier.
Lower-class children expected to quit school and go to work earlier.

Strictness of Regime

Middle-class children take naps in daytime more frequently.
Lower-class boys and girls allowed at movies alone earlier.
Middle-class boys and girls in house at night earlier.

Reproduced with permission from A. Davis and R. J. Havighurst (1946) Social class and color differences in child rearing, *Amer. sociol. Rev.*, **11,** p. 703.

also found that family-to-family differences, regardless of sociocultural background and race, were often potent influences in child rearing.

As we increase in ability to isolate the variables that are at work in feeding and other situations and as we gain knowledge of their present and delayed effects, such as the "sleeper effect", it will become possible to improve the precision of descriptive language. Although the construct of security may actually turn out to be worthwhile, it would not be surprising if the observations relating to it could be better conceptualized in terms of a number of specific concepts rather than one global term.

TABLE 23-2

Color Differences in Child Rearing

Feeding and Weaning

More Negro children are breast-fed only.
More Negro children are breast-fed for three months or more.
More Negro children are fed at will (lower class only).
More Negro children have pacifiers (middle class only).
More white children are weaned sharply (middle class only).
Weaning takes place earlier (on the average) among white children (middle class only).
More white children suck longer than 12 months (lower class only).

Toilet Training

Bowel training is begun earlier with Negro children.
Bladder training is begun earlier with Negro children.
Bowel training is completed earlier with Negro children (middle class only).
Bladder training is completed earlier with Negro children.
More Negro parents begin bowel training at 6 months or earlier (middle class only).
More Negro parents begin bladder training at 6 months or earlier (middle class only).
More Negro parents complete bowel training at 12 months or earlier (middle class only).
More Negro parents complete bladder training at 18 months or earlier (middle class only).

Father-Child Relations

White fathers spend more time with children (lower class only).
White fathers teach and play more with children (lower class only).
Negro fathers discipline children more (lower class only).

TABLE 23-2 (*Continued*)

Educational Expectations (Length of Education)

More Negro children expected to go to college (lower class only).

Age of Assuming Responsibility

Negro boys and girls cross street earlier (lower class only).
White girls cross street earlier (lower class only).
Negro boys go downtown alone earlier (lower class only).
Negro girls expected to dress selves earlier.
Negro girls expected to go to store earlier.
Negro girls expected to begin to cook earlier (lower class only).
Negro children expected to quit school and go to work later.

Strictness of Regime

Negro boys allowed to go to movies alone earlier.
White girls allowed to go to movies alone earlier.
White boys and girls in house at night earlier.

Reproduced with permission from A. Davis and R. J. Havighurst (1946), Social class and color differences in child rearing, *Amer. sociol. Rev.*, **11**, p. 704.

THE NEED TO CONFORM

How to get children to do the "right" things and to conform has always been a challenge to parents. However, as stated by L. E. Holt, Jr. (1929, pp. 189–190) almost as widespread as the child-rearing problems confronting parents have been the solutions recommended for them:

How may a child be trained to be regular in the action of the bowels?
By endeavoring to have them move at exactly the same time each day.
At what age may an infant be trained in this way?
Usually by the third or fourth month if training is begun early.
What is the best method of training?
A small chamber, about the size of a pint bowl, is placed between the nurse's knees, and upon this the infant is held, his back being against the nurse's chest and his body firmly supported. This should be done twice a day, after the morning and afternoon feedings, and always at the same hour. . . .
What advantage has such training?
The regular habit formed in infancy makes regularity in childhood much easier. It also saves the nurse much trouble and labor.

J. B. Watson (1928, pp. 121–122) has noted:

. . . The infant from 8 months of age onward should have a special toilet seat into which he can be safely strapped. *The child should be left in the bathroom without toys and with the door closed.* Under no circumstances should the door be left open or the mother or nurse stay with the child. This is a rule which seems to be almost universally broken. When broken it leads to dawdling, loud conversation, in general to unsocial and dependent behavior.

These quotations place in bold relief the contrast between value-laden, armchair, intuitive approaches to child behavior and contemporary, data-oriented approaches. Modern child psychologists are often reluctant to tell questioners how to get children to conform, to do the "right" things. This reluctance is a direct consequence of their awareness of the complexity of the variables that influence children's behavior. Let us look at some of the variables that have been uncovered in objective studies of conformity behavior.

In the preceding section we described the first social relationships of the infant in the feeding situation. We focused intensively on this situation because it seems prototypic of many mother-child interactions. Just as the feeding situation may be interpreted as central to "getting" behavior, so may the toilet training and cleanliness training situations be viewed as central to "giving" or conformity behavior. These are among the first situations in the socialization process that place demands on the child. It seems reasonable to hypothesize that the way in which the child is introduced to the concept of conformity may have a pervasive influence over many of his later social attitudes and reactions. It was essentially this possibility that contributed to Freud's hypothesis of an anal stage of development. He believed that premature and exaggerated emphasis by parents on toilet training might lead to fixations at and regressions to the anal stage (Chapter 2). However, it is difficult to make unequivocal predictions about the relationships between specific early experiences and later behavior. This difficulty arises because most specific early experiences are closely interlocked with the total experiential history of the individual. Furthermore, the influence of frustrations and trauma experienced at particular periods of life may be subjected to reinforcing or countervailing experiences later in life.

What this amounts to is a point implied in earlier discussions: While psychoanalytic theory seeks to provide a global, all-encompassing account of behavior, it is, in fact, lacking in sufficient explication to do this task successfully at the present time. What psychoanalytic theory has accomplished is the discovery of variables and dimensions of behavior that may play significant roles in a well-integrated system. It has dramatically brought to attention the importance, not only of the periods of infancy and childhood, but also of certain specific events that mark them. What is known at present of the anal period hypothesized by Freud, and the development of what we have described as conformity and giving behavior? Objective evidence concerning the events of this period is meager. Nevertheless, let us consider some of the hypotheses and data that seem to relate to this stage of development.

Our primary concern has been with individuality as it manifests itself in social relationships. From a developmental standpoint, what is the early history of the socialization process? Since there are wide differences among people in the types of social relationships they form, an historical approach would seem the best path to an understanding of their genesis. The socialization process may be viewed through two related classes of variables: (1) those pertaining to persons, and (2) those concerning situations and events. The former may be called personality variables, the latter, social contextual ones.

Personality variables are potentially relevant in every interaction between the child and the significant persons in his environment. The personalities of figures, such as the mother, are part and parcel of every such interaction. Since these interactions are situations, it would be desirable to isolate, classify, and study some of the more obvious ones. If we could do this, we might then proceed to analyze the effects on human development of the persons and events that influence the child and the contexts in which these influences occur. We have just described some of these joint effects with regard to the feeding situation; these were perhaps most apparent in the Heinstein (1963) study. Have similar effects been noted for the toilet-training and cleanliness-training situations?

The Sears, Maccoby, and Levin (1957) research is valuable because of the light it sheds on maternal attitudes that may relate to conformity training. These attitudes play roles in influencing particular child-rearing practices in the home. Regarding conformity training, Sears, Maccoby, and Levin found that the age at which toilet training was begun by mothers ranged from under five months to over 34 months. The duration of training (that is, the time between instituting and completing it) ranged from one or two months to over 17 months. In general, the duration was less the later the training began.

Of particular interest to our present inquiry was the relationship between the degree of a mother's anxiety over sex and the age at which toilet training was initiated. The greater the mother's anxiety over sex, the greater the likelihood that she would start toilet training early. This is especially suggestive in view of another finding reported by Sears, Maccoby, and Levin that the greater the sex anxiety of the mother, the greater was the likelihood that she would not breast feed her baby. It seems inescapable that what happens in the life of the child is quite directly related to the attitudes and preoccupations of persons in his environment.

This conclusion is further supported by findings in relation to the intensity or severity with which toilet training is pursued. By severity is meant the degree to which a child is scolded and punished for "accidents" and other transgressions. Sears, Maccoby, and Levin's findings suggest that the more severe the mother is in accomplishing toilet training, the greater the likelihood that the child will show signs of emotional upset. Further comparisons indicated that the upset shown by children who had received a relatively severe training regimen was greater when the mother appeared to be a relatively cold and hostile person than when she was a warm and affectionate one. One common symptom of emotional upset in children is that of bedwetting. Sears, Maccoby, and Levin found children trained by warm, affectionate mothers showed a much lower incidence of bedwetting than children whose mothers appeared to be cold and relatively aloof.

This evidence, gathered in exhaustive interviews with mothers, seems similar to the findings of Heinstein (1963) concerning feeding practices. Just as he had shown that a realistic approach to the feeding situation could not ignore the variable of the mother's personality, so Sears, Maccoby, and Levin demonstrated a similar interaction between the mother's personality and the social context of the toilet-training situation. Valuable as their data are, however, one cannot help wishing that Sears, Maccoby, and Levin had been in a position to obtain direct behavioral indices on the children in their study. The limits of their interview study did not permit this. Unfortunately, there is little evidence in the literature concerning direct behavioral consequences of different toilet-training procedures.

One study of these consequences was conducted by Bernstein (1955). His research was carried out on 47 five-year-old children. The data gathered consisted of children's records at a well-baby clinic, play interviews, and direct behavioral observations. Bernstein was interested in finding indications of the behavioral consequences of severe toilet training. His criteria for severity were early beginning of training, and punishment for noncompliance with training requirements. His results showed that severity of toilet training was related to separation anxiety, as inferred from willingness of the child to leave a room in which the mother was present, to negativeness, uncommunicativeness, and behavioral immaturity. Bernstein's findings concerning children's negativism appear to have been corroborated by Wittenborn (1956), who found coerciveness of toilet training to be related to children's aggressiveness at age five and also at ages eight and nine.

There would appear to be considerable value in relating children's experiences at particular periods in their lives to their subsequent attitudes and behavior. However, before these relationships can be specifically spelled out it will be necessary to improve and expand the methods used to study this sort of problem. Whereas interview data such as those presented by Sears, Maccoby, and Levin are of undeniable value, additional types of data are needed.

Observations made following experimental manipulations are valuable data. These manipulations might be discrete treatments administered over a short time period, such as children's interactions with their mothers in a playroom populated by different numbers of enticing toys, or long-term treatments, such as children's reactions to different child-rearing techniques taught to parents. Additional types of data include: (1) behavioral observations of mothers in a variety of situations, and especially in situations involving the mother and her child; (2) behavioral observations of the child in situations involving the mother, father, siblings, peers, and others; and (3) repeated observations over time of the mother and father and their offspring, through interviews, tests, and specially devised situations.

These latter data seem particularly relevant to conjectures about the effects of particular early childhood experiences such as feeding and toilet-training situations on later behavior. In view of the "sleeper effect" noted in longitudinal studies, it may be that differences in particular childhood regimens may not manifest themselves continuously throughout life, but may have impacts only at certain developmental periods. To evaluate these sorts of possibilities would suggest the need for more longitudinal research conceived and carried out to test specific hypotheses about (1) the significant events that occur in early childhood, and (2) the relationship between these early events and later personality functioning.

Returning now to the topic of conformity behavior, it is possible to approach the problem from a slightly different angle. To do this, we must begin with the fact that most children acquire a wide variety of conformity responses. Of course, initially these responses develop almost exclusively within the family setting. An interesting question suggested by the children's adherence to and actual adoption of standards set within the family is: What are the factors within the family that strengthen the emission of conformity responses? Let us consider some of the factors that may bear on this process of acquisition.

COMPETENCE MOTIVATION. White (1959) has suggested competence motivation as a factor both in personality formation and in the development of abilities (Chapter 3). He has argued that the child's acquisition of a variety of skills suggests a need or motive on the part of the child to explore and gain mastery over his environment. For example, why does the young child insist upon feeding himself with a spoon when his hunger would be more quickly and efficiently reduced by having his mother feed him? Anyone who has observed the young child struggling to place the spoon in his mouth has probably wondered why the child persists in the battle. White contended that the child's persistence was a function of his curiosity about his environment and his motivation to manipulate objects in it.

If one conceives of competence motivation in a broad sense, it is possible to include the acquisition of conformity responses within the large class of competencies acquired by the child. Just as the child makes a significant step toward competence when he learns to cope with a spoon, so he shows progress when he is successful in performing functions such as independently using the toilet and washing his own hands. Continuing this extension of competence motivation to conformity behavior leads to the conclusion that the conformity process is not simply a matter of coercing the child to do what adults want him to do. Although environmental pressures to conform are undeniable, there may also be strong pressures within the child that make acquisition of some conformity responses satisfying experiences.

IMITATION AND IDENTIFICATION. Regardless of what form a theory of conformity might take, it would seem likely that within it some mention would have to be made of the concepts of imitation and identification. When one imitates, one adopts or displays responses made by another person, a model. For example, when the child begins to feed himself, he may be quite attentive to the manner in which his mother and father feed themselves. Imitation may be thought of as a process through which the behavior of a model is reproduced. The reproduction is, of course, limited by the capabilities of the imitator (Bandura, 1965) (See Chapters 4, 18, and 22).

Related to the concept of imitation is that of identification. Some writers have questioned the need for both a concept of imitation and of identification. Certainly imitation plays a role in identification. It does seem, however, that identification as a developmental process possesses sufficient practical value to merit continued usage. It might be said that whereas imitation refers to a person's reproduction of a specific response made by a model, identification connotes a more general process whereby an individual comes to be like a significant person in his life. This process of "coming to be like" may be much more complex than the simple imitation of particular aspects of a model's behavior. It involves, in addition, an emotional relationship between two persons. The role of identification seems particularly apparent in the development of conformity. Children just do not conform to standards set for them. They also take as their own the standards, values, and attitudes of the persons with whom they identify.

Identification may involve both selectivity and ambivalence. Selectivity in identification may be observed when a child is like one parent in some respects and like the other parent in other respects. The child does not indiscriminately imitate all responses made by all potential models. Ambivalence in identification may be observed when the child reaches the point in development at which he can respond cognitively to the identifications that he has formed. Everyone has probably had contact with persons who have made remarks such as: "It's too bad I take after my father." This would suggest that although a boy may become like his father, he may also have significant affective and cognitive reactions to the acquired behaviors in his repertory.

Although it would be possible to discuss the concepts of imitation and identification in much greater detail, it is desirable to relate them to the topic with which we are presently concerned, conformity behavior. We have pointed out that the child's conformity to the standards prevalent within the family and within his social milieu need not be viewed as a simple product of coercion. The child's competency motivation may actually contribute to his seeking the acquisition of certain conforming responses. The environmental models available for the acquisition process in all likelihood influence the particular responses that are acquired and the attitudes that the child has toward conformity (Bandura and Walters, 1963). For an adequate understanding of these attitudes, it is necessary to study, describe, and analyze environmental models, and their attitudes and affective relationships to the child. Parents who themselves unwillingly comply with external demands will probably communicate these attitudes to their offspring. These communications will in turn influence the child's perception of the meaning of conformity. Similarly, parents who see conformity as a beginning of the growth of independence in the child can be expected in subtle and obvious ways to communicate these attitudes to their offspring.

The development of conformity behavior in children is to a significant degree a function of the social makeup of the family. Involved in this makeup are the various and often complex emotional stresses and strains that characterize family life. This social makeup influences the types of models available to the child as he acquires new responses. It also influences the definition of the roles and behaviors expected of the child.

Psychologists in laboratory studies of learning have found that what happens after a subject has made a particular response affects the probability of its recurrence. These environmental events may be called reinforcements (see Chapters 4 and 17). Some of them increase the likelihood of recurrence (positive reinforcers); others decrease the likelihood of recurrence (negative reinforcers).

When a baby first approximates the sound "Mama," two observations may be easily noted. The first is that the baby's utterance has an obvious impact on its environment. Each utterance of "Mama" by the baby leads to a positive affective response on the part of the mother. Maternal smiles, hugs, and attention come to be discriminated by the baby as consequences of the sounds emitted. The second observation is that this influx of maternal love leads to a strengthening of the baby's "Mama" response. Just as the baby's emission of "Mama" appears to be positively reinforcing for the mother, the mother's consequent behavior is reinforcing for the child. Each of us can think of illustrations of discernible effects of reinforcement on the behavior of both children and adults. Questions that arise in the study of reinforcement are: What constitutes an effective reinforcer? What individual difference variables associated with human reinforcers influence their effectiveness? In child rearing, how does a parent decide which responses made by children should be reinforced? It will be remembered that we ran up against these sorts of questions in connection with the verbal conditioning literature (Chapter 17).

In the case of conformity behavior, an important question is the degree to which parents see their children's conformity in terms of the acquisition of skills. Parents who *expect* their children to conform may be quite different as reinforcing agents from parents who *want* their children to learn conformity skills. Thus two parents who both seemingly reinforce conformity behavior in their children may actually have quite different effects on their children by virtue of the attitudes associated with reinforcement and the manner with which the reinforcers are administered. One can say with confidence that reinforcement in such forms as attention, love, and rewards clearly can influence the acquisition of conformity responses. But this need not blind us to the complexity of the nature of reinforcement.

As we have seen, post-response events, reinforcements, can be both positive and negative. Punishment represents an important form of negative reinforcement and may be effective as a means of eliminating or modifying responses. But punishment may also have different effects on different people. A commonly observed effect of punishment is a marked increase in interorganism variability. In general, positive reinforcement is a more reliable means of strengthening responses than negative reinforcement is a means of weakening them (Solomon, 1964).

Punishment is important in human development because of its effects on the personality of the individual. Two basic questions are: What is the individual's interpretation of punishments administered to him? What is the impact of punishment on the individual's self-concept and attitudes? One frequent concomitant of punishment is heightened anxiety, which may be viewed as a generalized reaction to physical or psychological pain created by the punishment. The child who is severely punished because he has wet his pants may respond to a wide variety of conformity situations with fear and anxiety. This anxiety may become so pervasive as to affect his behavior in many situations that are perceived to entail adherence to standards. Another psychological concomitant of punishment may be heightened guilt. The child who does not become toilet trained as quickly as his parents deem desirable may experience guilt over failure to satisfy his parents. Failure to acquire conformity responses speedily can be interpreted as letting parents down. In addition to and often mixed up with this guilt may be generalized anger over the pressures to adhere to norms.

It seems clear that ambivalences and frustrations may be significant consequences of a history of negative reinforcement. This does not mean that parents should never punish their children. It does mean that they should be aware of some of the possible consequences of too strong a reliance on punishment as a child-training technique. No doubt there is an optimal positive reinforcement-negative reinforcement balance for each family context. A challenge to personality researchers is to shed light on the nature of this balance.

There are two final points that need to be emphasized in connection with the development of conformity behavior in the child. The first is that the concepts used to describe the process of acquiring conformity responses are by no means limited to conformity responses. Competence motivation, imitation, identification, and reinforcement (both positive and negative) are factors that influence virtually all aspects of the developing individual's behavioral repertory. Because of our present concern, we have talked about these concepts within the context of conformity behavior. It is clear that the acquisition of conforming responses represents an early and significant part of socialization and of the establishment of personal values.

The second point that requires emphasis is that the effects of competence motivation, imitation, identification, and reinforcement are not always easily observable. It is necessary to be aware of their effects on covert as well as overt behavior. It is not enough to be satisfied with the statement that Johnny, age three years, stopped spilling his milk as a result of having been punished for sloppy eating habits. It is also necessary to ask: What impact may these punishment experiences have had on his self-awareness, his self-concept, and his attitudes toward other people, particularly those who have administered the punishment?

If we ask this type of question we are not likely to have the narrow conception of the human organism as purely a doer. People both do *and* think. The things we do influence our thinking, and our thoughts influence our actions. Psychologists have made considerable progress in their study and classification of overt actions—for example, the work of Barker (1963) and his colleagues. Progress in the description of covert behavior has been slower and often more on a conjectural than an empirical level. That this should be so is not surprising. Progress in a field will usually be faster where the subject matter is more clearly observable and more tangible than where the data are less public, as is so in the study of personal conscious and unconscious events.

Because of their interest in the person, personality researchers have sought through empirical observations to draw inferences about these thought processes. Their efforts have often been directed toward understanding thought processes that are affective in nature and have implications for social development. In the next chapter we shall turn to a consideration of some of the constructs that have been approached from this point of view. These constructs represent an attempt to conceptualize the differentiation of emotional experience that occurs in the process of development.

24

Emotional Differentiation

Human development may be thought of as a continuum ranging from the relative simplicity of infancy to the relative complexity of adulthood. This seems particularly apparent in the ways in which affect and emotions are expressed. Perhaps the child and the adult may not differ quantitatively in experiencing emotions, but they certainly differ in the directness and obviousness with which they express them.

Consider the one-month-old infant. Most of his time is spent in sleep. This sleep may be interrupted by periods of activity and generalized excitement that sometimes may be quite intense. The observer does not see in the child of this age either differentiated emotions or subtlety in the expression of feelings. What he sees is a direct, uninhibited, unfettered output of apparently excited behavior.

Consider the adult. Here problems in developing a vocabulary with which to describe emotional experience and expression are many times more imposing than in the infant. The adult's emotional expression is not limited to the either-or alternatives of generalized excitement and, to use Sullivan's term, to blissful euphoria. What we see in the adult are overdetermined responses that may be complex functions of emotional states such as fear, anger, jealousy, and elation.

This progression in emotional expression from the simple to the complex suggests a process of differentiation. That is, out of an initial matrix of generalized emotion or excitement, particular varieties of emotional experience differentiate in the course of development—for example, jealousy, anger, and love. At present, we do not know much about the development of these experiences. Part of the problem is semantic. How do we go about formulating concepts that adequately refer to these emotional experiences?

One way of approaching the question is to recognize clearly that when we talk about emotions we are drawing inferences. Emotions are basically no different from any other characteristics or traits inferred from behavior. The explanatory value of a particular emotional attribute such as anger or love will stand or fall on the clarity with which it has been formulated and the contribution it makes to the explanation of observed behavior. A major problem arising from an inferred attribute is the delineation of the life situations that influence its development. Anger and jealousy, for example, do not manifest themselves in all situations. Nor is it likely that they develop alike. What life history factors, such as family and socioeconomic factors, increase the likelihood of jealous and angry reactions? In what sorts of behavioral contexts do these characteristics exert an influence? Carefully worked out histories of this sort of inferred characteristic are at present not readily available. However, there are some observational leads that may contribute to our understanding of the differentiation of emotional characteristics.

Let us consider two of these inferred characteristics, dependency and aggression. Both concepts have been employed in describing social development and needs that underlie social contacts. In examining the concepts of dependency and aggression, our main concern will be with the ways in which researchers have gone about investigating them.

DEPENDENCY

Observations of very young infants suggest that their generalized excitement usually occurs in response to discomfort. As infants develop, the people who respond to their needs come to be of great significance to them. The varied responses of these people, usually the parents, to the needs of the child affect the child's perception of the world. A virtually universal aspect of early parent-child relationships is the child's dependence on parental figures. During the early years, this dependence is in a very real sense total, and is a potent force in the development of conformity to family and social mores. The parents become the most highly cathected objects in the child's world and become involved in almost all aspects of their offspring's affective experience.

As the child becomes older and more proficient in skills and abilities, it develops the ability to venture forth on its own into fields beyond the parents and the home. There are, however, marked individual differences among children in the ease with which they make steps toward independence. Dependence and independence are aspects of the same developmental problem, the problem of the individual's ties with sources of love, protection, and authority, on the one hand, and the capacity for autonomy and the development of new personal relationships, on the other. Everyone displays seemingly dependent and independent behavior at various points in life. It seems possible that underlying dependency and independency needs may constitute important motivators of overt behavior. In their research, students of personality have sought to define these needs and to determine their relationships to overt behavior.

Some might argue that talking about dependency and independency in terms of covert needs or tendencies complicates the study of development. A perhaps better approach would limit the field of interest to the incidence of behaviors that bear on dependency and independency. If we accept this approach, we would not talk about behavior that stems from the individual's underlying dependency needs, but would refer to the number and varieties of dependent behaviors he emits. Unfortunately, the simplicity of this approach may not do justice to the complexity of the determinants of particular overt responses. For example, we might consider the seeker of adventure as an emitter of independent responses. What sort of statements could be made about the antecedents of this operationally defined independent behavior? It is conceivable that some adventurers behave as they do because of reactions against strong, but unacceptable covert dependency needs. Merely labeling responses as reflectors of independence will not necessarily help to isolate determinants of overt behavior.

It seems useful to be aware that the study of dependency, independency, and other characteristics must be approached from two related standpoints: What responses can justifiably and reliably be labeled dependent behavior and independent behavior? What are the possible determinants, both overt and covert, of these behaviors? Understanding dependent and independent behavior requires investigation of (1) covert tendencies that may predispose persons to make certain overt responses, and (2) the environmental conditions associated with these responses.

It is, of course, more feasible to observe the incidence and environmental determinants of overt responses than to infer their covert antecedents. Many researchers have sought to describe particular types of overt responses. For example, Heathers (1955) defined dependency in terms of seeking affection and seeking approval and then compared two- and four- to five-year-old children with regard to these behaviors. He found that seeking affection was less noticeable among four-year-olds than among two-year-olds. He also found that the way in which dependency was expressed varied as a function of age. The quest for affection and approval among two-year-olds was directed primarily toward their teacher. Comparable responses of four-year-olds were most noticeable in relation to peers. Related to these results are some reported by Marshall (1961) who found that the strength of the affectionate relationship between children and their nursery school teacher decreased between the ages of two- and-one-half to six-and-one-half years. It seems clear that the objects of dependency such as parents, teachers, or peers will vary as a function of the age of the individual and the conditions under which he is responding.

The variables of dependency and independency have been approached in a number of ways. Some studies have used naturalistic observation and classified children's responses in terms of dependency. Other studies have used observational techniques within the context of an experimental situation. This sort of study is concerned with determining the effects of experimentally manipulated variables on observed behavior. A third group of studies may be referred to as developmental. The aim of these investigations is to chart the course of a variable such as dependency. Let us examine an example of each of these approaches.

Observational Study

The Heathers (1955) study compared dependency and independency in two- and four- to five-year-old children. It was performed by having two observers record three minute samples of children's behavior in a nursery school setting. These records were then scored for the occurrence of emotionally dependent and emotionally independent behavior. Emotionally dependent behavior was defined as affection-seeking, approval-seeking, and clinging responses directed at either teachers or peers. Emotionally independent behavior was defined as attempts to influence the play of others, resistance to interference by others, and ignoring cues emanating from teachers and peers.

Heathers found that dependence on the teacher seemed to decline as a function of increasing age and dependence on peers seemed to increase. With regard to independence, which was defined to a considerable extent in terms of self-reliance, Heathers found that ignoring stimuli stemming from the teacher and attempts at influencing the play of other children increased with age. Presumably observations of children's behavior within naturalistic settings represent a useful taking-off point for categorizing classes of response. It is important, however, to be aware that the behavior recorded during sample time periods may not be representative of the total behavior of the child and may be influenced by immediately preceding events. Perhaps the most promising use of naturalistic observation is in studies of behavior not in just one, but in a variety of settings. Such research might focus, for example, on comparisons of behavior at home, at school, in the playground, and elsewhere. The work of Barker (1963, 1965) and his colleagues has been concerned with these sorts of comparisons.

Experimental Study

Hartup (1958) performed an experiment in which preschool children responded to learning tasks under experimental conditions. The subjects ranged in age from three years ten months to five years six months. After entering the experimental room all of the children were given a five-minute period during which the experimenter behaved in a nurturant manner. Nurturance was defined as affection displayed by the experimenter toward the child plus the rewards and encouragement provided the child by the experimenter.

At the end of this five-minute period the subjects were separated into two groups. Half of the children received another five minutes of nurturance. The remaining subjects experienced five minutes of nurturance withdrawal during which the experimenter withdrew and responded in as nonnurturant and nonrewarding a manner as possible. When approached by subjects under this condition the experimenter said essentially, "I'm busy." Following the nurturant and nurturant withdrawal conditions, all subjects learned two tasks, the reward for which was approval by the experimenter. It was found that children who had experienced nurturance withdrawal learned the task significantly more quickly than children who experienced only nurturance. It was also found that this facilitative effect of nurturance withdrawal was more noticeable in girls than in boys.

One aspect of Hartup's experiment remains to be mentioned. He categorized his subjects in terms of their dependence on adults. This categorization was based on (1) observations of the children during the experimental nurturant session, (2) ratings of their dependency by preschool teachers, and (3) ratings of their preschool behavior by persons other than teachers. Dependence was defined in terms of seeking recognition, physical contact, and attention.

What relationship was uncovered between dependence and learning in this experiment? Hartup found that highly dependent boys responded much as girls. Low dependent boys, however, did not show a similarity to girls. Thus, girls and highly dependent boys responded in similar ways to nurturance withdrawal. But, low dependent boys who received the "full dose" of nurturance (that is, who were not subjected to withdrawal of nurturance) learned more quickly than did boys who had been subjected to nurturance withdrawal.

The Hartup experiment illustrates a point made earlier: to understand overt behavior, it is necessary to know something about both a subject's personal characteristics and the situational conditions under which he behaves. In the Hartup experiment an inferred characteristic, dependency, was related to intellectual performance under certain environmental conditions. A non-inferred individual difference variable, sex, was also found to be related to performance. This suggests the value of (1) perfecting measures of individual differences, and (2) constructing meaningful experimental conditions in which these differences play a significant role.

Developmental Study

When individual differences in behavior are observed, one almost invariably wonders about their developmental history. This historical concern must be viewed as a necessary complement to knowledge acquired in observational and experimental settings. The Sears, Maccoby, and Levin (1957, pp. 141–142) research contained a contribution to the dependency literature, and we shall use it as an example of a study with an historical orientation. This research entailed content analysis of detailed interviews with mothers about their children's developmental histories and their own personal reactions to the experiences of motherhood.

Before turning to the relevant findings, let us look at these authors' theoretical conception of the mother-child relationship and dependency:

A mother and her child are a *dyad*. That is, each has expectancies about how the other should behave. If these are fulfilled, each is happy and comfortable. If expectations are *not* met, however, there is frustration. Both mother and child learn how to control each other, that is, how to produce in the partner those actions which will make for satisfactions. However, during the child's early life, he no sooner learns one way of behaving than his mother's expectancies change. Then he must learn a new way. For example, he learns to hug and kiss her, to express his affection openly. But then she begins to view such behavior as changeworthy; she wants him to *talk* his love more and *hug* it less. If she begins to be less responsive to his customary ways of seeking her affection and attention, his first reaction will be to redouble his efforts. That is, he will behave "more dependently." Ultimately, if his mother just never responds at all, we would expect these specific forms of supplication to be eliminated (because of non-reward).

There are two types of maternal behavior that can be examined as possible sources of the child's dependent behavior. One is the initial learning situation in infancy. What kinds of treatment create a strong dependency motive? Breast feeding? Warmth and affectionate demonstrativeness? Or do the psychological "distance" of bottle feeding and the lack of intimacy offered by a cool and reserved mother produce insecurity and renewed efforts to gain affection and attention?

The second place to look is in the mother's current handling of the changeworthy behavior. Does punishment reduce it, or just make it flame into desperation? Does a permissive attitude allow the child to retain his more infantile forms of interaction, or does it ease the pressure in some way?

Sears, Maccoby, and Levin defined children's dependency in terms of the frequency with which their mothers referred to their attention-seeking, clinging behavior and their anxiety over separation. Comparisons between the sexes with regard to dependency did not reveal significant differences. The variable of birth order, however, was found to be important. Only children objected more and showed more anxiety about separation from mother than other children.

A logical place to begin looking for antecedents of behavioral dependency is in early infancy. Sears, Maccoby, and Levin, however, found no significant relationships between infant experiences, as reported by mothers, and later dependency. This result might seem at first glance to negate the psychoanalytic emphasis on early infant experiences. However, we must be aware that Sears, Maccoby, and Levin employed only one particular definition of dependency, a definition with which psychoanalysts might disagree. Furthermore, the data obtained were subject to biases inherent in retrospective accounts of mothers. It would seem, then, that although one might have anticipated significant relationships between infancy experiences and dependency, the absence of such findings may not be decisive in evaluating predictions emanating from psychoanalytic theory.

The children involved in the study of Sears, Maccoby, and Levin were kindergartners. Although their dependent behavior did not seem traceable to infant experiences, there were clear individual differences among them with regard to dependency. How do mothers respond to their children's dependency? Much variability was found among mothers in their reactions to dependency in their children and in their tendency to reward or not reward dependent behavior. Mothers who were relatively tolerant of dependency tended to show more warmth to their offspring, to be gentler in toilet training, to use relatively less physical punishment, and to hold their husbands and themselves in higher esteem than mothers who were less tolerant of dependency in children.

These findings by Sears, Maccoby and Levin (1957, pp. 174–175) concerning the handling of dependency support a learning interpretation of dependency:

> Mothers who repeatedly domonstrate their affection for children are providing many supports for whatever actions the children have performed in order to obtain such demonstrations. These actions often involve smiling at her and talking, and keeping some kind of contact with her. These are the actions, of course, that we have labeled dependency.
>
> Once the child has developed these habitual ways of acting—and all children develop some—he may be expected to use them as devices for reassuring himself that his mother does love him. That is to say, if she shows signs of rejection, if she used withdrawal of love to discipline him, and if she is punitive toward his aggression, he may be expected to double his efforts to secure her affection. This will simply increase the frequency and persistence of the acts we have defined as dependent, and hence the mother will describe more of them.
>
> The influence of affectionate demonstrativeness, if we may suggest a theoretical point, is an influence on the *learning* of dependent behavior. The effect of withdrawal of love, punishment of dependency and aggression, and other behaviors that threaten the child's security, is an effect on performance of *action*. Therefore, the actual amount of dependency observed and reported by a mother is a product of both factors. It follows that the most dependent children should be those whose mothers express openly their affection for the child but repeatedly threaten the affectional bond by withholding love as a means of discipline and by being punitive toward his displays of parent-directed aggression.
>
> These relationships are exactly what we have found, but just which way the cause-and-effect arrows point is impossible to say. We are skeptical that there is any single direction of cause-and-effect relations in the child-rearing process. True, the mother's personality comes first, chronologically, and she starts the sequence of interactive behavior that culminates in the child's personality. But once a child starts to be overdependent—or is *perceived* as being so by his mother—he becomes a stimulus to the mother and influences her behavior toward him. Perhaps, within the present group of mothers, over-dependency of their children increased the mothers' rejective feelings, made them more angry and hence more punitive for aggression. The whole relationship could be circular. An enormous amount of painstaking research will be required to untangle these phenomena.

Stendler (1954) reported data that bears on the problem of overdependency. She studied 20 overdependent children, six of whom were reared by overprotective mothers. Table 24-1 presents Stendler's

TABLE 24-1

Evidences of Overprotection in Six Overdependent Children

	Evidences of Infantilization			Evidences of Prevention of Independent Behavior
Case	Onset of Weaning	Onset of Toilet Training	Independence in Dressing	Mother's Comments
Eliza	14 mo.	16 mo.	Mother dresses at 6 years	She's our only child and I've given all my time to her. She doesn't need other children. I watch her very carefully and don't let her do some things; that's why she's never had any accident.
Robert	14 mo.	16 mo.	Independent	He's mother's boy. I like him to stay close to me. That way I know what he's doing. I don't send him to kinder-garten because they catch everything there.
James	15 mo.	14 mo.	Mother dresses at 6 years	I don't send him on any errands. He's too small for that. They grow up and get away soon enough as it is. I know I give him too much time and attention but they're only young once.
Ronnie	15 mo.	9 mo.	Dependent	I've always kept him near me from the time he was born. Even when his younger brother was born he never seemed to need the attention this one does. I watch him pretty carefully and don't let him run with the others.

TABLE 24-1 (*Continued*)

Case	Evidences of Infantilization: Onset of Weaning	Onset of Toilet Training	Independence in Dressing	Evidences of Prevention of Independent Behavior: Mother's Comments
Louise	2 yr.	16 mo.	Independent	I like to keep her with me. She always goes where I go. I like to raise her just right and if she gets to going with other kids she'll learn rough ways.
George	3 yr.	14 mo.	Mother dresses at 6 years	His older brother is 27 years old. I guess I've spoiled him. I hated to send him to kindergarten, he seemed such a baby. I drive him back and forth to school each day. It's safer that way.

Adapted from Celia B. Stendler (1954), Possible causes of overdependency in young children, *Child Developm.*, **25,** 141.

data on her six overdependent children-overprotective mother cases.

What about the 14 overdependent children who did not have mothers high in overprotectiveness? Stendler found that these children were as independent as one could expect in terms of their ability to take care of themselves, as in dressing or performing chores. But they seemed to have an inordinately strong need for their mothers' physical presence. *One must be cautious in uncritically accepting any single criterion of dependency. Multiple criteria, which may be complexly related to childhood experiences, would seem to be preferable in approaching dependency.*

By the use of the complementary techniques of naturalistic observations, experimentation, and developmental histories in the study of dependency, researchers have just begun to scratch the surface of this hard and complex phenomenon. The developmental history technique (Sears, Maccoby and Levin, 1957) in particular requires supplementation by longitudinal studies that provide direct behavioral observations. The Fels research (Kagan and Moss, 1962) mentioned earlier (Chapter 22) illustrates this type of investigation. In it dependency was actually studied longitudinally and not simply in terms of retrospective accounts of mothers. Among the findings that resulted from this study are these: (1) childhood dependency was predictive of dependent behavior for women, but not for men; (2) maternal protection of sons during the first three years was predictive of dependent behavior in boys for the first ten years of life; (3) maternal protection of daughters was not as predictive of dependency in girls as in boys; (4) maternal hostility toward sons showed minimal relationships to dependency in boys; (5) maternal hostility toward girls during the first three years significantly predicted independence with regard to love objects and a reluctance to withdraw from stress during adult years.

One of the greatest needs at the present time is for the specification of (1) the particular variables that contribute to the shaping of dependent behavior, and (2) the effects of dependency on other aspects of behavior. Conceivably, one result of filling in existing gaps in our knowledge will be a decreasing usage of dependency and independency as general concepts and an increase in the number of specialized constructs of dependency and independency that are allied to particular classes of behavior, such as peer dependency, parent dependency, sibling dependency, and other dependent dyadic relationships.

AGGRESSION

Aggression, defined in terms of destructive, harm-inflicting, motivated behavior, constitutes one of the major personal and social problems of our times. Previously we emphasized the experimental study of aggression (Chapter 18). In the present section, we shall again refer to experimental methods, but within the context of the general question of the development of aggression.

It is not difficult to see why there are arguments about the meaning of aggression. On the one hand, aggressive behavior exhibited by persons such as sports figures, movie heroes, and neighborhood gang leaders may be the basis for admiration and adulation. On the other hand, aggressive behavior is often viewed as crude, undesirable, worthy of condemnation. Why is it that groups of individuals, even nations, may follow leaders who are decidedly aggressive in nature? Why are some pacificists occasionally extremely aggressive in championing their creed of nonviolence?

If the hypothesis that there is ambivalence concerning aggression is even partially correct, what impact does this ambivalence have on child-rearing practices and child development? If we knew the answer to this question, we would probably be well on the path to the solution of many personal and social ills. Before this complex question can be answered, more data gathering and theorizing than has occurred up to now will be needed. In this section we shall examine some of the ideas that have been offered concerning aggression and some of the empirical relationships that have been established.

Although the emotional life of the very young infant may be describable in terms of generalized excitement, within several months differentiated emotional expression becomes discernible. One of the first of these differentiated emotions is anger. Anyone who has observed temper tantrums in young children will attest to the validity of this assertion. When these outbursts occur, they usually involve a direct lashing out at objects in the environment. One wonders what chain of events leads from the obvious and destructive aggression of the child to the subtlety with which aggression is expressed in adulthood.

This metamorphosis occurs through a process of socialization. Many views have been expressed concerning the socialization of aggression. Some have contended that socialization simply involves extinction of objectionable aggressive tendencies and responses. Others have felt that socialization involves changes in the way in which the aggressive drive manifests itself. To resolve this sort of disagreement, systematic data gathering seems necessary in order to provide a reliable avenue of approach. Let us look at some examples of three types of empirical research that have been directed at the problem of aggression.

Observational Study

One of the most widely used settings in which children's behavior has been observed involves free play. Investigators usually use free-play situations to assess the effects on behavior of factors in the child's life, such as the permissiveness of parents, or experimental conditions.

Sears, Whiting, Nowlis, and Sears (1953) reported the results of one interesting study of the play behavior of children. They divided nursery school children into three groups. One group had mothers who seemed to be quite punitive when their offspring displayed aggression at home. The mothers of a second group appeared to be non-punitive. The mothers of the children in the third group were mildly punitive. The question asked by Sears, et al. was: Would children reared by mothers who differed in punitiveness display different amounts of aggression in a free-play situation?

The findings were that (1) children of nonpunitive mothers emitted relatively few aggressive responses during a free-play period, (2) children of mildly punitive mothers displayed quite a few free-play aggressive responses, and (3) severely punished children made the greatest number of aggressive responses. Sex differences were also uncovered. A positive relationship between punishment for aggression at home and free-play aggression was quite striking in boys. However, in girls, a high degree of punishment for aggression at home seemed to lead to passivity and inhibition in free play. It is possible that passivity in girls may simply be a function of a generally lower activity level for girls than for boys. Interestingly, when an effort was made to separate the effects of activity level, the positive correlation between punishment for aggression at home and aggression in free play was noted for girls as well as boys.

These results suggest that punishment of aggression in one situation may decrease the likelihood of aggressive responses occurring in that situation, but they may occur with high frequency in other situations. Careful description of the situation in which aggressive responses are observed is necessary in drawing inferences about a person's potentiality for emitting such responses. Many crimes of violence are committed by people whose parents, relatives, and friends profess amazement that they would commit antisocial aggression. Punishment of aggression in one context such as the home may reduce aggressive responses in that situation, but it may not reduce the underlying tendency or drive to express aggression. If a general aggressive drive is hypothesized, then behavior must be observed, not in one situation, but in several. We must also consider the many ways in which aggression might subtly manifest itself. These include not only overt aggression, but also aggressive fantasy and seemingly nonaggressive behavior, which symbolically may permit the expression of aggressive impulses.

Experimental Study

Earlier we described several experimental approaches to the study of aggression (Chapter 18). One of these dealt with the relationships of personality characteristics, past experience, and experimental conditions to aggression in fantasy. It may be possible to "get rid of" particular aggressive responses by means of punishment, but aggressive tendencies may be capable of remaining potent and may manifest themselves in subtle ways.

Another experimental approach to aggression has focused on the isolation of variables that increase aggressive, harm-inflicting behavior. Do reinforcements influence the occurrence of harm-inflicting responses? Does positive reinforcement, such as a father rewarding his son for winning a fight with a playmate, increase the probability of occurrence of aggressive responses?

Lovaas (1961) has reported an experiment related to these questions. In it, nursery school children were given two kinds of experiences, operating a lever that caused a doll to strike another doll on the head with a stick, and operating a lever that propelled a ball to the top of a cage. Following these two preliminary experiences, the children talked into a box on which a dirty and a clean doll had been placed. Half of the subjects were reinforced for making nonaggressive responses (saying "good doll"); the remaining subjects were reinforced for aggressive responses (saying "bad doll"). Following selective reinforcement of their verbal responses, the children were again placed in the situation in which they could press the two levers.

Lovaas' experiment is noteworthy on two counts. First, it was successful in influencing children's use of verbally aggressive and nonaggressive responses. Children reinforced for aggressive responses increased their usage of them, while children reinforced for nonaggressive responses increased their usage of these. Second, it was found that children who had been reinforced for verbally nonaggressive responses made more nonaggressive motor responses (manipulating the lever which led to the propulsion of the ball up the cage) than children reinforced for verbally aggressive responses. Thus it was shown that positive reinforcement is an important variable in increasing the rate of emission of aggressive responses. It is interesting to note that in another experiment (Hollenberg and Sperry, 1951) negative reinforcement (verbal punishment) of aggressive responses was found to decrease their frequency of occurrence. However, negative reinforcement of aggression had only a temporary retarding influence.

It seems unlikely that reinforcement alone can adequately account for all of the observed individual differences in aggression. It will be remembered Bandura found that imitation may play a decisive role in the incidence of aggressive responses (Bandura, Ross and Ross, 1963*a*; Bandura and Walters, 1963). Another variable that must be considered in studying aggressive behavior is the strength of the subject's aggressive tendencies before he enters the experimental situation. Highly aggressive people may respond quite differently from passive, intropunitive individuals to the reinforcement of aggression and to the aggressive behavior of models. It would seem desirable to assess subjects' aggressive tendencies prior to studying them in experimental situations. It would also be enlightening to study the generalization effects of procedures, designed to increase of decrease aggressive responses. For example, if it were possible to demonstrate convincingly that negative reinforcement led to a decrease in the emission of a particular type of aggressive response, would other types of aggressive responses be similarly affected? Would aggression "go underground"? Overt aggressive responses might decline, at least temporarily, but covert aggression might increase.

Developmental Study

The suggestion that measures of individual differences be incorporated into the design of experiments on aggression reflects the belief that assessment approaches and experimental approaches to personality are of greatest value when they complement each other. One researcher may be primarily interested in devising measures of inferred individual differences, such as personality characteristics. Inevitably he must face the question: Do persons differing on such characteristics as dependency or aggression vary in their reactions to situations? The experimental method provides a powerful tool for devising and controlling situations that relate to personal characteristics. Another researcher might be primarily interested in investigating behavior within particular experimental contexts. But can he avoid wondering about the characteristics of individuals that bear on their observed behavior? It would seem necessary for him to regard individual differences as variables that can help account for the behavior of subjects in experiments.

We have also seen the value of proceeding one step beyond the assessment of characteristics: What is the developmental history of the characteristics that assessors define and measure? Although the Sears, Maccoby, and Levin study of children was based solely on the reports of mothers, rather than on experimental or assessment procedures employed with children, it provides suggestions of the histories behind observed or reported behaviors. From a psychological standpoint, a person's history is simply not a chronicle of *acts* that he has performed, but also a chronicle of the *experiences* and *environments* to which he has been subjected.

Sears, Maccoby, and Levin noted in connection with aggression what we saw earlier in relation to dependency. That is, there are discernible individual differences among mothers in reaction to aggressive or hurting behavior developed by their children. On the basis of interviews with mothers, Sears, Maccoby, and Levin (1957, pp. 234–236) found that 38 per cent of the mothers were not at all permissive when their children behaved aggressively. On the other hand, 11 per cent of the mothers described themselves as being quite permissive in relation to their children's aggressive behavior. One question asked of the mothers was:

Sometimes a child will get angry at his parents and hit them and kick them or shout angry things at them. How much of this sort of thing do you think parents ought to allow in a child of (his, her) age? How do you handle it when (child's name) acts like this?

Here is the response of one nonpermissive mother:

They never should allow him to hit them back. If he hits them, they should hit him right back. If you let him get away with it once he will always want to get away with it.

Here is the response of one permissive mother:

Well, he has done that a couple of times, and a few times he has said "I don't like you," because I punished him, and I just skipped it. I didn't even pay any attention and went right on with my work. And after he thought it over he realized he didn't feel that way at all, because he loves us very much and he knows that we love him. He gets a lot of attention and knows that we didn't mean anything. He'll tell me himself—I won't tell him he has to say he's sorry—he'll usually tell me himself.

In examining differences among mothers in response to children's aggressive behavior, Sears, Maccoby, and Levin found a negative correlation between mothers' permissiveness and their punitiveness when their children aggressed. Children who seemed to be low in aggressiveness had mothers who were low both in permissiveness and in the amount of punishment meted out when children aggressed. Children of mothers high on both permissiveness and punitiveness rated high in aggressiveness. Sears, Maccoby, and Levin's findings suggest that highly aggressive children often have mothers who may be quite tolerant of children's aggression but who, when their tolerance is at an end, react with a high degree of punishment. It may not be enough to characterize parents in terms of their punitiveness or permissiveness. It may be necessary also to specify the kinds and amounts of stimuli, such as the kind and amount of aggressive behavior displayed by children, which will evoke punitive responses from parents.

Support for this inference lies in another result obtained by these researchers. They discovered that permissiveness and punishment of aggression varied as a function of the object of the child's aggression. Mothers were more tolerant of children's aggression when the aggression was dircted at siblings and peers than when it was directed against themselves. The sex of the child also seems to matter. There was a positive correlation between punishment for aggression and aggressive behavior in girls, but not in boys. An earlier study found a similar positive correlation for boys (Sears, Whiting, Nowlis and Sears, 1953). In that study the index of aggressive behavior was based on actual nursery school behavior rather than on maternal reports.

Additional evidence on the relationship between parental aggression and children's aggressive behavior has come from a follow-up of the mothers studied by Sears, Maccoby, and Levin (Sears, 1961). The follow-up showed only slight correlations between mothers' punishment for aggression during the first five years of life and antisocial aggression at 12 years of age. Bandura and Walters (1959) studied a group of antisocial, aggressive boys and discovered that their parents used relatively more punitive disciplinary methods than had the parents of control boys. The aggressive boys were less aggressive at home than with peers and other adults. Another study (Eron, Walder, Toigo and Lefkowitz, 1963) found that children whose parents were high in punitiveness were described by peers as being higher in aggressiveness than children whose parents were less punitive. Finally, several investigators (Bandura and Walters, 1963; Davis, 1943) have shown that socioeconomic status is significantly and sometimes complexly related to children's aggression and parents' punitiveness and permissiveness.

As in dependency, longitudinal studies that utilize direct behavioral observations contribute much to an understanding of aggression. The Fels study (Kagan and Moss, 1962) uncovered these relationships: (1) whereas dependency showed greater stability over time for women than for men, aggressive behavior was stabler for men than for women; (2) childhood rage reactions predicted adult aggressive behavior for men but not for women; (3) a tendency toward rage reactions in young girls, while not predictive of aggression in women, did predict women's intellectual competitiveness, dependency conflicts, and masculine interests.

CONCLUDING COMMENTS CONCERNING DEPENDENCY AND AGGRESSION

Dependency and aggression can be viewed as outgrowths of a process of emotional differentiation. Recognizing dependency and aggression as inferences from behavior, rather than as self-evident phenomena, places them within the category of psychological constructs whose validities must be assessed and whose nomological networks must be delineated. We have seen that constructs have their beginnings in theoretical orientations and in fact gathering. This latter phase of construct validity is of the utmost importance. Whereas theoretical orientations provide impetus for investigation, it is the evidence gathered in such investigation that provides the building blocks for a truly scientific theory. Psychoanalytic and learning approaches to behavior have stimulated much of the data gathering on the dependency and aggression constructs. But the ultimate concern must be with the results and implications of empirical research rather than with the stimulus for that research.

At the present stage of knowledge, how might we summarize these results and their implications for the constructs of dependency and aggression? The shaping of dependency and aggression involves relationships among many variables. What are some of these? This is a partial list:

1. The reinforcement history of the child. To what degree was he positively reinforced for behaving in a dependent manner? To what degree may he have been negatively reinforced for responding aggressively?

2. The agents of reinforcement. Who was the primary reinforcer of the child's behavior, the mother or the father? What role do peers, siblings, and teachers play in the shaping of tendencies such as dependency and aggression?

3. The reinforcements themselves. Was the child positively rewarded by love and affection, or by money and tangibles? Was the child negatively reinforced through physical punishment or through withdrawal of affection?

4. Imitation and identification. To what extent are the child's dependency and aggressive tendencies results of the modeling of behavior of significant persons in his environment?

5. Frustration. To what extent are these tendencies a function of frustration and stresses experienced by the child?

6. Constitutional and genetic factors. To what degree may such factors as family background, body build, sex, and rate of physical maturation play roles in the expression of these tendencies? To what extent may they be a function of biologically rooted drives?

7. Situational factors. In what sorts of ways may tendencies like dependency and aggression manifest themselves? Are there general behavioral criteria of dependency and aggression or is their expression strongly influenced by situational factors? For different individuals,

may the same overt acts reflect varying degrees of dependency and aggression?

8. Overt and covert tendencies. To what degrees do dependency and aggressive tendencies function as covert influences of overt behavior? To what degree do factors such as anxiety and defense mechanisms modify the effects of aggression and dependency on overt behavior?

No construct of aggression or dependency, or for that matter, no personality construct, has been subjected to an analysis in which all of these factors have been simultaneously evaluated. Any construct is limited by the variables encompassed by it. One researcher interested in one set of variables will in all likelihood propound a different conception of aggression than another researcher concerned with a different set of variables. In the early stages of empirical work there is a multitude of approaches and operational definitions, each of which may contribute to a hoped-for general theory.

The theoretical issues and difficulties involved in the study of dependency and aggression are in principle the same as those involved in the study of other personality constructs. For our purposes, we selected dependency and aggression to illustrate constructs dealing with emotional expression in the developing child. Constructs such as those relating to anxiety and sex would have proved equally enlightening. In succeeding chapters, we shall refer to several other aspects of emotional differentiation. Generalizing from our study of dependency and aggression, we may say that when emotional aspects of behavior are studied, among the questions that loom large are: (1) How are they defined? (2) What relationships do they bear to observable responding? (3) How might these relationships be extended or clarified?

25

Ability Differentiation

An individual's emotional differentiation may be viewed through the greater subtlety and complexity of his affective involvements with objects in the environment. In discussing this differentiation we have focused primarily on social-learning variables that condition the evolution and expression of these involvements. Thus when we spoke in Chapter 24 of dependency and aggression, we referred to such variables as models for imitation, reinforcement, and family and social mores.

Although we have emphasized the roles of genetic, maturational, and organismic factors in personality development, this would seem to be a propitious place at which to reinforce this emphasis. Just as we have talked about affective or emotional differentiation, so may we refer to a differentiation of abilities. Ability differentiation, the broadening and refining of skills, is so easily observable in people, and particularly children, that its relationship to personality development may be either ignored or glossed over. What we, as students of personality, must keep before us is that the course of an individual's acquisition of abilities and skills may often exert powerful influences over his personality. Conversely, personal characteristics may influence the acquisition of abilities. Let us begin our consideration of ability differentiation by reference to three variables that influence it: (1) the individual's ability repertory, (2) his perception of his abilities, and (3) the reactions of others to his abilities. Then, following discussion of some biological factors and of perceptual and motor skills, we shall turn to the development of abilities in the spheres of language, thought, and intellect.

THE ABILITY REPERTORY

One of these variables concerns the individual's repertory of abilities at any given time. This repertory determines the responses that an organism is capable of making. For example, the infant may want to reach a toy on the floor, but may not yet have developed sufficient crawling skill to attain this goal. In some cases a person's ability repertory will permit him to act upon, or act out, his emotions and attitudes. This may be seen in the case of the adolescent bully who, because of superior physical development, can directly express his needs to be aggressive and dominant. On the other hand, the physically less well-developed child may have to resort to substitute means of expressing the same covert tendencies, such as being the intellectual know-it-all and bully of his class.

Too often in describing people we use such phrases as "highly intelligent," "low in intelligence," and "average in learning ability." Such descriptions, however, may be very misleading. A person described as "highly intelligent" might have quite low abilities in performing particular tasks. Someone said to be "average in learning ability" might learn certain tasks very quickly and other tasks very slowly. This means that it may be necessary to refer to groups of learning abilities rather than simply to over-all learning ability. For example, Gagné (1965) has described a number of specific types of learning. Among others he describes these: (1) Signal learning—learning to respond involuntarily to an environmental signal (putting one's foot on the brake when the light turns red). (2) Stimulus-response learning—learning to respond voluntarily, and with precision, to a stimulus (kicking a field goal). (3) Concept learning—learning to respond selectively to stimuli in terms of abstracted properties (shape, color, position). Persons might vary widely in their abilities to learn these sorts of tasks, and any individual might show more learning ability in one particular learning task than in others.

SELF-PERCEPTION OF ABILITIES

A number of writers such as Rogers (1951, 1959) and Allport (1960) have referred to the concept of self-perception. One group of stimuli which affects an individual's perception of himself are the things he can do, his own abilities. Individuals, at all developmental levels, react to their ability repertory. Self-confidence is often a direct function of one's interpretation of one's skills. It seems plausible to argue that a person's repertory of abilities is important both because it places a limit on the responses he can make and also because it serves as information that he can interpret and evaluate. These interpretations and evaluations in turn influence the goals that the individual sets for himself and the actual behaviors in which he engages.

Many of the concepts that we have considered can be interpreted in terms of the individual's perception of his abilities. Test anxiety, need for achievement, and the tendency toward conformity all seem linked to a person's awareness and interpretation of his abilities. The test-anxious student may experience tension in evaluative situations because of the dim view he takes of his abilities. The achievement-oriented person very likely sets imposing goals for himself, at least in part because his abilities make their attainment possible. The highly conforming person may be a follower in a group judgmental situation, in part because he lacks sufficient confidence to behave in an independent manner.

Examples of the effects on behavior of the individual's perception of his abilities abound during childhood. Children reared in homes in which there are pets are less likely to be fearful of animals than are children reared in homes without pets. The bases of this behavioral difference are obviously differential opportunities to develop skills in handling and responding to animals, and differences in self-confidence attributable to these opportunities. Exploratory behavior, submissiveness, and anger in children are often reactions to perceived inadequacies. These inadequacies may be exclusively a function of social learning. Quite likely, however, they are a function, at least partially, of the child's actual ability repertory and his interpretation of it.

SOCIAL RESPONSES TO ABILITIES

Just as the person's own evaluation of his abilities has an effect on his subsequent behavior, so do evaluations of persons in his environment. We saw earlier that the behavior of children is often a function of their parents' behavior and attitudes. Parental responses to children are in turn partly determined by the parents' interpretation of the behavior and abilities of their offspring.

The child with low motivation and a minimal level of aspiration may be reacting to attitudes of significant environmental figures. Similarly, the strongly achievement-oriented student may behave as he does owing to parental influences. In both cases, children's overt behavior at any given time may be related to interpretations by environmental figures of previously developed behavior and skills.

We see, then, that what a person does at a given point in time is limited by his ability repertory at that time, by his own reactions, and by the reactions of others to that repertory. It is necessary to keep in mind that abilities are multiply determined. Inherited tendencies, maturational level, and amount of training each play a role in the development of abilities.

It is also necessary to be aware that the term ability repertory refers to a complex of skills. Let us note some of the components of the ability repertory.

Factors in Ability Differentiation

PERCEPTUAL AND MOTOR SKILLS. These skills are among the first acquired by the young child. Responding to an environment requires (1) attention to and discrimination of its stimuli, and (2) the motor capacity to react to them. To the extent that these skills are not developed, ability to engage in normal personal relationships will be interfered with. This interference will result in a lack of development *per se* and in the reactions of the individual himself and of others to this lack.

The most dramatic illustrations of this sort of interference are individuals who are afflicted with major perceptual and motor handicaps and disabilities—for example, Helen Keller, who so heroically surmounted massive deprivations. Professional workers concerned with the adjustment problems of persons with varying degrees of perceptual and motor disabilities are well aware of the different ways in which these disabilities can affect personality and behavior. We shall not exhaustively review the multitude of major perceptual and motor handicaps. However, it is necessary to note the influence of major and minor handicaps on personality.

Imperfect vision, imperfect hearing, imperfect motor coordination, and various diseases are usually noted only when they result in an obvious behavioral deficit. Degrees of perceptual and motor skills, of course, occur on a continuum. Some people hear very clearly, others have slight auditory deficits, and still others may have profound deficits. Relatively slight deficits, which are at the edge of the normal range, might well influence the behavior of developing individuals. Examples of these possibilities include the child who misses portions of conversations owing to a hearing loss, or the student who cannot clearly see what the teacher writes on the blackboard, or the child whose motor coordination is poor.

Many of these minor deviations go unnoticed, but noticed or not, aberrent sensory-perceptual and motor abilities are potentially significant factors in the shaping of behavior. Awareness of them by the individual and by persons in his life can be important in terms of social adjustment. Their very existence may have implications for intellectual development. The ability to form concepts, to solve problems, and to use language is dependent on information gathered from the environment. Unless the developing individual can accurately receive, interpret, and respond to this information, his intellectual functioning and learning ability may suffer considerable loss.

PHYSICAL CHARACTERISTICS AND THEIR MATURATION. Reference has already been made to the relevance to personality development of the individual's bodily characteristics (Chapter 14). For example, although the relationships have not been unambiguously established, correlations do seem to exist between physique and temperament. Evidence for body type-personality correlations suggested by Sheldon (Sheldon and Stevens, 1942) seems clearest in the case of mesomorphy, which has been related to high energy level, assertiveness, and competitiveness. Evidence for the relationship of endomorphy to social introversion, and ectomorphy to fearfulness and lack of confidence is less impressive.

Walker (1962) reported one of the most comprehensive body type-personality studies with children. The results of his study with nursery school children tended to support Sheldon's hypothesis concerning the personality correlates of the three body types. Finding that body type-personality correlations are comparable for nursery school children and college students (the population most studied by Sheldon) leaves us with the task of developing a formulation with which these consistencies will be compatible. Although no such widely accepted formulation is yet available, some of the factors that must be incorporated within any that are propounded include (1) the bodily condition of the individual; (2) his learning experiences; and (3) his and society's reactions to his bodily condition.

The bodily characteristics of growing children are, of course, a function of their rates of physical maturation. Research dealing with this variable has been conducted using a variety of definitions for rate of maturation. Among the definitions used are maturity of skeletal structure, appearance of secondary sexual characteristics, and growth in terms of height and weight. Investigations of rate of maturation support the conclusion that it serves to limit the child's response repertory and functions as a stimulus to him and to others. Early maturing children seem to enjoy social and psychological advantages as compared with late maturing children. Although rate of maturation is partially a function of genetic factors, the experiences of children with different maturational rates clearly are powerful influences in accounting for behavioral differences among them. Thus, the frequently observed greater dependency and inferiority feelings of late maturing children seem to be a function of their relative physical inferiority, the interpretations that they make of their inferiority, and the responses of others to their inferiority.

Eichorn's (1963) survey of the literature on physical maturation indicates that at the present time the study of the psychological concommitants of physical maturation rates is at the point at which researchers need to focus particularly on the variables that may be tied to the maturational rate variable. Some of the questions that require clarification are: (1) What are the long-term effects on behavior—even after the child has "caught up"—of having been a late or early maturer as a child? (2) What are some of the social and environmental variables that alleviate or exacerbate the psychological consequences of different rates of physical growth? (3) What are the psychological, social, and biological histories of early and late maturers?

Although students of personality are primarily interested in psychological development, these questions concerning physical maturation indicate the need to conceive of development broadly and to expose correlations where they exist between physical and psychological events.

LANGUAGE, THINKING, AND INTELLECTUAL DEVELOPMENT

Language and Thinking

Linguistic communication represents a major component of social interactions. These interactions in turn contribute to the way in which many response tendencies and individual differences are formed. It is impossible to obtain verbal reports of subjective experience at very early age levels. Self-descriptions of adults may be inaccurate, but they do provide information that can be analyzed and interpreted. The infant, of course, cannot provide us with verbal reports. Interpretations of their subjective experiences must perforce rest even more on inference than on eventual interpretations of the personal life of the adult.

Numerous examples can be cited that suggest the vital role of language in personality development. The person who does not communicate verbally, for either biological or functional reasons, in effect suffers a degree of social ostracism. He is deprived of many social and emotional experiences. His life is much more restricted and private than that of verbally facile individuals. Many persons experience this enforced (or self-enforced) privacy, not because they cannot use language, but because they use language and linguistic symbols in unusual and atypical ways. The autistic child and the autistic adult present clinical problems because the ways in which they express themselves verbally are not consonant with commonly accepted modes of communication. We often simply do not understand what they are talking about. Disordered verbal communication leads not only to puzzled reactions from listeners, but often also to avoidance responses.

Language is not merely a convenient communication and cognitive tool. It is in addition a major factor in socialization. It is reasonable that the student of personality should be concerned with variables that contribute to the evolution of linguistic repertories. One of these students, Mowrer (1950*b*, pp. 699–700), has offered some provocative speculations about early human verbal development on the basis of observations of both birds and man:

It is very generally agreed, in all human societies, that a good mother is one who is loving and attentive to the needs of her child, and it is also a common expectation that mothers will coo and make other gentle noises when caring for their young. These two practices—loving care combined with vocalization—presumably create in the infant a predisposition to react with emotional satisfaction, first to the vocalizations of others and later to his own vocalizations. Since the sound of the mother's voice has often been accompanied by comfort-giving measures, it is to be expected that when the child, alone and uncomfortable, hears his own voice, it will likewise have a consoling, comforting effect. In this way it may be supposed that the infant will be rewarded for his own first babbling and jabbering, without any necessary reference to the effects they produce on others.

Gradually, from what the infant probably perceives as an inarticulate murmuring or warbling on the part of the mother, certain specific, recognizable words emerge which are especially welcome and reassuring, so that when, in the course of random vocalization, the child hits upon a sound that is recognizably like a sound which the mother (or possibly the father) makes, the child is motivated to reproduce that noise over and over and to try to perfect it, since a perfect reproduction of it is more satisfying than is an imperfect one. If one wishes to call this a kind of self-contained trial-and-error learning, there can be no objection, provided we remember that it has been preceded by important emotional conditioning and that the success of the infant's efforts at vocalization is not necessarily dependent upon the reactions of others. *It is the child's own reactions to the sounds he makes which seem all-important at this stage.*

In suggesting that the utterance of world-like noises occurs first on a purely autistic basis, I mean, specifically, that when a child or a bird is lonely, frightened, hungry, cold, or merely bored, it can comfort and divert itself by making noises which have previously been associated with comfort and diversion. These sounds have become "sweet music"; and they are reproduced, not because of their social effectiveness, but because of the intrapsychic satisfaction they provide. . . . Later, once particular sounds have been learned on this autistic basis, the stage is set for them to function instrumentally, in connection with the child's (or bird's) interactions with the external world; but this appears to be a second stage in language learning, not the first one.

Two aspects of Mowrer's analysis seem especially provocative. First, he argued that the child's reactions to his own sounds were important factors in language development. Second, he argued that the child's increasing quantity of sounds and increasing approximation to adult sounds was due to reinforcement he derived from speaking like the rewarding parent. The emphasis on the role of imitation and reinforcement in language development is consistent with a learning approach to behavior and the fact that languages are learned. Children whose parents talk to them and reinforce their utterances tend to speak at earlier ages than children whose parents are less responsive and less reinforcing. Relatively neglected institutionalized children develop linguistic repertories later than children reared in normal home settings. It would appear that the concepts of imitation and identification can contribute to an understanding of differences in language development as a function of environmental conditions. Children, particularly at certain stages of development, are imitators of the first order. But imitation cannot occur in the absence of models. The acquisition of language is at least in part a function of the child's exposure to models. As the child develops identifications with persons in his environment, these identifications may serve as motivation for the acquisition of language skills.

As McCarthy (1960, p. 9) states, there is reason to believe that verbal responses are as much influenced by personality differences and social-context variables as are other types of responses:

Studies indicate that it is not merely the amount of contact with the mother which is important, but also that the quality of the mother-child relationship has a significant influence on the acquisition of language. This factor is difficult to measure, but it is necessary to understand what the qualitative differences are and to learn how to measure and evaluate them. The mother reflects her own personality in the kind of nurture she gives her baby. The very way she approaches motherhood is significant. Whether she welcomes or dreads the child's arrival; whether she feels adequate to care for him; whether she is tense, worried, and uncertain in everything she does for him; whether she is happy and talks to him as she goes about her tasks or pushes the baby carriage; whether she is silent and preoccupied while giving mere physical care, or is impersonal and allows the child to vegetate most of the time are the kinds of things which are important in determining whether his language development will thrive, or be stunted and distorted in some unfortunate way.

There is clearly good reason to emphasize the social context within which the child comes to use language. Recent linguistic research, however, would seem to caution against exclusive concern with social-learning variables in language development. Weir (1962, pp. 131–132) has analyzed the presleep monologues of her two-and-one-half-year-old child, Anthony. The analysis suggested that during presleep periods of solitude Anthony essentially carried on conversations with himself. His monologues consisted of imaginary dialogues with people he knew or toys he owned or statements addressed to no one in particular. Here is one example of Anthony's presleep linguistic behavior:

(1) *Find it*
(2) *With juice* [2 times]
(3) *Drink it* [2 times]
(4) *Juice*
(5) *That's the right way*
(6) *Right way*
(7) *Where you going*
(8) *I'm going*
(9) *Shoe fixed*
(10) *Talk to Mommy*
(11) *Shoe fixed*
(12) *See Antho*
(13) *Anthony*
(14) *Good night*
(15) *See morrow morning*
(16) *Shoe fixed* [4 times]
(17) *Fix it*
(18) *Shoe fixed*
(19) *It took it*
(20) *Bring it back*
(21) *Took them*
(22) *Took it down* [4 times]
(23) *He took it* [2 times]
(24) *I'm going*
(25) *Yellow one*
(26) *Another one* [2 times]
(27) *Take a book*
(28) *Another book*
(29) *A phone call*
(30) *Phone call book*
(31) *This phone call book* [3 times]
(32) *This is the* [2 times]
(33) *Book*
(34) *Another phone call book*
(35) *This is light*
(36) *One light*
(37) *This is light on it*

Although Anthony was alone during his presleep monologues, it seems certain that environmental stimulation and particular events during the day influenced their content. Nevertheless, his solitary linguistic activities may well be as significant in their own right as they are reflections of prior experience. Weir's analysis of her son's presleep behavior showed that he engaged in such seemingly purposeful activities as drilling himself on consonant clusters, correcting his own pronunciation, and practicing the construction of sentences. Evident in the data she presents is the fun that Anthony derived from his verbal play.

Weir's data whet one's appetite for answers to such questions as: What do children know about the language they speak? What does language mean to them? What a child is thinking of and how he interprets events in his life are revealed by the things he says and the way in which he behaves. There seems little question that at the human level language and thought are intimately interrelated. In view of this, it seems clear that our understanding of thought processes will increase in proportion to our knowledge of linguistic phenomena, such as the developmental stages in language usage and communication, and language disabilities.

Human thought processes can be conceived as inferred events mediating between the information or stimuli available to the individual and his overt behavior. One might attempt to categorize these events on a variety of bases. Thinking can be concrete or abstract, rational or irrational. Freud (Chapter 2) believed that with development, primary process or irrational thinking played a diminishing role in determining action and that this diminution occurred in proportion to the child's increase in interest in the world about him. Whereas originally the infant is completely egocentric and preoccupied with his own biological processes, gradually objects and phenomena about him become important to him. What are the child's interpretations of his widening horizons? How does he perceive the world? How does he relate himself to this world?

While precise answers to these questions are not available now, it is clear that language is of great significance in the knowing process. This is particularly true of children. For example, in a series of experiments, Bruner (1964, p. 13) has shown that for children between the ages of 4 and 12 language ". . . shapes, augments, and even supersedes the child's earlier modes of processing information." The following comments by Bruner (1964, p. 14) suggest the role of language in both cognitive development and in what Freud called ego development:

> Once language becomes a medium for the translation of experience, there is a progressive release for immediacy. For language, as we have commented, has the new and powerful features of remoteness and arbitrariness:

It permits productive, combinatorial operations in the *absence* of what is represented. With this achievement, the child can delay gratification by virtue of representing to himself what lies beyond the present, what other possibilities exist beyond the clue that is under his nose. The child may be *ready* for delay of gratification, but he is no more able to bring it off than somebody ready to build a house, save that he has not yet heard of tools.

Piaget (1928, 1929, 1952, 1957; Flavell, 1963), an influential experimenter and writer, has been greatly concerned with the problem of children's cognitive responses to reality. He has investigated such problems as the evolution of the child's awareness and interpretation of causality in the physical world, the child's increasing sophistication in "thinking through" mathematical and geometric problems, and the child's changing schemes for classifying and labeling objects about him. As a result of his investigations, Piaget evolved a developmental theory of the growth of intelligence. He defined intelligence as the ability to adapt to the environment and has hypothesized a series of levels of adaptation to reality. He has spoken of two broad stages of intellectual development: sensorimotor intelligence, which occurs during the first two years of life, and conceptual intelligence, which occurs from age two to maturity.

During the first months of the sensorimotor stage innate reflexes such as sucking movements to a nipple become efficient. With maturation the infant moves from a neonatal, reflexive world in which there is little self-world differentiation to a relatively coherent world in which sensorimotor skills become perfected vis-à-vis the environment. The child comes to coordinate his actions with his perceptions, responds in different ways to the same object depending on the circumstances, and begins to evaluate his actions before acting.

The era of conceptual intelligence is an era of symbolic activity in which the child progresses from (1) the ability to attach meaning to stimuli, to (2) the ability to elaborate concepts, to (3) the ability to conceptualize in the face of perceptual changes such as recognizing that the number of beads in a one-quart container does not change when the beads are placed in a one and one-half quart container, to (4) the ability to think and reason abstractly. Piaget regarded linguistic responses as dependent variables and cognitions or thoughts as independent variables. Language, for him, is a symptom of underlying intellectual events and the ability to reason is the critical process in intellectual development.

Piaget's research has not been limited to a narrow band of intellectual activities. His efforts to understand thought processes led him to investigate such areas as the child's conception of the physical world and the acquisition by the child of a moral code. With regard to moral development, Piaget specified periods of childhood during which the child's conception of morality underwent change. The child between approximately 4 and 8 years of age possesses a morality that Piaget calls *heteronomous*. By heteronomous is meant subject to external standards and mores. The child who displays a heteronomous morality guides his behavior on the basis of adult authority and sanctions. The *autonomous* child, on the other hand, has developed his own law based on growth in awareness of the need for social cooperation and respect for others. Although the growth from heteronomous to autonomous morality as described by Piaget bears a resemblance to Freud's notion of introjection of parental and societal standards (Chapter 2), there is one important distinction that must be made. That is, for Freud the superego is acquired from the outside as it were—from others (the child introjects parental standards of morality); for Piaget autonomous morality is a product of the child's spontaneous efforts to organize a moral code for himself.

The level of specificity of many of Piaget's hypotheses has been criticized by some writers on the grounds that age norms can be deceptive (Flavell, 1963; Mussen, Conger, and Kagan, 1963). There is great variability among children, and particularly among young children, in the acquisition of skills. From the vantage point of the student of personality, it does seem that perhaps in Piaget's work personality differences are not awarded the role they merit. Piaget, however, has contributed enormously to the broad investigation of the child's intellectual development.

The adult is the person he is because of his genetic heritage, his environmental experiences, his personal needs and motivations, and the ways in which he construes the world about him. What these construing processes are and how they relate to the solution of problems constitute major problems for psychological investigation (Berlyne, 1965). If there are individual differences in various types of cognitive processes, it would seem necessary to expose and assess them. On the basis of factor analytic research, Guilford (1956, 1959*b*) has presented some provocative ideas in this regard. He has suggested that there are at least five types of cognitive processes. These are: (1) recognition of or sensitivity to environmental stimuli; (2) retention or recollection of information; (3) divergent thinking or the ability to conjure up numerous hypotheses or courses of action in problem-solving situations; (4) convergent thinking or the ability to integrate divergent ideas into a unified plan; and (5) decision making, or the ability to make firm decisions for action on the basis of convergent ideas.

The impacts on cognitive processes of environmental experiences and idiosyncratic motivations are ultimately related to the individual's actual problem-solving behavior. We know that these impacts vary with chronological age. Just as we may approach the discrimination between a square and a circle as a problem mediated through cognitive processes, so may we approach the problem, as expressed by Sullivan (1947, 1953; Mullahy, 1949), of the "good me" and the "bad me," or the problem of the "loving father" and the "rejecting father." One of the most frequently occurring frustrations experienced by parents, clinical workers, and researchers is their inability to discern what the world means to the child, and how he puts two and two together to get four or three or five. Children engage in classifying behavior with regard to objects (geometric shapes), persons (mother, father), and themselves ("good me," "bad me"). An exciting and challenging task, as yet barely begun, is that of understanding the child's construction of his life space. This is a difficult task, exceedingly so with very young children, because investigators are dependent on the language of subjects in order to infer their cognitions. However, such an understanding seems necessary in order to come to grips with the development of thought processes and their implications for behavior.

Intelligence and Its Assessment

Intelligence is an inference drawn from observed behavior. Definitions of it will vary according to the observations made. Thus there are as many definitions of intelligence as there are intelligence tests. Common to all of these is the aim of assessing human abilities. These abilities may be viewed as related to or functions of cognitive processes. Studies of intelligence and thought processes therefore show much overlap.

Since there are many different measures of intelligence, one might ask: Are they not all simply getting at different aspects of a trait of general intelligence? Is it not true that we tend to employ general labels such as "bright," and "dull," "smart" and "slow" in characterizing individuals?

The work of Spearman (1927) and the British school of factor analysis has provided evidence that supports the idea that a sizable component of human abilities can be accounted for with a concept of general intelligence. The research of Thurstone (1946; Thurstone and Thurstone, 1950) and a number of American factor analysts has shown that there are a number of significant, fairly specific intellective abilities that are not explicable simply in terms of general intelligence. Although heated argument persists over the nature of intellectual abilities, we may reasonably assume on a tentative basis that there is a general intelligence factor as well as specific ones (McNemar, 1964).

How "pure" is intelligence? Too often we tend glibly to distinguish between intelligence and personality as if they were two different entities. It is important to keep in mind that both personality and intelligence are constructs and that they may involve the same types of variables. Let us consider some of the factors that have been found to relate to both intellectual and personality functioning.

Perhaps environmental influence best illustrates the sort of variable that relates to both intelligence and personality. We have seen the powerful influences that environmental factors exert over personality and emotional expression. If environmental factors did not exert a modifying influence over intellectual abilities, one might expect intelligence tests to show relative constancy from one time to another. In fact, intelligence test scores are subject to change owing to modifications in environmental conditions (Sontag, Baker, and Nelson, 1958). Studies of intellectual change resulting from enriching educational socioeconomic experiences have shown that these experiences do raise IQ levels. For example, it has been found that the longer Negro children have been in northern schools the greater is the likelihood that their IQs will be within the normal range (Klineberg, 1935). This would suggest that intelligence as inferred from psychometric instruments increases with increases in educational opportunities, and that the better the schools, the brighter the students.

Another source of information about the relationship of environment to intelligence comes from research on identical twins who have been separated and reared apart (McCandless, 1961; Mussen, Conger, and Kagan, 1963). These studies indicate that despite a common genetic heritage, separated identical twins show sizable differences in assessed intelligence when there are marked differences in educational opportunities. Research with foster children has also shown the factor of educational opportunities to be a significant determinant of assessed intellectual ability. Still further evidence in support of an hypothesized relationship between experimental factors and intelligence comes from studies of the effects of nursery school experiences on intellectual development. Research in this area suggests that educational preschool experiences have a salutary effect on intellectual performance.

Turning from experiential variables, one sees additional indications of the role of nonintellective factors in intellectual performance. Both the variables of test anxiety and need for achievement have been examined in relation to intellectual performance (Chapter 15). There is reason to believe that measures of need for achievement, such as McClelland's (McClelland, 1955, 1965*b*; Atkinson, 1958*a*) are positively related to intellectual performance. High scores on measures of test anxiety appear to be associated with relatively poor performance on intelligence tests; low test-anxiety scores seem to be associated with relatively high levels of performance on intelligence tests (I. G. Sarason, 1960). It is worth recalling, however, that a negative correlation between test anxiety and intellectual performance may not be operative in all situations (I. G. Sarason, 1960). The less testlike and the less stressful the test situation is made to seem, the greater is the likelihood that high test-anxious subjects will not perform more poorly than low test-anxious subjects.

This relationship supports skepticism about distinctions between intellective determinants of performance, on the one hand, and motivational or personality factors, on the other. Although standardized intelligence tests are helpful predictors of achievement, there are numerous examples of discrepancies between assessed ability and actual achievement. MacKinnon (1962, p. 493) who has directed a series of studies of creativity, has come to these conclusions concerning the contribution of assessed intelligence and personality to creative talent:

> Our findings concerning the relations of intelligence to creativity suggest that we may have overestimated in our educational system the role of intelligence in creative achievement. If our expectation is that a child of a given intelligence will not respond creatively to a task which confronts him, and especially if we make this expectation known to the child, the probability that he will respond creatively is very much reduced. And later on, such a child, now grown older, may find doors closed to him so that he is definitely excluded from certain domains of learning. There is increasing reason to believe that in selecting students for special training of their talent we may have overweighted the role of intelligence either by setting the cutting point for selection on the intellective dimension too high or by assuming that regardless of other factors the student with the higher IQ is the more promising one and should consequently be chosen. Our data suggest, rather, that if a person has the minimum of intelligence required for mastery of a field of knowledge, whether he performs creatively or banally in that field will be crucially determined by nonintellective factors. We would do well then to pay more attention in the future than we have in the past to the nurturing of those nonintellective traits which in our studies have been shown to be intimately associated with creative talent.

Each of us can probably think of at least a few people who by any objective intellectual index are very bright, but who, for personality reasons, have not attained achievement levels commensurate with their assessed intelligence. There are also cases of individuals who do not appear to be intellectually dazzling, but who achieve acceptable and often outstanding levels of performance. Ability-achievement discrepancies are often explicable in terms of the particular situations and tasks with which persons are confronted. The findings concerning test anxiety support this view, since differences in the levels of performance between subjects differing in test anxiety have been found to be attributable to the conditions under which performance takes place, and to the particular tasks on which subjects labor. At a practical level, this would suggest that personality assessment techniques may have much to recommend them as tools in vocational and educational counseling.

Knowing that personality factors are related to intellectual performance and achievement leads one to wonder what role life history variables may play in this relationship. The family comes to mind as one significant determinant of characteristics that influence achievement. The relationship between events within the family and the intelligence and achievement of offspring may be thought of in terms of two questions: What sort of family experiences have noticeable effects on the abilities and achievement of children? What effects do exceptional children, either intellectually superior or retarded, have on the functioning of families?

FAMILY EXPERIENCES

In reference to the first question we can say that the attitudes acquired by individuals seem important in the translation of abilities into achievement. The desire to compete, to gain intellectual mastery, and to achieve strongly influences performance. Family experiences are probably predominant in the formation of these attitudes. Illustrative of this is the fact that children reared in lower-class family settings tend to obtain lower IQ scores on tests, and tend to be underachievers. That is, their actual intellectual achievement is lower than what might be predicted on the basis of their assessed abilities. Two questions raised by this sort of relationship are: (1) Are there cultural biases in intelligence tests? (2) What types of child-rearing practices lead to underachievement?

Several attempts have been made to develop culture-free intelligence tests (Davis, 1951; Haggard, 1954, p. 150). The following are examples of items on conventional tests, and items on a revised "culture-free" test:

Item No. 24 (Standard):

Cub is to bear as gosling is to

1 ( ) fox, 2 ( ) grouse, 3 ( ) goose, 4 ( ) rabbit, 5 ( ) duck.

Item No. 24 (Revised):

Puppy goes with dog like kitten goes with

1 ( ) fox, 2 ( ) goose, 3 ( ) cat, 4 ( ) rabbit, 5 ( ) duck.

Item No. 34 (Standard):

A weighs less than B.

B weighs less than C. Therefore

( ) B weighs more than C.

( ) A's weight is equal to B's and C.

( ) A weighs less than C.

Item No. 34 (Revised):

Jim can hit harder than Bill.

Bill can hit harder than Ted, so

( ) Ted can hit harder than Bill.

( ) Bill can hit as hard as Jim and Ted.

( ) Jim can hit harder than Ted.

Haggard (1954) found that although the performances of both middle- and lower-class children were facilitated by the culture-free test, the gap between them narrowed when this type of test was employed. The construction of culture-free intelligence tests is a particularly challenging one because the ways in which cultural factors bias performance are not yet well understood. It is understandable, of course, that lower-class children should, by and large, be less motivated to achieve the goals and stereotypes of a middle-class society. The family is the predominant agency, at least during childhood, for the transmission of these goals and stereotypes, and parents who have not adopted them cannot be very effective in transmitting them to their children.

An example of how the environment created by parents influences intellectual and achievement motivations is found in the Fels research (Kagan and Moss, 1962). Researchers found that mothers' concern about the developmental progress of their offspring during the first three years of life was positively correlated with IQs obtained by the children between the ages of 6 and 10. The mothers who were concerned about and who quite likely reinforced early talking and walking in their offspring had children who excelled intellectually. Interestingly, this positive correlation between maternal attitudes and children's intellectual performance was greater for girls than for boys.

One family variable that may be significantly related to children's intellectual progress is the identification models available. Girls tend to model themselves after their mothers, and boys tend to imitate their fathers. But it is understandable that children's motivation—for example, to achieve on intellectual tasks—may follow one parent in some cases, and the other parent in other cases. In still other cases identification with persons outside the home may be of decisive importance. Middle-class children may benefit from modeling their parents' intellectual behavior whereas lower-class children may require models outside the home.

Sarason, Davidson, Lighthall, Waite, and Ruebush (1960) have reported an investigation in which parental attitudes and behavior were studied in relation to children's anxiety and worry over taking tests. Their results were consistent with the hypothesis that high-anxious children came from less favorable home backgrounds than low-anxious children. Mothers of high-anxious children tended to be less permissive of aggression by their children and more defensive in interview situations than mothers of low-anxious children. There were more working mothers in the high- than in the low-anxious group. It was also found that fathers of high-anxious children had less formal education than fathers of low-anxious children. Furthermore, there were greater disparities in educational background among spouses who had high-anxious children than in those who had low-anxious children. An interesting over-all result was that fathers' descriptions of their children's anxieties tended to be more accurate than mothers' descriptions. This provides further support for the suggestion that developmental studies should pay more attention to the study of fathers.

EXCEPTIONAL CHILDREN

Just as there is reason to believe that the characteristics of parents and the environment they create influence children's motivations and intellectual development, there is reason to believe that the stimulus of the child, and particularly the exceptional child, can be a powerful force within the family. Perhaps one of the most extreme examples of this is the mentally retarded child. The response repertory of the retarded individual is quite limited. Its delimited character often arouses conflicting attitudes and emotions among family members. Parents are often pathetically torn between a strong desire to protect and care for a retarded child and a desire to rebel against the frustrations and inconveniences connected with rearing a retarded child. Not only does this ambivalence have an effect on the retarded child and his parents, but it also influences the lives of other children in the family.

At the other end of the continuum, the exceptionally bright and talented child poses other, albeit not quite so compelling, problems. If his abilities are far superior to those of significant persons in his milieu, his community of interests with them may not be great. He may be regarded as an "egghead" and arouse ambivalence in others. This ambivalence may reflect admiration for the superior individual, jealousy, and perhaps fear of his prowess. From the point of view of the gifted person, there may be conflict between pride in his talents and rejection of his talents because of the social isolation that may result from them. Ambivalence to talented individuals of persons in their lives is not an inevitable consequence of superior intellectual ability. Many myths and tales abound concerning the oddities that characterize creative individuals. Some people, apparently using as prototypes figures like Van Gogh, have contended that the demarcation between genius and insanity is very fine and tenuous. Actually, there is no evidence to support this position. In fact, Terman's (1925; Terman and Oden, 1947) study of gifted children and adults, one of the best pieces of research on the problem, showed that persons who were intellectually superior were better adjusted and more socially effective than other people in the population.

In general, the extent to which deviations from the average in intellectual ability may present personality problems depends on the extent and nature of the deviation and the response of the environment to it. The following study by Dearborn (1949, pp. 195–196) illustrates this point:

. . . in this case, the socio-economic, cultural, and occupational background, the personality, character, and industry of the student were all "tops," but the scholastic rating (amply tested) was around an IQ of 98 and the scholastic achievement was of a corresponding order. When one of the most esteemed and experienced headmasters of one of the best preparatory schools of this country advised the boy's parents that the boy, who was then seventeen and according to the classification in his school a year from college, was not "college material," the parents were extremely disappointed and sought the advice of the Harvard Psycho-Educational Clinic. The father was a leading practitioner of medicine and had for years hoped that in due course his son would take over his practice. The boy, not only as a dutiful son, but also of his own free will and desire, was of the same intention. After conferring with the boy and his parents and confirming the above statements, I, as Director of the Clinic, advised that, if he had the grit and really wanted to become a physician, was not too exacting about his choice of a college, and had the patience to stick with the job, his and his parents' ambitions could be accomplished. After another year at school, his record was not good enough to enter college on certificate and admission by college board examinations seemed out of the question. At this time the headmaster did me the honor of paying a visit to say that I was making a mistake in encouraging the boy to go on to college and professional school . . . , that a boy of his sterling character and integrity, set up in business or in farming in a small community, would come to be one of the leading citizens and tower of strength in the affairs of his community and withal a happier man than he would be if he should persist in his efforts to follow in his father's footsteps. Who can say?

By registering for extension and night courses in an urban university he finally gained admission to regular standing, but after a couple of years he gave up the effort and took a blind alley job in a department store. Pretty well discouraged and near to a nervous breakdown, he found or was helped to a job as athletic coach in a small preparatory school. Here in association with instructors who were college graduates, he was encouraged to make another try and four years ago this June, after ten years of effort, was graduated from a leading college of medicine.

Then, after two years in the service, he took up the practice of medicine in his father's office, where he is associated with a younger brother—a more recent graduate in medicine. This June he is to be married, and will, we shall assume, live happily ever afterwards.

In this instance, the student's socio-economic, cultural, and occupational background was a relatively more important factor than the more usually primary criteria—scholastic aptitude, rank in school, scholastic achievement, and headmaster's recommendation.

The concepts of intelligence and personality seem definitely intertwined. The task of unraveling them presents challenging problems that require careful and imaginative inquiry. At present it seems clear that a high IQ is no guarantee that a person will function originally and creatively. Similarly, a relatively low IQ does not necessarily mean a lack of ingenuity. It has been suggested that perhaps a distinction between intelligence and creativity would be sensible. Tests of the former (which yield IQs) usually call upon the subject to engage in such activities as defining words, solving arithmetic problems, and memorizing verbal material. But is there not a difference between the ability to define words and the ability to use language creatively? Is there not a difference between the ability to solve arithmetic problems of the type encountered in school, and the ability to think creatively in quantitative terms? Getzels and Jackson (1962, p. viii) have raised questions like these on the basis of research conducted by themselves, Guilford (1956, 1959*b*), and others. They have explicitly called for an effort to develop psychometric indices of two hypothesized traits, intelligence and creativity:

Once we accept the notion, however provisionally, that creativity and intelligence as measured by the IQ are not necessarily synonymous—that the number of words an individual can define or his ability to memorize digits backwards may tell us very little about his ability to produce new forms and to restructure stereotyped situations—an almost limitless number of exciting problems present themselves for systematic study. We may, for example, ask what might otherwise seem an egregious question: can we identify individuals who are outstanding in one of these functions but not in the other? Specifically, can we identify children who are very high in intelligence but not concomitantly high in creativity, and children who are very high in creativity but not concomitantly high in intelligence? If this can be done, we may raise all manner of relevant issues regarding the behavior of these children—the answers to which may yield significant insights not only into the children themselves but into the character of specific cognitive processes. Such issues would include: What is the relative performance of these children in school? What is the nature of their fantasies and imaginative productions? Their family background? Their values and aspirations? The reactions of others to them?

Another writer, Barron (1963), has sought to explore the nature of creativity and to place the creative act within its organismic and historical context. All too frequently when we speak of creativity—for example, Beethoven's *Eroica* Symphony, Einstein's theory of relativity—we think only of the product of the creative act. From a psychological point of view, however, the relationship of the personality and life history of the creative person to his product is perhaps the paramount question. Barron (1963, pp. 139–140) has expressed this point very clearly:

There has been a marked tendency in psychological research on originality to focus attention upon the single original act in itself, rather than upon the total personality of the originator. This is understandable, for the birth and development of the original idea are usually more immediately interesting and dramatically vivid than the birth and history of the man who had the idea. Newton's apple and Archimedes' tub and the well of Eratosthenes are thus naturally the circumstances with which we associate the remarkable insights of these original geniuses; we do not often ask ourselves whether these men were for the most part disposed to express or to suppress erotic impulses, or whether their emotions were fluent or turgid, or how subject to intense anxiety they were, or how much given to violent action. We tend to disembody the creative act and the creative process by limiting our inquiry to the creator's mental content at the moment of insight, forgetting that a highly organized system of responding lies behind the particular original response which, because of its validity, becomes an historical event.

There is good reason for believing, however, that originality is almost habitual with persons who produce a really singular insight. The biography of the inventive genius commonly records a lifetime of original thinking, though only a few ideas survive and are remembered to fame. Voluminous productivity is the rule and not the exception among individuals who have made some noteworthy contribution. Original responses, it would seem, recur regularly in some persons, while there are other individuals who do not ever depart from the stereotyped and the conventional in their thinking.

A CONCLUDING COMMENT CONCERNING PERSONALITY AND ABILITY DIFFERENTIATION

With increasing understanding of the relationships among personality, intelligence, and creativity, psychologists may be able to make significant social and educational contributions. These contributions may take the form of recommendations concerning family and social environments that maximize the effectiveness of persons as they develop. Even more specifically, they may take the form of new and better educational techniques of benefit to students of varying age and ability levels.

26

The School Experience

School experiences are probably second only to family experiences in their importance as molders of men and women. Much that we have discussed has direct relevance to the educational process. Research on test anxiety in relation to intellectual performance suggests that taking a test in school can for some children be a frightening and possibly traumatic event. Studies of need for achievement suggest that individual differences regarding this need are associated with differences in performance. Socioeconomic status and level of aspiration also have implications for the acquisition of intellectual and social skills within a school setting.

These characteristics are attributes of individuals. They are determined not only by the individual himself, but also by his family, school, and cultural experiences. Thus, for example, in thinking about the effects of test anxiety on school achievement, it is not sufficient to consider only what the student brings with him to the classroom. In addition, it is necessary to inquire into the characteristics of the classroom as a stimulus (Sarason, Davidson and Blatt, 1962). Can modifications in classroom procedures be devised that will reduce the incidence of anxiety? (Spielberger and Weitz, 1964). What can be done within the classroom to strengthen the academic motivations of children from lower socioeconomic backgrounds? Questions such as these argue for the psychological study of the school and classroom in the same sense as the psychological study of the family. Recent educational research has concentrated more and more on the role of the teacher in the classroom and the relationship he forms with individual students (Biddle and Ellena, 1964; Gage, 1963).

THE TEACHER-STUDENT RELATIONSHIP

Teachers and parents share many of the same roles and attributes. Both of these adult figures are for the child sources of knowledge and reinforcement. They are, in addition, significant influencers of the child's conceptions of himself and of others. Teachers and parents alike contribute to the intellectual and personality growth of young people. But what is the nature of this contribution? Our analysis of the dynamics of the family suggested that researchers were beginning to discover some of the relevant variables involved in the parent-child relationship. But, at present the gaps in our knowledge remain sizable and serve as challenges to scientific inquiry. This evaluation seems as applicable to the teacher-student as to the parent-child relationship (Sears and Hilgard, 1964).

A popular model of parents and teachers conceives of parents as persons who "bring up" children, provide adult control, and inculcate ethical values. Within this model teachers are imparters of knowledge about rather well-defined subject matter areas, reading, writing, and arithmetic. Such a model, however, is an oversimplification of reality. It is certainly true that teachers are not parents. It is also true that they are not psychiatrists and often not scholars. But they do or should have some of the qualities that characterize these roles. The characteristics of the fine teacher are not easily defined. It is important to recognize this and the fact that the roles of teachers are to a large extent determined by the society in which they work and by their own upbringing. As the values and goals of society change, so do the tasks assigned to teachers. An answer to the question, "What is the teacher's role?" must therefore be found in terms of the aspirations and attitudes of the citizenry and the characteristics of the students who are under the supervison of the teacher. As described by Havighurst (1964, p. 160), these observations by a visitor to a school in a poor urban area, suggest that the role played by a teacher may go far beyond that of a transmitter of wisdom:

> I stood with the principal on the playground during the upper-grade recess. Across the street stood five or six older boys who, according to the principal, were drop-outs. He stated that many times these boys enter the school, annoy the teachers, stand outside the windows and shout, or come around during recess time and set their sights on the older girls. Two other boys joined the group and a group of seven or eight girls drifted over to the unfenced sidewalk and moved across the street to join the boys. One of the four teachers on recess duty saw the girls leave the yard and went to

tell them to return. From across the street insults were shouted at the teacher by the boys, while the girls engaged in a form of catch-me-if-you-can, dashing back and forth in front of the teacher, taunting her. They moved slowly back into the playground in this fashion.

When teachers attempt yard control, the children completely ignore them, running out of the playground onto the street and into the lot next door. When I independently moved among the children, there were hostile glances and taunts directed toward me. Apparently I was taken for a substitute or a new teacher. When the bell rang, the children completely ignored it and continued to play despite the entreaties of the teacher to line up and pass inside the school. I timed the movement in and it took eighteen minutes from the time the bell rang to the time the last boy and girl reluctantly and belligerently crossed the door into the school.

Psychologists can be helpful to society by providing knowledge about human behavior that has relevance to the educational process. In this sense psychological study of the person and his thought processes can be of practical value. Comments made in Chapter 25 concerning intellectual creativity suggest such practical questions as: How does the teacher identify and respond to originality and intuitive sensitivity in school children? The discussions (Chapters 18 and 22) of the influence of the behavior of models on the behavior of children suggest the question: How can the middle-class teacher function as a meaningful model for the culturally and economically deprived student?

The teacher is as important when he is a diagnostician and reinforcer of students' behavior as when he is a communicator of knowledge. Bruner (1960, pp. 67–68) provided a provocative discussion of this point within the context of the problem of the response of teachers to students' insights and intuitive perceptions of relationships in the world. He emphasized:

. . . the intuitive confidence required of the poet and the literary critic in practicing their crafts: the need to proceed in the absence of specific and agreed-upon criteria for the choice of an image of the formulation of a critique. It is difficult for a teacher, a textbook, a demonstration film, to make explicit provision for the cultivation of courage in taste. As likely as not, courageous taste rests upon confidence in one's intuitions about what is moving, what is beautiful, what is tawdry. In a culture such as ours, where there is so much pressure toward uniformity of taste in our mass media of communication, so much fear of idiosyncratic style, indeed a certain suspicion of the idea of style altogether, it becomes the more important to nurture confident intuition in the realm of literature and the arts. Yet one finds a virtual vacuum of research on this topic in educational literature.

The warm praise that scientists lavish on those of their colleagues who earn the label "intuitive" is major evidence that intuition is a valuable commodity in science and one we should endeavor to foster in our students. The case for intuition in the arts and social studies is just as strong. But the pedagogic problems in fostering such a gift are severe and should not be overlooked in our eagerness to take the problem into the laboratory. For one thing, the intuitive method, as we have noted, often produces the wrong answer. It requires a sensitive teacher to distinguish an intuitive mistake—an interestingly wrong leap—from a stupid or ignorant mistake, and it requires a teacher who can give approval and correction stimultaneously to the intuitive student. To know a subject so thoroughly that he can go easily beyond the textbook is a great deal to ask of a high school teacher. Indeed, it must happen occasionally that a student is not only more intelligent than his teacher but better informed, and develops intuitive ways of approaching problems that he cannot explain and that the teacher is simply unable to follow or re-create for himself. It is impossible for the teacher to properly reward or correct such students, and it may very well be that it is precisely our more gifted students who suffer such unrewarded effort. So along with any program for developing methods of cultivating and measuring the occurrence of intuitive thinking, there must go some practical consideration of the classroom problems and the limitations on our capacity for encouraging such skills in our students. This, too, is research that should be given all possible support.

There are and have been many fine teachers in our schools. However, making explicit and communicable what teachers do to their students will contribute to an over-all improvement of the effectiveness of teachers. Ryans (1960) has described one of the most extensive studies of the characteristics of teachers reported in the literature. It was concerned with the identification of characteristics of teachers in general, but especially of the very able teachers. In the course of the research, 6,000 teachers in 1,700 schools and 450 school systems were studied. Observations were made in classrooms, responses to personality inventories were recorded, interviews were conducted, and life history information was gathered. Emphasis was placed upon both the intellectual and personality assessment of the subjects.

One aspect of the research on the superior teacher involved the study of 25 women teachers who had been rated by a group of experts to be outstanding in the ways in which they handled classroom situations. Detailed assessment of these women indicated that these personal qualities characterized them: a strong liking for children and interest in their development; personal admiration for such human characteristics as friendliness, permissiveness, and fairness; strong satisfaction with the job of teaching; "dreams" of becoming a teacher prior to college enrollment; and superior personal achievement in schools. Study of teachers rated low in effectiveness suggested that they possessed these characteristics: a critical attitude toward others; less interest in social relationships; and less favorable attitudes toward pupils. Their emotional adjustment and intellectual endowment appeared to be lower than that of highly effective teachers.

In general, the group of teachers rated as superior seemed to be exceptional with regard to intellectual ability, personality adjustment, and social interest and effectiveness. It would seem that the characteristics of these women seemed to cohere. Their designations as superior teachers seemed to have reliability and validity, but it is necessary to be aware of the relative nature of judgments of teacher effectiveness. In addition to the role that society plays in the evaluation of quality in teaching, two other factors make comparisons among teachers quite relative: the characteristics of the educational setting, and the characteristics of pupils.

The factor of the educational setting involves the relationship of the teacher to his subject matter and the teaching task assigned to him. The characteristics of the successful teacher of middle-class pupils may be quite different from those of the teacher of lower-class pupils. Some teachers with otherwise favorable characteristics may not be as effective as might be expected because of the topic they must teach. The outstanding teacher of art might be quite pedestrian as a science teacher. The teacher who is excellent with second graders might not be effective with high school children. More knowledge is needed concerning the ways in which teacher characteristics mesh with the particular kinds of situations in which they find themselves.

The characteristics of students would have to be a prominent factor in an attempt to analyze the teacher and the job he seeks to perform. Other important factors are the teacher's social status and the gap between his social status and that of his students. It is almost a cliché to state that the teacher-student relationship is at the heart of the educational experience. Examples abound from the sphere of higher education that show the profound impact certain teachers have on certain students. At lower educational levels, case after case could be cited in which the course of a child's academic career was drastically changed for the better because he "found himself" under the tutelage of a particular teacher. Precisely what the personal dynamics of these instances may be is usually a matter of conjecture, since, often, only partial knowledge of teacher and student characteristics is available.

Despite the many gaps in understanding what goes on within the classsroom, one may venture some opinions that relate to what is already known. One of these is that the teacher-pupil relationship bears much in common with the parent-child relationship. In psychoanalytic terms, one may think of the transference and countertransference relationships at work within the classroom. In learning terms, one thinks of the child's opportunity to develop identifications with his teachers, and the kinds of models that the teacher provides for him. Whereas the child's contacts with teachers lack the continuity and intensity of his contacts with his parents, there is every reason to believe that an understanding of personality and educational development can be increased by knowledge of the dynamics of the classroom. Psychologically, what goes on in the classroom is not just the learning of knowledge and skills. In addition, the classroom provides a matrix within which attitudes toward oneself, others, and scholarship are formed, esthetic appreciations are developed, and social outlooks are shaped. The psychology of personality can contribute to a broader conception of classroom learning that includes processes such as these. The evolution of this contribution can be aided by assessment studies of teachers and their students, observations of their interactions, and, where possible, experimentation within the classroom.

THE CHANGING CHARACTER OF THE SCHOOL EXPERIENCE

The school experience is a complex one because it influences behavior beyond the classroom and because experiences beyond the classroom influence behavior in school. Examples of the latter experiences are those involving siblings, peers, and neighborhood children. Examples of the former include the changing tasks that the school presents to the child.

One of the more obvious characteristics of school experiences is that they change noticeably as the child proceeds through grade levels. Let us consider some of the educational hurdles and events that seem of particular importance to the student of personality.

To begin at the beginning, the kindergartner is confronted with the need to participate in activities away from home for relatively long periods of time. There are marked differences in attitude among children upon entering school. The gamut runs from extreme elation and positive anticipation to high degrees of fear and dread. These individual differences in initial attitudes and anticipations concerning school may be attributable in part to the attitudes of parents toward the education of their children and their (the parents') responses, both conscious and unconscious, to this important step by the child outside the home. The favorableness of the child's adjustment to school, then, would seem to be a function of his already established relationship to parental figures. Levy's (1943) work on maternal overprotection suggests that the child who has developed too dependent and symbiotic a relationship with his mother may be quite unprepared for the personal independence required to make an adequate adjustment to the school situation. Separation anxiety upon entering school indicates the need to inquire not only into the nature of children's concerns, both reality-based and fantasy-based, about the meaning of going to school, but the concerns of mothers and fathers as well. It would seem desirable to avoid sharp conceptual distinctions between school and family experiences. Each exerts impacts on the other, and these influences may be quite pervasive.

Observation of the child's early school experiences can make it possible to place him on a number of important continua. One of these is the extent to which the child integrates himself into the classroom group. The ability to adopt and enjoy a useful group role is an important step in the process of socialization. Another dimension of group membership is the capacity for cooperation and the ability to inhibit personal needs and impulses in order to satisfy a group need. Yet another aspect of early school experiences that is related to socialization is the capacity to follow directions, rules, and conventions. Some children respond to authority with blatant disregard and others overly conform to perceived demands of authority figures. The response of the child to school authority can be interpreted as a consequence of his prior contacts with authority figures (usually parents), the personality of the teacher, and the way in which he wields authority.

The child's success in his school career is, of course, not simply a matter of learning to cooperate, adhere to authority, and become integrated into social groups. The prime business of education is the development of intellectual skills and motivations. In the course of developing cognitive abilities in children, it becomes necessary for both educational and administrative reasons to gauge the achievements and aptitudes of pupils. This process of intellectual assessment usually takes the form of tests or examinations, either written or oral. It rather quickly becomes apparent to students that these tests are for purposes of evaluation and that scores on them have implications for their status *vis-à-vis* teachers, peers, and parents. The successes, the failures, and generally the sorts of reinforcements that are administered to children as a consequence of their test performance markedly influence the anticipations they acquire with regard to tests and to school work.

The effects of test anxiety and need for achievement on intellectual performance have already been discussed. It is not difficult to see that these tendencies might greatly affect generalized responses to competition and to encounters that eventuate in success-failure evaluation. The classroom situation is probably one of the most decisive contexts for shaping aspiration levels and attitudes of fear of failure and hope of success in competition. However, it is necessary to recognize that factors such as socioeconomic status may place barriers and upper limits to certain kinds of competitive strivings.

An increasingly potent force in the lives of children in and out of school is their peers. During the preschool years, parents play a predominant role in the lives of children. During the early school years, teacher influence becomes a significant factor. Throughout the school years, and particularly in the later ones, peer influences become highly influential. These influences are frequently of two types that may at first glance seem contradictory. One is the strong need that children develop to conform to the standards, strictures, and mores of their peer groups. This need to conform to "what the other kids are doing" is frequently a source of great concern to parents who see their children come under the often stern influence of relatively immature individuals. With the need to receive acceptance and approval from peers, there develops at the same time a need to be successful in competition with peers. As the child's repertory of abilities expands, there is usually a concomitant tendency to make use of it and to excel. To the extent that this develops, the child will find himself in competition with peers. Although the needs to excel and to receive recognition may not always manifest themselves in the spheres of learning and knowledge, very often they do. To the extent that this occurs, the student's academic achievement may be facilitated or hindered. Individual differences in school progress would seem partly to be the consequence of the interweaving of conformity and competitive reactions to peers.

As previous discussions would imply, the form taken by conformity and competitive strivings of school children is determined to a significant degree by the cultural milieu in which they are reared. The academic and intellectual goals of lower-class children may be quite at variance with those of middle-class children and also, it is important to note, with those of their teachers, who come primarily from the middle class (Pettigrew, 1964). One way of interpreting this situation is to say that strivings in school are a function of the value system of the child. Personal values, in turn, arise out of the individual's cognitive processes and his perceptions of the world about him. Thus the idea of scholastic preparation for college for children reared in impoverished circumstances may be so far removed from their day-to-day world as to make it impossible for them to adopt usual middle-class educational goals. An important educational challenge would be to organize school curricula so that the goals that seem realistic to the student can be realized, and so that the cultural horizons of deprived children can be broadened. This, one hopes, would lead to a situation in which perceived, realizable goals would undergo constant upgrading and eventuate in social mobility upward.

If one were to sum up the goal of education, the development of a sense of independence comes to mind. An equally important goal is an awareness of one's interdependence with others. Without this awareness, the individual in his struggle for independence might well prove socially maladaptive and a nuisance to society. Steps toward independence begin in nursery school, kindergarten, and the early elementary grade levels in which emphasis is placed on the development of work and study habits, cooperation, and respect for rules. This is usually done within a context designed to be as pleasureful and gratifying to the child as is possible. Emphasis in the later elementary grades on homework and self-responsibility is expected to accelerate the growth of independence and social effectiveness.

The advent of high school, for many pupils, represents a rather drastic change from the protected elementary school environment. Independent study is emphasized much more than in elementary school. The protective role of the teacher in elementary school evolves into a more tutorial and professorial one. Increased emphasis is placed on the student's planning his own program. Extracurricular activities become increasingly available. These activities often come to be highly absorbing for high school students. Steps toward independence within the academic setting are related to the process of liberation from the family—a hallmark of the adolescent period. More and more, the social involvements of the high school student extend beyond a few extra curricular activities and one or two post-school play hours. Afternoons, evenings, and entire days may be spent in social activities outside the home without the guidance and supervision of parental figures.

Restricting ourselves for the present to intellectual and scholastic aspects of the high school period, one problem becomes more and more pressing for the student. That problem is the future. In elementary school the child begins to learn how to plan activities and to anticipate the future. But that future is not very distant. On the other hand, third- and fourth-year high school students must do some hard thinking about the adult lives that they will build for themselves. The better the adolescent is able to project himself into the future, the more likely will he be able to maximize the gain from high school experiences.

Planning for the future has important implications for the development of appropriate curricula for teenagers. Modern society seems to be moving with increasing acceleration toward specialization in vocational training and jobs. This trend toward specialization becomes quite noticeable in high school. Is the student headed in the direction of skilled mechanical work? Is preparation for college a reasonable and feasible course of action for a particular student? Answers to these questions are determined by such factors as the abilities and aptitudes of the student, the training facilities available within the school system, the sort of vocational counseling available to him at school and within the home, and his socioeconomic level. Yet another determining factor is that of peer influence: "What are the other kids planning to do when they get out?"

More and more the answer to this question is, "Go to college." Indeed, it might even be said that for many adolescents the high school experience is not as vocationally decisive as it might otherwise be because concrete vocational training and plans are not expected to be made until the collegiate years. Going to college means something quite different today from what it did a few decades ago. For broad segments of the population it is now the usual rather than the unusual thing to do.

What undergraduate education was to the society of 50 years ago, graduate and postgraduate training is to our present society. With the increasing need for highly trained technical and professional workers, there is every reason to believe that the trends toward specialization and the prolongation of education and training will continue to grow. This growth has implications both for the communication of knowledge and for the personal lives of individuals who pursue studies leading to Ph.D., M.D., and other advanced degrees. One consequence of specialization is that more and more people come to know more and more about narrower and narrower subject-matter areas. The constant refinement and definition of areas of specialization make it increasingly difficult for different types of specialists to communicate with one another at levels of discourse that are not superficial. With regard to the personal and social consequences of the pursuit of graduate and postgraduate training, it is obvious that the longer it takes a student to reach the point at which he can occupy a job, the longer will it be before he can function independently.

Functioning independently means involvement in the usual trappings of adult life: financial independence, marriage, and child rearing. The problem for the graduate student is that of establishing a rapprochement between intellectual thirst and vocational ambitions on the one hand, and personal needs and desires, such as having a family, on the other. Such conflicts require difficult choices, and reasonable compromises may not always be readily available.

Psychological researchers can contribute to the understanding of the personal and social implications of lengthening periods of education. Assessment of the personal needs and motivations of individuals who seek advanced university training could prove of great value in explaining their pursuit of knowledge. Analysis of the reinforcements that sustain or might sustain this pursuit would also be very enlightening, particularly with regard to able but unmotivated students.

PROGRAMMED INSTRUCTION: AN EXAMPLE OF THE CHANGING SCHOOL EXPERIENCE

We have been talking about the changing character of the school experience from the standpoint of the developing individual—child, adolescent, and adult. The school experience can be viewed also in terms of changes in the technology of education. The child as a person changes as he proceeds through grades in school, and the educational experiences afforded him change as new knowledge and techniques infiltrate the classroom. A dramatic example of this infiltration is the growing interest and research on programmed instruction (Glaser, 1965). Programmed instruction involves an interaction between a pupil and a device or book that is programmed to give him prompt feedback concerning the correctness of responses he makes in the course of learning.

A teaching machine may be thought of as a self-contained system for presenting information to a pupil, for providing "comments" about the pupil's responses and progress, and for guiding the pupil to a specific goal, for example, knowledge of the principles of electricity. One might believe that a device such as a teaching machine lacks sufficient sensitivity and flexibility to "comment" adeptly about the pupil's progress. If the development of computerized systems is carefully studied, however, one realizes that such an estimation is not altogether correct. For example, a computerized teaching machine called the "Socratic System" (Swets and Feurzeig, 1965, p. 573) has been developed which states a problem to the student and then provides a framework in which the student can proceed to a solution, and form concepts, on his own terms. The progression of the lesson is flexible and almost fully under the student's control. The student does not merely generate responses on cue; he can ask, as well as answer, questions. The emphasis of the system is not on stamping in responses, but on facilitating study.

The computer engages the student in "conversation" while he attempts to solve the problem that is posed. The conversation is accomplished by means of an electric typewriter. The student types a question or an assertion, and the computer responds by typing an answer or comment or, possibly, a question in return. Limited only by a specified vocabulary on a list given him, which can be extensive, the student can request information, or propose a solution, whenever he likes. The computer responds in natural English; the response is determined by the student's actions up to that time and by the information he has at that point, and may depend not only on all the previous interchanges but also on their order. The subject-matter specialist and the computer programmer devise conditional strategies so that the computer answers good questions, reproves hasty conclusions, acknowledges perceptive decisions, questions the grounds of inference, suggests new approaches, and develops interesting contingencies to the appropriate depth.

An illustrative protocol obtained with the first problem prepared is reproduced below. More a guessing game than a problem intended to help form complex concepts, it was devised by Judith R. Harris principally for use in debugging the computer program. It shows, however, that the responses of the computer can be of some interest in even a simple situation, and it has some properties that will serve as useful contrasts in discussing more complex problems.

The student (or player) is to try to guess a letter of the alphabet. The questions he can ask of the computer pertain, for the most part, to simple geometric characteristics of a printed letter, such as the number of horizontal, vertical, oblique, or curved line segments in the standard drawing of the letter. In the dialogue given here . . . the student's questions and assertions are in capital letters and indented to distinguish them from the computer's responses, which have only an initial capital and are not indented. In the original transcript the student's comments are typed in black and the computer's in red.

Start when ready.
  CURVES?
One.
  LOOSE ENDS?
Two.
  OBLIQUES?
Zero.
  C.

You don't have enough information yet to get the right answer. How do you know it isn't J, for example?

J.

You don't have enough information yet. How do you know it isn't C, for example?

HORIZONTALS?

Zero. That was a wasted question. It did not eliminate any possibilities.

VERTICALS?

Zero. Good question.

G.

Wrong. Your guess is inconsistent with the information you've been given. You must have forgotten that the right letter hasn't any *horizontal lines.* The letter you guessed can't be right—it has too many *loose ends.*

CURVES?

The answer is still: one.

X.

Wrong. Your guess is inconsistent with the information you've been given. I think you only made that guess to see what I would say.

C.

Yes, you've done it. Good work. If you want to play again, start right in.

Programmed instructional devices such as the "Socratic System" are of relevance to the student of personality because of his interest in the conditions under which behavior occurs and becomes modified. We have suggested that the personality of the teacher is an important factor in the acquisition of knowledge and skills by pupils. Without involving ourselves in the "personality" of the teaching machine, we can ask to what extent the relatively impersonal character of programmed instruction influences the learning of subject matter. If, as seems quite possible, different types of students (for example, students differing in test anxiety and need for achievement) tend to respond differentially to particular kinds of educational situations, the student of personality can contribute to the process of education by shedding light on the question of the optimal conditions of learning for persons with particular sets of characteristics. The personal characteristics of learners must be considered in adopting and evaluating any method of instruction.

A CONCLUDING COMMENT CONCERNING PERSONALITY AND THE SCHOOL EXPERIENCE

This review of some of the highlights of the educational process makes clear that school experiences are not independent of or divorced from the major determinants of personality. The school is probably second only to the family as an influence in the lives of growing children. It is possible to show many parallels between home and school as social institutions. There is, however, one practical difference between them that cannot go unnoticed. This difference is that opportunities for conducting research on psychological problems of relevance to personality development are often much greater in school settings than within the home.

This is particularly true when direct observations of behavior and experimentation are required. Although there are obstacles to carrying out controlled research in any social or institutional setting, they are particularly formidable in research related to the family setting. Direct observation of and experimentation with the family is not only difficult to envision from a practical point of view, but researchers are also loathe to make of themselves intrusive factors within the home.

Contrast this situation with that of the classroom. It is somewhat easier for a researcher to sit in and make observations of what occurs at a class meeting than it is for him to do the same thing in a family's living room. It is also much more feasible to manipulate variables experimentally in the school setting than in the home. Because of the realization that intellectual development and personality development are aspects of the same process of human growth, researchers interested in the educational process are increasingly attending to both of these facets in their work. It is likely that there will be more attention paid in the future to the effects on school behavior of such variables as the personal characteristics of students and teachers, and to the direct observation of classroom activities. More attention will probably also be given to significant determinants of behavior within the family that interact with the school in shaping the motivations and lives of children.

27

Development through the Life Span

Three psychological problems stand out as having particular relevance to an understanding of man as a social animal. One concerns the individual's changing perception of the world about him. How much of the physical environment becomes part of the individual's personally relevant environment? Looking at development with this question in mind, we can see the socialization process as a function of the individual's changing interpretations of the world about him. As we have seen, changes in interpretations of reality are related to maturation and to the types of experiences that characterize a given life. Thus, for example, the interests of the offspring of poor sharecroppers and those of middle-class, white-collar workers can be expected to be quite different. Similarly, the high school gang member and the middle-class honor student will perceive society differently and observe different kinds of behavior in family, social, and sexual situations.

Implied in these examples is a second problem, that of changes in personal attachments during development. This is a problem with which psychoanalysis has been especially concerned. Which environmental objects come to be highly cathected by the individual? What is the course of change of cathexis throughout life? For the student of personality it would seem important to focus attention on the relationship of the person's experiential history to his interpretation of the world about him and to the personal attachments that he develops as he proceeds through life. Studies of the socialization process support this concentration on both social perception and social behavior. An adequate understanding of social behavior requires an understanding of the cognitive context in which it occurs. Thus, although there is strong evidence that social groups differ in modes of expressing affection, aggression, and sexual impulses, there is no obvious reason why these differences occur. These differences may partly be explained by the meanings attached by people to their behavior.

In addition to interpreting reality and establishing cathexes, individuals also develop attitudes, beliefs, and values with regard to themselves and to others. These are by no means static, but change in relation to prior experience and current conditions. Thus, a third facet of the study of social development may be viewed as the delineation of those variables that shape attitudes, values, and beliefs. It is important to bear in mind that the suggestion that social development can be considered in terms of interpretations of reality, the establishment of cathexes, and the formation of attitudes does not imply that these processes are in any way independent of one another. Indeed, there is every reason to believe that they are intimately related to one another (Miller and Swanson, 1960).

There are many important environmental determinants of social development. As the child develops, his personal world enlarges, his independence and autonomy increase, and his sense of responsibility grows. The family, the school, and peers are clearly very influential in determining the psychological growth of the individual. As the child becomes more independent, the last-named factor, peers, becomes increasingly potent (Campbell, 1964). Adequate understanding of its role in socialization requires knowledge of the dynamics of friendships and peer cultures, their relationship to the broader social context, and the impacts that they exert on family life.

Another influence that should not be ignored is the culture in which a child is reared and the peculiar sets of circumstances that affect his life at various stages. While governmental policies and sociocultural influences do not exert such direct and obvious impacts on development as do the family, the school, and peers, their roles may be quite pervasive. All environmental pressures on the individual, be they subtle or obvious, exert their influence as part of a gestalt of forces. They do not occur *in vacuo*.

Unfortunately, knowledge of the effects of prior experience on present behavior diminishes as an individual's age increases. Although there are many gaps in our understanding of the first few years of life, the fund of information about behavior during this period is greater than what is known about developmental processes in adults. It is interesting to note that while child psychology can be delineated as a major substantive area within the field of psychology, other periods of life have been comparatively neglected. Why this should be so may not be immediately obvious. Perhaps the psychoanalytic emphasis on the durability of the personality formed during the early years of life has contributed to relative neglect of the study of development during later years. Certainly Allport's (1961) critique of psychoanalysis would seem to rest heavily on this emphasis.

Despite the absence of a truly developmental approach to behavior through the life span and regardless of the reasons that may account for this absence, there are indications that psychologists and other students of behavior are awakening to problems of development beyond the first several years of life. The more we can find out about the ways in which the personality of the individual changes as he becomes older, the better shall we be able to appreciate the complex relationships that characterize social interactions among persons. One step in this direction would be a comprehensive analysis of the family as an evolving and dynamic structure. It is one thing to study the impact of the mother's personality on her offsprings' behavior, and it is quite another to study developmentally the complex called the family. Another step would be a clearer understanding of the evolution of social and cultural organizations that impinge on the developing person. A third step toward a more truly developmental approach to behavior through the life span would be to hypothesize about and study personal events and circumstances that occur in adult behavior.

It is possible to conceive of many of these events and circumstances as developmental hurdles. Some of the hurdles of early childhood revolve around the acquisition of elemental skills such as speaking, bladder and bowel control, and the capacity to interact meaningfully with other children. A number of writers, notably Freud, Sullivan, and Erikson, (Chapters 2 and 3) have made clear the direct relevance of these hurdles to social development. We have seen how successful adjustment to the school situation constitutes another hurdle that has implications for social behavior, for the development of a sense of responsibility, and for the strengthening and weakening of particular attitudes toward self and others. School experiences are especially significant because they occur over such a long period of time and because this time period is marked by significant biological changes.

The period of adolescence dramatically illustrates this confluence of intellectual and biological progress (Moore and Holtzman, 1965). Multiple hurdles characterize this period (Elkin and Estley, 1955; Jersild, 1963). The adolescent is simultaneously faced with planning for the future, deciding on vocational objectives, adjusting his self-concept from that of a child to that of an adult, coming to terms with adult sexual urges, changing his social life in light of sexual maturation and his growing independence, and modifying his relationships to each of his parents from that of child to adult to that of adult to adult. A number of questions come to mind about these events of adolescence. What is the relationship of preadolescent personality to the ease with which adolescent hurdles are surmounted? How may we account for individual differences among adolescents in their adjustment to this period? What is the relationship of the degree of *sturm und drang* in adolescence to adult personality functioning and social behavior? In what ways do family and sociocultural factors influence youngsters' reactions to puberty and adolescence? Gottlieb and Ramsey (1964) have pointed to parents' lack of awareness of the developmental hurdles confronting the adolescent, and society's lack of clear definition of norms of adolescent behavior as exacerbating factors in the tensions of adolescence in Western society. It is interesting that in many primitive societies there are unambiguous *rites de passage* that help make explicit the roles of the adolescent and the adult (Whiting and Child, 1953).

With attainment of adulthood and with the end of the period of formal education, the individual finds himself in a world of adults in which he is, at least theoretically, accepted as an equal. This equality carries with it the rights and privileges of adulthood, but its responsibilities and tribulations as well. Whereas parents are often assigned the blame for imperfections of ability and character in their children, the imperfections of adults are usually considered to be their own. Early adulthood is of far-reaching importance as a developmental stage because ability to surmount its various hurdles directly affects the individual's conception of his place in the world, his vocational success, his social effectiveness, and his capacity for mature heterosexual relationships.

Marriage, of course, constitutes a major and sometimes traumatic developmental hurdle. Success in marriage does not appear to be an easily accomplished goal in our society. The high divorce rate strikingly attests to the validity of this assertion. We need to know much more than we do about the natural history of marriage and the variables that influence a person's decisions to marry and to select a particular marital partner. How does the relationship between marital partners change over time? How does the entry of children into the family affect the lives of husband and wife? Our discussion of human development has now come full circle. In our early discussion of child development, we emphasized the parents as an independent variable. We asked: How do the parents influence the child's behavior? Now we find ourselves confronted with the question: What does the advent of the child to his parents and their relationship to each other?

Child rearing, of course, is not an end point in the psychological development of parents. Parents experience constantly changing relationships with their children. They are also involved in their own social, vocational, and avocational interests. These preoccupations change with changes in age and in biological makeup. We tend to refer rather glibly to "middle age," "period of maturity," and "old age." To what events do these terms refer? Although we may be able arbitrarily to mention chronological age demarcation points that correspond to these terms, there may actually be only a weak correlation between an increase in chronological age and the occurrence of various biological and psychological events. Faced with the prospect of increasing numbers of older persons in our population, we find that it is becoming increasingly necessary to gain a better, fuller picture of the aging process from both biological and psychological standpoints. The following aspects of this process seem particularly relevant to the study of personality: (1) changes in goals, values, interests and motivations; (2) changes in self-perceptions; and (3) changes in perceptions of other—wife, child, and mankind generally.

At present we can say with confidence that 60-year-old men are less alert, less strong, and in many respects less able than are men of 30. But we can say with equal confidence that there are marked individual differences among people in the speed with which they "get old." While it is obviously a gross oversimplification to say, "You are as old as you feel," there remains a core of truth in this cliché.

In addition to knowing how intellectual and physical abilities change with increasing age, we also need to know what "getting old" and the threat of death mean to individuals. As the following comments by a group of older men recorded by Reichard, Livson, and Petersen (1962, pp. 127, 143, 153, 160, 157) suggest, "getting old" and death may mean quite different things to different people:

I haven't been hunting for about three years—too much climbing around the mountains and things like that. I'm getting too old for that. . . . Now just as soon stay home and watch television as go out to nightclubs and things. . . . When you're sixty-seven, you're not a kid any more; might as well face it. . . .

I think they shouldn't call middle-aged people old, even if they're not as young as they used to be. I don't call myself old!

Retired people can be useful in lots of ways. I'm not exactly able to express it like I would like to. There's different things that they could do to help out in all ways, many ways, to help themselves and help the community at large. No doubt there's lots of things that they could do, but I can't think of any. . . .

What are the advantages of getting older? That is the sixty-four-dollar question. Well, the satisfactions—if you've accomplished anything; if you haven't, I don't know what advantages there is to it.

Losing your health, that is a terrible thing to happen. It's terrible to be lame, bedridden—that's terrible. An old man laying there helpless, lifelong partner passed on. I think he should be done away with.

The need to comprehend the aging process has stimulated many speculations about development during the adult years. Most writers have seen aging as a "negative process." It will be remembered (Chapter 3) that Jung saw the middle and later years of life as ones in which man's spiritual and philosophical potentialities approached fruition. The problems of "getting old" and of death are universal. Personality researchers should be able to shed considerable light on the multifarious solutions to these problems that people reach (Birren, 1964; Chown and Heron, 1965; Feifel, 1959; Kuhlen, 1964; Neugarten et al., 1964; Williams, Tibbitts and Donahue, 1963).

In recent years progress has been made in describing the process of "getting old." This has led to a number of hypotheses about the meaning of aging. One of these has been called the disengagement theory of aging (Cummings and Henry, 1961; Havighurst, 1957; Neugarten et al., 1964). This theory postulates that the basic differences between the middle-aged and the old can be thought of in terms of social involvement, the middle-aged being fully engaged in life outside of themselves and the old being relatively disengaged. Support for this theory has come from evidence that the transition from middle age to old age is marked by increasing introversion, reduction in measurable interests and social relationships, decline in intellectual capacity, increase in preoccupation with self, and a general shrinkage in the psychological life of the individual (Neugarten et al., 1964). The concept of disengagement has been provocative and is consistent with many facts of life in old age. But a number of questions must be answered before its utility can be definitively assessed. What is the correlation between chronological age and disengagement? Individual differences among people of a given age are almost always large. What personality processes underlie social disengagement? The social behavior of persons must be recognized as being in relationship with their personalities, self-awareness, and attitudes. What are the biological correlates of disengagement? What are the socioeconomic correlates?

PROBLEMS IN DEVELOPMENTAL RESEARCH WITH ADULTS

We have noted the relative paucity of systematic and developmental studies of people during the adult years. There are many reasons for this state of affairs. Very important among these is the fact that carrying out research on adults often presents exceedingly difficult methodological problems. Most of the subject used in psychological investigations come from "captive populations." That is, they may come, for example, from a particular school or camp or hospital. It is much easier to obtain subjects under the age of 25 from defined populations such as these than to obtain the cooperation of autonomous adults or families.

This problem of obtaining the cooperation of individual adults is particularly pressing where the research aim is longitudinal comparison. Studies of changes in personality characteristics, interests, and values during the adult years have been carried out by several investigators (E. L. Kelly, 1955; Strong, 1943; Williams, Tibbitts and Donahue, 1963). One frustration associated with these studies is that it is virtually impossible to assess longitudinally the characteristics of the same group of people over time periods as short as a few years. People move, lose interest, and die, and because of these happenings, developmental studies suffer attrition in the samples of subjects investigated.

Despite these difficulties, there has been in recent years increased interest in normative, cross-sectional, and longitudinal research with adults (Birren, 1964; Neugarten et al., 1964; Williams, Tibbitts and Donahue, 1963).

A CONCLUDING COMMENT CONCERNING DEVELOPMENT THROUGH THE LIFE SPAN

This review of personality development has emphasized the role of personal factors at various stages of life. It has shown that although there are many gaps in our knowledge, there has been both conceptual and methodological progress. The relationship of theory to the actual process of data gathering was seen quite clearly in our consideration of early situations such as those involving feeding and toilet training. Although the results of many studies of these situations often lead to questions concerning the validity of existing hypotheses, the fact remains that these hypotheses have provided stimuli for much fruitful empirical work. On the other hand, the absence of exciting theoretical issues seems to have contributed to the relative paucity of evidence bearing on adult personality development. It may be that increased social concern and intensified efforts at gathering information about the adult years will stimulate provocative theoretical controversies.

Part 5

DEVIANT BEHAVIOR

THE STUDY OF BEHAVIOR immediately raises the matter of human variability. People perform the same acts in a different manner and vary in how often they perform certain kinds of acts, such as climbing mountains, answering telephones, and saying "thank you." A great deal of deviant human behavior is neither pathological nor earth-shaking; for example, saying "thank you" in a particular way. Some types of deviant behavior, however, constitute powerful sources of psychological and social concern. These are responses by individuals that either pose threats to others or to themselves, or lead to profound personal and social ineffectiveness. Emission of these responses provides the stimulus for the activities in research of many professional workers and laymen.

One set of behaviors with which we shall be concerned in Part 5 consists of responses that arouse anxiety in the responding individual. Although it may seem somewhat paradoxical, people often are pathetically troubled by their own behavior. That this is true gives the lie to clichés that describe man as the master of his own destiny. Why should a person be troubled by his own behavior? If he is troubled, why does he not modify his behavior so that he will be more satisfied with himself? These questions are simple and straightforward. They are, in fact, good questions. They are good questions not because answers to them are readily available, but because they pose significant challenges to the study of human behavior. They are poignant questions because they confront us directly with the phenomenon of human suffering. Sad to say, there are many, many people in this world who see their behavior as being deviant in some sense and who experience profound anxiety over this perception. For both scientific and humanitarian reasons, it seems necessary for the student of personality to come to grips with personally devalued behavior that arouses anxiety (Arieti, 1959; Wolman, 1965).

Part 5 will also be concerned with behavior that is noteworthy primarily because of its effect on society and its agencies. Whereas each person is free to evaluate subjectively his own behavior, society has public codes and standards of conduct that are applicable to all, and that define the limits of behavioral deviancy. A social problem may be said to be created by the behavior that deviates beyond these limits. Thus deviations perceived by either the individual or by society can pose problems that require psychological study, treatment, and research. A common situation is a combination of personal dissatisfaction on the part of an individual and concern expressed over his behavior by others, such as relatives, friends, and agencies of society.

Contributions to the understanding of deviant devalued behavior have come from many research directions. Many of these have involved applications of methodologies developed in studies of personality. Following a survey of the present-day classifications of deviant behavior, we shall turn our attention to some of these lines of empirical inquiry. In surveying research on psychopathology, we shall consider the three approaches with which we are already familiar: personality assessment, the experimental study of personality, and the developmental analysis of behavior.

28

Deviant Behavior and Its Classification

Both the individual and the society in which he lives evaluate his behavior. Depending on the evaluation, either the individual himself or society may make efforts to modify or at least control his behavior. Evaluating deviant behavior is a far from simple task. There is first the question of how an individual or a society decides that a given response is deviant, and then the question of whether a given deviant response requires control or modification. These questions may be closely related but they are not identical. Assuming that we could easily decide upon which responses emitted by people were deviant or abnormal, and which were not, we would still be left with the problem of how noteworthy the defined deviations were. It seems obvious that there are many behavioral abnormalities that either are no source of concern for the individual and society or are actually a source of pride. A man may be deviant in the style of clothing that he chooses. At worst, this deviation would be considered an eccentricity. Another person may be a scientific wizard. His behavior, although clearly unusual and deviant, would surely not be viewed as a source of concern either to himself or to the society in which he lives. There are also behavioral deviations that society frowns upon but which may not constitute clearly definable personal and social dangers. For examples, transvestites, persons who wear clothing appropriate to the opposite sex, are clearly violating societal customs. But to what extent are such practices "dangerous"? A similar question might be raised concerning homosexuality. There are complicated social and legal aspects to the concept of deviancy. Because of the complexity of human behavior and of social norms there are no simple formulae that can be applied uniformly in the evaluation of particular types of conduct.

Though recognizing the social and legal implications of evaluating the degree and significance of deviancy, the student of behavior can profitably direct his attention toward the broad challenge of understanding the determinants of behavior that individuals and society define as deviant, maladaptive, undesirable, and a source of concern. When an individual is concerned over his own behavior, the object of study is his anxiety and subjective reactions to himself and the world about him. Possible sources of personal anxiety are numerous. Many persons feel dissatisfied with their family, social, or occupational status. Some persons experience quite specific anxieties over perceived imperfections in themselves and the effect that they see these imperfections have on others. Others experience intense and pervasive anxiety whose basis may be unclear to them. Any one or a combination of these conditions can pose life adjustment problems. They contribute to the presence of a large number of unhappy people who lack the ability to solve personal problems. One recourse taken by some of these troubled people is professional psychological help.

However, there are many, many people who have personal problems and experience strong anxiety but who do not attempt to make contact with a psychiatrist, psychologist, or social worker. There are a number of reasons why unhappy people might not seek professional treatment or advice. People differ in the severity of the life stresses they experience and in the impacts these stresses have on their thoughts and behavior. They also differ with regard to the availability of nonprofessional individuals who may provide needed emotional support and advice. Wives, husbands, friends, family physicians, ministers, and teachers may perform these supportive functions. In studying the debilitating effects of anxiety and stress on behavior, it is necessary to attend both to strengths inherent in a person's personality and to stabilizing forces within the social milieu.

Whether or not an individual feels a need for assistance in coping with the problems of life, society has a stake in these problems to the extent that they influence the individual's overt behavior. In discussion here, society is conceived broadly and includes not only official governmental agencies, but also other individuals and informal social groups. A person can become a "case" when he unilaterally presents his personality problems to a qualified professional worker or when his family, a friend, a physician, or an employer has urged and brought him to the point of seeking help.

A person may also be seen clinically for diagnosis and treatment because a formally constituted instrument of society, such as a court or welfare agency, directs that this occur. This type of active intervention in the life of a citizen is attempted if it can be shown that an individual is a potential danger to himself or to others. The degree of governmental involvement in the life of an individual is determined by the nature and degree of the behavioral deviation manifested by him. In some cases in which a person commits an illegal act for the first time, he may not be punished through incarceration but may be permitted to remain in society on the condition that he seek treatment. This might happen, for example, in a case of indecent exposure where the first offender appears to the judge to be capable of rehabilitation and where the first offender's history suggests that a second offense is unlikely. In other cases, the judicial decision might be to require that an individual be rehabilitated through placement in a mental institution. When this decision is made, the individual is said to have been committed to a mental hospital. Such a decision is, of course, much more far-reaching than merely requiring an individual to seek professional help on his own. The committed individual is deprived of many of his civil liberties and of his autonomy as a citizen. He is essentially placed in the charge of the institution to which he has been sent.

It is important to note, however, that not all patients in mental hospitals are there because they have been subject to commitment proceedings. Many persons voluntarily seek hospitalization. There are many personal situations in connection with which voluntary hospitalization might appear to be the most appropriate course of action. Not the least important of these are situations in which the individual feels unable to cope either with the world about him or with his own feelings and thoughts. While the stereotype of the mental hospital is far from pleasant or desirable, for many troubled individuals the mental hospital may be viewed not only as a haven, but also as a last resort in achieving a semblance of self-satisfaction and happiness. For the lost individual who is unable to act responsibly or who may be on the verge of irresponsible behavior, a hospital may be the only possible alternative, which can provide both careful control and observation of his actions and an environment in which personality integration might take place.

Over the years, the concept of the mental institution has undergone rapid change. If one traces the history of society's response to the problem of mental disorder, one finds that as recently as the nineteenth century the mental hospital was conceived not as a therapeutic facility but as a place where people were "put away." This, of course, is not very different from the common contention that persons with communicable diseases must be placed in isolation in order that society be protected from them. That isolation of disturbed persons in the nineteenth century did not necessarily imply thoughtless or cruel treatment is suggested by these observations made by Charles Dickens (1842, pp. 105–111) of the dignified, exhortative, moral treatment given patients at Boston State Hospital:

The state Hospital for the insane [is] admirably conducted on those enlightened principles of conciliation and kindness, which twenty years ago would have been worse than heretical. . . .

Each ward in this institution is shaped like a long gallery or hall, with the dormitories of the patients opening from it on either hand. Here they work, read, play at skittles, and other games; and when the weather does not admit of their taking exercises out of doors, pass the day together. . . .

Every patient in this asylum sits down to dinner every day with a knife and fork; and in the midst of them sits the gentleman [the superintendent]. . . . At every meal, moral influence alone restrains the more violent among them from cutting the throats of the rest; but the effect of that influence is reduced to an absolute certainty, and is found, even as a means of restraint, to say nothing of it as a means of cure, a hundred times more efficacious than all the strait-waistcoats, fetters, and hand-cuffs, that ignorance, prejudice, and cruelty have manufactured since the creation of the world.

In the labour department, every patient is as freely trusted with the tools of his trade as if he were a sane man. In the garden, and on the farm, they work with spades, rakes, and hoes. For amusement, they walk, run, fish, paint, read, and ride out to take the air in carriages provided for the purpose. They have among themselves a sewing society to make clothes for the poor, which holds meetings, passes resolutions, never comes to fisty cuffs or bowie-knives as sane assemblies have been known to do elsewhere; and conducts all its proceedings with the greatest decorum. The irritability, which would otherwise be expended on their own flesh, clothes, and furniture, is dissipated in these pursuits. They are cheerful, tranquil, and healthy.

Once a week they have a ball, in which the Doctor and his family, with all the nurses and attendants, take an active part. Dances and marches are performed alternately, to the enlivening strains of a piano; and now and then some gentleman or lady (whose proficiency has been previously ascertained) obliges the company with a song; nor does it ever degenerate, at a tender crisis, into a screech or a howl; wherein, I must confess, I should have thought the danger lay. At an early hour they all meet together for these festive purposes; at eight o'clock refreshments are served; and at nine they separate.

Immense politeness and good-breeding are observed throughout. They all take their tone from the Doctor; and he moves a very Chesterfield among the company. Like other assemblies these entertainments afford a fruitful topic of conversation among the ladies for some days; and the gentlemen are so anxious to shine on these occasions, that they have been sometimes found "practicing their steps" in private, to cut a more distinguished figure in the dance.

It is obvious that one great feature of this system is the inculcation and encouragement, even among such unhappy persons, of a decent self-respect.

As concepts of mental disorders have changed, so have concepts of the mental hospital. The twentieth century has seen a clear-cut change from an emphasis on incarceration to an emphasis on therapeutic intervention with disturbed persons. Associated with this change has been burgeoning research and experimentation, designed to increase knowledge both of the factors that give rise to disturbed behavior and the factors that may serve to reduce its occurrence. There has been increasing recognition of the desirability of keeping individuals, even some rather disturbed ones, in their communities whenever this is possible. This does not mean that hospitalization of individuals with personality problems is undesirable. It means that if a person can be treated successfully without requiring him to make a total break with his community, this seems preferable to hospitalization.

There are two major aspects of this change of emphasis. One is the development of new types of treatment and treatment facilities that can be offered to disturbed persons in their home communities. Two such developments are the community mental hygiene clinic and the halfway house. The idea underlying the community clinic is that if easily accessible treatment facilities are available in home communities, problems that might increase in intensity and in time require hospitalization can be treated at relatively lower levels of behavioral impairment. The idea behind the halfway house is that in perhaps most instances persons do not become totally disabled by their personality problems. For example, some people may get along tolerably while at work during the day, but during the evening and night hours may experience intense and disabling anxiety. With the availability of a halfway house facility, individuals may continue to function in society and at the same time be assisted by a supportive semihospital type of social institution.

The second major aspect of the change of emphasis in dealing with mental disorders where they occur in the communities of the individuals affected concerns the attitudes of communities. It is well and good to say that whenever possible an individual with a psychological problem should be treated in his community. But what if the community is an unwilling or hesitant host? Many persons fear and avoid individuals who behave in "strange" ways. If the community mental health concept is to be effectively implemented, a change in both public and private attitudes toward mental illness seems necessary. How the fears of the layman concerning those who are psychologically troubled can be reduced, and how the layman's tolerance of behavioral diversity can be strengthened, are problems that probably equal in scope those of increasing tolerance and acceptance of racial and religious diversity. In this regard, it is worth noting that just as the psychiatrist and clinical psychologist are especially involved in the study of deviant behavior from the point of view of the patients' problems, social psychologists are concerned with society's response to deviancy.

THE SCOPE OF THE MENTAL HEALTH PROBLEM

Although the nature of emotional deviations is not well understood, there are objective facts that may be of value in gauging their prevalence. The number of persons in mental hospitals, prisons, and clinics can be counted. The amount of money expended in treating behavior deviations can in many cases be accurately established. This sort of factual information together with judgments of experts in the field of mental health can provide a reasonable basis for estimating the scope of the problem.

In any given year there are approximately 750,000 patients in mental hospitals in the United States. Yet hospital facilities for the treatment of disturbed persons are not nearly adequate enough to cope with the needs of the population. It has been estimated that were such facilities available the number of persons hospitalized might be of the order of 1,500,000 (Cameron, 1963).

There are some additional suggestive statistics. During the Second World War, of approximately 15,000,000 men who were given medical examinations, almost 2,500,000 were judged to have neuropsychiatric problems. During 1957, 2,500,000 persons, adults and children, were treated in mental hospitals, psychiatric clinics, and the consulting offices of psychiatrists and clinical psychologists. It has been said that half of the hospital beds in this country are assigned to persons who exhibit severe behavior deviations. Nearly half of all patients seen by physicians suffer from emotional disturbances. The following estimate (Coleman, 1964) of persons in the United States who exhibit various types of behavioral deviations is illuminating:

Persons considered to be chronic alcoholics	1,000,000
Persons considered to be drug addicts	60,000
Persons considered to be psychotic	700,000
Persons considered to be neurotic	10,000,000
Persons considered to be mentally retarded	5,500,000
Persons considered to be criminals and psychopaths	300,000

One need not exhaustively survey all the facts and estimates of the incidence of psychopathology to reach the conclusion that psychological disturbances are the most far-reaching of the health problems confronting the nation. Students of personality and of other disciplines have sought to contribute to the understanding of these disturbances through the conduct of controlled and imaginative research. *The major aim of Part 5 is to show how ideas and methods described in our study of personality can be applied to mental health problems.* Thus the topics covered in Chapters 29 to 32 will include applications to the study of deviant persons of assessment, experimental methods, and developmental concepts. However, before examining these applications let us acquire some perspective of the variety of mental health problems that come to the attention of clinical workers. The remaining portions of this chapter will be devoted to a descriptive survey of some of these problems. No attempt will be made to study exhaustively all the varieties of psychopathology. Our survey will, however, put us in a favorable position to appreciate the challenge and significance of research on psychopathology.

VARIETIES OF PSYCHOPATHOLOGY

We shall use the terms psychopathology, mental disorder, and behavior deviation in talking about cases dealt with by workers in the mental health field. These cases may be categorized in terms of the individual's behavioral deviation and symptoms—for example, does the patient hallucinate, that is, report events that, in fact, do not occur? Or they may be classified on the basis of etiology of the deviation, its prognosis or probable course, and the treatment indicated for it. These categorizations or diagnoses are typically made using the classification system devised by the American Psychiatric Association (*Diagnostic and Statistical Manual of Mental Disorders*, 1952). The examples of psychopathology that we shall present will be described in terms of this classification system. But as suggested earlier, we shall make no effort to present a detailed and systematic introduction to psychiatric diagnosis. Our goal will be limited to characterizing several significant types of behavioral problems.

These will include (1) behavioral deviations related to impaired brain function; (2) mental deficiency; (3) psychoses; (4) psychoneuroses; and (5) psychosomatic disorders.

Psychopathology from Impaired Brain Functioning

Behavior deviations may be attributable primarily to some sort of impairment of brain tissue. The degree of brain damage may vary from slight to great. Other things being equal, the degree of psychopathology or deviant behavior among persons with brain tissue damage is usually proportional to the amount of impairment.

Acute and chronic brain disorders are recognized as the two general types of psychopathology attributable to the impairment of brain tissues. Acute brain disorders are those in which impairment is temporary and reversible. Chronic brain disorders are behavioral deviations related to relatively permanent damage of tissue. Acute brain disorders include, among others, those stemming primarily from such conditions as head injuries, as might be suffered in automobile accidents, certain types of alcoholic, drug, or poison intoxications, and intracranial infections. Chronic brain disorders include, among others, those stemming from damage to the central nervous system, syphilitic infection, cerebral arteriosclerosis, permanent damage inflicted by head injuries, and senile brain deterioration.

Patients whose behavioral impairment is attributable to disturbance of brain function may present any of a wide variety of symptoms and problems. This very variety of symptomatology frequently makes diagnosis or classification a difficult task. This is particularly true when the symptoms are not severe. There are, however, a number of behavioral symptoms that tend to characterize persons suffering from impaired brain functioning. These include disorientation with regard to time and place, loss of memory and intellectual efficiency, impairment of judgment, and emotional shallowness and lability. Behavioral deficits owing to brain disorders may have sudden or gradual onsets. Acute conditions such as those induced by head injuries incurred in automobile accidents may have quite dramatic onsets, while chronic conditions such as brain deterioration attributable to senility may be gradual.

Study of patients with organically determined deviations in behavior has proved of considerable value to students of psychopathology. It has served to emphasize some of the complexities inherent in the study of personality, because many behavioral aberrations found in cases of organic brain damage are also found in persons who are not suffering from organic brain damage. Also many persons who are known to have undergone a degree of brain damage may not show these aberrations to any significant degree.

How might we account for this state of affairs? One way is to consider any symptom or set of symptoms within its proper personal and social context. Everyone has probably on many occasions made comments such as, "Jack is a very good patient," or "Jim is a very poor patient." What do we mean by statements such as these? Probably what we mean is that given a situation in which both Jack and Jim are equally sick with some physical problem, such as influenza, pneumonia, or head injury, Jack might be expected to adjust better to the role of the sick person and to withstand better the rigors and debilitations of illness than Jim. We probably also mean that Jack could be expected to return to work more quickly than Jim. Why might this be the case? It is possible that Jack is a more robust man than Jim. Because of this, he might be expected to "roll with the punches" of illness better than Jim. It is also possible that Jack and Jim differ in their psychological reactions to illness. As was shown in some of the experimental studies of personality discussed previously, there are often marked individual differences among people in their reactions to the same stress (Chapters 14, 15, 16, and 20).

One can regard chronic or acute brain impairment as an intrusive force in an environment, that environment being the afflicted person. The effect of this force depends on the nature of the environment. The behavioral consequences of trauma like a head injury can be expected to be different for persons with histories of emotional inadequacy, physical debilitation, or seemingly normal adjustment patterns. Psychological description and analysis of behavior require that the total behavior pattern of individuals be attended to rather than only the most obvious or salient features. In this connection, the results of several experimental studies cited earlier come to mind (Chapters 15 and 21). These studies showed that organisms' responses were not made simply in relation to a specific stimulus that an experimenter might have systematically manipulated, but were made to that stimulus within the context of the total configuration of stimuli that constituted the experimental situation.

Mental Deficiency

The term mental deficiency or mental retardation applies to persons who show a noticeable degree of intellectual deficit. It will be remembered that the symptoms displayed by persons whose brain tissue is impaired often involve drastic reductions in intellectual effectiveness. The term mental deficiency was not used, however, to describe them.

It is generally restricted to those cases of intellectual deficit believed to be present since birth. In a large number of cases the basis for this deficit is unknown. Many cases involve intellectual deficit that runs in families. For this reason they have been labeled as familial or hereditary. Some cases of retardation, particularly those that are severe, often relate to biological anomolies and malfunctions. Usually the degree of mental deficiency is classified as mild, moderate, or severe, with the individual's tested IQ and his overt behavior providing the basis for classifying the degree of deficit.

Describing mental deficiency in particular instances may pose quite complicated problems. While there are "pure" cases of retardation with no complicating conditions, many cases involve the interplay of sociocultural, physical, and personality factors. In certain cases intellectual deficit may be the primary problem, but there may be pervasive personality problems associated with it. In other cases, intellectual retardation may be secondary to a disturbance of personality. In all cases of intellectual deficit, it is necessary to pay attention not only to the particular psychometric test used in assessing intellectual ability, but also to the conditions under which intelligence is measured.

One of the most encouraging recent developments in the area of behavior deviations has been the reawakening of interest in mental deficiency. For many years there was a strong tendency to regard intellectual deficit as an unfortunate problem not susceptible to significant improvement. Training schools were regarded usually as terminal placements for retarded persons. Basic research on two fronts has changed this conception. One of these relates to the biological bases of mental deficiency, the other to sociocultural and environmental factors that may contribute to intellectual deficit. From a psychological standpoint, there would seem to be two particularly pressing problems: (1) To what degree can intellectual deficits be diminished? (2) To what degree can persons with intellectual deficits be helped to live happier and more effective lives?

It is becoming increasingly clear that placing an individual in an institution for retarded people, benevolent as that institution may be, does not necessarily represent the best therapy for him (S. B. Sarason, 1959). It is true that the severest cases of intellectual deficit do require the constant attention and care provided by an institution. It is equally true that many presently institutionalized persons could, with changes in public attitudes, the diminution of private fears of citizens, and increased psychological and biological knowledge of their condition, live more nearly normal lives in their home communities.

Research evidence strongly suggests that institutionalized retarded persons tend to have been deprived of adequate social experiences and to have inordinately strong motivation for contact with and approval from others (Shallenberger and Zigler, 1961; Zigler, 1963).

Functional Psychoses

Our discussions suggest that similar behaviors may be referable to different antecedent conditions. In acute and chronic brain disorders psychopathological reactions, such as inappropriate affect and confused thought, are often observed. However, many persons who display these sorts of reactions are not suffering from any biological condition that can be identified. Let us turn our attention to these functional or psychogenic behavior deviations.

The functional psychoses comprise a heterogeneous group of behavior disorders. Despite this, the conditions in this classification have a number of common characteristics. Perhaps the two most important are profound defects of thought and affect. Persons not considered psychotic may at times suffer from mild forms of these defects, but their behavior usually can be expected to show a measure of intactness not found among psychotics. The neurotic individual may at times display considerable anxiety and even show some signs of thought disorder and inappropriate affect, but he can usually be expected to avoid the profound personality disintegration of psychosis.

What do we mean when we state that thought and affective aberrations are characteristics of psychosis? With reference to thought defects, one can describe the psychotic as thinking in ways that do not make much sense to a disinterested observer. Thoughts and concepts that most people would consider to be unrelated may be complexly related by the psychotic individual. Thus, a psychotic individual might, through some chain of logical and illogical reasoning, conclude that two plus two equals five. Or he might conclude that he is Napoleon Bonaparte, or that his mission in this world is to destroy all animals. Consider this self-description from *A Mind That Found Itself* (Beers, 1908, pp. 57–58):

> Most sane people think that no insane person can reason logically. But this is not so. Upon unreasonable premises I made most reasonable deductions, and that at the time when my mind was in its most disturbed condition. Had the newspapers which I read on the day which I supposed to be February 1st borne a January date, I might not then, for so long a time, have believed in special editions. Probably I should have inferred that the regular editions had been held back. But the newspapers I had were dated about two weeks *ahead*. Now if a sane person on February 1st receives a news-

paper dated February 14th, he will be fully justified in thinking something wrong, either with the publication or with himself. But the shifted calendar which had planted itself in my mind meant as much to me as the true calendar does to any sane business man. During the seven hundred and ninety-eight days of depression I drew countless incorrect deductions. But, such as they were, they were deductions, and essentially the mental process was not other than that which takes place in a well-ordered mind.

The balance between logic and illogic varies from case to case. By and large, however, psychotic persons display irrationality to the point of causing serious problems of life adjustment.

Another way of describing the psychotic's irrationality is to say that his mechanisms for testing reality have undergone impairment. A STOP sign to most people is simply an impersonal direction. To the psychotic, it may indicate a message from God. Reality testing is impaired in the psychotic individual because his world is such a private and personalized one that he cannot achieve a proper separation or distance between events going on within himself and events occurring in his environment. It is interesting in this connection that inability to discriminate between self and not-self is characteristic of all children during early stages of their development. The similarity between the psychotic's deficient reality testing and the reality testing of the child has caused observers frequently to describe the psychotic as a regressed individual, that is, an individual whose reality testing has regressed or degenerated to a level observed in children.

The psychotic's impairment of affect may be viewed as a consequence of his thought disorder. Observations of cases of severe psychosis lead to these sorts of questions: Why does the psychotic display inappropriate affect? Why does he laugh at the wrong time? What explanation can be offered for his seemingly inappropriate anxieties and hostilities? One rationale is that the inappropriate affect of the psychotic manifests itself because of poor ability in discriminating between his private cognitive world and his environment. Stimuli in the environment that strike him as hilarious or frightening do so because of the private meanings he attaches to them.

There is another facet to affective impairment in psychosis that is frequently quite dramatic and provides a formidable barrier to treatment. The inappropriateness of affect in psychotic individuals makes it likely that they will not be able to form sustained personal relationships that are at all meaningful and warm. Because of the often strange behavior and irrational thinking of the psychotic, persons in his environment, even family members, are unable to empathize with and accept him. Because his private preoccupations keep him from making psychological contact with others, the psychotic individual frequently experiences not only psychological but also physical isolation. This isolation in turn serves to strengthen the tendency to withdraw into an idiosyncratic personal world. Let us mention some of the specific diagnostic classifications among the functional psychoses.

SCHIZOPHRENIC REACTIONS. Psychological and physical isolation are seen very clearly in persons who display schizophrenic reactions. Of all persons admitted and readmitted to mental hospitals, the classification of schizophrenia accounts for approximately 25 per cent of the cases. It is the commonest form of psychotic reaction, and is perhaps the most poorly understood. These factors contribute to making schizophrenia a health and scientific problem of the first order. The tragedy of schizophrenia is heightened by the fact that it occurs most commonly in relatively young people (ages 20 to 40 years) and often requires long periods of hospitalization.

Schizophrenic persons suffer from disturbances in reality testing. These disturbances are tied together with a generalized retreat from reality. This self-description given by one patient suggests the generalized retreat from reality in schizophrenia (Milici, 1937, p. 55):

Voices are constant from day to day, very continuous. They seem to have no end and it is well nigh impossible to avoid them. They are clear and distinct and very, very well understood. I try not to pay attention to voices, yet without paying attention know what is said. They come from without, from persons close to me who yet appear unconcerned, or even from persons out of sight, from a distance, from people I am thinking about, seeking knowledge or giving answers to my questions. I hear too continuous voices inwardly, so rapid at times I can't remember all that's said. Voices upset my equilibrium altogether. They are rarely good and can't be changed. They have no regard for anyone or anything.

Retreats from reality may take a variety of forms and may affect not only the schizophrenic's relationships with the emotionally toned aspects of reality, but also with seemingly "neutral" reality. The following was written on a Christmas card sent by a hospitalized schizophrenic (Rosen and Gregory, 1965, p. 307):

I am privileged to write & associate with you in ways. I have a brother that looks quite a bit like you and similaritys in character are crudely the same. I never knew what it meant to have friendship like that until the last log of the old book closed in the fulfillment of the WAR #II dispensational reafirmation, after War II. & it was the #1 conditions that inspired my interest in C.B.A. that was about the same but not quite such an old story. about all I knew about any of it was the (concords and strains) of occasional that rose me up to myself once in a while. Certification in desolation & Innosence & chastity. after last slaudye, I don't feel runtly in spite of LIMITations. I do have this & that. Persent Productive the advent, it'll mean a golden success to me & an encoureagement to others.

associated #

With this sort of retreat in mind, Cameron has provided this definition of schizophrenic reactions: "Schizophrenic reactions are regressive attempts to escape tension and anxiety by abandoning realistic interpersonal object relations and constructing delusions and hallucinations" (Cameron, 1963, p. 584). Implied in Cameron's definition is the idea that the pathology of schizophrenia is a result of problem-solving efforts to cope with anxiety. The regressive behavior and withdrawal of schizophrenics is thus interpreted as a response, albeit an ineffective one, to anxiety.

Because there is so much variability in the response patterns of persons considered to be schizophrenic, efforts have been made to classify them in terms of the type of deviant behavior manifested. Although there is broad overlap among types, several groups of persons diagnosed as schizophrenic do appear to exhibit a fair degree of homogeneity in behavior. Let us review some of these forms of schizophrenia.

Simple schizophrenia is perhaps closest to the stereotype of the schizophrenic process. Its onset, which is gradual, is usually noticed in late adolescence and early adulthood. Its psychopathology is the least dramatic of all forms of schizophrenia. Often neither hallucinations nor delusions are evident. Most commonly the simple schizophrenic displays an increasing tendency to withdraw into his own private world, to "fade into the wallpaper." He is usually the antithesis of the troublemaker, does not bother people, and seemingly just wants to be left alone. Many simple schizophrenics can live in society on a marginal level, but the extent to which this is possible depends on how well protected and lacking in threat the environment is.

It probably goes without saying that there is really nothing simple about simple schizophrenia. The withdrawal and impoverishment in human relationships observed in this type of schizophrenia represent significant challenges to behavioral researchers concerned with understanding psychopathology. Equally challenging are the more bizarre forms of behavior to be seen in other types of schizophrenic reactions. The schizophrenic who evinces what is called a hebephrenic reaction may exhibit grossly inappropriate affect, such as silly giggling, excessive motor activity and excitement, and shallowness in emotional expression. Delusions, hallucinations, and childlike behavior are commonly noted in behavioral descriptions of hebephrenics. The catatonic schizophrenia is characterized especially by an often vegetable level of existence and by either excessively inhibited or excessively excited motor activity. Characteristic examples of catatonic reactions are mutism, stuporous behavior, extreme negativism, and waxy flexibility in motor responding. The paranoid schizophrenic displays markedly autistic and unrealistic thinking and may have a variety of delusional thoughts. Examples of these include delusions of grandeur and persecutory delusions. In some paranoid schizophrenics delusions may be quite expansive and may pervade most of their life experiences.

If one wished to do so, it would be possible to cite other types of schizophrenic reaction patterns. For our purposes, the foregoing descriptions seem sufficient to indicate the variety of reaction patterns to be seen among persons labeled as schizophrenic. It is necessary, though, to realize that persons given diagnostic labels such as paranoid, catatonic, and simple schizophrenic show considerable overlap in their behaviors.

The most prevalent current view of schizophrenia is that it is a functional disorder, a disorder that comes about as a result of the life experiences of the individual and his reactions to them. Cameron (1963) has used the term "pseudocommunity" to refer to the schizophrenic's reconstruction of reality. Within this pseudocommunity, he may seek to solve life's problems, cope with anxieties, and experience the mastery that is denied him in the real world. It is quite clear that in order to proceed from the level of presenting simply a description of schizophrenic behavior to a level of producing a more theoretical explanation, it will be necessary to accumulate perceptive insights into the personal world of the disturbed individual, and to investigate the nature of the disturbances that he evinces in language and thought.

In addition to exploring the nature of inadequate thought processes, it seems important also to investigate the life histories of individuals who display various types of thought disorder. Clinical studies of the development of schizophrenic individuals suggest a history of disturbed family relationships in which the preschizophrenic has often been subjected to rejection by members of his family, particularly by parents, and most particularly by mother figures (Chapter 32).

That schizophrenia might be approached from the point of personality development is suggested also by its occurrence most frequently during the adolescent and postadolescent years. The young adult is confronted with the problem of paving an independent path for himself in life. He must learn to stand on his own feet. A child who has experienced a marked absence of reinforcement for independent behavior and whose mother has closely tied him to herself is unlikely to assume suddenly the independent role of the young adult.

Although the currently prevalent view of schizophrenia is that it is a product of disturbed personal relationships and affectional impoverishment in childhood, many investigators have sought to discover organic bases of schizophrenia. Research on organic factors in schizophrenia has followed two courses. In one type of study, the physiological responses and bodily reactions of schizophrenics have been compared with those of nonschizophrenics. In a second type of study the role of hereditary factors in schizophrenia has been explored.

There have been literally hundreds of studies in which endocrine functioning, cardiovascular responses, and biochemical reactions of schizophrenic, neurotic, normal, and other types of individuals have been compared. Though some of these researches have found differences among selected diagnostic categories, firm generalizations are difficult to support. This is true because there have been many inconsistencies in findings and failures to replicate previously reported positive results.

The second major path of investigation of organic factors in schizophrenia relates to a possible hereditary basis. Many writers have suspected that schizophrenia is determined at least in part by genetic factors. Kallmann (1959, 1962) conducted several systematic investigations of the genetics of schizophrenia. On the basis of his studies, he has concluded that schizophrenia is related to the inheritance of a recessive gene and that the likelihood of a person's becoming schizophrenic is directly proportional to the closeness of his blood relationship to a schizophrenic individual. The highest incidence of schizophrenia, according to Kallmann, occurs in those cases where there are monozygotic twins of two schizophrenic parents. This genetic trend has not been observed in other forms of psychopathology.

Although Kallmann's findings are impressive, their interpretation is not easy. We may know that schizophrenia runs in families, but why? Is it because of the common environment of each family, or is it due to the genes that are common to the family? At the present time, it would probably be most reasonable to conclude that both the environment of the individual and his genetic predispositions combine to influence the type of behavior that he manifests. Unfortunately, too often argument centers around the question of what is *the* source of schizophrenia. There seems no need to simplify a phenomenon as complex as schizophrenic behavior. It seems prudent at the present time to continue to investigate intensively the possible environmental, genetic, and other biological factors in schizophrenia.

This discussion of the schizophrenic reaction has dwelt primarily on a description of its behavioral manifestations and their interpretation. On a behavioral level, perhaps the outstanding characteristic of the schizophrenic's personality is the broad impact his thought disorder exerts on virtually all aspects of his life. The individual is disabled, not just in certain isolated spheres, but in all aspects of his behavior. This disability is a product of thought processes that not only are different from normal ones, but are also quite difficult to comprehend.

Related to the schizophrenic's idiosyncratic and regressive use of thought and language is his inability to express emotions and affect in a manner that is at all conventional. The comments concerning emotional expression in schizophrenia that are most often mentioned pertain to its flatness. This, however, cannot be taken as meaning that the schizophrenic does not experience emotion. Indeed, basic to most psychological explanations of schizophrenia is the assumption that emotional conflict is at the root of the disturbance. The schizophrenic's problem is not that he fails to experience emotion, but that he is unable to cope effectively with the emotional side of his life.

Before leaving the topic of schizophrenia, a few words are in order about the prognosis and treatment of schizophrenic reactions. Unfortunately, anything approaching a cure for schizophrenia is at the present time unavailable. This being so, the long-term prognosis in schizophrenia is decidedly unfavorable. Psychotherapy with some schizophrenics has resulted in marked improvement. It is, however, quite easy to cite many cases that have been unresponsive to psychotherapy. From the standpoint of the study of behavior deviations, the fact that there have been a few successfully treated cases may suggest that "talking therapy" designed to rethink and revamp life patterns and habits can, if perfected, provide a path to the reconstruction of schizophrenic personalities.

Although the picture in schizophrenia may be unfavorable in terms of a cure, there are a number of clinical techniques that are effective in bringing schizophrenic patients into closer contact with reality and that make them easier to handle from a management standpoint. Electric shock and other shock methods have often been found to lead to improved behavior and more reality-oriented thinking in schizophrenics. These positive effects, however, often obtain only for short periods of time. Tranquilizing drugs have also been of value in temporarily improving the level of adjustment of the schizophrenic patient. The salutary effects of tranquilizers are perhaps most noticeable in cases involving aggressive and destructive behavior. Patients exhibiting this sort of reaction pattern previously contributed greatly to the populations of "back wards." These wards are now largely extinct because persons previously placed in them can now either be placed in more socially active wards or be discharged from hospitals. These drugs, which have been in widespread medical use for little more than a decade, are enabling many previously hospitalized disturbed psychotic individuals to achieve at least marginal adjustments in hospitals and in their communities.

PARANOID REACTIONS. Although schizophrenia represents the most prevalent form of psychosis, there are other ways in which psychotic reactions may become manifest. One of these, paranoid reactions, is in some ways similar and in some ways dissimilar to the paranoid schizophrenic syndrome. The word paranoid is derived from Greek roots that literally refer to a "mind beside itself." The major similarity is that in both paranoid schizophrenic reactions and paranoid reactions, delusions are present as important symptoms. The major dissimilarity is that the delusions of the schizophrenic occur within a framework of fragmented thinking, whereas the delusions of the paranoid are highly systematized, and despite their bizarreness may even suggest a degree of logical intactness.

It is interesting to note a social-class difference between schizophrenics and paranoids. Whereas schizophrenic reactions may be observed at all social strata, a preponderance of schizophrenics seem to come from lower socioeconomic environments and to have deficient educational backgrounds. Paranoids, on the other hand, tend to come from higher socioeconomic groups and to be relatively well-educated people.

The thinking of the paranoid individual can best be viewed within the context of a definition of the word "delusion." A delusion is a persistent belief that is in conflict with what is in fact the case. In this sense all of us are probably to some degree delusional. Every person makes some incorrect assumptions about how the world works. The paranoid schizophrenic harbors delusions that are noteworthy for their bizarreness—for example, "I am Jesus Christ." This sort of bizarre delusion or assumption is usually patently ridiculous and cannot be buttressed by rationalizations that are even seemingly logical. The paranoid personality, on the other hand, harbors delusions that may be surprisingly systematic. Granting his delusional assumptions, we recognize that the paranoid's behavior may seem quite logical. Whereas the schizophrenic may simply state without supporting evidence that he is being persecuted by the F.B.I., the paranoid, making the same assertion, will attempt, sometimes perhaps successfully, to make a convincing case for his belief.

Paranoid psychotics typically do not show the flatness and withdrawal seen in the schizophrenic. Rather, their affect is appropriate to the assumptions and beliefs contained within their delusional system. Intellectually their effectiveness is much greater than that of schizophrenics. The complexities of their delusional systems usually develop gradually as "data" that feed into them become available. In some cases the delusional system is quite successfully encapsulated. For example, the individual who feels that the F.B.I. is after him may not seem to be suffering from delusional thinking unless he is engaged in conversation concerning the F.B.I. or matters related to police and governmental investigation.

Paranoid disorders are relatively rare, constituting less than 2 per cent of first admissions to mental hospitals. Paranoia, by which is meant cases involving slowly developing, stable, and highly intricate delusional systems, is a particularly rare phenomenon. Relatively more frequent in occurrence are paranoid states that involve delusional systems that are less detached and intricate and that may persist for short, and sometimes recurring, periods of time. Because of their degree of intellectual intactness, paranoids are often successful in avoiding contact with mental hospitals and clinics. Indeed, they may temporarily be quite successful in their endeavors, to wit, Hitler and Mussolini. Cases of paranoid reactions that do come to the attention of clinical workers often involve delusional systems that have expanded to the point at which encapsulation is difficult, and that intrude on the individual's personal relationships. The following autobiographical account suggests both the systematic nature of paranoid delusions and their enveloping character (Courtney, 1901, pp. 141–145):

> I call attention to a great crime, which has hardly its equal in history. . . . Fate, however, is fickle and deceitful. A conspiracy was inaugurated against me, unparalleled by anything heard of before. It was conducted by cunning and unscrupulous emissaries or agents who considered me a means by which they could extort money from wealthy people.
>
> So cunning is their work that no one can ever find them out. . . . The question must naturally arise: How in all the world is it possible that such a conspiracy, which is a real mockery of all human and divine laws, could exist . . . for fully ten years, and in a civilized commonwealth at that? . . . It is a custom in this country to use . . . the services of so-called private detectives . . . who are heartless and unscrupulous, who will ruin a man if they can only profit by it. . . .
>
> . . . They organized themselves into a permanent, regular corps of observation, watching all my steps and doings by day and night, and succeeded in running, and keeping me down. . . .

I was often kept in a state of stupor, which deprived me of power of acting and thinking. Often had I been wondering why I did not do what I ought to have done or the reverse, and what it was that could cause such a condition.

They must have given me internally some chemical mixtures, and I have reason to believe that also hypnotism or something similar was brought into use against me. I remember distinctly, for instance, that one evening when, on a visit in the Catskill Mountains during the summer, I tried to get up in order to join a party, I was powerless to do it.

I have often been trying to greet some person or speak to him, but, as if my arms and tongue were paralyzed, I was not able to take off my hat or to utter a single word.

I soon observed that I was closely watched by agents. I was given to understand from different sides that the proprietor of a hotel would like me to marry his daughter. . . . I declined the offer.

On some business, I once met some gentlemen in an office on Broadway, but suddenly one of these crafty emissaries or agents caused some chemical odors to penetrate into the room.

Owing to this mean trick I began to stammer like a drunken man, and was unable to utter a distinct word or grasp a single thought. Thus, . . . time again my plan for building up a future for myself was shamelessly destroyed by the combined effects of these agents.

Now, wherever I go, these diabolical agents are following me. They not only injure me in business, but are molesting every one who may come in contact with me. They place chemical odors in every room where I may be. The effects of these odors upon my system are as numerous as they are painful. Now and then I lose, almost, my consciousness, and with the utmost efforts can keep my eyes open.

Often, again, I experienced a feeling as if my whole body was pierced with needles. At night, especially, these merciless agents pour such chemical odors or gases into my room that I have a choking sensation, and I am unable to breathe. Pain seems to squeeze my eyes out of the sockets, and visions arise before me.

Just as in schizophrenic reactions, paranoid reactions have an unfavorable prognosis. Long-term psychotherapy has been attempted with some patients. But because this method of treatment is costly, and because of the paranoid's great resistance to modifying his delusional system, the number of successfully treated paranoids is quite small. As a result many hospitalized paranoids constitute primarily management and maintenance problems, with tranquilizing drugs and shock treatments as helpful adjuncts.

AFFECTIVE REACTIONS. One group of psychotic persons presents a picture that is almost the antithesis of the flatness of affect attributed to many schizophrenics. Such affective reactions are marked by an inability to cope with the experience of intense emotions. They are characterized by overt expression of intense emotion and by disturbance of mood. The two most easily identified reactions of this type are mania and depression. As with all forms of psychopathology, both manic and depressive reactions may vary with regard to severity.

In manic reactions, one observes extreme irritability, excitement, and elation. Behavioral indicators of mania include overtalkativeness, heightened motor activity, and flight of ideas. Although manic reactions vary widely in intensity, clinical workers have found it useful to distinguish between them and hypomanic reactions, which show less severe symptomatology. In acute manic episodes the patient may display such behavior as extreme boastfulness, expansive and unrealistic ambitions, boisterousness, and violence. Such patients require hospitalization to contain their psychomotor hyperactivity and to protect other people from their destructiveness and irritability. The high level of energy expenditure of the manic individual may reach a point at which his hyperactivity prevents him from sleeping and from performing simple functions such as sitting at a table in order to eat a meal. In severe manic episodes, both delusions and hallucinations may be in evidence. This description of an acute manic reaction illustrates many of the symptoms of this disorder (Karnosh and Zucker, 1945, p. 78):

> On admission she slapped the nurse, addressed the house physician as God, made the sign of the cross, and laughed loudly when she was asked to don the hospital garb. This she promptly tore into shreds. She remained nude for several hours before she was restrained in bed. She sang at the top of her voice, screamed through the window, and leered at the patients promenading in the recreation yard. She was very untidy and incontinent, smearing her excreta about the floor and walls. Frequently she would utter the words, 'God, Thou Holy One,' cross herself, laugh, and then give vent to vile expletives while she carried out suggestive movements of the body. She yelled for water, and, when this was proffered, she threw the tin cup across the room.

Acute manic episodes often have relatively sudden onsets. The primary precipitating factor usually appears to be a sudden reality demand or conflict that brings to the fore latent feelings of insecurity and lack of confidence. Manic episodes often appear to be distorted flights into reality. Whereas both the schizophrenic and the paranoid retreat into themselves, the manic person overtly lashes out in all directions to conquer the world and his felt inadequacy.

In depressive reactions, almost all of the symptoms of manic reactions are reversed. In these cases extreme depression of mood, motor retardation, uneasiness, apprehensiveness, and intense dejection are observed. Self-deprecation, self-condemnation, and guilt in a psychotic depression often reach delusional proportions. The result of these tendencies may be extreme regression in behavior and the very real danger of suicide. This self-description was provided by a person who experienced a psychotic depression (Custance, 1952, pp. 76–79):

> If I were asked to characterise in the briefest possible way, the whole experience of the depressive phase, I would describe it as a total reaction of repulsion between those fundamental poles of all being as we perceive it, which can be roughly and variously designated as the individual and the environment, the "I" and the "Not I," the ego and "the other," the perceiver and the perceived (including inner perceptions), or even as the soul and God. The basis of that repulsion seems to be fear, or "anxiety," to use the word generally employed to translate the Freudian concept of "Angst." And in the last analysis, as I have tried to show, the fear or anxiety seems to resolve itself at the climax into the fear of physical pain in the most terrifying form.
>
> There is something quite logical about this. . . . Certainly it seems to me that my reactions in the depressive phase are crude . . . or "total" . . . . There is little or no discrimination; everything is abhorrent to me, everything repels me, everything frightens me. My consciousness has, as it were, regressed to that earliest stage of the simple organism which, finding its environment unpleasant, wants to get away at all costs. I want to get away into the nothingness of annihilation, hence my suicidal impulses. Yet the unpleasantness of my situation thrusts itself upon my consciousness with all the intensity and with all the endless variety and refinement of torture made possible with the vast and intricate development of the nervous system in man. Infinite possibilities of horror and pain occur to me. If I have the slightest pain, that pain becomes in anticipation infinite and increasing, absorbing my whole consciousness. Every unpleasant reaction or thought is magnified to the limit. . . .
>
> . . . the sense of sin . . . in depression is dominating and all-pervading . . . . I can reach incredible extremes. . . . As far as I can analyze it, the sense of sin . . . was dominated by two factors. The first factor was a tremendous sense of repulsion . . . and guilt . . . . The second factor was an overwhelming sense of sexual sin.

An important difference between psychotic depressions and normal mourning reactions is that people recover from normal mourning reactions without the need for psychiatric help, and psychotic depressions show regression and delusional thoughts ("He died because of my evil thoughts about him"). What may be said concerning the prognosis and treatment of affective disorders? In general, the younger the individual, the more recent the outbreak of symptoms, and the more obvious the precipitating factors, the better is the prognosis. In general also, the prognosis for affective disorders is more favorable than for schizophrenia. Although both manic and depressive episodes tend to recur, there is usually a fair likelihood that they will subside and lead to a return to productive living. Somatic therapies such as electric shock treatment and drugs are often effective in dealing with affective psychoses. Electric shock therapy may show quite sudden improvements in depressed individuals.

The concept of affective disorders covers a wide territory. Some cases appear to have either obvious manic or depressive reactions to fairly specific and sudden precipitating factors. In others, disorders may occur within the context of a long history of obvious maladjustment reflected in manic or hypomanic, depressed, or other types of unusual reactions. In certain cases there may be cycles of manic and depressive reactions. The fact that manic-depressive cyclic reactions have been observed in the same individuals has suggested to some that the psychodynamics of manic and depressive reactions are similar.

INVOLUTIONAL REACTIONS. These disorders, which formerly went by the name of involutional melancholia, usually involve depressive or paranoid reactions, or both, during the middle and later years of life. They are discriminated not so much by their particular symptomatology as by the age of the individuals so diagnosed. Thus the involutional depressive individual who is 50 years of age may, in terms of his reactions, not appear markedly different from a younger person who is experiencing a depression of psychotic proportions. The American Psychiatric Association's classification system (*Diagnostic and Statistical Manual of Mental Disorders*, 1952) specifies that the diagnosis of involutional psychotic reaction is indicated in cases of psychosis in middle age which do not involve a history of prior overt psychotic manifestations.

Why depressive and paranoid reactions mark the middle years of life for many people is an interesting question. It seems reasonable that the events occurring during this period of life may be significant predisposing and precipitating factors. Most obvious of these is the biological slow down and deterioration that occurs in the 40s, 50s, and 60s. There are two facets to this slow down. First, there are the discernible biological changes within the individual, and second, the individual's interpretation of the deterioration in his physical capacities. Combined with his perception of his bodily changes during this period are other significant factors. For example, there usually is a decline in the socioeconomic status of the older person. Psychologically of greatest relevance is the fact that during these declining years the degree to which the individual's ambitions have been realized and his personal and social needs satisfied becomes evident. Death is a universal phenomenon. It is a termination of a life. How the person reacts to this impending event will be influenced by his underlying personality structure and the success he feels he has made of his life.

Although involutional psychotic reactions may not require a special set of explanatory principles, they do represent an increasingly pressing social problem. The number of older persons in society is progressively increasing. Concomitant with this, an increase in the incidence of involutional psychosis may be expected. Increased understanding of the nature of psychopathology and improvement in the acceptance and status of older people in our society will contribute to the solution of the problem of psychotic reactions during the middle years (Chapter 27).

CONCLUDING COMMENTS ON FUNCTIONAL PSYCHOSES. In the functional psychoses, as in organic psychotic reactions, there is a pathetic disintegration of behavioral competence. In organically based psychoses, there are known bodily disturbances; in functional ones, convincing organic bases are not in evidence. This, of course, does not mean that they may not be identified in the future. But for the present the functional psychoses are regarded as psychogenic disturbances, products of the interaction between individual differences in personality and the environments of childhood and adult life.

Clinical workers have frequently interpreted functional psychoses as reactions, albeit complex ones, to intense anxiety. As we shall presently see, a prime symptom in neurosis is anxiety of which the individual is well aware, and which may be perceived by him to be his major difficulty. In contrast, many psychotics do not show the usual indicators of anxiety, tension, and stress. When queried they may even deny feeling anxious and troubled. Indeed, when queried, they may be totally unresponsive. A prevalent assumption in the field of psychiatry is that the psychotic did experience intense anxiety in the past. This anxiety, it is believed, was warded off by means of immature defense mechanisms, such as denial or projection.

Fortunately or unfortunately, these defenses were reinforced because they reduced anxiety. It may not be desirable for a child to retreat into fantasies in order to escape the pressures of reality, but retreat may be the only avenue open to the novice. The troubled child may "solve" his problems in one special situation, for example, within the family, but he may be totally unprepared to cope with crises that come to the fore in other contexts. In this regard, it is interesting to note that the schizophrenic's problems tend to become acute when he reaches the late teens and early adulthood. Unless special circumstances are created that enable him to continue to lead the marginal life he had led within the family, he may be totally unable to adapt to a new and needed role, that of being an adult.

One hypothesized outcome of the premature defensive maneuvers of the potential psychotic is a severely impaired capacity to engage in meaningful social relationships, and what is more, an inability to derive any sense of pleasure from contacts with people. The complex fantasy life and psuedocommunity that many psychotics evolve may be for them a much safer and controllable stage upon which to act out and express thoughts and emotions than reality.

Psychoneurotic Disorders

Although diagnostic groupings are not mutually exclusive, there are many noticeable differences in the behaviors exhibited by psychoneurotic and psychotic persons. Most evident is the degree of psychopathology. Psychotic individuals display more maladjusted behavior than neurotics, and their ability to function without professional care and treatment is less than that of neurotics. Hallucinations and delusions, common characteristics of psychosis, occur infrequently in neurosis.

Granting that overt response patterns of persons described as neurotic and psychotic may differ widely, observers of deviant behavior have asked the question: Can these patterns be analyzed within a common frame of reference? Although neurotic and psychotic processes may ultimately be found to be basically different, it seems reasonable and parsimonious at the present time to consider that all overt behavior, regardless of degree of deviancy, can be understood in terms of a common set of principles and constructs. Most present-day clinical workers seem to believe that the behavior of the functional psychotic or neurotic is a product of inadequate techniques for coping with conflict and anxiety. The question thus arises: How might we account for the wide variability in degree of deviancy and maladjustment observed among neurotics and psychotics?

This question has often been approached by interpreting differences in degree of overt behavioral deviations as a function of (1) the amount of conflict and anxiety experienced by the individual, and (2) past learning and prior experience. We know from everyday life experiences that extreme conditions of stress often call forth extreme forms of behavior. In this sense, an hallucination or a retreat into fantasy might be conceived as one aspect of some individuals' solutions to psychological stress. It might be hypothesized that the more conflict and frustration (resulting in greater anxiety) present in the life of the individual and the less adequate his opportunities for acquiring adaptive responses, the greater will be the likelihood of regressive, socially inappropriate behavior occurring.

We have noted that anxiety may be either overt or covert. Psychotic individuals may appear to be surprisingly lacking in overt anxiety symptoms. That is, they do not show either the usual physiological signs of overt anxiety such as accelerated heart rate, perspiration, and fatigue, or the usual psychological signs of excessive worrying, feelings of inadequacy, and indecision. Overt anxiety is, however, one of the commonest symptoms of psychoneuroses.

ANXIETY REACTIONS. The condition called the anxiety reaction is marked by intense tension, which, however, may not be explicable in terms of discrete, immediate, traumatic stimuli. The person suffering from an anxiety reaction experiences diffuse and pervasive anxiety that permeates virtually every aspect of his day-to-day living. There are two major facets to this anxiety, one psychological and one physical. Psychologically, there is a state of chronic apprehension, fear, and dread of nameless dangers. The person with an anxiety reaction is well aware of his anxiety, but its bases for him are enigmatic. One is reminded of Franz Kafka's (1946) novel, *The Trial,* in which the hero is confronted with a trial, but is not informed of the charges brought against him. In the anxiety reaction the individual feels himself in danger, but he is unable to determine what that danger may be. Bodily there usually are many of the physiological concomitants of chronic, consciously experienced dread. These include sleeplessness, heightened autonomic activity, and disturbed digestive and sexual functioning.

Although persons with anxiety reactions may not be able to explain why they respond with anxiety to such a wide variety of situations, clinical workers have often inferred that this occurs because generalized environmental cues reinvoke previously repressed internal conflicts. Among the types of stimuli and situations that conceivably might evoke anxiety reactions are: (1) an increase in the likelihood of a breakthrough into consciousness of erotic or aggressive impulses; (2) reinvocation of prior traumatic experiences; (3) arousal of guilt and fear of retribution for transgressions; and (4) threats to affectional needs. These cases described by Cameron (1963, pp. 246–247) illustrate both the symptoms present in anxiety reactions and the use of psychotherapy in their treatment:

> A young man complained of feeling that something terrible was about to happen to him. For several months he had been continually fatigued. He had had pains in his head, his back and his legs. He suffered from frequent nightmares. Every once in a while he had sudden attacks of cardiac palpitation, in which he thought he was dying. During the course of psychotherapy it soon came out that he hated working for his aggressive, domineering father, but that he felt too afraid and too guilty to face up to the situation and quit his job. When psychotherapy brought this state of affairs out, the young man was soon able to face his father with the fact that he wanted another job and was determined to look for it. It goes without saying that the situation was complicated; but the psychotherapeutic help removed the young man from it, and his anxiety reactions disappeared.
>
> A young woman, whose fiance had postponed their wedding for the third time, began having bad dreams from which she would awaken frightened and sometimes crying. During the day she felt tense, angry and preoccupied. Her hands and feet became chronically cold and clammy. She developed a noticeable tremor in her fingers. Her menstrual periods became irregular. When, with the aid of psychotherapy, she recognized that her fiance was afraid of marrying her for his own personal reasons, she was able to handle the situation successfully.

What are the methods available to clinical workers in their efforts to overcome the symptoms of anxiety neurotics? Tranquilizing drugs have been found to be quite useful as a means of reducing many symptoms of overt anxiety. This pharmacological therapy, however, does not constitute a cure since its withdrawal results in reinstatement of the original symptoms. Psychotherapeutic intervention has been employed to reorient the thought processes and emotional life of the individual so that a relatively permanent resistance to symptoms will result. Persons with anxiety reactions often seem to benefit from psychotherapy, although a long period of treatment may be necessary in order to help patients overcome their maladaptive problem-solving techniques.

PHOBIC REACTIONS. The person with an anxiety reaction usually can tell only in vague terms what he is fearful of. He is perpetually anticipating a disaster but is unable to suggest what the nature of the disaster may be. The phobic individual presents a striking contrast to this situation. A phobia is a particular, irrational fear, and the person who has one is able to describe the basis for his discomfort.

The source of a phobia may be a situation, a person, or an object. There is probably no aspect of the environment that is exempt from the possibility of generating an intense dread. Among the commonest phobias are those involving fear of high places, enclosed spaces, open spaces, syphilis, dirt, and animals.

Everyone probably has a "pet" fear or two, which does not intrude very noticeably on day-to-day functioning. Children, particularly at certain ages—for example, the fourth and fifth years—may be prone to acquiring phobias. Phobias reach clinical proportions when they interfere with the individual's personal effectiveness. It is one thing to be afraid of dogs and another to be unable to walk down the street without being overcome by dread that a dog may appear. In the following example (Geer, 1964, p. 642) a 17-year-old girl developed a morbid fear of contracting a case of nits in her hair:

> The patient was reported as becoming anxious when she was in any "danger situation." Miss G.'s anxiety or fear continued until she told her mother about the event. When Miss G. told her mother about the "dangerous" event, a reduction of anxiety occurred even though a quarrel often began as her mother was agitated by these conversations. This unfortunate situation placed the patient in conflict between not telling her mother and feeling anxious or telling her mother and reducing the anxiety. The anxiety surrounding the phobic event was so strong, however, that she usually would tell her mother even though a quarrel often resulted.
>
> The phobia was of sufficient intensity that it interfered with Miss G.'s social life. Dating young men was restricted to those few she knew well enough to be sure they were neat and not a potential source of lice. Places where crowds gathered, such as movie theaters and dances, were avoided. In general, interpersonal relationships with strangers were avoided because they were anxiety arousing.
>
> There are two pieces of information relevant in explaining the possible etiology of the phobia. Miss G. had contracted a case of lice about 1.5 years prior to coming to the clinic. Her mother, a former beautician, successfully treated the condition which did not recur. The lice phobia began approximately 1 month following this experience. A second possible etiological factor is that the patient's mother is known to fear bugs. There have been instances when in the performance of her janitorial duties she has summoned help to remove a bug from a room before she could continue cleaning. It is quite likely that she reinforced her daughter's phobia in many subtle ways.

As with any symptom, there is usually no single, unambiguous cause of a phobia. Several factors usually contribute to the manifestation of symptoms. These include the present personality characteristics of the individual, his present status in life, and his history of prior experiences. An understanding of phobias requires an awareness of the complexity of these contributing factors. The history of the individual seems especially important because of the possibility that irrational fears may be conditioned responses.

Phobias have been treated by means of psychotherapy, the aim of which is to bring the individual to an awareness of the underlying needs and conflicts that result in the development of symptoms. As in all mental disorders, the more sudden the onset of symptoms, the more favorable is the prognosis. It is believed that a major hurdle in overcoming phobias through psychotherapy is the possibility of severe anxiety reactions coming to the fore as latent motivations come to the surface. Phobias have also been dealt with through support, reassurance, and re-education. Re-education often amounts essentially to desensitization through training and learning. In the desensitization process, the patient gradually becomes acclimated to stimuli associated with the phobic situation until he comes to respond appropriately. The goal of such re-education is to bring the patient to the point at which he can comfortably respond in the presence of previously phobic stimuli. Efforts to attain this level of comfort usually entail helping him to relax in situations that represent increasing intensities of the phobic stimulus. For example, in the case of the girl with a phobia about nits (Geer, 1964, p. 644) the patient was aided progressively to relax while thinking of the following situations:

1. Writing the words bug and lice.
2. While reading in school you notice a small bug on your book.
3. While walking down the sidewalk you notice a comb in the gutter.
4. You are at home watching television when an ad concerning dandruff removing shampoo comes on.
5. You are reading a *Readers Digest* article that goes into detail concerning the catching and curing of a case of lice.
6. You look at your desk top and notice several bobby pins and clips upon it.
7. You are in a department store, and the saleslady is fitting a hat on you.
8. At a store you are asked to try on a wig and you comply.
9. You are watching a movie and they show a scene where people are being deloused.
10. At school, in hygiene class, the teacher lectures on lice and bugs in people's hair.
11. A girl puts her scarf on your lap.
12. In a public washroom you touch the seat of a commode.
13. You are in a beauty shop having your hair set.

14. A girl sitting in front of you in school leans her head back on your books.

15. While sitting at home with your sister, she tells you that she used someone else's comb today.

16. While sitting in the local snack bar a friend tells you of her experiences when she had a case of lice.

17. You are combing your hair in the washroom when someone asks to borrow your comb.

18. A stranger asks to use your comb and continues to ask why not when you say no.

19. While standing looking at an ad in a store window, someone comes up beside you and puts their head near yours to see too.

20. A stranger in the washroom at school hands you her comb and asks you to hold it for her.

21. Your sister is fixing your hair when she drops the curlers on the floor, picks them up, and uses them in your hair.

22. A stranger notices a tangle in your hair and tries to help you by combing it out with her comb."

The desensitization phase was completed in 11 sessions. The procedure consisted of having the patient relax deeply and while remaining relaxed visualize the items in the hierarchy. The order of presentation of the items was from least frightening to most frightening. If the scene elicited anxiety, the patient signaled by raising a finger; and the scene was immediately discontinued. When a scene in its most frightening form had been visualized with no reported anxiety for three successive presentations, the item was discontinued and the next item begun.

Three months following the last interview and just prior to the writing of this report, Miss G. was contacted for a follow-up. At that time she reported that her phobia had not returned; she felt that it had lessened even more. She gave several examples of things that had occurred during the 3 months which formerly would have evoked considerable anxiety; however, they did not bother the patient. As one example, she reported that her new boyfriend had upon one occasion run his comb through her hair, yet she had felt only momentary anxiety which quickly disappeared. She also reported that two weeks prior to the interview she had been operated upon for appendicitis. She did not feel anxious sleeping in the hospital gowns and sheets that she knew strangers had used. She did report a feeling of anxiety when she anticipated placing her head on the pillow of the hospital bed. The anxiety rapidly passed, and she said that she had laughed with her mother over the incident.

The contrast between this learning or re-education approach to the treatment of phobias and the approach that emphasizes the need for the patient to achieve insight into his personal problems raises interesting questions: If phobic symptoms can be removed directly through desensitization or reinforcement of appropriate responses to phobic stimuli, why is the study of unconscious processes by means of often long periods of psychotherapy necessary? Is it necessary to go beyond the symptoms that the patient presents? If a person who is afraid of enclosed spaces can be brought, through re-education, desensitization, and reinforcement to enter comfortably and stay in them, need a behavior modifier or psychotherapist concern himself with the disturbances of thought and affect that may have given rise to the symptom in the first place?

Some researchers who study the modification of deviant behavior appear to have answered in the negative (Lundin, 1965; Krasner and Ullmann, 1965; Ullmann and Krasner, 1965). They feel that symptom removal or modification of behavior is the core problem of therapy with psychologically disturbed persons. For them the major techniques are those that researchers, active in the study of learning, have been developing for a number of years. These techniques first require careful study of the stimuli that give rise to deviant behavior and then experimental manipulation of environmental conditions that increase the frequency of appropriate responses by the patient.

This learning approach to behavior modification is appealing, parsimonious, and deserving of further exploration. Whether it is an altogether adequate approach to deviant behavior cannot be decided at the present time. A more dynamic position, such as psychoanalysis, also requires further study. This position emphasizes the relationship between overt behavior, such as a symptom, and covert behavior, thoughts, and conflicts of the individual. These two points of view can be integrated by focusing attention on both observable environmental stimuli associated with a particular response, and private thoughts and conflicts that may be antecedent to or correlated with deviant behavior. Such integration seems particularly reasonable when one considers that learning is important not only in the acquisition of overt responses but also in the development of a person's internal responses such as thoughts, fantasies, and conflicts. Core problems of a learning approach to deviant behavior involve accounting for the acquisition of both overt symptoms and internal, mediating responses that are related to symptoms.

OBSESSIVE-COMPULSIVE REACTIONS. A behavioral symptom may be viewed as a product of an individual's efforts to solve problems and to deal with anxieties aroused by conflicts and frustrations. Just as man exhibits creativity in the intellectual and esthetic spheres, he seems to use ingenuity in problem solving. We have observed that in anxiety reactions conflicts and anxiety have broad, pervasive behavioral consequences, and that in phobias anxiety seems to become channelized into well-circumscribed areas, namely those associated with fear-arousing stimuli such as tall buildings or dogs. Obsessive-compulsive reactions are characterized less by avoidance of certain external stimuli than by the recurrence of particular thoughts and actions.

What is common to both obsessions and compulsions is motivated repetition, either of words and ideas or of rituals and response patterns. Although some cases may show a picture mainly of obsessive thinking and others a picture predominantly of compulsive acts, one characteristic permits us to consider them as manifestations of the same process. This characteristic is the irrational nature of the repetitive events. What rational basis might there be for a person's inability to get the cliché, "East, west, home's best," out of his mind? What rational basis might there be for the need to step on every third crack in the sidewalk? Clearly this sort of response is neither planful nor rational. Furthermore, it does not seem easily interpretable as a product of a simple learning process. As described by Sherman (1938, pp. 226–227) this case of a 13-year-old boy illustrates many of the characteristics of obsessive-compulsive neuroses:

This boy's excessive cleanliness first showed itself at the age of thirteen, when it was noticed that he washed his hands many times during the day. Later he began to bathe frequently. Frequently he stayed two or three hours in the bathtub. On a number of occasions he daubed iodine on his hands and face. He told his parents that he had scratched himself and wanted to prevent an infection. In addition to iodine, he had bought mercurochrome and other antiseptics for use in "emergencies." He also used a boric acid solution to wash his eyes every evening. The parents stated that he refused to play ordinary games with other children because he did not want to soil his hands. When asked to explain his concern regarding cleanliness, he stated that he realized that he washed more than other boys, but that in his case there were real reasons. He believed that his skin was of such a texture that it retained dirt and germs, and he therefore was forced to wash and scrub himself.

No amount of persuasion was successful in deterring the boy from this behavior until his original conflicts began to be solved. He stated that he had been greatly worried about his guilt regarding his previous activities with other boys. His parents discovered that he took part in sex play and had punished him. They had frequently lectured him on the evils of "immoral" behavior and on one occasion, when he was nine, made him sign a pledge never to smoke or drink even beer. They also told him how some terrible diseases result from masturbation. . . . He stated that he had "sworn off" masturbating on many occasions, and after each time he masturbated he felt thoroughly ashamed of himself. He also believed that he was deficient in character and will-power because he could not stop. He stated, "I know it's a dirty habit and if anyone finds me out they will think terrible things about me." After many interviews and much discussion, he began to change his attitude regarding the immorality of his past behavior and the possible consequences of his supposed moral transgressions. His excessive cleanliness gradually decreased, and he was able to take part in the activities of other boys without feelings of unpleasantness from soiling his hands and clothes.

Phobias are in many ways similar to obsessive-compulsive patterns and, in fact, the two patterns may comprise the syndrome of particular persons. A phobia, after all, is a fear of an external object. Obsessions and compulsions, in the same vein, may be viewed as fears of the consequences of not thinking certain thoughts and of not performing certain acts. Clinical study of persons suffering from obsessive-compulsive reactions has suggested that their lives are frequently characterized by strong conflicts over conformity, the necessity to learn rigid, uncompromising standards of morality and self-evaluation, and the need for expiation of guilt over failure to adhere fully to social and family mores. Observations of the overt behavior of obsessive-compulsive persons suggest a picture of extreme conscientiousness, rigidity, and conventionality. Intensive clinical study of such personalities indicates that they have strong barriers to acceptance of their own wishes and fantasy life.

Consider the dutiful and loving son who cannot stop thinking about finding his mother murdered or stabbed. It is not difficult to imagine the guilt that such a thought might stimulate. Then why does the individual persist in its repetition? Does not this sort of horrifying thought seem completely out of context within the framework of the dutiful and loving son? Indeed, it does. It may be that through such repetitive, unacceptable thoughts an individual may actually be expressing a wish or motivation which, if consciously recognized and accepted, would result in overwhelming anxiety.

From a treatment standpoint, obsessive-compulsive disorders are often difficult to modify. It seems clear that the development of effective therapeutic techniques for the reduction of obsessive-compulsive behavior will require increased understanding of (1) thought processes and fantasies that may produce them, and (2) complex learning processes, which may lead to the attachment of unconscious conflicts to conscious obsessive thoughts and compulsive acts. This understanding will be enhanced when a number of pressing general questions can be answered: What sort of stresses exacerbate behavioral symptoms? To what extent are symptoms learned reactions? What historical variables, such as parental characteristics, environmental events, and socioeconomic background, are correlated with the development of different types of symptoms?

NEUROTIC DEPRESSIVE REACTIONS. Neurotic depressive reactions are often referred to as reactive depressions, that is, depressions that are reactions to environmental setbacks and stresses. Both neurotic and psychotic depressions are affective disturbances. They are marked by extreme dejection, self-deprecatory thoughts, and anxiety. Depressed individuals are low in self-confidence and they tend to regard themselves as unworthy, unlikable people. Neurotic depressives, however, do not experience the delusional thoughts characteristic of psychotic depressives and their ideation is less disordered.

An important point of difference between these two types of depressive reactions relates to precipitating factors. In neurotic depressives the precipitating factors are much more easily identifiable than in psychotic ones. The specific precipitating factors of neurotic depressions show considerable variety. Separation from or permanent loss of persons toward whom the individual has a strong attachment, social and vocational setbacks, and increases in responsibilities often appear to set off neurotic depressive reactions. Stimulated by such precipitating conditions, neurotic depressives may respond with behavioral regression as well as with characteristic dejection and masochistic self-accusations.

The onset of a neurotic depression often comes as a surprise to friends and relatives. Prior to its occurrence, an individual may appear to be quite well-adjusted and adequate in his social relations. Because of the suddenness of symptom onset and because of these patients' susceptibility to emotional support from others, short-term psychotherapy is often quite effective. As for all types of depressions, suicide must be considered as a possible result. Electric shock treatments are often dramatically effective in helping the severely depressed patient to "snap back" from his moroseness. Although most neurotic depressives do not require hospitalization, it becomes necessary in severe cases.

CONVERSION REACTIONS. The four types of neurotic disorders so far considered can, at some risk of oversimplification, be divided into two groups. Anxiety and depressive reactions, which constitute one of these groups, involve relatively high levels of consciously experienced anxiety and guilt. These reactions are at times set off by quite specific precipitating events and are marked by tension and feelings of dejection and worthlessness. Another group of neurotic reactions, which includes phobias, obsessions, and compulsions, does not seem to involve such high levels of affective output. These reactions may be quite pervasive and seemingly unrelated to specific precipitating factors. Anxiety and depressive reactions seem similar in that overt expressions of affect and emotion are present in both and this group of patients is generally more responsive to reassurance and affection than are phobic and obsessive-compulsive patients. The latter group seem to develop fairly specific thoughts and overt responses which may contribute to the reduction of anxiety. These individuals of both groups are susceptible to overconcentrating their tensions in one area, and their neurotic maneuvers may result in rigid patterns of living; and in view of the unpredictability of life stresses they may ultimately be unsuccessful in avoiding anxiety. But it does seem true that, at least over the short term, the symptoms of phobic and obsessive-compulsive patients do succeed in reducing conscious anxiety.

Another group of neurotics, persons who show conversion reactions, is perhaps even more successful at warding off conscious anxiety. The term conversion reaction, which is synonymous with the term conversion hysteria, refers to cases where no actual organic basis for bodily symptoms is evident. The following case described by Coon and Raymond (1940, pp. 224–225) illustrates this type of reaction:

> Since a child, this young woman cherished vague and beautiful ideas of her own charm, refinement and artistic ability. Her ambitions were stimulated and fostered by an admiring family circle, a protected life, and a group of friends whose admittance to friendship, consciously or unconsciously, depended on their uncritical admiration. The more or less deliberate purpose of her striving was to insure and magnify the admiration and uncritical affection of her friends through the talented use of a great voice. . . .
>
> Now the day approaches when her voice is to be tested, not by the admiring circle, but by a critical professional teacher who is to determine the course of her vaguely planned career. This day has approached before, but she has always had a severe headache or a bad throat or some other rather sudden but not infectious ailment which has prevented her meeting the test. . . .
>
> Finally, an act of will, or perhaps an access of ambition . . . and she actually goes to the test. She passes the earlier and simpler parts of the audition with fair credit, though with some trepidation. Then comes a more crucial, a more important, and far more difficult step in the trial, involving an uncompromising test of real quality of voice and real ability of technique. Something happens. Her voice cracks at the very beginning of this important step, her throat hurts, she has suddenly become hoarse. It is impossible

to carry the test further. She explains quite honestly to the teacher that she has a very delicate throat and that she did not realize it was in such shocking condition; furthermore, she ought not to have attempted the test. She goes home to much genuine and deserved sympathy. She becomes voiceless for several days or weeks.

. . . . and she rationalizes the episode as follows: The test, because she took it when her throat was in poor condition, has strained her voice. Of course, the teacher should have known better. Even after she refers to it sadly as the time when her voice was strained by an injudicious and premature test to which she was led by her inexorable courage and ambition. Furthermore, she says now, that because of this accident she is unable ever to sing well, the inference being that she did sing well before, which is probably not the fact, as her voice, though apparently quite normal, is of very small calibre and mediocre quality. However, the automatism of escape has "saved her face." It has saved the pretty picture of her great artistic ability, and has transferred the vision of her powerful and charming performance from the future to the past and, furthermore, it has given her a perfectly satisfactory explanation and justification in perpetuity for the manifest discrepancy between the greatness of her talent and the hopeless mediocrity of her best possible performance.

The symptoms of conversion reactions fall into three broad categories. Some conversion reactions involve sensory defects, such as complete or partial loss of vision and hearing. Still others involve motor disabilities such as loss of speech, tremors, and paralyses. A third set of symptoms are visceral in nature, for example, the presence of a persistent lump in the throat, headaches, and difficulty in breathing. Are there characteristics common to these types of hysterical or conversion symptoms? Conversion reactions are often misdiagnosed. In the purest cases in which there are not the slightest organic complications, misdiagnosis is not as likely. But in many instances some organic factors, albeit often peripheral and minimal, may be present. In such cases, it may not be easy to distinguish with certainty between psychologically motivated and organically determined symptoms.

There are several characteristics that seem to hold regardless of the particular conversion symptoms manifested. One of these, which helps to simplify the problem of diagnosis, is the degree to which the symptoms observed seem "illogical" from a medical standpoint. For example, certain kinds of anesthesias (loss of sensitivity) are quite inexplicable in terms of the way in which the nervous system is understood to function. Often these anesthesias seem to be more related to articles of clothing associated with parts of the body than to neurological functioning, for example, glove, stocking, and skull cap anesthesias.

Another general characteristic of conversion symptoms is that they may cease to be present under certain conditions. For example, areas of the body that may be relatively insensitive to painful stimuli during waking hours may respond normally when the individual is asleep. Also, hysterical symptoms may disappear as a result of hypnotic suggestions. Perhaps the most frequently mentioned characteristic of conversion reactions is *belle indifference.* Conversion neurotics seem to show a rather matter-of-fact, grin-and-bear-it type of reaction to their somatic disturbances. For example, whereas most persons who experience a loss of perceptual sensitivity or motor capability show considerable anxiety, conversion patients seem to be more intellectually than emotionally aware of their troubles. It is this *belle indifference* that has suggested to many clinical workers that conversion symptoms may be defensive in nature and may serve to reduce overt anxiety.

All of us at one time or another display varying degrees of anxiety, depression, phobias, obsessions, and compulsions; psychologically based somatic symptoms are also common occurrences. However, neurotic conversion symptoms are usually quite dramatic, relatively long lasting, and result in much more debilitation and dependence on others, as in hysterical blindness, than do more "normal" conversion reactions. Reference is commonly made to the role of secondary gain in conversion reactions, as contrasted with the hypothesized primary gain of anxiety reduction. It is also true that some conversion reactions are effective in removing individuals from personally threatening situations. Among the most dramatic cases in which this has been observed are those that were referred to during the First World War as shell shock cases. These cases involved a variety of types of conversion reactions among men who had been subjected to combat. Whereas in the First World War such cases often led to the decision to remove disabled, shell shocked soldiers from battle permanently, experience gathered during the Second World War suggested that short-term psychotherapy and short-term removal from combat often led to a speedy return to combat effectiveness.

Because persons with conversion tendencies tend to be highly suggestible, hypnotic suggestions are often employed to remove or reduce the severity of conversion symptoms. The patient, subject to psychotherapy that is designed to give him insight into possible unconscious bases for his conversion symptoms, often requires treatment over an extended period of time. Conversion neurotics may be very resistant to modifying their behavior because their symptoms are, despite the high price, so successful in reducing anxiety and also in providing secondary gain.

DISSOCIATIVE REACTIONS. Dissociative reactions are in many ways similar to conversion reactions. In fact, until fairly recently both were referred to diagnostically as forms of conversion hysteria or hysterical disorders. However, the characteristics of patients who display dissociative patterns seem sufficiently distinctive to merit separate consideration.

The symptoms of dissociative reactions are indeed distinctive and dramatic. Cameron has defined dissociative reactions as ". . . attempts to escape from excessive tension and anxiety by separating off some parts of personality function from the rest" (Cameron, 1963, p. 341). The form of this separation determines the particular symptom pattern that becomes manifest. As in conversion reactions, symptom formation in dissociative states has been interpreted in terms of the failure of defenses to keep intense covert conflicts from intruding upon day-to-day functioning. It has been hypothesized that in conversion reactions, internal conflict is expressed symbolically in the form of bodily symptoms. Clinical data suggest that in dissociative reactions, conflict resolution may take the form of escape or estrangement either from oneself or from reality. The following case described by Rosen and Gregory (1965, p. 241) illustrates this dissociative estrangement:

An extroverted, flirtatious, rather immature 21-year-old married woman, the mother of a young infant, on awakening from the anesthetic after an appendectomy, experienced complete amnesia for the previous five years. At 16 she had been briefly unconscious following an automobile accident and she now believed that she was hospitalized because of the accident. Taken home a few days after the appendectomy, she did not recognize her husband or child. When told who they were she did not challenge their identities and said they were "nice." While convalescing, she greatly enjoyed reading magazines designed for teen-agers. The amnesia and five-year regression were responses to an immediate stress situation: her husband was about to graduate from college and take a job in the family business in his native city. She did not want to leave her friends and she feared living under the watchful eye of her mother-in-law, a very dominant and critical woman. Just before the surgery, the mother-in-law had come to stay with the family and help them get ready to move. She had been outspokenly critical of her daughter-in-law's housekeeping habits and juvenile manner of dress. The amnesic episode psychologically eliminated the mother-in-law's existence, for if the patient had never married there could be no mother-in-law. There were also no marital responsibilities, no child to take care of and no need to leave her friends; instead she could live the teen-age existence that corresponded to her personality structure. The amnesia cleared up readily, however, with hypnotic treatment after administration of Sodium Amytal.

Dissociative reactions include some of the most exotic forms of deviant behavior. Cases of psychogenic or neurotic amnesia exhibit total or partial loss of memories of past events and experiences. Fugue states also involve loss of memory, but for present rather than for past experiences. In the fugue state the individual flees from his conflicts not only through forgetting but also through actual flight from his present environment. Cases of split or multiple personality perhaps best exemplify Cameron's definition of a dissociative reaction. In them, the individual may alternately exhibit two or more quite different patterns of personality and behavior, the Dr. Jekyll and Mr. Hyde type of personality alternation.

The most striking and general characteristic in dissociative states is the splitting off of certain mental processes from the rest of psychological functioning. Thus in the amnesic person, conspicuous segments of his life may be inaccessible to him. In fugue states, the individual may take up a totally new life which is apparently independent of past activities and responsibilities. In multiple personalities, the individual seems to contain within himself two or more personalities whose contact with one another is seemingly minimal or nonexistent. In somnambulism, the sleepwalker may emit behavior over which he appears to have little or no control.

An interesting comparison exists between dissociative patterns and conversion reactions. The latter contains the development of somatic symptoms which the individual places on exhibition and which may provide considerable secondary gain. In the former, the outstanding characteristic is total escape from conflict through the isolation of certain memories and thought from the rest of psychological functioning. In the adult dissociated personality, as in the young child, reality and unreality may seem to live side by side. All persons probably show some minimal symptoms of dissociation. Usually, however, tendencies toward dissociation are not overwhelming and may be manifest only in occasional daydreams and fantasies. In the seriously dissociated individual, particularly in cases of multiple personality, fantasy material may actually be directly acted out when stress becomes intense. A person who tends to isolate affect and impulses and to deny reality may, under the pressure of anxiety-arousing events, display blatant dissociation. Thus, a fugue may occur when an individual is suddenly confronted with new and pressing responsibilities, as in marriage, or the birth of a child; or an amnesic episode may ensue upon loss of a personally meaningful relationship, as in the death of a parent.

The behavior of dissociated individuals reflects much more of break with reality than the behavior of those with other disorders considered to be neurotic. Although dissociated personalities and persons who develop conversion reactions may have a number of characteristics in common, such as a high degree of egocentricity and naiveté, it is clear that the former manage to maintain social and affectional ties, whereas the latter may not be able to achieve this social stability. Because of the bizarre quality of their adaptive devices, dissociated individuals seem in some respects to be closer to psychotic than to neurotic persons. But as the bizarre mechanisms of dissociated individuals usually show up as sharp eruptions rather than as permanent social disabilities, one must be cautious in placing such individuals in either category. At the present time, knowledge of the meaning and treatment of symptoms of dissociation is not well developed and empirical study of the symptoms constitutes an intriguing challenge for experimental psychopathologists.

Psychosomatic or Psychophysiologic Disorders

Psychosomatic or psychophysiologic reactions have come under intensive study only in recent years. What is particularly dramatic and intriguing about them is that they seem to be psychological conditions that lead to disturbances in bodily functioning and result in actual tissue damage. Thus, they are to be distinguished from conversion reactions, which do not result in organic damage. Symptoms in psychosomatic disorders have a clearly delineated physiological basis and usually are referable to a particular organ system. Thus, gastrointestinal, psychosomatic reactions may involve the development of peptic ulcers and problems in elimination as well as other difficulties related to the digestive system. Cardiovascular reactions are exemplified by hypertension, fainting spells, and frequent and debilitating headaches. Numerous psychophysiologic skin, musculoskeletal, respiratory, and other systemic disorders have also been described in the literature. The following is an example described by Cameron (1963, p. 680) of a gastrointestinal reaction:

> A businessman, aged thirty-five, had been working hard under great pressure to build up his advertising agency. He was a typical "achiever" or "go-getter," full of energy, initiative and push, never able to relax, and driving himself to the limit. When one of his close associates left the firm to establish a rival agency, the patient developed a peptic ulcer. To a psychiatric consultant he at first presented a bland picture of indifference; but after reaching the point where he was able to express angry resentment over what he considered a betrayal by his former associate, his medical course showed marked improvement.

Present conceptions of psychosomatic disorders suggest that they develop in response to emotional stress in interaction with the bodily condition of the person. From this point of view, the organ system most affected by stress would be expected to be the one that is the weakest constitutionally. Another, not antithetical, interpretation of psychosomatic disorders centers on this question: Are there different personality characteristics associated with various types of psychosomatic reactions? This question has led to efforts to isolate problems and conflicts peculiar to particular disorders. For example, persons suffering from duodenal ulcers have been described in terms of having an overt ambitiousness and a covert need for dependency gratification. Hypertensive cases have been described in terms of chronic underlying hostility associated with overt friendliness and self-control. Although these interpretations may be correct, it seems desirable at the present time to emphasize that a particular psychosomatic disorder is probably a joint function of the biology of the individual, his personality development, and the social roles in which he finds himself involved. These three factors may be operative in varying proportions from case to case.

Perhaps the major contribution of recent research in psychosomatics is evidence that suggests that emotional reactions of the individual may lead to irreversible physical symptoms, and that subjective experiences, thoughts, and feelings may have consequences for the ways in which the body functions. One might raise the question: In what ways do psychosomatic disorders differ from other classifications of deviant functioning? Those displaying psychoneurotic disorders seem to have much in common with individuals displaying psychosomatic disorders. Both those with psychosomatic ailments and neurotics seem to be in good contact with reality and to experience relatively high levels of anxiety. But the dramatic difference between them is that whereas neurotics seem to express their conflicts symbolically in the form of behavioral symptoms, psychosomatic symptoms are physiological in nature.

PERSONALITY AND THE CLASSIFICATION OF BEHAVIOR

In our treatment of psychopathology we have not sought to include every part of the spectrum of deviant behavior. We have not endeavored to examine in depth all forms of psychopathology or to review completely their many interpretations. What is the meaning of the symptoms of the mentally disturbed person? Is deviant behavior an outgrowth of deviant thinking and an affective life of turmoil? Or may symptoms be viewed simply as acquired responses susceptible to change, as are other types of overt behavior? One interpretation of deviant behavior is that its understanding requires exploration of the inner life of the individual and its modification requires reorganization of that inner life. Most of the theorists considered in Part 1 share this interpretation, even though they may disagree sharply on the nature of the inner life of the individual. Thus, for example, Freudians and Rogerians disagree on many questions of tactics in psychotherapy but they share the belief that the exploration of deviant behavior requires analysis of the cognitive and emotional aspects of the personal world of the individual (Chapters 2 and 5).

Many of the learning views described in Chapter 4 are based on the assumption that neurotic, psychotic, or other types of deviant behavior are acquired in ways similar to the acquisition of less troublesome deviant behavior (Ban, 1964; Bandura and Walters, 1963; Krasner and Ullmann, 1965). The most extreme expression of this point of view is found among followers of Skinner who eschew study of the inner life of the individual in favor of direct attacks on undesirable behavior (Lundin, 1961, 1965; Skinner, 1953). Although most learning theorists do not go this far, most tend to emphasize changing overt behavior directly rather than through a process of personal insight and cognitive reorganization.

The type of rapprochement possible between these insight and direct-action orientations will be determined by future research on psychopathology. It is an interesting fact that in recent years theoretical efforts have been made to integrate them. It seems possible that forms of psychopathology can be approached meaningfully in terms of the combination of the determinants of a disordered inner life and of particular learning experiences. The relative importance of each of these determinants can be viewed as varying from case to case. This might suggest the need for combinations of reflective and direct-action therapeutic strategies (Haley, 1963; London, 1964; Mowrer, 1960*a*, 1960*b*, 1965).

A primary aim of this chapter has been to introduce the student of personality to deviant behavior as a concept and to describe several classifications of behavioral deviance. Why is it desirable to classify deviant behavior? Classification accomplishes two practical objectives. First, it provides a common terminology, which facilitates communication among clinical workers. Second, a common descriptive language makes it possible for these workers in the field to keep records and statistical tabulations of the incidence of mental disorder. Why is it desirable to employ the particular classification system propounded by the American Psychiatric Association (*Diagnostic and Statistical Manual of Mental Disorders,* 1952) in the United States? This question probably cannot be answered in a totally satisfying way. The answer most frequently given is that this system, although it has many obvious shortcomings, is the best descriptive system so far developed. Although we would not deny the legitimacy of this answer, it is necessary to be aware of the gaps between the present system and the perfect one toward which we aspire.

Diagnosis of an individual case in terms of the American Psychiatric Association system has four aims. One is to present a description of the problem involved and an indication of the severity of the symptoms. Another is to suggest the etiology or basis for the symptoms. Two additional aims are to provide indications of the prognosis or likely outcome of the disorder and of the treatment appropriate to the case. A weakness of the system stems from the fact that evidence concerning the many facets of maladjustment is often either meager or nonexistent. Clinical usage of the present classification seems justified primarily on the practical grounds of the need to respond to the mental health problems that people manifest and to develop a common professional vocabulary.

From a scientific point of view, the most urgent necessity is for intensive research into the nature of deviant behavior, its antecedents, and sequels. If this research can expand our knowledge of the various forms of psychopathology, more reliable and useful diagnostic categories can eventually be evolved. Work toward this end could proceed in any of a number of directions. One direction might involve attempts to analyze carefully cases that have been diagnosed in terms of the present classification system. This might take the form of intensive study of one or a few types of persons, for example, paranoid schizophrenics. One reason for ambiguity in the American Psychiatric Association system is that it does not do justice to the complex of characteristics that define a given case. If research can break down the heterogeneity that exists among persons presently considered to be in the category of paranoid schizophrenics, improvements in classifications could be expected to follow.

Efforts toward increasing the understanding of deviant behavior need not necessarily proceed within the context of the American Psychiatric Association or any other existing comprehensive system of classification. In view of the complexities involved in the nature and evaluation of deviant behavior, more molecular research might also be attempted. Such research might be directed toward understanding particular types of responses, such as suicidal attempts, delusions, and irrational fears, irrespective of existing diagnostic categories. The psychological study of complex human behavior is in an early stage of development and new approaches to it on a number of conceptual levels would seem to be desirable.

29

Personality Assessment and Deviant Behavior

The clinician requires considerable contact with a patient in order to make efficient use of the present psychiatric classification system. He may interview, observe, and study the patient for varying periods of time. From his impression of the patient's condition and the etiology, prognosis, and indicated method of treatment, he forms a diagnosis of the problem. Because different clinicians use various diagnostic procedures and because their theoretical orientations are often quite distinctive, the reliability of their assessment procedures may be disturbingly low. The diagnosis of schizophrenia, for example, is presented more often in some hospitals than in others. Are there more reliable and convenient personality assessment procedures than the present classification system?

Psychometric indices of personality may very well prove to be an effective vehicle for this purpose. Researchers in assessment seek to improve classification through the identification and measurement of variables that have predictive power. But that inevitable stumbling block appears: By what criterion or criteria does one judge predictive power? Assume the construction of a test to tap the level of consensual validation or contact with reality among persons who display deviant behavior. If the scoring system is both convenient and reliable, of what value is the test? By what standard shall its usefulness be evaluated?

For most personal characteristics there is no single criterion of predictive power that is superior to all other potential criteria. One's interests and the problems perceived to be important usually determine the predictions attempted. Thus, we might concern ourselves with the relationship of individual differences in reality testing to the ability to earn a living or the ability to live outside a hospital setting or the ability to control hallucinatory tendencies. Whether any of these relationships prove to be of practical predictive value, in the sense of being immediately useful to practicing clinical workers, is not crucial from a scientific standpoint. *What is decisive is that attempts at relating measures of individual differences to behavior increase our understanding of behavior that requires clinical attention.*

In a sense the relationship of personality assessment methods to psychopathology is comparable to the relationship of assessment methods to human development. Assessment procedures are used to study the development of children and significant persons in their lives, such as parents and teachers. The aim of these procedures is to shed light on variables that may be important in our understanding of how behavioral and attitudinal changes eventuate over time. In psychopathology, similar procedures may be employed to shed light on behavioral and attitudinal factors correlated with the emergence of deviant behavior. Thus while personality assessment can be considered as a somewhat distinct field investigation, it may also be viewed as a methodology that is applicable to a wide variety of psychological problems. Let us review some examples of personality assessment that have been applied to problems of psychopathology.

PERSONALITY ASSESSMENT APPROACHES TO PSYCHOPATHOLOGY

A Study of Duodenal Ulcers

Duodenal ulcers result from consumption of tissue in the duodenum by digestive juices. Clinical evidence suggests that the presence of duodenal ulcers in people is related to their gastric secretions, their psychological make-up, and the life stresses they experience. Although one never knows when traumatic events may occur in the life of an individual, it *is* possible to assess at any given time his physiological and psychological make-up. Would it not be of considerable interest and value to use these assessments as a basis for estimating probabilities of the incidence of ulcers in people? Were it possible to do this it would surely be both a practical and theoretically useful accomplishment.

Weiner, Thaler, Reiser, and Mirsky (1957) have reported a psychological investigation of duodenal ulcers that bears directly on this possibility. These investigators noted that many patients suffering from duodenal ulcers secreted more pepsinogen, one of the gastric juices, than persons not so afflicted. There is reason to believe, however, that though hypersecretion of pepsinogen is a significant factor in the incidence of duodenal ulcers, it is not the sole determinant. On the basis of past evidence concerning duodenal ulcers, Weiner et al. reasoned that predicting the occurrence of duodenal ulcers would require knowledge of individuals' psychological and physiological characteristics and knowledge of traumatic environmental events which might precipitate duodenal lesions.

To evaluate this interpretation of duodenal ulcers, Weiner et al. measured the pepsinogen secretions of over 2,000 army inductees. Two groups of these men were selected for intensive psychological assessment, those inductees whose pepsinogen secretion levels were in the upper 15 per cent and lower 9 per cent of the total subject pool. These groups were considered to consist of hypersecretors and hyposecretors, respectively. The assessment process involved two phases. Hyper- and hyposecretors were subjected to intensive medical study of their gastrointestinal tracts and were administered a battery of personality tests. These tests included both projective and self-report instruments. In addition, the social histories of subjects were obtained.

Medical study of the hyper- and hyposecretors of pepsinogen confirmed the relationship of the level of secretion of digestive juices to the incidence of ulcers. Every one of the inductees found to have gastrointestinal ulcers belonged to the group of hypersecretors. Having established this medical relationship, the researchers next asked: Do hyper- and hyposecretors differ in terms of psychological make-up as assessed through personality tests? As a result of their findings and clinical observations, Weiner et al. considered the hypersecretor group to include persons prone to the development of duodenal ulcers and the hyposecretor group to include persons not prone in this respect. Could assessment data permit correct identification of persons in these two groups?

Based on hypotheses from previous research and clinical experience, they set up a number of tentative criteria, or scoring categories, of responses on the personality tests that might accomplish this task. Although a number of these turned out not to be predictors of hyper- and hyposecretors, a group of 20 criteria was remarkably useful in the prediction task. Of 120 men in the two extreme pepsinogen groups only 18 could not, on the basis of blind or independent personality assessment, be identified as hyper- or hyposecretors. It is important to realize this highly significant separation of the two groups was due, not to one or a few assessed characteristics, but to a constellation of 20 variables. Thus, it is clear that the researchers who carried out this study were confronted with and were aware of the fact that the problem under study was multidimensional rather than unidimensional.

The evidence gathered suggested that hyper- and hyposecretors did not differ simply with regard to level of psychological adjustment. They differed with regard to the types of anxieties, conflicts, and defenses that seemed to be important in their adjustments to life. The psychological make-up of hypersecretors appeared to include strong dependency feeling toward others and a need to be compliant and passive in relation to authority figures. Hyposecretors, on the other hand, seemed to be people with strong needs to express hostile impulses and a greater capacity to express anger overtly. An interesting difference between the two groups was that hyposecretors were more prone on self-report indices than hypersecretors to indicate preoccupation with bodily complaints.

Since all the subjects in this research had been studied in the early stages of induction, one might legitimately wonder whether some might develop ulcers during the often stressful period of basic training, and if so, whether personality assessment procedures could identify them. In fact, all of the men who developed duodenal ulcers during the period of basic training had been classified correctly on the basis of psychological characteristics.

Reviewing their suggestive findings, Weiner, Thaler, Reiser, and Mirsky (1957, pp. 8–9) came to the following conclusions:

> The data . . . reveal a remarkable correlation between the concentration of pepsinogen in the serum and specific personality characteristics of a group of young men inducted into the army. The group of subjects with high serum pepsinogen concentrations show intense needs that are principally "oral" in nature and which are exhibited in terms of wishing to be fed, to lean on others, and to seek close bodily contact with others. Satisfaction of these needs for external support and external sources for satiation is attempted by many means. When such attempts fail, the resultant frustration arouses anger that cannot be expressed lest there ensue a loss of supply for their needs. Consequently these subjects usually do not make complaints or express any feelings of anger.
>
> In contrast to the above, the subjects with low concentration of pepsinogen in the serum exhibit fewer problems about and less dependency on external sources of supply and support. They are more narcissistic and exhibit more problems relative to internal, bodily discomfort, and react to the sources

of the discomfort with intense hostility which they express relatively freely. They show evidences of a disturbance in language style that is characterized by elaboration and pretentiousness. Some of the subjects show a hostile feminine identification which they defend themselves against by a masculine overcompensation. Projective defenses against anxiety are common. . . .

Although it is possible to postulate that the inherited secretory capacity of the stomach plays a role in determining not only the psychological development of the infant but also his physiological predisposition, it does not account for the marked individual differences that characterize the manner in which the needs described above are handled. Study of these individual differences suggest that the vagaries of each person's life experiences determine the manner in which impulses and life experiences determine the manner in which impulses and wishes are mastered, whereas the hypersecretor's persistent wishes for support and succor from the external environment are determined by early childhood factors. The manner in which he handles these wishes is determined by all his life experiences, that is, by the factors that determine his integrative capacity.

The research of Weiner et al. nicely illustrates the value of multileveled approaches to behavior and shows the relationships of psychological and situational factors in one specific psychosomatic symptoms complex, duodenal ulcers. It suggests the possibility of practical application of personality assessment techniques to the prediction of psychopathology. An important contribution of this research would appear to be the questions it raises for future investigation. What is the contribution of body chemistry to individual differences in personality? What are the historical behavioral antecedents of characteristics assessed through psychological techniques?

A Quantitative Study of Deviant Behavior

The foregoing investigation involved analysis of the relationship of personality and physiological characteristics to the specific medical problem of duodenal ulcers. This level of specificity is not characteristic of most functional disorders. In both neuroses and psychoses, symptomatology and behavioral characteristics may be quite diffuse.

We have described the American Psychiatric Association classification system as an effort to develop a means of describing patients' characteristics. It was observed, however, that there is reason for dissatisfaction with the reliability of usual clinical diagnostic procedures. A series of personality assessment studies carried out by Lorr, Klett, and McNair (1963) illustrates one psychological approach to improvement of the diagnostic process. Defining a syndrome as a set of related symptoms and deviant behaviors, Lorr, Klett, and

McNair devised objective procedures with which to define a number of diagnostic groupings. In carrying out their research they dwelt primarily on behavior deviations of rather extreme psychotic proportions. Building on prior studies, they hypothesized the existence of ten psychotic syndromes or symptom complexes. To tap these ten syndromes they devised a rating scale, the Inpatient Multidimensional Psychiatric Scale (IMPS), checked it for reliability, and factor analyzed the ratings. The results of their work indicate that IMPS provides a reliable vocabulary for the description of psychotic behavior. What was this vocabulary and what assessment procedures were related to it? Let us answer the first part of this question. Then we shall proceed to a presentation of the diagnostic language it generated.

The IMPS consists of 75 brief rating scale items to each of which a rater responds with "yes" or "no." Raters who fill out IMPS are clinicians who have interviewed the patients under study. They respond to IMPS following 30 to 45 minute interviews with patients, and there is wide latitude concerning the form the interviews can take. (It should be noted that the requirement of the interview makes IMPS inapplicable in instances where the patient cannot be interviewed, as in cases of mute individuals.) All of the items on IMPS refer to observable responses of individuals, such as: (1) Is the patient critical of others? (2) Does he exhibit unusual facial expressions? (3) Is his speech labored? (4) Does he show overt signs of tension? (5) Does he seem to be apathetic?

The patient samples used in the development of IMPS were so selected as to be representative of most of the diagnostic categories represented in the American Psychiatric Association Diagnostic Manual (1952). The statistical procedures of factor analysis were employed to determine the minimum number of concepts or variables, which would account for the variability among test scores. In the case of the Lorr, Klett, and McNair (1963, pp. 23–24) study, the test scores were clinical ratings of patients' behavior in interview situations. Ten factors were discovered through which the ratings could be described reliably and parsimoniously. Each factor was found to be associated with a relatively homogeneous set of items. The factors, together with their abbreviations or codes and their defining properties, were as follows:

A. *Excitement* (EXC). The defining characteristics are excess and acceleration of speech and motor activity. Mood level and self-esteem are high. Restraint in expression of emotion and feeling is lacking.

B. *Hostile Belligerence* (HOS). Manifest and verbal hostility, expressions of resentment, and an attitude of suspicion of others' intentions are characteristic of the syndrome. There is much complaining and irritability and a tendency to blame others for their difficulties.

C. *Paranoid Projection* (PAR). This syndrome is defined by morbid beliefs that attribute hostility, persecution and even a controlling influence to others.

D. *Grandiose Expansiveness* (GRN). This syndrome is marked by delusions of grandeur, an attitude of self-importance, and at times, a conviction of having a divine mission.

E. *Perceptual Distortion* (PCP). This grouping is characterized by hallucinations that threaten, accuse, demand, or extol.

F. *Anxious Intropunitiveness* (INP). This syndrome is marked by anxiety, fears, lowered mood level, and self-depreciation. Guilt, remorse, and self-blame for real or imagined faults are equally prominent.

G. *Retardation and Apathy* (RTD). The defining behaviors are slowed and reduced motor activity, ideation, and speech. Apathy and disinterest are also characteristic.

H. *Disorientation* (DIS). This symptom cluster represents a measure of disorientation for time, place, and person.

I. *Motor Disturbance* (MTR). Rigid bizarre postures, grimacing, and repetitive movements are the main behaviors defining this syndrome.

J. *Conceptual Disorganization* (CNP). Irrelevant, incoherent, and rambling speech as well as neologisms and stereotyped use of words and phrases characterize this syndrome.

Although the development of the IMPS proved to be challenging and time consuming, its construction must be regarded as only a setting of the stage for the task of validation. Through factor analysis its developers were able to show that on the IMPS there were ten sets of homogeneous items that tended to cohere. The content of each set of items suggested a set of behavioral characteristics. But the question remains: What is the validity of these sets of items? The problem of determining criteria by which validity is to be assessed must also be considered. As we have seen, the validity of certain tests can be determined by the results obtained from their correlation with recognized, unambiguous criteria. For example, a test to predict ability to sell life insurance might be validated through its correlation with the amount of insurance sold by insurance salesmen. But for most personality characteristics such obvious, tangible criteria are lacking. Rather, validation must proceed through the accumulation of empirical evidence and the expansion of a nomological network.

Lorr, Klett, and McNair fully recognized the need to validate the constructs of their ten IMPS scales and they have made several beginning steps in this direction. In one study they hypothesized that highly disturbed patients would receive higher scores than less dis-

TABLE 29-1

Syndrome Scores of Open and Closed Ward Patients

	Open Ward (N = 61)	Closed Ward (N = 146)
Syndrome	Mean	Mean
Excitement	20.1	33.5
Hostile belligerence	16.7	36.7
Paranoid projection	15.9	34.2
Grandiose expansiveness	4.5	11.8
Perceptual distortion	6.9	10.9
Motor disturbance	15.4	25.2
Conceptual disorganization	8.7	16.4

Adapted from M. Lorr, C. J. Klett and D. M. McNair (1963), Syndromes of psychosis, p. 101, Macmillan, New York.

turbed patients on the ten IMPS syndromes. They tested this hypothesis by comparing open- and closed-ward patients according to ratings given them on the IMPS. This procedure seemed reasonable since patients on closed or locked wards are considered to be more disturbed than those on open wards in which patients have considerable freedom of movement. Table 29-1 presents the mean IMPS syndrome scores for the open- and closed-ward patients on seven scales of the IMPS on which there were significant statistical differences. Although there were three scales that did not discriminate between open- and closed-ward patients, there clearly was a tendency for differences in the expected direction. Thus, the IMPS seems to be sensitive to the degree of psychopathology exhibited by patients.

In other studies, it has been shown that the IMPS is related to prominent indices of psychopathology, to diagnoses based on conventional psychiatric procedures, and to the reaction of patients to tranquilizing drugs. But as Lorr, Klett, and McNair well recognized, much work remains to be done and many relationships between IMPS scores and the behavior of patients are yet to be uncovered. The goal underlying assessment work in the area of psychopathology is to improve upon existing clinical diagnostic procedures. The IMPS, with its objectivity, convenience, and firm statistical basis, would appear to be a promising prospect as a basis for describing and classifying the behavior of deviant persons.

Social Competence, Social Status, and Mental Disorder

The contribution of Lorr, Klett, and McNair (1963) was the construction of a multidimensional instrument of potential value in the description and prediction of behavior. A series of investigations by Phillips and Zigler (1961; Zigler and Phillips, 1962), which were less broad in scope but equally provocative, involved biographical as contrasted with psychometric assessment of individuals. These workers focused on one concept, social competence, and devised an over-all quantitative index of it in terms of these factors: extent of the individual's education, his occupational skills, his ability to hold a job, and the adequacy of his heterosexual relationships. They were concerned primarily with establishing the relationship of social competence to (1) clinical diagnoses, and (2) patients' observed behavior.

Their research has shown that patients who are relatively high in assessed social competence tend to be diagnosed as neurotics or manic-depressives. Patients low in assessed social competence tend to receive clinical diagnoses of schizophrenia and character disorders. It has also been shown that there is a positive correlation between social competence and prognosis in schizophrenia. The higher the social competence index, the greater is the likelihood of improvement in schizophrenic patients. Other evidence suggests that less socially competent males have been subjected to relatively high degrees of maternal dominance, punitiveness, restrictiveness, and paternal inadequacy (Phillips, 1953). Male patients low in social competence seem to have had in their development a paucity of adult male figures with whom socially appropriate masculine identifications could have been developed.

It would appear that the Phillips-Zigler index of social competence, based upon life history information, is a useful contribution to the understanding of the antecedents of behavior deviations in general and schizophrenia in particular. The work on social competence may be contrasted in one respect with that of Lorr, Klett, and McNair. Whereas the latter aimed at a new psychometrically based diagnostic system, Phillips and Zigler focused on the relationship of one variable, social competence, to existing psychiatric diagnoses. Both approaches seem reasonable and worthy of exploration. Whereas Lorr, Klett, and McNair are working towards a new classification system, Phillips and Zigler appear interested in introducing into the existing diagnostic system a variable that may increase the reliability of psychiatric classification. The question of whether or not the ultimate solution to problems of classifying deviant behavior will involve the development of a totally new system or a revision of the existing one can be answered only by the results of research directed along both lines.

The assessment of patients is worthwhile whether it leads to a new classification scheme or a revision of an existing one. It is important that as much evidence as possible concerning individual differences that may be correlated with the incidence of deviant behavior be presented. An example of this sort of descriptive contribution has been reported by Hollingshead and Redlich (1958). Hollingshead, a sociologist, and Redlich, a psychiatrist, were concerned with deviant behavior in that it posed a significant social problem. They reasoned that to the extent that the social milieu affected the prevalence of forms of psychopathology, identification of significant social variables would contribute to the understanding of these disturbances. The rationale and hypotheses presented by Hollingshead and Redlich (1958, pp. 10–11) were as follows:

After several months of preliminary work, the central questions of this research emerged, namely: (1) Is mental illness related to class in our society? (2) Does a psychiatric patient's position in the status system affect how he is treated for his illness?

The first query is related to the etiology of mental illnesses. The psychodynamic concept of unconscious conflict between instinctual forces and the demands of the environment is crucial for many attempts at explanation of most neurotic and psychotic illnesses. Knowing that the different social classes exhibit different ways of life, we conjectured that emotional problems of individuals might be related to the patterns of life characteristic of their class positions.

The second question is focused on treatment. Our observations and experiences with psychiatric treatment led us to think that the kind of treatment a patient receives is not a function solely of the state of medical knowledge which is embodied in the art and science of making a diagnosis and prescribing treatment. Subtle and powerful psychological and social processes appear to be important determinants in the choice of treatment and its implementation. We are interested particularly in finding out whether the various psychiatric treatments patients receive are affected by class status.

Working Hypotheses

The third major step in the formulation of our research plans was taken when we crystallized our thoughts on these questions around a series of tentative hypotheses. Eventually, five working hypotheses were written into the research design. Each hypothesis connected the two major concepts of the research, namely, social class and mental illness, in such a way that the resulting proposition could be tested empirically. The several hypotheses were phrased thus:

Hypothesis 1. The prevalence of treated mental illness is related significantly to an individual's position in the class structure.

Hypothesis 2. The types of diagnosed psychiatric disorders are connected significantly to the class structure.

Hypothesis 3. The kind of psychiatric treatment administered by psychiatrists is associated with the patient's position in the class structure.

Hypothesis 4. Social and psychodynamic factors in the development of psychiatric disorders are correlative to an individual's position in the class structure.

Hypothesis 5. Mobility in the class structure is associated with the development of psychiatric difficulties.

In order to carry out their research, it was necessary for Hollingshead and Redlich to assess the social class of persons. To do this they employed an index of social position. This index permitted the social status classification of individuals on the basis of place of residence, occupation, and educational level. The index permitted the placement of an individual in one of five groups ranging from the highest ranking stratum of the social class structure (Class I) to the lowest (Class V). With the social status index in hand, the researchers proceeded to (1) enumerate persons receiving psychiatric treatment in the New Haven, Connecticut area, (2) make a sample census of the general population in that area, and (3) classify psychiatric patients and persons in the general population in terms of social class status.

Hollingshead and Redlich found that the individual's social class position and his becoming a psychiatric patient were strongly associated. The lower the social class, the greater was the proportion of patients in the population. This relationship held even when the factors of sex, race, age, religion, and marital status remained constant. The one exception to this generalization was the finding that social class and mental disorder were uncorrelated for individuals between the ages of 15 through 24 years.

If social class is related to the over-all incidence of mental disorder, might it not also be related to the incidence of specific types of behavior deviation? Evidence gathered concerning this possibility showed that type of diagnosed psychiatric disorder was correlated with social class. Whereas certain diagnoses were unrelated to social class (for example, senile psychoses), some were more characteristic of persons in the upper socioeconomic strata (affective psychoses and character neuroses), while others were most common among lower-class individuals (hysterical reactions and organic psychoses). Figure 29-1 shows the prevalence of neurotic and psychotic disorders per 100,000

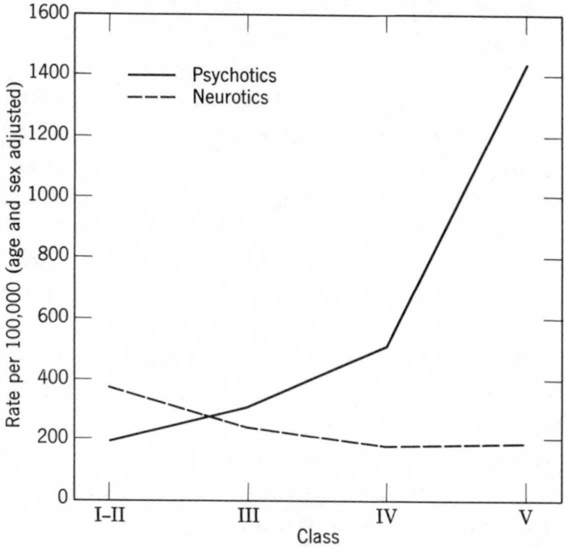

Figure 29-1 Prevalence of neurotic and psychotic disorders per 100,000 adjusted for age and sex—by class (after Hollingshead and Redlich, 1958, p. 230).

persons in the population (Classes I and II are the highest and Class V the lowest social status groups). It is clear that the incidence of psychosis increases as one proceeds down the social status scale.

Hollingshead and Redlich investigated not only the incidence of mental disorders, but also the ways in which they are treated by psychiatrists. Their findings showed that the social class status of a patient had a great deal to do with the treatment given him. For example, in neurosis, the higher the social class the greater was the likelihood that psychotherapy was employed by the psychiatrist. On the other hand, lower social class neurotics tend to be treated with organic therapies such as drugs and electric shock treatment. It seems possible that the social gulf between middle- and upper-class psychotherapists and lower-class patients bore significantly on the relatively low incidence of psychotherapy as a treatment technique with these patients.

The argument, supported by Hollingshead and Redlich's data, that social class and mental illness are related has been further strengthened by evidence that has come to the fore since publication of their findings. For example, the Midtown Manhattan project involved detailed interviews with 1700 adults between the ages of 20 and 59 who resided in New York City's Yorkville district (Langner and Michael, 1963; Srole et al., 1962). Analysis of the data gathered suggested that four out of five people in the survey had noteworthy psychiatric symptoms and that one out of four had symptoms judged to be severe. With respect to social class, it was found that one out of two adults living on poverty level incomes was judged to be severely disturbed psychologically. Only one out of eight persons living on at least moderate income levels was believed to be severely disturbed.

The Hollingshead and Redlich and Midtown Manhattan studies include many implications, two of which are that future research might profitably be directed at the discovery of factors in children's social development that are influenced by social class variables, and that social mobility, that is, changes in social class status, may well contribute to the incidence of certain types of mental disorders. When one considers the total picture presented by available research findings, it seems clear that the assessment of social class characteristics is a relevant part of the diagnostic process. The gulf in social status, attitudes, and values between therapist and patient may constitute a serious factor in the selection of a therapy technique and may prove to be a deterrent to clinical improvement. Finally, it would seem necessary that one be aware of the variable of social class when conducting research on the treatment of psychiatric patients. The possibility of devising treatment procedures that are specific to the problems of people belonging to particular social strata would then be increased.

CONCLUDING COMMENTS CONCERNING PERSONALITY ASSESSMENT AND DEVIANT BEHAVIOR

Although the studies reviewed are but a small sample from a growing body of literature, they suggest the range of applications of assessment procedures to the study of deviant behavior. Assessment may involve as straightforward and relatively uncomplicated a procedure as Hollingshead and Redlich's (1958) determination of social class status or as complex a methodology as Lorr, Klett, and McNair's (1963) factor analytic technique. It may involve the prediction of behavior on the basis of combinations of patients' scores on personality tests as in the Weiner, Thaler, Reiser, and Mirsky (1957) study, or it may be done in terms of psychiatric diagnosis based on clinical impressions.

Personality assessment aims at isolating relevant characteristics of individuals and then relating these to significant aspects of overt behavior. Many of the major issues in this field revolve around the ways in which this can best be achieved. Let us review within the context of the study of deviant behavior some of the problems involved in this endeavor.

1. THE NATURE OF THE CONSTRUCTS STUDIED. Many descriptive statements about persons seem quite straightforward and do not require complex hypotheses concerning internal processes. Social class status, as studied by Hollingshead and Redlich, would appear to be a variable of this type. Birth order, which has been found to be significantly related to the incidence of schizophrenia, is another variable of this type (Schooler, 1964). But what of such concepts as latent hostility, schizoid personality, and psychotic trends? These concepts are based on inferences from behavior, and because all persons may not draw the same inferences from observed behavior, controversy often results. We have pointed out that, for example, different clinicians often use the various diagnostic labels with varying frequencies. In all likelihood, this inconsistency results from the different meanings that may be attached to the various diagnostic categories. As a consequence, investigators such as Lorr, Klett, and McNair have sought to devise new and more reliable means of describing patients.

The problems connected with the assessment of inferred characteristics are those of construct validation. To achieve success in efforts at construct validation requires that we have valid personality theories. As we have seen, however, there are at present no personality theories that are scientifically valid *in toto*. There are, however, various theoretical orientations and formulations that may be valuable if they succeed in generating constructs whose validity may be determined empirically. Thus the seeds of constructs may be found in theoretical formulations and conjectures. As the constructs stemming from particular theoretical orientations come to be (1) stated unambiguously, and (2) shown to relate meaningfully to behavior, it becomes possible to speak of the validity of personality theories.

2. INDICES OF CONSTRUCTS. If a construct concerning covert response tendencies has been unambiguously stated, the problem of obtaining an index of the tendency yet remains to be solved. Two researchers may be in agreement concerning the usefulness of developing a construct, and yet they may differ in the ways in which they assess the tendency. Thus a given conception of anxiety or persuasibility or schizophrenia might be approached from an assessment standpoint in a variety of ways, for example, in terms of interview

responses, projective test responses, and paper-and-pencil test responses.

3. ANALYSIS OF ASSESSED CHARACTERISTICS. Let us assume that we have available for a group of patients indices of a large number of the characteristics believed to be important in personality description. Having these indices, we might then aim to make predictive statements concerning aspects of the future behavior of these patients. It is rare that an index of a single characteristic will by itself prove predictive of complex behavior. To predict how well a patient will respond to psychotherapy therefore requires knowledge of many things about him; for example, his age, social status, level of anxiety, degree of defensiveness, tendency to intellectualize his emotional conflicts.

What is the best way of integrating such multidimensional data? Some researchers have argued that the clinical worker, confronted with a mass of data about an individual, cannot be expected to integrate and interpret reliably and correctly all the information available to him. Others (Goldberg, 1965; Meehl, 1954) maintain that the development of statistical and computer methodologies that would permit impartial analysis and interpretation of the information available would be more desirable. Other researchers have contended that the skilled clinician can often be more perceptive than a computer in assessing subtle patterns of behavior (Holt, 1958).

This controversy, which has raged for many years, has been referred to in the literature as that of clinical versus statistical prediction. Its resolution has not yet been achieved. On the one hand, an impartial handbook which would provide objective predictions based on a set of assessed characteristics would be of immense value. On the other hand, at the present time, it would seem that much can be learned from the subjective problem-solving of master clinicians who are particularly skillful in gathering and interpreting evidence about persons (Lindzey, 1965). It seems likely that related efforts at (1) developing objective means for integrating large amounts of data about persons, and (2) studying the inferential processes of clinicians will maximize the likelihood of achieving scientifically based personality description and useful prediction methods.

That these efforts have produced worthwhile results has been demonstrated in one study directed at the prediction of maladjustment among college students (Kleinmuntz, 1963). On the basis of criteria used by an adept MMPI specialist, objective rules for classifying college students were arrived at and a computer program was written. This program proved highly successful in ordering the level of adjustment of college students. Thus it would appear that the skills of the individual clinician and the objectivity and "memory" of the computer can supplement each other in achieving efficient assessment.

4. THE CRITERION PROBLEM. Much of the impetus for research on personality assessment stems from the need to predict the future behavior of persons. Will the patient get better? Will he be able to live a relatively comfortable life after discharge from a hospital? These questions, significant as they are, contain within them yet further questions. By what criteria or standards may "getting better" be judged? What are the behavioral concomitants of a "relatively comfortable life"?

The criterion problem, simply put, is the problem of deciding on the standards whereby the value of assessment procedures may be determined. The use of the word "standards" rather than the word "standard" is significant. If one were interested in devising a test to measure schizophrenic tendencies, one would not be satisfied with a single criterion, such as the presence of hallucinations, the inadequacy of the individual's social life, his inability to hold a job, or his delusional thinking. One would be concerned with the relationship of test scores to these criteria of schizophrenia and to other criteria also.

Although there might be widespread agreement that validation of personality assessment procedures requires multiple criteria, there might not be similar agreement concerning the particular criteria to be employed. The word multidimensional can therefore be applied to two aspects of personality assessment. One is the multidimensionality of predictors of behavior (the many MMPI scale scores) and the other is the multidimensionality of behavior to be predicted (the various indices of degree of recovery from a neurotic depression).

30

Experimental Psychopathology

As we have seen, the experimental approach to personality entails a conscious effort to devise interventions and conditions that would change the behavior of subjects. Moreover, assessment and experimental approaches can be complementary. For instance, the researcher who is interested in studying eating habits may use any one of three methods. He might decide to assess the eating habits of subjects through psychometric techniques, such as self-reports of eating habits, or actual observation of eating behavior. He might decide to expose subjects to different experimental conditions, such as various time periods of food deprivation, in order to determine their influence on eating behavior. He might incorporate both assessment and experimental methods into his research design by exposing subjects, selected on the basis of previously assessed attitudes toward eating, to particular experimental conditions such as periods of food deprivation.

In the preceding chapter we explored some of the ways in which assessment might be applied to the study of deviant behavior. Let us now consider the role of experimentation in the study of psychopathology and the joint use of assessment and experimental methods in research on deviancy.

The experimental study of behavior may be viewed as having two objectives. One is to develop controlled and reliable conditions that will permit researchers to test their hypotheses. These hypotheses might be the result of study of existing theories, conjectures, and hunches. The other objective emphasizes not only how subjects respond under defined conditions, but also how experimental interventions outside the experimental room exert influences on subjects. The major aim of researchers who stress this latter issue is usually the modification of the person's behavior (Bachrach, 1962; Eysenck, 1961a). Thus one might conceive of the psychotherapy situation as an experimental one in which variables designed to influence the attitudes and behavior of patients are manipulated. In this sense, problems of psychotherapy are experimental problems. A study of research in psychopathology, which will be illustrated in this chapter, will provide examples of experimentation directed at the testing of hypotheses. Chapter 31 will provide examples of experimental efforts at achieving lasting behavior modification.

EXAMPLES OF RESEARCH ON EXPERIMENTAL PSYCHOPATHOLOGY

Censure and Conceptual Deficit in Schizophrenia

Schizophrenia is the major health problem of the nation. It is very poorly understood. If we define schizophrenic behavior as inadequate or deficient behavioral response patterns, we must ask the following question: What stimulus conditions give rise to this type of response? Rodnick and Garmezy (1957) and Rodnick (1963) have reported a series of investigations of schizophrenics that was motivated largely by this question.

The intent of this research seems comparable to that of the research on anxiety (Chapter 15). Much research on anxiety has dwelt on the problem of the specificity of anxiety. Are persons who obtain high scores on anxiety questionnaries generally inferior in level of performance to low-anxious scorers on difficult conceptual tests, or is their inferiority a result of specific stimuli associated with the tests? A review of the literature related to this question led to the conclusion that differences in performance levels between high- and low-anxious subjects could be explained by reference to the conditions under which testing took place. Similarly, Rodnick and Garmezy sought to determine whether the level of performance of schizophrenic patients was generally inferior to that of normal persons, or inferior only under certain conditions.

Their focus on this question was a result of the formulation of an hypothesis concerning the determinants of behavior in schizophrenia. They conceived of schizophrenic behavior as in part a psychological response to environmental stimuli. The stimuli of particular relevance to schizophrenia seemed to be those that included censure of an individual consequent to his behavior. To say that exposure to censure will lead to schizophreniclike behavior would obviously be a patent oversimplification. Rodnick and Garmezy did not make this assertion. They asked: How does censure influence the behavior of persons diagnosed as schizophrenic? Viewing the problem in this way, they hoped to make more explicit the conditions that increase and decrease the likelihood of psychological deficit among schizophrenics. One of the conclusions drawn from their research that has long-term effects is that if conditions that decrease the likelihood of defective behavior among schizophrenics can be isolated, it might ultimately be possible to devise therapeutic procedures for the improvement of patients.

Before turning to some of the specific experiments carried out by Rodnick, Garmezy, and their colleagues, let us consider one additional question: On what basis did these investigators select the variable of censure versus noncensure as the major one in their experiment? The selection of the censure-noncensure variable was based on clinical observations of schizophrenics and their families and hunches about the etiology of schizophrenia. It seemed possible that a link could be established between censure administered to an adult schizophrenic in an experimental setting and censure to which he might have been subjected as a child. In other words, if censure within the home had been an important factor in the development of the social and performance deficits of schizophrenics, might it not also be a factor responsible for the functioning of the adult patient?

Garmezy (1952) reported a study in which both acute schizophrenic patients and normal subjects were presented with an auditory discrimination task. The task required the subject to pull a switch lever following the presentation of a "training" tone and to push the lever in response to four other tones that varied in pitch. Under this arrangement it could be expected that there would be more erroneous "pull" responses to tones that were similar to the training tone than to those that were dissimilar. For both the schizophrenic and normal groups there were two experimental conditions. Under one, correct responses were followed by the lighting of a box reading "R." Under the other condition, "R" appeared for correct responses, but "W" appeared for incorrect ones. Under both conditions, subjects received informational feedback concerning the correctness of their responses, but there was more comprehensive feedback under the R-W condition than under the R condition.

One way of interpreting the two experimental conditions is to say that under the R condition, subjects received rewards for correct responses and under the R-W condition they received rewards for correct and punishment for incorrect responses. Rodnick and Garmezy emphasized this interpretation because they noted that clinical reports of schizophrenic behavior suggested that schizophrenics were especially sensitive to disapproval, censure, and threats of censure. If generalizations could be made from these reports to the experimental situation, it might be expected that under the R-W condition, which involves a degree of punishment or censure, a group of schizophrenic subjects would show poorer discrimination than a group of normal subjects. In general, one would expect poorer performance among schizophrenics than among normal subjects under censure conditions.

Garmezy's findings supported these expectations. He noted that under the R condition schizophrenics learned the discrimination task as well as normal persons. Normal subjects under the R-W condition showed superior discrimination to those under the Right condition. This was not found to be so for schizophrenics. Garmezy's experiment showed that under a social approval condition (R for correct responses) schizophrenics discriminate as well as normal persons, but that under a partial social disapproval condition schizophrenics do not discriminate as well as normal subjects.

Another experiment in this series of studies, carried out by Webb, (1952, 1955) shed further light on the problem of the effects of censure or social disapproval on the behavior of schizophrenics. Webb used a task quite different from the one employed by Garmezy. It was a conceptual one in which the subject was presented with two concepts and was asked to state in what ways the concepts were similar (table-chair, arm-toe). The experimental procedure called for two comparable series of similarities, each involving 20 pairs of concepts. In each series, the 20 items were graded in level of difficulty. However, in presenting them to subjects, the similarities items were so arranged that in each group of four there was a range of difficulty from easy to quite hard.

Webb (1952, 1955) studied two groups of schizophrenic patients. The control group was administered the first series of 20 similarities items, and the adequacy of its performance was not indicated. Then, after a brief interpolated task, which was irrelevant to the similarities task, a parallel, comparable form of the similarities test was administered. The experimental group was given mild criticism of its performance on the first series of tests. This social disapproval occurred immediately after performance of the first series and before that of the second series.

Webb wanted to know whether criticism and disapproval would effect schizophrenics' ability to respond to the conceptual similarities task. He analyzed his data by comparing the number of correct responses on the second series with those on the first. He found that the control group showed a noticeable trend of improvement on the second series of similarities. This was clearly not the case for the schizophrenics who had been subjected to mild censure. As the test session progressed the differences between the two groups of patients increased. While the control group improved, the experimental group showed a progressive deterioration in performance.

What implications grow out of these findings? Perhaps the most important one relates to the term "thought disorder," which is usually used to describe schizophrenia. What is meant by the statement, "Patient X is suffering from a schizophrenic thought disorder." One explanation might be that schizophrenia involves a basic, pervasive conceptual deficit. Rodnick and Garmezy (1957), on the other hand, argued that this deficit might not be as pervasive as initially it seemed to be. They contended that the conceptual deficit in schizophrenia could often be interpreted in terms of reactions to particular motivational stimuli, such as censure and social disapproval. Webb's results appear to support this contention.

After reviewing the Garmezy and Webb experiments one feels that if they extended their work to stimuli of more obvious social significance than tones and similarities test items they might produce more valuable conclusions. Another experiment in the Rodnick-Garmezy research program, carried out by Dunn (1953, 1954), was directed to such a study. Subjects were presented with a discrimination task that was basically the same as that employed by Garmezy. However, instead of using tones as stimuli, Dunn employed a series of pictures of personal scenes. His experiment seems particularly relevant in the light of observations and hypotheses about the genesis of schizophrenic behavior. Why does censure have the impact that it appears to have on adult schizophrenics? Could it be that adult schizophrenics are affected by censure because of early traumatic experiences associated with social censure? Might their mothers have been rejecting, dominating women who were extravagant in the censure of their children?

In Dunn's experiment four standard pictorial stimuli were presented to subjects. One was a silhouetted scene in which a mother was scolding a young boy. Two other scenes showed the mother and boy in feeding and physical punishment whipping situations. A fourth standard stimulus, a control stimulus, was a picture of a tree and a house.

For each standard stimulus there were five pictures that included slight variations from the standard. The task for the subject was to decide, after seeing the standard, whether a second picture shown was also the standard or one of the variations. Dunn wished to determine the degree to which schizophrenics might differ from normal persons in their discriminations concerning the three personal stimuli and the one control stimulus.

The results of his experiment showed that schizophrenics and normal subjects did not differ in their discriminations regarding the control picture and the whipping and feeding pictures. However, there was a sizable difference in the discrimination of the patients and that of the normal subjects on the scolding or censure picture, the schizophrenics showing less adequate discrimination than the control subjects. It would therefore appear that differences in discrimination between normal and schizophrenic subjects can be demonstrated either when censure is applied in the experimental situation, as in Garmezy's experiment, or when censure is communicated symbolically, as in Dunn's experiment.

Dunn followed up his experimental findings by gathering life history data for two groups of schizophrenics. Selecting a group of patients who did relatively well and a group of patients who did relatively poorly on the scolding discrimination task, he compared them with regard to the life history information available. The comparisons suggested that poor discrimination on the scolding pictures was correlated with a high degree of conflict between patients and their mothers. Rodnick and Garmezy (1957, pp. 130–131) have interpreted Dunn's results in this way:

> These results are of interest because they represent a successful effort to relate deficit behavior in a laboratory task involving essentially the symbolic representation of certain traumatic life history antecedents to such veridical experiences. The specificity of Dunn's findings supports our proposition that the most critical situations for the study of behavioral deficits in schizophrenia are those which have marked cue relevance for the patient and can thus serve as a more distinctive stimulus for eliciting maladaptive patterns of response. . . .
>
> The observations of many clinicians of a traumatogenic mother-child relationship in schizophrenia would certainly lend support to an interpretation of Dunn's data in terms of a reaction sensitivity of his patients to cues of criticism, ignoring, and domination. For normal Ss [subjects] the stimulus scenes which were used apparently merely possessed informational properties which resulted in self-corrective modifications in behavior and the selective direction of attention to what was necessary for satisfactory task performance. For the schizophrenic patient, however, environmental stimuli possessing properties of censure or rebuff may have served as signals for the arousal of personal ruminations, preoccupations, anxiety, and withdrawal responses or fantasied behaviors.

As a means of incorporating into their experiments an individual difference measure that would reflect the life experiences of schizophrenic persons, Rodnick and Garmezy employed the scale of premorbid adjustment developed by Phillips and Zigler (1961; Zigler and Phillips, 1962; Phillips, 1953); (Chapter 29). A reanalysis of Dunn's data in terms of this scale showed that schizophrenics with poor premorbid (prepsychotic) adjustments showed discrimination deficits on the scolding picture, but that patients with relatively good premorbid adjustments discriminated as well as normals. Findings related to this measure of premorbid adjustment suggest that the prior experiential history of schizophrenics greatly influences the adequacy with which they respond to learning situations, conceptual tasks, and socially symbolic stimuli.

The several studies reviewed seem to have uncovered valuable knowledge about schizophrenia. They have shown convincingly that not only do schizophrenics differ from normal persons on a variety of tasks, but that also within the schizophrenic group, good and poor premorbid histories are predictive of levels of performance. They have also shown that the stimulus properties of experimental situations, such as censure, influence the magnitude of these differences. Although the problem of the determinants has many facets (Buss and Lang, 1965; Garmezy, 1964; Lang and Buss, 1965), Rodnick and Garmezy have contributed importantly to its understanding.

An Experimental Approach to Criminal Behavior

Despite the obvious social problem posed by criminal behavior, relatively little is known about its determinants. The most common psychological approaches to this sort of behavior have taken the form of attempts to assess the personalities and histories of varieties of criminals. Emphasis has usually been given to assessment of characteristics believed to set criminals apart from other groups of individuals. Schachter and Latané (1964) have reported a suggestive series of studies of criminals that are distinctly experimental in nature. Their studies are particularly valuable because they provide illustrations of a new area of investigation, psychopharmacology. This area represents a coming together of two disciplines, pharmacology and psychology, and concerns itself with the effects of pharmacological agents, drugs, on thoughts, emotions, and overt behavior (Holliday, 1965).

The research of Schachter and Latané is an outgrowth of a general interest in the ways in which cognitive and physiological factors influence emotional states. The extent to which a person describes himself as experiencing an emotional state can be considered a function of his degree of physiological arousal and his interpretation of this arousal. Much study in recent years has been devoted to the effects of drugs on physiological arousal (Dews, 1962; Schachter, 1964). One drug, epinephrine, has been shown to be effective in producing physiological arousal comparable to that produced by active discharge of the sympathetic nervous system. The subject taking epinephrine experiences a more intense feeling of euphoria, irritation, or anger, depending on the environmental stimuli, than he would without taking the drug. Another drug, chlorpromazine, a commonly used tranquilizer, is known to be a sympathetic depressant and to suppress sympathetic nervous system centers in the brain. Let us observe how Schachter and Latané made use of these drugs in their experimental study of the behavior of criminals.

It has been reported that under fear-inducing environmental conditions, such as the simultaneous presentation of a buzzer, bell, and flashing light, rats injected with epinephrine are more frightened than chlorpromazine injected rats (Singer, 1963). Under non-fear-arousing stimulus conditions, the drugs did not appear to have differential effects on the rats' behavior. Schachter and Latané (1964, p. 223) felt that a variety of emotions might be manipulated in both rats and human subjects through drugs that affect the level of physiological arousal. Furthermore, they believed that this influence had relevance for criminal behavior:

> Given a criminal impulse, given the existence of restraining, fear-inducing conditions, the likelihood that a crime will occur can be manipulated by the manipulation of sympathetic activation.

With this as an hypothesis they carried out two experiments. One involved the relatively minor infraction of cheating in a school situation. The other involved the behavior of persons convicted of serious criminal acts.

The design of the academic cheating experiment was quite straightforward. College students took a test under highly motivating conditions; they were told that points would be added to their course grades if they did well. They then took a drug, chlorpromazine, and finally were given an opportunity to grade their own test papers. The orally administered chlorpromazine was described not as a tranquilizer, but as a vitamin. The vitamin (it was called suproxin) was described to subjects as one that might help individuals to perceive better.

After receiving the drug, the subjects spent 55 minutes working on apparently scientific perception tasks. In fact, the experimenters were not interested in subjects' performance during this period. The 55 minutes of contrived activity was needed to allow the chlorpromazine enough time to have its effect. The contrived experimental period served one other function. Under the guise of darkening the room in order to do the perception part of the experiment, the experimenter was able to remove the answer sheets to the previously administered test, to make reproductions of their answer sheets, and then return the originals without the subjects being aware of what had happened.

When the "perception experiment" was completed the experimenter passed the subjects' answer sheets back to them and asked them to score their own papers. After he had put the scoring key on the blackboard, he then left the room. It is important to note that the 11-minute test had consisted of 30 items, which for most subjects could not be completed during the allotted time. Finally, the key given the subjects was, in fact, incorrect. For six questions, answers that were actually incorrect were scored as correct. There was, then, ample opportunity for cheating in the scoring of the tests.

For half of the subjects, the vitamin was chlorpromazine; for the remaining subjects, it was a placebo. It is worth noting that the amount of chlorpromazine administered was small. When pulse rate and other measurements were recorded, it was found that some subjects were affected by chlorpromazine and others were not. This finding is what one might expect with small dosages of a drug given to persons who differ in bodily processes. Because of this differential reactivity to the drug, three groups of subjects were compared: (1) those who received the placebo, (2) those on whom chlorpromazine had a physiological effect, and (3) those on whom chlorpromazine did not have an effect.

The findings were these. Approximately 40 per cent of the subjects on whom the drug worked actually cheated. Only 20 per cent of the placebo subjects cheated. Six per cent of the subjects on whom the drug failed to work cheated. This latter group was actually a numerically small number of subjects compared with the other two groups. It appears, then, that when chlorpromazine is physiologically effective, it facilitates cheating.

Building on preliminary studies of the effects of drugs on animals and persons and on the cheating experiment, Schachter and Latané (1964) performed an experiment in which the subjects were not normal persons who had committed minor infractions but imprisoned criminals. In planning their study, they reasoned that there were two broad types of crimes, those attributable to passion and intense motivation and those attributable to either inadequate deterrents to crime or lack of fear of being caught. Criminals who can be described as chronically lacking this sort of fear are often called sociopaths or psychopaths. It is generally felt that they suffer from pervasive social impoverishment. Cleckley (1955, p. 427) who has studied many psychopaths intensively, has said:

> . . . that the psychopath fails to know all those more serious and deeply moving affective states which make up the tragedy and triumph of ordinary life, of life at the level of human personality . . . no normal person is so uninvolved, no ordinary criminal so generally unresponsive and distorted, but that he seems to experience satisfaction, love, hate, grief, a general participation in life at human personality levels, much more intense and more substantial than the affective reactions of the psychopath.

Lykken (1957) reported an experiment designed to test the hypothesis that sociopaths were unable to experience a strong affect, anxiety. His experiment employed an avoidance learning paradigm. The results showed that sociopaths not only obtained lower scores on psychometric measures of anxiety than neurotic criminals and normal subjects, but also demonstrated less avoidance of punished responses in the learning situation. The experiment carried out by Schachter and Latané employed a procedure similar to that used in the Lykken experiment and supports these findings.

The apparatus used was a cabinet on which a counter, two pilot lights, and four switches were mounted. The subject's task was to solve a complicated mental maze that had 20 choice points. The subject could proceed from one choice point to the next by pressing an arbitrarily designated correct switch. If the subject pressed the correct switch a light came on. If he made an error it was recorded on the counter. Each subject was instructed to complete the maze as quickly as possible. Twenty-one trials were given in which the correct switches were similar for all trials.

As far as the subjects were concerned, the task was simply a maze learning task. There was, however, one significant additional feature. At each choice point one of the three incorrect switches was programmed to deliver a moderately painful electric shock to the subject. The instructions to the subject had indicated that occasional random shocks would be administered to maintain his motivation. By avoiding the incorrect shock switches, the subject could avoid receiving shocks.

The criminals studied were inmates of maximum security prisons. Their case records were studied and their prison histories carefully reviewed. Special attention was paid to indications of emotionality. Three groups of criminals were finally selected for study, a group of sociopaths, a group of mixed cases in which there were some indications of sociopathic tendencies but also indications of a capacity to experience strong emotions, and a control group consisting of criminals whose misbehavior did not seem attributable to sociopathic tendencies. If escape from prison is taken as an index of psychopathic or sociopathic fearlessness, then it is interesting to note that 33 per cent of the sociopaths used in the experiment had made attempts, 20 per cent of the mixed cases had tried to escape, and none of the control prisoners had sought to escape.

There were two independent variables in the experiment. One was the assessed characteristic of sociopathic tendencies and the other was the experimental element of injection of either epinephrine (adrenalin) or a placebo prior to a subject's performance on the maze. Let us see how these variables affected the behavior of the three groups of criminals in the experimental situation.

An appropriate starting point is to consider the ease with which the subjects learned the maze. It will be remembered that this was the task defined for the subjects. Schachter and Latané found that the three groups did not differ significantly in ability to learn the maze. This finding replicates a previous one by Lykken (1957). It was also found that whether subjects received epinephrine or the placebo had no significant relationship to learning. It is important to note that so far we have said nothing about the subjects' ability to learn the "incidental" shock avoidance task. The findings considered so far indicate the subjects' ability to learn correct responses to the maze but not their ability to learn avoiding incorrect switches that led to shock.

Lykken, in his experiment, had found that sociopaths, when compared with normals, were remarkably poor at learning to avoid receiving shocks in the course of working on the maze. If this was a stable finding, it would seem reasonable to make a prediction about the subjects who received placebos (no drugs were administered in the Lykken experiment). That is, incarcerated sociopaths should be less adequate in learning to avoid electric shocks than the mixed and normal or control prisoners. Figure 30-1 shows the avoidance learning curves of the three groups. The abscissa of this curve represents thirds of the number of errors made by subjects during the experiment. The first point on the abscissa therefore represents the first third of

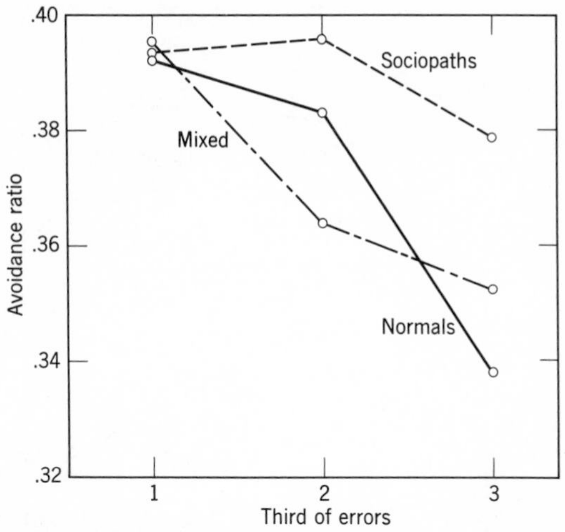

Figure 30-1 Avoidance ratio under placebo by thirds of errors (after Schachter and Latané, 1964, p. 248).

the number of errors made by subjects and the third point represents the third of the number of subjects' errors that occurred toward the end of the experimental session. The ordinate of the graph represents an avoidance ratio, the number of shocked errors divided by the total number of errors.

Figure 30-1 indicates that the sociopaths showed only a slight tendency to reduce the number of shocks that they received as the experiment progressed. The tendency to avoid errors was much greater among the mixed and normal subjects. Thus, the placebo data seem to replicate Lykken's results. We can conclude that sociopaths and control subjects did not differ in ability to learn the maze, but differed in their ability to carry out the avoidance learning task.

Figure 30-2 (subjects who had been administered epinephrine) presents curves comparable to those in Figure 30-1. As can be seen, the drug had strikingly different effects on the sociopaths and the other two groups. Under epinephrine, sociopaths not only learned to avoid electric shocks, but they also did this much more quickly than the mixed and normal subjects.

Schachter and Latané (1964, p. 252) offered this interpretation of their findings:

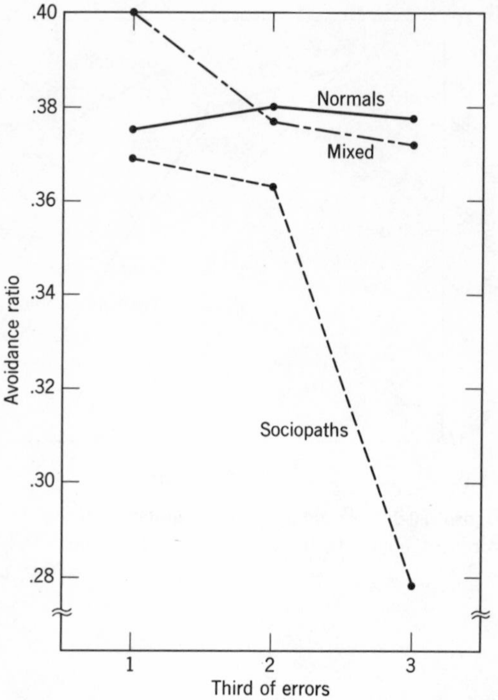

Figure 30-2 Avoidance ratio under adrenalin by thirds of errors (after Schachter and Latané, 1964, p. 250).

If we reconstruct the rough, semi-intuitive line of thought that led to this replication, with a pharmacological twist, of Lykken's work, the simple-minded chain of reasoning would run something like this: emotional states, fear among them, can be manipulated by manipulation of sympathetic arousal; fear or anxiety is presumed to be a major deterrent of antisocial impulses; sociopaths, notoriously antisocial, are presumed by the clinicians, notably Cleckley and Lykken, to be emotionally flat and anxiety-free. Given this chain of speculation and fact, the next steps are virtually self-evident—perhaps there is something amiss in the sympathetic activity of the sociopath and perhaps adrenalin [epinephrine] can remedy the effect. At this point adrenalin [epinephrine] does appear to be a remedy, but a remedy for what?

One possibility that Schachter and Latané's findings suggest is that sociopaths are less sympathetically reactive than other people. Available evidence suggests that not only are sociopaths more responsive to epinephrine but that they are also more autonomically responsive to stressful conditions than normals. This relationship is seemingly not consistent with the nonemotional, cool character usually described as the sociopath. If available evidence is correct, it would appear that high autonomic activity is characteristic both of persons who are high in anxiety and overemotionality, such as anxiety neurotics, and those who are extremely low in anxiety and overt emotionality, such as sociopaths. Schachter and Latané have inferred that sociopaths are persons of high autonomic reactivity but that they have learned *not* to apply emotional labels to their states of arousal. According to this view, the autonomic reactivity of the sociopath is due to an innate sensitivity to epinephrine whereas the reactivity of the person suffering an anxiety reaction is cognitively determined.

The conclusion of Schachter and Latané (1964, pp. 270–271) provides provocative hypotheses for future studies:

> The formulation of the criminal act that prompted this series of studies is based on the relative magnitudes of the impulse to commit a crime and the restraints against doing so. In Lewinian terms, if the magnitude of the driving force is greater than the magnitude of restraining forces, a crime will be committed. If the reverse relationship holds, it will not. Obviously the two experiments [the cheating and avoidance learning experiments] have been deliberately designed to manipulate the magnitude of the restraints. The circumstances of both studies have been so structured that the manipulation of sympathetic arousal has served to manipulate the state of anxiety. What about the impulse to commit a crime? Should it be similarly manipulable? Indeed it should. In studies described earlier, it has proven simple to manipulate such states as anger, euphoria, and fear by the manipulation, in proper cognitive circumstances, of sympathetic activation. There seems to be no reason that such states as hate, rage, lust, and jealousy could not be similarly manipulated. Conceive of an experiment in which a subject is injected with either adrenalin or a sympatholytic agent, a gun is shoved into his hand, he is taken by the arm and thrust into a room where he finds his wife in bed with a stooge. Undoubtedly the reader will agree that under such circumstances a subject whose head suddenly starts pounding, face flushing, and body trembling will be more likely to shoot than will a subject who contemplates this disturbing scene in a state of manipulated physiological quiescence. Why such an outcome rather than, as in the cheating experiment, the reverse? Because the situation has been so structured as to virtually force the immediate cognitive-emotive sequence: "I have been betrayed, I hate them, I could kill them," and the intensity of the state will be a function of the degree of physiological arousal.
>
> It is possible, then, to conceive of situations in which the manipulation of physiological arousal will, depending on cognitive factors, serve to manipulate either the impulse to commit a crime or the restraints against doing

so. Given this analysis, one may ask why the sociopath is a chronic troublemaker. His presumed emotional flatness should dampen both the restraints against committing a crime and the intensity of the impulses to commit one. If he is indeed emotionally flat, he should be as free of the emotional flare-ups that can precipitate a crime as of the anxiety that can inhibit it and his reputation as a troublemaker should be no more serious than any normal person's. This should, of course, be the case if the impulses to criminal activity were purely emotionally generated but such is obviously not true. Crimes are committed not only out of passion but to satisfy simple needs for necessities and comforts, and there is certainly no reason to assume that sociopaths feel any less hungry, cold, or covetous than do normals. If these considerations are correct, one should, however, anticipate different patterns of crime for normals and sociopaths.

It is interesting to note that in examining the subjects used in the avoidance learning experiment researchers found that the sociopaths were generally chronic burglars, con men, and similar types of criminals. On the other hand, control subjects were often the committers of crimes of passion such as assault or rape.

The Schachter and Latané research seems especially significant for two reasons. It has shed light on the correlates and antecedents of criminal behavior, and perhaps of greatest significance, it has contributed to knowledge of the interaction in individuals of both physiological factors and cognitive processes.

CONCLUDING COMMENT CONCERNING EXPERIMENTAL PSYCHOPATHOLOGY

The research of Rodnick and Garmezy and of Schachter and Latané shows that controlled experimentation can provide a fruitful basis for drawing meaningful inferences about the behavior of deviant persons. In each set of studies, persons categorized in a particular way performed tasks under special sets of conditions. In each case these conditions were dictated by hypotheses under consideration.

The following chapter has as its subject that of the present one, experimental psychopathology. However, the research described in Chapter 31 was devised not just to test hypotheses but also to contribute to the discovery of effective therapeutic responses to mental illness. In Chapter 31 a more practical approach to deviant behavior is outlined.

31

Behavior Modification

Two types of experimental efforts characterize research in psychopathology. One of these seeks to test hypotheses whereas the other, in addition to testing hypotheses, endeavors to develop practical clinical techniques. Psychologists hope that through the use of these techniques, they will be able to modify behavior and help subjects in social adjustment. The first type of research is reflected in the Rodnick-Garmezy (1957) and Schachter-Latané (1964) investigations, which sought to illuminate the nature of schizophrenia and sociopathy but did not attempt to develop therapeutic procedures. The second type of research comprises studies of methods of modifying behavior. This chapter is devoted to the latter type of undertaking.

EVALUATING PSYCHOTHERAPY

Psychotherapy is a form of treatment that takes place in a personal setting and involves a professional worker and an individual who presents certain symptoms. To use Freud's expression, the treatment is a "talking therapy." Usually it is designed to reduce symptomatology and improve personal development through uncovering latent anxieties and conflicts. Although it is difficult to state an exact date when psychotherapy was first practiced Freud's psychoanalytic formulations certainly gave this practice tremendous impetus. Much of the development of psychotherapeutic theories and practices has been clinical rather than formally experimental. That is, individual psychotherapists have tried to find out about and experiment with a number of techniques, but usually they have been more concerned with helping their patients than with testing hypotheses and procedures rigorously through scientific controls.

One approach to psychotherapy is to study the effects of psychotherapy on behavior. While the practice of psychotherapy is of interest and importance, the question is: Does it work? Eysenck (1952, 1961*b*, pp. 719–720) surveyed the literature to find out how effective psychotherapy was in curing or helping patients. He concluded that there was no evidence to support the contention that "talking therapy" works:

1. When untreated neurotic control groups are compared with experimental groups of neurotic patients treated by means of psychotherapy, both groups recover to approximately the same extent.
2. When soldiers who have suffered a neurotic breakdown and have not received psychotherapy are compared with soldiers who have received psychotherapy, the chances of the two groups returning to duty are approximately equal.
3. When neurotic soldiers are separated from the Service, their chances of recovery are not affected by their receiving or not receiving psychotherapy.
4. Civilian neurotics who are treated by psychotherapy recover or improve to approximately the same extent as similar neurotics receiving no psychotherapy.
5. Children suffering from emotional disorders and treated by psychotherapy recover or improve to approximately the same extent as similar children not receiving psychotherapy.
6. Neurotic patients treated by means of psychotherapeutic procedures based on learning theory improve significantly more quickly than do patients treated by means of psychoanalytic or eclectic psychotherapy, or not treated by psychotherapy at all.
7. Neurotic patients treated by psychoanalytic psychotherapy do not improve more quickly than patients treated by means of eclectic psychotherapy, and may improve less quickly when account is taken of the large proportion of patients breaking off treatment.
8. With the single exception of the psychotherapeutic methods based on learning theory, results of published research with military and civilian neurotics, and with both adults and children, suggest that the therapeutic effects of psychotherapy are small or non-existent, and do not in any demonstrable way add to the non-specific effects of routine medical treatment, or to such events as occur in the patients' everyday experience.

Needless to say, this conclusion aroused a great deal of controversy, and to this day the argument rages. Why should the argument continue if Eysenck's review of available evidence provided an objective basis for his conclusion? One reason is the heterogeneity among the researches that Eysenck attempted to integrate. The many studies varied widely with respect to scientific adequacy, psychotherapeutic procedures employed, patients studied, and indices of patient improvement utilized. By what criterion or standard of judgment shall the effectiveness of psychotherapy be judged: patients' subjective reports, clinical impressions of psychotherapists, removal or reduction of observable symptoms, or ability of patients to hold jobs and to be well-adjusted socially? Each of these criteria in itself seems reasonable but it is difficult to produce a single, composite criterion. A small number of well-controlled, comprehensive studies have also been made of the efficacy of psychotherapy and it is difficult at the present time to state with confidence the degree to which particular forms of psychotherapy, such as psychoanalytic or Rogerian, are efficacious.

Any final evaluations of psychotherapy as a technique for the modification of behavioral problems is a consideration for the future. This raises the question of what clinical workers and experimental psychopathologists should be doing at the present time to bring about this evaluation. Some might conclude that since psychotherapeutic techniques have not yet been thoroughly validated they should be abandoned until their validity has been assessed. This seems neither a likely nor a wise solution to the problem. Patients coming to psychiatrists, clinical psychologists, and social workers will not be satisfied by statements that these professional workers are busy with validation studies. What is more, the picture need not be as gloomy as Eysenck's report would suggest. It is true that completely objective validation of psychotherapy has not been accomplished, but there are two important pieces of data worth thinking about. One is that most clinical workers, on the basis of their experience, believe that psychotherapy is effective, at least with certain types of patients (Hollingshead and Redlich, 1958). The other is that subjective reports of many patients suggest that they feel they were helped by psychotherapy. Obviously, biases creep into subjective judgments. The psychotherapist who is professionally committed to the practice of psychotherapy may unconsciously be too optimistic about the fruits of his labor. The patient who has spent a large amount of money on psychotherapy may subtly push himself to feel he made a wise expenditure.

Considering (1) the mental health needs of the population, (2) the judged utility of at least some types of psychotherapeutic intervention, and (3) the absence of a therapy demonstrably superior to psychotherapy, we may assume that the practice of psychotherapy will continue. However, students of personality believe that other activities must be carried out concurrently. These are research activities that focus on a number of problems. One of these problems pertains to the choice of criteria. Though it may never be possible to come up with a single, composite index of the effects of psychotherapy, it should be feasible to study the relationship of various criteria of therapeutic success. Another problem involves analysis of the nature of psychotherapeutic intervention. If psychotherapy is effective, what makes it work? How do different methods of psychotherapy affect the behavior of clinicians, and ultimately of patients? Does it make a difference whether psychotherapists agree or disagree with regard to theoretical orientations and views? Available evidence suggests that there are individual differences among psychotherapists that are correlated with the effectiveness of their methods, but these differences are more attributable to their history of experiences, personal characteristics, and nontheory-motivated behavior than to their views about the process of psychotherapy (Betz, 1962; Fiedler, 1950, 1951; Krasner, 1962). Because this evidence has implications for research on personality, let us examine it a bit further.

If it is true that the personalities, mannerisms, behavior, and attitudes of particular psychotherapists are more powerful in modifying patients' attitudes and behavior than their theories of psychotherapy, it would seem logical to study the psychotherapist's characteristics intensively as independent variables in research on psychotherapy. It is interesting that this emphasis on the therapist as an independent variable in the clinical situation bears striking resemblance to the emphasis previously placed on the role of the experimenter in the experimental situation. Of course, one need not limit the social psychology of situations to those that occur in experimental or clinical settings. Many relatives, friends, and associates of people may in informal and often subconscious ways perform therapeutic functions. Advice and assistance from one person may be much more helpful to an individual than comparable advice and assistance from another person. It has been suggested that psychotherapy be viewed as an institutionalized vehicle for the purchase of friendship (Schofield, 1964). It has been shown that in some instances a group of minimally trained, college-educated, mature, married women with children functioned in roles of psychotherapists as effectively as professional psychotherapists (Rioch, 1963; Rioch et al., 1963). Our previous concern with the interplay between the experimenter and the subject, and our present concern with the therapist as an independent variable are two of the general problems of personality and behavioral research.

One significant attitudinal variable, the expectation of therapist and patient concerning psychotherapy, has been reviewed by Goldstein (1962). Patients and therapists differ in their expectations concerning the rate at which patient improvement should occur and how much over-all improvement should be anticipated. Therapists who are indecisive and lack confidence in their abilities can be expected to communicate this to patients. Similarly, patients who basically are resistant to modifying their behavior may communicate this tendency to their therapists. When we realize that there are many other attitudinal factors besides expectations in patient-therapist interactions, the complexity of the psychotherapeutic process becomes evident.

One example that emphasizes this is the problem of control groups in psychotherapy research. If we adopt the model of the individual therapist as an independent or experimental variable in a clinical situation, we must ask the question: What constitutes a control group in clinical research? Let us assume that we are conducting an experiment on the effects of psychotherapy in a clinic, and that, after initial evaluation, half of the persons who come to the clinic are accepted for psychotherapy and the remaining persons are not. Let us assume that at a later date a number of persons in both these groups are studied to determine the level of improvement. In one sense the nontreated persons might be regarded as a control group and the accepted persons as an experimental group. But would this control group really be a nontreated control group? It may be true that this group of people did not receive treatment from any formal clinical agency. But some nonaccepted patients may have managed at least partially to establish therapeutic relationships with persons in their community, such as friends, clergymen, and employers. Thus, students of behavior modification must study not only formally defined helping institutions but informal ones as well.

We have so far considered two approaches to psychotherapy. In one, existing forms of psychotherapy may be studied in terms of how acceptable they are when compared with one another. The question here is: Do they work? The other approach involved the study of personal processes in psychotherapy. The questions here are: What happens in psychotherapy? What are the independent variables that can be isolated, manipulated, and controlled in psychotherapy situations?

A third type of research in the area of behavior modification includes efforts to invent and develop new forms of therapy for behavioral disorders. In recent years a growing number of researchers have been concerned with treating deviant behavior through other means than that of the patient and psychotherapist in verbal, social interaction.

Examples of this are the various medical therapies. Individual and group psychotherapy are both based on the assumption that deviant behavior, although sometimes based on constitutional factors, is more often a product of social learning and of the deleterious effects of the environment on thoughts and feelings. Medical therapies, on the other hand, seek to effect behavior change not through exposure of patients to social situations but through somatic interventions. The two most widely used somatic therapies are shock treatment and drugs. Electroshock, the most common form of shock therapy, has proved to be effective in achieving symptom removal for a variety of neurotic and psychotic disorders, and is particularly effective in cases marked by depression. Drugs used in treating psychologically disturbed persons are of two types, tranquilizers and energizers. Tranquilizers have been used widely and often have dramatic effects in alleviating various disturbances, particularly those in which patients suffer from anxiety, hallucinations, and delusions.

From a research standpoint, the major questions concerning somatic therapies center on their effectiveness and safety, and the mechanisms through which they have their effects. Several somatic therapies have been discovered more by accident than as a consequence of a theory of how the body functions. It is hoped that as research on somatic therapies proceeds, basic contributions to understanding the physiology of behavior will result.

Examples of more purely psychological efforts at uncovering new procedures for treating emotional problems include psychodrama and role-playing techniques (Moreno, 1959), in which patients are asked to act out spontaneously many of their personal preoccupations; hypnosis (Moss, Logan, and Lynch, 1962; Orne, 1962*a*), in which patients are placed in trancelike states in order to help them come to grips with their problems; and conditioning and desensitization techniques designed to elicit specific adaptive response to replace maladaptive ones (Jones, 1961; Lang and Lazovik, 1963; Paul, 1964). For example, the symptom of enuresis (bedwetting) has been attacked by using simple classical conditioning principles. When this is done, an electrical device is incorporated into the child's bed so that when he urinates a bell sounds and awakens him. After a number of trials, the child responds to the sensations of bladder distention before the bell sounds and becomes conditioned to awaken when stimulated by the distention.

Lang and Lazovik (1963) have stated succinctly the view referred to earlier (Chapters 4 and 30) that behavior modification in the case of maladjustment is a matter of symptom removal through learning. They based their conclusion on a study carried out with subjects who had phobic fears of snakes. They used a desensitization training procedure that involved teaching phobic persons to respond in a relaxed manner to stimuli that progressively approximated the phobic stimuli. Through this training these researchers were able to reduce greatly the severity of many phobias. Lang and Lazovik (1963, p. 525) concluded:

1. It is not necessary to explore with a subject the factors contributing to the learning of a phobia or its "unconscious meaning" in order to eliminate the fear behavior.
2. The form of treatment employed here does not lead to symptom substitution or create new disturbances of behavior.
3. In reducing phobic behavior it is not necessary to change basic attitudes, values, or attempt to modify the "personality as a whole." The unlearning of phobic behavior appears to be analogous to the elimination of other responses from a subject's behavior repertoire.

Because applications of learning principles seem promising in strengthening appropriate responses and weakening inappropriate ones, examples of them will be presented in the following section.

EXPERIMENTAL APPROACHES TO BEHAVIOR MODIFICATION

Consider this question: What brings about the response patterns of organisms and how can these patterns be modified? From a behavioristic approach this question might be answered by saying that the environment must be recognized as a very powerful, if not the most powerful influence on behavior. If this is true, it follows that when behavior at any level of deviancy requires modification, it should be possible to manipulate the environment so that undesirable or unwanted behavior may be replaced by desirable or wanted behavior.

One group of researchers that espouses this view of behavior has emphasized particularly the events contingent on the responses made by organisms. That is, what happens after an organism has made a response will influence the probability of that response being emitted again. These response-contingent events function as reinforcers that increase or decrease probability of response. Experiments with animals and persons have provided support for this expectation (Broadhurst, 1961).

In recent years efforts have been made to extend this mode of behavior acquisition and change to deviant behavior. For example, one paper has reported a study of two severely psychotic patients who were classified as schizophrenics (Isaacs, Thomas, and Goldiamond, 1960). These patients had been mute for periods of 19 and 14 years.

Through reinforcement techniques, it was possible in both cases to reinstate some verbal behavior.

In making behavioristic approaches to deviant behavior, one must analyze carefully the response contingencies that impinge on individual patients in particular contexts. Let us consider some examples of individual cases that have been subjected to an experimental behavioristic analysis.

A Behavioristic Approach to Autistic Behavior in Children

Among the most poorly understood types of deviant behavior are those found in children. This is due in part to young children's lack of verbal facility in describing their thoughts and feelings. It is due also to the tendency of parents not to bring their children's behavior problems to qualified professional workers unless or until they become completely unmanageable. Moreover, descriptive language for characterizing children's emotional problems and their etiology has not been well developed.

Severe cases are, of course, more easily recognized than mild ones. In particular, autistic behavior has been subjected to increasing study (Rimland, 1964). Autistic children exhibit a marked inability to relate to persons in their environment and to their environment generally. They are often described as "living within a shell." Within this encapsulated psychological world, the autistic child lives with his fantasies. Retardation in speech and language is usually marked. Indeed, the verbal behavior of autistic children often seems completely nonsensical.

Ferster and DeMyer (1962, p. 90) have studied from an experimental standpoint one major deficiency of the autistic child, his very narrow repertory of appropriate responses to environmental events. The question that they sought to answer was: Could this impoverished behavioral repertory be expanded through reinforcement contingencies in the environment? They selected simple responses, such as pressing a key, and determined to what degree it would be possible to create an environment in which the child would emit and increase emission of the selected responses. They used three subjects in their study:

Thomas, aged 10 and hospitalized 3 years, has been studied for 12 months. He had a normal motor and speech development, speaking short sentences until he was 2½, when he developed severe rage reactions, wandering away from home, gradual loss of speech, an excessive reaction to changes in his daily routine, and withdrawing to a corner where he would remain for weeks.

The second child, Margie, 11 years old and hospitalized 4 years, has been studied for 6 months. Margie had a slower than normal motor development.

The parents cannot recall with sureness any motor development milestones except her walking at 19 months. Her speech was definitely advanced, beginning before her first birthday and proceeding quickly to well-formed sentences with good diction. Speech began regressing when she was 3 years old, gradually dropping off until she was mute. When speech was regained, it was not used socially but as a means of entertaining herself. At 3 years she was cutting with scissors but lost this skill, lost bowel and bladder training, and control over her affect. She has never developed any peer relationships.

Patrick, the third child, aged 3½, was hospitalized 14 months. He has been studied for 4 months. In his first year he showed normal motor development but abnormal emotional development. He didn't like to be held by his mother, would not look her in the eye, would not respond to his name, and shunned the approaches of his sibling. Changes in routine brought rage reactions. He has never developed speech.

Each of these children showed the narrow range of responses that Ferster and DeMyer were interested in studying. The lower portion of Figure 31-1 presents a schematic diagram of the experimental room. As the diagram indicates, the room contained such devices as a pinball machine, a picture viewer, a pigeon and monkey both trained to perform only when the animal compartments were lighted, a television set, and an eight-column vending machine that dispensed candy. Each of the devices could be operated either by a coin or a direct key. The room was so arranged that each time the child pressed a key or inserted a coin some rewarding consequence followed; for example, the television set would turn on, or the animals would perform. Coins were available to the child when he pressed the key to the coin dispenser. The subjects were deprived of all food between meals. The entire experiment was programmed so that all of the responses of interest could be automatically recorded.

During the initial phases of the experiment, the major goal was to observe the rate at which the children performed the various simple tasks. Later it was found that simple activities in the artificial environment created by the experiment could be sustained through reinforcement. When this was accomplished, the next step was to introduce progressive complexities into the artificial environment. For example, after the child was responding at a frequent rate, it was arranged that the reinforcements, the coins, would be delivered only when the plastic panel on which the response key was mounted lighted up. At a later stage, coin insertions were reinforced only when the coin slot was lighted. Since coins inserted in the unlightened coin slots were wasted, the children learned to save their coins until the appropriate light was on. Thus there appeared to be the development of progressively more complex discriminations.

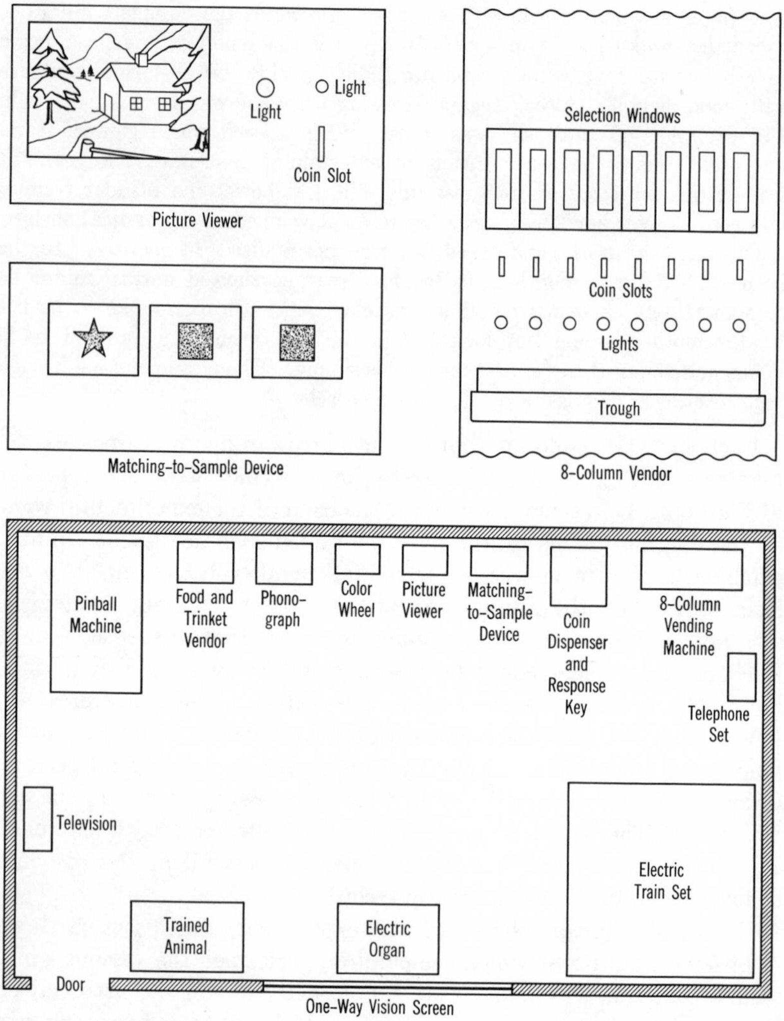

Figure 31-1 Schematic diagram of the experimental room. Each device had a coin slot, coin light and light that was on whenever the device was operating. The detail of the picture viewer illustrates the typical arrangement. Also shown in detail are the matching-to-sample device and the coin slot, coin light arrangement on the 8-column vendor (after Ferster and DeMyer, 1962, p. 92).

At a still later stage, a matching-to-sample device was introduced (see Figure 31-1). This device was programmed so that if the child touched the center window, a figure matching the one in the center window would appear to its left or right. When the child touched the matching figure a coin was dispensed. Otherwise, the child received no reinforcement. After the child learned to cope with the initial, simple matching-to-sample problem, more complex ones were progressively introduced. Ferster and DeMyer's data show that complex behavior, directly related to events in their environment, can be developed by severely disturbed children. Ferster and DeMyer concluded that if the laboratory procedures were capable of modifying the children's behavior, it might be possible also to modify behavior in the social millieu.

A Behavioristic Approach to Adult Psychotic Behavior

Lindsley (1960, 1963) has reported a series of operant conditioning experiments with adult psychotics that are similar to the experiment performed by Ferster and DeMyer (1962). By directly manipulating the behavior of patients in artificial environments, he hoped to contribute to the modification of deviant behavior. One group of studies dealt with the response of pulling a plunger. He found that the operant rate of plunger pulling for hospitalized mental patients was typically much lower than for normal persons. But why might an investigator use the plunger-pulling response as part of a therapy program for disturbed individuals?

It has been shown that when plunger pulling is reinforced with candy or cigarettes, the rate at which psychotic patients pull the plunger is negatively correlated with the rate of emission of psychotic responses such as hallucinations. That is, in the experimental situation, plunger pulling appears to interfere with psychotic behavior. It has also been noted that the display of psychotic symptoms by patients outside of the experimental room decreases under a reinforcement regimen. Thus, there seem to be a generalizing effect of reinforcement from the artificial laboratory environment to that of hospital wards.

Not all of Lindsley's severely disturbed patients responded positively to reinforcement procedures. One interesting case has been reported which suggests that, for some patients, combinations of behavior therapy in artificial environments and of the more traditional forms of psychotherapy may be more effective than either technique alone. One chronic schizophrenic patient had had 659 sessions of reinforcement for plunger pulling. Intermittent reinforcements (candy) had

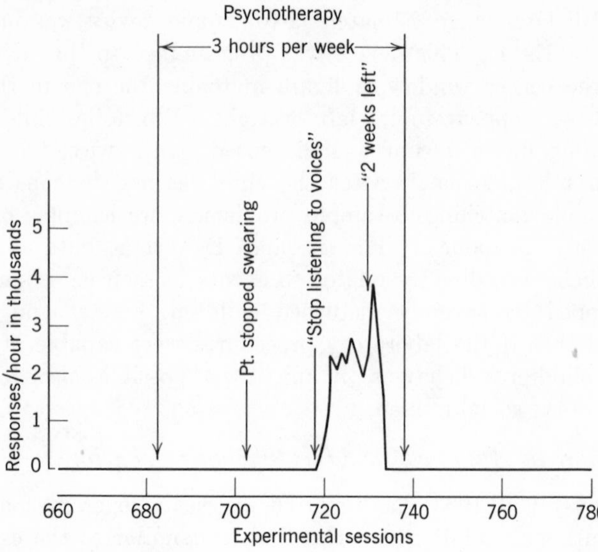

Figure 31-2 Effect of psychotherapy sessions on free-operant response rate of a chronic schizophrenic (after Lindsley, 1963, p. 52).

failed to increase his rate of plunger pulling. Following these sessions a student nurse began to see the patient three times a week for ten weeks in a form of psychotherapy. Figure 31-2 shows the way in which the talking therapy involving the student nurse influenced the patient's plunger-pulling response.

The first arrow indicates the beginning of the student nurse-patient interactions. At the second arrow, the patient stopped swearing at the student nurse. At the third arrow the student nurse became quite directive and told the patient to stop listening to his voices. The fourth arrow indicates the point at which the student nurse told the patient she would, in two weeks, not be able to see him any longer since her affiliation with the hospital would end at that time. The fifth arrow shows that in the session following the departure of the student nurse the patient's rate of plunger pulling declined to zero.

A few comments seem appropriate in relation to this case. It seems clear that the plunger-pulling behavior of the patient increased as a result of the development of the social relationship with the student nurse. Two facts are worth noting. One is that the patient-student nurse interactions did not take place in the experimental room. The other is that the patient's social relationship with the student nurse ended after only 10 weeks of contact. This is a relatively short period of time. Furthermore, the student nurse was by no means experienced in dealing with patients and in the conduct of psychotherapy. A number of promising possibilities come to mind in light of this one study with one patient. What effect would the presence of the student nurse or some other person in the experimental room have on plunger-pulling behavior? Could the patient be brought to the point at which he would pull the plunger in order to hear or see or talk to the other person? What might be the relative effects on ward behavior of psychotherapy alone and of psychotherapy and other methods based on behavior theory? What effects might somatic therapies have on operant responding?

A Social Psychological Experiment in Treating Mental Illness

The two experiments described so far in this chapter were aimed at modifying the behavior of hospitalized mental patients. But they were conducted in the laboratory rather than in the hospital ward; they involved very special sets of conditions and focused on specific responses of the solitary patient. Might experimental behavior modification efforts prove productive if applied to disturbed persons living together within the social structure of the mental hospital?

A group of psychologists led by Fairweather at the Palo Alto, California Veterans Administration Hospital sought to answer just this question by attempting to modify the behavior of a group of chronically hospitalized mental patients (Fairweather, 1964). These patients were men who had not benefited from traditional psychiatric therapies. Fairweather and his colleagues believed that the failure of these patients to find niches for themselves in their community was due to inability to play useful and appropriate roles in social contacts. These investigators reasoned that perhaps the ward of the mental hospital could be used as a mechanism for strengthening the social behavior of chronic mental patients. In their experiment they sought to rehabilitate severely socially constricted persons by creating a total social situation within the hospital ward that would approximate situations found in the community. In this environment the chronically hospitalized mental patient might acquire skills and learn to play social roles that would contribute to a return to society.

The Palo Alto experiment involved two groups of chronic patients. At the outset of the research these groups seemed quite comparable. Table 31-1 presents a breakdown of the types of patients living in the traditional or control ward and in the experimental, small group

TABLE 31-1

Number of Patients in Each of the Four Diagnostic Groups for the Two Treatments

Diagnostic Group	Traditional Ward	Small-Group Ward	Total
Nonpsychotics	7	13	20
Psychotics, 0–2 years	33	49	82
Psychotics, 2–4 years	18	22	40
Psychotics, over 4 years	26	27	53
Total	84	111	195

Adapted from G. W. Fairweather (Ed.) (1964), *Social psychology in treating mental illness: An experimental approach*, p. 39, John Wiley, New York.

ward. The table shows that 20 nonpsychotic and 175 psychotic patients participated in the experiment. Among the latter group were 82 men who had had 0 to 2 years of hospitalization prior to the experiment, 40 who had had 2 to 4 years, and 53 who had had more than 4 years of prior hospitalization.

Table 31-2 outlines the similarities and differences between the conditions to which the experimental and control groups were exposed. As the table reveals, the small group and traditional ward schedules were similar except for a few time periods. During one of these periods (8:00 to 9:00 A. M.) the patients on the experimental ward did ward housekeeping as a group. During another (11:00 to 12:00) the group discussed and made decisions and recommendations about group members.

Each patient on the small group ward was required to go through four steps in the experimental treatment program. A patient at Step 1 had to attain an acceptable level of personal care, punctuality on assignments, and activity in orienting new group members. At Step 1 a patient received $10.00 and a one-day pass each week. Step 2 required adequate performance in Step 1 and, in addition, qualitatively acceptable work on job assignments. The Step 2 group member was eligible for $15.00 a week and overnight passes every other week. Step 3 members received $20.00 a week and overnight passes for three of every four weekends. To attain this step a patient had to show good judgment in recommending issuance of money and passes. Step 4 permitted a patient unlimited withdrawal of money from an account and unlimited use of passes. Patients preparing to depart from the hospital were at the Step 4 level.

If one were to summarize the major differences between the small group and traditional ward group, one would have to emphasize the fact that patients of the latter were carefully supervised by staff members, while patients of the experimental group were given a high degree of personal choice and assigned responsibility for themselves. Fairweather (1964, pp. 31, 173) notes:

TABLE 31-2
Daily Ward Schedule

		Small-Group Ward	Traditional Ward
A. M.	6:00–6:30	Lights on in dormitory	Lights on in dormitory
	6:30–7:30	Bedmaking, shaving, bathing	Bedmaking, shaving, bathing
	7:30–7:55	Breakfast	Breakfast
	7:55–8:00	Medication	Medication
	8:00–9:00	Task group ward housekeeping	Individual work assignments
	9:00–10:00	Ward meeting hour	Individual work assignments
	10:00–11:00	Recreation hour	Ward meeting hour
	11:00–12:00	Autonomous meetings of task groups	Recreation hour
P. M.	12:00–12:05	Medication	Medication
	12:05–12:30	Free time	Free time
	12:30–1:00	Lunch	Lunch
	1:00–4:00	Individual work assignments	Individual work assignments
	4:00–5:30	Ward activity—patients' choice (recreation, shower, socialize, etc.)	Ward activity—patients' choice (recreation, shower, socialize, etc.)
	5:30–6:10	Dinner	Dinner
	6:10–9:00	Off-ward recreation, i.e., library, dance, etc.	Off-ward recreation, i.e., library, dance, etc.
	9:00–9:05	Medication	Medication
	9:05–10:00	Free time	Free time
	10:00	Bedtime	Bedtime

Adapted from G. E. Fairweather (Ed.) (1964), *Social psychology in treating mental illness: An experimental approach*, p. 28, John Wiley, New York.

In the traditional program, all problems regarding the patient are taken up with him as an individual matter. His role is very clearly a subordinate one in which he relies upon the staff for their final decisions without any voice about possible courses of action. On the other hand, the social system of the small-group threatment program clearly delineates the patient's role as that of participant in group discussion and recommendations. Although the final decision regarding such recommendations rests with the staff, each patient's task group has the responsibility and is rewarded for recommending realistic and meaningful courses of action for each of its members, with particular emphasis on daily living and future plans.

On four days a week the small group held its discussion meetings without the presence of staff members. The fifth meeting per week was attended by staff personnel:

No staff member was allowed to enter this room except when specifically requested by the task group for consultation. Consultations, as it will be developed, meant only that the staff could divulge information to the group which would allow the group to make adequate decisions. On the fifth day, the staff evaluated the degree to which each group had met its obligation to make adequate recommendations about problems presented to it. For the evaluation, the staff entered the task group room at a given time and was seated. Usually the task group leader, who had emerged in the process of the group's autonomous meetings, began presenting the group's evaluation. This constituted a review of the task group's recommendations about the step level to which each of their members should be assigned, an estimate of the over-all group morale, the manner in which the group had handled problems which had been presented to them by the staff during the week, recommendations concerning the money and passes for each of the individual members, and a progress report on the departure plans for every member who was in the fourth step level. Frequently, the task group spontaneously handed in a written report of their weekly recommendations to the staff, following the staff-patient evaluation session.

Immediately after this meeting the staff adjourned to their own room and discussed the task group's evaluation. Each recommendation of the task group was taken in turn and resolved by vote. All staff members, except the staff leader, a psychologist, had a vote on each of the task group recommendations. The psychologist did not vote except in case of a tie because it was believed that an adamant position by him might unduly influence the votes of other staff members who frequently looked to him for advice. For this reason, his role was that of discussion leader.

The following is an excerpt from one verbatim log of the experimental small group (Fairweather, 1964, pp. 185–186):

Monday: The group spent considerable time discussing Mr. Watson since he has become something of a problem to the group. In the desire of the group to help Mr. Watson as much as possible, it was decided to defer any action until Mr. Watson had conferred with Dr. Jones. Mr. Watson was given permission of the group to consult Dr. Jones. The group would like to know whether there is any medical or mental reason that Mr. Watson cannot take a more active part in the group discussion.

Action on Mr. Edwards. Mr. Edwards received a note stating that he did not get up in time to shave. It was noted by the group that Mr. Edwards had not shaved for the second day since receiving the note. Since this is negligence on the part of Mr. Edwards, the group decided that he be reduced in step from step 3 to step 2. The vote was as follows: Unanimous with the exception of Mr. Watson, that Mr. Edwards be reduced to step 2. A change in the pass list for that week was made by the group secretary.

Tuesday: By unanimous vote Mr. Watson was reduced to step 1 with privileges. It was noted by the group that Mr. Watson was unable to obtain help from his interview with Dr. Jones, and the group felt that his lack of response in the group business left no other alternative.

Mr. Thompson had been given permission of the group to be absent in order to obtain an interview with the Social Security representative.

Wednesday: It was decided by the group that Mr. Jacobs would submit plans in preparation for entering step 4. Mr. Jacobs submitted a plan for family care, but this plan was rejected by the group for its lack of long range planning during home care and after.

Mr. Williams was also under discussion but action is deferred until after the next report on his IT (hospital job) assignment. Mr. Williams has decided that he will try to obtain employment with Brewster Aviation after his ME (patient employment) has expired. The plan met with the approval of the group.

Thursday: It was decided by the group that a card would be purchased and sent to the Salvation Army. The suggestion was made by Mr. Scheerer. It was also decided that a card would be sent to each member discharged to show the discharged patient that he had the well wishes of the group. Money for the cards is donated by members of the group.

Mr. Parsons left on 90 day TV (trial visit). Mr. Parsons will be missed by the group to whom he gave his every service. Mr. Martin was unanimously elected to fill his post as secretary.

Friday: Group advancements as follows: Mr. Jacobs to remain in step 3 until he has forwarded a better detailed plan for the future (by majority vote). Mr. Graybeal to remain in step 3 until he has advanced plans for his future action. Mr. MacConnell, Lyons, Maddox, Thompson, Scheerer, Rollins, to be advanced to step 3. Unaminous vote. Mr. Watson to remain in step 1. Unanimous vote. Mr. Martin and Mr. Williams to remain in step 4, there being no change in future plans and their plans meeting the approval of group and staff. Mr. Edwards reduced to step 2.

This excerpt clearly suggests the social involvements engendered in the experimental ward. Patients of this ward were decision makers for themselves and others and initiators to a degree unheard of in traditional psychiatric hospitals. They were made to live in an environment much more comparable to the workaday world than to that of the protective and undemanding mental hospital. As might be expected, many chronic patients expressed preferences for the traditional over the experimental ward. This is not surprising since most chronic mental patients *are* chronic precisely because of social inertia and lack of work motivation. Let us look now at some of the behavioral comparisons made between the experimental and control groups.

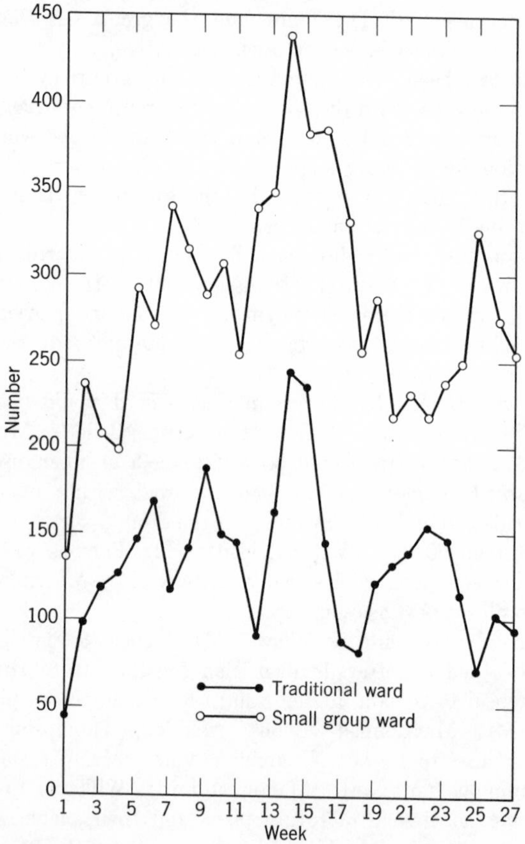

Figure 31-3 Mean number of speeches directed to other patients for each treatment program (after Fairweather, 1964, p. 84).

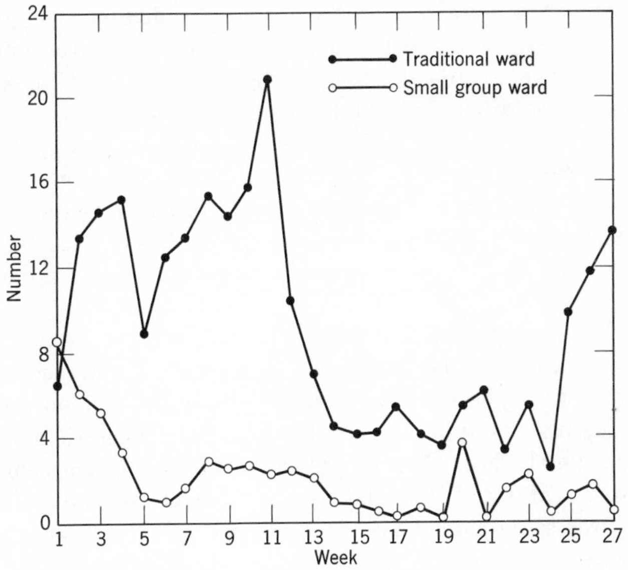

Figure 31-4 Mean number of speeches directed to the discussion leader for each treatment program (after Fairweather, 1964, p. 85).

Did the small group ward have a facilitating effect on the social behavior of chronic mental patients? Figure 31-3 shows the mean number of speeches at group meetings directed by patients to other patients. Figure 31-4 shows the mean number of speeches directed to the discussion leader. It is clear that small group members engage in many more verbal interchanges among themselves than do traditional ward patients. But traditional ward patients direct their verbal output to the discussion leader to a much greater extent than do small group members. This suggests that at group meetings on the traditional ward, verbal output may to a considerable extent be a collection of two-way interchanges between patient and leader. At group meetings on the experimental ward, the patients seem relatively active in responding to one another. Thus Figures 31-3 and 31-4 provide a basis for the conclusion that the experimental group did achieve a higher level of social interaction than the control group. Comparison of the two groups on other measures of social involvement also supported this conclusion.

A gross but important index of the success of a treatment program is its discharge rate. Did the experimental and treatment groups differ in total number of days spent in the hospital prior to discharge? The Palo Alto researchers found that patients in the small group program spent an average of 109.01 days in the hospital. The comparable mean for the traditional ward patients was 149.96. There was a difference of 40.95 days per patient between the two groups. Furthermore, there was no tendency for patients discharged relatively early in their hospitalizations to require rehospitalization more quickly than patients discharged relatively late. On the contrary, those who were discharged more quickly were most successful in remaining longer in their communities.

Although the results of the Palo Alto project seem encouraging, they should not be overstated. The small group ward discharged patients more quickly than the traditional ward. Its patients upon discharge were successful in staying out of the hospital longer than patients on the traditional ward. But its patients were usually not completely rehabilitated. Many of them did require rehospitalization. This was especially true of patients whose psychological problems were the most chronic.

The Palo Alto study cannot be regarded as either definitive or successful in every respect. But it represents a major step forward in experimentation within clinical settings. Much more must be found out about the causes of chronic illness and the factors that help and hinder hospital adjustment and return to the community (Schwartz and Schwartz, 1964). Much more research will be needed to perfect the techniques developed at Palo Alto. For example, Fairweather (1964, p. 284) speculated about the possibility that:

> . . . groups which have been trained in decision making within the hospital might be moved as units into the community. It can be supposed that this would provide a stable social system in which the former chronic patient would have an established role and status. However, the activities of such a group of patients would, of necessity, have to be consonant with the role requirements of citizens in the community. If one allows his fantasy free rein, it is but one logical step to see that the role requirements of patients in task groups are identical with role requirements of group membership in any problem-solving group in the community, whether it be industrial, educational, recreational, or whatever.

Experiments on deviant behavior need not be limited to the laboratory, or to specially created environments. They can also be carried out in the clinical setting and, as the work of Fairweather and his colleagues suggests, can contribute directly to the rehabilitation of human lives.

PSYCHOTHERAPY WITH SCHIZOPHRENIC PATIENTS

We have noted that many of the phenomena of psychotherapy such as transference, resistance, and countertransference may be quite general, and that the personal characteristics of psychotherapists seem to be perhaps the most significant single factor in determining their success with patients. It might be conjectured that the best matching, in terms of personal characteristics, of therapists with patients would produce the best results of psychotherapy encounters.

In reviewing diagnostic categories we commented upon the responsiveness of certain kinds of patients to psychotherapy. High anxiety and motivation to change behavior are usually taken as positive indicators in favor of attempting psychotherapy. Although the characteristics of patients in psychotherapy have long been explicitly recognized as factors relating to its efficacy, therapist characteristics have been discussed only in quite general terms such as countertransference. In recent years there has been explicit recognition that psychotherapy cannot be meaningfully discussed without incorporation of the psychotherapist and his personal characteristics as independent variables (Betz, 1962; Krasner, 1962).

In operant conducting experiments conducted in artificial environments, independent variables can be easily and objectively defined; for example, reinforcement with particular kinds and amounts of candy. These objective, standardized reinforcements may in a sense be regarded as the treatment in behavior therapy. It is a much more difficult assignment to define the treatment given by a psychotherapist. Psychotherapists, by virtue of being human, are not standardized, and to give explicit definition or description of their characteristics is a major challenge. Can characteristics of therapists be determined and the relationship of these characteristics to patients' behavior be observed? Viewed in terms of this question, assessment and experimental approaches to personality merge with each other.

An influential program of psychotherapy research from this standpoint has been carried out by Whitehorn and Betz at the Henry Phipps Psychiatric Clinic of the Johns Hopkins Hospital. Betz (1962) described its methods and reported on some of its findings. The general aim of the research was to ". . . establish with definite reliability what makes a difference in the treatment of schizophenic patients" (Betz, 1962, p. 41). In attempting to achieve this aim, Whitehorn and Betz intensively studied both participants in psychotherapy, the patient and the therapist.

The patients studied were considered to be suffering from schizophrenia, the most serious of the mental disorders and, as we have seen, a disorder that often becomes chronic to the point of total social incapacity. For many years, this incapacity had been regarded as a contraindication for the use of psychotherapy. Recently, clinical workers have come to feel more hopeful about the responses of at least some schizophrenics to psychotherapeutic experiences. However, a perennial question has been: Why are most schizophrenics resistant to forming meaningful relationships with psychotherapists, even with those who are quite skilled ones?

In preliminary studies, Whitehorn and Betz isolated one characteristic of schizophrenics related to their involvement in psychotherapy. They observed that in case after case schizophrenics' problems centered on their reactions to persons they interpreted as authority figures. It also seemed that much of the withdrawn attitude of schizophrenics could be interpreted as a fear of being hurt and controlled by perceived authority figures. Since psychotherapy, to be effective, requires establishment of a bond of trust between patient and therapist, it is not surprising that schizophrenics are difficult to treat. Whitehorn and Betz were challenged by the task of discovering attributes of therapists that might facilitate the establishment of a sense of trust by schizophrenic patients.

The therapists studied at the Phipps Clinic were psychiatric residents. Do different therapists, in fact, have different effects on schizophrenic patients? Using discharge from the clinic because of improvement as a criterion of success in psychotherapy, Whitehorn and Betz found strong indications that this was the case. They were able to define two groups of therapists. One group achieved an improvement rate of 75 per cent with schizophrenic patients, while the other achieved an improvement rate of only 25 per cent. When a second group of therapists was studied, it was possible again to define two groups of psychiatric residents, one who achieved an improvement rate of 82 per cent and the other that of 34 per cent. These are certainly large differences in therapist effectiveness that do not seem to be artifacts of systematically assigning easier or less severe cases to some therapists than to others.

Were Whitehorn and Betz able to isolate differences between the relatively successful and unsuccessful therapists? Successful therapists were more capable of grasping the meaning of the verbal communications of schizophrenics and the motivations behind them than were unsuccessful ones. Successful therapists tended to be oriented toward assisting their patients in specific ways so that they could achieve better adjustment patterns. Relatively unsuccessful therapists, on the other hand, tended to focus on the nature of the patients' psychopathology and existing symptoms. Successful therapists also tended to be more expressive in their interactions with patients than unsuccessful therapists. The unsuccessful, as compared with the successful, tended to be passively permissive and formal in such matters as interpreting to patients the meaning of their behavior.

Having established that in their treatment of schizophrenic patients therapists display individual differences to which the personal styles of therapists contribute significantly, Whitehorn and Betz next turned to the possibility of predicting which therapists would be relatively unsuccessful in working with schizophrenics. In this study, the Strong Vocational Interest Blank (Strong, 1943) was employed. By obtaining subjects' responses to the Strong Inventory, the investigators were able to compare the subjects' interests with those of persons who actually entered 45 different vocations. The Strong Inventory had previously been shown to be of value in predicting the areas of specialization selected by doctors (Strong, 1943). The group used in the Phipps prediction study consisted of 72 therapists whose effectiveness with schizophrenic patients was known and for whom Strong Vocational Interest Blank scores were available.

In one of their studies involving 15 relatively successful and 11 relatively unsuccessful therapists, the Phipps investigators found that the two groups differed with respect to four particular vocational groups in similarity of interests. The interests of the relatively successful therapists were significantly similar to those of lawyers and certified public accountants. On the other hand, the interests of the relatively unsuccessful therapists were similar to those of printers and teachers of mathematics and physical science. When scores on the Strong keys, which discriminated between the two groups of therapists, were applied to a second group of therapists, it was found that the printer, mathematics-physical science teacher, lawyer, and accountant keys again discriminated between relatively successful and unsuccessful therapists.

Each of the 400 individual items on the Strong Inventory was studied by the researchers so that the psychological meaning of the Strong scores might be understood. Twenty-three of the items were answered in significantly different ways by the two groups of therapists. Table 31-3 shows the items characteristic of the two groups of therapists. The A therapists referred to in this table were those therapists who were relatively successful in treating schizophrenics; the B therapists were those who were relatively unsuccessful.

TABLE 31-3

Characteristic Responses to Individual Strong Vocational Interest Test Items Which Differentiate 15 Known A Physicians from 11 Known B Physicians; Differences Are at Levels of Statistical Significance of between .02 and .05 by the Chi Square Test

Responses characterizing the A doctors (but not the B doctors):		
"Like"	*311	President of a society or club
	*356a	Many women friends
"Yes"	367	Accept just criticism without getting sore
	375	Can correct others without giving offense
"Dislike"	59	Marine engineer
	*60	Mechanical engineer
	*68	Photoengraver
	*90	Specialty salesman
	94	Toolmaker
	*185	Making a radio set
"No"	*368	Have mechanical ingenuity
Responses characterizing the B doctors (but not the A doctors):		
"Like"	17	Building contractor
	*19	Carpenter
	*87	Ship officer
	121	Manual training
	122	Mechanical training
	187	Adjusting a carburetor
	189	Cabinet making
	216	Entertaining others
	218	Looking at shop windows
"Dislike"	151	Drilling in a company
	290	Interest public in a new machine through public addresses
	*381	Follow up subordinates effectively

Adapted from Barbara J. Betz (1962), Experiences in research in psychotherapy with schizophrenic patients. In H. H. Strupp and L. Luborsky (Eds.), *Research in psychotherapy*, Vol. 2, p. 48, American Psychological Association, Washington, D.C.

* The asterisk indicates items used in constructing the predictive screening measure.

When a special Strong scale consisting of the 23 items in Table 31-3 was applied to a second group of A and B therapists it was similarly found to discriminate significantly between them. When the prediction procedures were applied to a group of therapists at another institution, similar results were obtained.

Integrating their quantitative assessments of therapists with all of the other available information on them, Whitehorn and Betz suggested that A (successful) therapists placed high value on self-determination, on being perceptive of patients' inner experiences, and on being individualistic in their own approach to life. As suggested earlier, the B (unsuccessful) therapists seemed to view patients as having inadequacies that require correction and to value deference and conformity. The A therapists seemed to be spontaneous and open with patients; the B therapists seemed to be formal and to keep a protective distance between themselves and patients. In view of what was said earlier about the schizophrenic's fear of authority figures, it does not seem surprising that the more authoritarian B therapists would have difficulty in involving schizophrenics in a trusting relationship. Betz (1962, pp. 53–54) states:

> The concept of "psychotherapy," if kept too abstract, can lead to needless pitfalls or ambiguity. Ambiguity can be reduced by focusing on the following specific considerations: "psychotherapy of whom?" "By whom?" "To what end?" Although the *goals in studying* psychotherapy may vary in a wide range, the *goal of psychotherapy* itself seems simply stated: *to assist a patient with a psychiatric disability to a state of improved well-being.* That is, the purpose of psychotherapy is favorable patient outcome. Success in efforts to achieve this purpose, the procedure taken toward it, even concepts of what "it" is may vary. But it is the presence of this purpose that determines that a "psychotherapeutic situation" exists. The nature of a two-person professional relationship is intrinsically distinguishable as one that is "psychotherapeutic" or one that is "nonpsychotherapeutic" by whether this purpose is present or absent.
>
> Minimum requirements for research in psychotherapy, therefore, include a focus on three basic variables: (a) the patient, (b) the therapist (as the focal point of the therapeutic situation), and (c) patient outcome.

Each of these variables has been referred to in previous discussions. It is clear that future research relating to patient and therapist variables must be directed towards meaningfully defining these variables. It is worth noting that the A and B therapists did not differ in the treatment results that they achieved with depressed and neurotic patients. This would suggest caution in broadly generalizing about the characteristics of relatively effective and ineffective therapists. It would be better to speak of particular behavior problems in particular types of patients treated by therapists whose personal characteristics are known.

The goal of psychotherapeutic endeavors is clearly patient improvement. Whereas criteria may vary widely, it is important that they be defined clearly and judged reliably. Criteria of improvement will vary according to the severity of the problems presented. Results of treating by psychotherapy severely disturbed and disabled patients should be considerably different from those of treating patients with mild behavioral and social difficulties. Criteria of patient improvement must not be subject to the biased judgments of the therapists who treat the patients under study. In the Phipps study, the therapists did make judgments of their patients' improvement but two supervising psychiatrists also independently made judgments. It was therefore possible to minimize errors that were made because of the therapists' closeness to the psychotherapeutic interaction. In addition to using psychiatric judgments of patient outcome, a number of other indices were employed in the Phipps studies. These included the disposition of the case (did the patient go from the Phipps Clinic to another hospital or to the community?), rating of patient behavior, and patients' ability to participate in the clinic's activity program.

In view of the evidence of the Phipps study, the conclusion stated by Betz (1962, p. 59) seems reasonable and suggestive of useful directions for future research in psychotherapy:

> . . . psychotherapeutic change is conceived as the solution of specific personal problems and the activation of latent inner potentialities for more healthy functioning, brought about through meaningful human experience provided along specific lines through the relationship with the therapist. For the schizophrenic patient this is a profound, personal experience, superseding that with any previous interpersonal partners. It is customarily an absorbing professional experience for the doctor. It is the goal of research in psychotherapy to contribute to a body of knowledge about how these profound changes can be brought about so that they can be produced by more doctors for more patients with a high probability of success.

CONCLUDING COMMENTS

The studies considered in this chapter and the preceding one suggest the role that experimentation can play in increasing knowledge of deviant behavior. They show that experimental methods can illuminate some of the determinants and maintainers of personal maladjustment. Furthermore, they indicate that behavior modification techniques such as psychotherapy can be viewed as experimental methods whose procedures and effects can be objectively evaluated.

In terms of our view of the study of personality, an experimental approach to deviant behavior and its modification represents a logical extension of concepts and methods already considered. The use of experimental methods, such as the methods of personality assessment, need not be limited to the study of nonclinical cases. Each of these methods contributes to the confirmation or nonconfirmation of judgments and hunches that are the result of clinical work. On the basis of the evidence reviewed, it seems reasonable to conclude that, whenever possible and appropriate, personality assessment and experimental manipulations be used jointly in testing hypotheses and techniques.

Using scientific methods in the study of maladjusted individuals in no way, of course, represents a panacea. One can use reliable methods in unimaginative, mundane ways. Such an approach will not produce any breakthrough or discoveries of new relationships. Moreover, scientific methods cannot be expected to eliminate the necessity for prudently interpreting data and imaginatively building upon existing information. These cautions are relevant to the study of personality generally, and in the present case to psychopathology specifically. When the number of firmly established facts is not great, controversies centering on the judgments and biases of investigators may abound. Rosenthal (1963) has shown this to be so in the role expectations play in experimenters' determination of empirical findings. What one's hypotheses are and how they are tested will influence experimental findings (Holt, 1965).

It is worthwhile to note that controversies among researchers may ultimately lead to significant empirical contributions, if not to rapprochement among differing points of view. This becomes evident in the behavior therapy versus psychotherapy controversy. Practitioners of psychotherapy stress the uncovering and understanding of unconscious anxieties and conflicts as a step toward symptom removal. Many behavior therapists regard this concern as an unnecessary, indeed as a sidetracking, preoccupation. Regardless of how we may feel individually about this issue, it seems possible that, with the issue clearly stated, experimental and clinical comparisons of the two approaches can be achieved (Breger and McGaugh, 1965). The results of these empirical tests may not be as simple or as clear-cut or as universally applicable as one might wish, but they should increase understanding of the nature of behavioral maladjustment and rehabilitation.

32

Developmental Aspects of Psychopathology

Even such widely divergent groups as psychoanalysts and behavior therapists agree on the importance of the historical antecedents of behavior. In Part 4 we talked about methods of studying personality development. These methods include assessment techniques, experimentation, and longitudinal studies. Assessment and experimental research are cross-sectional in nature. For example, selected subjects varying in age are tested or studied in experimental situations and their behavior is compared. An example of this sort of investigation would be the administration of a personality inventory to children of 10, 12, and 14 years of age in order to compare their scores. An elaboration of this paradigm would be to select children 10, 12, and 14 years of age, assess both of them and their parents, and then make desired comparisons. Experimental studies of development would involve placing subjects differing in a developmental characteristic in an experimental situation, and then comparing their reactions to it. For example, children at ages three, four, and five might be placed in an experimental play room with and without the presence of their mothers in order to compare the effects of the mothers' presence on the behavior of children who differ in age.

We also saw that longitudinal approaches to development require follow-ups of subjects studied. There might be one follow-up or many. We have seen that longitudinal research, in which subjects are studied, not in retrospect but as development proceeds, is especially valuable in shedding light on the history of personal characteristics. The Fels studies (Kagan and Moss, 1962) exemplify this type of investigation.

In examining longitudinal studies one soon realizes that they are among the most challenging, difficult, expensive, and time-consuming types of psychological research. However, children grow up to be the kind of people they are, to a large extent, because of their contact with their environment. Unfortunately, the number of longitudinal studies of development necessary to provide adequate description of these contacts and their impacts have not been made. The need for studies that permit observations of the same individuals over periods of time is a pressing one. Some characteristics may show a high degree of continuity in an individual's life history; others may change significantly. We not only need to know whether characteristics of people change over time, we also need to have an understanding of how continuities and changes eventuate.

These needs are perhaps even greater in persons who display deviant and bizarre behavior than in normal individuals. One need not have the opinion, often unfairly attributed to psychoanalysts, that adult behavior is determined by a small number of particular types of childhood experiences in order to appreciate the impact of environment on maladjusted persons. But useful as these data are, the paucity of ambitious longitudinal studies of personality development of normal persons is less glaring than that of similar studies of persons who require clinical attention.

The reason for this state of affairs is not difficult to comprehend. In longitudinal studies of normal children, subjects are selected either at random or in terms of certain characteristics such as socioeconomic status and intelligence. Regular follow-up contacts are then made with the subjects over a period of time. The problem of doing longitudinal research with persons who display particular types of psychopathology is this: they usually do not become identified until seen in a clinical setting. Once the patient has come to a clinic, hospital, or consulting office he can be identified as someone on whom we might like to make longitudinal assessments and observations. But from the standpoint of longitudinal research it is then too late.

A possible but not feasible way of undertaking longitudinal research on deviant individuals would be to assess a group of subjects large enough to include some who could be expected to develop identifiable behavioral maladjustments. Such a study would require a group many times larger than any involved in previous longitudinal studies. For this reason, researchers interested in gathering information about the histories of maladjusted persons have been forced to resort to a variety of less than ideal tactics. Some have carried out retrospective "longitudinal" studies through case histories based on interviews with patients. Others have sought to observe and interview the parents of patients. Still others have conducted psychometric assessments of patients and their parents.

Several investigators have studied schizophrenics and their parents in the same social situation. This latter approach, although clearly not longitudinal, seems quite useful because it does at least provide investigators with an opportunity to observe directly social interactions among family members. Finally, mention should be made of a type of follow-up suggested in a previous context. These are follow-ups of patients after they have been discharged from a clinic or hospital (Chapter **29**). These particular studies are usually designed to determine how effective different methods of treatment have been. Except for postclinical follow-ups, which have the specific purpose of describing clinical results, the other methods mentioned must be regarded primarily as suggestive and valuable in generating hypotheses.

A CASE STUDY OF SCHIZOPHRENIC QUADRUPLETS

There are many longitudinal "substitutes" designed to provide sets of data as objective and comprehensive as possible in order to reconstruct the experimental backgrounds of persons. Opportunities for attempts at this type of reconstruction vary according to clinical facilities. There is therefore a catch-as-catch-can element to behavioral reconstructions. One of the most provocative examples of this kind of effort has been provided by Rosenthal (**1964**) and a group of his colleagues at the National Institute of Mental Health (NIMH). It followed the format of a case study. It was, in fact, a case study not only of a patient but of an entire family in the context of its community.

The major protagonists in this study were four postadolescent, genetically identical sisters each of whom had been diagnosed as schizophrenic. They were treated at NIMH over a period of three years. One of the quadruplets, Nora Genain, was diagnosed as a schizophrenic reaction, catatonic type. She was quiet, withdrawn, and seemed at times to hallucinate. At discharge she was considered to have improved, but still to have the major characteristics of a catatonic schizophrenic and still to require hospitalization. Her sister, Hester, was similarly diagnosed upon admission and seemed more inaccessible than Nora. Although she had periods of improvement during her stay at NIMH, shortly before her discharge she became increasingly suspicious and anxious. She was the only one of the four sisters who explicitly expressed an interest in remaining at NIMH. She was discharged with the same diagnosis as that given upon admission and it was recommended that she receive further hospitalization.

Iris also was diagnosed and discharged as catatonic schizophrenic. Her symptoms included some of the most easily recognized indications of catatonia such as standing motionless for long periods of time. Upon discharge, further hospitalization was recommended. However, it was felt that she had improved during her stay at NIMH. Myra, upon admission, was given the same diagnosis as had been assigned her sisters. She was tense and anxious and showed psychomotor retardation. However, she was better integrated than her sisters and seemed to be the leader among them. In contradistinction to her sisters, Myra showed a strongly positive response to therapy. During her stay, in fact, she worked part time in a laboratory on the grounds. During her third year she made great progress. Although she experienced difficulties in leaving NIMH, she was able to pass a civil service examination, and a driver's license examination as well. She showed an ability to hold a job, dated, and was able to engage in a variety of social activities. She was discharged as distinctly improved and there was optimism about her future.

The girls' father, Mr. Genain, objected to their stay at NIMH. He often threatened to take them out of the hospital. He seemed to be a man who, although at times cooperative and cordial, had considerable hostility toward people. His wife reported that he had tried to choke her on several occasions and that she had considered leaving him at a number of points. At times he accused his wife of having sexual relationships with his daughters' psychiatrists. During the girls' stay at NIMH he came to accept the *fait accompli* of their hospitalization. During their third year at the hospital he died.

Mrs. Genain seemed to welcome the hospitalization of her daughters. In contrast to her husband she seemed cheerful and sociable and was the person in the family who most often showed strength and stability. However, during the first visit to her daughters, she behaved quite bizarrely and appeared to be having a psychotic episode. She recovered from the episode, was brought into contact with an NIMH social worker, and through this relationship seemed to maintain an effective level of adjustment. When her daughters were discharged she approached her many problems with realism and competence.

These are some of the facts concerning the girls and their stay at NIMH. They were treated by different psychiatrists and no somatic therapies were employed. When their parents visited them for periodic week-long stays, the family lived together as a unit at NIMH. In the reconstruction of the history of the Genain family, Mrs. Genain functioned as the primary informant. To gather the needed information over 100 interviews were necessary. We have suggested that the depth of investigation in the Genain case exceeded by far what is characteristic of most case studies. In addition to data gathered in the psychotherapy of the girls, observations of them at NIMH, and the history obtained from Mr. Genain, much biological, psychological, and sociocultural data were uncovered. Thus, for example, sociologists objectively assessed the community in which the Genains lived. Prior to the quads' admission to the NIMH Clinical Center, a psychiatrist visited and observed the family in the home. The history of the family was examined to check for the incidence of mental disorder. The degree to which the quads were actually monozygotic was carefully checked, and it was concluded that they were genetically identical. Their intellectual and physical development was carefully analyzed. Numerous measures of the family members' biological and psychological characteristics were recorded, and some of these were obtained on several different occasions. Because of Mr. Genain's resistence to the quads' treatment, it was not possible to study him as intensively as Mrs. Genain. Among the data recorded were: electroencephalographic records, indices of GSR reactivity, reaction time, and scores on a battery of psychological tests. Ratings of the quads' behavior at NIMH and observations of their patterns of social interaction were also obtained.

We mentioned that Kallmann (1959, 1962) and others have shown that schizophrenia, more than any other supposed functional psychosis, tends to run in families. One theory about schizophrenia is that this disorder is a specifically inherited disease. This view assumes that schizophrenia comes about because of the presence of a mutant gene. It is often further assumed that this gene leads to a disturbance in metabolism whose cause is as yet unknown. Another theory of schizophrenia assumes that what is inherited is a constitutional predisposition to schizophrenia. This view is more ambiguous or more complex than the specific gene hypothesis, since it does not state the specific basis for the predisposition. It assumes that a variety of predispositions may be inherited, some of which may eventuate in schizophrenia. A widely held view in the United States is that schizophrenia is a result of persons' life experiences rather than their genetic or constitutional make-up. The major determinants of schizophrenia from this latter point of view are direct and indirect learning during development and conscious and unconscious anxiety and conflict.

The Genain study is significant because its subjects were four schizophrenics who were genetically identical. This provided Rosenthal and his colleagues the rare opportunity to gather evidence relevant to controversies that exist concerning the roles of heredity and environment in the development of schizophrenia. Let us now look at some of the evidence in the Genain study that bears on current theoretical issues.

Electroencephalographic (EEG) studies of the Genains showed brainwave abnormalities, but not of the type most characteristic of schizophrenics. Myra, who showed the least psychopathology, evinced the greatest EEG disturbance. Hester, who was clinically the most disturbed of the sisters, showed the least slowing of EEG brain waves.

There is evidence in the literature that suggests that hereditary factors influence the introversive-extroversive dimension of personality (Shields and Slater, 1961). It appears, however, that schizophrenics who are strongly introversive are but one of many subtypes of introverted persons. In the case of the Genains, the girls were all markedly introverted. The important question, which unfortunately cannot be answered conclusively is: Were they introverted because of their heredity or because of their life experiences? The evidence available supports the view that both nature and nurture made them the persons they became. From what is known generally about the hereditary influences in introversion and in schizophrenia, together with the Genain data, the hypothesis of a genetic predisposition seems defensible. The case history data of the Genains support the idea that their life experience profoundly influenced their development. As children they were described as being solitary and submissive. Mrs. Genain exerted a tremendous influence over them in terms of the roles they played at home and in the community. The following description (Rosenthal, 1964, pp. 463–465) suggests the powerful influence she had in shaping her daughters' characteristics:

> Each characteristic served as the theme of a life-role which Mrs. Genain unconsciously assigned to her daughters, these themes reverberating in her own intraphysic life. The central theme of the role she assigned to Nora was the "protected (dependent) positive." Mrs. Genain related to Nora by protecting her, even from herself. According to her mother's formulation, Nora would have no inner emotional life, since all influences came from outside and, often, from Mother. Mrs. Genain's unfulfilled needs for maternal nurturing found expression in her closeness to Nora. It was the symbiotic tie of mother and infant, one in which the mother does not see the infant as a separate individual but as a part of herself. Mrs. Genain equated Nora's appeasement of Mr. Genain with dependency. Nora showed no evidence of striving for the protected positive position with her mother, nor did she move

against it; she was enveloped in it. In her adult psychosis, she caricatured her mother's friendly façade and stereotyped sweetness. The closeness between them supported a report that Nora was not only her father's "favorite," but her mother's also. The earliest evidence for this was that Nora was always the first of the babies to be burped after feeding; the most recent evidence was that Nora was the daughter Mrs. Genain took home first for trial visits from the hospital, although Iris' adjustment was also appropriate for home visits.

The central role for Myra was the "independent positive." Mrs. Genain identified Myra with her own independent strivings and actions, encouraging her to be independent and to establish herself away from home. She hoped and planned for Myra in these directions. Myra was the daughter upon whom Mrs. Genain was prone to lean in times of stress, who often strove for the favored position (which in this family was the protected one) with her mother. Her communications to her mother about physical problems may have been an avenue toward such closeness with her. Concomitantly, she tried to live out the role her mother assigned to her of becoming independent, and the dependent-independent conflict became acute for her when she tried to move out on her own. This conflict posed a dilemma: how was she to live out her mother's unconscious aims for her and satisfy her own strivings toward independence at the same time? The former would diminish her own idividuality, while the latter required her sense of identity to be consolidated and developed. Myra concerned and interested her mother, but she could not displace Nora from first position. Myra had an approximate two-thirds positive and one-third negative on the continuum.

The central theme of the role Mrs. Genain assigned to Iris was the "repressed" one. She identified in Iris her own feeling that she must put up with anything, and in her psychosis, Iris caricatured this aspect of her mother's personality. The more pronounced Iris' catatonic symptoms were, the more repressed was her functioning. Later, when she improved, she made occasional sarcastic remarks to her mother which Mrs. Genain described as being like Iris' pre-psychotic behavior and as being hostile to her. When Iris confided in her mother about her soma, an area in which they shared confusion about the distinction between somatic and emotional feelings, her mother could respond and was interested in her. But in areas that concerned Iris as an individual, e.g., her abilities and appearance, Mrs. Genain was neither concerned nor interested. On the continuum, Iris had third place, with a rough measure of two-thirds negative and one-third positive.

The central theme assigned to Hester was the "negative" one. It was as though Hester personified that which Mrs. Genain regarded as undesirable—hostility and sexuality for examples. The perception of these feelings in Hester appeared to have blocked her mother's perception of other human qualities in her, and this perceptual pattern began the day she brought Hester home from the hospital. Why was Hester selected? The baby's crying appeared to have triggered her mother's hostility, a feeling which Mrs. Genain never could tolerate in herself. As a child, Hester fought back, but the total negation of her own personality was too much for her. In her adult psychosis, she lives in a small world dominated by fear, anxiety, and anger. She was the last to be regarded as sick (she had been "bad"), and she was not hospitalized before coming to the Clinical Center. Later Mrs. Genain did not even consider a time when Hester might come for home visits from the hospital. Hester had the end position on the continuum.

Mr. Genain's own dependency and various inadequacies offered the weakest possible counter to Mrs. Genain's influence. Thus the combination of Mrs. Genain's overprotective, enveloping way of interacting with her daughters was, if anything, exaggerated by her husband's distant role. It would appear that the girls' development was not shaped by one environmental factor but by a constellation of them and this constellation in turn interacted with existing genetic factors.

A very interesting facet of the Genains concerns the different treatment outcomes of the quads. Why did Myra show such a favorable response and her three sisters such minimal ones? While the fact that the sisters all became schizophrenic is in line with a purely genetic interpretation of schizophrenia, the different outcomes do not appear to be easily compatible with such an interpretation. Not only did the girls differ in their reactions to treatment but they also behaved differently at home. For example, although the four sisters greatly feared their father, Myra reacted by avoiding him whereas Hester was unable to make this anxiety-reducing adjustment.

If one looks selectively at the body of the Genain data, evidence for each of the three theories of schizophrenia, the monogenetic, genetic predisposition, and the life experiential views, can be found. But it does not seem possible to argue that all of the Genain data fit one and only one of these viewpoints. It seems, rather, that schizophrenia in these quarduplets was a joint function of their genetic heritage and of their family and social environments. Perhaps the major contribution of this study is the damage it has done to one-factor theories such as the purely genetic and purely environmental ones. It suggests that the combination of two factors, the environment in which the individual is reared and his biological makeup shape personality (Meehl, 1962). The study of the Genains indicates the need for future research directed toward objective description of this combination.

A STUDY OF PHYSICAL HEALTH, PSYCHOLOGICAL ADJUSTMENT, AND THE SOCIAL ENVIRONMENT

The Genain quadruplets were patients in a mental hospital and were diagnosed as schizophrenics. They were intensively studied clinically at NIMH and retrospectively studied as part of an effort to reconstruct aspects of their development. Unless one is actually able to assess persons over a long period of time, the next best approach would appear to be to study as many of them as possible through reconstruction methods. Such methods require the most objective means of obtaining and analyzing available data. The aim of this type of reconstructive investigation, as we saw in the Genain family, is to go beyond the assessment of the present status of the individual to include data concerning prior events that may have contributed to his present status.

An interesting large-scale reconstructive assessment study has been carried out by Hinkle and Wolff (1957) and Hinkle (1959). It differs from most of the examples mentioned in this section in that the major concern of the study is not just mental illness, but the whole sweep of illnesses that can beset man. It was based on the assumption that illness is a product of the relationship of organisms and their environment. Conceiving of illness as a form of biological behavior these researchers asked the question: What characteristics discriminate between healthy and unhealthy persons? Degree of health was defined in terms of the frequencies of illnesses of various degrees of severity.

The subjects in the study belonged to six population groups. The groups and the numbers of persons in the groups were as follows: (1) Semiskilled American working women ($N = 1700$); (2) skilled American working men ($N = 1527$); (3) Chinese graduate students and professional ($N = 100$); (4) Hungarian refugees ($N = 76$); (5) recent graduates of American colleges ($N = 132$); and (6) American supervisors and foreman ($N = 84$).

Each of these groups consisted of persons who seemed relatively homogeneous. The two major groups, the American working groups, were selected because health, work, and performance records were available for them. The other groups may be considered as comparison groups. The individuals in these six groups were studied over a period of several years. Family histories and biographies were obtained for them. Psychologists, sociologists, psychiatrists, and internists studied them. They were administered a battery of intelligence and personality tests. Reports from family members, associates, and employers were obtained. Much data relevant to the health of the subjects were obtained. These included medical records kept over as long as 25-year periods, laboratory diagnostic tests, physical examinations, psychiatrist interviews, direct observation of health patterns, and reports of private physicians and hospitals. In addition to all of these data, comprehensive work-attendance and personnel records over as long as 25 years were available.

One group of subjects that was of special interest to Hinkle and Wolff was a set of 336 semiskilled working women who had more than 20 years of unbroken employment. Ninety-six of these women were studied with especially great comprehensiveness. The initial question in studying them was: What is their record of disabling illnesses over a 20 year period from approximately age 20 to age 40? It was found that one-quarter of the women accounted for 50 per cent of all illnesses. It seemed clear that these women, similar in other respects to the other women, differed from them in the tendency to become ill. Furthermore, those who had the greatest number of episodes of illness had more disease syndromes, more illness due to various etiologies, and were more likely to have major illnesses and disturbances of mood, thought, and behavior.

Hinkle and Wolff found that a group of exceptionally healthy women had been disabled, on the average, only 33 days in 28 years, whereas a group of unhealthy women had been disabled, on the average, approximately four years over a similar period of time. When these two groups of women were assessed, it was found that there were many nonmedical characteristics that seemed clearly associated with each. The healthy women tended to be dowdy, dressed in a styleless manner, were relaxed, pleasant, contented, and concerned with themselves and their own welfare. The unhealthy women tended to be neat, young-looking women who dressed fashionably, were tense, full of doubts, suspicious, hostile, discouraged, and worried about their jobs and families. The healthy women did not appear to be intensely involved with themselves and others; the unhealthy women were deeply involved in their personal preoccupations and with others. Thus, it appeared that less ambitious and less aware women had better health records than women who were relatively low on these characteristics.

It should be mentioned that these two groups did not differ either with regard to the health records of their families or with regard to social and economic background factors. One noticeable difference was that the healthy women seemed, when compared with the unhealthy women, to be low in heterosexual drive and tended to have little desire to get married. They had settled into a rather dull routine life for which they seemed well suited. On the basis of this evidence Hinkle and Wolff conjectured that healthy persons were those best suited for the particular ecological niche in which they found themselves.

What tendencies did these investigators uncover among relatively healthy and unhealthy men drawn from the large group of working men? In general, they discovered a striking parallel to the findings for women. The more intense, conscientious, and striving men tended to have poorer health records than those who were relatively more placid, satisfied, and contented. In studying the group of Chinese subjects, further verification of the findings for women was obtained. Unhealthy Chinese people seemed to be intensely involved with others and to experience feelings such as anxiety, hate, and love more often than Chinese people who were quite healthy. The latter seemed to be "emotionally insulated" and not to be affectively preoccupied with others.

The studies carried out by Hinkle and Wolff seem to support the view that persons with relatively poor health records tend to see their life experiences as more demanding and conflict-laden than persons with relatively good health records. The Hinkle and Wolff study is valuable because it suggests the psychological side of the general phenomenon of illness. The techniques they employed would seem to be quite useful with more specific reference to behavior disorders (Langner and Michael, 1963; Srole et al., 1962).

One facet of their findings bears a striking parallel to the Genain study which, of course, dealt with a different sort of problem. The evidence gathered in studying the Genains suggested that any ultimate explanation of schizophrenia would require knowledge of both the biology of the individual and the environment in which he lives. The evidence gathered by Hinkle and Wolff seems to support a similar hypothesis, that the health of an individual is a product of what might be called his degree of compatibility with his environment. Might we then conclude that the level of maladjustment of the individual, be the maladjustment physical, psychological, or some combination of these, is a function of the degree to which he is hampered in achieving a niche in life compatible with his biological and psychological characteristics?

CONCLUDING COMMENTS CONCERNING DEVELOPMENTAL ASPECTS OF RESEARCH ON PSYCHOPATHOLOGY

The process of development must be of direct interest to anyone who believes that the individual is a product of his history of life experiences. Cases of psychopathology are usually identified only after behavior deviations reach clinical proportions. Earlier we mentioned some of the reasons for the paucity of studies of persons *before* they manifest extreme behavioral deviations. These included difficulty in identifying these persons prior to illness. Mentioned also were practical problems connected with studying large-scale groups of persons, some of whom could be expected to develop deviations in the future.

In the absence of direct observations of mentally disturbed persons during their development, researchers have resorted to various kinds of reconstruction tasks. These include, as we have seen, the case study method and the survey method. Both may be viewed as applications of assessment techniques. In the study of the Genains by the NIMH group and the ecological work of Hinkle and Wolff we saw how reconstruction assessment research can be worthwhile and provocative.

One research approach to the problems of personality development and psychotherapy that seems promising is the follow-up study of clinical cases (Sherman et al., 1964). As indicated earlier, the aim of this sort of study is often the practical one of finding out the long-term effects of treatment procedures. For example, in what ways does psychotherapy influence the later behavior of patients? One need not, however, look at the follow-up study from only this particular point of view. In addition, these studies can be viewed as developmental ones which permit assessments and direct observations of behavior starting at one selected point in time.

Among the most valuable kinds of follow-up studies are those of children who display psychopathological manifestations. These studies are of particular value for a number of reasons. First, the younger the person is, the longer the potential follow-up period. Second, the younger the person, the greater is the likelihood that development during formative years can be observed. And third, among the most poorly understood forms of deviant behavior are those that occur in childhood. In this latter connection, it is worth noting that there is a trend toward increasing attention to psychological disorders of childhood.

But valuable as case studies, surveys, and follow-ups are, the need to study individuals longitudinally prior to their display of overt symptoms of psychopathology seems compelling. Through longitudinal studies we can come to know more precisely in what ways personal and social adjustment and maladjustment come about.

A CONCLUDING COMMENT CONCERNING DEVIANT BEHAVIOR

We began our study of psychopathology by considering the need for a reliable and meaningful language with which to describe it. We next reviewed some examples of currently employed descriptive classifications. The review indicated that present psychiatric classifications, though perhaps adequate in terms of existing knowledge of deviant behavior, leave much to be desired. This state of affairs suggested that the major scientific challenge concerning deviant behavior was to understand the reasons for such behavior and to evolve effective techniques for modifying it.

We have focused on three approaches to an understanding of disturbed persons. These are the applications of reliable assessment methods, the experimental method, and a developmental orientation to psychopathology. Our study of these applications showed that personality aberrations may be subject to objective research. There are, however, many problems and frustrations that beset the curious and rigorous inquirer into maladjustments. Among the most poignant of these is the communication gulf between the psychologically troubled individual and the scientists and clinicians who seek to understand and help him. The following (Pierce and Pierce, 1929, p. 54; Raymond, 1946, pp. 152–153; Custance, 1952, p. 61) are suggestive comments on this problem:

> But how impossible, how futile, to try to put any of the diverse horrors of a neurosis into words. Words—that is *all* they are, when set down on paper, just words. Words lacking the peculiar connotation of sick, blind terror with which every real neurosis is fraught; wording lacking, I fear (or should I rejoice?) the power of transmitting even a vestige of that emotion over onto their readers. Only those who have gone through it, can know; the others, the untouched, will have to accept it on faith as truth—dark truth.

> The loneliness of the insane! The insane are surely the most lonely people in the world . . . from the very nature of their illness the insane are shut out from all communication to others of what is happening to them . . . . A great gulf separates each and all of the patients: they wander round and round, shut off completely from one another, unable to explain themselves or their actions . . . and to this is added the last cruelty . . . the suffering of the insane arouses quite often a feeling of revulsion—so morbid, so full of the strange and unknown is it.

> I seem shut into myself, withdrawn from real contact with the outer world as also from contact with God; the sun does not really shine, the trees and fields are not really green; I am shut in with my thoughts, always of a depressing and melancholy nature.
>
> This sense of isolation, of being cut off from God, one's fellows and the world, seems to me to be the paramount feature underlying the whole state . . . .
>
> Moral tension returns in full force. I am haunted by a sense of guilt, my conscience gives me no rest, even when there do not seem to be any particularly grievious sins upon it. Whatever I am doing I feel I ought to

be doing something else. I worry perpetually about my past sins and failures; not for a moment can I forget the mess I seem to have made of my life. However I may pray for and think of forgiveness, no forgiveness comes. Eventually the terrors of Hell approach.

Human suffering and anguish evoke human sympathy and the wish to help. Individuals and society can help in a variety of ways. With dispassion and perseverence, the psychological inquirer strives to make his contribution.

A Final Comment

We have attempted to show that personality is neither a thing nor an unknowable essence but, rather, a rubric that includes concepts that refer to man's individuality. These concepts may be found in every one of the preceding chapters. Their concentration was greatest in Part 1 in which a number of influential theoretical orientations were reviewed. Were the study of personality no more than the study of concepts, Part 1, in itself, might have provided an adequate introduction to this field. But, as we have seen in Parts 2, 3, 4, and 5 a scientific study of personality requires as much preoccupation with methods as with concepts. Scientific endeavors require not just concepts but concepts, operations, and reliable observations.

The operations and observations made by personality researchers comprise two broad categories, assessment and experimentation. Assessment involves recording data under standard or control conditions. Experimentation involves recording and observing behavior under conditions that are varied systematically. We have seen that these two approaches to behavior are not incompatible. Rather, they complement each other and together aid the researcher in his study of both the characteristics of individuals and the conditions to which they react. We have also seen that these approaches are highly adaptable. The study over time of selected individuals, the study of development generally, and the study of deviant behavior may all be described in terms of these two general methodologies.

Our study of personality has given as much emphasis to problems, ambiguities, and inadequacies as to existing knowledge. A reasonably accurate reflection of this field could not be accomplished in any other way. An objective study of personality is not for the faint-hearted, nor for the impatient, nor for the person who is uncomfortable with uncertainty. It is much like a young child—developing rapidly, at times clumsy and frustrating, at times remarkably perceptive, fascinating, and promising.

Bibliography

Aas, A. (1958) *Mutilation fantasies and autonomic response.* Oslo, Norway: Oslo University Press.

Aborn, M. (1953) The influence of experimentally induced failure on the retention of material acquired through set and incidental learning. *J. exp. Psychol.,* **45**, 225–231.

Ader, R., Tatum, R., & Beels, C. C. (1960) Social factors affecting emotionality and resistance to disease in animals: I. Age of separation from the mother and susceptibility to gastric ulcers in the rat. *J. comp. physiol. Psychol.,* **53**, 446–454.

Adler, A. (1927*a*) *Understanding human nature.* New York: Chilton.

Adler, A. (1927*b*) *Practice and theory of individual psychology.* New York: Harcourt, Brace.

Adler, A. (1930) Individual psychology. In C. Murchison (Ed.), *Psychologies of 1930.* Worcester: Clark University Press.

Adorno, T. W., Frenkel-Brunswik, Else, Levinson, D. J., & Sanford, R. N. (1950) *The authoritarian personality.* New York: Harper.

Allport, F. H. (1955) *Theories of perception and the concept of structure.* New York: Wiley.

Allport, G. W. (1937) *Personality: A psychological interpretation.* New York: Holt.

Allport, G. W. (1942) *The use of personal documents in psychological science.* New York: Social Science Research Council.

Allport, G. W. (1960) *Personality and social encounter.* Boston: Beacon Press.

Allport, G. W. (1961) *Pattern and growth in personality.* New York: Holt, Rinehart, & Winston.

Allport, G. W., & Vernon, P. E. (1933) *Studies in expressive movement.* New York: Macmillan.

Angyal, A. (1941) *Foundations for a science of personality.* New York: Commonwealth Fund.

Angyal, A. (1965) *Neurosis and treatment: A holistic theory* (Eugenia Hanfmann and R. M. Jones, Eds.). New York: Wiley.

Ansbacher, H. C., & Ansbacher, Rowena R. (Eds.) (1956) *The individual psychology of Alfred Adler.* New York: Basic Books.

Arieti, S. (Ed.) (1959) *American handbook of psychiatry* (2 vols.). New York: Basic Books.

Arlow, J. A., & Brenner, C. (1964) *Psychoanalytic concepts and the structure of theory.* New York: International Universities Press.

Asch, S. E. (1946) Forming impressions of personality. *J. abnorm. soc. Pschol.,* **41**, 258–290.

Asch, S. E. (1956) Studies of independence and conformity: I. A minority of one against a unanimous majority. *Psychol. Monogr.,* **70**, Whole No. 416.

Atkinson, J. W. (Ed.) (1958*a*) *Motives in fantasy, action, and society.* Princeton, New Jersey: Van Nostrand.

Atkinson, J. W. (1958*b*) Towards experimental analysis of human motivation in terms of motives, expectancies, and incentives. In J. W. Atkinson (Ed.), *Motives in fantasy, action, and society.* New York: Van Nostrand, pp. 288–305.

Atkinson, J. W. (1964) *An introduction to motivation.* Princeton, New Jersey: Van Nostrand.

Auld, F., Jr., & Murray, E. J. (1955) Content-analysis studies of psychotherapy. *Psychol. Bull.,* **52, 377–395.**

Ax, A. F. (1953) The physiological differentiation between fear and anger in humans. *Psychosom. Med.,* **15, 433–442.**

Bachrach, A. J. (Ed.) (1962) *Experimental foundations of clinical psychology.* New York: Basic Books.

Baldwin, A. L. (1955) *Behavior and development in childhood.* New York: Dryden Press.

Baldwin, A. L. (1960) The study of child behavior and development. In P. H. Mussen (Ed.), *Handbook of research methods in child development.* New York: Wiley, pp. 3–35.

Ban, T. A. (1964) *Conditioning and psychiatry.* Chicago: Aldine.

Bandura, A. (1961) Psychotherapy as a learning process. *Psychol. Bull.,* **58,** 143–159.

Bandura, A. (1962) Social learning through imitation. In M. R. Jones (Ed.), *1962 Nebraska symposium on motivation.* Lincoln: University of Nebraska Press, pp. 211–269.

Bandura, A. (1965) Vicarious processes: A case of no-trial learning. In L. Berkowitz (Ed.), *Advances in experimental social psychology.* Vol. 2, New York: Academic Press.

Bandura, A., Lipsher, D., & Miller, Paula E. (1960) Psychotherapists' approach-avoidance reactions to patients' expressions of hostility. *J. consult. Psychol.,* **24,** 1–8.

Bandura, A., & McDonald, F. J. (1963). Influence of social reinforcement and the behavior of models in shaping children's moral-judgments. *J. abnorm. soc. Psychol.,* **67,** 274–281.

Bandura, A., Ross, Dorothea, & Ross, Sheila A. (1961) Transmission of aggression through imitation of aggressive models. *J. abnorm. soc. Psychol.,* **63,** 575–582.

Bandura, A., Ross, Dorothea, & Ross, Sheila A. (1963*a*) Imitation of film-mediated aggressive models. *J. abnorm. soc. Psychol.,* **66, 3–11.**

Bandura, A., Ross, Dorothea, & Ross, Sheila A. (1963*b*) Vicarious reinforcement and imitation. *J. abnorm. soc. Psychol.,* **67, 601–607.**

Bandura, A., & Walters, R. H. (1959) *Adolescent aggression.* New York: Ronald.

Bandura, A. & Walters, R. H. (1963) *Social learning and personality development.* New York: Holt, Rinehart, & Winston.

Barker, R. G. (Ed.) (1963) *The stream of behavior: Explorations of its structure and content.* New York: Appleton-Century-Crofts.

Barker, R. G. (1965) Explorations in ecological psychology. *Amer. Psychologist,* **20,** 1–14.

Barker, R. G., Dembo, Tamara, & Lewin, K. (1941) Frustration and regression: An experiment with young children. *Univ. Iowa Stud. Child Welf.* **18,** No. 1, 1–314.

Barker, R. G., & Wright, H. F. (1951) *One boy's day.* New York: Harper.

Barron, F. (1953) An ego-strength scale which predicts response to psychotherapy. *J. consult. Psychol.,* **17,** 327–333.

Barron, F. (1963) The disposition towards originality. In C. W. Taylor and F. Barron, (Eds.), *Scientific creativity: Its recognition and development.* New York: Wiley, pp. 139–152.

Barry, H., III, and Miller, N. E. (1962) Effects of drugs on approach-avoidance conflict tested repeatedly by means of a "telescope alley." *J. comp. physiol. Psychol.,* **55,** 210.

Basowitz, H., Persky, H., Korchin, S. J., & Grinker, R. R. (1955) *Anxiety and stress.* New York: McGraw-Hill.

Baughman, E. E. (1958) The role of the stimulus in Rorschach responses. *Psychol. Bull.,* **55,** 121–147.

Baumrind, D. (1964) Some thoughts on ethics of research: After reading Milgram's "Behavioral study of obedience." *Amer. Psychologist,* **19,** 421–423.

Beck, S. J., Beck, A. G., Levitt, E. E., & Molish, H. B. (1961) *Rorschach's test, Vol. 1: Basic processes* (3rd. rev. ed.). New York: Grune & Stratton.

Becker, W. C., Peterson, D. R., Hellmer, L. A., Shoemaker, P. J., & Quay, H. C. (1959) Factors in parental behavior and personality as related to problem behavior in children. *J. consult. Psychol.,* **23,** 107–118.

Beers, C. W. (1908) *A mind that found itself.* New York: Longmans, Green.

Behrens, Marjorie L. (1954) Child rearing and the character structure of the mother. *Child Developm.,* **25,** 225–238.

Bellak, L. (1956) Freud and projective techniques. *J. proj. Tech.,* **20,** 5–13.

Bellak, L., & Bellak, S. S. (1949) *Children's apperception test and manual.* New York: CPS Co.

Bender, Lauretta A. (1938) A visual motor gestalt test and its clinical use. *Res. Monogr. Amer. Orthopsychiat. Ass.,* No. 3.

Berelson, B. (1954) Content analysis. In G. Lindzey (Ed.), *Handbook of social psychology,* Vol. I. Cambridge, Mass.: Addison-Wesley, pp. 488–522.

Bergmann, G. (1943) Psychoanalysis and experimental psychology: A review from the standpoint of scientific empiricism. *Mind,* **52,** 122–140.

Berkowitz, L. (1959) Anti-semitism and the displacement of aggression. *J. abnorm. soc. Psychol.,* **59,** 182–187.

Berkowitz, L. (1962) *Aggression: A social psychological analysis.* New York: McGraw-Hill.

Berkun, M. M., Bialek, H. M., Kern, R. P., & Yagi, K. (1962) Experimental studies of psychological stress in man. *Psychol. Monogr.,* **76,** No. 15.

Berlyne, D. E. (1965) *Structure and direction in thinking.* New York: Wiley.

Bernstein, A. (1955) Some relations between techniques of feeding and training during infancy and certain behavior in childhood. *Genet. psychol. Monogr.,* **51,** 3–44.

Betz, Barbara J. (1962) Experiences in research in psychotherapy with schizophrenic patients. In H. H. Strupp & L. Luborsky (Eds.), *Research in psychotherapy,* Vol. 2. Washington, D. C.: Amer. Psychological Assoc., pp. 41–60.

Biddle, B. J., & Ellena, W. J. (1964) *Contemporary research on teacher effectiveness.* New York: Holt, Rinehart & Winston.

Birren, J. E. (1964) *The psychology of aging.* Englewood Cliffs, New Jersey: Prentice-Hall.

Block, J. (1961) *The Q-sort method in personality assessment and psychiatric research.* Springfield, Ill.: Charles C Thomas.

Block, J. (1965) *The challenge of response sets.* New York: Appleton-Century-Crofts.

Bower, P. A., Testin, R., & Roberts, A. (1960) Rorschach diagnosis by a systematic combining of content, thought process, and determinant scales. *Genet. psychol. Monogr.,* **62,** 105–183.

Breger, L., & McGaugh, J. L. (1965) Critique and reformulation of "learning-theory" approaches to psychotherapy and neurosis. *Psychol. Bull.,* **63,** 338–358.

Brehm, J., & Cohen, A. R. (1962) *Explorations in cognitive dissonance.* New York: Wiley.

Brenner, C. (1955) *An elementary textbook of psychoanalysis.* New York: International Universities Press.

Breuer, J., & Freud, S. (1895) *Studies in hysteria.* Boston: Beacon Press, 1950.

Broadhurst, P. L. (1961) Abnormal behavior. In Eysenck, H. J. (Ed.) *Handbook of abnormal psychology.* New York: Basic Books, pp. 726–763.

Bronfenbrenner, U. (1958) Socialization and social class through time and space. In Eleanor E. Maccoby, T. M. Newcomb, & E. L. Hartley (Eds.), *Readings in social psychology* (3rd. ed.). New York: Holt, Rinehart, & Winston, pp. 400–424.

Brown, J. S. (1948) Gradients of approach and avoidance responses and their relation to level of motivation. *J. comp. physiol. Psychol.,* **41,** 450–465.

Bruner, J. S. (1960) *The process of education.* Cambridge, Mass.: Harvard University Press.

Bruner, J. S. (1964) The course of cognitive growth. *Amer. Psychologist,* **19,** 1–15.

Bruner, J. S., & Tagiuri, R. (1954) The perception of people. In G. Lindzey (Ed.), *Handbook of social psychology.* Cambridge, Mass.: Addison-Wesley, pp. 634–654.

Brunswik, E. (1955) The conceptual framework of psychology. In *International Encyclopedia of Unified Science,* combined edition, 1, Part 2. Chicago: University of Chicago Press, pp. 656–760.

Brunswik, E. (1956) *Perception and the representative design of psychological experiments.* Berkeley: University of California Press.

Bugental, J. F. T. (1965) *The search for authenticity: An existential-analytic approach to psychotherapy.* New York: Holt, Rinehart, & Winston.

Buss, A. H. (1961) *The psychology of aggression.* New York: Wiley.

Buss, A. H., & Durkee, Ann (1957) An inventory for assessing different kinds of hostility. *J. consult. Psychol.,* **21,** 343–348.

Buss, A. H., & Lang, P. J. (1965) Psychological deficit in schizophrenia: I. Affect, reinforcement, and concept attainment. *J. abnorm. Psychol.,* **70,** 2–24.

Byrne, D. (1964) Repression-sensitization as a dimension of personality. In B. A. Maher (Ed.), *Progress in experimental personality research,* Vol. 1. New York: Academic Press, pp. 115–169.

Byrne, D., & Sheffield, J. (1965) Response to sexually arousing stimuli as a function of repressing and sensitizing defenses. *J. abnorm. Psychol.,* **70,** 114–118.

Cameron, N. A. (1963) *Personality development and psychopathology: A dynamic approach.* Boston: Houghton Mifflin.

Campbell, D. T. (1950) The indirect assessment of social attitudes. *Psychol. Bull.,* **47,** 15–38.

Campbell, D. T. (1960) Recommendations for APA test standards regarding construct, trait, or discriminant validity. *Amer. Psychologist,* **15,** 546–553.

Campbell, D. T., & Fiske, D. W. (1959) Convergent and discriminant validation by the multitrait-multimethod matrix. *Psychol. Bull.,* **56,** 81–105.

Campbell, J. D. (1964) Peer relations in childhood. In M. L. Hoffman and Lois W. Hoffman (Eds.), *Review of child development research,* Vol. 1. New York: Russell Sage Foundation, pp. 289–322.

Carrigan, Patricia M. (1960) Extroversion-introversion as a dimension of personality: A reappraisal. *Psychol. Bull.* **57,** 329–360.

Cartwright, D. (1959) Lewinian theory as a contemporary systematic framework. In S. Koch (Ed.), *Psychology: A study of a science,* Vol. 2. New York: McGraw-Hill, pp. 7–91.

Casler, L. (1961) Maternal deprivation: A critical review of the literature. *Monogr. Soc. Res. Child Developm.,* **26,** No. 2.

Cattell, R. B. (1950) *Personality.* New York: McGraw-Hill.

Cattell, R. B. (1956) Personality and motivation theory based on structural measurement. In J. C. McCary (Ed.), *Psychology of personality.* New York: Logos Press, pp. 63–120.

Cattell, R. B. (1957*a*) *The sixteen personality factor questionnaire* (rev. ed.) Champaign, Ill.: Institute of Personality and Ability Testing.

Cattell, R. B. (1957*b*) *Personality and motivation: Structure and measurement.* New York: Harcourt, Brace & World.

Chasdi, Eleanor H., & Lawrence, Margaret S. (1955) Some antecedents of aggression and effects of aggression in doll play. In D. McClelland (Ed.), *Studies in motivation.* New York: Appleton-Century-Crofts, pp. 517–528.

Child, I. L., & Waterhouse, I. K. (1952) Frustration and the quality of performance: I. A critique of the Barker, Dembo, and Lewin experiment. *Psychol. Rev.,* **59,** 351–362.

Child, I. L., & Waterhouse, I. K. (1953) Frustration and the quality of performance: II. A theoretical statement. *Psychol. Rev.,* **60,** 127–139.

Chown, Sheila M., & Heron, A. (1965) Psychological aspects of aging in man. In P. R. Farnsworth (Ed.), *Annual review of psychology,* Vol. 16. Palo Alto: Annual Reviews, Inc., pp. 417–450.

Christie, R., Havel, Joan, & Seidenberg, B. (1958) Is the F Scale irreversible? *J. abnorm. soc. Psychol.,* **56,** 143–159.

Christie, R., & Jahoda, Marie (Eds.) (1954) *Studies in the scope and method of "The Authoritarian Personality."* Glencoe, Illinois: Free Press.

Cleckley, H. (1955) *The mask of sanity.* St. Louis: Mosby.

Cline, V. B. (1964) Interpersonal perception. In B. A. Maher (Ed.), *Progress in experimental personality research.* New York: Academic Press, pp. 221–284.

Cline, V. B., & Richards, J. M., Jr. (1960) Accuracy of interpersonal perception—A general trait? *J. abnorm. soc. Psychol.,* **60,** 1–7.

Cofer, C. N., & Appley, M. H. (1964) *Motivation: Theory and research.* New York: Wiley.

Coleman, J. C. (1964) *Abnormal psychology and modern life* (3rd ed.). Chicago: Scott, Foresman.

Combs, A. W., & Snygg, D. (1959) *Individual behavior* (rev. ed.). New York: Harper.

Conger, J. J., Sawrey, W. L., and Turrell, E. S. (1958) The role of social experience in the production of gastric ulcers in hooded rats placed in a conflict situation. *J. abnorm. soc. Psychol.,* **57,** 214–220.

Conners, C. K. (1963) Birth order and needs for affiliation. *J. Pers.,* **31,** 408–416.

Coon, G. P., & Raymond, Alice F. (1940) *A review of the psychoneuroses at Stockbridge.* Stockbridge, Mass.: Austin Riggs Foundation.

Courtney, J. E. (1901) Dangerous paranoics—With autobiography of one. *Alien. and Neurol.,* **22,** 139–149.

Crandall, V. (1951) Induced frustration and punishment-reward expectancy in thematic apperception stories. *J. consult. Psychol.,* **15,** 400–404.

Crockett, H. J. (1962) The achievement motive and differential occupational mobility in the United States. *Amer. sociol. Rev.,* **27,** 191–204.

Cronbach, L. J. (1946) Response sets and test validity. *Educ. Psychol. Measmt.,* **6,** 475–494.

Cronbach, L. J. (1949) Statistical methods applied to Rorschach scores: A review. *Psychol. Bull.,* **46,** 393–429.

Cronbach, L. J. (1960) *Essentials of psychological testing* (2nd ed.). New York: Harper & Row.

Cronbach, L. J., & Meehl, P. E. (1955) Construct validity in psychological tests. *Psychol. Bull.,* **52,** 281–302.

Crowne, D. P., & Marlowe, D. (1964) *The approval motive: Studies in evaluative dependence.* New York: Wiley.

Crutchfield, R. S. (1955) Conformity and character. *Amer. Psychologist,* **10,** 191–198.

Cummings, Elaine, & Henry, W. E. (1961) *Growing old.* New York: Basic Books.

Custance, J. (1952) *Wisdom, madness, and folly: The philosophy of a lunatic.* London: Victor Gollancz.

Dahlstrom, W. G., & Welsh, G. S. (1960) *An MMPI handbook: A guide to use in clinical practice and research.* Minneapolis: University of Minnesota Press.

David, P. R., & Snyder, L. H. (1962) Some interrelationships between psychology and genetics. In S. Koch (Ed.), *Psychology: A study of a science,* Vol. 4. New York: McGraw-Hill, pp. 1–50.

Davids, A., DeVault, S., & Talmadge, M. (1961) Anxiety, pregnancy, and childbirth abnormalities. *J. consult. Psychol.,* **25,** 74–77.

Davis, A. (1943) Child training and social class. In R. G. Barker, J. S. Kounin, and H. F. Wright (Eds.), *Child behavior and development.* New York: McGraw-Hill, pp. 607–620.

Davis, A. (1951) Socio-economic influences upon children's learning. *Understanding the Child,* **20,** 10–16.

Davis, A., & Havighurst, R. J. (1946) Social class and color differences in child rearing. *Amer. sociol. Rev.*, **11**, 698–710.

Dearborn, W. F. (1949) The students' background in relation to school success. In Wilma T. Donahue, C. H. Coombs, and R. M. W. Travers (Eds.), *The measurement of student adjustment and achievement.* Ann Arbor: University of Michigan Press, pp. 191–200.

Denenberg, V. H. (1964) Critical periods, stimulus input, and emotional reactivity: A theory of infantile stimulation. *Psychol. Rev.*, **71**, 335–351.

DeNike, L. D. (1964) The temporal relationship between awareness and performance in verbal conditioning. *J. exp. Psychol.*, **68**, 521–529.

Deutsch, M., & Collins, Mary E. (1951) *Interracial housing and a psychological evaluation of a social experiment.* Minneapolis: University of Minnesota Press.

Dews, P. B. (1962) Psychopharmacology. In A. J. Bachrach (Ed.), *Experimental foundations of clinical psychology.* New York: Basic Books, pp. 423–441.

Diagnostic and statistical manual of mental disorders. (1952) Washington, D.C.: American Psychiatric Association.

Dickens, C. (1842) *American notes for general circulation* (3rd ed.), Vol. 1. London: Chapman and Hall, 1842, pp. 105–111.

DiMascio, A., Boyd, R. W., Greenblatt, M., & Solomon, H. C. (1955) The psychiatric interview: A sociophysiologic study. *Dis. nerv. System,* **16**, 2–7.

Diven, K. (1937) Certain determinants in the conditioning of anxiety reactions. *J. Psychol.*, **3**, 291–308.

Doidge, W. T., & Holtzman, W. H. (1960) Implications of homosexuality among Air Force trainees. *J. consult. Psychol.*, **24**, 9–13.

Dollard, J., Doob, L. W., Miller, N. E., Mowrer, O. H., & Sears, R. R. (1939) *Frustration and aggression.* New Haven: Yale University Press.

Dollard, J., & Miller, N. E. (1950) *Personality and psychotherapy.* New York: McGraw-Hill.

Duffy, Elizabeth, & Lacey, O. L. (1946) Adaptation in energy mobilization: Changes in general level of palmar skin conductance. *J. exp. Psychol.,* **36**, 437–452.

Dulaney, D. E., Jr. (1962) The place of hypotheses and intentions: An analysis of verbal control in verbal conditioning. In C. W. Eriksen (Ed.), *Behavior and awareness.* Durham: Duke University Press, pp. 102–129.

Dunn, W. L., Jr. (1953) Changes in the visual discrimination behavior of schizophrenic subjects as a function of the meaning content of the stimulus. Unpublished Ph.D. thesis, Duke University.

Dunn, W. L., Jr. (1954) Visual discrimination of schizophrenic subjects as a function of stimulus meaning. *J. Pers.*, **23**, 48–64.

Dykman, R. A., Ackerman, Peggy, T., Galbrecht, C. R., & Reese, W. G. (1963) Physiological reactivity to different stresses and methods of evaluation. *Psychosomatic Med.,* **25**, 37–59.

Edwards, A. L. (1953*a*) The relationship between the judged desirability of a trait and the probability that the trait will be endorsed. *J. appl. Psychol.,* **37**, 90–93.

Edwards, A. L. (1953*b*) *Edwards Personal Preference Schedule.* New York: Psychological Corporation.

Edwards, A. L. (1957) *The social desirability variable in personality research.* New York: Dryden.

Edwards, A. L. (1961) Social desirability or acquiescence in the MMPI? A case study of the SD scale. *J. abnorm. soc. Psychol.,* **63,** 351–359.

Eichorn, Dorothy (1963) Biological correlates of behavior. In H. W. Stevenson (Ed.), *Child Psychology: Sixty-second yearbook of the National Society for the Study of Education, Part 1.* Chicago: University of Chicago Press, pp. 1–61.

Einstein, A. (1940) Considerations concerning the fundaments of theoretical physics. *Science,* **91,** 487–492.

Elizur, A. (1949) Content analyses of the Rorschach with regard to anxiety and hostility. *Rorschach Research Exchange and J. proj. Tech.,* **13,** 247–284.

Elkin, F., & Estley, W. A. (1955) The myth of adolescent culture. *Amer. sociol. Rev.,* **20,** 680–684.

Epstein, S. (1961) Food-related responses to ambiguous stimuli as a function of hunger and ego strength. *J. consult. Psychol.,* **25,** 463–469.

Epstein, S. (1962) The measurement of drive and conflict in humans: Theory and experiment. In M. R. Jones (Ed.), *1962 Nebraska symposium on motivation.* Lincoln: University of Nebraska Press, pp. 127–206.

Eriksen, C. W. (1952) Defense against ego-threat in memory and perception. *J. abnorm. soc. Psychol.,* **47,** 230–235.

Eriksen, C. W. (1954) The case for perceptual defense. *Psychol. Rev.,* **61,** 175–182.

Eriksen, C. W. (1958) Unconscious processes. In M. R. Jones (Ed.), *Nebraska symposium on motivation.* Lincoln: University of Nebraska Press, pp. 169–227.

Erikson, E. H. (1950) *Childhood and society.* New York: Norton.

Erikson, E. H. (1964) *Insight and responsibility.* New York: W. W. Norton.

Eron, L. D. (1950) A normative study of the Thematic Apperception test. *Psychol. Monogr.,* **64,** No. 9.

Eron, L. D. (1953) Responses of women to the Thematic Apperception Test. *J. consult. Psychol.,* **17,** 269–282.

Eron, L., Walder, L. O., Toigo, R., & Lefkowitz, M. M. (1963) Social class, parental punishment for aggression, and child aggression. *Child Develpm.,* **34,** 849–867.

Ervin, Susan M. (1964) Language and TAT content in bilinguals. *J. abnorm. soc. Psychol.,* **68,** 500–507.

Eysenck, H. J. (1952) The effects of psychotherapy: An evaluation. *J. consult. Psychol.,* **16,** 319–324.

Eysenck, H. J. (1957) *The dynamics of anxiety and hysteria.* New York: Praeger.

Eysenck, H. J. (Ed.) (1961*a*) *Handbook of abnormal psychology.* New York: Basic Books.

Eysenck, H. J. (1961*b*) The effects of psychotherapy. In H. J. Eysenck (Ed.), *Handbook of abnormal psychology.* New York: Basic Books, pp. 697–725.

Eysenck, H. J. (Ed.) (1964) *Experiments in motivation.* New York: Macmillan.

Fairweather, G. W. (Ed.) (1964) *Social psychology in treating mental illness: An experimental approach.* New York: Wiley.

Farber, I. E. (1963) The things people say to themselves. *Amer. Psychologist,* **18,** 185–197.

Feather, N. T. (1961) The relationship of persistence at a task to expectation of success and achievement-related motives. *J. abnorm. soc. Psychol.,* **63,** 552–561.

Feifel, H. (Ed.) (1959) *The meaning of death.* New York: McGraw-Hill.

Fenz, W. D. (1964) Conflict and stress as related to physiological activation and sensory, perceptual, and cognitive functioning. *Psychol. Monogr.,* **78,** No. 8.

Ferguson, L. W. (1939) Primary social attitudes. *J. Psychol.,* **8,** 127–223.

Ferster, C. B., & DeMeyer, M. K. (1962) A method for the experimental analysis of the behavior of autistic children. *Amer. J. Orthopsychiat.,* **32,** 89–98.

Feshbach, S. (1955) The drive-reducing function of fantasy behavior. *J. abnorm. soc. Psychol.,* **50,** 3–11.

Feshbach, S. (1961) The stimulating versus cathartic effects of a vicarious aggressive activity. *J. abnorm. soc. Psychol.,* **63,** 381–385.

Feshbach, S. (1964) The function of aggression and the regulation of aggressive drive. *Psychol. Rev.,* **1,** 257–272.

Festinger, L. (1957) *A theory of cognitive dissonance.* Evanston, Illinois: Row, Peterson.

Festinger, L., & Carlsmith, J. M. (1959) Cognitive consequences of forced compliance. *J. abnorm. soc. Psychol.,* **58,** 203–210.

Fiedler, F. E. (1950) A comparison of therapeutic relationships in psychoanalytic, non-directive, and Adlerian therapy. *J. consult. Psychol.,* **14,** 436–445.

Fiedler, F. E. (1951) Factor analyses of psychoanalytic, non-directive, and Adlerian therapeutic relationships. *J. consult. Psychol.,* **15,** 32–38.

Fischer, S. (1964) Sex differences in body perception. *Psychol. Monogr.,* **78,** No. 14.

Fischer, S., & Cleveland, S. E. (1958) *Body image and personality.* Princeton: Van Nostrand.

Flavell, J. H. (1963) *The developmental psychology of Jean Piaget.* Princeton: Van Nostrand.

Ford, D. H., & Urban, H. B. (1963) *Systems of psychotherapy.* New York: Wiley.

Frank, J. D. (1961) *Persuasion and healing.* Baltimore: Johns Hopkins Press.

Frank, L. K. (1939) Projective methods for the study of personality. *J. Psychol.,* **8,** 389–413.

Freedman, S. J., Grunebaum, H. U., Stare, F. A., & Greenblatt, M. (1962) Imagery in sensory deprivation. In L. J. West (Ed.), *Hallucinations.* New York: Grune & Stratton, pp. 108–117.

Frenkel-Brunswik, Else (1949) Intolerance of ambiguity as an emotional and perceptual personality variable. *J. Pers.,* **18,** 108–143.

Freud, Anna (1946) *The ego and the mechanisms of defense.* New York: International Universities Press.

Freud, S. (1900) *The interpretation of dreams.* London: Hogarth, 1953.

Freud, S. (1904) *Psychopathology of everyday life.* New York: New American Library, 1951.

Freud, S. (1905) *Three essays on sexuality.* London: Hogarth, 1953.

Freud, S. (1923) *The ego and the id.* London: Hogarth, 1947.

Freud, S. (1926) *Inhibitions, symptoms, and anxiety.* London: Hogarth, 1948.

Freud, S. (1938) *The basic writings of Sigmund Freud* (A. A. Brill, Ed.). New York: Random House.

Freud, S. (1950*a*) *Beyond the pleasure principle.* New York: Liveright.

Freud, S. (1950*b*) *Collected papers.* London: Hogarth.

Freud, S. (1953–1955) *The standard edition of the complete psychological works.* (Strachey, J., trans.). London: Hogarth.

Friedman, C. J., Johnson, C. A., & Fode, K. (1964) Subjects' descriptions of selected TAT cards via the semantic differential. *J. consult. Psychol.,* **28, 317–325.**

Fromm, E. (1941) *Escape from freedom.* New York: Rinehart.

Fromm, E. (1947) *Man for himself.* New York: Rinehart.

Fromm, E. (1955) *The sane society.* New York: Holt, Rinehart & Winston.

Fromm, E. (1959) *Sigmund Freud's mission.* New York: Harper.

Funkenstein, D. H. (1955) The physiology of fear and anger. *Scient. American,* **192, 74–80.**

Gage, N. L. (Ed.) (1963) *Handbook of research on teaching.* Chicago: Rand McNally.

Gagné, R. M. (1965) *The conditions of learning.* New York: Holt, Rinehart & Winston.

Gardner, R. W., Holzman, P. S., Klein, G. S., Linton, Harriet, & Spence, D. P. (1959) *Cognitive control: A study of individual consistencies in cognitive behavior. Psychol. Issues,* **1,** No. 4.

Garmezy, N. (1952) Stimulus differentiation by schizophrenic and normal subjects under conditions of reward and punishment. *J. Pers.,* **21, 253–276.**

Garmezy, N. (1964) Some determiners and characteristics of learning research in schizophrenia. *Amer. J. Orthopsychiat.,* **34, 643–651.**

Geer, J. H. (1964) Phobia treated by reciprocal inhibition. *J. abnorm. soc. Psychol.,* **69,** 642–645.

Gerard, R. W. (1959) Material aspects of mental disease. *Diseases of the nervous system.* Monogr. supplement, **20,** sections **2,** 5, pp. 33–40.

Gesell, A. (1954) The ontogenesis of infant behavior. In L. Carmichael (Ed.), *Manual of child psychology.* New York: Wiley, pp. 335–373.

Getzels, J. W., & Jackson, P. W. (1962) *Creativity and intelligence: Explorations with gifted students.* New York: Wiley.

Ghiselli, E. E. (1963) Moderating effects and differential reliability and validity. *J. appl. Psychol.,* **47,** 81–86.

Glaser, R. (1965) *Teaching machines and programed learning:* II. Washington, D.C.: National Education Association.

Glueck, S., & Glueck, Eleanor T. (1956) *Physique and delinquency.* New York: Harper.

Goldberg, L. R. (1965) Diagnosticians vs. diagnostic signs: The diagnosis of psychosis vs. neurosis from the MMPI. *Psychol. Monogr.,* **79,** No. 9.

Goldstein, A. P. (1962) *Therapist-patient expectancies in psychotherapy.* New York: Pergamon Press.

Goldstein, K. (1939) *The organism:* New York: American Book Co.

Goldstein, K. (1940) *Human nature in the light of psychotherapy.* Cambridge: Harvard University Press.

Goldstein, M. J., Jones, R. B., Clemens, T. C., Flagg, G. W., and Alexander, F. G. (1965) Coping style as a factor in psychophysiological response to a tension-arousing film. *J. pers. soc. Psychol.,* **1, 290–302.**

Gottesman, I. I. (1963) Heritability of personality: A demonstration. *Psychol. Monogr.,* **77,** No. 9.

Gottlieb, D., & Ramsey, C. (1964) *The American adolescent.* Homewood, Illinois: Dorsey Press.

Gough, H. G. (1957) *California Psychological Inventory Manual.* Palo Alto: Consulting Psychologists Press.

Gough, H. G., and Hall, W. B. (1964) Prediction of performance in medical school from the California Psychological Inventory. *J. appl. Psychol.,* **48,** 218–226.

Greenspoon, J. (1955) The reinforcing effects of two spoken sounds on the frequency of two responses. *Amer. J. Psychol.,* **68,** 409–416.

Gronlund, N. E. (1959) *Sociometry in the classroom.* New York: Harper & Row.

Guilford, J. P. (1956) The structure of intellect. *Psychol. Bull.,* **53,** 267–293.

Guilford, J. P. (1957) A revised structure of intellect. *Rep. Psychol. Lab.,* No. 19. Los Angeles: University of Southern California, pp. 1–27.

Guilford, J. P. (1959*a*) *Personality.* New York: McGraw-Hill.

Guilford, J. P. (1959*b*) Three faces of intellect. *Amer. Psychologist,* **14,** 469–479.

Guilford, J. P., & Zimmerman, W. S. (1956) Fourteen dimensions of temperament. *Psychol. Monogr.,* **70,** No. 10.

Gump, P. V., Schoggen, P., & Redl, F. (1963) The behavior of the same child in different milieus. In R. G. Barker (Ed.), (1963) *The stream of behavior: Explorations of its structure and content.* New York: Appleton-Century-Crofts, pp. 169–202.

Haggard, E. A. (1954) Social-status and intelligence: An experimental study of certain cultural determinants of measured intelligence. *Genet. psychol. Monogr.,* **49,** 141–186.

Haley, J. (1963) *Strategies of psychotherapy.* New York: Grune & Stratton.

Hall, C. S. (1936) Emotional behavior in the rat: III. The relationship between emotionality and ambulatory activity. *J. comp. Psychol.,* **22,** 345–352.

Hall, C. S. (1941) Temperament: A survey of animal studies. *Psychol. Bull.,* **38,** 909–943.

Hall, C. S., & Lindzey, G. (1957) *Theories of personality.* New York: Wiley.

Haner, C. F., & Brown, P. A. (1955) Clarification of the instigation to action concept in the frustration-aggression hypothesis. *J. abnorm. soc. Psychol.,* **51,** 204–206.

Harlow, H. F. (1958) The nature of love. *Amer. Psychologist,* **13,** 673–685.

Harlow, H. F. (1962) The heterosexual affectional system in monkeys. *Amer. Psychologist,* **17,** 1–9.

Harris, J. G., Jr., & Baxter, J. C. (1965) Ambiguity in the MMPI. *J. consult. Psychol.,* **29,** 112–118.

Hartmann, H. (1958) *Ego psychology and the problem of adaptation.* New York: International Universities Press.

Hartmann, H. (1964) *Essays on ego psychology: Selected problems in psychoanalytic theory.* New York: International Universities Press.

Hartmann, H., & Kris, E. (1945) The genetic approach in psychoanalysis. In *The Psychoanalytic study of the child,* Vol. I. New York: International Universities Press, pp. 11–29.

Hartmann, H., Kris, E., & Lowenstein, R. M. (1946) Comments on the formation of psychic structure. In *The Psychoanalytic study of the child,* Vol. 2. New York: International Universities Press, pp. 11–38.

Hartmann, H., Kris, F., and Lowenstein, R. M. (1964) *Papers on psychoanalytic psychology. Psychol. Issues,* **2,** No. 2 (monogr. 14).

Hartup, W. W. (1958) Nurturance and nurturance-withdrawal in relation to the dependency behavior of pre-school children. *Child Developm.,* **29,** 191–201.

Hathaway, S. R., & McKinley, J. C. (1942) A multiphasic personality schedule (Minnesota): I. Construction of the schedule. *J. Psychol.,* **10,** 249–254.

Hathaway, S. R., & McKinley, J. C. (1943) *Manual for the Minnesota Multiphasic Personality Inventory.* New York: Psychological Corporation.

Hathaway, S. R., & Monachesi, E. D. (Eds.) (1953) *Analyzing and predicting juvenile delinquency with the MMPI.* Minneapolis: University of Minnesota Press.

Hathaway, S. R., & Monachesi, E. D. (1961) *An atlas of juvenile MMPI profiles.* Minneapolis: University of Minnesota Press.

Hathaway, S. R., & Monachesi, E. D. (1963) *Adolescent personality and behavior.* Minneapolis: University of Minnesota Press.

Havighurst, R. J. (1957) The social competence of middle aged people. *Genet. psychol. Monogr.,* **56,** 297–375.

Havighurst, R. J. (1964) *The Public Schools of Chicago.* Chicago: Board of Education of the City of Chicago.

Heathers, G. (1955) Emotional dependence and independence in nursery school play. *J. genet Psychol.,* **87,** 35–57.

Hebb, D. O., & Thompson, W. R. (1954) The social significance of animal studies. In G. Lindzey (Ed.), *Handbook of social psychology,* Vol. 1. Cambridge, Mass.: Addison-Wesley Publishing Co., pp. 532–561.

Heinstein, M. I. (1963) Behavioral correlates of breast-bottle regimes under varying parent-infant relationships. *Monogr. Soc. Res. Child Develpm.,* **28,** no. 4.

Helson, H. (1964) *Adaptation-level theory: An experimental and systematic approach to behavior.* New York: Harper & Row.

Henry, W. E. (1956) *The analysis of fantasy.* New York: Wiley.

Henry, W. E., & Farley, J. (1959) The validity of the Thematic Apperception Test in the study of adolescent personality. *Psychol. Monogr.,* **73,** No. 17.

Heron, W. (1957). The pathology of boredom. *Scient. American,* **196, 52–56.**

Hilgard, E. R. (1949) Human motives and the concept of the self. *Amer. Psychologist,* **4,** 374–382.

Hilgard, E. R. (1952) Experimental approaches to psychoanalysis. In E. Pumpian-Mindlin (Ed.), *Psychoanalysis as science.* Stanford: Stanford University Press, pp. 3–45.

Hilgard, E. R. (1956) *Theories of learning* (2nd ed.). New York: Appleton-Century-Crofts.

Hilgard, E. R. (1962*a*) The scientific status of psychoanalysis. In E. Nagel, P. Suppes, and A. Tarski (Eds.), *Logic, methodology, and philosophy of science: Proceedings of the 1960 International Congress.* Stanford: Stanford University Press, pp. 375–390.

Hilgard, E. R. (1962*b*) *Introduction to psychology* (3rd ed.). New York: Harcourt, Brace and World.

Hinkle, L. E., Jr. (1959) Physical health, mental health, and the social environment: Some characteristics of healthy and unhealthy people. In R. H. Ojemann (Ed.), *Recent contributions of biological and psychosocial investigations to preventive psychiatry.* Iowa City: State University of Iowa, pp. 80–103.

Hinkle, L. E., Jr., & Wolff, H. G. (1957) Health and the social environment: Experimental investigations. In A. H. Leighton, J. A. Clausen, and R. N. Wilson (Eds.) *Exploration in social psychiatry.* New York: Basic Books, pp. 105–132.

Hoffman, Lois W., & Lippitt, R. (1960) The measurement of family life variables. In P. H. Mussen (Ed.), *Handbook of research methods in child development.* New York: Wiley, pp. 945–1013.

Hokanson, J. E. (1961) The effects of frustration and anxiety on overt aggression. *J. abnorm. soc. Psychol.,* **62,** 346–351.

Hokanson, J. E., & Shetler, S. (1961) The effect of overt aggression on physiological arousal level. *J. abnorm. soc. Psychol.,* **63,** 446–448.

Hollenberg, Eleanor, & Sperry, Margaret (1951) Some antecedents of aggression and effects of frustration in doll play. *Personality,* **1,** 32–43.

Holliday, Audrey R. (1965) A review of psychopharmacology. In B. B. Wolman (Ed.), *Handbook of clinical psychology.* New York: McGraw-Hill, pp. 1296–1322.

Hollingshead, A. B., & Redlich, F. C. (1958) *Social class and mental illness: A community study.* New York: Wiley.

Holt, L. E., Jr. (1929) *The care and feeding of children: A catechism for the use of mothers and children's nurses.* New York: Appleton-Century-Crofts.

Holt, R. R. (1956) Gauging primary and secondary process in Rorschach responses. *J. proj. Tech.,* **20,** 14–25.

Holt, R. R. (1958) Clinical and statistical prediction: A reformulation and some new data. *J. abnorm. soc. Psychol.,* **56,** 1–2.

Holt, R. R. (1965) Experimental methods in clinical psychology. In B. B. Wolman (Ed.), *Handbook of clinical psychology.* New York: McGraw-Hill, pp. 40–77.

Holt, R. R., & Havel, Joan (1960) A method for assessing primary and secondary process in the Rorschach. In Maria A. Rickers-Ovsiankina (Ed.), *Rorschach psychology.* New York: Wiley, pp. 263–315.

Holtzman, W. H., Thorpe, J. S., Swartz, J. D., & Herron, E. W. (1961) *Inkblot perception and personality.* Austin: University of Texas Press.

Horney, Karen (1937) *Neurotic personality of our times.* New York: Norton.

Horney, Karen (1939) *New ways in psychoanalysis.* New York: Norton.

Horney, Karen (1950) *Neurosis and human growth.* New York: Norton.

Hovland, C. I., & Weiss, W. (1951) The influence of source credibility on communication effectiveness. *Publ. Open. Quart.,* **15,** 635–650.

Howes, D. H., & Solomon, R. L. (1950) A note on McGinnies' "Emotionality and perceptual defense." *Psychol. Rev.,* **57,** 229–234.

Howes, D. H., & Solomon, R. L. (1951) Visual duration threshold as a function of word probability. *J. exp. Psychol.,* **41,** 401–410.

Hull, C. L. (1952) *A behavior system.* New Haven: Yale University Press.

Isaacs, W., Thomas, J., & Goldiamond, I. (1960) Application of operant conditioning to reinstate verbal behavior in psychotics. *J. speech hear. Disord.,* **25,** 8–12.

Jackson, D. N., & Messick, S. (1958) Content and style in personality assessment. *Psychol. Bull.,* **55,** 243–252.

Jaffe, J. (1963) Electronic computers in psychoanalytic research. In J. H. Masserman (Ed.), *Science and psychoanalysis,* Vol. 6. New York: Grune & Stratton, pp. 160–170.

Janis, I. L., Terwilliger, R. F. (1962) An experimental study of psychological resistances to fear arousing communications. *J. abnorm. soc. Psychol.,* **65,** 403–410.

Jersild, A. T. (1963) *The psychology of adolescence* (2nd ed.). New York: Macmillan.

Jessor, R., & Hammond, K. R. (1957) Construct validity and the Taylor Anxiety Scale. *Psychol. Bull.,* **54,** 161–170.

Jones, E. (1953–1957) *The life and work of Sigmund Freud* (3 vols.). New York: Basic Books.

Jones, E. E. (1964) *Ingratiation: A social psychological approach.* New York: Appleton-Century-Crofts.

Jones, H. E. (1958) Problems of method in longitudinal research. *Int. J. human Develpm.,* **1,** 93–99.

Jones, H. G. (1961) Applied abnormal psychology: The experimental approach. In H. J. Eysenck (Ed.), *Handbook of abnormal psychology.* New York: Basic Books, pp. 764–781.

Jung, C. G. (1918) *Studies in word-association.* London: Heinemann.

Jung, C. G. (1933) *Psychological types.* New York: Harcourt, Brace.

Jung, C. G. (1938) *Psychology and religion.* New Haven: Yale University Press.

Jung, C. G. (1953) *Two essays on analytical psychology.* In *Collected Works,* Vol. 7. New York: Pantheon.

Jung, C. G. (1959) *The basic writings of C. G. Jung* (V. de Laszlo, Ed.). New York: Random House.

Kafka, F. (1946) *The trial.* New York: Alfred A. Knopf.

Kagan, J. (1964) Acquisition and significance of sex typing and sex role identity. In M. L. Hoffman, and Lois W. Hoffman (Eds.), *Review of child development research,* Vol. 1. New York: Russell Sage Foundation, pp. 137–167.

Kagan, J., & Moss, H. A. (1962) *Birth to maturity: A study in psychological development.* New York: Wiley.

Kahn, R. L., & Cannell, C. F. (1957) *The dynamics of interviewing.* New York: Wiley.

Kallmann, F. J. (1959) Psychogenetic studies of twins. In S. Koch (Ed.), *Psychology: A study of a science,* Vol. 3. New York: McGraw-Hill, pp. 328–362.

Kallmann, F. J. (Ed.) (1962) *Expanding goals of genetics in psychiatry.* New York: Grune & Stratton.

Karnosh, L. J., & Zucker, E. M. (1945) *Handbook of psychiatry.* St. Louis: Mosby.

Kassebaum, G. G., Couch, A. S., & Slater, P. E. (1959) The factorial dimensions of the MMPI. *J. consult. Psychol.,* **23,** 226–236.

Katz, I., Roberts, S. O., & Robinson, J. M. (1965) Effects of task difficulty, race of administrator, and instructions on digit-symbol performance of Negroes. *J. pers. soc. Psychol.,* **2,** 53–59.

Keller, F. S., & Schoenfeld, W. N. (1950) *Principles of psychology.* New York: Appleton-Century-Crofts.

Kelley, H. H. (1953) *Communications and persuasion: Psychological studies of opinion change.* New Haven: Yale University Press.

Kelly, E. L. (1954) Theory and techniques of assessment. In *Annu. Rev. Psychol.,* Vol. 5, pp. 281–310.

Kelly, E. L. (1955) Consistency of the adult personality. *Amer. Psychologist,* **10,** 659–681.

Kelly, G. A. (1955) *The psychology of personal constructs.* (2 vols.) New York: Norton.

Kenny, D. T. (1964) Stimulus functions in projective techniques. In *Progress in experimental personality research,* Vol. 1 (B. A. Maher, Ed.). New York: Academic Press, pp. 285–354.

Keys, A., Brozek, J., Henschel, A., Mickelson, O., & Taylor, H. L. (1950) *The biology of human starvation.* Minneapolis: University of Minnesota Press.

Kissel, S., & Littig, L. W. (1962) Test anxiety and skin conductance. *J. abnorm. soc. Psychol.,* **65,** 276–278.

Klein, G. S. (1956) Perception, motives and personality. In J. L. McCary (Ed.), *Psychology of personality.* New York: Logos Press, pp. 121–200.

Klein, G. S. (1958) Cognitive control and motivation. In G. Lindzey (Ed.), *The assessment of human motives.* New York: Rinehart, pp. 87–118.

Kleinmuntz, B. (1963) MMPI decision rules for the identification of college maladjustment: A digital computer approach. *Psychol. Monogr.,* **77,** No. 14.

Klineberg, O. (1935) *Negro intelligence and selective migration.* New York: Columbia University Press.

Klopfer, B., Ainsworth, Mary D., Klopfer, W. G., & Holt, R. R. (1954) *Developments in the Rorschach technique,* Vol. 1. New York: Harcourt, Brace & World.

Koch, Helen L., (1956) Some emotional attitudes of the young child in relation to characteristics of his sibling. *Child Developm.,* **2,** 393–426.

Kogan, N., & Wallach, M. A. (1964) *Risk taking: A study in cognition and personality.* New York: Holt, Rinehart & Winston.

Kohs, S. C. (1923) *Intelligence measurement.* New York: Macmillan.

Krall, Vita (1953) Personality characteristics of accident repeating children. *J. abnorm. soc. Psychol.,* **48,** 99–107.

Krasner, L. (1962) The therapist as a social reinforcement machine. In H. H. Strupp and L. Luborsky (Eds.), *Research in psychotherapy,* Vol. 2. Washington, D.C.: American Psychological Association, pp. 61–94.

Krasner, L., & Ullmann, L. P. (1965) *Research in behavior modification: New developments and implications.* New York: Holt, Rinehart & Winston.

Krech, D., & Crutchfield, R. (1948) *Theory and problems of social psychology.* New York: McGraw-Hill.

Krech, D., Crutchfield, R. S., & Ballachey, E. L. (1962) *Individual in society.* New York: McGraw-Hill.

Kretschmer, E. (1925) *Physique and character.* London: Routledge & Kegan Paul.

Kris, E. (1947) The nature of psychoanalytic propositions and their validation. In S. Hook and M. R. Konvitz (Eds.), *Freedom and experience: Essays presented to Horace Kallen.* Ithaca, New York: Cornell University Press, pp. 239–259.

Kuhlen, R. G. (1964) Personality change with age. In P. Worchel, and D. Byrne (Eds.), *Personality change.* New York: Wiley, pp. 524–555.

Lacey, J. I. (1950) Individual differences in somatic response patterns. *J. comp. physiol. Psychol.,* **43,** 338, 350.

Lacey, J. I. (1956) The evaluation of autonomic responses: Toward a general solution. *Ann. N.Y. Acad. Sci.,* **67,** 123–164.

Lacey, J. I., Bateman, D. E., & Van Lehn, R. (1952) Autonomic response specificity and Rorschach color responses. *Psychosom. Med.,* **14,** 256–260.

Lacey, J. I., & Van Lehn, R. (1952) Differential emphasis in somatic responses to stress. *Psychosom. Med.,* **14,** 71–81.

Lakin, M. (1957) Personality factors in mothers of excessively crying (colicky) infants. *Monogr. Soc. Res. Child Develpm.,* **22,** No. 1.

Lang, P. J., & Buss, A. H. (1965) Psychological deficit in schizophrenia: II. Interference and activation. *J. abnorm. Psychol.,* **70,** 77–106.

Lang, P. J., & Lazovick, A. D. (1963) Experimental desensitization of a phobia. *J. abnorm. soc. Psychol.,* **66,** 519–525.

Langner, T. S., & Michael, S. T. (1963) *Life stress and mental health.* New York: Free Press.

Lazarus, R. S. (1964) A laboratory approach to the dynamics of psychological stress. *Amer. Psychologist,* **19,** 400–411.

Lazarus, R. S., Deese, J., & Osler, Sonia F. (1952) The effects of stress upon performance. *Psychol. Bull.,* **49,** 293–317.

Lazarus, R. S., & McCleary, R. A. (1951) Autonomic discrimination without awareness: A study of subception. *Psychol. Rev.,* **58,** 113–122.

Lazarus, R. S., Speisman, J. C., Mordkoff, A. M., & Davison, L. A. (1962) A laboratory study of psychological stress produced by a motion picture film. *Psychol. Monogr.,* **6,** No. 34.

Lesser, G. S. (1961) Custom-making projective tests for research. *J. proj. Tech.,* **25,** No. 34.

Levine, R., Chein, I., & Murphy, G. (1942) The relation of the intensity of a need to the amount of perceptual distortion: A preliminary report. *J. Psychol.,* **13,** 283–293.

Levy, D. M. (1928) Finger-sucking in and accessory movements in early infancy: An etiologic study. *Amer. J. Psychiat.,* **7,** 881–918.

Levy, D. M. (1934) Experiments in the sucking reflex and social behavior of dogs. *Amer. J. Orthopsychiat.,* **4,** 203–224.

Levy, D. M. (1942) Psychosomatic studies of some aspects of maternal behavior. *Psychosom. Med.,* **4,** 223–227.

Levy, D. M. (1943) *Maternal overprotection.* New York: Columbia University Press.

Lewin, K. (1935) *A dynamic theory of personality.* New York: McGraw-Hill.

Lewin, K. (1938) *The conceptual representation and the measurement of psychological forces.* Durham, North Carolina: Duke University Press.

Lewin, K. (1951) *Field theory in social science.* New York: Harper.

Lewin, K. (1954) Behavior and development as a function of the total situation. In L. Carmichael (Ed.), *Manual of child psychology* (2nd ed.). New York: Wiley, pp. 918–983.

Liddell, H. S. (1944) Condition reflex method and experimental neurosis. In J. McV. Hunt (Ed.), *Personality and the behavior disorders.* New York: Ronald, pp. 389–412.

Lindsley, O. R. (1960) Characteristics of the behavior of chronic psychotics as revealed by free-operant conditioning methods. *Dis. nerv. System,* monogr. supplement, **21,** 66–78.

Lindsley, O. R. (1963) Free-operant conditioning and psychotherapy. In *Current psychiatric therapies,* Vol. 3. New York: Grune & Stratton.

Lindzey, G. (1959) On the classification of projective techniques. *Psychol. Bull.,* **56,** 158–168.

Lindzey, G. (1961) *Projective techniques and cross-cultural research.* New York: Appleton-Century-Crofts.

Lindzey, G. (1965) Seer versus sign. *J. exp. res. in Pers.,* **1,** 17–26.

Lindzey, G., Lykken, D. T., & Winston, H. P. (1960) Infantile trauma, genetic factors, and adult temperament. *J. abnorm. soc. Psychol.,* **61,** 7–14.

Linton, Harriet B. (1955) Dependence on external influence: Correlates in perception, attitudes, and judgment. *J. abnorm. soc. Psychol.,* **51,** 502–507.

Linton, Harriet, & Graham, Elaine (1959) Personality correlates of persuasibility. In I. L. Janis et al. *Personality and persuasibility.* New Haven: Yale University Press, pp. 69–101.

Lipsitt, L. P. (1963) Learning in the first year of life. In L. P. Lipsitt, and C. C. Spiker (Eds.), *Advances in child development and behavior.* New York: Academic Press, pp. 147–196.

Littig, L. W., & Yeracaris, C. A. (1965) Achievement motivation and intergenerational occupational mobility. *J. pers. soc. Psychol.,* **1,** 386–389.

London, P. (1964) *The modes and morals of psychotherapy.* New York: Holt, Rinehart & Winston.

Lorr, M. C., Jenkins, R. L., & O'Connor, J. P. (1955) Factors descriptive of psychopathology and behavior of hospitalized psychotics. *J. abnorm. soc. Psychol.,* **50,** 76–86.

Lorr, M., Klett, C. J., & McNair, D. M. (1963) *Symposium of psychosis.* New York: Macmillan.

Lovaas, O. I. (1961) Interaction between verbal and nonverbal behavior. *Child Developm.,* **32,** 329–336.

Lowell, E. L. (1952) The effect of need for achievement on learning and speed of performance. *J. Psychol.* **33,** 31–40.

Lundin, R. W. (1961) *Personality: An experimental approach.* New York: Macmillan.

Lundin, R. W. (1965) *Principles of psychopathology.* Columbus, Ohio: Charles E. Merrill, 1965.

Lykken, D. T. (1957) A study of anxiety in the sociopathic personality. *J. abnorm. soc. Psychol.,* **55,** 6–10.

Lynn, D. B., & Sawrey, W. L. (1959) The effects of father-absence on Norwegian boys and girls. *J. abnorm. soc. Psychol.,* **59,** 258–262.

Lyons, J. (1963) *Psychology and the measure of man.* New York: Free Press.

Machover, Karen (1949) *Personality projection in the drawing of the human figure.* Springfield, Illinois: Charles C Thomas.

MacKinnon, D. W. (1962) The nature and nurture of creative talent. *Amer. Psychologist,* **17,** 484–495.

Maier, N. R. F. (1949) *Frustration: The study of behavior without a goal.* New York: McGraw-Hill.

Mandler, G., Mandler, Jean M., Kremen, I., & Sholiton, R. D. (1961) The response to threat: Relations among verbal and physiological indices. *Psychol. Monogr.,* **75,** No. 9.

Mandler, G., & Sarason, S. B. (1952) A study of anxiety and learning. *J. abnorm. soc. Psychol.,* **47,** 166–173.

Marsden, G. (1965) Content-analysis studies of therapeutic interviews: 1954 to 1964. *Psychol. Bull.,* **63,** 298–321.

Marshall, Helen R. (1961) Relations between home experiences and children's use of language in play interactions with peers. *Psychol. Monogr.,* **75,** No. 5.

Masling, J. (1960) The influence of situational and interpersonal variables in projective testing. *Psychol. Bull.,* **57,** 65–85.

Maslow, A. H. (1954*a*) The instinctoid nature of basic needs. *J. Pers.,* **22,** 326–347.

Maslow, A. H. (1954*b*) *Motivation and personality.* New York: Harper.

Maslow, A. H. (1956) Personality problems and personality growth. In C. G. Moustakas (Ed.), *The Self: Explorations in personal growth.* New York: Harper, pp. 232–256.

Mason, W. A. (1964) Sociability and social organization in monkeys and apes. In L. Berkowitz (Ed.), *Advances in experimental social psychology,* Vol. 1. New York: Academic Press, pp. 278–305.

Mason, W. A., Saxon, S. V., & Sharpe, L. B. (1963) Preferential responses of young chimpanzees to food and social rewards. *Psychol. Rec.,* **13,** 341–345.

Masserman, J. H. (1943) *Behavior and neurosis.* Chicago: University of Chicago Press.

Masserman, J. H., & Siever, P. W. (1944) Dominance, neurosis, and aggression: An experimental study. *Psychosom. Med.,* **6,** 7–16.

Matkom, A. J. (1963) Impression formation as a function of adjustment. *Psychol. Monogr.,* **77,** Whole No. 568.

May, R. (Ed.), (1961) *Existential psychology.* New York: Random House.

McCandless, B. R. (1961) *Children and adolescents: Behavior and development.* New York: Holt, Rinehart & Winston.

McCarthy, Dorothea (1960) Language development. In Nancy E. Wood (Ed.), Language development and language disorders: A compenium of lectures. *Monogr. Soc. Res. Child Develpm.,* **25,** No. 3, pp. 5–14.

McClearn, G. E. (1964) Genetics and behavior development. In M. L. Hoffman and L. W. Hoffman (Eds.), *Review of child development research,* Vol. 1. New York: Russell Sage Foundation, pp. 433–480.

McCleary, R. A., & Lazarus, R. S. (1949) Autonomic discrimination without awareness. *J. Pers.,* **18,** 171–179.

McClelland, D. C. (1951) *Personality.* New York: Sloane.

McClelland, D. C. (Ed.) (1955) *Studies in motivation.* New York: Appleton-Century-Crofts.

McClelland. D. C. (1961) *The achieving society.* Princeton: Van Nostrand.

McClelland, D. C. (1965*a*) Achievement and entrepreneurship: A longitudinal study. *J. pers. soc. Psychol.,* **1,** 389–392.

McClelland, D. C. (1956*b*) Toward a theory of motive acquisition. *Amer. Psychologist,* **20,** 321–333.

McClelland, D. C., & Atkinson, J. W. (1948) The projective expression of needs. I: The effect of different intensities of the hunger drive on perception. *J. Psychol.,* **25,** 205–222.

McClelland, D. C., Clark, R. A., Roby, T. B., & Atkinson, J. W. (1949) The projective expression of needs: IV: The effect of the need for achievement on thematic apperception. *J. exp. Psychol.,* **39, 242–255.**

McGee, R. K. (1962) Response style as a personality variable: By what criterion? *Psychol. Bull.,* **59, 284–295.**

McGinnies, E. (1949) Emotionality and perceptual defense. *Psychol. Rev.,* **56,** 244–251.

McGinnies, E. (1950) Discussion of Howes' and Solomon's note on "Emotionality and perceptual defense." *Psychol. Rev.,* **57, 235–240.**

McGuigan, F. J. (1963) The experimenter: A neglected stimulus object. *Psychol. Bull.,* **60, 421–428.**

McGuire, W. J. (1960) Cognitive consistency and attitude change. *J. abnorm. soc. Psychol.,* **60,** 345–353.

McKee, J. P., & Honzik, Marjorie P. (1962) The sucking behavior of mammals: An illustration of the nature-nurture question. In L. Postman (Ed.), *Psychology in the making.* New York: A. A. Knopf, pp. 585–661.

McNeil, E. B. (Ed.) (1965) *The nature of human conflict.* Englewood Cliffs, New Jersey: Prentice-Hall.

McNemar, Q. (1964) Lost: Our intelligence? Why? *Amer. Psychologist,* **19,** 871–882.

Meehl, P. E. (1945) The dynamics of structured personality tests. *J. clin. Psychol.,* **1,** 296–303.

Meehl, P. E. (1954) *Clinical vs. statistical prediction.* Minneapolis: University of Minnesota Press.

Meehl, P. E. (1962) Schizotaxia, schizotypy, schizophrenia. *Amer. Psychologist,* **17,** 827–838.

Milgram, S. (1963) Behavioral study of obedience. *J. abnorm. soc. Psychol.,* **67,** 371–378.

Milgram, S. (1964) Issues in the study of obedience: A reply to Baumrind. *Amer. Psychologist,* **19,** 848–852.

Milgram, S. (1965) Liberating effects of group pressure. *J. pers. soc. Psychol.,* **1,** 127–134.

Milici, P. (1937) Graphocatharsis in schizophrenia. *Psychiat. Quart.,* **11,** 44–73.

Miller, D. R., & Swanson, G. E. (1960) *Inner conflict and defense.* New York: Holt, Rinehart & Winston.

Miller, N. E. (1948) Theory and experiment relating psychoanalytic displacement to stimulus-response generalization. *J. abnorm. soc. Psychol.,* **43,** 155–178.

Miller, N. E. (1951) Learnable drives and rewards. In S. S. Stevens (Ed.), *Handbook of experimental psychology.* New York: Wiley, pp. 435–472.

Miller, N. E. (1961) Some recent studies of conflict behavior and drugs. *Amer. Psychologist,* **16,** 12–24.

Miller, N. E., & Bugelski, R. (1948) Minor studies of aggression. II: The influence of frustrations imposed by the in-group on attitudes expressed toward out-groups. *J. Psychol.,* **25,** 437–442.

Miller, N. E., & Dollard J. (1941) *Social learning and imitation.* New Haven: Yale University Press.

Mingione, Ann D. (1965) Need for achievement in Negro and white children. *J. consult. Psychol.,* **29,** 108–111.

Mirsky, A. F. (1960) Studies on the effects of brain lesions on social behavior in *macca mulatta:* Methodological and theoretical considerations. *Ann. N.Y. Acad. Sci.,* **85,** 785–794.

Mirsky, I. A., Miller, R. E., & Murphy, J. V. (1958) The communication of affect in rhesus monkeys: I. An experimental method. *J. Amer. Psychoanal. Ass.,* **6,** 433–441.

Moore, Bernice M., & Holtzman, W. (1965) *Tomorrow's parents: A study of youth and their families.* Austin: University of Texas Press.

Moreno, J. L. (1959) Psychodrama. In S. Arieti (Ed.), *American handbook of psychiatry,* Vol. 2. New York: Basic Books, pp. 1375–1396.

Morgan, C. D., & Murray, H. A. (1935) A method for investigating fantasies: The Thematic Apperception Test.. *Arch. neurol. & Psychiat.,* **34,** 289–306.

Moss, C. S.. Logan, J. C., & Lynch, Dorothy (1962) Present status of psychological research and training in hypnosis: A developing professional problem. *Amer. Psychologist,* **17,** 542–549.

Mowrer, O. H. (1950*a*) *Learning theory and personality dynamics: Selected papers.* New York: Ronald Press.

Mowrer, O. H. (1950*b*) On the psychology of "talking birds"—a contribution to language and personality theory. *Learning theory and personality dynamics.* New York: Ronald, pp. 688–726.

Mowrer, O. H. (Ed.) (1953) *Psychotherapy: Theory and research.* New York: Ronald.

Mowrer, O. H. (1960*a*) *Learning theory and behavior.* New York: Wiley.

Mowrer, O. H. (1960*b*) *Learning theory and the symbolic processes.* New York: Wiley.

Mowrer, O. H. (1965) Learning theory and behavior therapy. In B. B. Wolman (Ed.), *Handbook of clinical psychology.* New York: McGraw-Hill, pp. 242–276.

Mullahy, P. (Ed.) (1949) *A study of interpersonal relations.* New York: Hermitage House.

Munn, N. L. (1954) Learning in children. In L. Carmichael, (Ed.), *Manual of child psychology* (2nd ed.). New York: Wiley, pp. 374–458.

Munroe, Ruth (1955) *Schools of psychoanalytic thought.* New York: Dryden.

Murphy, G. (1947) *Personality: A biosocial approach.* New York: Harper.

Murphy, Lois B. (1962) *The widening world of childhood.* New York: Basic Books.

Murray, E. J. (1954) A case study in a behavioral analysis of psychotherapy. *J. abnorm. soc. Psychol.,* **49,** 305–310.

Murray, E. J., Auld, F., & White, A. M. (1954) A psychotherapy case showing progress but no decrease in the discomfort-relief quotient. *J. consult. Psychol.,* **18,** 349–353.

Murray, H. A. (1938) *Explorations in personality.* New York: Oxford University Press.

Murray, H. A. (1943) *Thematic Apperception Test.* Cambridge, Massachusetts: Harvard University Press (set of cards and manual.)

Murstein, B. I. (1961) The role of the stimulus in the manifestation of fantasy. In J. Kagan and G. Lesser, (Eds.), *Contemporary issues in thematic apperceptive methods.* Springfield, Illinois: Charles C Thomas, pp. 221–273.

Mussen, P. H. (1961) Some antecedents and consequents of masculine sex-typing in adolescent boys. *Psychol. Monogr.,* **75,** No. 2.

Mussen, P. H., Conger, J. J., & Kagan, J. (1963) *Child development and personality* (2nd ed.). New York: Harper & Row.

Nelson, C. L. (1961) Thematic apperception as a function of sleep deprivation, set, and goal availability. Unpublished doctoral dissertation, University of Massachusetts.

Nelson, J. T., & Epstein, S. (1962) Relationships among three measures of conflict over hostility. *J. consult. Psychol.,* **26,** 345–350.

Neugarten, Bernice L. and associates. (1964) *Personality in middle and late life: Empirical studies.* New York: Atherton Press.

Oeser, O. A. (1961) Review of G. W. Allport, Personality and social encounter: selected essays. *Contemporary psychology,* **6,** 450–451.

Office of Strategic Service Assessment Staff (1948) *Assessment of men.* New York: Holt, Rinehart & Winston.

Olds, J., & Milner, P. (1954) Positive reinforcement produced by electrical stimulation of septal area and other regions of rat brain. *J. comp. physiol. Psychol.,* **47,** 419–427.

Orne, M. T. (1962*a*) Implications for psychotherapy derived from current research on the nature of hypnosis. *Amer. J. Psychiat.,* **118,** 1097–1103.

Orne, M. T. (1962*b*) On the social psychology of the psychological experiment. *Amer. Psychologist,* **17,** 776–783.

Orne, M. T., & Scheibe, K. E. (1964) The contribution of nondeprivation factors in the production of sensory deprivation effects: The psychology of the "panic button." *J. abnorm. soc. Psychol.,* **68,** 3–13.

Osgood, C. E., Suci, G. J., & Tannenbaum, P. H. (1957) *The measurement of meaning.* Urbana: University of Illinois Press.

Paul, G. L. (1964) Effects of insight, desensitization, and attention—placebo treatment of anxiety: An approach to outcome research in psychotherapy. Unpublished doctoral dissertation, University of Illinois.

Payne, D. E., & Mussen, P. H. (1956) Parent-child relations and father identification among adolescent boys. *J. abnorm. soc. Psychol.,* **52,** 358–362.

Penfield, W. (1954) Some observations on the functional organization of the human brain. *Proc. Amer. Phil. Soc.,* **98,** 293–297.

Penfield, W., & Roberts, L. (1950) *Speech and brain-mechanisms.* Princeton: Princeton University Press.

Peterson, D. R., Becker, W. C., Hellmer, L. A., Shoemaker, D. J., & Quay, H. C. (1959) Parental attitudes and child adjustment. *Child Develpm.,* **30,** 119–130.

Pettigrew, T. F. (1964) *A profile of the Negro American.* Princeton, New Jersey: Van Nostrand.

Phillips, L. (1953) Case history data and prognosis in schizophrenia. *J. nerv. ment. Dis.,* **117,** 515–525.

Phillips, L., & Zigler, E. (1961) Social competence: The action-thought parameter and vicariousness in normal and pathological behaviors. *J. abnorm. soc. Psychol.,* **63,** 137–146.

Piaget, J. (1928) *Judgment and reasoning in the child.* New York: Harcourt, Brace.

Piaget, J. (1929) *The child's conception of the world.* New York: Harcourt, Brace.

Piaget, J. (1952) *The origins of intelligence in children.* New York: International Universities Press.

Piaget, J. (1957). *Logic and psychology.* New York: Basic Books.

Pierce, S. W., & Pierce, J. T. (1929) *The layman looks at doctors.* New York: Harcourt, Brace.

Pribram, K. H. (1962) Interrelationships of psychology and the neurological disciplines. In S. Koch (Ed.), *Psychology: A study of a science,* Vol. 4. New York: McGraw-Hill, pp. 119–157.

Raimy, V. C. (1948) Self-reference in counselling interviews. *J. consult. Psychol.,* **12,** 153–163.

Ramer, J. (1963) The Rorschach barrier score and social behavior. *J. consult. Psychol.,* **27,** 525–531.

Rank, O. (1929) *The trauma of birth.* London: Routledge & Kegan Paul.

Rapaport, D. (1942) *Emotions and memory.* Baltimore: Williams and Wilkins (2nd unaltered ed., 1950). New York: International Universities Press.

Rapaport, D. (1959) The structure of psychoanalytic theory: A systematizing attempt. In S. Koch, (Ed.), *Psychology: A study of a science,* Vol. 3. New York: McGraw-Hill, pp. 55–183.

Raphelson, A. C. (1957) The relationships among imaginative, direct verbal, and physiological measures of anxiety in an achievement situation. *J. abnorm. soc. Psychol.,* **54,** 13–18.

Raymond, E. (Ed.) (1946) *The autobiography of David—.* London: Gollancz.

Reichard, Suzanne, Livson, Florine, & Petersen, P. G. (1962) *Aging and personality: A study of eighty-seven older men.* New York: Wiley.

Rheingold, Harriet L. (1956) The modification of social responsiveness in institutional babies. *Monogr. Soc. Res. Child Develpm.,* **21,** No. 2.

Rheingold, Harriet, L. (1960) The measurement of maternal care. *Child Develpm.,* **31,** 565–575.

Rheingold, Harriet L. (1961) The effect of environmental stimulation upon social and exploratory behavior in the human infant. In B. M. Foss, (Ed.), *Determinants of infant behavior,* New York: Wiley, pp. 143–171.

Ribble, Margaret A. (1943) *The rights of infants: Early psychological needs and their satisfaction.* New York: Columbia University Press.

Rickers-Ovsiankina, Maria A. (1960) Synopsis of psychological premises underlying the Rorschach. In Maria A. Rickers-Ovsiankina (Ed.), *Rorschach psychology.* New York: Wiley, pp. 3–24.

Rimland, B. (1964) *Infantile autism.* New York: Appleton-Century-Crofts.

Rioch, Margaret J. (1963) *Selection and training in the pilot project in training mental health counselors.* Paper presented at 1963 meeting of American Psychological Association.

Rioch, Margaret, J., Elkes, C., Flint, A. A., Usdansky, B. S., Newman, R. G., and Silber, E. (1963) National Institute of Mental Health Pilot Study in training mental health counselors. *Amer. J. Orthopsychiat.* **33,** 678–689.

Rodnick, E. H. (1963) Clinical psychology, psychopathology, and research on schizophrenia. In S. Koch, (Ed.), *Psychology: A study of a science,* Vol. 5. New York: McGraw-Hill, pp. 738–779.

Rodnick, E. H., & Garmezy, N. (1957) An experimental approach to the study of motivation in schizophrenia. In M. R. Jones (Ed.), *Nebraska Symposium on motivation.* Lincoln: University of Nebraska Press, pp. 109–184.

Rogers, C. R. (1951) *Client-centered therapy.* Boston: Houghton Mifflin.

Rogers, C. R. (1959) A theory of therapy, personality, and interpersonal relationships, as developed in the client-centered framework. In S. Koch, (Ed.),

Psychology: A study of a science, Vol. 3. New York: McGraw-Hill, pp. 184–256.

Rogers, C. R., & Dymond, Rosalind F. (Eds.) (1954) *Psychotherapy and personality change: Co-ordinated studies in the client-centered approach.* Chicago: University of Chicago Press.

Rohde, Amanda R. (1957) *The sentence completion method.* New York: Ronald.

Rorer, L. G. (1965) The great response-style myth. *Psychol. Bull.,* **63,** 129–156.

Rorschach, H. (1942) *Psychodiagnostics.* (P. Lemkau, and B. Kronenberg, trans.) (2nd. ed.). Bern: Huber.

Rosen, A. (1958) Differentiation of diagnostic groups by individual MMPI scales. *J. consult. Psychol.,* **22,** 453–457.

Rosen, E., & Gregory, I. (1965) *Abnormal psychology.* Philadelphia: Saunders.

Rosenthal, D. (Ed.) (1963) *The Genain quadruplets: A case study and theoretical analysis of heredity and environment in schizophrenia.* New York: Basic Books.

Rosenthal, R. (1963) On the social psychology of the psychological experiment. *Amer. Scientist,* **51,** 268–283.

Rosenthal, R. (1964) Experimenter outcome-orientation and the results of the psychological experiment. *Psychol. Bull.,* **61,** 405–412.

Rosenthal, R., & Lawson, R. (1964) A longitudinal study of the effects of experimenter bias on the operant learning of laboratory rats. *J. psychiat. Res.,* **2,** 61–72.

Rosenthal, R., Persinger, G. W., Kline, Linda V., & Mulry, R. C. (1963) The role of the research assistant in the mediation of experimenter bias. *J. Pers.,* **31,** 313–335.

Rotter, J. B. (1951) Word association and sentence completion methods. In H. H. Anderson and Gladys Anderson (Eds.), *Introduction to projective techniques.* New York: Prentice-Hall, pp. 279–311.

Rotter, J. B. (1954) *Social learning and clinical psychology.* New York: Prentice-Hall.

Rotter, J. B., Rafferty, J. E., & Schachitz, F. (1949) Validation of the Rotter Incomplete Sentences Blank for college screening. *J. consult. Psychol.,* **13,** 348–356.

Rubinstein, E. A., & Parloff, M. B. (Eds.) (1959) *Research in psychotherapy,* Vol. 1. Washington, D.C.: American Psychological Association.

Ruesch, J., & Bateson, G. (1951) *Communication: the social matrix of psychiatry.* New York: Norton.

Ryans, D G. (1960) *Characteristics of teachers.* Washington, D.C.: American Council on Education.

Salzinger, K. (1959) Experimental manipulation of verbal behavior: A review. *J. gen. Psychol.,* **61,** 65–94.

Salzinger, Suzanne, Salzinger, K., Portnoy, Stephanie, Eckman, Judith, Bacon, Pauline M., Deutsch, M., & Zubin, J. (1962) Operant conditioning of continuous speech in younger children. *Child Develpm.,* **33,** 683–695.

Sanford, N. (1963) Personality: Its place in psychology. In S. Koch (Ed.), *Psychology: A study of a science,* Vol. 5. New York: McGraw-Hill, pp. 488–592.

Sanford, R. N. (1936) The effects of abstinence from food upon imaginal processes: A preliminary experiment. *J. Psychol.,* **2,** 129–136.

Sanford, R. N. (1937) The effects of abstinence from food upon imaginal processes: A further experiment. *J. Psychol.,* **3,** 145–159.

Sarason, B. R. (1956) The effects of verbally conditioned response classes on post-conditioning tasks. Unpublished doctoral dissertation, Indiana University.

Sarason, I. G. (1958) Interrelationships among individual difference variables, behavior in psychotherapy, and verbal conditioning. *J. abnorm. soc. Psychol.,* **56,** 339–344.

Sarason, I. G. (1960) Empirical findings and theoretical problems in the use of anxiety scales. *Psychol. Bull.,* **57,** 403–415.

Sarason, I. G. (1961) The effects of anxiety and threat on the solution of a difficult task. *J. abnorm. soc. Psychol.,* **62,** 165–168.

Sarason, I. G. (Ed.) (1965a) *Science and theory in psychoanalysis.* Princeton: Van Nostrand.

Sarason, I. G. (Ed.) (1965*b*) *Psychoanalysis and the study of behavior.* Princeton: Van Nostrand.

Sarason, I. G. (1965*c*) The human reinforcer in verbal behavior research. In L. Krasner and L. P. Ullmann (Eds.), *Research in behavior modification: New developments and their clinical implications.* New York: Holt, Rinehart & Winston, pp. 229–243.

Sarason, I. G., & Ganzer, V. J. (1962) Anxiety, reinforcement, and experimental instructions in a free verbalization situation. *J. abnorm. soc. Psychol.,* **65,** 300–307.

Sarason, I. G., & Minard, J. (1963) Interrelationships among subject, experimenter, and situational variables. *J. abnorm. soc. Psychol.,* **67,** 87–91.

Sarason, S. B. (1954) *The clinical interaction.* New York: Harper.

Sarason, S. B. (1959) *Psychological problems in mental deficiency* (3rd ed.). New York: Harper and Row.

Sarason, S. B., Davidson, K. S., & Blatt, B. (1962) *The preparation of teachers. An unstudied problem in education.* New York: Wiley.

Sarason, S. B., Davidson, K. S., Lighthall, F. F., Waite, R. R., & Ruebush, B. K. (1960) *Anxiety in elementary school children.* New York: Wiley.

Sarason, S. B., & Mandler, G. (1952) Some correlates of test anxiety. *J. abnorm. soc. Psychol.,* **47,** 810–817.

Sarason, S. B., Mandler, G., & Craighill, P. C. (1952) The effect of differential instructions on anxiety and learning. *J. abnorm. soc. Psychol.,* **47,** 561–565.

Schachtel, E. G. (1945) Subjective definitions of the Rorschach test and their effect on test performance. *Psychiatry,* **8,** 419–448.

Schachtel, E. G. (1951) Notes on Rorschach tests of 500 juvenile delinquents and a control group of 500 nondelinquent adolescents. *J. proj. Tech.,* **15,** 144–172.

Schachter, S. (1959) *The psychology of affiliation: Experimental studies of the sources of gregariousness.* Stanford: Stanford University Press.

Schachter, S. (1964) The interaction of cognitive and psychological determinants of emotional state. In L. Berkowitz (Ed.), *Advances in experimental social psychology,* Vol. 1. New York: Academic Press, pp. 49–80.

Schachter, S., & Latané, B. (1964) Crime, cognition and the autonomic nervous system. In D. Levine (Ed.), *Nebraska symposium on motivation.* Lincoln: University of Nebraska Press, pp. 221–273.

Schaefer, E. S., & Bayley, Nancy (1963) Maternal behavior, child behavior, and their intercorrelations from infancy through adolescence. *Monogr. Soc. Res. Child Develpm.*, **28,** 3.

Schafer, R. (1954) *Psychoanalytic interpretation in Rorschach testing.* New York: Grune & Stratton.

Schaffer, H. R., & Emerson, Peggy E. (1964) The development of social attachments in infancy. *Monogr. Soc. Res. Child Develpm.*, **29,** no. 3.

Schaller, G. B. (1963) *The mountain gorilla: Ecology and behavior.* Chicago: University of Chicago Press.

Schofield, W. (1964) *Psychotherapy: The purchase of friendship.* Englewood Cliffs, New Jersey: Prentice-Hall.

Schooler, Carmi (1964) Birth order and hospitalization for schizophrenia. *J. abnorm. soc. Psychol.*, **69,** 574–579.

Schwartz, B. J. (1956) An empirical test of two Freudian hypotheses concerning castration anxiety. *J. Pers.*, **24,** 318–327.

Schwartz, M. S., & Schwartz, Charlotte G. (1964) *Social approaches to mental patient care.* New York: Columbia University Press.

Scodel, A., & Mussen, P. (1953) Social perceptions of authoritarians and non-authoritarians. *J. abnorm. soc. Psychol.*, **48,** 181–184.

Scott, J. P. (1958) *Aggression.* Chicago: University of Chicago Press.

Scott, J. P., & Fuller, J. L. (1965) *Genetics and the social behavior of the dog.* Chicago: University of Chicago Press.

Sears, Pauline S., & Hilgard, E. R. (1964) The teacher's role in the motivation of the learner. In E. R. Hilgard (Ed.), *Theories of learning and instruction.* (Sixty-third Yearbook of the National Society for the Study of Education.) Chicago: National Society for the Study of Education, pp. 182–209.

Sears, R. (1933) Psychogalvanic responses in arithmetical work. *Arch. Psychol., N.Y.*, No. 155.

Sears, R. R. (1943) *Survey of objective studies of psychoanalytic concepts.* New York: Social Science Research Council.

Sears, R. R. (1961) Relation of early socialization experiences to aggression in middle childhood. *J. abnorm. soc. Psychol.*, **63,** 466–492.

Sears, R. R., Maccoby, Eleanor E., & Levin, H. (1957) *Patterns of childrearing.* Evanston, Illinois: Row, Peterson.

Sears, R. R., Whiting, J. W. M., Nowlis, V., & Sears, Pauline S. (1953) Some child-rearing antecedents of aggression and dependency in young children. *Genet. Psychol. Monogr.*, **47,** 135–234.

Sears, R. R., & Wise, G. W. (1950) Relations of cup-feeding in infancy to thumb sucking and the oral drive. *Amer. J. Orthopsychiat.*, **20,** 123–138.

Seward, J. P. (1963) The structure of functional autonomy. *Amer. Psychologist*, **18,** 703–710.

Shakow, D., & Rapaport, D. (1964) *The influence of Freud on American psychology. Psychol. Issues,* **4,** No. 1 (Monogr. No. 13).

Shallenberger, Patricia, & Zigler, E. (1961) Rigidity, negative reaction tendencies, and cosatiation effects in normal and feebleminded children. *J. abnorm. soc. Psychol.*, **63,** 20–26.

Sharp, A. A. (1938) An experimental test of Freud's doctrine of the relation of hedonic tone to memory revival. *J. exp. Psychol.*, **22,** 395–418.

Sheldon, W. H., Dupertius, C. W., & McDermott, E. (1954) *Atlas of men.* New York: Harper & Row.

Sheldon, W. H., & Stevens, S. S. (1942) *The varieties of temperament.* New York: Harper & Row.

Sheldon, W. H., Stevens, S. S., & Tucker, W. B. (1940) *The varieties of human physique.* New York: Harper & Row.

Sherif, M. (1935) A study of some social factors in perception. *Arch. Psychol.,* No. 187.

Sherif, M., & Cantril, H. (1947) *The psychology of ego-involvement: Social attitudes and identification.* New York: Wiley.

Sherman, L. J., Moseley, E. C., Ging, Rosalie, & Bookbinder, L. J. (1964) Prognosis in schizophrenia: A follow-up study of 588 patients. *Archives of Gen. Psychiatry,* **10,** 123–130.

Sherman, M. (1938) *Mental conflicts and personality.* New York: Longmans, Green.

Shields, J., & Slater, E. (1961) Heredity and psychological abnormality. In H. J. Eysenck (Ed.), *Handbook of abnormal psychology.* New York: Basic Books, pp. 298–343.

Shipley, T. E., Jr., & Veroff, J. (1952) A projective measure of need for affiliation. *J. exp. Psychol.,* **43,** 349–356.

Short, J. B., Jr., Tennyson, R. A., & Howard, R. A. (1963) Behavior dimensions of gang delinquency. *Amer. sociological Rev.,* **28,** 411–428.

Simkins, L. (1961) Generalization effects of hostile verb reinforcement as a function of stimulus similarity and type of reinforcer. *J. Pers.,* **29,** 64–72.

Singer, J. E. (1963) Sympathetic activation, drugs, and fear. *J. comp. physiol. Psychol.,* **56,** 612–615.

Singer, R. D. (1961) Verbal conditioning and generalization of prodemocratic responses. *J. abnorm. soc. Psychol.,* **63,** 43–46.

Skinner, B. F. (1953) *Science and human behavior.* New York: Macmillan.

Skinner, B. F. (1954) Critique of psychoanalytical concepts and theories. *Scientific Monthly,* **79,** 300–305.

Skinner, B. F. (1956) What is psychotic behavior? In *Theory and treatment of the psychoses.* St. Louis: Washington University.

Slater, E. (1953) Psychotic and neurotic illness in twins. Great Britain, *Medical Research Council Special Report Series,* No. 278, Part 2.

Smith, W. (1922) *The measurement of emotion.* London: Kegan Paul.

Snyder, W. U. (1961) *The psychotherapy relationship.* New York: Macmillan.

Snyder, W. U. (1963) *Dependency in psychotherapy: A casebook.* New York: Macmillan.

Solomon, R. L. (1964) Punishment. *Amer. Psychologist,* **19,** 239–254.

Sontag, L. W. (1944) War and the fetal-maternal relationship. *Marriage fam. Liv.,* **6,** 1–5.

Sontag, L. W., Baker, C. T., & Nelson, V. L. (1958) Mental growth and personality development: A longitudinal study. *Monogr. Soc. Res. Child Develpm.,* **23,** serial No. 68, No. 2.

Spearman, C. (1927) *The abilities of man.* New York: Macmillan.

Speisman, J. C., Lazarus, R. S., Mordkoff, A., & Davison, L. (1964) Experimental reduction of stress based on ego-defense theory. *J. abnorm. soc. Psychol.,* **68,** 367–380.

Spielberger, C. D. (1962) The role of awareness in verbal conditioning. In C. W. Eriksen (Ed.), *Behavior and awareness.* Durham: Duke University Press, pp. 73–101.

Spielberger, C. D., DeNike, L. D., & Stein, L. S. (1965) Anxiety and verbal conditioning. *J. pers. soc. Psychol.,* **1,** 229–239.

Spielberger, C. D., Levin, S. M., & Shepard, Mary C. (1962) The effect of awareness and attitude toward the reinforcement on the operant conditioning of verbal behavior. *J. Pers.,* **30,** 106–121.

Spielberger, C. D., & Weitz, H. (1964) Improving the academic performance of anxious college freshmen. *Psychol. Monogr.,* **78,** No. 13.

Srole, L., Langner, T. S., Michael, S. T., Opler, M. K., & Rennie, T. A. C. (1962) *Mental health in the metropolis: The Midtown Manhattan Study.* New York: McGraw-Hill.

Stanton, A. H., & Schwartz, M. S. (1954) *The mental hospital.* New York: Basic Books.

Steele, J. R. (1961) Personality, defense and task performance. Unpublished Ph.D. thesis, University of Washington.

Stendler, Celia B. (1954) Possible causes of overdependency in young children. *Child. Develpm.,* **25,** 125–146.

Stephenson, W. (1953) *The study of behavior.* Chicago: University of Chicago Press.

Stern, G. G., Stein, M. I., & Bloom, B. S. (1956) *Methods in personality assessment.* Glencoe, Illinois: Free Press.

Stolz, Lois M. (1954) *Father relations of war-born children.* Stanford: Stanford University Press.

Stone, P. J., Bales, R. F., & Namenwirth, J. (1962) The general inquirer: A computer system for content analysis and retrieval based on the sentence as a unit of information. *Behavioral Science,* **7,** 1–15.

Strong, E. K., Jr. (1943) *Vocational interests of men and women.* Stanford: Stanford University Press.

Strong, E. K., Jr. (1951) Permanence of interest scores over 22 years. *J. appl. Psychol.,* **35,** 89–91.

Strupp, H. H., & Luborsky, L. (Eds.) (1962) *Research in psychotherapy,* Vol. 2. Washington, D.C.: American Psychological Association.

Sullivan, H. S. (1947) *Conceptions of modern psychiatry.* Washington, D.C.: William Alanson White Psychiatric Foundation.

Sullivan, H. S. (1953) *The interpersonal theory of psychiatry.* New York: Norton.

Sumerwell, Harriet, B., Campbell, Marjorie M., & Sarason, I. G. (1958) The effect of differential motivating instructions on the emotional tone and outcome of TAT stories. *J. consult. Psychol.,* **22,** 385–388.

Swets, J. A., & Feurzeig, W. (1965) Computer-aided instruction. *Science,* **150,** 572–576.

Symonds, P. M. (1948) *Symonds Picture-Story Test.* New York: Columbia University Teachers' College, Bureau of Publications.

Taffel, C. (1955) Anxiety and the conditioning of verbal behavior. *J. abnorm. soc. Psychol.,* **51,** 496–501.

Taft, R. (1959) Multiple methods of personality assessment. *Psychol. Bull.,* **56,** 333–352.

Tagiuri, R., & Petrullo, L. (Eds.) (1958) *Person perception and interpersonal behavior.* Stanford: Stanford University Press.

Taylor, Janet A. (1951) The relationship of anxiety to the conditioned eyelid response. *J. exp. Psychol.,* **41,** 81–92.

Taylor, Janet A. (1953) A personality scale of manifest anxiety. *J. abnorm. soc. Psychol.*, **48**, 285–290.

Technical recommendations for psychological tests and diagnostic techniques. (1954) *Psychol. Bull. Supplement* **51, 2,** Part 2, 1–38.

Terman, L. M. (1925) *Genetic studies of genius. Mental and physical traits of a thousand gifted children,* Vol. 1. Stanford: Stanford University Press.

Terman, L. M., & Oden, M. H. (1947) *The gifted child grows up: Twenty-five years follow-up of a superior group.* Stanford: Stanford University Press.

Thorndike, E. L., & Lorge, I. (1944) *The teacher's word book of 30,000 words.* New York: Bureau of Publications, Teacher's College, Columbia University.

Thurstone, L. L. (1946) Theories of intelligence. *Scientific Monthly,* **62,** 101–112.

Thurstone, L. L., & Thurstone, Thelma G. (1950) *Primary mental abilities scales: Primary, elementary, and intermediate.* Chicago: Science Research Associates.

Tillmann, W. A., & Hobbs, G. E. (1949) The accident-prone automobile driver. *Amer. J. Psychiat.*, **106**, 321–331.

Timmons, E. O. (1959) Experiments in conditioning operant verbal behavior. Unpublished doctoral dissertation, University of Tennessee.

Truax, C. B. (1957) The repression response to implied failure as a function of the hysteria-psychasthenia index. *J. abnorm. soc. Psychol.*, **55**, 188–193.

Turner, W. S. (1963) Correlation between test scores, life data, and behavior during testing. Unpublished Ph.D. thesis, University of California.

Ullmann, L. P., & Krasner, L. (1965) *Case studies in behavior modification.* New York: Holt, Rinehart & Winston.

Vandenberg, S. G. (1962) The hereditary abilities study: Hereditary components in a psychological test battery. *Amer. J. human genetics,* **14,** 220–237.

Vernon, M. D. (1952) *A further study of visual perception.* Cambridge: Cambridge University Press.

Verplanck, W. S. (1955) The control of the content of conversation: Reinforcement of statements of opinion. *J. abnorm. soc. Psychol.*, **51**, 668–676.

Von Bonin, G. (1962) Brain and mind. In S. Koch (Ed.), *Psychology: A study of a science,* Vol. 4. New York: McGraw-Hill, pp. 100–118.

Walker, R. N. (1962) Body build and behavior in young children: I. Body build and nursery school teachers' ratings. *Monogr. Soc. Res. Child Develpm.*, **27**, No. 3.

Wallach, M. A. (1962) Commentary: Active-analytical vs. passive-global cognitive functioning. In S. Messick and J. Ross (Eds.), *Measurement in personality and cognition.* New York: Wiley, pp. 211–215.

Watson, J. B. (1928) *Psychological care of infant and child.* New York: Norton.

Webb, W. W. (1952) Conceptual ability of schizophrenics as a function of threat of failure. Unpublished Ph.D. thesis, Duke University.

Webb, W. W. (1955) Conceptual ability of schizophrenics as a function of threat of failure. *J. abnorm. soc. Psychol.*, **50**, 221–224.

Weiner, H., Thaler, Margaret, Reiser, M. F., & Mirsky, I. A. (1957) Etiology of duodenal ulcer: I. Relation of specific psychological characteristics to rate of gastric secretion (serum pepsinogen). *Psychosom. Med.,* **19,** 1–10.

Weir, Ruth H. (1962) *Language in the crib.* The Hague: Mouton & Co.

Weiss, W., & Fine, B. J. (1955) Opinion change as a function of some interpersonal attributes of the communicatees. *J. abnorm. soc. Psychol.,* **51,** 246–253.

Welsh, G. S., & Dahlstrom, W. G. (Eds.) (1956) *Basic readings on the MMPI in psychology and medicine.* Minneapolis: University of Minnesota Press.

White, R. W. (1959) Motivation reconsidered: The concept of competence. *Psychol. Rev.,* **66,** 297–333.

White, R. W. (1963) *Ego and reality in psychoanalytic theory. Psychological Issues,* **3,** No. 3, (Monogr. No. 11).

Whiting, J. W. M., & Child. I. L. (1953) *Child training and personality.* New Haven: Yale University Press.

Wiener, M. (1955) Word frequency or motivation in perceptual defense. *J. abnorm. soc. Psychol.,* **51,** 214–218.

Williams, Juanita H. (1964) Conditioning of verbalization: A review. *Psychol. Bull.* **62,** 383–393.

Williams, R. H., Tibbits, C., & Donahue, Wilma (Eds.) (1963) *Processes of aging* (2 vols.). New York: Atherton Press.

Williams, R. L., & Krasnoff, A. G. (1964) Body image and physiological patterns in patients with peptic ulcer and rheumatoid arthritis. *Psychosom. Med.,* **26,** 701–709.

Winkel, G. H., & Sarason, I. G. (1964) Subject, experimenter, and situational variables in research on anxiety. *J. abnorm. soc. Psychol.,* **68,** 601–608.

Wishner, J. (1960) Reanalysis of "Impressions of personality," *Psychol. Rev.,* **67,** 96–112.

Wittenborn, J. R. (1955) *Wittenborn psychiatric rating scales.* New York: Psychological Corporation.

Wittenborn, J. R. (1956) A study of adoptive children. *Psychol. Monogr.,* **70,** 93–115.

Wolman, B. B. (Ed.) (1965) *Handbook of clinical psychology.* New York: McGraw-Hill.

Wolpe, J. (1958) *Psychotherapy through reciprocal inhibition.* Stanford: Stanford University Press.

Wolpe, J. (1962) The experimental foundations of some new psychotherapeutic methods. In A. J. Bachrach (Ed.), *Experimental foundations of clinical psychology.* New York: Basic Books, pp. 554–575.

Woodworth, R. S. (1919) *Personal data sheet.* Chicago: C. H. Stoelting.

Wright, H. F. (1960) Observational child study. In P. H. Mussen (Ed.), *Handbook of research methods in child development.* New York: Wiley, pp. 71–139.

Wright, M. E. (1942) Constructiveness of play as affected by group organization and frustration. *Character and Personality,* **11,** 40–49.

Yarrow, L. J. (1960) Interviewing children. In P. H. Mussen (Ed.), *Handbook of research methods in child development.* New York: Wiley, pp. 561–602.

Yarrow, L. J. (1964) Separation from parents during early childhood. In M. L. Hoffman and Lois W. Hoffman (Eds.), *Review of child development research,* Vol. 1. New York: Russell Sage Foundation, pp. 89–136.

Yarrow, L. J., & Yarrow, Marian R. (1964) Personality continuity and change in the family context. In P. Worchel and D. Byrne (Eds.), *Personality change.* New York: Wiley, pp. 489–523.

Yates, A. J. (1962) *Frustration and conflict.* New York: Wiley.

Zeigarnik, Bluma (1927) Über das Behalten von erledigten und unerledigten Handlungen. *Psychol. Forsch.,* **9,** 1–85.

Zeller, A. F. (1950*a*) An experimental analogue of repression: I. Historical summary. *Psychol. Bull.,* **47,** 39–51.

Zeller, A. F. (1950*b*) An experimental analogue of repression: II. The effect of individual failure and success on memory measured by relearning. *J. exp. Psychol.,* **40,** 411–422.

Zigler, E., & Phillips, L. (1962) Social competence and the process-reactive distinction in psychopathology. *J. abnorm. soc. Psychol.,* **65,** 215–222.

Zigler, E., & Williams, Joanna (1963) Institutionalization and the effectiveness of social reinforcement: A three year follow-up study. *J. abnorm. soc. Psychol.,* **66,** 197–205.

Zubin, J., Eron, L. D., & Sultan, Florence (1956) Current status of the Rorschach test: I. A psychometric evaluation of the Rorschach experiment. *Amer. J. Orthopsychiat.,* **26,** 773–782.

Zubin, J., Eron, L. D., & Schumer, Florence (1965) *An experimental approach to projective techniques.* New York: Wiley.

Author Index

Subject Index